Communications
in Computer and Information Science   1546

More information about this series at https://link.springer.com/bookseries/7899

Amita Dev · S. S. Agrawal · Arun Sharma (Eds.)

Artificial Intelligence and Speech Technology

Third International Conference, AIST 2021
Delhi, India, November 12–13, 2021
Revised Selected Papers

Editors
Amita Dev
Indira Gandhi Delhi Technical University for
Women
Delhi, India

S. S. Agrawal
Kamrah Institute of Information Technology
Gurgaon, India

Arun Sharma 🆔
Indira Gandhi Delhi Technical University for
Women
Delhi, India

ISSN 1865-0929   ISSN 1865-0937 (electronic)
Communications in Computer and Information Science
ISBN 978-3-030-95710-0   ISBN 978-3-030-95711-7 (eBook)
https://doi.org/10.1007/978-3-030-95711-7

This Springer imprint is published by the registered company Springer Nature Switzerland AG
The registered company address is: Gewerbestrasse 11, 6330 Cham, Switzerland

Preface

There has been tremendous advancement and innovation in artificial intelligence (AI), which is incomparable to the artificial intelligence that emerged traditionally. Artificial intelligence has greatly enhanced machine learning, natural language processing (NLP), and deep learning, enabling new developments in various specialized domains including speech technology. Artificial intelligence is widely used for various speech-related solutions including speech analysis, representation and models, spoken language recognition and understanding, affective speech recognition, interpretation and synthesis, speech interface design and human factors engineering, speech emotion recognition technologies, and audio-visual speech processing, amongst others.

This volume contains papers presented during the Third International Conference on Artificial Intelligence and Speech Technology (AIST 2021), organized by the Indira Gandhi Delhi Technical University for Women (IGDTUW), India, and held during November 12–13, 2021. Like the previous two editions of the conference (AIST 2019 and AIST 2020), this third edition of AIST was a great success, with the participation of experts and authors from countries including Japan, Germany, Australia, France, and almost all corners of India.

The aim of the conference was to serve as a forum for discussions on the state-of-the-art research, development, and implementations of artificial intelligence and speech technology. AIST 2021 was dedicated to cutting edge research that addressed scientific needs of academic researchers and industrial professionals to explore new horizons of knowledge related to artificial intelligence and speech technology. Researchers presented their work revealing the latest and relevant research findings on almost all the aspects of these domains.

The Technical Program Committee of AIST 2021 is extremely grateful to the authors who showed an overwhelming response to the call for papers, with over 180 papers received. All submitted papers went through a single-blind peer review process, and finally 55 papers were accepted for publication in the Springer CCIS series. We are thankful to the reviewers for their efforts in assessing the high-quality papers.

The AIST 2021 conference included prominent keynote addresses by Satoshi Nakamura (NAIST, Japan), S. Umesh (IIT Madras, India), S. S. Agrawal (CSIR, India), Rajkumar Buyya (University of Melbourne, Australia), S. Sakti (JAIST and NAIST, Japan), Laurent Besacier (Naver Labs Europe, France), and Tanja Shultz (University of Bremen, Germany). It also included Technical Sessions chaired by eminent experts from AI and speech technologies including Samudra Vijay (IIT Guwahati, India), Karunesh Arora (C-DAC, India), Poonam Bansal (MSIT, India), Monica Mehrotra (Jamia Millia Islamia, India), D.K. Vishwakarma (DTU, India), Mani Madhukar (IBM Research, India), Anurag Jain (GGSIPU, India), D P Mohapatra (NIT Rourkela, India), and P K Behera (Utkal University, India).

We are sincerely thankful to the Department of Science and Technology, Government of India, for their support in establishing the Centre of Excellence in AI at IGDTUW, under whose banner AIST 2021 was organized.

We are sure that this colloquy of researchers and experts from academia and industry will greatly benefit researchers, students, and faculty. Young scientists and researchers will find the contents of the proceedings helpful to set roadmaps for their future endeavors.

November 2021

Amita Dev
S. S. Agrawal
Arun Sharma

Organization

Honorary Chair

Satoshi Nakamura   NAIST, Japan

General Chair

Amita Dev   IGDTUW, India

General Co-chair

Anupam Shukla   IIIT Pune, India

Technical Program Committee Chair

S. S. Agrawal   CSIR, India

Conference Secretary and Convener

Arun Sharma   IGDTUW, India

Organizing Committee Chair

R. K. Singh   IGDTUW, India

Technical Program Committee Co-chairs

Gianluca Valentino	University of Malta, Malta
K. Samudravijaya	IIT Guwahati, India
Odette Scharenborg	Delft University of Technology, The Netherlands
S. Sakti	NAIST, Japan
Win Pa Pa	University of Computer Studies Yangon, Myanmar

Publicity Chair

Jasdeep Kaur   IGDTUW, India

Publicity Co-chair

Deepti Chabbra   IGDTUW, India

Keynote Speakers

Laurent Besacier   Naver Labs Europe, France
Rajkumar Buyya   University of Melbourne, Australia
S. Sakti   JAIST and NAIST, Japan
Satoshi Nakamura   NAIST, Japan
S. S. Agrawal   CSIR, India
S. Umesh   IIT Madras, India
Tanja Shultz   University of Bremen, Germany

Technical Program Committee

A. K. Mohapatra   Delhi Police, India
Adesh Pandey   KIET, Ghaziabad, India
Ahmed A. Elngar   Beni-Suef University, Egypt
Ajish Abhraham   AIISH, India
Akash Tayal   IGDTUW, India
Alexey Karpov   SPIIRAS, Russia
Amardeep Singh   Punjabi University, India
Amit Prakash Singh   GGSIPU, India
Amita Dev   IGDTUW, India
Anil Ahlawat   KIET, Ghaziabad, India
Anuj Garg   IBM India Pvt. Ltd., India
Anup Girdhar   Sedulity Solutions, India
Anupam Shukla (Director)   IIIT Pune, India
Archana Singh   Amity University, Noida, India
Arun Kumar   IIIT Delhi, India
Arun Kumar   Jubail University College, Saudi Arabia
Arun Solanki   Gautam Buddha University, India
Ashish Khanna   MAIT, India
Ashish Seth   Inha University in Tashkent, Uzbekistan
Ashwni Kumar   IGDTUW, India
Avadhesh Kumar   Galgotias University, India
Ayu Purwarianti   Bandung Institute of Technology, Indonesia
B. B. Sagar   BITS Noida, India
B. K. Murthy   Deity, India
Barbara Zitova   Institute of Information Theory and Automation,
                             CAS, Czech Republic
Bhawna Narwal   IGDTUW, India

Bin Ma	Institute for Infocomm Research, Singapore
Biplob Ray	CQUniversity Australia, Australia
Brian Mak	Hong Kong University of Science and Technology, China
Burlea Schiopoiu Aiana	University of Craiova, Romania
Chai Wutiwiwatchai	NECTEC, Thailand
Chandra Prakash	NIT Delhi, India
Charl Van Heerden	SPbSU, Russia
Charu Gupta	IGDTUW, India
Chhaya R. Kant	IGDTUW, India
Chiu Yu Tseng	Institute of Linguistics, Academia Sinica, Taiwan
Christopher Cieri	University of Pennsylvania, USA
Claudia Soria	ILC-CNR, Italy
D. K. Tayal	IGDTUW, India
Deepak Garg	Bennett University, India
Deepak Gupta	MAIT, India
Deepti Mehrotra	Amity University, India
Dirk Van Compernolle	Katholieke Universiteit Leuven, Belgium
Durga Toshniwal	IIT Roorkee, India
Ela Kumar	IGDTUW, India
Emmanuel Dupoux	EHESS-ENS, France
Eric Castelli	MICA, Vietnam
Etienne Barnard	North-West University, South Africa
Gabriella Casalino	University of Bari Aldo Moro, Italy
Gagan Tiwari	Galgotias University, India
Gaurav Ina	IGDTUW, India
Gerard Bailly	GIPSA Lab, CNRS, France
Gianluca Valentino	University of Malta, Malta
Gilles Adda	CNRS, France
Girish Nath Jha	JNU Delhi, India
Haizhou Li	National University of Singapore, Singapore
Hemant Patil	DA-IICT, India
Hiroya Fujisaki	Tokyo University, Japan
Hsin-Min Wang	IIS, Academia Sinica, Taiwan
Jasdep Kaur	IGDTUW, India
Joseph Mariani	LIMSI and IMMI-CNRS, France
Kalpana Yadav	IGDTUW, India
Kamini Malhotra	SAG, DRDO, India
Kapil Sharma	DTU, India
Karunesh Arora	C-DAC, Noida, India
Khalid Choukri	ELDA, France
Khundmir Syed	IBM India Pvt. Ltd., India

Kirti Tyagi	Inha University in Tashkent, Uzbekistan
Kranti Athalye	IBM India Pvt. Ltd., India
Kusum Deep	IIT Roorkee, India
Laurent Besacier	Naver Labs Europe, France
Laxmi Ahuja	Amity University, Noida, India
Lori Lamel	LIMSI, France
Luong Chi Mai	IOIT, Vietnam
M. N. Hoda	BVICAM, India
Mahesh Chandra	BIT Mesra, India
Mani Madhukar	IBM India Pvt. Ltd., India
Manoj Kumar	MCNUJ, India
Manoj Soni	IGDTUW, India
Mansaf Alam	Jamia Millia Islamia, India
Mansi Sharma	IIT Madras, India
Marcin Paprzycki	Polish Academy of Sciences, Poland
Marelie Davel	North-West University, South Africa
Mariko Kondo	Waseda University, Japan
Mayank Singh	Consilio Research Lab, India
Milan Stehlic	Johannes Kepler University Linz, Austria
Mirna Adriani	University of Indonesia, Indonesia
Mohona Ghosh	IGDTUW, India
Mona Bharadwaj	IBM India Pvt. Ltd., India
Munish Trivedi	NIT Agartala, India
Nemeth Geza	Budapest University of Technology and Economics, Hungary
Nick Campbell	Trinity College Dublin, Ireland
Nidhi Goel	IGDTUW, India
Nisheeth Joshi	Banasthali University, India
Niyati Baliyan	IGDTUW, India
O. P. Sangwan	GJU Hisar, India
Odette Scharenborg	Delft University of Technology, The Netherlands
Omar Farooq	AMU, India
P. S. Grover	GGSIP University, India
P. K. Das	IIT Guwahati, India
P. K. Saxena	PSA, Government of India, India
P. C. Ching	Chinese University of Hong Kong, Hong Kong
Pedro Moreno	Google, USA
Peri Bhaskararao	IIIT Hyderabad, India
Pooja	Sharda University, India
Poonam Bansal	MSIT, India
Poornima Iyengar	IBM India Pvt. Ltd., India
Pratishtha Mathur	Sikim Manipal University, India

Purushottam Sharma	Amity University, Noida, India
R. K. Singh	IGDTUW, India
Rajesh Kumar	Thapar University, India
Rajesh Tyagi	SRM University, Delhi-NCR, India
Rajiv Sangal	IIIT Hyderabad, India
Rajkumar Buyya	University of Melbourne, Australia
Ranu Gadi	IGDTUW, India
Ratnadeep Deshmukh	BAM University, India
Ruchika Gupta	IBM India Pvt. Ltd., India
S. R. N. Reddy	IGDTUW, India
S. S. Agrawal	CSIR, India
S. Umesh	IIT Madras, India
S. K. Jain	CFSL, India
S. Sakti	JAIST and NAIST, Japan
Samudra Vijaya K.	IIT Guwahati, India
Sandeep Chauhan	Bank of America, India
Sangeeta Arora	AKTU Lucknow, India
Sanjay Gupta	NXP Semiconductors, India
Sanjay Misra	Covenant University, Nigeria
Sanjay Singla	IET Bhaddal, India
Satoshi Nakamura	NAIST, Japan
Sebastian Stüker	KIT, Germany
Seeja K. R.	IGDTUW, India
Selvamani K.	Anna University, India
Shakir Khan	Al-Imam University, Saudi Arabia
Shalini Arora	IGDTUW, India
Shikha Maheshwari	IBM India Pvt. Ltd., India
Shrrdha Sagar	Galgotias University, India
Shweta Bansal	Amity University, Noida, India
Shweta Sinha	KIIT, India
Shyamal K. Das Mandal	IIT Kharagpur, India
Sin Horng Chen	NCTU, Taiwan
Somnath Chandra	MEITY, Government of India, India
Sourabh Bharti	IGDTUW, India
Steven Bird	Charles Darwin University, Australia
Subhash Bhalla	University of Aizu, Japan
Sudip Sanyal	BML Munjal University, India
Sunil Tyagi	Indian Navy, Delhi, India
Sunita Yadav	AKGEC, India
Swaran Lata	MEITY, Government of India, India
Syed Hussain	University of Liberal Arts Bangladesh, Bangladesh

Tan Tien Ping	USM, Malaysia
Tanja Schultz	University of Bremen, Germany
Thang Vu	University of Stuttgart, Germany
Tiziana Margaria	University of Limerick, Ireland
V. K. Arora	Anveshan Foundation, India
Vijai Kumar	Ciena, India
Vineet Kansal	AKTU Lucknow, India
Vinod Shukla	Amity University, Dubai, UAE
Vipin Tyagi	JUIT, India
Vishal Bhatnagar	NSUT East Campus, India
Win Pa Pa	University of Computer Studies Yangon, Myanmar
Xavier Anguera	Telefonica, Spain
Yoshinori Sagisaka	University of Waseda, Japan
Zuraida Mohd Don	UPSI, Indonesia

Sponsors

Department of Science and Technology, Government of India

IGDTUW-Anveshan Foundation, India

AI Club, IGDTUW, India

Contents

AI Techniques

Speech and Natural language Processing

A Critical Insight into Automatic Visual Speech Recognition System

Kiran Suryavanshi[1]([⊠]), Suvarnsing Bhable[1], and Charansing Kayte[2]

[1] Department of Computer Science & IT, Dr. Babasaheb Ambedkar Marathwada University, Aurangabad, MH, India
[2] Government Institute of Forensic Science, Aurangabad, MH, India

Abstract. This research paper investigated the robustness of the Automatic Visual Speech Recognition System (AVSR), for acoustic models that are based on GMM and DNNs. Most of the recent survey literature is surpassed in this article. Which shows how, over the last 30 years, analysis and product growth on AVSR robustness in noisy acoustic conditions has progressed? There are various categories of languages covered, with coverage, development processes, Corpus, and granularity varying. The key advantage of deep-learning tools, including a deeply convoluted neural network, a bi-directional long-term memory grid, a 3D convolutional neural network, and others, is that they are relatively easy to solve such problems, which are indissolubly linked to feature extraction and complex audiovisual fusion. Its objective is to act as an AVSR representative.

Keywords: Speech recognition · AVSR · MFCC · HMM · CNN · DNN

1 Introduction

Human-computer collaboration is a pursuit of HCI as human-computer communication for the interaction between humans and computers (HCI). Given the rapid advancement and promotion of computer intellectualization in Artificial Intelligence, HCI technology is presently confronted by more challenges and complexity than before. With this in mind, a most effective and humanized audio perception method appears feasible when dealing with large HCI issues, whether the devices run in a nice work surrounding or in a noisy working environment. ASR is an effective link between the two components of humans and machines; ASR (Audio speech recognition) is an effective link [1, 2].

The AVSR may be utilized in many settings, including ground vehicle signal recognition, mobile text translation, lip-reading for persons with hearing impairments, voice identification of speakers out of a lot of persons speaking simultaneously time, etc. [3].

The AVSR's historical period in that we summarized the conventional and deep learning-based methods used in AVSR systems by mathematically representing the AVSR operation. Meanwhile, we compared the existing AVSR dataset with the mission, testers, corpus, perspective (or view), and so on, and explain our ideas in practical scenarios of open-source audiovisual databases [4].

A. Dev et al. (Eds.): AIST 2021, CCIS 1546, pp. 3–11, 2022.
https://doi.org/10.1007/978-3-030-95711-7_1

We focused on two major issues when constructing AVSR anatomy. The function extraction (in terms of audio/visual modality) and complex audiovisual fusion are both thoroughly investigated in theory. Extractors based on convolutional neural networks (CNNs) that allow efficient feature extractions and advanced neural networks [5].

For continuous number digits registered in the TIDIGIT database, the speech recognition rate for the MFCC-based ASR system is higher than the speech recognition rate for the PLP-based ASR system. In the same report, however, PLP-based ASR systems outperformed MFCC-based ASR systems in terms of accurate phoneme accuracies for speech data from the TIMIT database [6].

2   Related Work

The deep neural network hidden Markov model (DNN-HMM) Sanskrit speech recognition using HTK is one of the most promising implementations of DNNs in ASR. For extraction, MFCC and two states of HMM were used, yielding 95.2% and 97.2% precision, respectively [7]. For Hindi words, a real-time speaker recognition system was created. MFCC was used to remove features using the Quantization Linde, Buzond Gray (VQLBG) algorithm. To break the silence, the Voice Activity Detector (VAC) was suggested [8].

Technology is used. Linear Predictive Coding (LPC) and Gaussian Mixture Model were used to remove features (GMM). A total of 100 words were reported 1000 times, yielding an accuracy of 84% [9].

Auto HTK language recognition. Isolated terms are used to identify HMM topology speech in 10 states that generated 96,61% [10]. A Hidden Markov Model Toolkit is an automated voice recognition framework for isolated and associated Hindi words (HTK). Hindi terms are used with MFCC datasets and 95% isolated words and 90% in related words are used with a recognition scheme [11].

A successful speech recognition system experimented with a 98% precision Mel Frequency Cepstrum Coefficients (MFCC), Vector Quantization (VQ) [12], HMM. The index is made up of five words spoken ten times by four voices. We need a sense of how the voice is generated to grasp the relationship between the auditory sound and the associated visual signals which can be perceived on the speaker's mouth/lips. The two areas of grammar that research sounds of human language are phonetics and phonological science. Phonetics investigates the language's actual speech sounds, and how the sound is produced, communicated, and seen. On the other hand, phonology is a formal analysis of the organization of speech sounds to create sound structures. Phonetics is linked to acoustic research by using a great deal of sound processing technically employed by acoustics [13].

The development of a broad-based Hindi language recognition system using a hybrid approach combining rule-based and statistical approaches through Kaldi toolkits. The initial attempt was based on the Hindi language to automatically detect spoken sentences in Indian languages. In 1998, a hierarchical speech recognition device was reported which could recognize the Hindi phrases spoken with intervals [14] (Fig. 1).

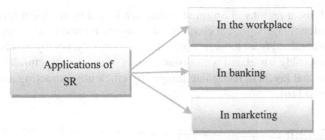

Fig. 1. Applications of speech recognition

3 Applications of Speech Recognition

3.1 In the Workplace

- Look for reports or papers on your computer;
- Make a graph or tables out of data
- Dictate the information you wish to include in a document.
- On-demand printing of documents
- Begin holding video conferences.
- Arrange meetings
- Record minutes.
- Make travel plans

3.2 In Banking

- Request information about your balance, transactions, and spending trends without opening your phone.
- Make payments
- Receive information about your transaction history

3.3 In Marketing

Voice-search has the potential to change the way marketers communicate with their customers. Marketers should be on the lookout for emerging trends in user data and behavior as people's interactions with their gadgets evolve.

4 Convolutional Neural Network

Speech recognition device that recognize words. For feature, A CNN is a DNN version often used for issues with image classification. In order to maintain spatial invariance, CNNs combine three design ideas: local receptive, mutual weights, and spatial subsampling. Consequently, CNNs are useful in three different ways relative to standard entirely linked feed-forward networks [15].

Only small local regions of an input image are linked by the local reception fields in the convolutional layers. Visual elements such as orientation borders, endpoints, and corners can be obtained from local receptive fields. Typically, nearby pixels are strongly correlated and weakly correlated with distant pixels. Thus it is structurally beneficial to stack convolutional layers to recognize images by efficiently extracting and mixing the features obtained [16].

5   Kaldi Toolkit

A scheme for the understanding of audio-visual speech using the toolkit for recognizing the Kaldi language. Kaldi was a first step in the AI conversation pipeline, which was launched at the University of Johns Hopkins in 2009 to improve technology to minimize the expense and time needed to establish speech recognition systems. This is an open-source software platform for language processing. Since then, Kaldi has been the community's de facto toolkit that allows millions of people to use expression every day. In three key steps, the standard languages to text workflow seen in the diagram below take place: extraction of features (conversion of a raw audio signal to machine learning features), acoustic modeling, and linguistic modeling. Acoustic models today at Kaldi are replaced by recurrent, convolutions-based neural networks with Gaussian Mixture (GMM) and Hidden Markov Models (HMM), to effectively simulate states, which leads to state-of-the-art outcomes [17].

6   Proposed Methodology

Propose a method to build Automatic Visual Speech Recognition System for Marathi Language (Fig. 2).

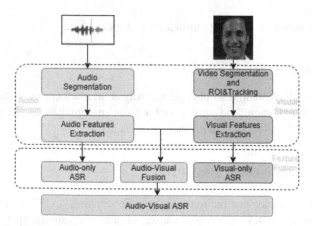

Fig. 2. Block diagram of a typical audio-video speech recognition

6.1 Combining Residual Networks with LSTMs for Lipreading

ResNets and LSTMs are the machine vision and NLP game-changers. In these books, the writers sought to offer the cumulative advantages of long and short-term memory networks in spacetime convolution, residual and bidirectional. They suggested an end-to-the-end architecture of deep learning to recognize words on visual expression, which is educated and tested on the Lip-reading In-The-Wild dataset [18].

6.2 Deep Word Embedding

The Residual and bidirectional LSTM network and the in-the-wild Lipreading database are trained. The findings reveal an average error rate of 11.92% in the 500-word language. Probabilistic Linear Discriminatory Analysis (PLDA) is used to design the embedding on words not seen during testing to make low-shot learning. The studies have shown that word-level visual perception of speech is possible even though the target words are not included in the training package [19].

6.3 Lrw-1000

A wild, naturally distributed wildlife lip-reading benchmark called LRW-1000 has been developed for researchers, containing 1,000 classes of 718,018 samples, compiled by over 2,000 single speakers. Each class corresponds to a Mandarin word syllable consisting of one or more Chinese characters [20].

Table 1. Marathi vowels

Devanagari	Transliterated	IPA
अ	a	/ə/
आ	ā	/aː/
इ	i	/i/
ई	ī	/iː/
उ	u	/u/
ऊ	ū	/uː/
ऋ	ṛ	/ru/
ए	e	/e/
ऐ	ai	/əi/
ओ	o	/o/
औ	au	/əu/
अं	aṃ	/əm/
अः	aḥ	/əɦə/

6.4 Marathi Language Vowels and Consonants

The Marathi-language phoneme inventory is like that of many Indo-Aryan languages. The following is an IPA map of Marathi (Table 1).

7 Features Extraction

The videos are captured in QuickTime File Format (.MOV) with a sampling rate of 22.050 Hz using the iPhone 5. Each video has a 24-bit RGB face view of 720 × 1280 pixels. The video only captures the face of the respondent (Table 2). The participants were asked to remove eyewear or face gear during their filming procedure, and all the videos were taken in bright and dynamic environments. Audio and visual data were separated from the raw video dataset. Five visual frames taken from the video show the visual detail for each video clip. A total of 1000 video samples were taken, 1000 audio samples of 2-s length, and 5,000 visually extracted from the video samples recorded [21].

7.1 Visual Preprocessing

In order to delete data unrelated to voice and upgrade those features, visual streams must be pre-processed in order to improve speech recognition accuracy prior to application to the recognizer for testing or recognition purposes. Face identification and mouth detection and ROI extraction are the first stages in vision preprocessing. The picture that the camera has taken is an RGB picture. The picture should be changed to the gray-level picture before visual preprocessing is applied to the file. Gray-level photographs are known as monochrome images or one color. They just provide details about brightness. The standard picture consists of 8 bit/pixel (data) which allows for different levels of luminosity (0–255). The 8-bit rendering is usually because the byte that matches 8 bits of data is the tiny standard unit in the modern computing world [22].

7.2 Region of Interest (ROI) Extraction

The ROI supplies raw input data for visual function extraction and thus is affected by the correct ROI extraction in the overall output of an audiovisual automated speech recognition (AVASR) system. Due to its high deformation of the lip structure and to changes in the mouth area material due to the appearance or absence of tongue, teeth, and mouth opening and closing during the voice, the detection of ROI is made more difficult. The differences in lighting conditions and changes in speaker posture and orientation often affect ROI detection approaches. ROI extraction is often affected by the appearance or lack of a barb or mustache [23].

7.3 Visual Feature Extraction

The purpose of the extraction function is to preserve as much spoken knowledge in a relatively limited number of parameters from the original images of the speaker as possible.

Table 2. Marathi consonants

क	ख	ग	घ	ङ
ka /kə/	kha /kʰə/	ga /gə/	gha /gʱə/	ṅa (/ŋə/)
च	छ	ज	झ	ञ
ca /tɕə/	cha /tɕʰə/	ja /dzə/	jha /dzʱə/	ña (/ɲə/)
ट	ठ	ड	ढ	ण
ṭa /ʈə/	ṭha /ʈʰə/	ḍa /ɖə/	ḍha /ɖʱə/	ṇa /ɳə/
त	थ	द	ध	न
ta /tə/	tha /tʰə/	da /də/	dha /dʱə/	na /nə/
प	फ	ब	भ	म
pa /pə/	pha /pʰə/ or /fə/	ba /bə/	bha /bʱə/ or /və/	ma /mə/
य	र	ल	व	श
ya /jə/	ra /rə/	la /lə/	va /ʋə/	śa /ʃə/
ष	स	ह	ळ	क्ष
ṣa /ʂə/	sa /sə/	ha /ɦə/	ḷa /ɭə/	kṣa /kɕə/
ज्ञ				
jña /gɲə/				

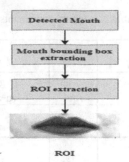

Fig. 3. ROI extraction form frame.

A variety of techniques for transformation, such as a discrete cosine transform (DCT), Discrete Wavelets Transform (DWT), and a Linear Discriminant Analytical analysis (LDA), are employed for visual feature extraction. The three detailed images are deleted and, by combining columns, the average subset image is transformed into a vector. This vector is used for the purposes of image classification as an image representation. By applying LDA, the average image in the form of ROI vectors is reduced to 30 dimensions. The DWT method in the ROI picture is shown in Fig. 3 [24].

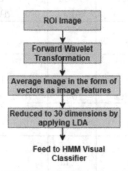

Fig. 4. DWT and HHM visual classifier

8   Conclusion

A systematic review of the current and past visual automatic speech recognition system literature (Fig. 4). What are the methodologies used up to now in this article, the original use of the Visual Speech Recognition system in this survey? It will be useful in future work to explore how the automatic visual speech recognition system can be developed for Marathi language.

References

1. Grudin, A.J.: A Moving Target—The Evolution of Human-Computer Interaction. Taylor and Francis, New York (2012)

2. Ruchika, K., Amita, D., Archana, B., Ashwani, K.: Machine learning techniques in speech generation: a review. J. Adv. Res. Dyn. Control Syst. **11**, 1095–1110 (2019). https://doi.org/10.5373/JARDCS/V11SP11/20193141
3. Hassanat, A.: Visual Speech Recognition. InTech, London (June 2011)
4. Noda, K., et al.: Audio-Visual Speech Recognition Using Deep Learning. Springer Science+Business Media, New York (2014). https://doi.org/10.1007/s10489-014-0629-7
5. Sterpu, G., Saam, C., Harte, N.: Attention-based Audio-Visual Fusion for Robust Automatic Speech Recognition. arXiv:1809.01728v3 [eess.AS]. Accessed 1 May 2019
6. Tamazin, M., Gouda, A., Khedr, M.: Enhanced automatic speech recognition system based on enhancing power-normalized cepstral coefficients. Appl. Sci. **9**, 2166 (2019)
7. Deshmukh, A.M.: Comparison of Hidden Markov Model and Recurrent Neural Network in Automatic SpeechRecognition. EJERS Eur. J. Eng. Res. Sci. **5**(8), 958–965 (2020)
8. Panda, A.K., Sahoo, A.K.: Study of Speaker Recognition Systems (2011)
9. Akkas Ali, M.D., Hossain, M., Bhuiyan, M.N.: Automatic speech recognition technique for Bangla words. Int. J. Adv. Sci. Technol. **50** (2013)
10. Gales, M., Young, S.: The application of hidden Markov models in speech recognition. Sign. Process. **1**(3), 195–304 (2007)
11. Dua, M., Saini, P., Kaur, P.: Hindi automatic speech recognition using HTK (June 2013)
12. Bansal, P., Dev, A., Jain, S.B.: Automatic speaker identification using vector quantization. Asian J. Inform. Technol. **6**(9), 938–942 (2007)
13. Mahalakshmi, P., Muruganandam, M., Sharmila, A.: Voice recognition security system using Mel-frequency cepstrum coefficients. Innovare Acad. Sci. **9**(Suppl), 3 (2016)
14. Kumar, M., Rajput, N., Verma, A.: A large-vocabulary continuous speech recognition system for Hindi. IBM J. Res. Dev. **48**(5.6), 703–715 (2004)
15. Gu, J., et al.: Recent Advances in Convolutional Neural Networks. arXiv:1512.07108v6 [cs.CV]. Accessed 19 Oct 2017
16. Chelaru, M.I., Dragoi, V.: Negative correlations in visual cortical networks. Cereb Cortex. **26**(1), 246–256 (2016)
17. https://kaldi-asr.org/doc/history.html
18. Young, T., Hazarik, D., Poria, S., Cambria, E.: Recent Trends in Deep Learning Based Natural Language Processing. arXiv:1708.02709v8 [cs.CL]. Accessed 25 Nov 2018
19. Stafylakis, T., Tzimiropoulos, G.: Zero-shot keyword spotting for visual speech recognition in-the-wild. In: 15th European Conference, Munich, Germany, Proceedings, Part IV, 8–14 Sept (2018)
20. Yang, S., et al.: LRW-1000: A Naturally-Distributed Large-Scale Benchmark for Lip Reading in the Wild. arXiv:1810.06990 [cs.CV]. Accessed 24 Apr 2019
21. Pramuk, B.: Proposal of a review valuable advices on the theory of sup- of cosmetics items. In: Proceedings of 2019 4th International Conference on Information Technology (2019)
22. Hassanat, A.B.: Visual Words for Automatic Lip-Reading. arXiv:1409.6689 [cs.CV]. Accessed 17 Sep 2017
23. Lu, Y., Li, H.: Automatic lip-reading system based on deep convolutional neural network and attention-based long short-term memory. Appl. Sci. **9**(8), 1599 (2019)
24. Gautam, B.: Image Compression Using Discrete Cosine Transform and Discrete Wavelet Transform (2010)

Speaker Independent Accent Based Speech Recognition for Malayalam Isolated Words: An LSTM-RNN Approach

Rizwana Kallooravi Thandil[✉] [iD] and K. P. Mohamed Basheer [iD]

Sullamussalam Science College, Areekode, Kerala, India

Abstract. Automatic speech recognition (ASR) has been a very active area of research for the past few decades. Though there are great advancements in ASR in many languages accent-based speech recognition is an area that is yet to be explored in many languages. Speech recognition by humans is an intuitive process and so is a tough process to make the computers automatically recognize human speech. Although speech recognition has achieved promising achievements for many languages; speech recognition for the Malayalam language is still in infancy. The scarcity of the datasets makes it researchers difficult to do the experiments. Here in this paper, we have experimented with Long Short-Term Memory (LSTM) a Recurrent Neural Network (RNN), for recognizing the accent-based isolated words in Malayalam. The datasets we used here have been constructed manually under a natural recording environment. We used Mel Frequency Cepstral Coefficient (MFCC) methods to extract the features from the audio signals. LSTM with RNN is used to train and build the model since this technology significantly outperforms all other feed-forward deep neural networks and other statistical methodologies.

Keywords: Malayalam speech recognition · Accent-based ASR · LSTM · RNN · MFCC

1 Introduction

ASR has been traditionally modeled using the Hidden Markov Models (HMM) and Gaussian Markov Model (GMM) based models which could yield considerably good performance in speech recognition. But the performance of ASR has been drastically improved by the introduction of deep neural networks (DNN). Even though there are many advancements in the ASR techniques by the introduction of neural networks, the state of the art of building ASR for languages, low-resourced ones to be specific is extremely complicated.

Malayalam is a language spoken in Kerala, a southern state, and in the Lakshadweep Islands in India. Malayalam is one of the most inflicted languages with more than 10 dialects across the state. The language is composed of 53 letters with 37 consonants and 16 vowels.

A. Dev et al. (Eds.): AIST 2021, CCIS 1546, pp. 12–22, 2022.
https://doi.org/10.1007/978-3-030-95711-7_2

Automatic Speech Recognition (ASR) is the intelligence imparted on machines to understand and act upon spoken commands in natural languages. Commands given in the form of text were the only way of communication between humans and machines for the past many decades. The speech recognition system has been an active area of research for the last few decades. Active research is happening in speech recognition for many languages and there are many promising advancements in the quality of speech recognition for those languages. On the other hand, ASR for the Malayalam language has drawn little attention due to the complexity of the language. And accent-based ASR for the Malayalam language will add more complexity to the researchers. It requires high expertise and dedication by the researchers to develop accent-based ASR for the same. Malayalam is one of the low-resourced languages in terms of dataset availability for performing the research. The work is proposed to model a novel method for accent-based speech recognition for Malayalam words using deep long short-term memory, for identifying the spoken words in Malayalam by different speakers.

In this experiment, we have collected 3070 speech samples from 29 speakers. The age of the speakers ranges from six to eighty with 10 males and 19 females. Many different speech recognition experiments were done using the studio environment. But here in this work, a speech corpus of 1.705 h was constructed in a normal noisy environment using the crowdsourcing method. An application was built online to collect data from different speakers across the globe.

In summary, this paper makes the following contributions.

- A Malayalam accent-based dataset was created.
- A Malayalam word-based embedding was constructed for building the association between utterances and textual words.
- An LSTM-RNN based acoustic model was constructed for recognizing accent-based Malayalam speech.

2 Related Work

Major development in Speech recognition happened in late 1930s at the world fair in the New York city which simply synthesized human speech by imitating the signals from the human vocal cord. The first ASR that belongs to AI was developed in 1952 at the Bell labs that could identify small sections of spoken digits from zero to nine. Ten years later IBM introduced Shoebox that could identify sixteen spoken words in English. It was during the early1980s the speech recognition had a great breakthrough when the scientists began to use mathematical and probabilistic models like HMM for ASR that produced better results.

Some of the major problems faced by the ASR are noise, echo, accents, and similarity in sounds. The scientists had to deal with speech signals that are infected by these problems. Disorganized speech is yet another challenge faced by the researchers working in ASR. So, for most of the experiments, the researchers use data recorded in the studio recording environment that reduces the above-mentioned challenges. There are still certain challenges specific to certain languages which require additional effort in building the ASR systems.

2.1 Accent Based Speech Recognition Using RNN in Literature

Accent-based ASR systems are found to be more efficient when the model is constructed using LSTM-RNN models which use sequential information. RNN is a neural network that stores sequential information in a memory that influences predictions. The memory in the network makes RNN unique from other neural networks. So using traditional neural networks in speech recognition will not yield good results when compared to the one with RNN [3].

Jinyu Li et al. in their work proposed an FT--LSTM architecture to model the spectrogram. They proposed a method that first used F-LSTM that performs a frequency recurrence that in turn summarizes the frequency-wise patterns which will be then fed into T-LSTM. The experiment had better performance and a reduced word error rate when there was a reasonable number of memory cells in the F-LSTM [1].

Yajie Miao et al. [2] has used Eesen framework that is deep bidirectional RNNs trained with the connectionist temporal classification (CTC) objective function for simplifying the ASR process. They used CTC for the association between speech signals and label sequences. The experiment yielded lower error rates when compared with the DNN systems.

Krishna Ramachandran et al. [7] proposed a work for Malayalam speech using GMM and they could build a model with a reduced error rate. The authors also verified the performance of multivariate Gaussian mixtures.

Wangyang YING et al. [8] had combined HMM with LSTM-RNN to develop a model for Sichuan accent-based speech recognition. The authors in their work concluded that context in HMM is required for speech recognition. Praveen Edward James et al. [9] proposed a speech recognition system using LSTM in MATLAB. Muneer V.K et al. [10] had done a detailed review on text processing in the Malayalam language for constructing models for recommender systems in the travel domain. The authors throw light on the methodologies that shall be adopted for developing a voice assisted recommender system in the Malayalam language.

3 Proposed Methodology and Design

The proposed work aims at creating a model that identifies accent-based human speech in the Malayalam language and converts it into corresponding text. The model is trained to understand 20 classes of isolated Malayalam words. Ten of which include Malayalam digits and the other ten some random Malayalam words. Technically the model must learn all the different classes of utterance it has been trained for and convert the speech into the standard text in Malayalam (Fig. 1).

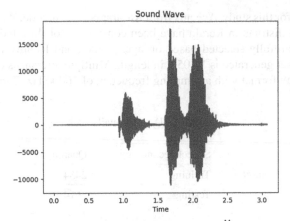

Fig. 1. Speech signal for utterance പുസ്തകം..

3.1 The Blueprint of the Model

Figure 2 shows the diagrammatic representation of the model. The steps involved in the proposed system are:

i.   Record the speech signal
ii. Develop the dataset
iii. Extract the features from the inputted speech signal
iv. Build the model using LSTM-RNN
v.   Build the language model
vi. Search for the matching word for the input speech signal.

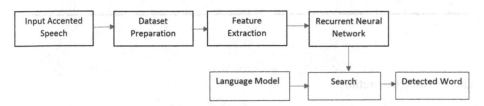

Fig. 2. Workflow of proposed system.

3.2 Dataset

Dataset construction is the most crucial step in all experiments, especially when working with neural network systems. Accent-based speech data from people of various age groups have been recorded for this work. The speech corpus of 3070 recordings has been constructed using the crowdsourcing method in the natural recording environment. A web application has been developed for this purpose. We have considered speech with different accents for this study. Accents from Kasaragod, Kozhikode, Wayanad, Kannur, and Malappuram districts in Kerala have been considered for this study. Twenty-nine members were carefully selected based on age, gender, and locality for building the dataset. The dataset generated is 1.705 h in length. Multiple utterances of the words are converted into.wav format with a sampling frequency of 16000 Hz (Tables 1 and 2).

Table 1. Dataset details.

	Speech technology	Quantity
Dataset	Training	2454
	Testing	614

Table 2. Example classes used in the experiment.

Uttered word	IPA	Uttered word	IPA
പൂജ്യം	puːjjam	പുസ്തകം	pusṭakam
ഒന്ന്	oṉṉə	വരയ്ക്കുക	ʋarajkkuka
രണ്ട്	raɳṭə	അറിവ്	ariʋə
മൂന്ന്	muːṉṉə	പഠിക്കുക	paʈʰikkuka
നാല്	ɳaːl	ലൈബ്രറി	laibrari
അഞ്ച്	aɲʧə	വായിക്കുക	ʋaːjikkuka
ആറ്	aːrə	സ്കൂൾ	skuːḷ
ഏഴ്	eːɻə	വിദ്യാർഥി	ʋidʲjaːrṭṭʰi
എട്ട്	eʈʈə	അധ്യാപകൻ	adʰjaːpakan
ഒമ്പത്	oṉpaṭə	എഴുതുക	eɻuṭuka

3.3 Feature Extraction

The next step in the experiment is to extract the features from the speech signals. Appropriate feature selection could lead to a better-trained model, while inappropriate features would significantly hinder the training process. Librosa audio library used for feature extraction process. Specifically, here in this experiment, we have used Mel Frequency Cepstral Coefficients (MFCC) algorithm for the feature extraction purpose. We have considered 20 prominent features from each signal. A text file and a CSV file has been generated to store the extracted features which will be then split into train and test set for building the model. Figure 3 shows the 20 features that have been extracted from the speech signals.

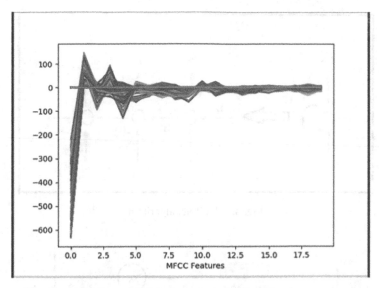

Fig. 3. MFCC features of the speech signals used for the experiment

3.4 Model Building Using LSTM_RNN

The entire model is designed using Python. Audio signals are preprocessed to regain the elements which is utilized for preparing the model. The LSTM-RNN is prepared on the dataset and planned onto the word models. The extracted features from test set will be ordered by the trained network as indicated by the classes that have been already described. The training signals are vectorized utilizing a one-hot encoding method and forwarded to the LSTM network. The training phase is responsible for comparing these values with the target class and updating the weights accordingly which will enable the network to predict the result.

Figure 6 shows the visualization of the computational steps that clearly show the flow from train inputs to loss and predictions. The input to the network is the width and height of the accented speech signals. Width data are the features of the signals extracted using the MFCC algorithm. Height data is the maximum height of the signals which has been set to 1000 in the experiment. There are 20 classes of isolated words in the experiment.

Even though there are many neural networks available, RNNs are used for doing speech recognition experiments since it is proven by many scientists that RNN outperforms all other neural networks when used to work with speech recognition [5, 6].

Steps involved in the RNN algorithm are [5]:

- x_t is the input at time t, $x_t - 1$ is the past input and $x_t + 1$ is the future input (sampled speech signal).
- s_t is the hidden state and the hidden memory which is calculated as $s_t = f(U*x_t + W * x_t - 1)$.

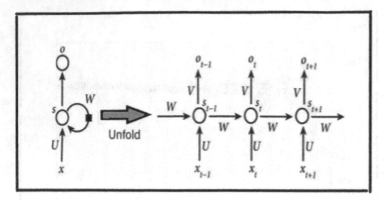

Fig. 4. The RNN algorithm

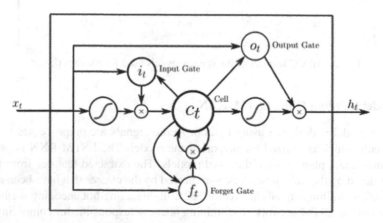

Fig. 5. A long-short term memory cell.

- o_t is the output at step t. It is the vector of probabilities across the vocabulary and calculated as $o_t = \text{softmax}(V * s_t)$ (Fig. 4).

LSTMs are the most used RNNs. The cell state in LSTM makes the information flow through the network possible. The input gate, output gate and the forget gates are the three gates in LSTM. The sigmoid function in the LSTM has only two outputs. Either the entire information received at the input or no information (Fig. 5).

To work on accent-based speech recognition system in this work we have collected speech samples from five districts in Kerala. The data collected was not free from noise since it was recorded in a natural recording environment. A web application was incorporated for the data collection procedure. Speech samples from twenty-nine speakers were collected over the internet while a few were collected directly from the natural recording environment. The collected speech is sampled to 16000 Hz frequency and converted the speech files into.wav format for further processing. The samples collected can be shown as (Table 3)

Table 3. Statistics of the data collection

Age group	No. of samples collected
Below 10	459
11 to 20	460
21 to 40	1290
41 to 60	590
61 to 80	271
Total	3070

Eighty percent of the entire dataset of 3070 speech samples are split for the training purpose. The model using RNN has been built with a total of 2454 speech samples. The remaining twenty percent that constitutes 614 speech samples used for testing the model.

The classification loss is high at the beginning of the training process. Later it gets reduced when the algorithm keeps learning in each step. The algorithm validates each step and displays the classification loss. It took 738000 steps to train the model. The experiment took over 12.5 h of training to build the model over GPU. The total loss calculated according to the classification loss and validation loss. The total loss decreases to 0.25 towards the last steps when the algorithm learns more over the computation.

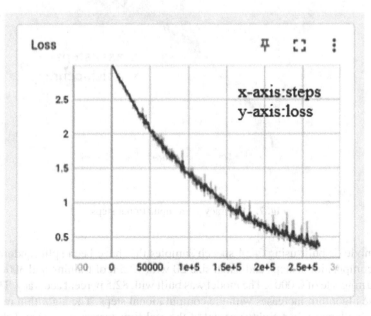

Fig. 6. Total loss vs computational steps

Figure 7 describes the total loss versus the computational steps. Model will be better when the loss is lower. The faded line shows the original classification loss whereas the darker line is found after using a smoothing of 0.6.

4   Result and Discussion

This experiment is aimed at developing a novel method for accent-based speech recognition of Malayalam isolated words. We have adopted the LSTM-RNN algorithm which is known best for speech recognition experiments. A dataset of 3070 speech samples has been constructed for this purpose. Twenty-nine speakers from various age groups and five different districts have been considered for collecting the samples. Speakers are asked to record multiple recordings of the same words in the natural recording environment. People of age group 21 to 40 constitute 42 percent of the entire data for the experiment. This category has been wisely chosen with an expectation to contribute high-quality data. Eighty percent of the data is split randomly for training the model.

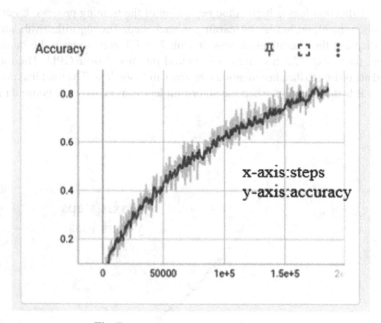

Fig. 7. Accuracy vs computational steps

The model is built using 2454 speech samples that have been split randomly with 7,38000 computational steps and batch size 20 with 12.5 h of training and 3000 epochs with a learning rate of 0.0001. The model was built with 82.5 percent accuracy. The accuracy of the algorithm increases with the computational steps. The algorithm responded accurately with more than eighty percent of the real-time test cases. Figure 7 shows the accuracy obtained through the computational steps. The accuracy gets increased as the algorithm learns from the computations.

5   The Performance Evaluation Metrics

Accuracy is the most common method of evaluation in classification problems. It is computed as the ratio of correct predictions made by the model to all predictions made by the model. F1-score is the weighted average of precision and recall.

The evaluation metrics of the work is shown below (Table 4).

Table 4. The performance evaluation metrics

Evaluation metric	Value in percentage
Accuracy	82.5
Micro Precision	82
Micro Recall	82
Micro F1-score	82
Macro Precision	84
Macro Recall	83
Macro F1-score	83
Weighted Precision	83
Weighted Recall	82
Weighted F1-score	82

6   Conclusion

We attempted to create an accent-based dataset to address the scarcity of accent-based data in the Malayalam language. An accurate and efficient model for accent-based speech recognition in Malayalam has been developed by the authors. The proposed work is one of the prominent areas of research in ASR using LSTM-RNN. Even though the model is accurate for most of the real-time test cases the model had some false positive predictions. Size of dataset may be the reason. The data considered is accent based which might increase the complexity in building the accurate model.

Currently, this work had focused only on twenty classes of isolated words which is very small when considering the Malayalam language. The authors are planning to extend the research in accent-based speech recognition for continuous speech in the Malayalam language in the future.

References

1. Li, J., Abdelrahman Mohamed, A., Zweig, G., Gong, Y.: LSTM time and frequency recurrence for automatic speech recognition. In: 2015 IEEE Workshop on Automatic Speech Recognition and Understanding (ASRU) (2015)

2. Miao, Y., Gowayyed, M., Metze, F.: EESEN: end-to-end speech recognition using deep RNN models and WFST-based decoding. In: 2015 IEEE Workshop on Automatic Speech Recognition and Understanding (ASRU) (2015)
3. Yashwanth, H., Harish, M., Suman, D.: Automatic speech recognition using audio visual cues. In: IEEE India Annual conference, pp. 166–169 (2004)
4. Aditya, A., Parikshit, A., Gaurav Deshmukh, G., Piyush, D.: Speech recognition using recurrent neural networks. In: 2018 International Conference on Current Trends Towards Converging Technologies (ICCTCT) (2018)
5. Bhushan, C.K.: Speech recognition using artificial neural network. Proc. Int. J. Comput. Commun. Instrum. Engg. (IJCCIE) **3**(1) (2016)
6. Shrawankar, U., Thakare, V.: Techniques for feature extraction in speech recognition system: a comparative study, (IJCAETS), pp. 412–418, ISSN 0974-3596 (2010)
7. Krishna Ramachandran, L., Elizabeth, S.: Generation of GMM weights by dirichlet distribution and model selection using information criterion for Malayalam speech recognition. In: Tiwary, U.S. (ed.) IHCI 2018. LNCS, vol. 11278, pp. 111–122. Springer, Cham (2018). https://doi.org/10.1007/978-3-030-04021-5_11
8. Ying, W., Zhang, L., Deng, H.: Sichuan dialect speech recognition with deep LSTM network. Frontiers Comput. Sci. **14**, 378–387 (2019)
9. James, P.E., Kit, M.H., Vaithilingam, C.A., Chiat, A.T.W.: Recurrent neural network-based speech recognition using MATLAB. Int. J. Intell. Enterp. **7**(1/2/3), 56–66 (2020)
10. Muneer, V.K., Mohamed Basheer, K.P.: The evolution of travel recommender systems: a comprehensive review. Malaya J. Matematik **8**(4), 1777–1785 (2020)

A Review on Speech Synthesis Based on Machine Learning

Ruchika Kumari$^{(\boxtimes)}$, Amita Dev, and Ashwni Kumar

Indira Gandhi Delhi Technical University for Women, Delhi, India

Abstract. Recently, Speech synthesis is one of the growing techniques in the research domain that takes input as text and provides output as acoustical form. The speech synthesis system is more advantageous to physically impaired people. In execution process, there arise some complications by surrounding noises and communication style. To neglect such unnecessary noises various machine learning techniques are employed. In this paper, we described various techniques adopted to improve the naturalness and quality of synthesized speech. The main contribution of this paper is to elaborate and compare the characteristics of techniques utilized in speech synthesis for different languages. The techniques such as support vector machine, Artificial Neural Network, Gaussian mixture modeling, Generative adversarial network, Deep Neural Network and Hidden Markov Model are employed in this work to enhance the speech naturalness and quality of synthesized speech signals.

Keywords: Text to speech · Syllables · Database · Artificial neural network · Gaussian mixture modeling · Deep neural network · Hidden Markov model

1 Introduction

Speech synthesis is the synthetic simulation of human language using computers or other types of equipment. Many verbal communication technologies are employed for speech synthesis systems [1]. In speech synthesis, the text information is converted to audio information for speech recognition which is now frequently employed to improve the human–machine connections such as in mobile and audio enabled applications, remote access and communication purposes. Mainly speech synthesis is helpful for visually impaired individuals for reading the text [2]. The conversion of written language to speech is the TTS (Text to Speech) framework. The conversion of orthographic text into audio signals is done in two segments and these two segments perform different operations like pre-processing and segmentation. In the front end of TTS synthesis, the complications like higher-level linguistic characteristics and text analysis are managed [3]. In addition to this, it translates the orthographic text and delivers phonetic transcription. It is also known as pre-processing or text normalization which handles homographs and neglects the lack of word clarity [4]. At the next level, the text information is converted to sound series by the computer using phonemes. In the back end of TTS synthesis, the obtained phonetic transcription is converted to speech by using

A. Dev et al. (Eds.): AIST 2021, CCIS 1546, pp. 23–35, 2022.
https://doi.org/10.1007/978-3-030-95711-7_3

the techniques of sound-generation techniques and manual recordings [5]. The official Hindi language is an Indo-Aryan language spoken extensively by Indian people [6, 7]. The Hindi language contains 13 vocals and 33 consonants while speaking both are combined. Many research works are done for other languages in speech synthesis but less in the Hindi language due to the lack of pronunciation rules and standard datasets [8–11]. The speech synthesis technique for Hindi language is used widely in different sectors like railways and airports for ticket reservations [12]. TTS relies on the intended syllable for processing the sequential approach.

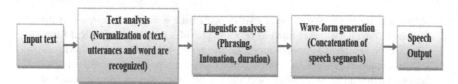

Fig. 1. Speech synthesis block diagram

Figure 1 represents the block diagram of the TTS System. Text analysis consists of normalization of the text, utterances and words are recognized. The linguistic analysis part of the speech contains phrasing, intonation and duration linked with syllables and phoneme. The next step is the waveform generation corresponding to the text. Furthermore, the audio recognition syllable-based system is faster than text-based systems due to the division of syllables into multiple units [13]. The main features of Hindi language comprise nasalization, germination, retroflexed and aspiration. However, the language undergoes certain complications by natural language and speaker characteristics [14]. Precise segmentation and labeling are important features for developing TTS. Hindi is syllable-centric based language and is considered an appropriate section for labeling. But manual labeling is more problematic which utilizes a longer period of time and is liable to cause mistakes [15–17]. Here, the main contribution of speech synthesis is to convert the verbal expression into sequential textual structure unaffected by the ambient environment and speaker characteristics [18].

2 Literature Survey

Numerous relevant research works have been put forward to analyze the speech synthesis of various indo-Aryan languages like Tamil, Hindi, Marathi, Urdu, etc. using various machine learning techniques. The significant intention of these techniques is to generate high-quality and natural-sounding speech to obtain an effective and sensitive outcome of natural speech. The methods employed in this section are support vector machine, Artificial Neural Network, Gaussian mixture modeling, Generative adversarial network, deep neural network and Hidden Markov Model to improve the audio signals by neglecting the unwanted noises thereby increasing the quality and fidelity of audio. Few research works based on speech synthesis using the above-mentioned techniques are discussed as pursues.

2.1 Support Vector Machine (SVM) Based Speech Enhancement Systems

For the generation of high-quality and natural-sounding speech, Jalin et al. (2020) [19] suggested the speech synthesizer using SVM for the Tamil language. Despite most powerful approaches like Gaussian mixture (GMM) and Hidden Markov (HMM) models existing, SVM (support vector machine) mechanism was utilized for its effective and sensitive outcome of natural speech. The SVM classifier works under training and testing phases. Here, the speech samples are aggregated from the dataset with reference to Unicode and generate the label output in numeral value. First, many words are assigned to the training phase and each of these words was trained by SVM. It creates net value and each letter of word was assigned with numeral values. The Unicode and consequent audio signals are saved in the database. Here, the Tamil language was signified in Tamil Unicode. The audio samples are merged to form the words by using the Unicode and audio samples that are recovered from the database. After delivering the unicodes, the label value was produced in the testing phase. Using tool audacity with a high-quality microphone, the words are recorded. The performance was evaluated in terms of recall, precision, accuracy, specificity and sensitivity to check the robustness. In comparison with HMM and GMM methods, the described SVM technique enhances the accuracy level to 90% and achieves superior naturalness. But this technique failed to apply neural networks in the decision-making process. The improvement of the speech system (noise-canceling system) is described by Kinoshita et al. (2021) [20] using the support vector machine-based classifier to accomplish high performance of generalization. This SVM method was utilized to determine whether the sound was natural or announcement. In this, the kernel function was employed to design the data provided in a large dimension. For evaluation, the classifier uses 60 sentences that contain 30 sentences as natural sound and 30 as announcement sound. The frequency level of the sound sample was 96000 Hz along three types of speakers were employed for output generation. Finally, the output showed that the SVM classifier categorized the two classes of sound with an accuracy of 96% and was also best suited for the intended condition. But the complexities were unable to check the required audio length for classification and inapplicable for large data processing.

2.2 Neural Network Based Text to Speech Synthesis Technique

For high performance classification, an efficient artificial neural network (ANN) based TTS synthesizer was evaluated by Kumari et al. (2021) [21] for the Hindi language. The ALO-ANN (Ant Lion Optimization) technique was implemented to predict the basic frequency level of syllable sequence which was determined by employing the Mel Frequency Cepstrum coefficient (MFCC). The time taken to record the speech is represented by 16-bits. The database includes intensity, phrasing and duration of the speech. Using the group delay algorithm, the audio signals are segmented and labeled. By subjective evaluation, the naturalness and intelligibility of the synthesized speech were measured. The ALO-ANN model is compared with ANN/SVM, GMM, HMM and DNN techniques to evaluate the performance. The comparison result proved that the ALO-ANN method had accomplished enhanced prediction of prosodic sequential syllable models. The mean distribution bias is reduced by post and pre-processing approaches. Thus, the

ALO-ANN model gains an accuracy of about 92.97% than other existing techniques Lui et al. (2021) [22] demonstrated the neural speech synthesis-based architecture, Graphspeech. In Natural language processing, the Graphspeech serves an important part while the graph model was infused with neural TTS architecture is Graphspeech. In this, verbal and linguistic knowledge was included in the input to the encoder. Graphspeech includes three phases; they are relation encoder, graph encoder and decoder. In the relation encoder phase, the syntax text is transformed into a syntax graph which provides a word to reach directly to other relevant words by creating two-way connections. In the graph decoder, the input character and relation embeddings are converted to syntactical character embeddings. In the decoder, the obtained character embedding expression was taken as input that generates the natural audio feature as output. The database was obtained from the LJSpeech which contains 13,100 short records. The performance was evaluated by comparing the Graphspeech with the TTS framework. The suggested Graphspeech technique accomplished superior performance like prosody naturalness and audio quality.

2.3 Multi -level Speech Synthesis Based Gaussian Mixture Modeling

The multi-level Gaussian Mixture Model (GMM) based cross-lingual audio conversion technique was introduced by Ramani et al. (2016) [23] for the polyglot speech synthesis. The mixed language utilizes a multilingual synthesizer that delivers the human-understandable language and this synthesized audio depicts speaker switching. It was overcome by converting the multilingual corpus to polyglot speech. Here, the over-smoothing effect occurred in the GMM based audio conversion system which was reduced by employing multi-level GMM technique. This technique was implemented for Indian and foreign languages like Tamil, Indian English, Malayalam, Telugu and Hindi. These languages were considered to have the same phones but have different frequencies. During the process of tokenization, the source language was utilized in place of the target language. The quality of speech signals from the original sound was determined using the mean opinion score. It showed enhancement in the value of about 0.49 to 0.77 for the described multi-level GMM approach. But this technique had limited speaker switching in comparison with the multilingual synthesizer. Popov et al. (2020) [24] worked to improve the overall performance of TTS by implementing the Gaussian LPCNet technique for the multi-sample speech synthesis. The multisampling Gaussian LPCNet was an enhanced method of LPCNet vocoder that provides unlimited 16-bit signals and also independently forecasts two excitation samples at once. Modified LPCNet vocoder was 1.5 times faster and provides better efficiency, good quality of synthesized speech. The database was collected from the 16 kHz frequency of short audio clips. The performance is evaluated by considering the efficiency of time and memory and a comparison process takes place among the original LPCNet vocoder and Gaussian LPCNet technique. Real-time factor and sum of non-zero parameters were computed respectively to determine the time and memory efficiency of speech synthesis. The disadvantage was that the suggested technique is unsuitable for operating the audio signals with a frequency greater than 16 kHz and generates low numbers of excitation values.

2.4 Speech Synthesis Using Generative Adversarial Network

To improve the reading capacity of children Zhou et al. (2020) [25] established speech synthesis using the generative adversarial network method. This technique helps the teachers to accelerate recuperation that makes the child spell the word correctly. GAN technique employs optimized Mel generative adversarial network to work with original voice in Mel-spectrograms and the process continues until the optimal outcome is accomplished. Here, the 5 to 8-year-old children were assisted by taking 300 fundamental 2 or 3 Hindi words as input. The words were recorded in the dictionary and were repeated until the child pronounces correctly. The databases were gathered from SC09 and Google. Moreover, the MeiGAN approach was utilized to generate the audio signals from raw audio samples which had a lengthy process. For the comparison process, the minimum optimum score is calculated. In the training phase, positive outcomes were generated by layering and filtering the audio a number of times. It automatically increases the audio time generation but decreases the audio naturalness. Kaliyev et al. (2021) [26] introduced the Couple-Agent Acoustic Generative Adversarial Network (CAAG-GAN) based acoustic model for Kazakh language speech synthesis. A new GAN framework was introduced to enhance the fidelity of audio and consisted of a generator and a pair of discriminators. The generator generates sound parameters and a pair of discriminators enhances the audio accuracy of speech synthesis. By providing the discriminator with extra lingual parameters, it was capable of capturing the connection between auditory and lingual parameters, if not provided with additional parameters causes complications in the system. To avoid such undesirable conditions, the GAN technique is expanded with a couple agent structure. The quality of speech synthesis is measured by MOS (mean optimum score) score and performance test. The suggested approach had enhanced accuracy but prosodic features were not examined in this approach.

2.5 DNN Based Speech Synthesis Technique

Inoue et al. (2021) [27] suggested the modern architecture to promote the emotional terms in the deep neural network (DNN) based text to speech synthesis. The employed architecture models were parallel model, serial model, auxiliary input model and hybrid model. By the combination of emotional and speaker factors, the emotional speech was generated. In the parallel model, the linear summation of both emotional and speaker factors was given as output. In the serial model, these two factors are sequentially arranged in two different layers and due to the presence of sigmoid function; both the factors were added non-linearly. In an auxiliary input model, the rate of input vector was forwarded by using the implicitly models. In hybrid models two kinds such as the combined form of PM and AIM, combined form of SM and AIM were used based on a diverse input and output layer. The extrapolation performance was evaluated by conducting subjective and objective analysis of open emotion and closed emotion tests. The databases were gathered from two Japanese speech corpuses with 500 and 130 sentences which were uttered by male and female speakers. Moreover, the conveying accuracy gains in subjective analysis in parallel models than objective analysis. But this technique requires additional consideration in collecting the emotional speech expressions. Imene Zangari et al. (2021) [28] presented a duration modeling for Arabic speech synthesis using a Deep

Neural network (DNN) architecture. They are training the DNN classifier for different sound classes such as simple consonants, short vowels, long vowels, and geminated consonants. The germination and vowel quality are introduced to enhance the performance of Arabic parametric speech synthesis. The enhancement in the Arabic speech synthesis helps to handle different Arabic sound classes and fits the phone duration into its appropriate pheromone classes. The drawback associated with this technique is processing large vowels which needs knowledge in the phoneme type modeling domain. Lorenzo et al. (2017) [29] investigated the different modeling and controlling approaches for emotional speech using deep neural network (DNN) based speech synthesis. This technique was carried out to determine the better path for annotating the emotional speech information and representing the emotional speech data into labels. The performance analysis was made by employing different 156 evaluators of crowd-sourced perceptual evaluation. As a result, it showed improved modeling efficiency and provided closeness of natural speech with 0% confusion rate. This technique works by capturing the emotional speech but fails to capture the expressive speech. V. Ramu Reddy (2016) et al. [30] made an imperative part in enhancing the nature of text to-speech synthesis (TTS) framework. The elements identified with the linguistic and the production requirements were utilized for displaying the prosodic parameters, for example, duration, intonation and intensities of the syllables. The phonetic imperatives were spoken to by positional, contextual and phonological elements, and the generation limitations were spoken to by articulatory components. Neural system models were investigated to catch the certain term, F0 and force learning utilizing previously mentioned highlights.

2.6 Speech Synthesis Techniques Based on HMM

Maeno et al. (2014) [31] demonstrated the enhancement of prosodic variations utilizing the unsupervised labeling technique for HMM based speech synthesis. The prosodic features and linguistic information were generated from Hidden Markov Model (HMM) training using the conventional labels. In this technique, the typical variations among the raw audio and the synthesized audio were computed and categorized as three phases with high, neutral and low frequency rates. The databases were collected from two types of Japanese speech data; they are appealing speech by three female speakers and fairy tale speech by single male speaker. By subjective and objective analysis, the HMM based speech synthesis technique produces a fundamental frequency (F0) contour which is closer to the original voice than other existing techniques. But the drawback was there was no consideration of time duration and power context in evaluating the test data with small variations. Houidhek et al. (2018) [32] developed an HMM based speech synthesis technique (HTS) to evaluate the speech unit modeling for Arabic language. The application of hidden Markov models in Arabic language necessitates the description of contextual features. The two main constituents of this technique were based on vowel quantity and germination. Here, four modeling systems were introduced and the dataset obtained from the Arabic corps with 1806 utterances with 4-h speech recording. The recording of audio carried out by software pro tools with a frequency rate about 48 kHz. The duration of speech units was evaluated in subjective analysis and the quality of speech signals were evaluated in objective analysis. The evaluation result showed that there was no great difference among varied modeling approaches. So, identification of long vowels and geminated consonants was not necessary in HTS for modern standard Arabic language. Yan-You Chen (2016) et al. [33] concentrated on a hybrid way to deal with natural-sounding speech synthesis in light of applicant extension, unit determination, and prosody alteration utilizing a little corpus. The utilized technique was more particular to tonal language, specifically Mandarin. In traditional speech combination ponders the nature of orchestrated speech depends intensely on the extent of the speech corpus. Notwithstanding, it was profoundly tedious and work serious to set up a substantial named corpus. Here, hopeful extension was proposed to recover potential applicants that were probably not going to be recovered utilizing just phonetic elements. The ideal unit arrangement was then acquired from the extended competitors by utilizing the unit selection mechanism at the phoneme and prosodic word levels. At last, a prosodic word-level prosody modification was utilized to enhance the continuity and smoothness of the prosody of the synthesized speech. R. Karhila (2014) et al. [34] distinguished examinations on utilizing boisterous adjustment information to make customized voices with HMM-based speech synthesis. They explore how natural clamor influences feature extraction and CSMAPLR and EMLLR adaptation. They explore impacts of relapse trees and information amount and test noise-robust feature for arrangement and NMF-based source partition as preprocessing. Speaker- adaptive HMM-TTS framework was vigorous to direct ecological noise.

2.7 Multilingual Text to Speech Synthesis

The multilingual byte2speech model was evaluated by He et al. (2021) [35] for scaling the neural speech synthesis. In this, 43 source languages with diverse phonemes and human scripts are selected as database. Linguistic similarities on resource adaption and source language along with their phonetic traits, pronunciation, lexicons were verified which efficiently displays the adaption capabilities. The performance metrics such as character error rate and mean square error computed to determine the efficiency of model. Thus, the multilingual byte2speech model achieved better intelligibility for higher resource language. This method also possesses enhanced performance on low resource adaption whereas has reduced few shot performances. Yang et al. (2021) [36] introduced the multilingual TTS system based lifelong learning technique. This technique enhances both the learning baseline and quality of synthesis. Four languages such as Dutch, German, Japanese and Chinese are chosen as datasets which are trained initially; final 20 samples of all languages are selected for validation and testing. The dual sampling process alleviates the over-fitting process and addresses the language imbalance. This learning technique accomplished 43% of Mel-Cepstral Distortion reduction compared with other approaches while the naturalness of speech gets affected. de Korte et al. (2020) [37] suggested the neural speech synthesis of multilingual modeling and examined the ability of low resource data when combined with foreign language data. The naturalness of low resource data is severely affected by training both low and high resource language data in combination which tends to cause language imbalance. Here, the computational cost becomes less due to re-weighting function. But the Naturalness of target language gets affected when it combined with auxiliary non-target language data.

3 Comparative Analysis and Discussion of Speech Synthesis Framework

Table 1 depicts the comparative performances of diverse approaches based on speech synthesis, techniques employed by authors, its databases, merits and demerits are also tabulated in the following table.

Table 1. Comparative analysis of speech synthesizer employed in various techniques

Author's name and year	Databases	Techniques employed	Merits	Demerits
Jalin et al. (2020) [19]	High quality microphone dataset recorded using Tamil speaker	Support Vector Machine (SVM)	Improved naturalness of synthesized speech and accuracy	Failed to apply neural networks in decision making process
Kinoshita et al. (2021) [20]	Train announcement	Support Vector Machine (SVM)	Classifies two classes of sound with higher accuracy	Unable to detect audio duration for classification and inapplicable for large databases
Kumari et al. (2021) [21]	Speech signal of Hindi language	Ant-Lion Optimization Artificial Neural Network (ALO-ANN)	Achieve higher prediction of prosodic sequential syllables with greater accuracy	Poor linguistic resources
Liu et al. (2021) [22]	LJS speech database	Graphspeech framework	Better prosody naturalness and audio quality and improved TTS audio rendering	High computational process
Ramani et al. (2016) [23]	Speech signal of Tamil sentences	Multi-level Gaussian Mixture Model (GMM)	Reduces over-smoothing and high accuracy of word prediction	Inadequate speaker switching and over-fitting process
Popov et al. (2020) [24]	LJS speech, CSS10 database	Gaussian LPCNet technique	Enhanced time duration and memory efficiency of speech	Unsuitable for audio signals with frequency greater than 16 kHz

(continued)

Table 1. (*continued*)

Author's name and year	Databases	Techniques employed	Merits	Demerits
Zhou et al. (2020) [25]	SC09 for testing WaveGAN, normal voice commands and one train voice	Mel-Generative Adversarial Network (GAN)	Improves human–computer interaction system	Decreased audio naturalness
Kaliyev et al. (2021) [26]	50 sentences of Kazakh language	Couple-Agent Acoustic Generative Adversarial Network (CAAG-GAN)	Enhance the audio fidelity and naturalness	Prosodic features were not analyzed
Inoue et al. (2021) [27]	Emotional speech database with joy, sad and neutral	Deep neural network (DNN)	Gains accuracy of speech signal	Didn't consider emotional speech
Imene Zangari et al. (2021) [28]	Medium sized Arabic letters with 450 sentences	Deep neural network (DNN)	Handle different Arabic sound classes and fits the phone duration into pheromone classes	Difficult for processing large vowels
Lorenzo et al. (2017) [29]	Self-recorded three types of database: happy-sad, calm-insecure and excited-angry	Deep neural network (DNN)	Improved modeling efficiency and closeness of natural speech	Did not capture the expressive speech signals
V. Ramu Reddy (2016) et al. [30]	Bengali (10 h)	feedforward neural networks (FNNN)	prediction accuracy high and flexibility	Loss naturalness
Maeno et al. (2014) [31]	Japanese appealing and fairy tale speech	Hidden Markov Model (HMM)	Enhanced naturalness of synthesized speech	Time duration and power context was not considered

(*continued*)

Table 1. (*continued*)

Author's name and year	Databases	Techniques employed	Merits	Demerits
Houidhek et al. (2018) [32]	Arabic corps with 1806 utterances	Hidden Markov Model (HMM)	Identification fully-fledged phonemes was not necessary	Depletes the quality of signal
Yan-You Chen (2016) et al. [33]	Mandarin corpus with 5406 utterances	Hidden Markov Model (HMM)	improved quality and naturalness	Less prediction accuracy
R. Karhila et al. (2014) [34]	EMIME Finnish with 145 utterances with Noise	Hidden Markov Model (HMM)	Noise removed effectively and flexible	speech parameters excessively smoothed
He et al. (2021) [35]	43 Spoken languages such as English, German, telugu etc	Multi lingual Bype2speech model	Enhanced performance of low resource adaptation	Low few-shot performance
Yang et al. (2021) [36]	German, Chinese, Japanese and Dutch language datasets	Multi lingual TTS system	Improved quality of synthesis	Naturalness of synthesis gets affected
de Korte et al. (2020) [37]	14 foreign languages	Neural Multilingual speech synthesis	Increased the naturalness of low resource speech	Naturalness of target language gets affected when it combined with auxiliary non-target language data

The comparison analysis of speech synthesis for various languages employed in different machine learning techniques was illustrated above with their respective merits and demerits. The methods employed are support vector machine, Artificial Neural Network, Gaussian mixture modeling, Generative adversarial network, deep neural network, Hidden Markov Model to improve the audio signals by neglecting the unwanted noises thereby increasing the quality and fidelity of audio. In future work, the drawbacks such as poor linguistic resources, high computational cost, lack of specified expression consideration, quality improvement, excessive time duration, and signal quality depletion can be rectified using novel approaches designed for the particular domain.

4   Conclusion

Over the last few decades, the speech synthesis is in progress and gradually many research scholars have been carried out several researches based on numerous speech synthesis techniques. This review paper presented an overview to the latest ongoing advances based on current trends and past progress of speech synthesis. Here, diverse methods namely support vector machine, Artificial Neural Network, Gaussian mixture modeling, Generative adversarial network, deep neural network and Hidden Markov Model are employed to enhance the audio signals by neglecting the unwanted noises and to increase the quality of audio. In addition to this, the merits and demerits of diverse approaches are discussed to enhance the performance of speech synthesis in the future.

References

1. Kumari, R., Dev, A., Kumar, A.: Automatic segmentation of hindi speech into syllable-like units. Int. J. Adv. Comput. Sci. Appl. **11**(6), 400–406 (2020)
2. Kumari, R., Dev, A., Kumar, A.: Development of syllable dominated Hindi speech corpora. Int. Conf. Artif. Intell. Speech Technol. (AIST2019) **8**(3), 1–9 (2019)
3. Macchi, M.: Issues in text-to-speech synthesis. In: Proceedings of the IEEE International Joint Symposia on Intelligence and Systems (Cat. No. 98EX174), pp. 318–325 (1998)
4. Baby, A., Prakash, J.J., Subramanian, A.S., Murthy, H.A.: Significance of spectral cues in automatic speech segmentation for Indian language speech synthesizers. Speech Commun. **123**, 10–25 (2020)
5. Kumari, R., Dev, A., Bayana, A., Kumar, A.: Machine learning techniques in speech generation: a review. J. Adv. Res. Dyn. Control Syst. **9**, 1095–1110 (2019)
6. Balyan, A.: An overview on resources for development of Hindi speech synthesis system. New Ideas Concerning Sci. Technol. **11**, 57–63 (2021)
7. Bhatt, S., Jain, A., Dev, A.: Syllable based Hindi speech recognition. J. Inf. Optim. Sci. **41**, 1333–1351 (2020)
8. Ramteke, G.D., Ramteke, R.J.: Efficient model for numerical text-to-speech synthesis system in Marathi, Hindi and English languages. Int. J. Image Graphics Sig. Process. **9**(3), 1–13 (2017)
9. Begum, A., Askari, S.M.: Text-to-speech synthesis system for mymensinghiya dialect of Bangla language. In: Panigrahi, C.R., Pujari, A.K., Misra, S., Pati, B., Li, K.-C. (eds.) Progress in Advanced Computing and Intelligent Engineering, pp. 291–303. Springer Singapore, Singapore (2019). https://doi.org/10.1007/978-981-13-0224-4_27
10. Rajendran, V., Kumar, G.B.: A Robust syllable centric pronunciation model for Tamil text to speech synthesizer. IETE J. Res. **65**(5), 601–612 (2019)
11. Ramteke, R.J., Ramteke, G.D.: Hindi spoken signals for speech synthesizer. In: 2016 2nd International Conference on Next Generation Computing Technologies (NGCT), pp. 323–328. IEEE (2016)
12. Balyan, A., Agrawal, S.S., Dev, A.: Speech synthesis: a review. Int. J. Eng. Res. Technol. (IJERT) **2**(6), 57–75 (2013)
13. Keletay, M.A., Worku, H.S.: Developing concatenative based text to speech synthesizer for Tigrigna. Internet Things Cloud Comput. **8**(6), 24–30 (2020)
14. Reddy, M.K., Rao, K.S.: Improved HMM-based mixed-language (Telugu–Hindi) polyglot speech synthesis. In: Advances in Communication, Signal Processing, VLSI, and Embedded Systems, pp. 279–287 (2020)

15. Panda, S.P., Nayak, A.K.: Automatic speech segmentation in syllable centric speech recognition system. Int. J. Speech Technol. **19**(1), 9–18 (2016)
16. Balyan, A., Agrawal, S.S., Dev, A.: Automatic phonetic segmentation of Hindi speech using hidden Markov model. AI Soc. **27**, 543–549 (2012)
17. Balyan, A., Dev, A., Kumari, R., Agrawal, S.S.: Labelling of Hindi speech. IETE J. Res. **62**, 146–153 (2016)
18. Balyan, A.: Resources for development of Hindi speech synthesis system: an overview. Open J. Appl. Sci. **7**(6), 233–241 (2017)
19. Jalin, A.F., Jayakumari, J.: A Robust Tamil text to speech synthesizer using support vector machine (SVM). In: Advances in Communication Systems and Networks, pp. 809–819. Springer, Singapore (2020)
20. Kinoshita, Y., Hirakawa, R., Kawano, H., Nakashi, K., Nakatoh, Y.: Speech enhancement system using SVM for train announcement. In: 2021 IEEE International Conference on Consumer Electronics (ICCE), pp. 1–3 (2021)
21. Kumari, R., Dev, A., Kumar, A.: An efficient adaptive artificial neural network based text to speech synthesizer for Hindi language. Multimedia Tools Appl. **80**(2), 24669–24695 (2021)
22. Liu, R., Sisman, B., Li, H.: Graphspeech: syntax-aware graph attention network for neural speech synthesis. In: ICASSP 2021–2021 IEEE International Conference on Acoustics, Speech, and Signal Processing (ICASSP), pp. 6059–6063 (2021)
23. Ramani, B., Jeeva, M.A., Vijayalakshmi, P., Nagarajan, T.: A multi-level GMM-based cross-lingual voice conversion using language-specific mixture weights for polyglot synthesis. Circuits Syst. Sign. Process. **35**(4), 1283–1311 (2016)
24. Popov, V., Kudinov, M., Sadekova, T.: Gaussian LPCNet for multisample speech synthesis. In: CASSP 2020–2020 IEEE International Conference on Acoustics, Speech and Signal Processing (ICASSP), pp. 6204–6208 (2020)
25. Zhou, S., Jia, J., Zhang, L., Wang, Y., Chen, W., Meng, F., Yu, F., Shen, J.: Inferring emphasis for real voice data: an attentive multimodal neural network approach. In: Ro, Y.M., Cheng, W.-H., Kim, J., Chu, W.-T., Cui, P., Choi, J.-W., Hu, M.-C., De Neve, W. (eds.) MMM 2020. LNCS, vol. 11962, pp. 52–62. Springer, Cham (2020). https://doi.org/10.1007/978-3-030-37734-2_5
26. Kaliyev, A., Zeno, B., Rybin, S.V., Matveev, Y.N., Lyakso, E.: GAN acoustic model for Kazakh speech synthesis. Int. J. Speech Technol. **24**, 729–735 (2021)
27. Inoue, K., Hara, S., Abe, M., Hojo, N., Ijima, Y.: Model architectures to extrapolate emotional expressions in DNN-based text-to-speech. Speech Commun. **126**, 35–43 (2021)
28. Zangar, I., Mnasri, Z., Colotte, V., Jouvet, D.: Duration modelling and evaluation for Arabic statistical parametric speech synthesis. Multimedia Tools Appl. **80**(6), 8331–8353 (2021)
29. Lorenzo-Trueba, J., Henter, G.E., Takahashi, S., Yamagishi, J., Morino, Y., Ochiai, Y.: Investigating different representations for modeling multiple emotions in DNN-based speech synthesis. In: 3rd International Workshop on The Affective Social Multimedia Computing (2017)
30. Reddy, R., Sreenivasa, V., Rao, K.: Prosody modeling for syllable based text-to-speech synthesis using feedforward neural networks. Neurocomputing **171**, 1323–1334 (2016)
31. Maeno, Y., Nose, T., Kobayashi, T., Koriyama, T., Ijima, Y., Nakajima, H., Mizuno, H., Yoshioka, O.: Prosodic variation enhancement using unsupervised context labeling for HMM-based expressive speech synthesis. Speech Commun. **57**, 144–154 (2014)
32. Houidhek, A., Colotte, V., Mnasri, Z., Jouvet, D.: Evaluation of speech unit modelling for HMM-based speech synthesis for Arabic. Int. J. Speech Technol. **21**(4), 895–906 (2018)
33. Chen, C.-H., Wu, Y.C., Huang, S.-L., Lin, J.-F.: Candidate expansion and prosody adjustment for natural speech synthesis using a small corpus. IEEE/ACM Trans. Audio Speech Lang. Process. **24**(6), 1052–1065 (2016)

34. Karhila, R., Remes, U., Kurimo, M.: Noise in HMM-based speech synthesis adaptation: analysis, evaluation methods and experiments. IEEE J. Sel. Top. Sign. Process. **8**(5), 285–295 (2014)
35. He, M., Yang, J., He, L., Soong, F.K.: Multilingual Byte2Speech Models for Scalable Low-resource Speech Synthesis (2021). arXiv preprint arXiv:2103.03541
36. Yang, M., Ding, S., Chen, T., Wang, T., Wang, Z.: Towards Lifelong Learning of Multilingual Text-To-Speech Synthesis (2021). arXiv preprint arXiv:2110.04482
37. De Korte, M., Kim, J., Klabbers, E.: Efficient neural speech synthesis for low-resource languages through multilingual modelling (2020). arXiv preprint arXiv:2008.09659

Hindi Phoneme Recognition - A Review

Shobha Bhatt[1(⊠)], Amita Dev[2], and Anurag Jain[1]

[1] University School of Information and Communication Technology,
GGSIP University, New Delhi, India
anurag@ipu.ac.in
[2] Indira Gandhi Delhi Technical University for Women, New Delhi, India

Abstract. A review for Hindi phoneme recognition is presented to address Hindi speech recognition. Different issues related to Hindi phonemes such as Hindi speech characteristics, features used in phoneme recognition, and classification method highlighted. Related work was also presented to highlight issues concerned with feature extraction, classification, and distinct features. Earlier reviews mostly addressed speech recognition technologies. This work is an early research study presented for Hindi phoneme recognition. A phoneme-based system is used to overcome the constraint of the requirement of large training samples for word-based models. Phoneme-based systems are widely used for large vocabulary speech recognition, different issues related to consonants and vowels were also included. The comparative analysis is presented for different feature extraction and classification techniques with a recognition score. The research helps by presenting issues related to phoneme recognition.

Keywords: Review · Hindi · Phoneme · Features · Consonants · Vowels

1 Introduction

Speech recognition is the conversion of spoken words into text so that the machine can understand natural voice input to take further action based on the input. Different sub-word models are used in speech recognition to overcome the constraint of large training sample requirements of word-based models. A phoneme-based system is mostly used to overcome the constraint of word-based models due to large training data requirements [1]. Phoneme recognition is one of the fundamental issues in speech recognition. A phoneme is a basic unit for spoken language. The limited number of phonemes can be combined to generate all possible words in a language. Further, due to fewer phonemes, different rules and procedures can be applied for phonemes. Phoneme recognition technologies are applied in speech recognition, speaker identification, language identification, and speech synthesis also[2].

Figure 1 shows the process of speech recognition. The speech recognition systems based on phoneme obtain the highly probable phoneme series for given input speech features [3]. Researchers applied different feature extraction methods and classification methods to recognize the phonemes. Further phoneme recognition can be categorized based on vowel recognition and consonant recognition. The vowels are generated with

© Springer Nature Switzerland AG 2022
A. Dev et al. (Eds.): AIST 2021, CCIS 1546, pp. 36–46, 2022.
https://doi.org/10.1007/978-3-030-95711-7_4

an open vocal tract at any point above the glottis. Three articulatory features are high, backness, and roundness. Researchers presented reviews on evolving theories of vowel recognition [4]. Consonants are an important part of any phoneme-based system. Consonants are articulated in the presence of constriction or closure at some point along the vocal tract. The categories of consonants on the basis of place of articulation are bilabial, alveolar, velar, postalveolar, labiodental, and retroflex. Consonants are further categorized on the manner of articulation and voicing. The plosive or stop, fricative, approximant, and closure are grouped under the manner of articulation. The voicing sounds indicate the presence of a voiced region [5]. The recognition of consonants is a challenging task in speech recognition due to their production methods. Researchers made efforts to recognize the consonants using different techniques in the literature.

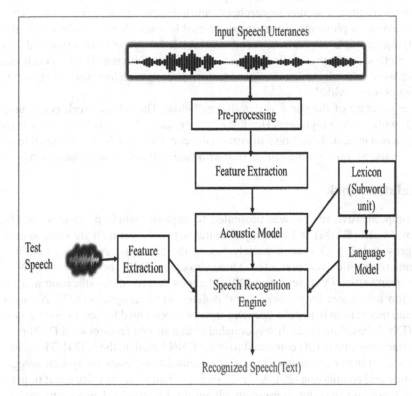

Fig. 1. Speech recognition block diagram

However, phoneme-based speech recognition faces contextual effects. The phonemes are categorized into vowels and consonants. The stop consonants are produced by obstruction of airflow and release. All the periods of stop consonants, such as during which the articulator moves, during which the articulator obstructs the airflow, and when articulators separate to release the air, are important and need to be addressed in the context of speech recognition. Further, recognizing semivowels is also challenging due to acoustically similar characteristics to vowels [6]. Nasalization also causes difficulty in detection due to antiresonance. Researchers attempted to reduce the contextual effect by using context-dependent triphones [7–9]. Researchers also used longer acoustic units to overcome the contextual effects [10].

Hindi speech recognition systems are discussed in the literature using various feature extraction techniques [2, 11–13]. Different researchers also presented phoneme recognition in Hindi to explore different categories of phonemes such as vowels and consonants. Researchers [2, 14–20] worked for phoneme recognition to find out different issues such as recognition for vowel, consonants, stop consonants, structural analysis, phoneme aspiration detection, retroflex effect, and dental using different feature extraction techniques and classification methods.

Earlier reviews presented for Hindi speech recognition are related to overall speech recognition. The research review in this paper presents different issues related to Hindi phoneme recognition so that researchers can understand underlying issues. The presented review on phoneme recognition will enable researchers to understand different underlying concepts of phoneme recognition related to feature extraction and classification methods to improve Hindi speech recognition. Different Hindi speech characteristics were defined. Further details of feature extraction techniques and classification techniques are provided.

The structure of the paper is detailed as below. The related work is discussed in Sect. 2, while Sect. 3 highlights Hindi language issues. The feature extraction methods are explained in Sect. 4. Section 5 illustrates the classifier, and Sect. 6 is related to results and analysis. Section 7 is the last section with future direction and conclusion.

2   Related Work

The comprehensive review was presented to explore Bangla phonemes for Hidden Markov Model (HMM) and multilayer neural network over a single layer neural network provided [21]. Comparative analysis was also presented. A review of the study of phoneme recognition was presented. Three classifiers HMM, neural network (NN) and vector quantization (VQ) reviewed [22]. Methods described classification and feature extraction techniques for phonemes and isolated word recognition [23]. A survey for phoneme recognition in popular speech corpus was presented for recent deep neural network (DNN) based methods. It was concluded that simple feed-forward DNN provides less phone error rate (PER) compared to other DNN based methods [24]. The study was conducted on important characteristics of pronunciation issues for speech recognition evaluation and comparison [25]. A survey on cross-language for voice onset time (VOT) was addressed for two-stop consonants /d/ and /t/. Finally, VOT was compared for the investigated languages to explore the differences for these stop consonants [26]. A survey was presented for phoneme recognition by the classifier support vector machine (SVM) [27]. A study was presented by using recurrent neural networks (RNNs). It was concluded that RNNs improved speech recognition [28]. A review was presented for landmarks detection such as VOT and burst release to detect stop consonants. It was stated that stop consonants are difficult to recognize due to low energy values, high variabilities, and random behavior [29]. Discriminative phonetic features (DPF) such as the way of phoneme representation were reviewed. It was concluded that Arabic is a Semitic language and needs more research related to DPF. Monophone and hybrid subword units were used in creating a speech recognition system [30]. The domain-based syntactic structures were also applied to improve speech recognition by reducing the search space during the recognition process. It was observed that maximum word accuracy of 88.54% was achieved with PLP with energy coefficients and a hybrid model. Research findings reveal that substitution errors mostly occurred. Hindi vowel recognition was explored in [2]. The speech recognition framework was implemented using MFCCs with five states of HMM-based modeling. The vowels were subgrouped into the front, back, and middle vowels. The average recognition score of 83.19% was recorded. The results show that accurate prediction of the consonant score was obtained for a broad range of signal-to-noise ratios. The researchers also presented a study to show how vowels and consonants shape the recognition process. It was demonstrated that lexical processing is more strongly connected to consonants in comparison to vowel processing. Acoustically vowels are continuous and long, while consonants are transitory in nature [31]. An extensive study on Hindi phoneme confusion analysis was presented by the researchers [32]. Experiments were carried out using HMM and PLP coefficients on Hindi continuous speech utterances. The results were reported for both consonants and vowels. The vowels attained 70% recognition accuracy. The palatal phonemes achieved the maximum recognition score of 94%.

3 Hindi Language

Hindi alphabets are properly defined [33]. Alphabets in the Hindi language are divided into consonants and vowels. Hindi has about fifty-eight phonemic letters, which include ten vowels, thirty-seven consonants, and an additional five nuktas taken from Farsi/Arabic [34]. Some of the dominant features in the Hindi language are aspiration, gemination, nasalization, and retroflexive [14, 35]. The sounds are voiced and unvoiced in the Hindi language. Hindi vowels are divided into short and long vowels. Table 1 shows the Hindi vowel acoustic classification. Table 2 presents Hindi consonants with IPA symbols [36]. Table 3 presents Hindi semivowels and fricatives with IPA symbols [37].

Table 1. Hindi vowel acoustic classification

Front		Middle		Back	
Hindi vowels	IPA	Hindi Vowels	IPA	Hindi Vowels	IPA
इ	ɪ	अ	ɑ	उ	ʊ
ई	i:	आ	ɑ:	ऊ	u:
ए	e:			ओ	o:
ऐ	ɛ:			औ	ɔ:

Table 2. Hindi consonants

Hindi Consonants	IPA	Label used	Hindi Consonants	IPA	Label
क	K	k	ञ	ɲ	nj
ख	kʰ	kh	ट	ʈ	t:
ग	G	g	ठ	ʈʰ	t:h
घ	gʰ	gh	ड	ɖ	d:
ङ	ŋ	ng	ढ	ɖʰ	d:h
च	tʃ	c	ण	ɳ	n:
छ	tʃʰ	ch	त	t̪	t
ज	dʒ	j	थ	t̪ʰ	th
झ	dʒʰ	jh	द	d̪	d
ध	d̪ʰ	dh	ब	b	b
न	n	n	भ	bʰ	bh
प	p	p	म	m	m
फ	pʰ	ph			

Table 3. Hindi semivowels and fricatives

Hindi semivowel	IPA	Label	Hindi fricatives	IPA
य	j	y	श	ʃ
र	r	r	ष	ʂ
ल	l	l	स	s
व	ʋ	v	ह	h

4 Feature Extraction Methods

The vowel recognition was presented using Mel Frequency cepstral coefficients (MFCCs) in [2]. Hindi consonants were classified using EMG-based sub-vocal features in [38] and Linear prediction coefficients [17]. For the recognition of Hindi, phoneme features used are wavelet sub-band based temporal features in [19] and MFCCs in [14]. Researcher work was also presented to develop a phoneme-based system for the Hindi language by using MFCCs, PLPs, and LPCs with their variants [39]. The results show that PLPs and MFCCs performed better than LPCs. The work was also presented using hybrid subword units using PLPs to improve phoneme-based speech recognition [30].

5 Classification Methods

For classification in speech recognition, two models, generative and discriminative, are generally used. The generative models learn from the joint probability distribution of the observed acoustic features and respective speech labels using Bayes rules. In contrast, discriminative training is used to optimize the model parameter [40]. The HMM is simple in design and practical in use for representing variability in speech. However, HMMs are not efficient when modeling nonlinear functions. In contrary to HMM, the ANNs allow discriminative training efficiently. Other research work also presented deep neural networks (DNNs) for improving speech recognition [41]. Several different methods, such as Gaussinization and based on discriminative training, were experimented [42]. Sequence to sequence acoustic modeling proposed for speech recognition [43]. Researchers applied different classification methods for speech recognition based on HMMs. Artificial neural network (ANNs) based classification was applied in [14]. Other works reported Gaussian Mixture Modeling (GMM) for vowel recognition [44]. For recognition of Hindi consonants, vector quantization was used in [17]. The researchers also used context-dependent HMM (CDHMM) for vowel classification [45]. Different matrices have been applied by the researchers to evaluate phoneme recognition. The matrices, such as phoneme error rate (PER), phoneme accuracy, and phoneme correctness, were applied by most of the developers. The phoneme accuracy and phoneme error rate (PER) were used by most of the researchers. The phoneme accuracy and PER are defined is as given below [5, 46, 47]. Hindi phonemes were characterized using time-delay neural networks (TDNNs) [48]. The queries related to Indian railways consisting of 207 Hindi vocabulary words were used in the experiment. Features used in the study were the MFCCs and cepstral mean normalization using the frame. Different TDDNs were trained and tested for Hindi phoneme categorization. Studies also presented to predict consonant recognition and confusion in background noise by using microscopic speech recognition [49].

6 Results and Analysis

The results indicate that researchers worked for the recognition of Hindi phonemes, consonants, and vowels. Most of the works are reported for vowel recognition. Some research findings indicate results for a small group of phonemes. The results were reported for different categories of phonemes. Researchers used different speech recognition systems. Phoneme recognition was also reported for different environmental conditions. The works were reported for a clean and noisy environment.

MFCCs, LPCs, and wavelet-based methods were applied. Feature extraction techniques based on wavelet sub-band and the combination of wavelet cepstral features with harmonic energy features improved speech recognition. The idea was presented that stops in speech signals are most difficult due to short-duration frequency bursts. Research work also presented different segmentation techniques. The researchers also experimented with subvocal speech recognition based on electromyography signal (EMG). Research also applied Gammatone frequency cepstral coefficients (GFCCs). The following Table 4 shows the list of features used in different research works. The comparative analysis was made based on extracted features, classification methods, phonemes types, and accuracy.

Table 4. Phoneme recognition comparative analysis

S.no	Reference	Features used	Classification method	Recognition	Accuracy
1	[48]	MFCCs	Time delay neural network (TDNN)	Hindi phoneme	Vowel: 99% Unvoiced stops: 87% Voiced stops: 82% Semivowel: 94.7% Fricatives: 96.4% Nasals: 98.1%
2	[2]	MFCCs	HMM	Hindi vowel	Vowel: 83.19%
3	[44]	MFCCs	GMM	Hindi vowel	Microphone recorded speech: 91.4% Telephonic speech: 84.2%
4	[45]	Gammatone frequency cepstral coefficients and formant	CDHMM	Hindi vowel	Speaker dependent: 99.15% Speaker independent: 98.5%
5	[38]	EMG based sub vocal features	HMM	Hindi alphabets	/Ka/: 75% /kha/: 78.05% /Ga/: 80.5% /Gha/: 81.3%

(continued)

Table 4. (*continued*)

S.no	Reference	Features used	Classification method	Recognition	Accuracy
7	[50]	Quantile-based dynamic cepstral normalization MFCC (QCN-MFCC)	HMM	Hindi vowel	Context dependent: MFCC: 89.7% QCN-MFCC: 92.7% Context Independent: MFCC: 87.6% QCN-MFCC: 92.7

Research findings reveal that researchers applied different classification methods. The classification methods used are HMM-based, ANN-based, GMM based, and using vector quantization. Different methods, such as based on backpropagation and time-delay neural network, were applied. Recognition results were presented using accuracy. It was also observed that vowel recognition was mostly explored.

7 Conclusion

A review of Hindi phoneme recognition is presented to understand the issues related to Hindi speech recognition. Different issues related to Hindi phonemes such as Hindi speech characteristics, features used in phoneme recognition, and classification with related work described. The classifiers based on HMM, ANN, GMM, and VQ were experimented. Feature extraction methods improved phoneme recognition. Researchers also worked on subcategories such as vowels and consonants in addition to phonemes. The research work on Hindi speech recognition was also presented using the deep learning method. Researchers also presented studies for phoneme confusion analysis to understand and improve speech recognition. It was also revealed that substitution errors have mostly occurred. Further research may include more studies exploring Hindi phonology and applying hybrid feature extraction methods and classification methods. The outcome of the study consists of that researchers worked mainly on the recognition of the vowels. Further research work may include more studies related to Hindi phonology.

Acknowledgements. The authors would like to acknowledge the Ministry of Electronics & Information Technology (MeitY), Government of India, for providing financial assistance for this research work through "Visvesvaraya Ph.D. Scheme for Electronics & IT".

References

1. Bhatt, S., Jain, A., Dev, A.: Acoustic modeling in speech recognition: a systematic review. IJACSA Int. J. Adv. Comput. Sci. Appl. **11**, 397–412 (2020)

2. Bhatt, S., Dev, A., Jain, A.: Hindi speech vowel recognition using hidden markov model. In: The 6th International Workshop on Spoken Language Technologies for Under-Resourced Languages, pp. 196–199 (2018)
3. Lopes, C., Perdigao, F.: Phoneme recognition on the TIMIT database. Speech Technol. (2011). https://doi.org/10.5772/17600
4. Strange, W.: Evolving theories of vowel perception. J. Acoust. Soc. Am. **85**, 2081–2087 (1989). https://doi.org/10.1121/1.397860
5. Vasquez, D., Gruhn, R., Minker, W.: Hierarchical Neural Network Structures for Phoneme Recognition. Springer, Berlin (2013). https://doi.org/10.1007/978-3-642-34425-1
6. Espy-Wilson, C.Y.: A feature-based semivowel recognition system. J. Acoust. Soc. Am. **96**, 65–72 (1994). https://doi.org/10.1121/1.410375
7. Bhatt, S., Jain, A., Dev, A.: CICD acoustic modeling based on monophone and triphone for HINDI speech recognition. In: International Conference on Artificial Intelligence and Speech Technology (AIST2019), 14–15th Nov (2019)
8. Mikolov, T., Zweig, G.: Context dependent recurrent neural network language model. In: 2012 IEEE Work Spoken Language *Technology* SLT 2012 – Proceeding, pp. 234–239 (2012). https://doi.org/10.1109/SLT.2012.6424228
9. Tüske, Z., Sundermeyer, M., Schlüter, R., Ney, H.: Context-dependent MLPs for LVCSR: TANDEM, hybrid or both? In: 13th Annual Conference of the International Speech Communication Association 2012, INTERSPEECH 2012, vol. 1, pp. 8–21 (2012)
10. Ganapathiraju, A., et al.: Syllable - a promising recognition unit for LVCSR. In: IEEE Workshop on Automatic Speech Recognition and Understanding Proceeding, pp. 207–214 (1997). https://doi.org/10.1109/asru.1997.659007
11. Kumar, K., Aggarwal, R.K., Jain, A.: A Hindi speech recognition system for connected words using HTK. Int. J. Comput. Syst. Eng. **1**, 25 (2012). https://doi.org/10.1504/ijcsyse.2012.044740
12. Sinha, S., Agrawal, S.S., Jain, A.: Continuous density Hidden Markov Model for context dependent Hindi speech recognition. In: International Conference on Advances in Computing, Communications and Informatics, pp. 1953–1958 (2013). https://doi.org/10.1109/ICACCI.2013.6637481
13. Pruthi, T., Saksena, S., Das, P.K.: Swaranjali: isolated word recognition for Hindi language using VQ and HMM. Int. Conf. Multimed. Process. Syst. **1**, 13–15 (2000)
14. Dev, A.: Effect of retroflex sounds on the recognition of Hindi voiced and unvoiced stops. AI Soc. **23**, 603–612 (2009). https://doi.org/10.1007/s00146-008-0179-9
15. Sharma, R.P., Khan, I., Farooq, O.: Acoustic study of Hindi unaspirated stop consonants in consonant-vowel (CV) context. Int. J. Eng. Tech. Res. **1**, 5–9 (2014)
16. Patil, V.V., Rao, P.: Detection of phonemic aspiration for spoken Hindi pronunciation evaluation. J. Phon. **54**, 202–221 (2016). https://doi.org/10.1016/j.wocn.2015.11.001
17. Das, P.K., Agrawal, S.S.: Machine recognition of Hindi consonants and distinctive features using vector quantization. J. Acoust. Soc. Am. **103**, 2779–2779 (1998). https://doi.org/10.1121/1.422255
18. Mishra, A.: Interlaced Derivation for HINDI phoneme- Viseme recognition from continuous speech. Int. J. Recent Res. Aspects **4**, 172–176 (2017)
19. Farooq, O., Datta, S., Shrotriya, M.C.: Wavelet sub-band based temporal features for robust hindi phoneme recognition. Int. J. Wavelets Multiresolut. Inf. Process. **8**, 847–859 (2010). https://doi.org/10.1142/S0219691310003845
20. Khan, M., Jahan, M.: Classification of myoelectric signal for sub-vocal Hindi phoneme speech recognition. J. Intell. Fuzzy Syst. **35**, 5585–5592 (2018). https://doi.org/10.3233/JIFS-161067
21. Tasnim Swarna, S., Ehsan, S., Islam, S., Jannat, M.E.: A comprehensive survey on bengali phoneme recognition. In: Proceedings of the International Conference on Engineering Research, Innovation and Education 2017 ICERIE 2017, pp. 1–7 (2017)

22. Kshirsagar, A., Dighe, A., Nagar, K., Patidar, M.: Comparative study of phoneme recognition techniques. In: Proceeding of 2012 3rd *International Conference* on *Computer* and *Communication Technologies* ICCCT 2012, pp. 98–103 (2012). https://doi.org/10.1109/ICCCT.2012.28

23. Yusnita, M.A., Paulraj, M.P., Yaacob, S., Abu Bakar, S., Saidatul, A., Abdullah, A.N.: Phoneme-based or isolated-word modeling speech recognition system? An overview. In: *Proceedings - 2011 IEEE 7th International Colloquium* on *Signal Processing* and *Its Applications*, CSPA 2011, pp. 304–309 (2011). https://doi.org/10.1109/CSPA.2011.5759892

24. Michálek, J., Vaněk, J.: A survey of recent DNN architectures on the TIMIT phone recognition task. In: Sojka, P., Horák, A., Kopeček, I., Pala, K. (eds.) Text, Speech, and Dialogue. TSD 2018. Lecture Notes in Computer Science, vol 11107. Springer, Cham (2018). https://doi.org/10.1007/978-3-030-00794-2_47

25. Strik, H., Cucchiarini, C.: Modeling pronunciation variation for ASR: a survey of the literature. Speech Commun. **29**, 225–246 (1999). https://doi.org/10.1016/S0167-6393(99)00038-2

26. AlDahri, S.S., Alotaibi, Y.A.: A crosslanguage survey of VOT values for stops (/d/, /t/). In: Proceeding - 2010 IEEE International Conference on Intelligent Computing and Intelligent Systems, ICIS 2010, vol. 3, pp. 334–338 (2010). https://doi.org/10.1109/ICICISYS.2010.5658744

27. Fathima Nazarath, P.A.: Survey on phoneme recognition using support vector machine. In: National Conference on Emerging Research Trend in Electrical and Electronics Engineering (ERTE 19), pp. 187–192 (2019)

28. Koizumi, T., Mori, M., Taniguchi, S., Maruya, M.: Recurrent neural networks for phoneme recognition. In: International Conference *Spoken language processing,* ICSLP, Proceeding, vol. 1, pp. 326–329 (1996). https://doi.org/10.1109/icslp.1996.607119

29. Nirmala, S.R., Upashana, G.: Advances in computational research a review on landmark detection methodologies of stop consonants. Adv. Comput. Res. **8**, 316–320 (2017)

30. Bhatt, S., Jain, A., Dev, A.: Monophone-based connected word Hindi speech recognition improvement. Sādhanā **46**, 1–17 (2021). https://doi.org/10.1007/S12046-021-01614-3

31. Nazzi, T., Cutler, A.: How consonants and vowels shape spoken-language recognition. Annu. Rev. Linguistics **5**, 25–47 (2018). https://doi.org/10.1146/annurev-linguistics

32. Bhatt, S., Dev, A., Jain, A.: Confusion analysis in phoneme based speech recognition in Hindi. J. Ambient Intell. Humaniz. Comput. **11**, 4213–4238 (2020). https://doi.org/10.1007/s12652-020-01703-x

33. Bansal, P., Dev, A., Jain, S.B.: Optimum HMM combined with vector quantization for Hindi speech recognition. IETE J. Res. **54**, 239–243 (2008). https://doi.org/10.4103/0377-2063.44216

34. Aarti, B., Kopparapu, S.K.: Spoken Indian language identification: a review of features and databases. Sadhana - Acad. Proc. Eng. Sci. **43**, 1–14 (2018). https://doi.org/10.1007/s12046-018-0841-y

35. Malviya, S., Mishra, R., Tiwary, U.S.: Structural analysis of Hindi phonetics and a method for extraction of phonetically rich sentences from a very large Hindi text corpus. In: Conference of the Oriental Chapter of International Committee for Coordination and Standardization of Speech Databases and Assessment Techniques, O-COCOSDA 2016. pp. 188–193 (2017). https://doi.org/10.1109/ICSDA.2016.7919009

36. Sadhukhan, T., Bansal, S., Kumar, A.: Automatic identification of spoken language. IOSR J. Comput. Eng. **19**, 84–89 (2017). https://doi.org/10.9790/0661-1902058489

37. Kachru, Y.: Hindi. John Benjamins Publishing, London (2006)

38. Khan, M., Jahan, M.: Sub-vocal speech pattern recognition of Hindi alphabet with surface electromyography signal. Perspect. Sci. **8**, 558–560 (2016). https://doi.org/10.1016/j.pisc.2016.06.019

39. Bhatt, S., Jain, A., Dev, A.: Feature extraction techniques with analysis of confusing words for speech recognition in the Hindi language. Wirel. Pers. Commun. **118**, 3303–3333 (2021). https://doi.org/10.1007/S11277-021-08181-0
40. Gales, M.J.F., Watanabe, S., Fosler-Lussier, E.: Structured discriminative models for speech recognition: an overview. IEEE Sig. Process. Mag. **29**, 70–81 (2012). https://doi.org/10.1109/MSP.2012.2207140
41. Wason, R.: Deep learning: evolution and expansion. Cogn. Syst. Res. **52**, 701–708 (2018). https://doi.org/10.1016/j.cogsys.2018.08.023
42. Liu, X., Gales, M.J.F., Sim, K.C., Yu, K.: Investigation of acoustic modeling techniques for LVCSR systems. In: ICASSP, *IEEE International Conference* on *Acoustics, Speech* and *Signal Processing I* (2005). https://doi.org/10.1109/ICASSP.2005.1415247
43. Zhang, J.X., Ling, Z.H., Liu, L.J., Jiang, Y., Dai, L.R.: Sequence-to-sequence acoustic modeling for voice conversion. IEEE/ACM Trans. Audio Speech Lang. Process. **27**, 631–644 (2019). https://doi.org/10.1109/TASLP.2019.2892235
44. Koolagudi, S.G., Thakur, S.N., Barthwal, A., Singh, M.K., Rawat, R., Sreenivasa Rao, K.: Vowel recognition from telephonic speech using MFCCs and Gaussian mixture models. In: Communications in Computer and Information Science, pp. 170–177 (2012). https://doi.org/10.1007/978-3-642-32112-2_21
45. Biswas, A., Sahu, P.K., Bhowmick, A., Chandra, M.: Hindi vowel classification using GFCC and formant analysis in sensor mismatch condition. WSEAS Trans. Syst. **13**, 130–143 (2014)
46. Moses, D.A., Mesgarani, N., Leonard, M.K., Chang, E.F.: Neural speech recognition: continuous phoneme decoding using spatiotemporal representations of human cortical activity. J. Neural Eng. **13**, 056004 (2016). https://doi.org/10.1088/1741-2560/13/5/056004
47. Gales, M., Young, S.: The application of hidden Markov models in speech recognition. Found. Trends Sig. Process. **1**, 195–304 (2007). https://doi.org/10.1561/2000000004
48. Dev, A., Agrawal, S.S., Choudhury, D.R.: Categorization of Hindi phonemes by neural networks. AI Soc. **17**, 375–382 (2003). https://doi.org/10.1007/s00146-003-0263-0
49. Zaar, J., Dau, T.: Predicting consonant recognition and confusions in normal-hearing listeners. J. Acoust. Soc. Am. **141**, 1051–1064 (2017). https://doi.org/10.1121/1.4976054
50. Mishra, S., Bhowmick, A., Shrotriya, M.C.: Hindi vowel classification using QCN-MFCC features. Perspect. Sci. **8**, 28–31 (2016). https://doi.org/10.1016/j.pisc.2016.01.010

Comparison of Modelling ASR System with Different Features Extraction Methods Using Sequential Model

Aishwarya Suresh[✉], Anushka Jain, Kriti Mathur, and Pooja Gambhir

Indira Gandhi Delhi Technical University for Women, Delhi, India
aishwarya100btit19@igdtuw.ac.in

Abstract. Speech recognition refers to a device's ability to respond to spoken instructions. Speech recognition facilitates hands-free use of various gadgets and appliances (a godsend for many incapacitated persons), as well as supplying input for automatic translation and ready-to-print dictation. Many industries, including healthcare, military telecommunications, and personal computing, use speech recognition programmes. In our paper, we are including the comparison between the different feature extraction methods (BFCC, GFCC, MFCC, MFCC Delta, MFCC Double Delta, LFCC and NGCC) using neural networks.

Keywords: Feature extraction method · Speech recognition · Neural network · FFT

1 Introduction

Speech recognition is a capability of computer software that allows it to turn human speech into text. In simple words, it means that when humans are speaking, a machine understands it. Speech recognition employs a wide range of computer science, linguistics, and computer engineering research. Speech recognition functions are included into many current gadgets and text-focused programmes to make using them easier or hands-free. Speech recognition, which is commonly mistaken with voice recognition, is concerned with converting speech from a verbal to a text format in a spoken language, whereas the biometric technique of voice recognition focuses only on recognising the voice of a certain individual. Traditional methods of interfacing with a computer, such as textual input through a keyboard, are being replaced by speech recognition. A good system can either eliminate or reduce the need for traditional keyboard input. By analysing the audio, breaking it down into parts, digitising it into a computer-readable format, and matching it to the most appropriate text representation using an algorithm, a computer programme translates the sound acquired by a microphone into a textual language that computers and people can comprehend (Fig. 1).

The most common method for building a speech recognition system is to create a generative model of language. Using language models, we create a certain sequence of words. Then, for each word, there's a pronunciation model that describes how to

© Springer Nature Switzerland AG 2022
A. Dev et al. (Eds.): AIST 2021, CCIS 1546, pp. 47–61, 2022.
https://doi.org/10.1007/978-3-030-95711-7_5

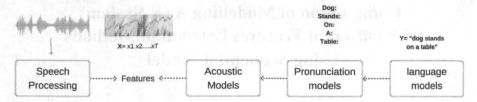

Fig. 1. A simple speech recognition model

pronounce the term. It's usually defined as a series of phonemes — basic sound units — but for the sake of our language, we'll just call it a series of tokens — which represent a collection of objects. The pronunciation models are then fed into an acoustic model, which determines the sound of a token. The data is currently described using these acoustic models. The data is x, which is a sequence of audio feature frames spanning from ×1 to xT in this case. Professionals in signal processing are usually the ones that decide on these characteristics (such as the frequency components of the audio waveforms that are captured).

Speech recognition software should adjust to the widely changeable and context-specific nature of human speech. Software algorithms that translate and organise audio into text are trained using a variety of speech patterns, speaking styles, languages, dialects, accents, and phrasings. The software distinguishes speech audio from the often-present background clatter. Speech recognition systems use two types of models to achieve these requirements: acoustic models and linguistic models. We used the acoustic model in our paper. Speech recognition software employs natural language processing (NLP) and deep learning neural networks. We employed convolutional neural networks, which are a sort of deep learning neural network. The flexibility and forecasting capacity of deep neural networks, which have lately become more accessible, are an advantage of deep learning for voice recognition. Another major issue in voice recognition is latency; in order to translate in real time, the model must properly predict words without knowing the entire sentence. Because of the increased context, some deep learning models profit greatly from using the entire sentence. To reduce latency, integrate restricted context in the model structure by allowing the neural network to access a little amount of data after a given word. Despite its difficulty, speech recognition is always present in a variety of industries. It allows a large number of individuals to readily access whatever material they wish. Speech recognition is a burgeoning field with numerous applications. Speech recognition research will almost certainly continue, and important practical applications will emerge. Despite the fact that speech recognition is a flourishing field, accuracy is a big challenge in this sector. The most accurate machine conceivable is continually being developed through research and development.

Speech recognition is achieved using a convolutional neural network because human speech signals are significantly variable due to various speaker features, speaking styles, and other sounds. Convolutional neural networks are a type of deep neural network that conducts little preprocessing, or learning the filter before doing the classification. When fed a huge number of signals as input, CNNs, which can have one or more layers, can do a lot of things. The Convolutional Neural Network (CNN) uses a subset of the data rather than the entire signal because it is difficult for a computer system to evaluate the entire signal. CNN is a type of neural network in which the input variables are connected spatially. The Xuejiao Li and Zixuan Zhou speech recognition system, which uses Google's Tensorflow's Speech command dataset, shows how CNN improves speech recognition. The models employed were the vanilla single-layer Softmax model, Deep Neural Network, and convolutional neural network, with the convolutional neural network surpassing the other two. CNN outperformed DNN and vanilla in terms of precision value, with an 18.6% relative improvement over DNN and a 72.3% relative improvement over Vanilla. A basic 2-layer ConvLayer CNN network beats Vanilla and DNN, with 31.43% and 66.67% comparitive improvements in test accuracy and 82% and 94.6% in loss, respectively, over DNN and Vanilla.

HMM and GMM are two must-learn voice recognition technologies that existed before the Deep Learning (DL) era. There are now hybrid systems that mix HMM with Deep Learning, as well as systems that do not use HMM. We now have more design options. HMM, on the other hand, is still important for many generative models. A Markov chain contains all of a system's possible states as well as the probability of changing states. The next state of a first-order Markov chain is solely determined by the current state. We call it a Markov chain for simplicity's sake. For sequential tasks like speech recognition, recurrent neural networks (RNNs), particularly long short-term memory (LSTM) RNNs, are effective networks. Because of their excellent learning potential, deeper LSTM models perform well on large vocabulary continuous speech recognition. A deeper network, on the other hand, is more difficult to train. For deeper LSTM models, we present a training architecture that includes layer-wise training and exponential moving average approaches.

MFCC, MFCC Delta, MFCC Double Delta, GFCC, BFCC, and LFCC are the feature extraction methods employed in our paper. For a certain dataset, their performance is compared. In the field of speech processing, the Gammatone Frequency Cepstral Coefficients (GFCCs) are a relatively novel characteristic. The GFCCs work on the basis of an auditory peripheral model that is similar to the human cochlear filtering system. They are a set of Gammatone Filter banks for creating auditory features. A Cochleagram, which is a frequency-time representation of the signal, can be created using the Gammatone filterbank output. The Gammatone filters are designed to emulate the processes of the human auditory system. Windowing the signal, using the DCT, and selecting the log of the magnitude are all part of the GFCC feature extraction approach. LFCC is as robust as MFCC in babbling noise, but not in white noise. LFCC consistently outperforms MFCC in female trials. LFCC has the same qualities as MFCC except for the frequency scale. Linear filter banks provide excellent resolution in higher frequency bands. Linear Frequency Cepstral Coefficient (LFCC) is a feature extraction method. In LFCC, the method for extracting features is the same as in MFCC. LFCC extraction differs from MFCC extraction in that it employs a linear filter bank rather than a mel filter bank. It functions in the same way that the human auditory system does. The linear filter bank has improved resolution in the higher frequency band. To compute LFCC features, first transform a windowed signal with the Fast Fourier Transform (FFT), which converts each frame of N samples from time to frequency dominion. After the FFT block, the power coefficients are filtered using linear frequency filter banks. Signal disintegration with a filter bank is the foundation of the MFCC algorithm. Windowing the signal is part of the MFCC feature extraction approach, also known as Mel Frequency Cepstral Coefficient. On each frame, a window is bored to taper the signal to the frame limits. Hanning or Hamming windows are commonly utilised. DFT is then used to transform the magnitude spectrum of each windowed frame. The Mel spectrum is calculated using the log of the magnitude and a Mel scale to bend the frequencies after passing a Fourier transformed signal through a Mel-filter bank of band-pass filters. A Mel is a measuring unit obtained from the human ear's perceived frequency and modified using the inverse Discrete Cosine Transform. On the Mel frequency scale, the MFCC generates a discrete cosine transform (DCT) of a short-term energy's real logarithm. MFCC is used to identify airline reservations, phone numbers, and speech recognition systems for security reasons. Understanding the dynamics of the power spectrum, or the trajectories of MFCCs over time, is critical for improving speech recognition, which is why delta (differential) and delta-delta (acceleration) coefficients are used. FFTs (fast Fourier transforms) are simple methods for quickly performing the discrete Fourier transform (DFT) on the basis of a finite abelian group. They are among the most important algorithms in engineering and applied mathematics, as well as computer science, with Signal processing and one- and multidimensional systems theory applications.

2   Related Work

In [1], Zhang Wanli and Li Guoxin used Mel frequency cepstral coefficients (MFCC) for speaker recognition. They worked on a study of MFCC-based feature extraction for speaker recognition. MFCCs outperform hidden Markov model-based MFCCs. [2] Dev Amita Agrawal, S.S., "A Novel MFCCs Normalization Technique for Robust Hindi Speech Recognition" 17th International Congress on Acoustics (ICA) Rome September 2–7, 2001. Nagajyothi and P. Siddaiah worked on Speech Recognition Using Convolutional Neural Networks [3]. They investigated the performance of a CNN-based ASR that uses raw speech signals as input to large vocabulary challenges in this research. Their research on wideband signals revealed that the CNN-based system outperforms the traditional Neural Network Techniques-based system. They employed the primary activation function in the first convolutional layer to provide fragments in a 2-D matrix. In [4] Jui-Ting Huang et al. worked upon an analysis of sequential Conv2D layer for speech recognition. They presented a detailed examination of CNNs in this paper. They showed that by analysing the localised filters acquired in the convolutional layer, edge detectors in multiple orientations may be automatically taught. CNNs outperformed FCNNs in four areas: channel-mismatched training-test conditions, noise reliability, remote speech recognition, and small-footprint models, according to the researchers. In [5] Ossama Abdel-Hamid et al. worked on FFN for Speech Recognition. They demonstrated how to apply CNNs in a novel method for speech recognition in which the CNN structure directly accommodates specific sorts of speech variability in this study. Using this strategy, they demonstrated a performance improvement over normal DNNs with equal amounts of weight parameters, in comparison to the more ambiguous findings of convolving along the axis of time, as CNNs have sought to use speech in the past. (about 6–10% relative error reduction). They improved performance on two ASR tasks:

TIMIT phone perception and an enormous-terminology voice search test, using a variety of Conv2D layer parameters and design choices. They discovered that integrating energy information improves feedforward neural network's recognition accuracy significantly. In [6], Phani Bhusan S et al. worked on stuttered speech recognition using Convolutional Neural Networks. They extracted features using the MFCC approach. They examined the scalability of a SSR based on CNN that accepts the raw speech signal as input in the proposed method. They were able to achieve 92% accuracy with only 7% validation loss in the suggested technique using CNN. Taabish Gulzar et al. surveys a correlative analysis of LPCC, MFCC and BFCC as feature extraction techniques and classifier as ANN in [7]. For database purposes, they used Hindi isolated, paired, and hybrid words. The results of their study reveal that MFCC outperforms the traditional LPCC and BFCC approaches. Using the Speech command dataset provided by Google's Tensorflow, the Xuejiao Li and Zixuan Zhou speech recognition system shows an improvement in speech recognition using CNN in [8]. The models used were the vanilla single-layer Softmax model, DNN, and feed forward neural network, with the Conv-2D layer surpassing the other two by obtaining an accuracy of 95.1% for six labels. The work of Mariusz Kubanek et al. proposes a unique technique to speech recognition established on the exact time-domain coding and frequency properties in [9]. Their plan was to combine three convolution layers: classic time convolution, feedforward neural network convolution, and spectrum convolution. Their research found that using the correct sound coding and pictures, effective speech recognition for isolated words may be achieved. To reduce noise impacts and raise robustness against various forms of environmental disturbances, Mohamed Tamazin et al. upgraded the (PNCC) system by combining gammatone channel clarity with channel bias minimization in [10]. At low SNR, the proposed method considerably improves recognition accuracy (SNR). Furthermore, in terms of recognition rate, the suggested method beats the GFCC [11] and PNCC methods. [12] Dr. Amita Dev, Sweeta Bansal, "Emotional Hindi Speech: Feature Extraction and Classification" published in IEEE Explorer, Computing for Sustainable Global Development (INDIACom), 2015 2nd International Conference (989-9-3805–4415-1), page(s): 1865–1868, 11–13 March 2015. In many languages, the accuracy of the identification evaluation for speaker recognition remains a key challenge. So, Ankur Maurya et al. in [13], used Conv-2D layer–vector quantization (MFCC-VQ) and Conv-2D layer–Gaussian mixture model (MFCC-GMM) for text dependent and text independent phrases to develop speaker detection for Hindi voice samples. In terms of text dependent recognition accuracy, MFCC-GMM surpassed MFCC-VQ by a significant margin. In [14], Pooja Gambhir and Amita dev reviewed different frontend feature extraction methods and DNN feature vectors for identification of context independent speaker voice.

3 Experiment Conducted

In this research, a sample from Tensorflow's Speech Commands Dataset [15] was used to compare the suggested method's performance to that of state-of-the-art approaches. Thousands of people contributed 65,000 one-second long utterances comprising 30 small words. Twenty of the words are core terms, while the remaining ten are auxiliary words that could be used as tests for algorithms to determine whether or not a speech contains triggers. A variety of background noise audio recordings is included with the 30 words. It was bifurcated into three subsets. The training set consisted of 51,094 audio clips, validation set consisted of 6,798 audio clips and testing set consisted of 6,835 audio clips. All audio files have a 16 k sample rate which means they capture up to 8 k Hz sound frequency. The feature extraction methods used- MFCC, GFCC, BFCC, LFCC, NGCC.

The MFCC feature extraction technique or Mel Frequency Cepstral Coefficient includes windowing the signal. A window is bored on each frame to taper the signal to the frame boundaries. Typically, Hanning or Hamming windows are used. The magnitude spectrum of each windowed frame is then transformed using DFT. On passing Fourier transformed signal via a Mel-filter bank of band-pass filters, the Mel spectrum is calculated using the log of the magnitude and a Mel scale to bend the frequencies. A Mel is a unit of measurement derived from the perceived frequency of the human ear, then transformed using the inverse Discrete Cosine Transform. Finally MFCCs are calculated as (Fig. 2):-

$$c(n) = \sum_{M=0}^{M-1} \log_{10}(s(m)) \cos\left(\frac{\prod n(m-0.5)}{M}\right) \tag{1}$$

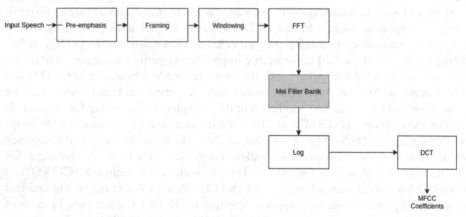

Fig. 2. A block representation of MFCC extraction

The cepstral coefficients are referred to as static features because they only carry information from a single frame. The 1st and 2nd derivatives of cepstral coefficients provide further information about the temporal dynamics of the signal. The first-order derivative is delta coefficients, while the second-order derivative is delta–delta coefficients. Delta coefficients represent the speech pace, while delta–delta coefficients represent the speech acceleration.

$$c(n) = \sum_{M=0}^{M-1} \log_{10}(s(m)) \cos\left(\frac{\prod n(m-0.5)}{M}\right) \tag{2}$$

LFCC feature extraction method is Linear Frequency Cepstral Coefficient. The approach for extracting features in LFCC is the same as in MFCC. The difference between MFCC and LFCC extraction is that the latter uses a linear filter bank rather than a Mel filter bank. It works in a similar way to the human auditory system. In the higher frequency band, the linear filter bank has more resolution. To compute LFCC features, first apply the Fast Fourier Transform (FFT) to a windowed signal, which turns each frame of N samples from time to frequency dominion. The power coefficients are filtered by linear frequency filter banks after the FFT block. Finally, utilizing the Discrete Cosine Transform, the log Mel spectrum is altered into time (DCT). The feature vector of LFCC uses 13 coefficients (Fig. 3).

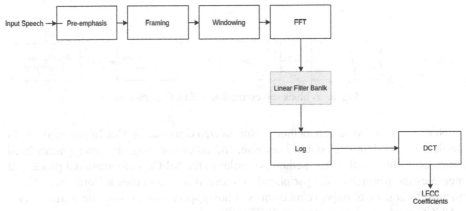

Fig. 3. A block representation of LFCC extraction

The Gammatone Frequency Cepstral Coefficients (GFCC) are a series of Gammatone Filter banks that are used to create auditory features. The Gammatone filterbank output can be used to create a Cochleagram, which is a frequency-time representation of the signal. The Gammatone filters are intended to mimic the human auditory system's processes. The GFCC feature extraction methodology primarily comprises windowing the signal, employing the DCT, picking the log of the magnitude. The below equation represents the GFCC extraction (Fig. 4)

$$g(n;\ u) = \left(\frac{2}{M}\right)^{0.5} \sum_{M=0}^{M-1} \left\{ \frac{1}{3} log\left(\underline{y}(n;\ i)\right) cos\left[\frac{\Pi u}{2M}(2i-1)\right] \right\} \tag{3}$$

The BFCC [16] extraction method is the Bark Filter Cepstral Coefficient method. To obtain the cepstral coefficients, the PLP processing of the spectra and the cosine transform are merged in the BFCC process. The Bark filter bank was employed instead of the Mel filter bank, and the MFCC-like features were given the same loudness pre-emphasis with an intensity to loudness power law. The implementation of BFCC is very similar to that of MFCC (Fig. 5).

$$f_{bark} = 6ln\left[\frac{f}{600} + \left[\left(\frac{f}{600}\right)^2 + 1\right]^{0.5}\right] \tag{4}$$

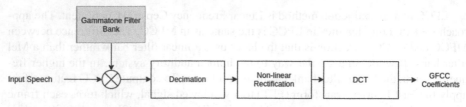

Fig. 4. A block representation of GFCC extraction

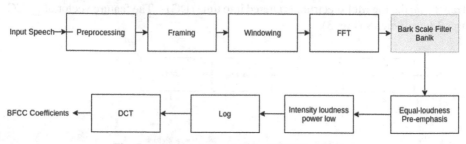

Fig. 5. A block representation of BFCC extraction

NGCC feature extraction method is Normalized Gammachip Coefficient method. To simulate the mechanism, NGCC uses a second order low-pass filter and a normalised gammachirp filterbank. This method is similar to the MFCC computational process. It integrates the features of the peripheral auditory system and uses a Normalized Gammachirp filter bank to improve robustness in noisy speech situations. The feature vector in NGCC used 13 coefficients as well (Fig. 6).

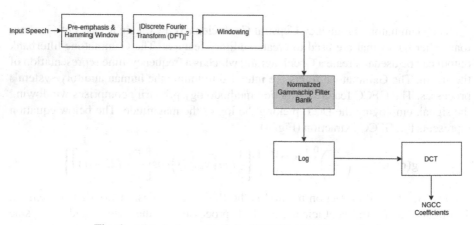

Fig. 6. A block representation of NGCC extraction method

To separate each syllable, 25.6 ms overlapping frames with 10 ms variations amongst frames were employed in the feature extraction method's design. A Hamming window was then applied to each frame. The FFT was then applied with a 256-bit resolution. For each approach, 13 features (cepstral coefficients) were collected in the final stage.

After applying CMN, Δ and $\Delta\Delta$ features were calculated' the total number of extracted features was 39 features. Despite the fact that higher order coefficients reflect increased spectral information, 12 to 20 cepstral coefficients are often appropriate for speech analysis, depending on the sampling rate and estimate method. The models become more complex when a high number of cepstral coefficients are chosen. For example, in order to effectively estimate the parameters of a Gaussian mixture model (GMM) to represent a speech signal with a large number of cepstral coefficients, we normally require more data.

A Sequential 2D Convolution Neural Network Model (2D CNN Model) was utilised to construct acoustic models for each type of feature extraction approach used. It comprises two completely linked layers and three 2D convolution layers, all with kernels of size 3 3. The number of channels in the first convolutional layer is assumed to be 30. The network is trained using a Soft max Loss function. Before being put to the test with both noise-free and loud utterances, all feature extraction algorithms were skilled on noise-free utterances (Fig. 7).

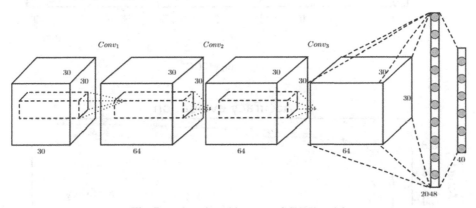

Fig. 7. Network architecture of CNN model

4 Results and Outcomes

The MFCC feature extraction method yielded the maximum accuracy; 88.20% for the sequential model, and the BFCC feature extraction method yielded the lowest accuracy; 68.65%. The best results are obtained with MFCC feature extraction, as shown in the following observations. This suggests that when training CNN models, MFCC is more efficient. With BFCC feature extraction, this is not the case. As a result, BFCC is shown to be the least accurate of all, making it less effective for training the sequential model (Fig. 8 and Table 1).

We can observe the rise and fall about this test validation performed on these features using CNN.

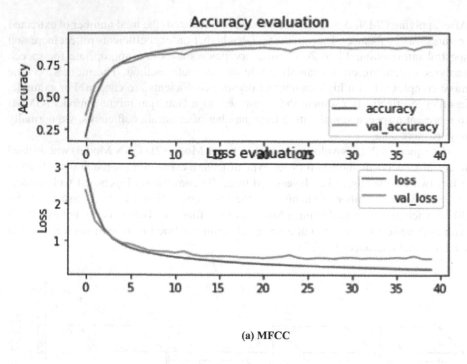

(a) MFCC

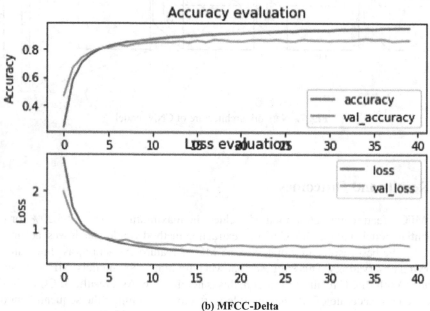

(b) MFCC-Delta

Fig. 8. Percentage accuracy and loss of each feature extraction method namely (a) MFCC, (b) MFCC-Delta, (c) MFCC Double Delta, (d) GFCC, (e) BFCC, (f) LFCC, (g) NGCC

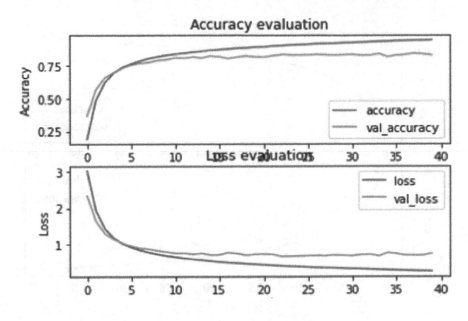

(c) MFCC-Double Delta

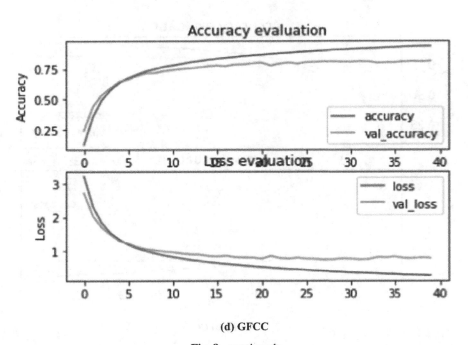

(d) GFCC

Fig. 8. continued

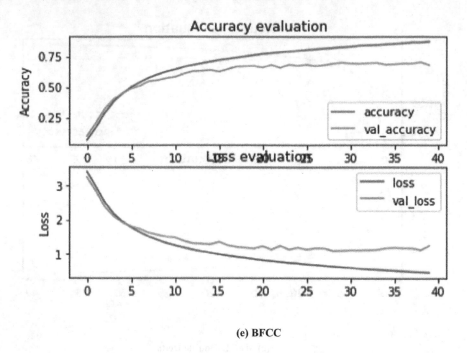

(e) BFCC

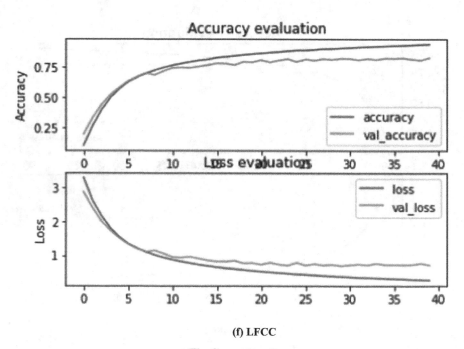

(f) LFCC

Fig. 8. continued

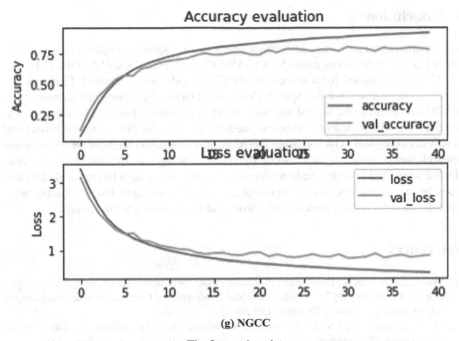

(g) NGCC

Fig. 8. continued

Table 1. Comparison between accuracy and loss of different feature extraction methods

Model	Feature extraction method	Test accuracy	Test loss
2D Sequential Convolution Neural Network Model	MFCC	88.20%	0.49
	MFCC-Delta	86.62%	0.57
	MFCC-Double Delta	83.01%	0.73
	GFCC	81.41%	0.77
	BFCC	68.65%	1.21
	LFCC	81.66%	0.73
	NGCC	78.11%	0.84

5 Conclusion

In this paper, a comparison of performance of automatic speech recognition between different feature extraction methods; MFCC, MFCC-$\triangle$, MFCC-Double$\triangle$, GFCC, BFCC, LFCC, NGCC trained for a sequential 2D CNN model was presented. Experimental results were acquired for the Speech Command Dataset by TensorFlow consisting of 65,000 wav files of one-second utterance of 30 short words. The highest accuracy was achieved for MFCC feature extraction method; 88.20% for the sequential model and lowest accuracy was achieved using BFCC feature extraction method; 68.65%. Future research would include a variety of modifications, testing, and experiments. For example, the suggested system's performance can be evaluated using a larger vocabulary and many language datasets. Noisier scenarios must also be evaluated, like resounding noise effects, colourful noises, background music, and mixtures of external noises.

References

1. Wanli, Z., Guoxin, L.: The research of feature extraction based on MFCC for speaker recognition. In: Proceedings of 2013 3rd International Conference on Computer Science and Network Technology, pp. 1074–1077. IEEE (Oct 2013)
2. Dev Amita Agrawal, S.S.: A Novel MFCCs Normalization Technique for Robust Hindi Speech Recognition 17th International Congress on Acoustics (ICA) Rome, 2–7 Sept (2001)
3. Kherdekar, V.A., Naik, S.A.: Convolution neural network model for recognition of speech for words used in mathematical expression. Turkish J. Comput. Math. Educ. (TURCOMAT) 12(6), 4034–4042 (2021)
4. Huang, J.T., Li, J., Gong, Y.: An analysis of convolutional neural networks for speech recognition. In: 2015 IEEE International Conference on Acoustics, Speech and Signal Processing (ICASSP), pp. 4989–4993. IEEE (Apr 2015)
5. Abdel-Hamid, O., Mohamed, A.R., Jiang, H., Deng, L., Penn, G., Yu, D.: Convolutional neural networks for speech recognition. IEEE/ACM Trans. Audio Speech Lang. Process. 22(10), 1533–1545 (2014)
6. Phani Bhushan, S., Vani, H.Y., Shivkumar, D.K., Sreeraksha, M.R.: Stuttered speech recognition using convolutional neural networks. Int. J. Eng. Res. Technol. (IJERT) NCCDS 9(12) (2021)
7. Gulzar, T., Singh, A., Sharma, S.: Comparative analysis of LPCC, MFCC and BFCC for the recognition of Hindi words using artificial neural networks. Int. J. Comput. Appl. 101(12), 22–27 (2014)
8. Li, X., Zhou, Z.: Speech command recognition with convolutional neural network. In: IEEE International Conference on Acoustics, Speech and Signal Processing (ICASSP) (2017)
9. Kubanek, M., Bobulski, J., Kulawik, J.: A method of speech coding for speech recognition using a convolutional neural network. Symmetry 11(9), 1185 (2019)
10. Tamazin, M., Gouda, A., Khedr, M.: Enhanced automatic speech recognition system based on enhancing power-normalized cepstral coefficients. Appl. Sci. 9(10), 2166 (2019)
11. Kanthi, A.N., Moinuddin, M.: Speaker Identification based on GFCC using GMM. Int. J. Innov. Res. Adv. Eng. 1(8), 224–232 (2014)
12. Dev, A., Bansal, S.: Emotional Hindi speech: feature extraction and classification. In: IEEE Explorer, Computing for Sustainable Global Development (INDIACom), 2015 2nd International Conference (989-9-805-4415-1), 11–13 Mar 2015, pp. 1865–1868 (2015)

13. Maurya, A., Kumar, D., Agarwal, R.K.: Speaker recognition for Hindi speech signal using MFCC-GMM approach. Procedia Comput. Sci. **125**, 880–887 (2018)
14. Gambhira, P., Devb, A.: A run-through: text independent speaker identification using deep learning. In: Artificial Intelligence and Speech Technology: Proceedings of the 2nd International Conference on Artificial Intelligence and Speech Technology, (AIST2020), 19–20 Nov 2020, Delhi, India, pp. 139. CRC Press (June 2021)
15. Warden, P.: Speech commands: A dataset for limited-vocabulary speech recognition (2018). arXiv preprint arXiv:1804.03209
16. Kumar, C., Ur Rehman, F., Kumar, S., Mehmood, A., Shabir, G.: Analysis of MFCC and BFCC in a speaker identification system. In: 2018 International Conference on Computing, Mathematics and Engineering Technologies. iCoMET 2018 - Invent, Innovate and Integrate for Socioeconomic Development: Conference Proceedings, vol. Jan–Dec, pp. 1–5 (2018)

Latest Trends in Deep Learning for Automatic Speech Recognition System

Amritpreet Kaur[1]([✉]), Rohit Sachdeva[2], and Amitoj Singh[3]

[1] Department of Computer Science, Punjabi University, Patiala, India
[2] Department of Computer Science, MM Modi College, Patiala, India
[3] Department of Computational Science, MRS PTU, Bathinda, India

Abstract. In the field of Computer Learning and Intelligent Systems research, Deep Learning is one of the latest development projects. It's also one of the trendiest areas of study right now. Computational vision and pattern recognition have benefited greatly from the dramatic advances made possible by deep learning techniques. New deep learning approaches are already being suggested, offering performance that outperforms current state-of-the-art methods and even surpasses them. There has been much significant advancement in this area in the last few years. Deep learning is developing at an accelerated rate, making it difficult for new investigators to keep pace of its many kinds. We will quickly cover current developments in Deep Learning in the last several years in this article.

Keywords: Deep Learning · Machine Learning · Neural Networks

1 Introduction

A person's ability to express themselves verbally is known as speech. Speech is made up of consonant and vowel segments, and each time individuals say something, they're using a speech segment. Human speech can be understood by machines thanks to Automatic Speech Recognition (ASR), which uses a machine-readable format to identify what people are saying. In the ASR process, a speech signal is converted into a series of words. The reliability of speech identification is affected by a variety of variables, including the style of speech, the speaker's dependence, the quantity of the vocab, and the form of recognition, such as a single word, a linked word, or a continuous word. There are numerous methods for recognising speech, including audible phonetics, pattern matching, support vector machines, and machine intelligence. The Gaussian mixtures based hidden Markov model is the most effective audible prototype for speaker identification (HMM). As can be seen in Fig. 1, a fast and accurate speech recognition system has the following general architecture: The ASR model is composed of extracting features, audible modelling, language modelling, vocabulary, and decoder. Modeling of the acoustic characteristics of a speech signal is the focus of Acoustic Modeling research. In 1986, the concept "Deep Learning" (DL) was first used in relation to Machine Learning (ML), and in 2000 it was applied to Artificial Neural Networks (ANN) [1,2]. To learn relevant

A. Dev et al. (Eds.): AIST 2021, CCIS 1546, pp. 62–72, 2022.
https://doi.org/10.1007/978-3-030-95711-7_6

data at various levels of analysis, deep learning methods use numerous layers of computation [3]. Complex concepts can be learned by building on easier things using deep learning approaches [4].

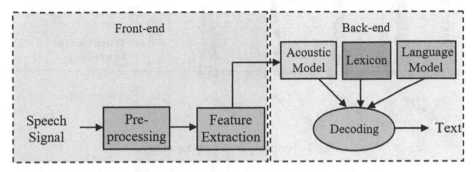

Fig. 1. General architecture of Automatic Speech Recognition System

To evaluate and investigate different features of ASR models provided throughout time, numerous survey articles have been published in the last few years. According to a newly released survey study, the difficulties in ASR that must be solved have been examined, as well as popular ASR models that have been reviewed and evaluated by [5]. It examines a wide range of issues, such as the method and manner of utterance, alternative speaker models, the quantity of vocabulary, and channel diversity.

2 Deep Learning

Automatic voice identification systems have been transformed by the Deep Neural Network (DNN) auditory model. DNNs have outperformed the conventional ASR system, according to [6]. For example, in ASR, DNN includes several hidden layers in addition to represent context-dependent variables effectively [7]. To simulate the observation signal probabilistic model, DNN substitutes the Gaussian Mixture Model (GMM), which is also used to model speech characteristic dispersion.

Hybrid Artificial Neural Networks (ANN)-HMM models have been used to provide complex results for almost two decades. Based on small frames of parameters, these systems used ANNs with non-linear kernel function with just one hidden layer of hidden units. However, at the time, neither the computing power nor the training methods available were sophisticated enough to train ANNs with numerous hidden units, making them ineffective. HMMs combined with Gaussian mixture auditory models have been extremely effective [8], however combined ANN-HMM models cannot replace them [9]. DNN-based auditory models are increasingly replacing conventional speech recognition systems [10–12].

Figure 2 compares deep learning's efficiency to that of more traditional learning methods in different domains. It's a measure of deep learning's effectiveness based on a massive quantity of data gathered across a wide range of industries, from military to

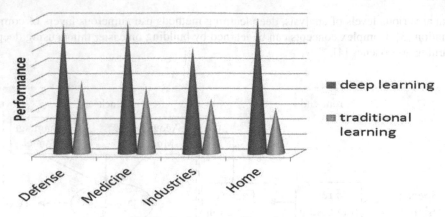

Fig. 2. Performance of Deep Learning

consumer electronics. This method uses neural network designs to categorize a database and is sometimes referred to as deep learning models.

In the following figures below Fig. 3(a) shows the classification using the traditional learning method and the Fig. 3(b) presents the deep learning method that automatically learns from the dataset. A conventional classification technique is shown in Fig. 3(a), whereas a deep learning method is shown in Fig. 3(b).

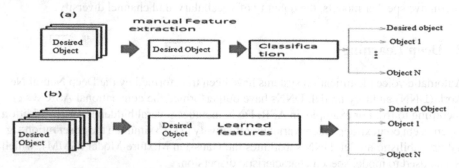

Fig. 3. Conventional and Deep Learning classification techniques

This section discusses the six most common deep learning models: -

There are many types of neural networks: Auto-Encoder (AE), Convolution Neural Network (CNN), Restricted Boltzmann Machine (RBM), GAN, and Deep Stacking Network (DSN) and LSTM. Out of above discussed methods, LSTM and CNN are two of the fundamental and the most commonly used approaches.

2.1 Auto-encoder

Data may be compressed into a smaller amount of storage space using an auto-encoder, which is a special kind of artificial system. The transmitter and receiver sub-models make up an auto-encoder. Compressing the input is done by the transmitter, and the receiver uses that digital copy to try to reconstruct the original. The transmitter model is kept and the receiver model is thrown away once training is finished. The encoder, code, and decoder are all parts of an auto-encoder. A compression algorithm is used to create a code, which is subsequently decoded by a different algorithm. A decoder, an encoding technique and a transfer functions to evaluate the product to the goal are all required to create an auto-encoder (Fig. 4).

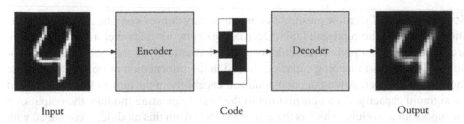

Fig. 4. Auto-encoder and decoder applied in image classification

2.2 Convolutional Neural Network

An image-processing technique known as a convolutional neural network (CNN) uses deep learning to distinguish between distinct features and objects in a picture. There is much less pre-processing needed when using a CNN than when using other classification methods. While filters are hand-engineered in basic techniques, CNN can learn these extensions with adequate training. A growing amount of focus is being placed on CNN-based voice recognition algorithms for end-to-end [13–16].

2.3 Generative Adversarial Network

Another DL model for improving voice quality is the GAN [17]. The convolution system and the generator system are combined in this design. The generative model is comparable to an auto-encoder in that it generates a comparable feature of the input data, but the convolution network functions as a binary filter trained to distinguish between a genuine and a false input model. It's hard to train DNNs in general, but here, two DNNs are being taught to operate together, which makes it much more difficult [18]. The use of GANs for speech augmentation and fine-tuning has also been shown to be ineffective at times.

2.4 Restricted Boltzmann Machine

An RBM is a deep learning tool that uses artificial neural networks to learn probabilistic models.

2.5 Deep Belief Network

Hinton created this deep learning approach for the first time, and it has been used effectively for techniques such as segmentation and pattern recognition [11]. DBN has been utilized as it's a building blocks and a linear model layer for forecast in an unstructured learning component.

2.6 Deep Stacking Network

Stacking layers of shallow presumption modules may convey complicated functions, as shown by [19], who represent DSN. Deep convex network is another name for it. There are three layers to a premise module: one for information, one for secrecy, and one for output. There is no mapping capacity utilized in the information or output layers since they are both direct. A fundamental nonlinear capability in the hidden layer is provided by sigmoid capacity. As a contribution to the next associating module, the output of a presupposition module, which is the expected labels from this module, is combined with the initial info information.

2.7 Long Short-Term Memory

Deep learning makes use of the LSTM, an enhanced recurrent neural system (RNS). A "widely helpful PC" is one that has input correlations like those seen in LSTM. In an LSTM, inputs are fed into state boxes that learn over time [20]. It is unable to digest just a single piece of information, but also large chunks of data. Unsegmented, related penmanship acknowledgement or speech recognition, for example, benefit greatly from the use of LSTM (Table 1).

Table 1. Deep neural networks: architectures and applications

Architecture	Major application areas
Auto-encoder	Analysis of basic language, comprehension of concise collected data
Convolutional neural networks	Face identification, picture analysis, language processing, and video analysis are all examples of document analysis
Deep belief networks	Fault detection and prevention, data retrieval, and language comprehension
Deep stacking networks	Speech recognition that is always active, information retrieval
LSTM/GRU network	Recognition of gestures, compression of natural language text, and recognition of voice
Recurrent neural networks	Identification of handwriting and speech
Restricted Boltzmann machine	Segmentation, prediction and topic modelling with machine learning

3   Related Work

According to Mohamed et al. [21], a pre-trained ANN/HMM for consistent speech recognition in a large vocab has been suggested in the paper and demonstrates a significant progress in speech processing over a GMM/HMM. Many related scenarios are suggested and presented in [22] With the interferences of speech identification and audible modeling, Manohar et al. [23] found that front-end speech evoking and beam forming combined with comprehensive i-vector extraction significantly improved speech recognition over the usual system while reducing error rates. (CNN+TDNN+LSTM). Speech recognition deep neural networks are summarised in Table 2, which can be found after the break.

Table 2. Frameworks of Deep Neural Networks for Speech Recognition

	Literature	Technology used	Features
Deep Neural Network in Speech Recognition	Deng et al. [24]	DNN	More languages may be extracted with ease with this method than with GMM
	Peddinti et al. [25]	TDNN+I vector based adaption	Enables you to train at fast speeds
	Zhang et al. [13]	CNN+CTC	Highly efficient in terms of computation End-to-end voice recognition that is computationally efficient
	Palaz et al. [26]	DBN+trained ANN/HMM	For a big document, continuous voice recognition is required
	Manohar et al. [23]	CNN+LSTM+TDNN	Speech recognition has enhanced, and the number of mistakes has decreased

4   Comparison Table

(See Table 3)

Table 3. Comparison table consisting various Deep Learning Techniques used by different authors during their research

Authors	DL architecture	Strengths	Limitations
Narasimhan et al. [27]	CNN	Did not take the temporal segmentation of bird relation between bird syllables recording to identify into account. Bio-acoustics for birds	Did not take the temporal relation between bird syllables into account
Zhang et al. [28]	RNN and BLSTM	Can accomplish over 10 percent of relative decrease in phone mistake rate	Not feasible with adaptation
Liu et al. [29]	CNN	Improvement of state of art approaches by applying several data set conditions for polyphonic transcription	Involves lots of steps
Hennequin et al. [30]	CNN	Good performance on large scale database and robustness to codec type and re-sampling	Small scale databases are not used
Badrinarayananet et al. [31]	CNN	SegNet provides good performance with competitive inference time Significantly smaller in the number of trainable parameters than other competing architectures	somewhat difficult to apply Kendall
Wang et al. [32]	DNN	Less speech distortion	Low frequency units are distorted

5   Characteristics of Deep Learning

Artificial intelligence (AI) and machine learning (ML) are both subsets of the larger field known as deep learning. A wide range of applications have seen great success using deep learning methods. There have been improvements in the efficiency and durability in new fields such as information synthesis and on-board portable devices. Deep learning has the following characteristics:

- Extremely useful tool in a wide range of areas based only on neural networks with an extra two layers and therefore referred to as deep.
- Possess a high level of aptitude for learning.
- Can make better use of datasets.
- Enhanced outcomes.
- Network topology, input vector, and statistical modeling all play a role in deep learning networks.
- A few parameters may describe characteristics with a great degree of variability.
- The accuracy of predictions may be significantly enhanced.
- Solve computationally intensive problems.
- No previous data or knowledge is used in deep learning networks.
- To comprehend the models, especially when dealing with huge amounts of unlabeled data, DNN uses novel techniques.
- These systems can extract complex characteristics because of their high degree of abstraction.

6 Motivation for Using Deep Learning

The above system believes that there are no intrinsic challenges to improve the efficiency of the applications. For example, speech recognition on computers reaches human levels of productivity just like faces and object identification. To be honest, handwriting recognition is where deep learning begins. The following facts provide motivation for using deep learning: -

a) Deep Learning will unquestionably help AI spread throughout the business world.
b) Artificial neural networks with various layers and high efficiency are the basis for machine learning, which consists of a variety of methods and techniques.
c) Because of its deep networking opportunities networks and support from graphical processing elements, deep learning sees significant growth.
d) Feed-forward artificial neural network with complexity and convolution layer make up the majority of deep learning models.
e) It doesn't matter what comes before or after it, because the inputs and outputs are unrelated.
f) In 2017, NVIDIA had a significant impact on the market because of their rich deep Learning ecosystem.
g) In terms of deep learning, Intel Xeon Phi methods are buried on the emergence.
h) Meta-learning will become more and more important to designers.
i) If this prediction is correct, then reinforcement learning will become more inventive.

7 Machine Learning vs. Deep Learning

The framework of deep learning is made up of many layers, each with various neurons. Machine learning framework is composed of numerous hidden layers and layers of neurons.

- Generalization and Diversity.
- Preparation of data.
- Pre - processing and normalisation of data are not required in deep learning.
- Changes in Activities over Time and Space.

8 Challenges of Deep Learning

Deep learning techniques have unquestionably proven their worth and have been used to solve a wide range of challenging problems involving multiple layers of complexity. It has a high degree of abstraction as well, of course. It's also widely agreed that deep learning systems have accuracy, acuteness, receptivity, and precision that's on par with or even better than human experts. So, here is a rundown of the difficulties that deep learning will have to face:

- Deep learning algorithms need to keep track of the input data all the time.
- Algorithms must guarantee that the conclusion is transparent.
- High-performance GPUs and storage requirements are resource-demanding technologies.
- Improved techniques for the analysis of large amounts of data. Deep networks are also known as black box networks because of their obscurity.
- Using Deep learning, computers may learn concepts and descriptions by using new tools and networks.

9 Conclusion and Future Aspects

Deep learning models, such as the ones described above, are very useful. Numerous jobs in computer science need them to demonstrate their capacity to recognize things like images and voice. They've done so in many other areas as well, including information and cyber security. Their accuracy is comparable to that of humans, and they may even outperform humans on occasion. In terms of drawbacks, these models need large amounts of data to train, as well as a lot of computing resources to classify and train the models. It's almost impossible to build these models without graphics processing equipment. Deep learning (DL) models in voice recognition have shifted the paradigm from statistical models to deep learning. They are now the standard. In a real-world situation, they outperform humans. We may attempt to make them simpler in the future so that they can be handled by humans instead of high-end machines.

References

1. Bhatt, S., Jain, A., Dev, A.: Acoustic modeling in speech recognition: a systematic review. Int. J. Adv. Comput. Sci. Appl. (IJACSA) **11**(4), 397–412 (2020)
2. Schmidhuber, J.: Deep learning in neural networks: an overview. Neural Netw. **61**, 85–117 (2015)
3. LeCun, Y., Bengio, Y., Hinton, G.: Deep learning. Nature **521**(7553), 436–444 (2015)
4. Goodfellow, I., Bengio, Y., Courville, A.: Deep Learning. MIT Press (2016)
5. Kaur, J., Singh, A., Kadyan, V.: Automatic speech recognition system for tonal languages: state-of-the-art survey. Arch. Comput. Meth. Eng. **28**(3), 1039–1068 (2021)
6. Seide, F., Li, G., Chen, X., Yu, D.:Feature engineering in context-dependent deep neural networks for conversational speech transcription. In: 2011 IEEE Workshop on Automatic Speech Recognition & Understanding, pp. 24–29. IEEE (2011)
7. Hinton, G., et al.: Deep neural networks for acoustic modeling in speech recognition: the shared views of four research groups. IEEE Sig. Process. Mag. **29**(6), 82–97 (2012)
8. Bansal, P., Kant, A., Kumar, S., Sharda, A., Gupta, S.: Improved hybrid moda of HMM/GMM for speech recognition. Inf. Sci. Comput. **2**, 69–74 (2008). Supplement to international Journal; "Information Technologies and Knowledge"
9. Bourlard, H.A., Morgan, N.: Connectionist Speech Recognition: A Hybrid Approach. Springer, Boston (2012). https://doi.org/10.1007/978-1-4615-3210-1
10. Graves, A., Mohamed, A., Hinton, G.: Speech recognition with deep recurrent neural networks. In: 2013 IEEE International Conference on Acoustics, Speech and Signal Processing, pp. 6645–6649. IEEE (2013)
11. Hinton, G.E., Osindero, S., Teh, Y.-W.: A fast learning algorithm for deep belief nets. Neural Comput. **18**(7), 1527–1554 (2006)
12. Deng, L., et al.: Recent advances in deep learning for speech research at Microsoft. In: 2013 IEEE International Conference on Acoustics, Speech and Signal Processing, pp. 8604–8608. IEEE (2013)
13. Zhang, Y., Chan, W., Jaitly, N.: Very deep convolutional networks for end-to-end speech recognition. In: 2017 IEEE International Conference on Acoustics, Speech and Signal Processing (ICASSP), pp. 4845–4849. IEEE (2017)
14. Zeghidour, N., Xu, Q., Liptchinsky, V., Usunier, N., Synnaeve, G., Collobert, R.: Fully convolutional speech recognition. arXiv preprint arXiv:06864 (2018)
15. Kriman, S., et al.: QuartzNet: deep automatic speech recognition with 1d time-channel separable convolutions. In: 2020 IEEE International Conference on Acoustics, Speech and Signal Processing (ICASSP), ICASSP 2020, pp. 6124–6128. IEEE (2020)
16. Li, J., et al.: Jasper: an end-to-end convolutional neural acoustic model. arXiv preprint arXiv: 03288 (2019)
17. Pascual, S., Bonafonte, A., Serra, J.: SEGAN: speech enhancement generative adversarial network. arXiv preprint arXiv:09452 (2017)
18. Mao, X., Li, Q., Xie, H., Lau, R.Y., Wang, Z., Paul Smolley, S.: Least squares generative adversarial networks. In: Proceedings of the IEEE International Conference on Computer Vision, pp. 2794–2802 (2017)
19. Sun, C., Ma, M., Zhao, Z., Chen, X.: Sparse deep stacking network for fault diagnosis of motor. IEEE Trans. Industr. Inf. **14**(7), 3261–3270 (2018)
20. Medsker, L.R., Jain, L.: Recurrent neural networks. Des. Appl. **5**, 64–67 (2001)
21. Mohamed, A., Hinton, G., Penn, G.: Understanding how deep belief networks perform acoustic modelling. In: 2012 IEEE International Conference on Acoustics, Speech and Signal Processing (ICASSP), pp. 4273–4276. IEEE (2012)

22. Balyan, A., Agrawal, S.S., Dev, A.: Automatic phonetic segmentation of Hindi speech using hidden Markov model. AI Soc. **27**, 543–549 (2012). https://doi.org/10.1007/s00146-012-0386-2
23. Manohar, V., Chen, S.-J., Wang, Z., Fujita, Y., Watanabe, S., Khudanpur, S.:Acoustic modeling for overlapping speech recognition: JHU CHiME-5 challenge system. In: 2019 IEEE International Conference on Acoustics, Speech and Signal Processing (ICASSP), ICASSP 2019, pp. 6665–6669. IEEE (2019)
24. Deng, L., Hinton, G., Kingsbury, B.:New types of deep neural network learning for speech recognition and related applications: an overview. In: 2013 IEEE International Conference on Acoustics, Speech and Signal Processing, pp. 8599–8603. IEEE (2013)
25. Peddinti, V., Povey, D., Khudanpur, S.:A time delay neural network architecture for efficient modeling of long temporal contexts. In: 16th Annual Conference of the International Speech Communication Association (2015)
26. Palaz, D., Doss, M.M., Collobert, R.:Convolutional neural networks-based continuous speech recognition using raw speech signal. In: 2015 IEEE International Conference on Acoustics, Speech and Signal Processing (ICASSP), pp. 4295–4299. IEEE (2015)
27. Narasimhan, R., Fern, X.Z., Raich, R.:Simultaneous segmentation and classification of bird song using CNN. In: 2017 IEEE International Conference on Acoustics, Speech and Signal Processing (ICASSP), pp. 146–150. IEEE (2017)
28. Zhang, Y., Pezeshki, M., Brakel, P., Zhang, S., Bengio, C.L.Y., Courville, A.:Towards end-to-end speech recognition with deep convolutional neural networks. arXiv preprint arXiv:02720 (2017)
29. Liu, P., Zhang, H., Zhang, K., Lin, L., Zuo, W.:Multi-level wavelet-CNN for image restoration. In: Proceedings of the IEEE Conference on Computer Vision and Pattern Recognition Workshops, pp. 773–782 (2018)
30. Hennequin, R., Royo-Letelier, J., Moussallam,M.: Codec independent lossy audio compression detection. In: 2017 IEEE International Conference on Acoustics, Speech and Signal Processing (ICASSP), pp. 726–730. IEEE (2017)
31. Badrinarayanan, V., Kendall, A., Cipolla, R.: SegNet: a deep convolutional encoder-decoder architecture for image segmentation. IEEE Trans. Pattern Anal. Mach. Intell. **39**(12), 2481–2495 (2017)
32. Wang, H., Wang, D.: Towards robust speech super-resolution. IEEE/ACM Trans. Audio Speech Lang. Process. **23**, 2058–2066 (2021)

Deep Learning Approaches for Speech Analysis: A Critical Insight

Alisha Goyal[1], Advikaa Kapil[2], Sparsh Sharma[3], Garima Jaiswal[1],
and Arun Sharma[1(✉)]

[1] Indira Gandhi Delhi Technical University for Women, Delhi, India
arunsharma@igdtuw.ac.in
[2] Sanskriti School, Chanakyapuri, New Delhi, India
[3] Delhi Technological University, Delhi, India

Abstract. The main objective of speaker recognition is to identify the voice of an authenticated and authorized individual by extracting features from their voices. The number of published techniques for speaker recognition algorithms is text-dependent. On the other hand, text-independent speech recognition appears to be more advantageous since the user can freely interact with the system. Several scholars have suggested a variety of strategies for detecting speakers, although these systems were difficult and inaccurate. Relying on WOA and Bi-LSTM, this research suggested a text-independent speaker identification algorithm. In presence of various degradation and voice effects, the sample signals were obtained from a available dataset. Following that, MFCC features are extracted from these signals, but only the most important characteristics are chosen from the available features by utilizing WOA to build a single feature set. The Bi-LSTM network receives this feature set and uses it for training and testing. In the MATLAB simulation software, the proposed model's performance is assessed and compared to that of the standard model. Various dependent factors, like accuracy, sensitivity, specificity, precision, recall, and Fscore, were used to calculate the simulated outputs. The findings showed that the suggested model is more efficient and precise at recognizing speaker voices.

Keywords: Speaker recognition system · Artificial intelligence · Whale optimization algorithm · Recurrent neural network

1 Introduction

Speaker recognition is considered a biometric technology that uses typical features collected from a user's speech sample to validate their claimed identification [1]. Recently, speaker recognition along with the technologies like depreciation and speech recognition is becoming a key component in speech analysis of audio and video content. Automatic subtitling, automatic metadata, and generation Query-by-voice for television and movies are considered instances of practical applications of these techniques [2]. Aside from physical distinctions, each speaker does have a distinct way of speaking, which includes the usage of a unique word, intonation style, pronunciation pattern,

A. Dev et al. (Eds.): AIST 2021, CCIS 1546, pp. 73–84, 2022.
https://doi.org/10.1007/978-3-030-95711-7_7

accent, choice, rhythm, etc. In speaker recognition system, speaker identification and verification is considered as the most essential parts [3] (Fig. 1).

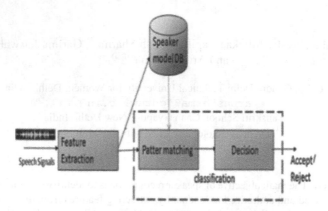

Fig. 1. Block diagram of standard speaker recognition system [8]

By utilizing module of feature extraction, speaker-specific elements of the speech signal are extracted. The speaker-specific elements of the speech signal are extracted using the feature extraction module. The characteristics are intended to offer the greatest possible separation amongst speakers in a group. Then after extracting features, the pattern recognition module matches the predicted characteristics of test speech samples to the system's speaker models [9]. This module matches the sample of a test speech to all of the stored models in a recognition task and returns a semantic similarity among the sample of test speech and all of the registered speaker models. The predicted features were calculated through an alternate model representing speakers besides the enrolled speakers in the task of the speaker authentication [10]. Furthermore, to make decisions, the decision module examines the semantic scores offered by the module of pattern matching. The decision module's outcome is determined by the mode and task type's for which the system is utilized. For instance, the decision module chooses the speaker model with the closest match to the test speech sample in closed-set mode [11]. A threshold value in the recognition task of open-set is needed to determine whether the match is good enough to recognize the speaker. Accuracy or the percentage of correct identifications is a performance criterion in an identification task. False Acceptance Rate (FAR) and False Rejection Rate (FRR) are the performance criteria in verification tasks. A high FAR gives the system unsafe to utilize, whereas a high FRR makes it inconvenient. In an ideal world, systems would be turned towards a low Total Error Rate (TER), which is equal to a low FAR + FRR. This state is obtained by altering the decision module's threshold value.

Forensics are considered a significant application of speaker recognition technology. In telephone conversations, a lot of data is transferred across two people, especially criminals, and there's been a growing interest in incorporating automatic speaker recognition to enhance semi-automatic and auditory analysis approaches [12–14]. The speaker recognition system can be modelled into two types Text-Dependent or Text-Independent system. Text-based recognition is used in situations where the user has a good command over the input [15]. Since the system is already familiar with the spoken content, this form of recognition provides improved system performance. Text-independent method is utilized to recognize any form of conversational speech or a phrase chosen by the user. The text-independent SRS does not have any previous knowledge of the text that the user has uttered. This is commonly utilized in applications when the user has less control over the input [16].

Recently, Artificial Intelligence (AI) has played a major role in speaker recognition, because AI provides various independent methods that utilize the unique characteristics to identify human voice. AI techniques like Support Vector Machine (SVM), Hidden Markov Modeling (HMM), Artificial Neural Networks (ANN), K-NEAREST NEIGHBOR (KNN), Convolutional Neural Network (CNN) etc. are useful in the In the areas of forensic voice verification, electronic voice eavesdropping, security and surveillance, mobile banking and shopping, etc. Other than this several researchers have proposed various techniques for speaker recognition that is described in the next section.

2 Related Work

For speaker identification, many researchers have developed a number of methods out of which some are discussed here: El-Moneim et al. [17] described the text-independent SRS in the presence of depletion factors like distortion and echoes. The suggested system by authors of this paper faced considerable difficulties in recognizing speakers in various recording situations. As a result, several speech improvement methods like wavelet denoising and spectrum subtraction were applied to increase recognition ability. **X. Zhao and Y. Wei** [18] investigated the SRS's performance as a function of input type and NN configuration, as well as the best feature parameters and NN architecture for an SRS. Additionally, traditional deep learning-based SR techniques like CNN and DNN, have been evaluated, and various enhanced deep learning-based models have been constructed and evaluated. The network model, when combined, has a greater recognition rate in speaker recognition than the standard network architecture.

Nammous et al. [19] integrated the prior research and implemented it to the issue of multi-speaker conversation speaker recognition. On Speakers in the Field, the authors tracked the performance and offered what they believe were the best described failure rates for this database. The suggested technique was also more resistant to domain shifts and produced results that were comparable to those acquired with a well-tuned threshold. Mobin et al. [20] developed a text-independent system relying on LSTM, with the goal of collecting spectral speaker-related data by working with standard speech attributes. For speaker verification, the LSTM framework was taught to build a discrimination space for verifying match and non-match pairings. When contrasted to other established approaches, the suggested design demonstrated its advantages in the text-independent domain. **S. Shon et al.** [21] presented an SRS is relying on CNNs for obtaining a reliable speaker embedding. With linear activation in the embedding layer, the embedding may be retrieved quickly. The frame level model permits authors to evaluate networks at the frame level, as well as perform additional analysis to enhance speaker recognition.

Jagiasi et al. [22],presented the development of an automatic speaker recognition system that incorporates classification and recognition of Sepedi home language speakers.

The performance of each model is evaluated in WEKA using 10-fold cross validation. MLP and RF yielded good accuracy surpassing the state-of-the-art with an accuracy of 97% and 99.9%, respectively; the RF model is then implemented in a graphical user interface for development testing. Mokgonyane et al. [23] in their work implemented a text-independent, language-independent speaker recognition system using dense & convolutional neural networks. The researcher of this paper explored a system that uses MFCC along with DNN and CNN as the model for building a speaker recognition system. Soufiane et al. [24] proposed a new technique to employ DNN (Deep neural network) in speaker recognition to understand the feature distribution. Experiments were carried out on the THUYG-20 SRE corpus, and excellent findings were obtained. Furthermore, in both noisy and clean situations, this innovative technique beated both i-vector/PLDA and their baseline approach. Mohammadi et al. [25] used the statistical properties of target training vectors to suggest a technique for balancing the framework and test. To analyze the system, the TIMIT database was employed. The experimental findings showed that using the suggested weighted vectors lowers the SVS's failure rate considerably. Duolin Huang et al. [26] presented a SRS technique depending on latent discriminative model learning. A reconstruction restriction was also added to develop a linear mapping matrix, making representation discriminative. Depending on the Apollo datasets utilized in the Fearless Steps Challenge at INTERSPEECH2019 and the TIMIT dataset, test findings showed that the presented approach surpassed common techniques.

After reviewing the literature it is concluded that the speaker recognition systems are playing important role in number of applications. Various researchers have proposed different approaches for recognizing the speaker from their voice. MFCC features are important feature model that are is recommended in most of the algorithms. Other than this there are few more features as frequency domain, time domain features that are also used in few of the studies. From the study it is concluded that the features processing is very crucial part of a recognition system, therefore selecting informative features can enhance the recognition rate. Very less studies are focus on feature selection models. Other than this artificial intelligence algorithms are the fundamental requirement of effective speaker recognition systems. Currently different machine learning algorithm such as SVM, ANN etc. are used for recognition applications, deep learning has reduced the system's complexity due to its high speed and better recognition capability. CNNs and RNNs are one of the examples of such models. But still the scope of modification and improvements are there, inspired from this the proposed scheme provides an improved speaker recognition system that is given in next section.

3   Proposed Work

To overcome the issues related to the traditional models, a novel and effective technique are proposed. The proposed work provides efficient algorithm to handle the complexity of the system and also gives a high recognition rate. Relying on WOA and Bi-LSTM, this research suggested a text-independent speaker identification algorithm. MFCC based features are extracted in the proposed model and using Whale optimization algorithm the informative feature are selected for all the speaker's audio samples. In addition to this, an upgraded variant of RNN that is BI-LSTM classification model is used for recognition.

The reason behind using the BI-LSTM network instead of conventional LSTM is the features of this model that are: It has two methods for dealing with inputs. It can not only process the inputs that have already passed through it, but it can also manage the inputs that have passed through it in the past. The simulation of the proposed model is done in MATLAB software by following the below written methodology.

Methodology
The proposed model's first step is to obtain input data from a dataset that is either available online or can be obtained in the real world. The dataset utilized in the suggested work was obtained from Kaggle.

Dataset Information
The audio sample of five famous political leaders can be found in the Kaggle dataset. The dataset comprises a collection of 500 audio samples, with 100 audio samples for each leader. Each audio file in the files is a PCM encoded one-second 16000 sample rate audio file. Figure 2 depicts a sample of audio signal collected from the dataset.

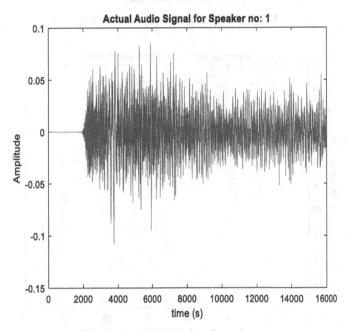

Fig. 2. Sample data taken from dataset

Following the collection of data, the signals must be processed and converted into a definite set of features. With 14 coefficients, the proposed model obtains MFCCs features. Figure 3 depicts each coefficient, which includes 100 characteristics.

Furthermore, in each audio signal sample, the average value of al 14 MFCC coefficients is determined and evaluated as represented in Fig. 4.

Moreover, other audio samples MFCC features are evaluated with their average MFCC coefficient of audio signals. At last, the WOA optimization method, as well as its

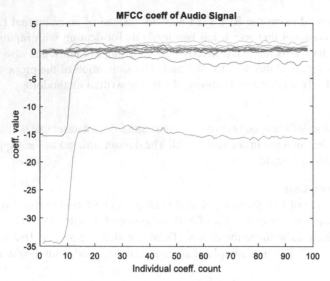

Fig. 3. MFCC features of 14 coefficients

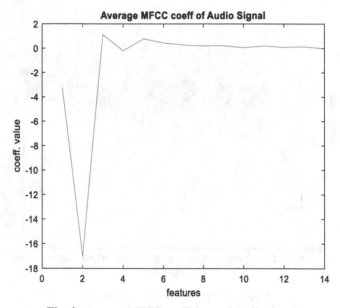

Fig. 4. Average MFCC coefficients of Audio signal

various parameters and their configurational values, must be initialized next to choose features from the available feature set. Table 1 shows the particular value of each and every parameter.

Then, the WOA algorithm only chooses the features that are essential for recognizing speaker from the available datasets. Only six of the 14 retrieved features are chosen as

Table 1. Configuration table for WOA feature selection model

WOA parameter	Value
Max Iteration	50
Population	10
Decision variable	6
Coefficient a	2 to 0
r	[0 1]
Population dimension	6

essential features with the highest fitness value. For each and every value, the optimal fitness value is evaluated by utilizing Eq. 1

$$Fitness = \frac{1}{mean(Std(SelectedFeatures))} \tag{1}$$

Following the creation of the final feature set, the proposed RNN-Bi-LSTM classification network is initialized by specifying different parameters like max epochs and threshold input size. Aside from that, the proposed network defines a number of other parameters, which are listed in Table 2.

Table 2. Configuration table for RNN BI-LSTM Classification model

Network's parameter	Value
Max epochs	150
Gradient threshold	1
Num of hidden Layer	120
Input size	1
No of layer	5
Min. batch size	10

For training and testing, the final feature set is send into the suggested RNN-BILSTM classification model. The model is trained by supplying trained data. At last, by supplying the testing data, the suggested model efficiency is tested. At last, the suggested model's efficiency is evaluated by supplying it with test data. The performance is assessed by using a number of performance parameters that are briefly described in the next section.

4 Results and Discussion

In the MATLAB simulation software, the proposed model's performance is simulated and examined. The simulation results were evaluated using a variety of performance metrics, including accuracy, sensitivity, specificity, precision, recall, and Fscore. Furthermore, the suggested model's performance is compared to that of the standard model, which is briefly addressed in this section.

- **Performance Evaluation**

The suggested model's efficiency is first assessed in terms of the convergence curve depicted in Fig. 5.

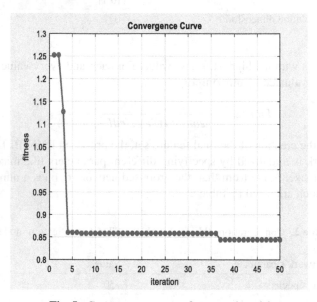

Fig. 5. Convergence curve of proposed model

The fitness graph obtained by the WOA algorithm during the feature selection process in the proposed model is shown in Fig. 5. The total number of iterations conducted is represented on the x-axis, while the fitness value is represented on the y-axis. The graph shows that the value of fitness is initially high, but as the number of iterations increases, the value of fitness drops dramatically, from 1.25 to 0.86 in just 4 iterations. After 50 iterations, the fitness value continues to decline and falls slightly below 0.85. This indicates that the suggested model is capable of extracting features efficiently and effectively.

The suggested model's performance is assessed using a variety of dependence variables such as accuracy, sensitivity, specificity, precision, recall, and Fscore. The suggested model's performance is first evaluated using several performance parameters, as illustrated in Fig. 6.

In Fig. 6 illustrates the several dependencies factors of the graphs that include the accuracy, sensitivity, specificity, precision, recall and Fscore of the proposed model. The blue, orange, and yellow colored bars represent the performance f-of accuracy, sensitivity, and specificity. The precision, recall, and Fscore performance are shown

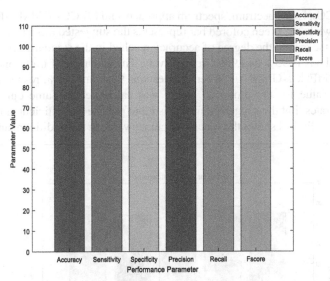

Fig. 6. Different performance parameters of proposed model

by purple, green, and sky-blue colored bars, respectively. The accuracy achieved in the suggested model is equivalent to 99% while the sensitivity and specificity achieved in the proposed model is equal to 98% and 99% respectively. Similarly, the suggested model examines the value of precision, recall, and Fscore, which come out to be 97%, 98%, and 98%, respectively. These results demonstrate that the suggested model is capable of reliably recognizing speakers. Table 3 shows the particular values of these parameters.

Table 3. Specific value of different parameters

Parameters	Values (% age)
Accuracy	99.2016
Sensitivity	98.9899
Specificity	99.2537
Precision	97.0297
Recall	98.9899
Fscore	98

In addition, the proposed model's accuracy is evaluated and compared to that of the standard model. Figure 7 represents the proposed model's comparison graph and proposed model in terms of accuracy.

Figure 7 illustrates the comparison of the suggested model and traditional MFCCs, Log-spectrum, spectrum technique, MFCCs-GMM-UBM models in terms of their accuracy value. Blue, orange, yellow, and purple colored bars represent the performance of the standard MFCCs, Log-spectrum, spectrum approach, and MFCCs-GMM-UBM models, respectively, while the green colored bar represents the suggested model's performance. According to the graph, the degree of accuracy reached in the standard MFCC and log-spectrum methods is 95% and 98%, respectively. The accuracy of traditional spectrum methods and MFCCs-GMM-UBM techniques was 98% and 94%, respectively. when the accuracy value for the proposed model was calculated, it came out to be 99%. This demonstrates that the suggested model is more precise and efficient at recognizing speaker signals. Table 4 shows the specific accuracy value in the traditional and proposed models.

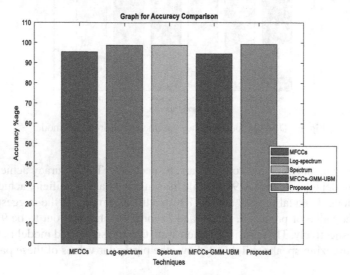

Fig. 7. Comparison graph of proposed and traditional model for accuracy

Table 4. Accuracy values in traditional and proposed model

Technique	Accuracy values (%age)
MFCCs	95.33
Log-spectrum	98.7
Spectrum	98.7
MFCCs-GMM-UBM	94.5
Proposed	99.2016

From graphs and tables, it is analyzed that the proposed model is more accurate and efficient in recognizing distinct speakers.

5 Conclusion

Nowadays, various researchers and experts have expressed their interest in automatic speech and speaker identification. Various scholars have developed a variety of methodologies, although the key problem for researchers is determine how precisely the system can identify and recognize speakers. The WOA and Bi-LSTM were used to suggest a model in this research. In terms of accuracy, sensitivity, specificity, precision, recall, and Fscore, the suggested model is compared to conventional MFCCs, Log-spectrum, spectrum method, and MFCCs-GMM-UBM models. The proposed model's sensitivity and specificity were calculated to be 98.9899% and 99.2537%, respectively. Furthermore, the precision, recall, and Fscore values were discovered to be 97.0297%, 98.9899%, and 98%, respectively. Furthermore, the traditional MFCCs and Log-spectrum accuracy values were 95.33% and 98.7%, respectively, but the traditional spectrum approach and MFCCs-GMM-UBM models accuracy values were 98.7% and 94.5%, respectively. The proposed model, on the other hand, achieved a value of accuracy of 99.2016%, demonstrating that it is more efficient and effective in recognizing distinct speakers.

References

1. Zilovic, M.S., Ramachandran, R.P., Mammone, R.J.: Speaker identification based on the use of robust cepstral features obtained from pole-zero transfer functions. IEEE Trans. Speech Audio Process. **6**, 260–267 (1998)
2. Tranter, S., Reynolds, D.: An overview of automatic speaker diarization systems. IEEE Trans. Audio Speech Lang. Process. **14**, 1557–1565 (2006)
3. Alexander, A., Botti, F., Dessimoz, D., Drygajlo, A.: The effect of mismatched recording conditions on human and automatic speaker recognition in forensic applications. Forensic Sci. Int. **146S**, 95–99 (2004)
4. Hansen, J., Hasan, T.: Speaker recognition by machines and humans: a tutorial review. Sign. Process. Mag. IEEE **32**, 74–99 (2015)
5. Jothilakshmi, S., Gudivada, V.N.: Large scale data enabled evolution of spoken language research and applications. Elsevier **35**, 301–340 (2016)
6. Kekre, H., Kulkarni, V.: Closed set and open set Speaker Identification using amplitude distribution of different transforms. In: 2013 International Conference on Advances in Technology and Engineering, pp. 1–8 (2013)
7. Mathu, S., et al.: Speaker recognition system and its forensic implications. Open Access Scientific Reports (2013)
8. Imdad, M.N., et al.: Speaker recognition in noisy environment. Int. J. Adv. Res. Comput. Sci. Electron. Eng. **1**, 52–57 (2012)
9. Imam, S.A., et al.: Review: speaker recognition using automated systems. AGU Int. J. Eng. Technol. **5**, 31–39 (2017)
10. Dhakal, P., Damacharla, P., Javaid, A.Y., Devabhaktuni, V.: A near real-time automatic speaker recognition architecture for voice-based user interface. Mach. Learn. Knowl. Extr. **1**, 504–520 (2019)
11. Varun, S., Bansal, P.K.: A review on speaker recognition approaches and challenges. Int. J. Eng. Res. Technol. (IJERT) **2**, 1581–1588 (2013)
12. Niemi-Laitinen, T., Saastamoinen, J., Kinnunen, T., Fränti, P.: Applying MFCC-based automatic speaker recognition to GSM and forensic data. In: Proceedings of the Second Baltic Conference on Human Language Technologies, pp. 317–322 (2005)

13. Pfister, B., Beutler, R.: Estimating the weight of evidence in forensic speaker verification. In: Proceedings of the 8th European Conference on Speech Communication and Technology, pp. 701–704 (2003)
14. Thiruvaran, T., Ambikairajah, E., Epps, J.: FM features for automatic forensic speaker recognition. In: Proceedings of the Interspeech 2008, pp. 1497–1500 (2008)
15. Hebert, M.: Text-dependent speaker recognition. Springer handbook of speech processing. Springer Verlag, pp. 743–762, 2008. https://doi.org/10.1007/978-3-540-49127-9_37
16. Nayana, P.K., Mathew, D., Thomas, A.: Comparison of text independent speaker identification systems using GMM and i-Vector methods. Procedia Comput. Sci. **115**, 47–54 (2017)
17. El-Moneim, S., Nassar, M., Dessouky, M.I., Ismail, N., El-Fishawy, A., Abd El-Samie, F.: Text-independent speaker recognition using LSTM-RNN and speech enhancement. Multimedia Tools Appl. (2020). https://doi.org/10.1007/s11042-019-08293-7
18. Zhao, X., Wei, Y.: Speaker recognition based on deep learning. In: 2019 IEEE International Conference on Real-time Computing and Robotics (RCAR), pp. 283–287 (2019)
19. Nammous, M.K., Saeed, K., Kobojek, P.: Using a small amount of text-independent speech data for a BiLSTM large-scale speaker identification approach. J. King Saud Univ.- Comput. Inf. Sci. (2020)
20. Mobin, A., Najarian, M.: Text-independent speaker verification using long short-term memory networks. arXiv:1805.00604 (2018)
21. Shon, S., Tang, H., Glass, J.: Frame-level speaker embeddings for text-independent speaker recognition and analysis of end-to-end model. In: 2018 IEEE Spoken Language Technology Workshop (SLT), pp. 1007–1013 (2018)
22. Jagiasi, R., Ghosalkar, S., Kulal, P., Bharambe, A.: CNN based speaker recognition in language and text-independent small scale system. In: 2019 Third International Conference on I-SMAC (IoT in Social, Mobile, Analytics and Cloud) (I-SMAC), pp. 176–179 (2019)
23. Mokgonyane, T.B., Sefara, T.J., Modipa, T.I., Mogale, M.M., Manamela, M.J., Manamela, P.J.: Automatic speaker recognition system based on machine learning algorithms. In: 2019 Southern African Universities Power Engineering Conference/Robotics and Mechatronics/Pattern Recognition Association of South Africa (SAUPEC/RobMech/PRASA), pp. 141–146 (2019)
24. Hourri, S., Kharroubi, J.: A deep learning approach for speaker recognition. Int. J. Speech Technol. **23**(1), 123–131 (2019). https://doi.org/10.1007/s10772-019-09665-y
25. Mohammadi, M., Mohammadi, H.R.S.: Weighted I-vector based text-independent speaker verification system. In: 2019 27th Iranian Conference on Electrical Engineering (ICEE), pp. 1647–1653 (2019)
26. Huang, D., Mao, Q., Ma, Z., et al.: Latent discriminative representation learning for speaker recognition. Front Inform. Technol. Electron. Eng. **22**, 697–708 (2021)

Survey on Automatic Speech Recognition Systems for Indic Languages

Nandini Sethi[✉] and Amita Dev

Indira Gandhi Delhi Technical University for Women, Delhi 110006, India
{nandini053phd20,vc}@igdtuw.ac.in

Abstract. For the past few decades, Automatic Speech Recognition (ASR) has gained a wide range of interest among researchers. From just identifying the digits for a single speaker to authenticating the speaker has a long history of improvisations and experiments. Human's Speech Recognition has been fascinating problem amongst speech and natural language processing researchers. Speech is the utmost vital and indispensable way of transferring information amongst the human beings. Numerous research works have been equipped in the field of speech processing and recognition in the last few decades. Accordingly, a review of various speech recognition approaches and techniques suitable for text identification from speech is conversed in this survey. The chief inspiration of this review is to discover the prevailing speech recognition approaches and techniques in such a way that the researchers of this field can incorporate entirely the essential parameters in their speech recognition system which helps in overcoming the limitations of existing systems. In this review, various challenges involved in speech recognition process are discussed and what can be the future directives for the researchers of this field is also discussed. The typical speech recognition trials were considered to determine which metrics should be involved in the system and which can be disregarded.

Keywords: Speech recognition · Acoustic modelling · Hidden Markov model · Dynamic time wrapping · Mel-frequency Cepstrum Coefficient

1 Introduction

Human voice has been the major mode of communication, interacting with machines has evolved a lot from identifying digits to the complex Automatic Speech Recognition (ASR) till date. The desire to automate simple tasks to complex tasks has necessitated human-machine interactions. Over the past decades, a lot of research has been carried out in order to create an ideal system which can understand and analyse continuous speech in real time and perform tasks accordingly. Some of which are Speech-to-text conversions, biometric identifications, home automation and has also highly benefited disabled persons. Advancements in the deep neural networks has made it all possible. Hidden Markov Model (HMM) hydride with Deep neural networks (DNN) and Recurrent Neural Networks has achieved remarkable performance in many large vocabulary speech recognition tasks [42].

But this was not as easy as what we see today. In terms of evolution, it can be organised and shown in Table 1.

© Springer Nature Switzerland AG 2022
A. Dev et al. (Eds.): AIST 2021, CCIS 1546, pp. 85–98, 2022.
https://doi.org/10.1007/978-3-030-95711-7_8

Table 1. Evolution of Speech Recognition Systems

Generation	Technology	Timeline
First generation	First attempt	1950s to 1960s
Second generation	Template based technology	1960s to 1970s
Third generation	Statistical modelling	1980s and 2000
Fourth generation	Advancements in deep Neural networks	after late 2000

1.1 First Generation

Earlier attempts in the field of ASR were made between 1950s to 1960s, when researchers were experimenting with the fundamental ideas of acoustic phonetics. In 1952, at Bell Laboratories in USA, David, Balashek and Biddulph built a system which could recognize digits for a single isolated speaker using formant frequencies measured during vowel regions of each digit. Further, at University College in England, Fry and Denies built a system which could recognize four vowels and nine consonants. This was the benchmark at that point of time in recognizing phonemes with much better accuracy as before. In the 1960s computers were not fast enough which was the limitation for the hardware. Other than this non-uniformity of time scales in speech was also a hurdle. To overcome this problem Martin and his colleagues at RCA labs developed a set of elementary time-normalised methods. This helped in reliably recognizing the start and end of a speech that reduced the variability of the recognition scores.

1.2 Second Generation

During the late 1960s and 1970s, ASR achieved many benchmarking milestones. Dynamic programming methods or Dynamic Time Wrapping (DTW) was introduced which helped in aligning a pair of speech utterances and also algorithms for connected word recognition. Many attempts were made during this time, for example, by IBM labs, AT & T Bell Labs, DARPA program and many more.

1.3 Third Generation

During the late 1980s, the focus was on building a more robust system which could recognize a fluently spoken string. A wide range of algorithms and experiments were performed to obtain a concatenated string of different words spoken. One of the key technologies developed during this time was the Hidden Markov Model (HMM). This technique was then boosted and was widely applied in every speech recognition research laboratory. Also, the idea of Neural networks was reintroduced in speech recognition. However, the concept was introduced earlier in the 1950s but was not useful because of practical limitations [44]. In the 1990s, after neural networks were reintroduced, many new innovations came in the area of pattern recognition.

1.4 Fourth Generation

For the past two decades, after so many successful attempts of improvising speech recognition systems, Deep Neural networks took speech recognition systems from just experimenting it on desk to some real-world applications for users. People can now interact and can make many tasks done just through voice command. For example, Ok Google, Siri, Alexa.

2 Speech Utterances

Based on the types of utterances, different speech recognition approaches are categorized into various groups in the way that they are capable to identify. Various types of speech utterances include Isolated speech, connected words, Continuous speech and spontaneous speech are shown in Fig. 1 and discussed below:

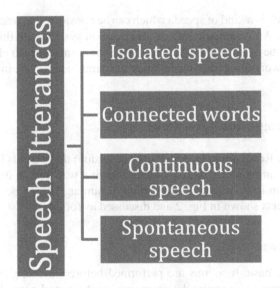

Fig. 1. Type of utterances

2.1 Isolated Speech

The recognizers which work with isolated speech requires every word to have noiselessness such as the absence of an audial signal on every side of the trial window. It accepts individual utterances at a specific point of time. This procedure includes two states named "Listen and Not-Listen", in which the user is required to pause among the words consistently carrying out the processing during the period of pauses. It can also be termed as Isolated Utterance.

2.2 Connected Words

In the case of Connected word, it requires a least gap among utterances to permit the flow of speech smoothly. These type of speech utterances are slightly similar to isolated speech.

2.3 Continuous Speech

The recognizers which work with Continuous speech allows the operators to speak nearly in a natural way, whereas the processor chooses the context. Primarily, it characterizes the computer transcription. This type of Recognizers which work with the continuous speech are supplementary hard to produce as they implement exclusive procedures to choose on the utterance boundaries.

2.4 Spontaneous Speech

Spontaneous speech is a kind of speech which can be considered as a natural speech, not as the trained one. An Automatic Speech Recognition system with this type of speech dimensions has to be capable to identify the owner of normal speech characters such as utterances which work altogether for instance the "ums" and "ahs", involves the minor stammers.

3 Speech Recognition Overview

Automatic Speech Recognition or ASR, is the procedure that permits humans to utilize their speeches to communicate with a system in such a way that, in its utmost cultured distinctions, be similar to natural conversation of humans. It can be divided into five different components shown in Fig. 2 and discussed as follows:

3.1 Pre-processing

In this step, some basic functions are performed before extracting any features. For Example, noise removal, endpoint detection, pre-emphasis and normalisation.

3.2 Feature Extraction

Features which will be used to differentiate between different phonemes and eventually to words and sentences are extracted. Most commonly extracted feature for ASR is Mel frequency cepstral coefficients (MFCCs) [43]. Since the mid-1980s MFCCs are the most widely used feature in ASRs. Discrete Wavelet Transform (DWT), Wavelet Packet Transform (WPT), Linear prediction cepstral coefficients (LPCC) and many more features are available with their strengths and weaknesses which can be used as required [40].

3.3 Classification

Numerous approaches have been done in order to find an optimal classifier which could correctly recognize speech segments under various conditions. Some of the classification techniques used are Artificial Neural Networks (ANNs), Hidden Markov Model (HMM).

3.4 A Language Model

Contains the knowledge specific to a language. This model is required to recognise phonemes and eventually represent meaningful representations of the speech signal [41].

3.5 Acoustic Modelling

Acoustic modelling establishes a relationship between acoustic information and language construct in SR [35].

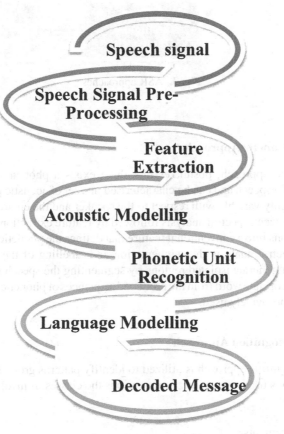

Fig. 2. Automatic speech recognition process

4 Speech Recognition Approaches

Speech Recognition has various techniques which can be further categorized into three major categories shown in Fig. 3 and discussed below:

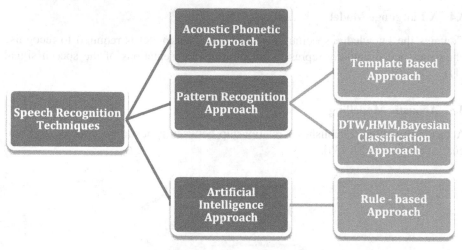

Fig. 3. ASR approaches

4.1 Acoustic Phonetic Approach

Acoustic phonetic approach, postulates that there exists a phoneme unit which is a building block of a speech and can be characterised in a set of acoustic properties. These properties are highly variable with respect to the speaker and the environment [36]. The very first step is speech spectral analysis followed by feature extraction which translates spectral dimensions into a conventional feature that defines the phonetics characteristics. After speech spectral analysis the segmentation and labelling of the speech signal is performed which generate isolated regions by segmenting the speech signal. Finally, it identifies the appropriate word from the produced sequences of phonetic labels. However, this approach is not widely used.

4.2 Pattern Recognition Approach

The pattern recognition approach is utilized to identify patterns grounded on convinced conditions which is used to categorize into various the classes. It involves various steps namely:

- feature measurements,
- pattern training,
- pattern classification and

- decision logic.

Various measurements are taken place to outline a test pattern on an input speech signal. Reference patterns are generated for each speech sound identified. Reference patterns can be generated with the help of speech templates or by using a statistical model such as HMM. The model can be functional to an utterance, a term or an idiom [46]. Finally, a comparison is performed among the unknown patterns and reference patterns in this pattern classification. And in Decision logic the identity of the unknown is determined. This approach is primarily used in ASR systems.

4.2.1 Template Based Approach

The essential thought of the Template based approach is elementary. A compendium of ideal patterns of speech is combined as reference patterns describing the vocabulary of candidate utterances. Afterwards, by toning the unnamed words with every reference pattern the recognition of word is performed and selects the kind of the finest matching form. All the words of the templates are configuring. One of the vibrant origins in this approach is to reach at a distinguishable sequence of speech frames for a word by means of firm averaging procedure and to be contingent on the arrangement of limited spectral distance metrics to evaluate and distinguish among the patterns [45]. An alternative vital concept is to implement a specific form of dynamic programming to briefly line up the patterns to reason for the alterations in the talking rates transversely the speakers as well across the repetitions of the term by the matching speaker.

Depending on the context, this approach handles the varying form of a nation-wide contour. It postulates an only sensible quantity of situations. This approach is considerable sturdier and long-range forecasters. The implementation of patterns is planned to detect and replicate the utmost significant syllable-level structures [39] of the outline without doing much smoothing. To depict the template form, this approach exploits the supple utterance arrangement. The benefit of using this approach is that, it can avoid the faults happened due to classification or segmentation of smaller adjustable components of illustration phonemes [38].

4.2.2 DTW, HMM Based Approach

In Dynamic time wrapping, various templates are used to represent every class which is to be recognized. To improve the speaker variability or the pronunciation modelling it is preferred to utilize two or more reference templates for each class. All through the process recognition, a gap among an experimental sequence of speech and class template is considered. The stretched and wrapped forms of the reference templates are also implemented in the gap calculation, to disregard the influence of duration discrepancy among the experimental sequence of speech and class template. The predictable word matches to the track over the model that reduces the total gap [41]. To improve the performance of dynamic time wrapping the number of class template variants can be increased and the wrapping constraints can be loosed but on the outflow of storing space and computational needs. Due to improved generalization features and lower memory necessities, HMM based approach is more widely used instead of dynamic time wrapping approach in various state of the art systems.

4.3 Artificial Intelligence Approach

Artificial Intelligence approach is the combination of both the pattern recognition and acoustic phonetic approaches. Few scholars established knowledge base of acoustic phonetic features for speech recognition system which classifies the rules for sound of the speech [37]. The methods based on templates provides slight intuition about humanoid speech processing, nevertheless these procedures have been very efficient in the development of a diversity of automatic speech recognition systems. On the contrary, verbal and phonic works providing intuitions about humanoid speech processing. Though, this method had only fractional accomplishment due to the complexity in computing proficient information.

5   Various Speech Recognition System

This study efforts to examine entirely all the published works for automatic speech recognition of various Indic languages. Works that denotes to speech recognition system in Indic languages or associated investigation on the Indian Automatic Speech Recognition datasets variety, investigational and non-experimental have been encompassed in this review paper. The necessity of the critical study is to identify the position of the investigation on automatic speech recognition. Various automatic speech recognition research studies for Indian languages emphasised on:

- LPC (Linear Predictive Coding),
- MFCC (Mel-frequency Cepstrum Coefficient),
- RASTA (Relative Spectra Processing)
- ZCPA (Zero Crossing with Peak amplitude), and
- Dynamic Time Wrapping (DTW) features.

Various ASR systems with their features and accuracy are discussed in Table 2.

Table 2. Survey-based on feature extraction technique

Authors	Feature extracted	Language	Accuracy
Thasleema TM et al. [1]	LPC, wavelet packet decomposition method	Malayalam	34% with LPC
			74% with wavelet packet decomposition method
Sinha et al. [2]	MFCC, PLP	Hindi	–
Dutta and Sarma et al. [3]	MFCC, LPC	Assamese	–
Kaur and Singh et al. [4]	MFCC, PLP, PNCC	Punjabi	WER of MFCC-13.19%
			WER of PLP-16.28%
			WER of PNCC-16.28%
Kadyan et al. [5]	LDA, SAT, fMLLR and MLLT	Punjabi	WER of 17.53
Ventateswarlu et al. [6]	LPCC and MFCC	Telegu	3–4% higher for MFCC instead of PLP
Kumar et al. [7]	MFCC and PLP	Hindi	MFCC-(92.0%)
			PLP – (73.36%)
Bharali and Kalita et al. [8]	MFCC	Assamese	81%
Bhowmik et al. [9]	MFCC	Bengali	86.19%
Mohamed and Lajish et al. [10]	MFCC	Malayalam	80.74%
ChellaPriyadharshini et al. [11]	MFCC, LDA, MLLT, fMLLR	Tamil	WER reduction of 15%
Manjunath and Rao et al. [12]	Afs (Articulatory Features)	Kannada, Telugu, Bengali, and Odia	(PER) of 10.4%
Darekar and Dhande et al. [13]	Cepstral, NMF and MFCC	Marathi	–

Various classification techniques are available for automatic speech recognition such as HMM, GMM, RNN, SOM, DE-HMM, DE-GMM, MPE, MMI and MLE. Techniques used in various research works with features extracted and language used is discussed in Table 3.

Table 3. Survey based on classification techniques

Author	Classifier used	Features extracted	Language
Kurian and Balakrishnan et al. [14]	HMM	–	Malayalam
Paul et al. [15]	ANN	MLP and LPC	Bangla
Sarma et al. [16]	ANN and SOM	MLP	Assamese
Sukumar et al. [17]	ANN	DWT	Malayalam
Bhuvanagirir and Kopparapu [18]	ANN	N/A	Malayalam
Dutta and Sarma [3]	RNN	LPC and MFCC	Assamese
Das et al. [19]	HMM	–	Bengali
Sarma et al. [20]	RNN, SOM and PNN	DWT	Assamese
Kumar et al. [21]	HMM and GMM	MFCC	Bengali and Odia
Patil and Pardeshi [22]	HMM	N/A	Devanagari
Patil and Pardeshi [23]	HMM	MFCC	Marathi
Hemakumar and Punitha [24]	HMM	LPC and RCC	Kannada
Patil and Rao [25]	HMM	acoustic–phonetic features	Hindi, Marathi
Dua et al. [26]	HMM	MFCC, PLP, MMIE, MME and MPE	Hindi
Bhat et al. [27]	Bayesian and HMM	–	Kannada
Pulugundla et al. [28]	TDNN and BRMN	–	Tamil, Telugu and Gujarati
Dua et al. [29]	HMM, GMM, DE-HMM, DE-GMM, MPE, MMI and MLE	MFCC, GFCC	Hindi
Samudravijaya et al. [30]	HMM, n-gram language modelling and RNNLM	MFCC	Hindi
Fathima et al. [31]	TDNN	Phonetic Features	Gujrati
Pandey and Nathwani [32]	DNN, DNN-HMM, KWS	Spectral and Prosodic features	Hindi
Pal et al. [33]	SGMM with LDA, MLLT and SAT	MFCC, delta and double delta features	Bengali

(*continued*)

Table 3. (*continued*)

Author	Classifier used	Features extracted	Language
Patel et al. [34]	GMM_HMM, DNN-HMM, KWS	–	Manipuri

6 Challenges and Future Directions in Speech Recognition

Robustness of an Automatic Speech Recognition system is the capability of the system to effectively deal with diverse characteristics of inconsistency in the speech (input) signal. The accuracy of a speech recognition system can be evaluated by a number of eminent factors. The utmost perceptible ones are: speaker, pronunciation, region, speech rate, context, channel and environment variability. In the development of ASR systems, these thought-provoking factors must be taken care and efficient models to be formed to deliver virtuous recognition precision regardless of these variabilities. In advanced level, ASR system development requires the accessibility of procedures or algorithms for instinctive generation of expression lexicons, instinctive generation of linguistic models for novel tasks, instinctive algorithms for speech segmentation, algorithm for finest utterance verification-rejection, attaining or exceptional humanoid presentation on ASR tasks. Some of the challenges and future directives are discussed below:

- Several Automatic Speech Recognition systems has absence of huge speech corpus. To build such a huge corpus must include tonal information, dialectal and prosodic information to perform more analytical processing of information.
- Language such as Punjabi, Bodo and Dogari are tonal Indic languages. An examination required to be accomplished by means of vocal tract information and pitch information about these dialects and their successive languages.
- Additional chief problem with vernaculars is a discrepancy of dialectal statistics. Rare studies were performed on mining the dialectal information of Indic dialects. This required to be united with speech methodologies to diminish Word Error Rate.
- Various works in this field implemented the bottle neck features. Various speech databases established in Indic dialects are grounded on noise free situation. In future, researchers can develop noisy datasets and develop speech recognition system on these datasets by utilizing various pitch characteristics and robust approaches to enhance the performance of the system.
- By utilizing the optimisation algorithm on model metrics, an effort can be made to improve the acoustical features. Very rare works has been worked on optimizing or refining the features. Study in other dialects emphases on previously recognized techniques of feature extraction such as MFCC. A limited studies have utilized hybridisation techniques of feature extraction for the refinement of feature.

7 Conclusion

Speech recognition is a standout amongst the utmost enabling zones of machine information since people do an ordinary movement of speech recognition. In this survey, various speech recognition techniques and their works are reviewed and tabulated different features extracted and classifier used on the (input) speech signal. Prominently, three distinct factors such as, approach, features extracted and accuracy measure were taken care for comparison and studying the prevailing works. The comprehensive analysis accomplished in this study will give the attainment happened in the field of automatic speech recognition to further articulate the research notions to overcome the existing yardstick outcomes for the scholars. At last, some of the research challenges and future directives are also addressed to lead the further research in the same direction. In future, researchers can develop noisy datasets and develop speech recognition system on these datasets by utilizing various pitch characteristics and robust approaches to enhance the performance of the system.

References

1. Thasleema, T.M., Kabeer, V., Narayanan, N.K.: Malayalam vowel recognition based on linear predictive coding parameters and k-NN algorithm. In: Proceedings of international conference on computational intelligence and multimedia applications (ICCIMA 2007), pp. 361–365 (2007)
2. Sinha, S., Agrawal, S.S., Olsen, J.: Development of Hindi mobile communication text and speech corpus. In: Proceedings of O-COCODSA, pp. 30–35 (2011)
3. Dutta, K., Sarma, K.K.: Multiple feature extraction for RNN-based Assamese speech recognition for speech to text conversion application. In: Proceedings of the international conference on communications, devices and intelligent systems (CODIS), pp. 600–603 (2012)
4. Kaur, A., Singh, A.: Optimizing feature extraction techniques constituting phone-based modelling on connected words for Punjabi automatic speech recognition. In: Proceedings of the 2nd International Conference on Advances in Computing, Communications and Informatics (ICACCI), Jaipur, India, pp. 2104–2108 (2016b)
5. Kadyan, V., Mantri, A., Aggarwal, R.K., Singh, A.: A comparative study of deep neural network-based Punjabi—ASR system. Int. J. Speech Technol. 22(1), 111–119 (2018)
6. Venkateswarlu, R.L.K., Teja, R.R., Kumari, R.V.: Developing efficient speech recognition system for Telugu letter recognition. In: Proceedings of International Conference on Computing, Communication and Applications, pp. 1–6 (2012)
7. Kumar, A., Dua, M., Choudhary, A.: Implementation and performance evaluation of continuous Hindi speech recognition. In: Proceedings of International Conference on Electronics and Communication Systems (ICECS), pp. 1–5 (2014a)
8. Bharali, S.S., Kalita, S.K.: Speech recognition with reference to Assamese language using novel fusion technique. Int. J. Speech Technol. 21(2), 251–263 (2018). https://doi.org/10.1007/s10772-018-9501-1
9. Bhowmik, T., Chowdhury, A., Mandal, S.K.D.: Deep neural network-based place and manner of articulation detection and classifcation for Bengali continuous speech. Procedia Comput. Sci. 125, 895–901 (2018)
10. Mohamed, F.K., Lajish, V.L.: Nonlinear speech analysis and modeling for Malayalam vowel recognition. Procedia Comput. Sci. 93, 676–682 (2016)

11. Chellapriyadharshini, M., Tofy, A., Srinivasa, R.K.M., Ramasubramanian, V.: Semi-supervised and active-learning scenarios: efficient acoustic model refinement for a low resource Indian language. In: Computer and Languages, pp. 1041–1045 (2018)
12. Manjunath, K.E., Sreenivasa Rao, K.: Improvement of phone recognition accuracy using articulatory features. Circ. Syst. Sig. Process. **37**(2), 704–728 (2017). https://doi.org/10.1007/s00034-017-0568-8
13. Darekar, R.V., Dhande, A.P.: Emotion recognition from Marathi speech database using adaptive artifcial neural network. Biol. Inspired Cognit. Archit. **23**, 35–42 (2018)
14. Kurian, C., Balakrishnan, K.: Speech recognition of Malayalam numbers. In: Proceedings of the World Congress on Nature and Biologically Inspired Computing, pp. 1475–1479 (2009)
15. Paul, A.K., Das, D., Kamal, M.: Bangla speech recognition system using LPC and ANN. In: Proceedings of the 7th International Conference on Advances in Pattern Recognition, pp. 171–174 (2009)
16. Sarma, B.D., Sarmah, P., Lalhminghlui, W., Prasanna, S.M.: Detection of Mizo tones. In: Proceedings of Sixteenth Annual Conference of the International Speech Communication Association, pp. 934–937 (2015)
17. Sukumar, A.R., Shah, A.F., Anto, P.B.: Isolated question words recognition from speech queries by using artifcial neural networks. In: Proceedings of international conference on computing communication and networking technologies, pp. 1–4 (2010)
18. Bhuvanagirir, K., Kopparapu, S.K.: Mixed language speech recognition without explicit identifcation of language. Am. J. Sig. Process. **2**(5), 92–97 (2012)
19. Das, B., Mandal, S., Mitra, P.: Bengali speech corpus for continuous automatic speech recognition system. In: Proceedings of the International Conference on Speech Database and Assessments, pp. 51–55 (2011)
20. Sarma, B.D., Sarma, M., Sarma, M., Prasanna, S.R.M.: Development of Assamese phonetic engine: some issues. In: Proceedings of the annual IEEE India Conference (INDICON), pp. 1–6 (2013)
21. Kumar, S.B.S., Rao, K.S., Pati, D.: Phonetic and prosodically rich transcribed speech corpus in Indian languages: Bengali and Odia. In: Proceedings of International Conference Oriental COCOSDA held Jointly with 2013 Conference on Asian Spoken Language Research and Evaluation (O-COCOSDA/CASLRE), pp. 1–5 (2013a)
22. Patil, P.P., Pardeshi, S.A.: Devnagari phoneme recognition system. In: Proceedings of the Fourth International Conference on Advances in Computing and Communications (ICACC), pp. 5–8 (2014b)
23. Patil, P.P., Pardeshi, S.A.: Marathi connected word speech recognition system. In: Proceedings of the First International Conference on Networks and Soft Computing (ICNSC), pp. 314–318 (2014a)
24. Hemakumar, G., Punitha, P.: Automatic segmentation of Kannada speech signal into syllables and sub-words: noised and noiseless signals. Int. J. Sci. Eng. Res. **5**(1), 1707–1711 (2014)
25. Patil, V.V., Rao, P.: Detection of phonemic aspiration for spoken Hindi pronunciation evaluation. J. Phon. **54**, 202–221 (2016)
26. Dua, M., Aggarwal, R.K., Biswas, M.: Discriminative training using heterogeneous feature vector for Hindi automatic speech recognition system. In: Proceedings of International Conference on Computer and Applications (ICCA), pp. 158–162 (2017)
27. Kannadaguli, P., Bhat, V.: A comparison of Bayesian and HMM based approaches in machine learning for emotion detection in native Kannada speaker. In: Proceedings of the IEEMA Engineer infinite conference (eTechNxT), pp. 1–6 (2018)
28. Pulugundla, B., et al.: BUT system for low resource Indian language ASR. In: Interspeech, pp. 3182–3186 (2018)

29. Dua, M., Aggarwal, R.K., Biswas, M.: Discriminative training using noise robust integrated features and refned HMM modeling. J. Intell. Syst. (2018). https://doi.org/10.1515/jisys-2017-0618

30. Samudravijaya, K., Rao, P.V.S., Agrawal, S.S.: Hindi speech database. In: Proceedings of the International Conference on Spoken Language Processing, pp. 456–464 (2002)

31. Fathima, N., Patel, T., Mahima, C., Iyengar, A.: TDNN-based multilingual speech recognition system for low resource Indian languages. In: Proceedings of the Inter-speech, pp. 3197–3201 (2018)

32. Pandey, L., Nathwani, K.: LSTM based attentive fusion of spectral and prosodic information for keyword spotting in Hindi language. In: Interspeech, pp 112–116 (2018)

33. Pal, M., Roy, R., Khan, S., Bepari, M.S., Basu, J.: PannoMulloKathan: voice enabled mobile app for agricultural commodity price dissemination in Bengali language. In: Interspeech, pp. 1491–1492 (2018)

34. Patel, T., Krishna, D.N., Fathima, N., Shah, N., Mahima, C., Kumar, D., Iyengar, A.: Development of large vocabulary speech recognition system with keyword search for Manipuri. In: Proceedings of Inter speech (2018). https://doi.org/10.21437/Interspeech.2018-2133

35. Bhatt, S., Jain, A., Dev, A.: Monophone-based connected word Hindi speech recognition improvement. Sādhanā **46**(2), 1–17 (2021). https://doi.org/10.1007/s12046-021-01614-3

36. Agrawal, S.S., Jain, A., Sinha, S.: Analysis and modeling of acoustic information for automatic dialect classification. Int. J. Speech Technol. **19**(3), 593–609 (2016). https://doi.org/10.1007/s10772-016-9351-7

37. Bhatt, S., Dev, A., Jain, A.: Effects of the dynamic and energy-based feature extraction on Hindi speech recognition. Recent Adv. Comput. Sci. Commun. **14**(5), 1422–1430 (2021)

38. Bhatt, S., Dev, A., Jain, A.: Confusion analysis in phoneme based speech recognition in Hindi. J. Ambient Intell. Humanized Comput. **11**(10), 4213–4238 (2020). https://doi.org/10.1007/s12652-020-01703-x

39. Kumari, R., Dev, A., Kumar, A.: Automatic segmentation of Hindi speech into syllable-like units. Int. J. Adv. Comput. Sci. Appl. **11**(5), 400–406 (2020)

40. Bhatt, S., Jain, A., Dev, A.: Feature extraction techniques with analysis of confusing words for speech recognition in the Hindi language. Wireless Pers. Commun. **118**(4), 3303–3333 (2021). https://doi.org/10.1007/s11277-021-08181-0

41. Bhatt, S., Jain, A., Dev, A.: Continuous speech recognition technologies—a review. In: Singh, M., Rafat, Y. (eds.) Recent Developments in Acoustics. LNME, pp. 85–94. Springer, Singapore (2021). https://doi.org/10.1007/978-981-15-5776-7_8

42. Kumari, R., Dev, A., Kumar, A.: An efficient adaptive artificial neural network-based text to speech synthesizer for Hindi language. Multimedia Tools Appl. **80**(16), 24669–24695 (2021)

43. Sethi, N., Prajapati, D.K.: Text-independent voice authentication system using MFCC features. In: Gupta, D., Khanna, A., Bhattacharyya, S., Hassanien, A.E., Anand, S., Jaiswal, A. (eds.) International Conference on Innovative Computing and Communications. AISC, vol. 1165, pp. 567–577. Springer, Singapore (2021). https://doi.org/10.1007/978-981-15-5113-0_45

44. Sethi, N., Kumar, A., Swami, R.: Automated web development: theme detection and code generation using Mix-NLP. In: ACM International Conference Proceeding Series, p. a45 (2019)

45. Sethi, D., Sethi, N., Gambhir, P., Anand, R.: E-Pandit: automated voice-based system for religious puja's. In: ICRITO 2020 - IEEE 8th International Conference on Reliability, Infocom Technologies and Optimization (Trends and Future Directions), pp. 174–181, 9197831 (2020)

46. Sethi, N., Agrawal, P., Madaan, V., Singh, S.K., Kumar, A.: Automated title generation in English language using NLP. Int. J. Control Theor. Appl. **9**(Specialissue11), 5159–5168 (2016)

Analytical Approach for Sentiment Analysis of Movie Reviews Using CNN and LSTM

Arushi Garg, Soumya Vats, Garima Jaiswal$^{(\boxtimes)}$, and Arun Sharma

Indira Gandhi Delhi Technical University for Women, Delhi, India
arunsharma@igdtuw.ac.in

Abstract. With the rapid growth of technology and easier access to the internet, several forums like Twitter, Facebook, Instagram, etc., have come up, providing people with a space to express their opinions and reviews about anything and everything happening in the world. Movies are widely appreciated and criticized art forms. They are a significant source of entertainment and lead to web forums like IMDB and amazon reviews for users to give their feedback about the movies and web series. These reviews and feedback draw incredible consideration from scientists and researchers to capture the vital information from the data. Although this information is unstructured, it is very crucial. Deep learning and machine learning have grown as powerful tools examining the polarity of the sentiments communicated in the review, known as 'opinion mining' or 'sentiment classification.' Sentiment analysis has become the most dynamic exploration in NLP (natural language processing) as text frequently conveys rich semantics helpful for analyzing. With ongoing advancement in deep learning, the capacity to analyze this content has enhanced significantly. Convolutional Neural Networks (CNN) and Long Short Term Memory (LSTM) is primarily implemented as powerful deep learning techniques in Natural Language Processing tasks. This study covers an exhaustive study of sentiment analysis of movie reviews using CNN and LSTM by elaborating the approaches, datasets, results, and limitations.

Keywords: CNN · LSTM · Movie reviews · Sentiment analysis

1 Introduction

In today's world, with ever-growing access to the internet and its many services, it has become easier for users to express their opinions and reviews about various topics, from political views to books. Movies are visual art that continues to grow and multiply over year and year [1]. Movies are a widely appreciated and criticized art form, with movie reviews by critics and regular people holding weightage in forming others' decisions about the same. The film industry is a booming industry and considerably contributes to the economy's growth, so customer feedback is essential for the improvement and growth of the industry. It helps the movie creators understand the content their viewers want to watch and helps other viewers choose what might interest them. When users express their views, they need to understand their requirements and make necessary changes

© Springer Nature Switzerland AG 2022
A. Dev et al. (Eds.): AIST 2021, CCIS 1546, pp. 99–115, 2022.
https://doi.org/10.1007/978-3-030-95711-7_9

to keep them as customers for longer [2]. It is humanly impossible and illogical to go through the thousands of reviews available on numerous rating websites, so automation is required. Machine learning can assist mainly in terms of effectiveness and efficiency.

Sentiment analysis of movie reviews is an automated categorization of movie reviews based on their polarity, i.e., 'Negative' and 'Positive.' Sentiment analysis using machine learning helps users choose what's best for them most efficiently and quickly and helps businesses handle customer feedback. They could utilize it to characterize and organize such feedback consequently and could subsequently decide, for instance, the percentage of happy client base without perusing any customer input. Sentiment analysis has perceived huge consideration since it transforms unstructured surveys of clients into valuable data. In simple terms, sentiment analysis is preprocessing the given textual data and extracting the emotion, also known as opinion mining [3]. Sentiment analysis is one of the essential parts of Natural Language processing, a component of AI [4, 36].

In this work, we have zeroed in on understanding the polarity of the given movie reviews by arranging whether it is positively polarized or negatively polarized. This issue can be acted like a multi-label classification task where the last assessment could be worse, bad, impartial, great, and brilliant. In this work, the issue is acted like a binary classification task where the last assessment can be either certain or negative. The surveys given by various individuals are of various lengths, with an alternate quantity of words in each audit. Sentence vectorization techniques are utilized to manage the fluctuation of the sentence length.

Natural-language-based sentiment classification has many applications, such as movie review classification, subjective and objective sentence classification, and text classification technology. Traditional text classification approaches were dictionary-based and basic machine learning techniques. Yet, as of late, they have been supplanted by more productive and precise profound learning techniques, for example, sequence-based long-term short memory (LSTM) and, all the more as of late, the convolution neural network (CNN) technique. LSTM is a worked-on recurring neural network (RNN) design that utilizes a gating instrument comprising of an input gate, forget gate, and output gate. These gates assist with deciding if information in the previous state ought to be held or forgotten in the present state. Subsequently, the gating system helps the LSTM address the issue of long-term information preservation and the vanishing gradient problem experienced by customary RNNs. The LSTM's incredible capacity to extricate progressed text data assumes a significant part in text classification. The extent of utilization of LSTMs has extended quickly as of late, and numerous researchers have proposed numerous ways of redoing LSTMs to work on their precision additionally. The present paper presents a sentiment analysis on movie reviews, illustrating the datasets, approach, results, and limitations for the work done by the researchers.

2   Related Work

With the growing trend in this domain, we studied the work done by the researchers from 2017 to 2021. The relevant papers were extracted from various online databases like Springer, Elsevier, Wiley, IEEE, ACM Digital Library, etc. We analyzed the approaches, results, datasets, and limitations of the methods implemented to analyze movie reviews using CNN and LSTM.

Recurrent neural networks (RNN) are incredible for modeling sequence data such as time series or natural language. The authors of [3] have shown that lower rank RNTN (Recursive Neural Tensor Network) attained approximate accuracies to standard RNTN much faster. Pouransari et al. [4] implemented a few classifiers, including random forest, SVM, and logistic regression, to perform the binary classification on the IMDB dataset procured from Kaggle and recursive neural tensor network executed in the second part to train a multi-sentiment analyzer. Thus, getting different accuracy values for various combinations of algorithms and obtaining the highest value for the RNN model. The author in [5] proposed a hybrid model of Bi-LSTM and CNN and solved the issue of data loss when the size of the training dataset increases and yields an accuracy of 91.41%. They also provided a different solution to the long-term dependency problem. In [6], the authors proposed a hybrid model of CNN and LSTM. Different features and advantages of both LSTM and CNN were combined to attain high accuracy, which is 91%. It closely examines traditional neural networking strategies and tentatively shows higher precision in neural network programs.

In [7], the authors have performed N-gram analysis on the IMDB dataset and applied the SVM and recursive neural network model. They have also used various combinations of algorithms to obtain high accuracy, and the highest accuracy is achieved by the model RNN-LM + NB SVM Trigram analysis, i.e. 92.57%. Yin et al. [8] utilized CNN and lexical assets to acquire an exactness of 87.9% and presumed that SCNN further develops sentiment analysis by utilizing word semantic implanting and sentiment analysis. Naive Bayes is a straightforward yet powerful and regularly utilized machine learning classifier. N-gram analysis and NBSVM were implemented in [9] to achieve an accuracy of 93.05% and hence concluded that when this model is combined with RNN-LSTM, it gives the best result among all the ensemble models.

Govindarajan et al. [10] concluded that the Genetic Algorithm performs better than NB. They concluded that hybrid classifiers are more accurate than single classifiers. The author in [11] proved that Naive Bayes achieved the highest accuracy compared to KNN and the Random forest algorithm. The classification algorithm for two-group classification problems is utilized by a supervised machine learning model called SVM (Support Vector Machine). A support vector machine (SVM) is a supervised machine learning model that utilizes classification algorithms for two-group classification problems. In the wake of giving an SVM model arrangement of labeled training data for every category, they're ready to classify new content. In the wake of giving an SVM model arrangement of labeled training data for every category, they're prepared to classify new content. The k-nearest neighbors (KNN) supervised machine learning algorithm may cover both characterization and regression issues. It's not difficult to execute and comprehend and is one of the most widely used for sentiment analysis. The algorithms of information gain and KNN were implemented in [1, 12]. These algorithms enabled them to achieve an accuracy of 96.80%.

Lexical analysis is the primary period of gathering. The altered source code is taken from language preprocessors that are written as sentences. The job of the lexical analyzer is to disintegrate the syntaxes into a series of tokens by eliminating any whitespace or comments in the source code. The authors adopted rule-based methodologies [13] that characterize many rules and information sources like classic natural language processing techniques, stemming, tokenization, a region of speech tagging, and contextualizing of machine learning for sentiment analysis. In [14], the authors showed that KNN achieved an accuracy of 60% without feature selection, but after using information gain, the accuracy was enhanced to 96.8%.

A composite model was proposed, which consists of a Probabilistic Neural Network (PNN) and a two-layered Restricted Boltzmann (RBM) in [15], which helped the author to achieve an accuracy of 85.6%. Nezhad et al. [16] came up with a deep learning model for Persian sentiment analysis. Their model had two learning stages, utilizing the Skip-gram model for learning vector representation of words and using two deep neural organizations (Bidirectional LSTM and CNN) separately in a supervised way. In [17], the authors consolidated RNN and LSTM, which gave the best outcome among all the ensemble models.

The authors of [18] observed that stacked bi-LSTM outperformed shallow machine learning techniques. But the authors did not work for multi-language movie reviews. Since most of the work done by different researchers' explored the English language only, there is a significant need to explore other languages - Arabic, Chinese, etc. In [19], a French (multilingual) dataset was used to improve generalization capabilities, and CNN was implemented for unseen data. The proposed model can jointly detect aspects and associated sentiments expressed by reviews at the same time.

A composite model [20] was proposed, which comprised a Probabilistic Neural Network (PNN) and a two-layered Restricted Boltzmann (RBM). The authors showed that feature selection methods, specifically information gain [21], can work on the precision of the SVM classifiers. Movie review data can be categorized into positive and negative reviews. A Bi-LSTM model was proposed in [22, 23]. Bidirectional LSTMs are a development of conventional LSTMs that can escalate model performance on sequence classification problems. In issues where inconsistent strides of the information arrangement are accessible, Bidirectional LSTMs train two instead of one LSTMs on the input sequence. Bi-LSTM models utilized along with CNN and attention mechanism [5] may yield higher precision. In [24], the authors explored CNN by setting the number of pooling and convolutional layers to one for analyzing the aspect level of sentiments, which also gave precise results.

Nghiem et al. [25] discussed a CNN-Tree-LSTM model, which achieved good results. Authors in [26, 27] also proposed a hybrid model of CNN and LSTM and experimentally showed that the results outperformed the pure neural network's performance. Continuous Bag of Words (CBOW) and skip-gram approach was deployed in [28] to increase the word vector accuracy and training speed. Bi-LSTM model and methods of Term Frequency and Inverse Document frequency were used to calculate the weight of vectors to enhance the accuracy further. The authors in [29] have shown that CNN surpassed the results of LSTM and CNN-LSTM, which depicted that LSTM performs well in NLP assignments where the syntactic and semantic structures are both significant. Jnoub et al. [30] experimentally demonstrated that neural networks work more efficiently than random forest and SVM as they extract robust features using vectorization methods. The author in [31] showed that neural networks aid in the estimation of sentiment analysis of literary data and aids in sentiment analysis of visual data. CNN helps by forming an inside association among text and picture and gives a predominant result in sentiment analysis.

Authors in [32] proposed lexicon integrated two channels CN-LSTM and CNN-BiLSTM model, whereas the authors in [33] used generic opinion lexicon to gain accuracy of 82.57%. The proposed approach performs sentiment analysis at the condition level to ensure that opinions for various viewpoints can be dissected independently. The framework processes the linguistic conditions of words in a sentence, partitions it into autonomous provisos. It ascertains the logical opinion score of every statement zeroing in on a particular angle. Dang et al. [35] experimentally demonstrated that hybrid models showed the best accuracy compared to all other models. It was also observed that SVM makes computational time much longer. Jain et al. [34] performed sentiment classification on Twitter Dataset and applied CNN model to achieve an accuracy of 74.42%.

Table 1 summarizes the work done by researchers for analyzing movie reviews. The dataset, approach, results, accuracy, and limitations are elaborated. From the table, it can be concluded that the IMDB dataset is the most widely used. Various preprocessing approaches were implemented by the researchers - Word2Vec, word embedding, encoding, and vectorization. The deep learning approaches outperform machine learning algorithms though they have limitations like time consumption, proneness to overfitting, and inability to handle emojis.

3 Dataset

Different datasets have been used in different projects to test and train the model and predict the accuracy and efficiency of the model. Some of the standard datasets explored are elaborated.

Stanford sentiment Treebank dataset of movie reviews is divided into two parts. Stanford sentiment treebank −1 contains movie reviews labeled as fine-grain labels as very positive, positive, neutral, negative, and very negative. The second part of the dataset, i.e., Stanford sentiment treebank −2, contains movie reviews labeled as only two categories, positive and negative. It contains 1250 movie reviews labeled as positive and 1250 movie reviews labeled as negative.

Cornell dataset of movie reviews contains 1000 positive and 1000 negative reviews. Sentibank contains around 20,000 image posts containing one image and a text description of the image for sentiment analysis.

IMDB is one of the largest datasets available on the internet. It contains 50,000 labeled movie reviews, 25,000 are positively polarized, and 25,000 are negatively polarized. The negative reviews have a score of $<= 4$ out of 10, and positive reviews have a score of $>= 7$ out of 10. The dataset also contains additional unlabeled data.

Amazon review dataset contains approximately 8 million reviews as of October 2012, and the review contains user information and product information, ratings, and plain text review. Around 7,911,684 reviews were given by 889,176 users for 253,059 products. Around 16,341 users have given more than 50 reviews on various products. The median no of words used per review lies around 101. These reviews were collected from Aug 1997 to Oct 2012.

Table 1. Comparative study on movie reviews analysis using CNN and LSTM.

Paper ID	DataSet	Approach	Accuracy	Results	Limitations
Bodapati et al. [3]	IMDB	MLP, SVM, CNN, DNN and LSTM	Logistic Regression-85.5%; LSTM + DNN-88.46%	• Comparative study between traditional and neural networks • LSTM with DNN showed the highest accuracy	Difficult to detect small emotions
Pouransari et al. [4]	IMDB	Bag of words, word2vec, SVM, Logistic regression, Random forest and Recursive neural network	Random forest - 84%; Logistic Regression classifier - 86.6%	• RNTN with lower ranks can accomplish equivalent accuracy to standard RNTN a lot quicker • RNTN with a lower rank allows us to train several models and use them for ensemble averaging	Nonlinear problems cannot be solved using this algorithm
Jang et al. [5]	IMDB	CNN, LSTM, And MLP	Hybrid model-89.06%; proposed model - 90.01%	• A hybrid model of CNN-LSTM is proposed to achieve higher accuracy • An elective solution for the drawn-out reliance and data loss issue while training a huge dataset is proposed	Large memory bandwidth is required
Rehman et al. [6]	IMDB, Amazon reviews	Word embedding using word2vec model, application of CNN and LSTM hybrid model	CNN + LSTM-91%	• Comparative research between traditional and neural networking methods • Word2vec used for word embedding • Experimentally shown higher accuracy in neural network algorithms	Inclined to overfit and it is hard to apply the dropout calculation to control this issue

(continued)

Table 1. (*continued*)

Paper ID	DataSet	Approach	Accuracy	Results	Limitations
Mesnil et al. [7]	IMDB	N-gram RNN-LM Sentence Vectors NB-SVM Trigram	State of the art 91.22%	• Compared accuracies of various combinations of traditional and neural network methods • Usage of N-gram analysis is discussed	Difficult to recognize and elucidate the final model
Yin et al. [8]	Stanford Sentiment Treebank	CNN, lexical resource	CNN-87.9%	• SCNN further develops sentiment analysis by leveraging word and semantic and sentiment embedding	Do not tell the position and orientation of the object
Dhande et al. [9]	IMDB, Amazon reviews	Naive Bayes, Neural Network Classifier	Naive Neural Classifier-80.65%	• In data mining, Naive Bayes and Neural Network classifiers are used for classification tasks	The algorithm faces the zero-frequency problem
Govind Rajan et al. [10]	IMDB	Naive Bayes, Genetic Algorithm	Hybrid NGB_GA Method-93.80%	• GA performs better than NB. The hybrid classifier is more accurate than single classifiers	Time-consuming and hence still less in art
Baid et al. [11]	IMDB	K-nearest neighbor, Random forest, Naive Bayes	Naive Bayes - 81.4%; Random forest - 78.65%	• Naive Bayes achieved the highest accuracy. A hybrid model is suggested	For better accuracy, a larger dataset need to be trained
Samat et al. [12]	IMDB	SVM, Stochastic pooling, Max pooling, Average pooling CNN	–	• Experiment on CNN with three different pooling level • Max Pooling and Stochastic Pooling improve when there is an increment in the quantity of convolutional and pooling layers	Lack of stability

(*continued*)

Table 1. (*continued*)

Paper ID	DataSet	Approach	Accuracy	Results	Limitations
Brar et al. [13]	TMDB	Machine Learning, Neural Language Processing, Sentiment Lexicon	ML-81.22%	• An online API for sentiment analysis for movie reviews with JSON yield to show results on any operating framework	Low accuracy due to the implementation of traditional machine learning algorithms
Mitra et al. [14]	–	Logistic Regression, Random Forest, Decision Tree, N-gram analysis	Logistic Regression-80%	• Classic natural language processing techniques, stemming from tokenization are used to process the data and conclude that the sentiment classification's strength relies upon the lexicon's scale	The model is not ready to capture complex relationships
Lei et al. [15]	Stanford Sentiment Treebank	CNN, SVM, LSTM	CNN+LSTM-84.35%	• LR-LSTM and LR-Bi-LSTM steadily beat RNTN, LSTM, BiLSTM, and CNN on datasets	Prone to overfitting
Nezhad et al. [16]	–	Word2vec, LSTM, CNN, RNTN, Max Pooling, GRU (Gated recurrent unit)	RNTM-85%	• CNN-LSTM works nearly better in collation with CNN-GRU • GRU is easier to train than LSTM and has fewer parameters	Inability to handle unknown words
Li et al. [17]	IMDB	N-gram analysis, NBSVM	NBSVM-93.05%	• When combined with RNN-LSTM, the model gives the best result among all the ensemble models	No guarantee that it will be able to represent all unseen instances

(*continued*)

Table 1. (*continued*)

Paper ID	DataSet	Approach	Accuracy	Results	Limitations
Ray et al. [18]	Twitter, Stanford Sentiment Treebank, SemEval Task	CNN, Rule-Based	Precision-88.6%; Recall-90.5%	• This blended methodology is presented for extricating and estimating the angle levels of assumptions. A seven-layer explicit profound CNN is created	A lot of manual work is required
Kane et al. [19]	French SemEval2016 annotated	CNN + LSTM	CLC-77.2%	• To improve generalization capabilities, CNN is applied to unseen data jointly to detect aspects and associated sentiments at the same time	Lack of resources and work done in French. More attention needs to be given to CLC. Need of developing ABSA to get rid of annotations
Ain et al. [20]	Twitter	CNN, SVM, LSTM,	85.60%	• A composite model has been proposed, which contain a Probabilistic Neural Network (PNN) and a two-layered Restricted Boltzmann (RBM)	Unable to detect emojis, images, and other multimedia
Maulauna et al. [21]	Cornell, Stanford dataset	SVM, Information Gain	SVM+IG-86.6%	• The accuracy of the SVM classifiers is enhanced by the utilization of the feature selection method	Long training time for dataset
Gupta et al. [22]	IMDB t	Senti_ALSTM, Bi-LSTM, KSTM, CNN	Senti_ALSTM-87.43%	• Comprises Glo-Ve 300 measurements word embedding which is superior to one hot embedding and devours less space for storing vectors	Execution of attention-based bidirectional LSTM can be utilized for upgrading results

(*continued*)

Table 1. (*continued*)

Paper ID	DataSet	Approach	Accuracy	Results	Limitations
Dashtipour et al. [23]	Cafecinema	Stacked-BiLSTM, MLP-Autoencoder	Stacked-BiLSTM-95.61%; Stacked LSTM-93.65%	• Stacked bi-LSTM outperformed shallow machine learning approaches	Multilingual reviews may be explored
Shen et al. [24]	IMDB	CNN, LSTM	CNN+LSTM-82.5%	• The number of pooling and convolutional layers is one, which performed best by comparison	Adjectives and adverbs that describe the feelings of the author are not being included for pre-processing
Van et al. [25]	Stanford Sentiment Treebank	CNN-Tree-LSTM	CNN-Tree-LSTM-89.7%	• CNN-Tree-LSTM outperforms most pure convolution • The use of RNN is superior to k-max pooling	A binary setting can be unsafe to Glove Amazon in the fine-grained setting
Minaee et al. [26]	IMDB	Ensemble of LSTM and CNN	LSTM+CNN-90%	• Performance is gained by the ensemble as compared to individual CNN and LSTM model	The accuracy needs to be further improved by jointly training the LSTM and CNN model
Kaur et al. [27]	IMDB, Wikipedia (January 2020)	CNN, LSTM	CNN+LSTM-95.01%	• The model gives better accuracy as compared to the baseline system for CNN	Emojis cannot be processed. Fake reviews cannot be distinguished
Xu et al. [28]	1500 hotel comment text from ctrip	Word2vec, CBOW, Skip-gram, LSTM	LSTM-92.18	• BiLSTM model proposed for higher accuracy • CBOW and skip-gram are used for increasing the accuracy of word vectors and training speed • TF and IDF weight calculation methods are used	Inability to handle short forms and emojis

(*continued*)

Table 1. (*continued*)

Paper ID	DataSet	Approach	Accuracy	Results	Limitations
Haque et la. [29]	IMDB	Word2vec, CNN, LSTM	CNN - 91%; LSTM-86%; CNN - LSTM -88%	• CNN has outperformed LSTM • LSTM performs really great in NLP tasks where the syntactic and semantic structure is of utmost importance	Inability to handle unknown words
Jnoub et al. [30]	IMDB, Amazon Restaurants review	CNN, SNN, DCC, Autoencoders	Autoencoders-70% SVM-77%;CNN-86	• Showed better results because neural models can extract robust features using vectors	Low performance is a disadvantage here
Cai et al. [31]	SentiBank	CNN	Test CNN-77%; Image CNN-72.3%;Multi CNN-79.6%	• An interior connection between text and picture helps in better execution in sentiment prediction	More investigation into multimedia is needed with substantially more mix among text, image, and social media
Li et al. [32]	Stanford sentiment Treebank	Lexicon integrated two-channel CNN-BiLSTM model	CNN-BiLSTM (sentiment Padding) - 49.8944%	• Proposed the sentiment padding method to ensure that the input data has consistency and size and to improve the proportion of information related to sentiments in the review	More focus on the factors that influence the coupling of two branches CNN and Bi-LSTM

(*continued*)

Table 1. (*continued*)

Paper ID	DataSet	Approach	Accuracy	Results	Limitations
Thet et al. [33]	IMDB dataset	Generic opinion lexicon	82.57%	• The proposed approach is compelling for aspect-based sentiment analysis of short reports, for example, message posts on conversation sheets • This approach focuses on providing the sentiment score of a clause or a sentence	Do not focus on feature extraction
Stojanovski et al. [34]	Twitter	Glo Ve, CNN	74.42%	• CNN that leverage on pre trained word vectors perform well on text classification	Low performance is a disadvantage here
Dang et al. [35]	IMDB dataset, Cornell movie reviews	CNN+LSTM, SVM	93.4%	• Hybrid models showed the best accuracy as compared to all other models • The effectiveness of the algorithm depends largely on the characteristics of the dataset	Using SVM makes computational time much longer

Wikipedia dataset comprises about 6000 reviews, out of which 2253 are highly positive, 1453 are positive, whereas 835 are negative and 1120 are highly negative and used for training od model. Also, around 300 different reviews were used for testing, and the other 400 reviews were used to develop the model.

Table 2 summarizes the details about datasets frequently used by various researchers for their research in this field of sentiment analysis of movie reviews. From this table, it can be easily observed that the IMDB dataset is the most widely used.

Stanford sentiment Treebank dataset of movie reviews are divided into two parts Stanford sentiment treebank −1 which contains movie reviews labeled as fine-grain labels as very positive, positive, neutral, negative, and very negative. The second part of the dataset i.e., Stanford sentiment treebank −2 contains movie reviews labeled as only two categories positive and negative. It contains 1250 movie reviews labeled as positive and 1250 movie reviews labeled as negative.

Cornell dataset of movie reviews contains 1000 positive and 1000 negative reviews. Sentibank contains around 20,000 image posts containing one image and a text description of the image for sentiment analysis.

IMDB is one of the largest datasets available on the internet. It contains 50,000 labeled movie reviews out of which 25,000 are positively polarized and 25,000 are negatively polarized. The negative reviews have a score of <= 4 out of 10 and positive reviews have a score of >= 7 out of 10. The dataset also contains additional unlabeled data.

Amazon review dataset contains approximately 8 million reviews as of October 2012, the review contains user information and product information, ratings, and plain text review. Around 7,911,684 reviews were given by 889,176 users for 253,059 products. Around 16,341 users have given more than 50 reviews on various products. The median of no of words used per review lies around 101. These reviews were collected in the time span of Aug 1997–Oct 2012.

Wikipedia dataset comprises of about 6000 reviews out of which 2253 are extremely positive, 1453 are positive whereas 835 are negative and 1120 are extremely negative and these are used for training od model. Also, around 300 different reviews were used for testing and the other 400 reviews were used for the development of the model.

Table 2 summarizes the details about datasets that are frequently used by various researchers for their research in this field of sentiment analysis of movie reviews. from this table, it can be easily observed that the IMDB dataset is the most widely used dataset.

Table 2. Comparative study on various datasets used for sentiment analysis of movie reviews.

S.No.	Dataset	Description	References
1	Stanford sentiment Treebank dataset	Dataset is divided into two parts. One contains movie reviews labeled as fine-grain labels and is divided into five categories, while the other contains movie reviews labeled as only two categories	[8, 15, 18, 25, 32]
2	Cornell dataset	The dataset contains about 2000 reviews, 1000 are positive, and the other 1000 are negative	[21, 35]

(*continued*)

Table 2. (*continued*)

S.No.	Dataset	Description	References
3	IMDB dataset	The dataset contains 50,000 reviews which are equally divided into negative and positive polarity	[3–7, 9–13, 17, 22, 24, 26, 27, 29, 30, 33, 35]
4	Amazon review dataset	The dataset contains 8 million reviews with user and product information, and these reviews were collected from Aug 1997 to Oct 2012	[9, 30]
5	Wikipedia dataset	The dataset comprises about 6000 movie reviews, out of which 300 are used for testing, 400 are used for model development, and the other is majorly used for training purposes	[27]
6	Sentibank	The dataset contains one image and a text description for that image	[18, 31]

4 Conclusion

Sentiment analysis is an emerging area, and it has different determinations in web-based media, for example, movie reviews. Artificial intelligence can be used to understand and generate results from the vast data of reviews present on the internet. With the advancement in deep learning, analyzing the polarity of sentiment expressed in reviews has become more accessible. In the present study, we have reviewed various hybrid models using deep learning (CNN and LSTM) techniques and machine learning algorithms. The results illustrated that the neural network models (CNN, LSTM, Bi-LSTM) combined with other machine learning algorithms (word2vec, bag of words) yielded better and promising results than traditional machine learning methods. CNN has a convolutional layer to extricate data by a more significant part of the text, so we work for sentiment analysis with the convolutional neural network, and we plan a basic convolutional neural network model and test it on the benchmark, the outcome shows that it accomplishes better precision execution on movie review sentiment analysis than traditional strategies like the SVM and Naive Bayes techniques.

For future work, existing sentiment analysis models may be extended with more semantic and reasonable information. Unsupervised approaches may be examined to remove the constraints of the dependencies. In addition to that, emojis need more understanding as they are indispensable parts for representing emotions. And the identity of the author of the reviews also needs to be considered to prevent fake reviews, which can manipulate the results. In the future, we also need to consider multimedia while deciding the polarity of the review and the social media platform. Moreover, more confounded neural network structures to form word embedding and sentiment embedding features may be explored to enhance the results. Future work might investigate more confounded neural network structures to form word embedding and sentiment embedding features.

References

1. Daeli, N.O., Adiwijaya, A.: Sentiment analysis on movie reviews using information gain and K-nearest neighbor. J. Data Sci. Appl. **3**(1), 1–7 (2020)
2. Lakshmi, B.S., Raj, P.S., Vikram, R.R.: Sentiment analysis using deep learning technique CNN with KMeans. Int. J. Pure Appl. Math. **114**(11), 47–57 (2017)
3. Bodapati, J.D., Veeranjaneyulu, N., Shaik, S.: Sentiment analysis from movie reviews using LSTMs. Ingenierie des Systemes d'Information **24**(1), 125–129 (2019)
4. Pouransari, H., Ghili, S.: Deep learning for sentiment analysis of movie reviews. CS224N Proj. 1–8 (2014)
5. Jang, B., Kim, M., Harerimana, G., Kang, S.U., Kim, J.W.: Bi-LSTM model to increase accuracy in text classification: combining Word2vec CNN and attention mechanism. Appl. Sci. **10**(17), 5841 (2020)
6. Rehman, A.U., Malik, A.K., Raza, B., Ali, W.: A hybrid CNN-LSTM model for improving accuracy of movie reviews sentiment analysis. Multimedia Tools Appl. **78**(18), 26597–26613 (2019)
7. Mesnil, G., Mikolov, T., Ranzato, M.A., Bengio, Y.: Ensemble of generative and discriminative techniques for sentiment analysis of movie reviews. arXiv preprint arXiv:1412.5335, 17 December 2014
8. Yin, R., Li, P., Wang, B.: Sentiment lexical-augmented convolutional neural networks for sentiment analysis. In: 2017 IEEE Second International Conference on Data Science in Cyberspace (DSC), June 26 2017, pp. 630–635. IEEE (2017)
9. Dhande, L.L., Patnaik, G.K.: Analyzing sentiment of movie review data using Naive Bayes neural classifier. Int. J. Emerg. Trends Technol. Comput. Sci. (IJETTCS) **3**(4), 313–320 (2014)
10. Govindarajan, M.: Sentiment analysis of movie reviews using hybrid method of naive bayes and genetic algorithm. Int. J. Adv. Comput. Res. **3**(4), 139 (2013)
11. Baid, P., Gupta, A., Chaplot, N.: Sentiment analysis of movie reviews using machine learning techniques. Int. J. Comput. Appl. **179**(7), 45–49 (2017)
12. Samat, N.A., Salleh, M.N., Ali, H.: The comparison of pooling functions in convolutional neural network for sentiment analysis task. In: Ghazali, R., Nawi, N., Deris, M., Abawajy, J. (eds.) SCDM 2020. AISC, vol. 978, pp. 202–210. Springer, Cham (2020). https://doi.org/10.1007/978-3-030-36056-6_20
13. Brar, G.S., Sharma, A.: Sentiment analysis of movie review using supervised machine learning techniques. Int. J. Appl. Eng. Res. **13**(16), 12788–12791 (2018)

14. Mitra, A.: Sentiment analysis using machine learning approaches (lexicon based on movie review dataset). J. Ubiquitous Comput. Commun. Technol. (UCCT) **2**(03), 145–152 (2020)
15. Lei, Z., Yang, Y., Yang, M.: SAAN: a sentiment-aware attention network for sentiment analysis. In: The 41st International ACM SIGIR Conference on Research & Development in Information, 27 June 2018, pp. 1197–1200 (2018)
16. Nezhad, Z.B., Deihimi, M.A.: A combined deep learning model for Persian sentiment analysis. IIUM Eng. J. **20**(1), 129–139 (2019)
17. Li, B., Liu, T., Du, X., Zhang, D., Zhao, Z.: Learning document embeddings by predicting n-grams for sentiment classification of long movie reviews. arXiv preprint arXiv:1512.08183, 27 December 2015
18. Ray, P., Chakrabarti, A.: A mixed approach of deep learning method and rule-based method to improve aspect level sentiment analysis. Appl. Comput. Inform. (2020)
19. Kane, B., et al.: ICAART, no. 1, pp. 498–505 (2021)
20. Ain, Q.T., et al.: Sentiment analysis using deep learning techniques: a review. Int. J. Adv. Comput. Sci. Appl. **8**(6), 424 (2017)
21. Maulana, R., Rahayuningsih, P.A., Irmayani, W., Saputra, D., Jayanti, W.E.: Improved accuracy of sentiment analysis movie review using support vector machine based information gain. J. Phys. Conf. Ser. **1641**(1), 012060 (2020)
22. Gupta, C., Chawla, G., Rawlley, K., Bisht, K., Sharma, M.: Senti_ALSTM: sentiment analysis of movie reviews using attention-based-LSTM. In: Abraham, A., Castillo, O., Virmani, D. (eds.) Proceedings of 3rd International Conference on Computing Informatics and Networks. LNNS, vol. 167, pp. 211–219. Springer, Singapore (2021). https://doi.org/10.1007/978-981-15-9712-1_18
23. Dashtipour, K., Gogate, M., Adeel, A., Larijani, H., Hussain, A.: Sentiment analysis of Persian movie reviews using deep learning. Entropy **23**(5), 596 (2021)
24. Shen, Q., Wang, Z., Sun, Y.: Sentiment analysis of movie reviews based on CNN-BLSTM. In: Shi, Z., Goertzel, B., Feng, J. (eds.) ICIS 2017. IAICT, vol. 510, pp. 164–171. Springer, Cham (2017). https://doi.org/10.1007/978-3-319-68121-4_17
25. Van, V.D., Thai, T., Nghiem, M.Q.: Combining convolution and recursive neural networks for sentiment analysis. In: Proceedings of the Eighth International Symposium on Information and Communication Technology, 7 December 2017, pp. 151–158 (2017)
26. Minaee, S., Azimi, E., Abdolrashidi, A.: Deep-sentiment: sentiment analysis using ensemble of CNN and Bi-LSTM models. arXiv preprint arXiv:1904.04206, 8 April 2019
27. Kaur, H.: Sentiment analysis of user review text through CNN and LSTM methods. PalArch's J. Archaeol. Egypt/Egyptology **17**(12), 290–306 (2020)
28. Xu, G., Meng, Y., Qiu, X., Yu, Z., Wu, X.: Sentiment analysis of comment texts based on BiLSTM. IEEE Access **9**(7), 51522–51532 (2019)
29. Haque, M.R., Lima, S.A., Mishu, S.Z.: Performance analysis of different neural networks for sentiment analysis on IMDb movie reviews. In: 2019 3rd International Conference on Electrical, Computer & Telecommunication Engineering (ICECTE), 26 December 2019, pp. 161–164. IEEE (2019)
30. Jnoub, N., Al Machot, F., Klas, W.: A domain-independent classification model for sentiment analysis using neural models. Appl. Sci. **10**(18), 6221 (2020)
31. Cai, G., Xia, B.: Convolutional neural networks for multimedia sentiment analysis. In: Li, J., Ji, H., Zhao, D., Feng, Y. (eds.) NLPCC 2015. LNCS (LNAI), vol. 9362, pp. 159–167. Springer, Cham (2015). https://doi.org/10.1007/978-3-319-25207-0_14
32. Li, W., Zhu, L., Shi, Y., Guo, K., Cambria, E.: User reviews: sentiment analysis using lexicon integrated two-channel CNN–LSTM family models. Appl. Soft Comput. **94**, 106435 (2020)
33. Thet, T.T., Na, J.C., Khoo, C.S.: Aspect-based sentiment analysis of movie reviews on discussion boards. J. Inf. Sci. **36**(6), 823–848 (2010)

34. Stojanovski, D., Strezoski, G., Madjarov, G., Dimitrovski, I.: Twitter sentiment analysis using deep convolutional neural network. In: Onieva, E., Santos, I., Osaba, E., Quintián, H., Corchado, E. (eds.) HAIS 2015. LNCS (LNAI), vol. 9121, pp. 726–737. Springer, Cham (2015). https://doi.org/10.1007/978-3-319-19644-2_60
35. Dang, C.N., Moreno-García, M.N., De la Prieta, F.: Hybrid deep learning models for sentiment analysis. Complexity **2021** (2021)
36. Bhatt, S., Jain, A., Dev, A.: Monophone-based connected word Hindi speech recognition improvement. Sādhanā **46**(2), 1–17 (2021). https://doi.org/10.1007/s12046-021-01614-3

Analysis of Indian News with Corona Headlines Classification

Janhavi Jain[✉], Debadrita Dey, Bhavika Kelkar, and Khyati Ahlawat

Indira Gandhi Delhi Technical University for Women, Madrasa Road, Opposite Street, James Church, Kashmere Gate, Delhi 110006, India
janhavi.j.98@gmail.com, debadrita3456@gmail.com, bhavika12.1999@gmail.com, khyatiahlawat@igdtuw.ac.in

Abstract. With the advent of the world wide web, the world has seen an explosion in the amount of information that is available online. People stay informed about the national and international affairs through online news which is readily available and portable allowing ease of access. These news pieces tend to shape people's thoughts and provoke emotions, which may be positive, neutral or negative, without them realizing their effect. The objective of this work is to create a hybrid model that can analyze the overall effect of digital news content in India. The hybrid approach of sentiment analysis encompasses lexicon and machine learning algorithms as well as a self-created scored corpus of corona related words to classify all sorts of headlines. The labelled dataset is used to train decision tree and random forest algorithms. They are evaluated based on their accuracy scores, classification reports and confusion matrices. The results prove that both the algorithms perform well on the dataset and that the Indian media highlighted neutral news the most. This finding can be very useful for the Indian news agencies since they can alter their reporting strategies to create an impact of their choice on the readers' minds and thus, increase the readership.

Keywords: Sentiment analysis · Lexicon · Corona corpus · Machine learning · Random forest · Decision trees

1 Introduction

News has always played a dynamic role in shaping a person's thoughts, vision and perception. It can affect people's emotions in a negative or a positive way on a large scale. Headlines alone can have a great impact on people's minds as most of the people just scan through the headlines and judge a news article. Ever since the advent of the internet, online media has also gained a great momentum among people, with the latest news just a click away. This has led to the need of analyzing online news content to understand what type of emotion is being spread by news organizations via a process of sentiment analysis. Sentiment analysis is a text classification process which highlights the sentiment behind a piece of information. It can help the public understand the sentiment behind any news being published and hence, alter their choice of newspapers.

© Springer Nature Switzerland AG 2022
A. Dev et al. (Eds.): AIST 2021, CCIS 1546, pp. 116–126, 2022.
https://doi.org/10.1007/978-3-030-95711-7_10

A lot of development has been made in the area of sentiment analysis of news articles but the work on Indian news and COVID-19 related news is very limited. There has been some progress in the area of sentiment analysis of news articles concerning COVID-19 news headlines since the outbreak of COVID-19. For example: the authors of [16] divided their research into two parts. In the first part they used the topic model to produce topics for each country and for the second part they used the RoBERTa model for sentiment classification of headlines. They examined key topics of English language COVID-19 news articles for 4 countries and analysed the associated sentiments. The authors of [17] studied and investigated the relation between the stock market and news sentiment related to COVID-19. Sentiment scores for COVID-19 related news were generated using BERT-based Financial Sentiment Index.

In this work, sentiment analysis has been done on the headlines of Indian news and the idea is driven by two primary things.

1. What are the emotions conveyed by the headlines and how they affect the audience?
2. How well the machine learning algorithms work in classifying these news headlines correctly?

Online news headlines of two leading Indian newspapers were collected for the period of September 2019 to September 2020 followed by their pre-processing to avoid any future inconsistencies. The preprocessed dataset was later classified into three classes of polarities (positive, negative and neutral) on the basis of the polarity scores received from a lexicon dictionary. A self-created scored corpus of corona related words was created and applied on the dataset to correctly classify covid-19 news headlines which were misclassified by the lexicon. The updated dataset was fed into two ML algorithms, decision trees and random forest, to check how well they could classify the news headlines. Their performance was measured based on metrics like accuracy, F1 score, precision, recall and confusion matrix.

2 Literature Survey

There has been significant work in analyzing sentiments of news headlines using lexicon and machine learning approaches.

The authors of [1] performed analysis of news related to the Coordinator Minister of Maritime Affairs period 2016–2019 using naïve bayes classifier, support vector machine and particle swarm optimization. Researchers of [2] tried to derive the degree of correlation between the information released by the Chinese government about coronavirus and the Chinese public opinion on the issue using BosonNlp sentiment dictionary. In paper [3], the authors studied the news articles reported on the BBC news website which were categorized in 5 classes (business, entertainment, politics, sport and tech). Sentiments were assigned using Wordnet dictionary and TF - IDF method, which fall under lexicon model. The work in [4] presented a way for enlarging small candidate seed lists of positive and negative words into larger lexicons using path-based analysis of synonym and antonym sets in Wordnet. The new seed lists were used to check public sentiments of each entity. The research done in [5] analyzed news articles associated with companies by preprocessing the data to give candidate words which were compared with the words in a positive and a negative dictionary to check for a match. A match led to accumulation of the words in specific classes. The task was accomplished using naïve bayes, Bernoulli naïve bayes and Laplacian smoothing. [6] focused on the effect of certain words used in political texts to influence the sentiments of the public in polls for 3 Indian political parties. The results obtained from SentiWordNet dictionary were compared to naïve bayes and support vector machine results. Researchers of [7] attempted to classify news comments into positive, negative and neutral classes using AFFIN-111 word list, TF-IDF, support vector machine and k-nearest neighbor algorithm. The results indicate better performance of the SVM model. The work accomplished in [8] provided a comparative study of the methods that can be used for analysis of quotations in newspaper articles. The idea involved using a bag of words approach and similarity approach. The labelled dataset became a training set for SVM classifier to determine sentiment classification. The authors of [9] proposed a technique to analyze sentiments of headlines using three models, namely linear SVM, TF-IDF and linear SVM, SGD and linear SVM. The results indicate better performance of TF-IDF and linear SVM for small datasets and of SGD and linear SVM for large datasets. The study conducted in [10] employed a lexicon-based approach to identify sentiments of news articles. Each article was considered a document and assigned polarity using WordNet dictionary. The results showed only a few articles under neutral class. In paper [11], the researchers tried to provide a platform to serve positive news to the public by eliminating negative sentiment news from a pool of articles. This was achieved using a news aggregator and processing engine, SentiWordNet for feature extraction, SVM model and filtering out negative polarity news. The work done in [12] involved sentiment classification of Indian news extracted from Indian journals. The approach was machine learning based and made use of recurrent neural networks with long short-term memory units. The author of [13] studied financial news articles to determine the effect on future stock trends. A dictionary of polarity words was created and applied on the news documents, which were converted into a set of vectors and classified using random forest and naïve bayes algorithms. An extensive study was conducted in [14] that aimed to determine the effect of mutual fund news in India on the investors, amidst covid-19 outbreak, and to create a model to forecast assets under management indicator. The articles extracted from Indian journals were assigned sentiments using the VADER lexicon tool. Assets under management values and sentiment scores were used as variables to train linear regression and multiple regression models. The results showed that sentiment scores and assets under management were generally directly proportional and a regression model could be used to predict assets under management. Researchers of [15] performed sentiment analysis on Punjabi news using a machine learning approach. The dataset was pre-processed and transformed using a TF-IDF vectorizer followed by application of SVM. The classifier first classified news into categories like crime, politics, entertainment, weather and sports and then sorted them into positive and negative classes with high accuracy.

3   Methodology

This study involves a hybrid approach which makes use of lexicon and machine learning techniques to determine overall polarity of Indian news headlines reported during a period of one year from September 2019 - September 2020. Figure 1 illustrates the flow diagram of the proposed work, which has been divided into several phases. Each of the phases has been discussed in detail in the following sections.

3.1 Dataset Collection

The headline texts for this study were collected from two leading Indian English newspapers, namely The Hindu and The Times of India. A python script was written using Beautiful Soup, a python package for parsing HTML and XML files, to scrape the headlines from the prints' website. All the scraped headlines were stored in a csv file for pre-processing.

3.2 Data Preprocessing

Data preprocessing was done to transform raw data into useful and effective format and to minimize the inconsistencies. The steps involved were:

- Removal of punctuations
- Tokenization
- Stop word removal
- Lemmatization
- Removal of duplicate and missing headlines

3.3 Lexicon Based Approach

In this phase, the unlabeled dataset was labeled using bag of words approach where each word was associated with an opinion value that contributes to the overall polarity score of a headline. Initially, TextBlob (a python library) was used to assign polarity to headlines using its polarity sentiment function. However, while skimming through the labeled dataset, many mislabeled tuples were found which led to the use of another python library, NLTK VADER. Its Sentiment Intensity Analyzer function was used to assign polarity scores and it gave an improved dataset. The labels were assigned according to the following rules:

$$\text{IF polarity\_score} < 0 \text{ THEN negative.} \tag{1}$$

$$\text{IF polarity\_score} = 0 \text{ THEN neutral.} \tag{2}$$

$$\text{IF polarity\_score} > 0 \text{ THEN positive.} \tag{3}$$

The work proceeded with the labelling executed by NLTK VADER.

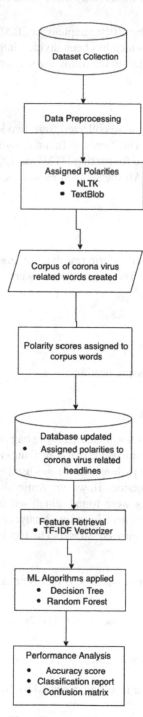

Fig. 1. Flow diagram of the research work.

3.4 Covid Headlines Classification

The NLTK VADER couldn't correctly classify most news headlines related to coronavirus. This was due to different interpretations of many words when used in general and when used in coronavirus context. The words had flipping polarities in both the scenarios. For example, the word "positive" when used in a sentence in general displays a positive sentiment but when used in coronavirus headlines it is rather negative. In such cases, VADER's classification of the headline as positive was a misclassification. To overcome this shortcoming and cater to the news related to coronavirus, a separate covid headlines classification function was created working around the idea of using a self-scored corpus.

Since the term covid19 is polyonymous, a corpus of words was generated containing alternate terms for covid19 and another corpus of words was created containing words that were wrongly classified by the sentiment VADER but were really commonly found with news related to covid-19. Polarity scores of words within the VADER corpus were modified in the new corona corpus so as to fit the coronavirus context such that headlines of covid19 could be correctly classified. Polarity scores assigned by sentiment VADER and polarity scores assigned using the self-created corpus were then compared on the following grounds:

$$\text{IF (Positive Score)}_{\text{Covid}} > \text{(Neutral Score)}_{\text{Vader}} + \text{(Negative Score)}_{\text{Vader}} \text{ THEN}$$
$$\text{(Compound Score)}_{\text{Vader}} = 1. \tag{4}$$

$$\text{IF (Negative Score)}_{\text{Covid}} > \text{(Neutral Score)}_{\text{Vader}} + \text{(Positive Score)}_{\text{Vader}} \text{ THEN}$$
$$\text{(Compound Score)}_{\text{Vader}} = -1. \tag{5}$$

$$\text{IF (Negative Score)}_{\text{Covid}} < \text{(Neutral Score)}_{\text{Vader}} \text{ AND (Negative Score)}_{\text{Covid}} >$$
$$\text{(Positive Score)}_{\text{Vader}} \text{ AND (Neutral Score)}_{\text{Vader}} - \text{(Negative Score)}_{\text{covid}} <= 0.5$$
$$\text{THEN (Compound Score)}_{\text{Vader}} = -1. \tag{6}$$

$$\text{IF (Positive Score)}_{\text{Covid}} < \text{(Neutral Score)}_{\text{Vader}} \text{ AND (Positive Score)}_{\text{Covid}} >$$
$$\text{(Negative Score)}_{\text{Vader}} \text{ AND (Neutral Score)}_{\text{Vader}} - \text{(Positive Score)}_{\text{covid}} <= 0.5$$
$$\text{THEN (Compound Score)}_{\text{Vader}} = -1. \tag{7}$$

Based on the above cases, the final polarity was updated in the database.

3.5 Decision Tree

This phase comprised application of decision tree algorithm on the dataset obtained from the lexicon phase. Decision tree was chosen for analysis of Indian headlines as there was less study done in this discipline. Due to the lack of ability of decision trees to work on textual data, a feature weighting technique TF-IDF, was used to give numeric scores to the text data. The dataset for classification was divided into 80% training and 20% testing data.

In this research, scikit-learn module's DecisionTree classifier was used with criterion Gini, that is CART algorithm of decision tree, and its various parameters were tuned to optimize the result of the classification. After drawing validation curves over a range of values for each parameter, the optimal values were chosen to avoid overfitting or underfitting and to obtain the best result.

3.6 Random Forest

This phase encompassed application of the random forest algorithm on the dataset since it is an ensemble technique for the decision tree algorithm and was less explored by the other researchers. Due to the textual nature of the data and the inability of ML algorithms to work on text, a feature weighting technique, TF-IDF, was applied to assign numeric scores to the text. Based on various observations, the default value of the maximum features parameter of the TF-IDF function was modified so as to omit the transformation of rare words in the vocabulary.

Later, the data was fed into the random forest classifier function provided by the scikit-learn module in python and performance metrics were obtained. The metrics had to be improved by tuning the hyperparameters and this task was achieved by plotting validation curves for each parameter. On studying the curves well, optimal values for each attribute were chosen such that overfitting and underfitting could be minimized and the algorithm's performance improved.

4   Results

4.1 Lexicon Phase

Post assignment of polarities by lexicon dictionaries TextBlob and NLTK Vader, the following results were obtained.

There were 72% neutral, 18% positive and 10% negative labels assigned by TextBlob which indicated that most of the data was neutral. While NLTK VADER labeling gave 50% neutral, 22% positive and 28% negative labels. Figure 2 gives a comparison of the results obtained by TextBlob and NLTK VADER.

4.2 Covid Headlines Classification

After using a scored corpus of words to correctly classify the covid19 headlines and modifying the polarity scores within VADER corpus, it was observed that the number of headlines under each label changed to a certain extent. The positive class saw a decrease of 139 headlines, the negative class experienced an increase of 342 headlines and the neutral class saw a decrease of 285 headlines. Table 1 provides a comparison of the total number of headlines under each label before and after the application of scored corpus. It lists down the changes in magnitudes accompanied by associated signs.

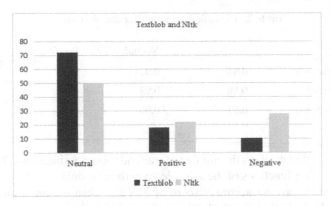

Fig. 2. Comparison of polarity classification done by TextBlob and NLTK.

Table 1. Comparison of total number of headlines before and after covid headlines classification function.

Polarity	Before	After	Change
Positive	23303	23018	−139
Negative	12099	12441	+ 342
Neutral	9760	9621	−285

4.3 Decision Tree

Decision tree algorithm performed in differing ways on each dataset. The results were analyzed using four metrics - accuracy, precision, recall and f1 score - to measure the classifier's results. Confusion matrix was also analyzed that displays the number of true and false classifications. These values were attained by using inbuilt functions of the scikit-learn python module.

Applying the algorithm on the dataset obtained from the lexicon phase without the covid headline classification function gave an accuracy score of 94% at the default values of parameters of the classifier. Decision tree tends to overfit at default values of hyperparameters thus, optimal values of hyperparameters were set to reduce overfitting.

The accuracy score after tuning the hyperparameters and using the modified dataset obtained is 93.05% along with high values of precision, recall and F1-score as shown in Table 2. These results show that the algorithm applied on the dataset functioned adequately.

4.4 Random Forest

The random forest algorithm performs differently on each dataset so it becomes imperative to analyze its performance via some functions. This study involved four metrics - accuracy, precision, recall and f1 score - to judge the classifier's results along with

Table 2. Classification report for decision tree.

	Negative	Neutral	Positive
Precision	0.96	0.92	0.92
Recall	0.86	0.99	0.87
F1-Score	0.91	0.96	0.89

confusion matrix that displays the number of true and false classifications. These values were obtained using functions of the scikit-learn python module.

The algorithm gave an accuracy score of 87.98% when executed on the dataset obtained after the lexicon phase. At that point, the covid headlines classification function was not applied on the headlines and the classifier had all its parameters set to their default values.

However, after all the optimizations, the classification of news headlines by random forest gave a promising accuracy score of 92.36%. It was supported by the high values of precision, recall and F1-score as shown in Table 3. These attributes indicate that the algorithm worked well on the dataset.

Table 3. Classification report for random forest.

	Negative	Neutral	Positive
Precision	0.93	0.92	0.94
Recall	0.87	0.98	0.86
F1-Score	0.90	0.95	0.90

5 Conclusion

In this research project, sentiment analysis on news headlines of Indian journals was successfully implemented using both lexicon and machine learning approaches. Amongst the two dictionaries used as part of the lexicon model, NLTK gave more convincing results than TextBlob. An effective corpus of covid-19 words was created to correctly classify coronavirus related news and the dataset thus formed, was fed to machine learning classifiers, decision trees and random forest. The algorithms gave good accuracy scores of 93.05% and 92.36% respectively along with high F1-scores, precisions and recalls. It was concluded that the Indian newspapers highlight neutral news the most, followed by negative and positive news in respective order.

This finding can be very useful for the Indian news agencies while targeting readers and contemplating their reporting strategies. If they report a lot of negative news then there could be a decrease in their sales and subscribers. Hence, they can study the effects of their reported news on the general public and alter their strategies for greater views and subscribers.

The public too can take advantage of the work by understanding sentiments behind Indian journalism and hence filtering the newspapers they want to read. They can skip or read a newspaper on the basis of the sentiment conveyed by its corresponding headlines. If it appears to be appealing and of a desiring sentiment then they can continue reading the newspaper, or else move to another one. This could be a way to avoid highly negative or depressing information.

The work can be further expanded to create a platform, or can be integrated with an application, to segregate news based on the sentiment choice of the user where filtered news is provided to the public based on the sentiment of their choice.

Corporate organizations can make use of this research to strategize their advertisement and branding of products as the language of advertisements in the news media forms a sentiment in a person's mind. A person forms an opinion about a product even before knowing its details. Thus, the opinion of people on a product through advertisement plays a major role in the sales of any product.

This study can be extended in other fields, such as analyzing the mental and behavioral effects of Indian news headlines/taglines, because the type of news affects the mental and psychological well-being of a person. Reading too much of a particular type of news can impact one's mind and thought process. It can make the brain perceive a certain type of information alone which can lead to unwanted emotions like fear, aggression, greed etc. The nature of news can also affect the behavior and actions of an individual since a person can copy or imitate things from the news both in positive or negative ways.

The research can be used to study the impact of news in promoting the art and culture of India since Indian journals contain extensive cultural information which helps people to form an opinion of India's culture, food, art, traditions etc. It lets a person form an opinion of a place they might or might not have visited and this opinion can considerably impact the tourism industry for the area.

References

1. Wardhani, N.K., et al.: Sentiment analysis article news coordinator minister of maritime affairs using algorithm naive bayes and support vector machine with particle swarm optimization. J. Theor. Appl. Inf. Technol. **96**(24), 8365–8378 (2018)
2. Yu, X., Zhong, C., Li, D., Xu, W.: Sentiment analysis for news and social media in COVID-19. In: Proceedings of the 6th ACM SIGSPATIAL International Workshop on Emergency Management using GIS, pp. 1–4. Association for Computing Machinery, Seattle Washington (2020)
3. Taj, S., Shaikh, B.B., Meghji, A.F.: Sentiment analysis of news articles: a lexicon based approach. In: 2nd International Conference on Computing, Mathematics and Engineering Technologies (iCoMET), pp. 1–5. IEEE, Sukkur, Pakistan (2019)
4. Godbole, N., Srinivasaiah, M., Skiena, S.: Large-scale sentiment analysis for news and blogs. In: Proceedings of the International Conference on Weblogs and Social Media, pp. 219–222 (2007)
5. Swati, U., Pranali, C., Pragati, S.: Sentiment analysis of news articles using machine learning approach. In: Proceedings of 20th IRF International Conference, pp.114–116 (2015)

6. Padmaja, S., Fatima, S.S., Bandu, S., Kosala, P., Abhignya, M.C.: Comparing and evaluating the sentiment on newspaper articles: a preliminary experiment. In: 2014 Science and Information Conference, pp. 789–792. IEEE, London (2014). https://doi.org/10.1109/SAI.2014. 6918276

7. Mukwazvure, A., Supreethi, K.P.: A hybrid approach to sentiment analysis of news comments. In: 2015 4th International Conference on Reliability, Infocom Technologies and Optimization (ICRITO) (Trends and Future Directions), pp. 1–6. IEEE, Noida (2015). https://doi.org/10. 1109/ICRITO.2015.7359282

8. Balahur, A., Steinberger, R., Van Der Goot, E., Pouliquen, B., Kabadjov, M.: Opinion mining on newspaper quotations. In: 2009 IEEE/WIC/ACM International Joint Conference on Web Intelligence and Intelligent Agent Technology, pp. 523–526. IEEE, Milan (2009). https://doi. org/10.1109/WI-IAT.2009.340

9. Rameshbhai, C.J., Paulose, J.: Opinion mining on newspaper headlines using SVM and NLP. Int. J. Electr. Comput. Eng. (IJECE) 9(3), 2152–2163 (2019)

10. Ahmed, J., Ahmed, M.: A framework for sentiment analysis of online news articles. Int. J. Emerg. Technol. 11(3), 267–274 (2020)

11. Haribhakta, Y., Doddi, K.S.: Categorization of news articles using sentiment analysis. Int. J. Sci. Res. Comput. Sci. Eng. Inform. Technol. 2, 52–60 (2017)

12. Prakashini, S., Vijayakumar, D.: Sentimental classification of news headlines using recurrent neural network. Int. J. Innovative Technol. Exploring Eng. (IJITEE) 9, 207–210 (2020)

13. Kirange, D.K., Deshmukh, R.R.: Sentiment Analysis of news headlines for stock price prediction. COMPOSOFT Int. J. Adv. Comput. Technol. 5(3), 2080–2084 (2016)

14. Sundaram, A.: Sentiment analysis of major mutual fund related news articles in India AMID the COVID-19 outbreak, to obtain investor sentiment in mutual funds & to forecast assets under management (AUM), a mutual fund market indicator. Int. J. Manage. 11(11), 117–127 (2020)

15. Kaur, G., Kaur, K.: Sentiment analysis on Punjabi news articles using SVM. Int. J. Sci. Res. 6(8), 414–421 (2015)

16. Ghasiya, P., Okamura, K.: Investigating COVID-19 news across four nations: a topic modeling and sentiment analysis approach. IEEE Access 9, 36645–36656 (2021). https://doi.org/10. 1109/ACCESS.2021.3062875

17. Costola, M., Nofer, M., Hinz, O., Pelizzon, L.: Machine Learning Sentiment Analysis, Covid-19 News and Stock Market Reactions. SAFE Working Paper No. 288 (2020)

Feature Extraction and Sentiment Analysis Using Machine Learning

Neha Vaish[1], Nidhi Goel[1]($\boxtimes$), and Gaurav Gupta[2]($\boxtimes$)

[1] Department of Electronics and Communication, IGDTUW, Delhi, India
[2] College of Science and Technology, Wenzhou-Kean University, Wenzhou, China

Abstract. The role of social networks has bought a tremendous change in the analysis of the opinions. Understanding people sentiments or opinion helps the business or organization to better understand their customers. There are several platforms where people can easily post their views about a service or products, these can be facebook, twitter e.t.c. Feature extraction or aspect extraction becomes important since one needs to know the qualities a product or a service have. In this research, we have analyzed hotel reviews by applying n-gram for feature. As the dataset is always noisy so basic preprocessing steps are applied before extraction. The features extracted are trained and tested by basic machine learning classifiers. Various machine learning algorithms like KNN, SVM, and random forest are used for the analysis of the performance. The evaluation measures are calculated at the end to validate the results. K-fold cross validation scheme is also applied on the dataset to improve the overall accuracy of the results.

Keywords: Feature · Sentiment · Polarity · Classifier · Machine learning

1 Introduction

With the phenomenal advancement in the field of internet and social media, it has become easy to gather lot of information. This information can be opinion, feelings or reviews of people towards an entity. Understanding people's sentiment towards an entity is sentiment analysis [1]. These sentiments can be in the form of rating from 1 to 5 or it can be an emoticon or it can simply be a text review. Customers always look upon the reviews before buying an entity. Sentiment analysis is on the data reviews based on polarity, i.e. analyzing and categorizing them as a positive or a negative review.

Sentiment analysis can be done in three different domains: document, sentence and aspect [2]. When a document is analyzed for polarity detection then it comes under document level. When a sentence is analyzed for polarity detection then it comes under sentence level. When we analyze and extract the aspects from the text then it comes under aspect level. Here aspect level analyses are performed on the dataset that consists of reviews of a hotel. Hotel may have different features like service, staff, ambience, location e.t.c.

Task of sentiment analysis is divided into two main tasks, feature extraction and sentiment classification [3]. Say a review is 'the location of the hotel was awesome'

© Springer Nature Switzerland AG 2022
A. Dev et al. (Eds.): AIST 2021, CCIS 1546, pp. 127–133, 2022.
https://doi.org/10.1007/978-3-030-95711-7_11

here, feature of the hotel is the 'location' and sentiment is 'awesome' i.e. a positive polarity. For feature extraction there are many existing techniques like frequency based approach, CRF, LDA, Gini index etc. In this paper n-gram approach [5] is used on the hotel dataset for feature extraction and for sentiment analysis machine learning classifiers are implemented. SVM, KNN and random forest techniques are used to classify the polarity of the reviews [4].

2 Related Work

This section reviews the work done in the field of aspect based sentiment analysis. Areas of focus are feature extraction and polarity detection. For feature extraction various approaches have been used in the past years.

Sarkar et al.[5] worked with multinomial naïve bayes with n-gram and senti Wordnet features for detecting the polarity for Bengali tweets.

Z. Jianqiang, G. Xiaolin [7] discussed the effects of text pre-processing method on sentiment classification performance in two types of classification tasks, and discussed the classification performances of six pre-processing methods using two feature models and four classifiers on five Twitter datasets. Naïve bayes and random forest proved to be better.

Yoon et al. [8] used topic model based techniques which is an unsupervised method for building the topics from the text. LDA (latent dirichlet allocation) and LSA are the two models used. This is a probabilistic approach of finding topics.

A survey on sentiment analysis [10] was conducted where various supervised algorithms and a sequence based neural network classifier was implemented.

Amplyo et al. [11] worked on the detection of the aspect terms by using two topic model approaches SA-ASM and SA-PSM, these were the unified models that were able to give good results by determining both the feature and the sentiments.

The limitations of these methods are they could not efficiently differentiate the implicit features. It is easy to find the explicit features which are already mentioned in the text but implicit feature extraction becomes difficult. For e.g. 'phone is little heavy' so heavy is a feature that is linking to the weight of the phone, so here weight is the feature of the entity phone which is implicitly mentioned.

3 Methodology

In this work, we have collected the dataset of the hotel reviews which are more than 35,000 in number from Kaggle.com. Python on Anaconda platform is used to work for sentiment analysis. Figure 1 shows the work flow for sentiment analysis.

3.1 Data Preprocessing

The dataset is processed by removing the stop words, unintended characters, punctuations, urls, hashtags [9]. It also includes stemming and lemmatizing the words. In preprocessing the hotel reviews are processed and we have converted uppercase to lower case, removed all unnecessary punctuations and characters. Stemming and lemmetization of words means if word is say 'boating' then it is stemmed to 'boat' and lemmatization looks for beyond word reduction say lemma of 'saw' is 'see'.

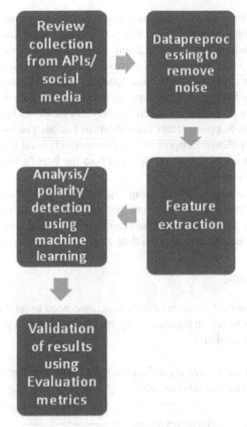

Fig. 1. Framework of sentiment analysis

3.2 Feature Extraction

After pre processing the reviews, features are extracted. In this work n-grams are used for feature extraction. N-gram are the set of co occurring words which are found in the text. In Uni-gram the n-gram size = 1 and in bi-gram this value is 2. For example a review 'food was good' is positive but 'food was not bad' might be predicted as negative due to the occurrence of word 'bad' in the text. Here bigram helps as it considers combination of two word tokens. Count frequency is used to see the occurrence of most frequent words that helps in giving out the features.

3.3 Polarity Detection

In order to find the polarity of the reviews basic classifiers like KNN (k-nearest neighbour), SVM and random forest are used to classify the reviews into positive or negative polarity.

KNN (K nearest neighbour)- KNN is a pattern recognition algorithm that utilizes the training data to look for the k closest relatives. Its main purpose is to utilize a dataset where the data points are separated into multiple classes to predict the classification of new sample points. Once the algorithm is trained the unknown data to be classified is assigned to a group that appear majorly in those K closest neighbours.

SVM- It is a supervised learning approach and known to be a good classifier with less error rate. It is known to be used for both regression as well as classification analysis. It transforms the data to a higher dimensional space in order to separate the data linearly. SVM classifier finds a hyperplane that separates the training data on the either sides of the plane such that the data gets separated linearly. SVM works both as binary as well as multiclass classifier. Support vector classification can also be used in order to work with the regression problems. Support vector regression is used in this paper. SVR has all the important features of SVM and helps to find the best fit line on the hyperplane that has maximum number of points.

Random Forest- It is a supervised learning algorithm, which is collection of trees. It basically develops various decision trees and then ultimately combines then to get a stable and an absolute value. This algorithm takes random data and creates a tree. Depending upon the threshold value it segregates the data as positive or a negative polarity.

3.4 Evaluation Metrics

In order to measure the performance of our model, we need to let it categorize the texts that are already known to which topic category they fall under, and see how it performed. The basic metrics analyzed are:

1. Accuracy: It tells how accurately a classifier functions. This means it should classify correctly, true as true and false as false.

$$Accuracy = \frac{TP + TN}{TP + FN + FP + TN} \tag{1}$$

2. Precision: It tells the proportion to which TP against all positive samples.

$$Precision = \frac{TP}{TP + FP} \tag{2}$$

3. Recall: It is the measure that tells the proportion of resulted outcomes that was correctly observed. It is also known as sensitivity.

$$Recall = \frac{TP}{TP + FN} \tag{3}$$

4. F-score: Instead of calculating different metrics like precision and recall, F-score combines them into single metrics and gives the harmonic mean of recall and precision. A perfect model has an F score of value 1.

$$F - score = \frac{2 * Precision * Recall}{Precision + Recall} \tag{4}$$

The various parameters used are defined below.

(a) True Positive (TP): The actual and predicted values are true.
(b) False Positive (FP): The actual values are false but predicted values are true.
(c) True Negative (TN): Both the values are false.
(d) False negative (FN): The actual values are true but the predicted are false.
      Lastly, the results are validated using K fold cross validation, with a value of K
   = 5.

4 Results and Discussion

The hotel reviews are analyzed by using machine learning classifiers. The raw dataset is
pre processed, n-gram is used for feature extraction along with count vectorizer. Results
are validated using evaluation metrics. The result of classifier performance is shown in
Table 1.

Table 1. Classifier performance

Classifier	Accuracy	Precision	Recall	F score
SVM	88.6	88.6	88.6	88.6
Random	89.1	89.1	89.1	89.1
KNN	83.7	83.7	83.7	83.7

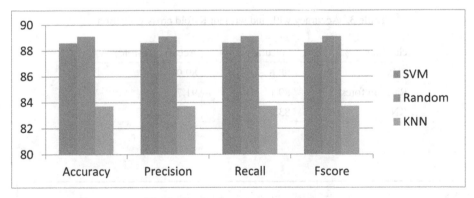

Fig. 2. Evaluation metrics comparison

   In Fig. 2 the graphical representation shows it clearly that random forest performs
the best amongst the three classifiers with 88.6% accuracy.
   Table 2 illustrates the accuracy comparison using two feature extraction with the
classifiers. Unigram performs better than bigram for hotel review dataset.
   Here, Fig. 3 shows that Unigrams worked better with random forest on the hotel
review dataset.
   Table 3 illustrates the comparison of accuracy of the classifiers with and without
using K fold cross validation (Fig. 4).

Table 2. Accuracy using Unigram and Bigram

Classifier	Unigram	Bigram
SVM	88.6	79.2
Random forest	89.1	76.3
KNN	83.7	72.1

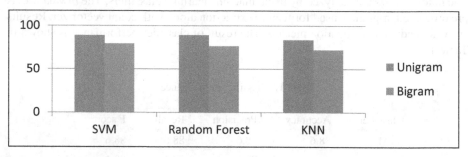

Fig. 3. Accuracy comparison with unigram and bigram.

Table 3. Accuracy with and without K-fold cross validation

classifier	Accuracy	Accuracy(k-fold)
SVM	88.6	89.9
Random forest	89.1	91.7
KNN	83.7	85.4

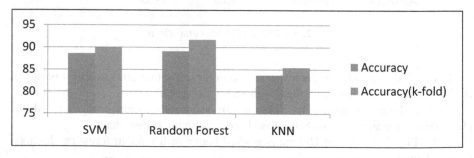

Fig. 4. Comparison with and without K-fold validation

It clearly shows that by implementing 5 fold validation the resulting accuracy have improved since k fold shuffles the dataset and make it more efficient.

5 Conclusion

This study helps to classify the hotel reviews collected from a source into positive and negative polarity. Unigram and bigram helped to extract the features. Different machine learning algorithms are used for classification. We have performed steps of preprocessing to clean our data, thereby performing feature extraction and sentiment classification. Later, for sentiment classification three different supervised machine learning algorithms helped to classify dataset. The results shown above indicate that random forest and SVM gives better results than KNN algorithm. Results were improved by k fold validation scheme where value of k = 5.

References

1. Pang, B., Lee, L., Vaithyanathan, S.: Sentiment classification using machine learning techniques. In: Proceedings of the Conference on Empirical Methods in Natural Language Processing, pp. 79–86 (2002)
2. Liu, B.: Sentiment analysis and subjectivity. In: Indurkhya, N., Damerau, F.J. (eds.) Handbook of Natural Language Processing, 2nd ed. CRC Press, Boca Raton (2010)
3. Cambria, E.: Affective computing and sentiment analysis. IEEE Intell. Syst. 31(2), 102–107 (2016). https://doi.org/10.1109/MIS.2016.31
4. Naz, S., Sharan, A., Malik, N.: Sentiment classification on Twitter data using support vector machine. In: Proceedings of IEEE/WIC/ACM International Conference on Web Intelligence (WI), Santiago, Chile, December 2018, pp. 3–6 (2018). https://doi.org/10.1109/WI.2018.00-13
5. Sarkar, K.: Using character N-gram features and multinomial Naïve Bayes for sentiment polarity detection in Bengali tweets. In: Proceedings of 5th International Conference on Emerging Applications of Information Technology (EAIT), Kolkata, India, January 2018, pp. 12–13 (2018). https://doi.org/10.1109/EAIT.2018.8470415
6. Zhou, L., Bian, X.: Improved text sentiment classification method based on BiGRU-attention. J. Phys. Conf. Ser. 1345, 032097 (2019)
7. Jianqiang, Z., Xiaolin, G.: Comparison Research on text pre-processing methods. In: IEEE Access, vol 5 (2017). https://doi.org/10.1109/ACCESS.2017.2672677
8. Yoon, H.G., Kim, H., Kim, C.O., Song, M.: Opinion polarity detection in Twitter data combining shrinkage regression and topic modeling. J. Informetrics 10(2), 634–644 (2016)
9. Pandey, S.V., Deorankar, A.V.: A study of sentiment analysis task and it's challenges. In: 2019 IEEE International Conference on Electrical, Computer and Communication Technologies (ICECCT), pp. 1–5 (2019). https://doi.org/10.1109/ICECCT.2019.8869160
10. Subramanian, R.R., Akshith, N., Murthy, G.N., Vikas, M., Amara, S., Balaji, K.: A survey on sentiment analysis. In: 2021 11th International Conference on Cloud Computing, Data Science & Engineering (Confluence), pp. 70–75 (2021). https://doi.org/10.1109/Confluence51648.2021.9377136
11. Amplayo, R.K., Lee, S., Song, M.: Incorporating product description to sentiment topic models for improved aspect-based sentiment analysis. Inf. Sci. 454–455, 200–215 (2018). https://doi.org/10.1016/j.ins.2018.04.079

A Neural Network Based Approach for Text-Level Sentiment Analysis Using Sentiment Lexicons

Gaurav Dubey[✉] and Pinki Sharma

ABES Engineering College, Ghaziabad, Uttar Pradesh, India

Abstract. There have been many discussions on forums, e-commerce sites, sites for reviewing products, social media which helps in exchanging opinions, thoughts through free expression of users. Internet as well as web 2.0 is overflowing with the data generated by users which provides a good source for various sentiments, reviews, and evaluations. Opinion mining more popularly known as sentiment analysis classifies the text document based on a positive or negative sentiment that it holds. This is an open research domain and this particular research paper puts forth a model called Artificial Neural Network Based Model i.e., ANNBM. The model is trained and tested through Information Gain as well as three other popular lexicons to extract the sentiments. It's a new approach that best utilizes the ANNBM model and the subjectivity knowledge which is available in sentiment lexicons. Experiments were conducted on the mobile phone review as well as car review to derive that this approach was successful in finding best output for sentiment-based classification of text and simultaneously reduces dimensionality.

Keywords: PSO · PSO-TVAC · Parameter tuning

1 Introduction

The Internet as well as Web 2.0 users have extensively increased and gathered the opinions, ideas, reviews and criticism that consumers provide in open-source platforms. Many researchers further claim through various studies conducted that even non-traditional mediums are used by consumers for exchanging information and opinions. Mediums like message forums, review sites and blogs are used by online users to access the opinions of others besides expressing their own. And these online reviews also are a substitution for word of mouth because those carry a persuasive impact on the reader. These reviews have a larger impact on the decision making of users and potential buyers who seek the easy advice of the internet, as a word from a current user is more trustable than a bit from a salesperson. Such reviews are easy to access in websites like Amazon.com, Epinions.com, IMDb etc. where the users share their point of views through their personal experiences for different products ranging from phones, cars, FMCG, tour packages, and movies.

Although, as useful as these customer insights are, its immense volume is overwhelmingly huge for brands to track the reviews for their own products. At the same

© Springer Nature Switzerland AG 2022
A. Dev et al. (Eds.): AIST 2021, CCIS 1546, pp. 134–150, 2022.
https://doi.org/10.1007/978-3-030-95711-7_12

time, it's also difficult and time consuming for the users to go through all opinions as they're segregated in various platforms/blogs/forums/social media. Therefore, there arises a need to automate the process which can extract the useful knowledge from these subjective reviews. Sentiment Analysis or opinion mining is useful in classifying the opinionated texts as per the positive or negative polarity. It does look similar to text classification but it has challenges of its own which calls for a lot of focussed research in the domain. To take an example where the text entered by the user isn't formatted and also contains mistakes, orthographic or otherwise, some abbreviations, idiomatic expressions or sarcastic/ironic statements. There also exists a temporal dynamism in the text content since the opinion has a tendency to change from time to time. Plus, sentiment analysis is very specific to the domain. It'll be done in a different manner for electronic products when compared to movie reviews. Hence, the process uniqueness makes sentiment analysis challenging as well as quite an interesting arena.

Through time, many different solutions have been showcased which are based on semantic approaches, machine learning, dictionary and statistics. The machine learning methods like SVM, Decision Trees, Naive Bayes, etc. have also helped in giving out fruitful results for classification tasks. When it comes to the dictionary approach, a pre-built dictionary is used like Opinions Lexicons and General Inquirer and are called sentiment lexicons. A score can further be calculated by polarizing the sentiments expressed through words which can be quantified and used for analysis. After the score is obtained, it can categories the text as positive or negative. The co-occurrence of words helps determine the sentiment polarity and statistical approaches play a good role in exploiting those features. Synonyms and antonyms are also used to find semantic relationships between the words which help in the calculation of polarities for analysis.

For the purpose of this research paper, ANNBM has been used i.e., Artificial Neural Network Based Model which is a model for classification of sentiments. For extracting the sentiments, popular lexicons like Information Gain and three others have been deployed which can be used to train and test the model ANNBM. It makes the methodology very unique since the classification performance of ANNBM is exploited and the lexicons provide the domain knowledge. The performance for the method used is compared against the Pang and Lee which is used as a benchmark dataset. This dataset is a repository of movie reviews from IMDb (Internet Movies Database). It also uses the dataset for reviews of hotels extracted from trip planning websites like Yatra and/or Trip Advisor.

The sections of paper have been delegated as follows: the Sect. 2 explains Related Work done so far on Sentiment Analysis. Section 3 describes the use of ANNBM and how it's applied to this paper. Section 4 deals with Experimental results and then Sect. 5, finally talks about conclusion.

2   Background Details and Related Work

In this area of sentiment analysis, various research has been conducted in the past years and earlier times witnessed the use of certain semantic orientation or the polarity which indicates the orientation of the text. This particular research paper has been restricted to finding out the subjective polarity for any document of text. When sentiment analysis is performed on a document, an overall opinion is found which could either be positive or negative. It takes an assumption into consideration that only the opinion is expressed for one object and only one subject at a time.

2.1 Document-Level Sentiment Analysis

When it comes to document level Analysis of sentiments be it through any online platform like blogs, news etc., a lot of research studies have been proposed dealing with supervised, semi-supervised and unsupervised algorithms. The first step of these approaches is to extract the adverbs and adjectives which was followed by calculating semantic orientations. This process used PMI i.e., Pointwise Mutual Information and after this the reviews were divided as per what the average of semantic orientations came out to be. Apart from PMI, LSA i.e., Latent Semantic Analysis is also used to find out the semantic orientations between the words, proposed by Turney and Littman. This particular research was worked further upon in order to find the semantic network WordNet when compared to a number of tagged words which came from Stanford Political Dictionary and the General Inquirer lexicon which puts forth the relations of lexicons in the adjectives.

The summaries for the purpose of product features based on the positive and negative sentiments were put forward by Hu and Liu (2004). There were certain opinionated texts which came into picture using the dictionary for the adjectives. The work proposed by Hu and Liu saw some improvement when it practiced giving a score to the opinion terms which were found on the basis of the distance that lied between the opinion term as well as the feature. A semi-supervised method for classification of the terms according to the semantic orientation was put forth by Esuli and Sebastiani. A basic assumption considered here was that the terms which have a similar orientation will have glosses also as similar.

A lexicon based on sentiment was proposed by Godbole and others which was based on the semantic methodology and the aim was to give a certain sentiment score to every entity in the data/ text which is followed by allotting a subjectivity score. An algorithm using lexicons using the WordNet polarity score was put forth and this research showed that the algorithms based on semantics are at par with some ML algorithms in terms of accuracy.

When it comes to ML methodologies, they started to be known for sentiment analysis inspired by seminal work conducted by Pang and Lee (2002). In the particular study, there were three supervised classifiers namely: maximum entropy (ME), Naive Bayes (NB) and then support vector machines (SVM) which were used for the purpose of experimentation. The best performance was shown by SVM conducted for the purpose of movie reviews corpus which displayed an average level of precision which was about 80% [25]. That particular study was extended by putting an emphasis on the feature selection which used the Laplacian smoothing method for Naïve Bayes, and this resulted in the accuracy of the classification to rise up to level of 87% [11]. In order to make the precision for the Naïve Bayes better, a subjectivity identification was followed in text which was proposed for the purpose of a pre-processing step to be conducted in some other study. The best level of accuracy was calculated to 87.2% and this was achieved for a dataset of movie reviews [22].

The multi-class problem of the sentiment classification was researched which used the Support Vector Machine for the purpose of multi-class OVA that is the one-versus-all. It was also used for the SVR which is the regression mode and this contained a feature of metric labelling [24]. The results that were concluded were such that, there's a combination of the SVM with other unsupervised categorization approaches and that resulted in better precision. This approach based on the SVM was extended in the studies carry forward which had to look for the support or opposition. This was conducted in reference to the political texts found online. The modelling of the relationships was conducted and an agreement was exploited between authors which showcased a 71% level of accuracy which was achieved through transcripts which were congressional and floor- debate [34].

There were certain other techniques of ML such as winnow, and generative models which are based on the language modelling as well as discriminative classifiers that employ a certain projection which are based upon the learning which have to be studied for the purpose of finding the sentiment analysis [10]. The experiment took place for 0.4 GB corpus which contained 100,000 of the product reviews extracted from the web and which showcased that the classifiers which are discriminative are what give the best outcomes. Such experiments conducted with the SVM, ME as well as NB for the movie, plus the reviews of car brands have shown a confirmation for a high performance exhibited by ML techniques which gave an accuracy up to a level of 90.25% [5]. The method for N-gram language with Naive Bayes has been in the studies for purpose of subjectivity and also for a polarity analysis at the document level which is performed on the legal Weblogs as well as the movie reviews, proposed by Conrad and Schilder [9].

Certain algorithms of ML such as the centroid classifier, Naïve Bayes, K-nearest, winnow classifier and the Support Vector Machine along with the many methods for feature selection have also been researched for the purpose of analysing the sentiment on the Chinese data/documents [33]. Those concluded that the IG i.e., Information Gain is a great indicator for the performance of the feature selection process and the SVM feature showcased the best performance for the sentiment analysis at document level. SVM when in a combination with the other classifiers such as the general inquirer-based classifier (GIBC), statistics-based classifier (SBC), the rule-based classifier (RBC), has been researched to classify the reviews [27]. This form of hybrid classification approach actually brings forth the best F-score which goes up till level of 91% accuracy when it is used with the dataset of movie reviews, Myspace comments, and product reviews classification. The supervised ML techniques when amalgamated with the lexicon-based methods are researched for the sentiment analysis of the comments which are extracted from the BBC Messages Boards and also from the website of social news [21]. The recent studies conducted concluded the effectiveness of the techniques of ML like Support Vector Machine [2] and also Naïve Bayes [19].

2.2 ANNBM for Mining Sentiments

The reviews by different researchers which contributed in writing the literature, concludes that the techniques of ML have been performing way better when comparing in the terms of accuracy with the lexicon as well as semantic based methods for the sentiment analysis. But, performance wise, the approaches of machine learning are highly interdependent on certain features, and the quantity and quality for the data used for the train set as well as the domain for the dataset. When considering the additional learning time which would be needed for the machine learning methods is an important point, as the lexicon or the semantic based method does not require the time to train. Hence, in order to get through the shortcomings of both of these methodologies, and also, I order to preserve the strengths they carry, this particular research paper aims to propose a method of Artificial Neural Network Based Model (ANNBM) which is derived on the approach which combines both advantages of the techniques of ML as well as the lexicon-based approaches.

This technique is very rarely seen as a task of sentiment analysis and it could definitely be verified from the surveys conducted recently on sentiment analysis. Some of the slides have seen ANN along with a certain semantic orientation index which possibly finds out the sentiment as expressed in the blogs [6] and the self-organizing maps (SOM) in order to cluster the microblogs posts [8]. But, all these observations in studies do not have experiments which are conclusive and that involve the selection feature which uses the sentiment lexicons. The ANNBM method has been used as a model for basic learners for the sentiment classification which was studied recently [4]. The performance of this as observed from the data is quite established. The use of ANNBM can be extended to solve a complex and difficult non-linear function derived from the observations for the purpose of pattern discovery in the datasets. This paper exhibits the ability on the extracted sentiment features. The most contribution that this work has provided has been the combination of ANNBM along with the sentiment lexicons to find out the sentiment-based classification particularly for reviews of the two varied domains.

3 Proposed Approach

The technique which is proposed here in this study has been presented in this particular section. The first point is that the text documents which are opinionated are gathered. Then, it is pre- processed. The Vector Space Model (VSM) is put to use in order to put forth a new set of words which represent each document. The document can be represented as part of a vector of the identifiers and every dimension actually corresponds to a different term in the vocabulary.

Now, the technique of stemming is conducted for reducing the words up till their root or till the stem is reached. This study uses the method of Porter Stemmer Algorithm in the English language [26]. In order to calculate a numerical representation derived from a user-generated and opinionated data (text), the residual tokens are then arranged according to their frequencies or the number of occurrences they have in the entire document set. The representation of term frequency is a very popular weighting scheme in the comparative study on the feature selection technique which has been reported that the information which is gained based on the feature selection is useful or not for text classification [30, 31]. Therefore, the topmost features with n-ranks are then chosen with the criteria of the information gain feature as well as the very frequently used words in the sentiment lexicons. These sentiment-bearing words in the text data can be found by using sentiment lexicons. After that the representative features of them may be used from therein. The findings of the last research have positively confirmed that in order to look after the high dimensionality, which is only a small set that represents the entire data can be put to use in the form of features. The degradation occurs in the performance of the classifier when the representative features are being used is negligible [20]. The final features that come as a result are then used for training ANNBM for the sentiment-based classification.

3.1 Use of Information Gain for Selecting Feature

The Information gain (IG) is a feature representing the goodness criterion, it has done quite well for the sentiment-feature selection [33]. Here, a feature is selected which is based on how much impact it has on the overall decreasing entropy. Entropy is the information which is expected that is supposed to be classified as an instance. Then, the attributes are ranked high according to the Information Gain score which minimizes the information which is important for the classification of instances into some predefined classes. This information gain for the feature w, for all the classes can be stated as:

$$
\begin{aligned}
IG(w) = & -\Sigma_{i=1}^{|c|} P(c_i) \log_2(c_i) + P(w) \Sigma_{i=1}^{|c|} P(c_i|w) \log_2 P(c_i|w) \\
& + P(\overline{w}) \Sigma_{i=1}^{|c|} P(c_i|w) \log_2 P(c_i|w))
\end{aligned}
\tag{1}
$$

Here, P(ci) is basically the probability which gives the random instance of the document which is from the class ci. The P(w) gives the probability indicating the occurrence for feature w when a random document is selected. Then, P(ci|w) refers to the probability when a document selected randomly which belongs to a class, ci when this document contains feature w. Then, P(w) refers to a probability wherein w is not appearing in the document which was chosen randomly. The P (ci|w) describes the probability of the chosen random document belonging to the class ci in case w is not occurring. This feature selection has the ability to improve the features in an overall manner. Henceforth, this way the efficiency of the classifier can be improved [30]. In the next section, certain fundamental concepts of BPANN are presented.

3.2 Artificial Neural Network Based Model (ANNBM)

The ANN i.e., Artificial Neural network is one of the well-known classifiers which are used for dealing with the linear categorization as well as non-linear text categorization problems. Some of the advantages include adaptive learning, pattern learning, parallelism, fault tolerance, sequence recognition, and also generalization because of which ANN is viewed as a great option for sentiment-based classification. The ANNs can be seen as one of the two: either it is feed-forward or it is feedback networks. Talking about feedforward ANN, the nodes in it are connected to each other in a unidirectional manner. It has been deployed in this paper because it has a superior ability for classification. Comparing the many training algorithms of the Artificial Neural Network, the BP i.e., error back propagation is considered to be the best among the known algorithms. The BP algorithm is iterative in nature and is a gradient algorithm which was proposed so that the MSE (mean square error) can be minimized. The MSE is said to be a measure which finds how much difference lies between the actual and the output desired for a multilayer and feed-forward neural network [28]. There are a minimum of three layers in Feed-forward ANNs which include input, output, and there is a minimum one layer which is hidden.

There are two passes in which the Back Propagation algorithm works. The forward pass as well as the backward pass. While the forward pass takes the inputs and the value for activation, the backward pass is responsible for adjusting the weights attached with the network nodes and also aids in minimizing MSE. Both these passes repeat themselves iteratively till the time the network has been converged.

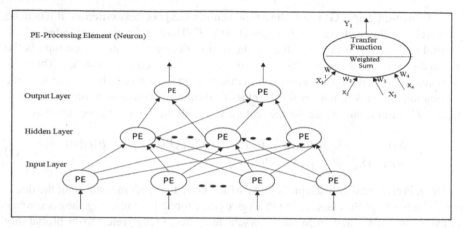

Fig. 1. ANN for classification of sentiments

Figure 1 shows ANNBM being represented through a network diagram which is made by nodes which are inter-connected and use directed edges which have been arranged into many different layers. Every layer in the ANNBM algorithm is made up of processing the neurons or elements which implement the two simple states sigmoid transfer functions. Every neuron finds a way to interact though the median of weighted connections. The associated weight value with each directed link is determined by minimizing the global error function propagated through backward error propagation. This is followed in a gradient descent learning process. There exist intermediate hidden layer(s) in between layers for input and output, and the neurons do not take the inputs directly. The processing on signals is performed by the hidden layers which are received from the previous one and which forward them towards the very next layer [29].

Every neuron goes through a very simple mathematical model. In case of the forward pass, there's a neuron which calculates the weighted sum for sample inputs which is then applied. Then an activation function is performed to this calculated sum which gives the final output. The input signal actually progresses via every layer by making use of a nonlinear function. The sigmoid function is deployed then as it's a well-known activation function [29]:

$$f(x) = 1/(1 + e - (2))$$ (2)

When the model is being trained, a modification is done in weights of every layer consisting of neurons which decreases the global error factor, in case the expected output comes out to be different from the actual output.

It is to be assumed that there are n layers in the network, which have been initialized as y_j^n, wherein that $y_{j_0}^n$ is the output calculated which has n layers and there are j nodes. In case of input layer, y_j^0 is equal to x_j, wherein the input is j. Let's assume that w_{ij}^n is a connection edge which has weight lying between y_i^{n-1} and y_j^n, then the threshold θ_j^n when the layer is n-th and node is j-th. These are the steps followed for the learning algorithm of neural networks:

Step 1. To be used for every train data (at the input layer taken in a random order):

Step 1.1. Apply the inputs to the network, then initialize the node connection with weights and some random values, also including some set of other parameters.

Step 1.2. Then the output is estimated for the case of each neuron, and is extracted from the input layer. It passes via hidden layer(s), and goes up till the output layer. This function is used at the network progression by the signal:

$$y_j^n = F\left(Sig_j^n\right) = F\left(\sum W_{ij}^n y_i^{n-1} + \theta_j^n\right) \tag{3}$$

Here, $F(Sig)$ is the function (i.e., the sigmoid transfer functions which is mentioned in the Eq. 2).

Step 1.3. Calculation of an actual output which works forward via the layers and through the error present at the output side. In case the desired output is D_j^k, the error can be given as:

$$\delta_j^n = y_j^n\left(1 - y_j^n\right)(D_j^k - y_j^n) \tag{4}$$

The value of the error in case of every neuron node for hidden or the last layer is dependent on the backward error propagation for every such layer (where $n = n, n-1...$ 1) and the formula is given as:

$$\delta_j^{n-1} = F\left(Sig_j^{n-1}\right) \sum W_{ij}^n \delta_i^n \tag{5}$$

Step 1.4. The error signals are put to use for the purpose of computation of the adjustment of weights. One has to work backward starting from the output layer, going via the hidden layers and is carried on as follows:

$$W_{ij}^n(p + 1) = W_{ij}^n(p) + \eta \delta_j^n y_i^{n-1} + \alpha[W_{ij}^n(p) - W_{ij}^n(p - 1)] \tag{6}$$

$$\theta_j^n(p + 1) = \theta_j^n(p) + \eta \delta_j^n + \alpha[\theta_j^n(p) - \theta_j^n(p - 1)] \tag{7}$$

4   Experimental Setup and Result

4.1   Corpora and Sentiment Lexicons

For the purpose of this research, we experimented with reviews of mobile and cars datasets. The datasets of the cars reviews have been collected through teambhp.com. This particular dataset is being used in many researches and is seen as a benchmark.

There have been as much as 750 positive and similarly 750 reviews which have been negative. This dataset which was delegated as a benchmark, for the cars reviews is also seen as a very difficult arena which is categorized as showcased by the sentiment of the dataset [36].

The dataset of mobile reviews is made by extracting reviews of different e-commerce sites like flipkart, amazon. This dataset has 450 positives as well as 450 negative reviews generated by customer for mobiles. These reviews were explained with independent subjects and were categorised as complete sentiment orientations as negative or positive. The response was taken on the 5-star rating for verification of the face validity of the content. Same approach was adopted by this study in [22] that mobile reviews were taken as positive for those whose rating is more than 3 stars and reviews of mobiles as being negative for those whose rating is less than 3 stars.

Moreover, we have removed the reviews with exact 3 stars as they restricted our work for binary sentiment analysis. Three most known lexicons i.e., Sentiment dictionaries were also used in this study. HM dataset, which is the first lexicon, was introduced by Hatzivassiloglou and McKeown [16]. There are 1300 adjectives which are further divided where 650 are positive and 650 are negative. GI dataset, which is the second lexicon, is the group of labelled words pulled out from the General Inquirer lexicon [32]. It contains 3596 adjectives, nouns, adverbs and also verbs, which contains 1614 positive and 1982 negative. The Opinion Lexicon has been adopted in reference to [17]. The words have been divided into positive and negative from which 2006 are positive and 4783 are negative words.

4.2 Performance Evaluation

Here, for performance evaluation metrics we have been using overall accuracy i.e., OA. For analysing the performance of the classifiers, we have used the confusion matrix discussed in Table 1.

Table 1. The confusion matrix.

	Predicted positives	Predicted negatives
Positive examples	Total true positive examples (TP)	Total false negative examples (FN)
Negative examples	Total false positive examples (FP)	Total true negative examples (TN)

$$\text{Overall Accuracy} = (TP + TN)/(TP + FP + TN + FN)$$

Precision and Recall are some other famous evaluation metrics which are denoted by ratios of the entries in the confusion matrix. The Recall & Precision are defined by:

$$\text{Precision} = TP/(TP + FN), \text{ Recall} = TP/(TP + FP)$$

4.3   Experiment and Results

Experiments done and the output which was obtained are described in this section. ANNBM was implemented with the help of an implementation based on Python which is on the platform of Microsoft Windows. The training of the ANNBM model needs some important parameter tuning that can be done by running multiple empirical tests. The information for the model parameter and its intimations is far beyond the work done so far and can also be found in reference [28]. The study conducted used the feed forward ANN with just one hidden layer. The input layer sets the input nodes lying between the number 50 and 950 just as research studies we have seen before in reference with [20]. The nodes which were hidden were taken as 15. The nodes for output were taken to be 2 for the binary classification. 500 iterations were deployed with a learning rate whose value comes out to be 0.01 and the momentum whose value is 0.8 for ANNBM. Out of all the datasets for reviews, 70% of the dataset were used to train and 30% were used to test ANNBM model.

Other ratios are also worked upon for the train and test sets which have opted for the best results that can be benchmarked with the previous studies. The ANNBM which is conducted using the gradient descent technique doesn't always converge [29]. In order to solve the issue of convergence to an optimal or to a satisfactory level, this study had a method of choosing optimal parameters after providing training to the candidate model several times (preferably over 3) by giving the model with various sets of weights that were randomly generated. Therefore, by repeatedly training the model while allotting some random values as initial weights is done to solve the issue of non convergence. Lastly, this paper uses the method of restricted iterations as an early stopping procedure to solve the problem of overclocking. Refer Section C for the remaining details of the experiment design.

4.3.1   Results on the Dataset of Car Reviews

We can note that Figs. 2, 3 and 4 give the accuracy, recall and precision for sentiment-based classification that was done on the dataset of car reviews. The hypothesised ANNBM gives the reliable accuracy based on the information gain-based feature selection and gives an impressive accuracy of 95% for the selected 800–1000 features. An 89% best accuracy was given for the movie review domain by the Opinion Lexicon. The General Enquirer lexicon was able to generate the best accuracy of 86% while the HM lexicon was the poorest in terms of all the given four feature selection methods.

The results that were gathered for the precision and recall of the dataset of cars reviews was also quite similar. Out of all the given methods, the IG-based feature selection was the best in terms of results. Due to great similarity of features in both the GI and Opinion lexicon, they gave results that were remarkably similar when we had selected top-n features (n = 50 to 1000) which were ordered according to their occurrences in the car reviews. Conversely, the HM lexicon had just 600 positive and 600 negative adjectives. Therefore, when we tried to get features using HM lexicon, the resulting feature matrix was highly sparse, which greatly impacted the performance of the ANNBM. The GI and Opinion lexicon had covered a large majority of the sentiment bearing features that were consistently seen in opinionated texts. Therefore, the GI and Opinion lexicon were

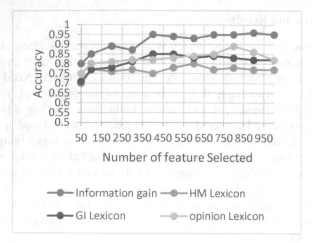

Fig. 2. Accuracy of ANNBM based sentiment analysis for cars reviews

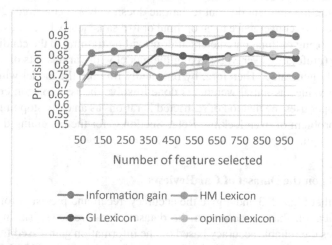

Fig. 3. Examination on precision of ANNBM with different feature selection for cars reviews

the more optimal choices when going in for a domain independent sentiment analysis system due to the fact that they have sentiment features, people usually adopt to explain their attitudes. The F1 score comparison for all the four feature selection methods can also be obtained from Fig. 2 and 3.

4.3.2   Results on the Dataset of Mobile Reviews

The Figs. 5, 6 as well 7 indicate the accuracy, precision and the recall in case of classification based on sentiment which is being conducted on mobile review dataset.

It is observed that in case of information gain, it's on the basis of feature selection which gives the best level of accuracy lying in the range of 89–90% for a sample of

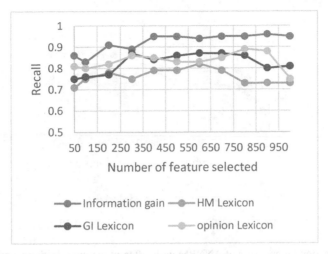

Fig. 4. Examination on recall of ANNBM with different feature selection for cars reviews

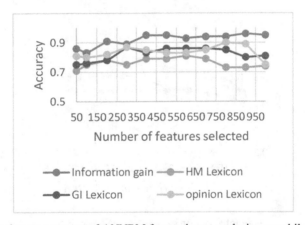

Fig. 5. Examination on accuracy of ANNBM for sentiment analysis on mobile reviews dataset

selected features between 800–1000. The best accuracy displayed so far is 85% by the opinion lexicon in case of the dataset of the mobile reviews. The best accuracy which was of the level 80.6% has been displayed by the General Enquirer lexicon. The worst performer among all the feature selection was the HM lexicon.

The output displayed so far in this particular arena has been shown as a function of the selected features which are extracted from the vocabulary on an overall basis. A comparison can be done this way covering all of the three sentiment lexicons which are then extracted from the sentiment features used to study the sensitivity behaviour of classification accuracy from the Back Propagation algorithm. Before the studies were conducted, this notion was also supported that a better value of accuracy is achievable when the number of inputs vary [30, 31]. When the experiment is carried out with

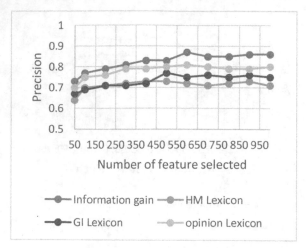

Fig. 6. Examination on precision of ANNBM with different feature selection on mobile reviews dataset

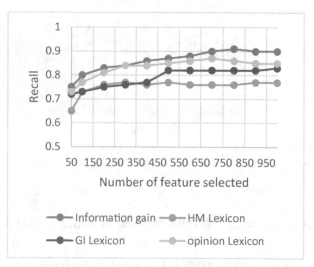

Fig. 7. Examination on recall of ANNBM with different feature selection on mobile reviews dataset

over 1000 features, there is no such significant improvement which is observed in the classification accuracy.

5   Discussion

The output shows clearly that ANNBM is quite suitable when used for the sentiment-based classification and it displays a comparable performance against the other machine learning methods/algorithms which have been studied before [11, 22, 24, 25, 34]. The

Information Gain (IG) seems to have performed better than the lexicon-based feature selection. These outputs complement the outputs that were put forth during the previous studies [30, 33] wherein it was found that IG is better when compared to mutual information, Relief-F, CHI statistics, and the feature selection based on the document frequency. When the report is considered for the output which was reported as a part of Sect. 4, there were certain observations that came into picture which are as follows:

1. Complexity for the model of ANNBM can be taken into control if some restriction is made on the number of the layers hidden which is mostly only one as well as for the number of neurons present in every hidden layer. When the experimentation is carried out, some random neurons are chosen in the hidden layer which varies from 10–50. This paper has deployed a very simplistic structure for the ANNBM which has some 15 neurons contained in just one hidden layer, which in turn suggested some satisfactory outputs.
2. For selection of over 1000 features which are based on the sentiment of lexicons, IG actually didn't result in any such improvement for the classification of output results. The Figs. 2, 3, 4, 5, 6 and 7 showcase the features which lie between 500 to 1000 and can act as a good enough trade-off amongst the learning time, the acceptable level of accuracy for classification and the computational effort required.
3. ANNBM is seen to be sensitive towards the total number of the train as well as the test data which when experimented with different sizes of datasets gives different outputs. However, when the input data is decreased, the dimensions which use the important feature selection (such as IG in this case), the ANNBM algorithm could be deployed to the tasks of sentiment analysis which is done at a mega level. The performance for the ANNBM is quite poor for the dataset on mobile reviews and this might be because of a large number of noisy terms when compared to the pre-processed dataset which has been benchmarked for the car reviews.
4. The ANNBM has been under some criticism because of not being able to converge to the optimal output and giving certain overfitting problems. The experiments conducted as a part of this study display that the training conducted on ANNBM a couple of times and by applying the same amount of the hidden layer nodes, however with a random value of initial weights given, plus by using of a predefined criteria for stopping can proved as a good way to solve the issues. But the strategy might actually be impractical in case the train time comes out to be a problem for the large scale of sentiment analysis. Although, the weaknesses which were discussed before in this paper conclude that the algorithm of ANNBM can be seen as a worthy approach when used for sentiment analysis.

6 Conclusion

This particular study puts forth a model for the sentiment classification which uses the artificial neural network based model (ANNBM). The Information gain along with the other three known approaches in the sentiment lexicons have been used for extracting of the sentiments which represent the features. These are then given as an input to the training and the test set in ANNBM. The output derived from the car reviews and for the mobile reviews have clearly displayed that this method has been successful to reduce the dimensionality factor as far as accuracy is concerned for the sentiment-based classification. When the input features are decreased, the one important work is for the ML based technique which is based on the sentiment classification. The Internet is growing rapidly and with Web 2.0, the size as well as the dimensionality for the opinionated textual data keeps growing in an exponential manner. Hence, the approach which has been proposed is a possible output which has an improved level of classification scalability and performance.

When we have a huge data set of the applications such as product reviews classification, the method that we have described would be extremely ideal. By using IG and the fissure selection based on sentiment lexicon, we were able to make sure that the method we had selected was not dependent on any one specific domain. Feature Selection based on Information Gain method gave the optimal outcome while HM lexicon lagged behind the optimality of the other two lexicons. Going forward we may look into extending this ANNBM based study to order and rank sentiments in different domain texts like Facebook, Blogs, and Twitter because this paper has had a restriction in its experimentation to be applicable only for the reviews of consumers. To study the efficiency of the approach that we have described, other studies can use varied domain data sets as part of their study.

References

1. Annett, M., Kondrak, G.: A comparison of sentiment analysis techniques: polarizing movie blogs. Adv. Artif. Intell. **5032**, 25–35 (2008)
2. Bai, X.: Predicting consumer sentiments from online text. Decis. Support Syst. **50**(4), 732–742 (2011)
3. Balog, K., Mishne, G., de Rijke, M.: Why are they excited?: identifying and explaining spikes in blog mood levels. In: Proceedings of EACL, Morristown, NJ, USA, pp. 207–210. ACL (2006)
4. Bespalov, D., Bai, B., Qi, Y., Shokoufandeh, A.: Sentiment classification based on supervised latent n-gram analysis. In: Proceedings of the 20th ACM International Conference on Information and Knowledge Management, Glasgow, Scotland, UK, 2011, pp. 375–382. ACM (2011)
5. Boiy, E., Hens, P., Deschacht, K., Moens, M.F.: Automatic sentiment analysis of on-line text. In: Proceedings of the 11th International Conference on Electronic Publishing, Vienna, Austria (2007)
6. Chen, L.S., Liu, C.H., Chiu, H.J.: A neural network based approach for sentiment classification in the blogosphere. J. Informet. **5**(2), 313–322 (2011)
7. Chevalier, J.A., Mayzlin, D.: The effect of word of mouth on sales: online book reviews. J. Mark. Res. **43**(3), 345–354 (2006)
8. Claster, W.B., Quoc, H.D., Shanmuganathan, S.: Unsupervised artificial neural nets for modeling movie sentiment. In: Proceedings of 2nd International Conference on Computational Intelligence, Communication Systems and Networks (CICSyN'10), Beppu, Japan, 349–354 (2010)
9. Conrad, J.G., Schilder, F.: Opinion mining in legal blogs. In: Proceedings of 11th International Conference on Artificial Intelligence and Law (ICAIL'07), New York, pp. 231–236. ACM (2007)

10. Cui, H., Mittal, V., Datar, M.: Comparative experiments on sentiment classification for online product reviews. In: Proceedings of AAAI, Boston, Massachusetts, 16–20 July 2006, pp. 1265–1270 (2006)
11. Dave, K., Lawrence, S., Pennock, D.M.: Mining the peanut gallery: opinion extraction and semantic classification of product reviews. In: Proceedings of the 12th International WWW Conference, Budapest, Hungary, 20–24 May 2003, pp. 519–528 (2003)
12. Decker, R., Trusov, M.: Estimating aggregate consumer preferences from online product reviews. Int. J. Res. Mark. **27**(4), 293–307 (2010)
13. Ding, X., Liu, B.: The utility of linguistic rules in opinion mining. In: Proceedings of the 30th Annual International ACM SIGIR Conference on Research and Development in Information Retrieval (SIGIR '07), pp. 811–812 (2007)
14. Esuli, A., Sebastiani, F.: Determining the semantic orientation of terms through gloss classification. In: Proceedings of the 14th ACM International Conference on Information and Knowledge Management (CIKM '05), pp. 617–624 (2005)
15. Godbole, N., Srinivasaiah, M., and Skiena, S. Large-scale sentiment analysis for news and blogs. In Proceedings of the International Conference on Weblogs and Social Media (ICWSM'07) 2007
16. Hatzivassiloglou, V., McKeown, K.R.: Predicting the semantic orientation of adjectives. In: Proceedings of the 35th ACL/8th EACL, pp. 174–181 (1997)
17. Hu, M., Liu, B.: Mining and summarizing customer reviews. In: Proceedings of the tenth ACM SIGKDD International Conference on Knowledge Discovery and Data Mining, Seattle, WA, USA. ACM (2004)
18. Kamps, J., Marx, M., Mokken, R.J., De Rijke, M.: Using wordnet to measure semantic orientations of adjectives. In: Proceedings of 4th International Conference on Language Resources and Evaluation, Lisbon, PT, pp. 1115–1118 (2004)
19. Kang, H., Yoo, S.J., Han, D.: Senti-lexicon and improved Naïve Bayes algorithms for sentiment analysis of restaurant reviews. Expert Syst. Appl. (2011). https://doi.org/10.1016/j.eswa.2011.11.107
20. Osherenko, A., André, E.: Lexical affect sensing: are affect dictionaries necessary to analyze affect? In: Paiva, A.C.R., Prada, R., Picard, R.W. (eds.) ACII 2007. LNCS, vol. 4738, pp. 230–241. Springer, Heidelberg (2007). https://doi.org/10.1007/978-3-540-74889-2_21
21. Paltoglou, G., Gobron, S., Skowron, M., Thelwall, M., Thalmann, D.: Sentiment analysis of informal textual communication in cyberspace. In: Proceedings of Engage'10, pp. 13–25 (2010)
22. Pang, B., Lee, L.: A sentimental education: sentiment analysis using subjectivity summarization based on minimum cuts. In: Proceedings of the 42nd annual meeting of the Association for Computational Linguistics (ACL), Barcelona, Spain, 21–26 July 2004, pp. 271–278 (2004)
23. Pang, B., Lee, L.: Opinion mining and sentiment analysis. Found. Trends Inf. Retr. **2**(1–2), 1–135 (2008)
24. Pang, B., Lee, L.: Seeing stars: exploiting class relationships for sentiment categorization with respect to rating scales. In: Proceedings of the 43rd Annual Meeting of the ACL, University of Michigan, USA, 25–30 June 2005, pp. 115–124 (2005)
25. Pang, B., Lee, L., Vaithyanathan, S.: Thumbs up? sentiment classification using machine learning techniques. In: Proceedings of the ACL-02 Conference on Empirical Methods in Natural Language Processing, vol. 10. ACL (2002)
26. Porter, M.F.: Snowball: a language for stemming algorithms (2001)
27. Prabowo, R., Thelwall, M.: Sentiment analysis: a combined approach. J. Informet. **3**(2), 143–157 (2009)
28. Rumelhart, D.E., McClelland, J.L.: Parallel Distributed Processing. MIT Press Cambridge and the PDP Research Group (1986)

29. Russell, S.J., Norvig, P., Davis, E.: Artificial Intelligence: A Modern Approach. Prentice Hall, Upper Saddle River (2010)
30. Sharma, A., Dey, S.: A comparative study of feature selection and machine learning techniques for sentiment analysis. In: Proceedings of the Proceedings of the ACM Research in Applied Computation Symposium, San Antonio, Texas, 2012, pp. 1–7. ACM (2012)
31. Sharma, A., Dey, S.: Performance investigation of feature selection methods and sentiment lexicons for sentiment analysis. IJCA Spec. Issue Adv. Comput. Commun. Technol. HPC Appl. **3**, 15–20 (2012)
32. Stone, P.J., Dunphy, D.C., Smith, M.S., Ogilvie, D.M.: The General Inquirer: A Computer Approach to Content Analysis. MIT Press, Cambridge (1966)
33. Tan, S., Zhang, J.: An empirical study of sentiment analysis for Chinese documents. Expert Syst. Appl. **34**(4), 2622–2629 (2008)
34. Thomas, M., Pang, B., Lee, L.: Get out the vote: determining support or opposition from congressional floordebate transcripts. In: Proceedings of the 2006 Conference on Empirical Methods in Natural Language Processing (EMNLP 2006), Sydney, pp. 327–335 (2006)
35. Tsytsarau, M., Palpanas, T.: Survey on mining subjective data on the web. Data Min. Knowl. Disc. **24**, 1–37 (2011)
36. Turney, P.D.: Thumbs up or thumbs down?: semantic orientation applied to unsupervised classification of reviews. In: Proceedings of the 40th Annual Meeting on ACL (ACL'02), Morristown, NJ, USA, pp. 417–424. ACL (2002)

Cross Linguistic Acoustic Phonetic Study of Punjabi and Indian English

Amita Dev[1], Shweta A. Bansal[2(✉)], and Shyam S. Agrawal[1]

[1] Indira Gandhi Delhi Technical University for Women, Delhi, India
[2] K.R. Mangalam University, Gurugram, India

Abstract. Punjabi and English are the languages that does not belong to the similar family. For instance, English belongs to the West German languages while Punjabi is a part of the Indo Aryan family. Regional languages have an impact on English in this borrowing and code-mixing process because borrowed words go through a make-up caused by phonetic features of the regional languages. In India, English is the medium of media, science, and technology & its influence on the native languages of the country is significant. This study shows how the regional dialects of the country have a significant influence on the way English is pronounced. It is an effort to define the phonemic changes in Punjabi and Indian English. The purpose of this study was to see if the sound pattern of Indian English varies depending on the speakers' native languages or if it is the same irrespective of the speakers' native languages and also to identify words that differ in pronunciation from Standard English and are clearly marked by an influence of the first language of the native Punjabi speakers of India.

Keywords: Acoustic phonetics · Indian English · Punjabi

1 Introduction

Punjabi is one of India's official languages. Punjabi is the primary official language in Punjab, and it is also spoken in Himachal Pradesh, Haryana and Delhi. Punjabi is considered to be a tonal language. It's because it uses tones to differentiate between words that are otherwise interchangeable [1]. Speakers may experience stress as a result of the influence of their native tongue, which does not have the same verbal delivery as English. According to Nadeem et al. [8], the primary reason of confusion is the natural tendency of first-language Punjabi speakers to utilise tones without specifying stressed syllables. It's an exploratory-qualitative study in which pronunciation discrepancies were suggested by constructing lists based on long-term observation of ignorant native Punjabi speakers. The research is exploratory in nature because no major studies on the same issue could be found (Fig. 1).

© Springer Nature Switzerland AG 2022
A. Dev et al. (Eds.): AIST 2021, CCIS 1546, pp. 151–159, 2022.
https://doi.org/10.1007/978-3-030-95711-7_13

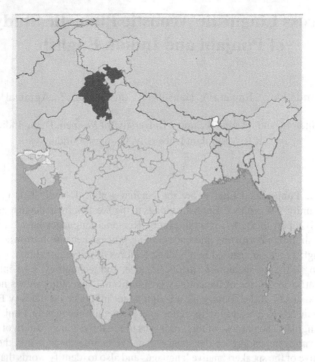

Fig. 1. Punjabi speaking region in India (highlighted in red) [7]. (Color figure online)

The variations of English which originated in the subcontinent of India are known as Indian English (IE). IE is now India's co-official language alongside Hindi. The impact of native language on the phonology of the Indian English was first studied by comparing English uttered by a specific group of Indians to British English [2]. Indian English (IE) has absorbed various traits from India's indigenous languages, according to these studies.

The recent experiments have studied the effects of various native languages on the phonology of IE [3, 4] Even though some differences are identified, the evidence supporting the notion that native speakers from various backgrounds produce a similar level of sound pattern for Indian English language is still strong.

Maxwell et al. studied the acoustic–phonetic properties of IE vowels in Hindi and Punjabi speakers. They were able to identify the differences in the two languages' vowel inventories. Although the IE vowels were produced little variations whereas more phonetic variety in their diphthongs were obtained in Punjabi speakers than those of Hindi speakers [5]. In addition, they found that the English pronunciation of Hindi and Punjabi speakers had the same vowel classifications. The consonant inventory of Punjabi and Indian English is shown in Fig. 2 and 3 respectively:

		Labial	Dental	Retroflex	Palatal	Velar	Glottal
Stop	Voiceless	p pʰ	t tʰ	ʈ ʈʰ		k kʰ	
	Voiced	b	d	ɖ		g	
Affricate	Voiceless				tʃ tʃʰ		
	Voiced				dʒ		
Fricative		(f)	s (z)		(ʃ)	(x)	ɦ
Nasal		m	n	ɳ	ɲ	ŋ	
Liquid			l r	ɭ ɽ			
Glide		ʋ			j		

Fig. 2. Consonant inventory of Punjabi language [9]

			Place of Articulation					
Manner of Articulation		Labial	Dental	Alveolar	Post-alveolar	Palatal	Velar	Glottal
Nasal		m		n			ŋ	
Stop	Unvoiced	p		t			k	
	Voiced	b		d			g	
Affricate	Unvoiced				tʃ			
	Voiced				dʒ			
Fricative	Unvoiced	f	θ	s	ʃ			h
	Voiced	v	ð	z	ʒ			
Approximant				l	ɹ	j	w	

Fig. 3. Consonant inventory of English language [10]

2 Current Study

In India, people learn Indian English phonology that has the influence of their own tongue or their native language. This argument does not rule out the possibility that IE phonology is influenced by original Indian languages; it only implies that these impacts are historical in nature. To study the perceptual and auditory similarities and variations of IE produced by native Punjabi speakers, who had all been educated in English medium since high school, we explored the perceptual and acoustical resemblances and differences of Indian English spoken by native Punjabi speakers.

3   Methodology

3.1   Development of Corpus for Acoustic–Phonetic Study

For this study, a phonemically balanced Indian English text database of 60 k words was prepared. Out of these words, we have created 200 phonetically rich Indian English sentences which include all the phonemes. These sentences were recorded by 50 native Punjabi speakers (25 male and 25 female) Punjabi. All the speakers have an educational background in their native language at least up to senior schooling. Speakers were provided with the English sentences and were instructed to speak in their own way of pronouncing the words. All these utterances were recorded using an electret microphone in an office environment by using "Goldwave" recording software at the sampling rate of 16 kHz/16 bit.

3.2   Cross-Language Phonemic Differences

After the perceptual analysis it can be concluded that the pronunciation of Punjabi speakers in the language varies considerably from the English standard in British or North American. Due to the tonal effect of Punjabi, the style of speaking English of native Punjabi speakers was modified and modifications in the sound patterns were discovered as shown in the Table 1.

Table 1. Deviate pronunciation of English phoneme by native Punjabi speakers

S.No.	Actual Phoneme	Deviate Phoneme	Example
1.	oʊ	ʊ	/ˌkoʊkʊ ˈkʊlɑ:/ is pronounced as /ˌkoʊkə ˈkoʊlə/
2.	æ	a:	/ˌtræns ˈfɔ:rmər/ is pronounced as /trɑ:ns ˈfɑ:rmər/
3.	e	/æ/	/meməri/ is pronounced as /ˈmæməri/
4.	/ɪ/	/ɪ:/	/ˈtemprəri/ is pronounced as /ˈtempəreri:/
5.	/ʌ/	/oʊ/	/ˈkʌmpəni/ is pronounced as /ˈkoʊmpni:/
6.	/eɪ/	/æ/	/leɪs / is pronouncesd as /læs /
7.	/ɔ:/	/a:/	/fɔ:rm/ is pronounced as /fɑ:rəm/

It has also been observed that /ə/sound is added by the native Punjabi speakers between the consonants s/p or s/t, for instance sprite (/spraɪt /) is pronounced along with tonal effect as /səpræt/ . Similarly, /ə/sound is added between various consonants such as horn /hɔ:rn/ is uttered as /hɑ:rən/ , wolf/wʊlf/ as / vʊləf/ etc.

The spectrograms in Fig. 4 and 5 depicts the pronunciation variation in the English word "college" which is pronounced as "Kaalej" by the native Punjabi speakers respectively.

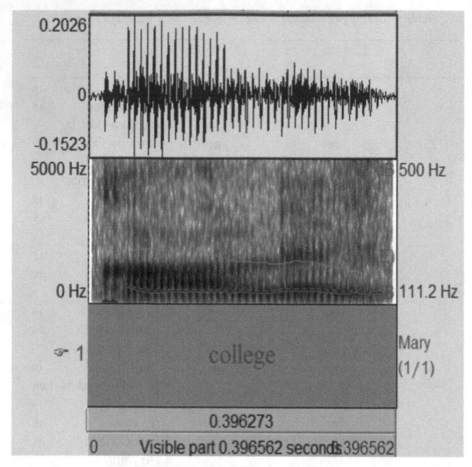

Fig. 4. Spectrogram of the word "College"

3.3 Acoustic Measurements

In the second experiment, impact of speaker background on the distinct segmental and supra-segmental attributes by performing acoustic measurements. The PRAAT speech processing software was used to display recorded utterances and segment them for vowel measurement. At the midpoint of every vowel, F1 and F2 values were extracted instantaneously. Formant values were generalised by using the Lobanov method to analyse the variability based on the vocal tract features of an individual speaker[6]. In the vowel analyses, the dependent variables were normalised F1 and F2, as well as the ratio of F1 to F2.

In Fig. 6, the IE and Punjabi vowels are plotted as a function of speaker background using normalised F1 and F2 values. A comparison of the various vowel spaces represented in the figure shows that, while IE varies due to influence of the speaker's background, the variations between IE and the native language are clearly evident. This analysis was carried out to determine the differences in the sounds that were uttered by

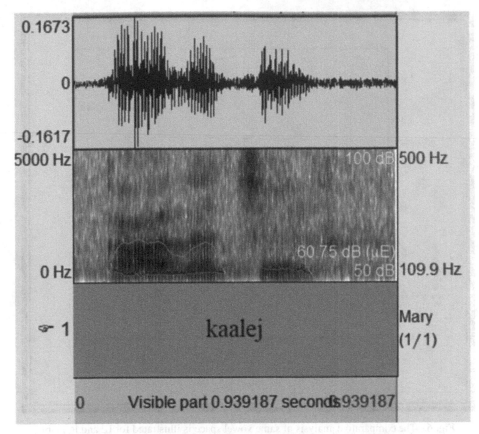

Fig. 5. Spectrogram of the word "Kaalej" spoken by native Punjabi speaker

different speakers. The F1 and F2 studies were carried out to investigate the impact of a language and a speaker background on the generation of certain vowels.

It has been observed from the Fig. 4 that the effect of background is most pronounced among Punjabi speakers. The effect of background on /u/ was most likely caused by the fronted articulation of Punjabi speakers (L1). On the other hand, the effect of language task was more centralized in IE than in L1. Also, the acoustic measurements determined the impact of native language on Indian English. It has been observed that due to the influence of L1 i.e. Punjabi the IE vowels /i/, /e/, /ɑ/, and /u/ get affected.

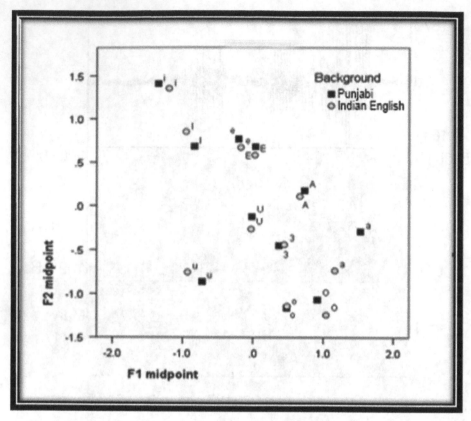

Fig. 6. The comparative analysis of same vowel space is illustrated for IE and Punjabi.

4 Conclusion

It can be inferred that native Punjabi speakers' pronunciation differs significantly from conventional British or American English. The supplemental sound "schwa" is generally added to the words at the initial, middle, and final positions by the Punjabi speakers. This study implies that native Punjabi speakers' pronunciation is punjabicized and distinct in its own manner. Investigating regionally based changes in IE that are independent of L1 would be a complementary future research work. For example, we will intrigued if the Indian English uttered by native Punjabi speakers in places outside the Punjab state differs from that uttered by native Punjabi speakers in Punjab. A study of this nature would help to clarify the distinction between psycholinguistic and sociolinguistic aspects.

References

1. Ghai, W.P., Singh, N.: Analysis of automatic speech recognition systems for indo-aryan languages: Punjabi a case study. Int. J. Softw. Comput. Eng. **2**(1), 379–385 (2012)

2. Bansal, R.K.: A phonetic analysis of English spoken by a group of well-educated speakers from Uttar Pradesh. CIEFL Bull. (Hyderabad) **8**, 1–11 (1970)
3. Maxwell, O., Fletcher, J.: Acoustic and durational properties of Indian English vowels. World Englishes **28**, 52–70 (2009)
4. Maxwell, O., Fletcher, J.: The acoustic characteristics of diphthongs in Indian English. World Englishes **29**, 27–44(. 2010)
5. Agrawal, S.S., Bansal, S., Sharan, S., Mahajan, M.: Acoustic analysis of oral and nasal Hindi vowels spoken by native and non-native speakers. J. Acoust. Soc. Am. **140**, 3338 (2016)
6. Erik, R.T., Kendall, T.: NORM: the vowel normalization and plotting suite (2007). http://ncs laap.lib.ncsu.edu/tools/norm/
7. https://en.wikipedia.org/wiki/Punjabi_Suba_movement
8. Rahman, G.: A comparative study of Pashto and English consonants. Pashto **45**, 11–27 (2016)
9. http://www.languagesgulper.com/eng/Punjabi.html
10. https://psyclanguage.pressbooks.tru.ca/chapter/consonants/

Prashn: University Voice Assistant

Priya Sharma[1], Sparsh Sharma[2], and Pooja Gambhir[1(✉)]

[1] Indira Gandhi Delhi Technical University for Women, Delhi, India
{priya003btcsai20,pooja001phd19}@igdtuw.ac.in
[2] Delhi Technological University, Delhi, India

Abstract. University websites are the best source to get information about a university. But each university has a different methodology for the implementation of its website and there is no common layout for finding specific information. This can be difficult for users, especially potential students who are trying to compare different universities to decide where to get admitted in. Natural Language Human-Computer Interaction (HCI) is trending these days due to its ease of use. Thus, implementing a chatbot on university websites can reduce a lot of time students spend looking for information they need like office timings, address, admission procedure, accommodation information, etc. Voice Assistants are the future of Natural language HCI. Prashn is a web application that allows users to get all the necessary information about Indira Gandhi Delhi Technical University for Women, Delhi either through a chat interface or through speech recognition.

Keywords: Voice assistant · University chatbot · CNN · Flask

1 Introduction

In this era, where everything ranging from international TV shows to buying groceries is just a tap or click away, students should be able to get all the information about universities easily too. But often, university websites are either not intuitive or not timely updated. Even if it has all the information about the university's administration and academics, it often lacks common answers about co-curricular activities or locations inside the campus. Sometimes, the website has information but it is buried deep under various hyperlinks and the lack of a search bar or a common platform often discourages the user to search through the website. People prefer asking their queries to other people in natural language so that they can get to the point answers to their queries.

Chatbots have become increasingly popular with every service opting to embed one on their website to help the users find what they are looking for with ease [1]. HDFC Bank's Eva, IRCTC's DISHA, BPCL's Urja are great examples of chatbots implemented on websites. Petter Bae Brandtzaeg et al. in their paper "Why do people use Chatbots" talked about various motivational factors in conversational interfaces that contribute to the design of a chatbot [2]. While the presence of chatbots is increasing day by day, there is still nothing better than finding a human who knows everything and talking to them. Humans cherish natural human interaction, especially voice conversations. This brings a need for Voice Assistants.

A. Dev et al. (Eds.): AIST 2021, CCIS 1546, pp. 160–170, 2022.
https://doi.org/10.1007/978-3-030-95711-7_14

Voice Assistants have grown exponentially in popularity since the first one developed in the 90s. They provide a more natural flow of conversation while harnessing the power to accurately provide information from a huge database [3].

Prashn is aimed to assist existing, as well as potential students, in finding all sorts of information about the University using machine learning [4]. A dataset that consists of frequently asked questions and information from the website is manually created and trained using the keras sequential model with a Conv1D layer. This model is used to predict the intents of every message sent by the user. The interface is then created using HTML, CSS, and JS and integrated with the backend using python's popular micro web framework - Flask. Google's Web Speech API is used to implement speech to text as well as text to speech functionality in the chatbot.

2 Related Work

Georgia State University introduced personalized text messaging with the help of main-stay (formerly AdminHub). This Chatbot was called "Pounce". Pounce was designed to assist students in their day-to-day academic tasks by giving timely reminders and answering commonly asked questions 24 × 7. With the help of the university, a random-ized controlled trial (RCT) was conducted where half of the incoming freshman class were given access to Pounce and the remaining were selected for the control group. By the program's end, 63% of all students within the treatment group had engaged with Pounce on a minimum of 3 separate days throughout the admission process and had sent an average of 60 messages. Around 1% of the queries required human support from Georgia State staff—the rest being handled by Pounce. The response was positive and students appreciated the casual language, approachability, and personalization of messages. One student said, "It was the easiest part of enrollment." The feeling of not being judged for asking what might seem like a "stupid" question was appreciated by the students, they also appreciated the instantaneous responses, especially when they asked questions at unconventional hours [5] (Fig. 1).

Ranoliya et al. designed a chatbot for university-related FAQs. The chatbot was based on AIML language and was proposed to be implemented at Manipal University. Its objective was to help students with information about the ranking of the university, administrative services, info about campus life, ongoing and upcoming events, and other academic information [6].

Saint Louis University leverages the popular voice assistant Amazon Alexa to help students with academic queries. They have set up 2,300 Echo Dots (smart speaker by Amazon that is Alexa-enabled) in student dorms. Each Echo Dot is equipped with an Alexa app, also known as a "Skill" called SLU. The skill helps students get answers to university specific queries via a popular voice assistant Alexa, leveraging their Natural Language Understanding (NLU) capabilities at the cost of customizability and privacy. Currently, the skill can answer over 150 questions related to the campus. This dataset is planned to be expanded in the future based on student feedback [7].

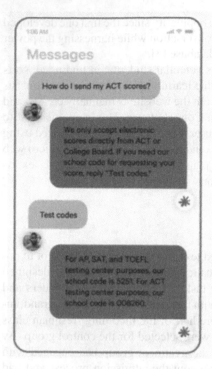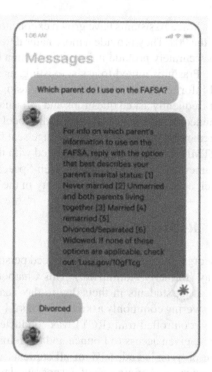

Fig. 1. Pounce helping out students with admission queries.

3 Experiment and Design

3.1 Creating the Dataset

A collection of 50 frequently asked questions ranging from ways to reach the university to Admission process queries is prepared in JSON format. The JSON file (intents.json) has questions grouped as intents with a separate tag for each intent that will be used for intent classification. Questions of the following categories were framed and stored -

- Small Talk and Chatbot Information
- Reach out - timings and location
- Information about Departments and HODs
- Hostel Information
- Admission Procedure for various courses
- Student Life FAQs

Sample Intent

```json
{
  "tag": "document",
  "patterns": [
    "document to bring",
    "documents needed for admission",
    "documents needed at the time of admission",
    "documents needed during admission",
    "documents required for admission",
    "documents required at the time of admission",
    "documents required during admission",
    "What document are required for admission",
    "Which document to bring for admission",
    "documents",
    "what documents do i need",
    "what documents do I need for admission",
    "documents needed"
  ],
  "responses": [
    "The marksheet of class 12th and 10th, Character cer-
tificate, caste certificate(if not general),School leav-
ing certificate, Two passpoert size photographs, Ad-
mit Card, Nta scores(B.Tech) and migration certificate"
  ],
  "context_set": ""
},
```

The intent object has four properties. A tag to classify the intent, an array of patterns that describe the intent, an array of possible responses, and the context set. Since this is not a contextual chatbot, the context set property is set to empty. This dataset was then parsed using the JSON module in python. It was then converted into a pandas dataframe for further processing (Tables 1 and 2).

Table 1. Patterns dataframe (Sample)

	Questions	Labels
50	Timing of college	hours
428	Which busstop station is closest	bus-stop
210	Syllabus for it	syllabus
126	Phd branch	Ph.D
11	Bye bye	goodbye

Table 2. Responses dataframe (Sample)

	Response	Labels
12	I'm Prashn aka IGDTUW's Chatbot	38
6	Come back soon	23
8	I was created by Ms. Priya Sharma, who is curr...	15
31	The university has an excellent placement reco...	41
64	IGDTUW was established in 2013	29

3.2 Text Pre-processing

Tokenization. It is the process where a given document is split into its smallest relevant component which is called a token. It can be a character, word, phrase, or sentence depending upon the context. Words are the most common tokens used in a text corpus.

Lemmatization. A common normalization technique in text pre-processing. Once a document is tokenized, each token is then replaced by its root word or word with a similar meaning. This helps us reduce redundancy and focus on important data [8] (Fig. 2).

Lemmatization

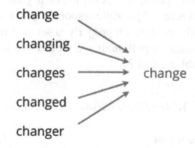

Fig. 2. Example of Lemmatization

After tokenizing and lemmatizing the dataset, a vocabulary of words used in training dataset is created. This vocabulary will be helpful when encoding the dataset.

Encoding and Decoding. Once the vocabulary of words is obtained, these tokens need to be encoded into machine readable format for further processing and training. There are various methods to achieve this, most common methods being count vectorizer, tf-idf, hashing etc. `Tensorflow.keras.text_to_sequence` is used to encode each token into a vector where the coefficient for each token will be binary, based on TF-IDF of the token in that document. This resulting vector is then padded with zeroes to ensure the length of vectors is equal.

TF-IDF (term frequency-inverse document frequency) is a statistical measure that decides the relevance of a word in a document based on its count and inverse document frequency in that document. TF-IDF vectorizer converts the tokens into a vector based on this measure.

TF-IDF vectorizer is known to yield slightly better results as compared to other vectorizers [9].

Train-Test Split. After encoding, the data is now ready to be split into training and testing sets. It is divided into four components – X_train – which has the features that are to be trained by the model, X_test – features that will be used for validation, Y_train – The labels corresponding to vectors in X_train and Y_test – the labels corresponding to vectors in X_test. This can be done using a stratified approach, whereby of the patterns in the tags are well represented in the testing set.

3.3 Model Used

This chatbot is trained on a deep learning model due to its state-of-the-art performance. The keras sequential API is used to build the model with various layers as discussed below.[10].

The dataset given as input to the model is a two-dimensional vector of dimensions (None, 11), in which 11 is the maximum length of padded sequences of the input dimension. As we are using keras sequential API, the data goes through a series of layers and thus a model is obtained. First, the data enters the embedding layer which converts each word into a into a fixed length vector of defined size. Then, it goes through one-dimensional convolution layer to further extract the features and obtain a three-dimensional output vector of size (None, 11, 600). Here, 600 is the size of the convolution layer filters. Then, the vector enters a pooling layer, which gives out a three-dimensional output vector of dimension (None, 1, 64). These vectors are then flattened (transposed to a single row of vectors) for the fully connected layer before compiling it with an Adam optimizer. This layer structure for the model is obtained after various iterations so that the model is optimized for our dataset. The figure below shows the model summary with details about various layers (Fig. 3).

3.4 Testing and Validation

Once the model is created, it is trained on the dataset with 50 epochs and reduced learning rate on plateau to prevent overfitting. The model is trained successfully with validation accuracy of 83.02% and a validation loss of 0.76. This was further verified by manually testing the model over 20 queries out of which, 18 were answered correctly. The graph below shows the learning curve of model with each epoch (Fig. 4).

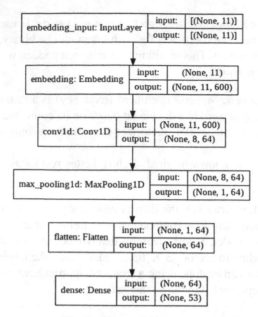

Fig. 3. The model summary

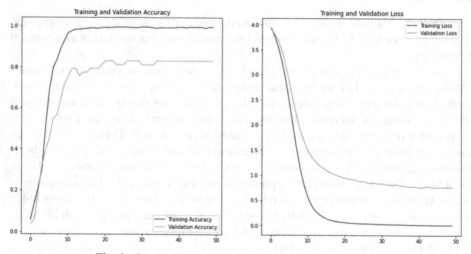

Fig. 4. Graph of Training and validation accuracy and loss

3.5 Creating the Interface

User Interface is a very crucial part of a chatbot since that is what the user interacts on. It needs to be appealing as well as accessible. Since Prashn is proposed to be implemented on the university website, the UI is a web application made using HTML, CSS and JavaScript for front-end design with flask being the micro web framework used to integrate backend. The interface is simple with a header and one-on-one text chat window. It is designed to feel like a normal messaging platform's interface. Since it is also a voice assistant, a mic button has been added which can be used to record voice and synthesize it to generate response.

Prashn's audio greeting is added to give users a warm welcome. An avatar is also added to the chatbot which is displayed when it responds to a query. This helps in making the chatbot look more like a human user and makes it approachable to users asking queries. Once the user asks a query, in the form of text or voice, the query is displayed in the chat window as a message from user. In the back-end, the query is pre-processed and encoded to be sent to the model for prediction. The model, which is pre-loaded via.h5 file during initialisation then uses the encoded message and sends the most accurate reply. The reply is shown as a text from the bot. This interface also keeps track of message history thus allowing support for contextual replies. The UI is responsive and can be easily adapted to be implemented as an overlay to the university website (Fig. 5).

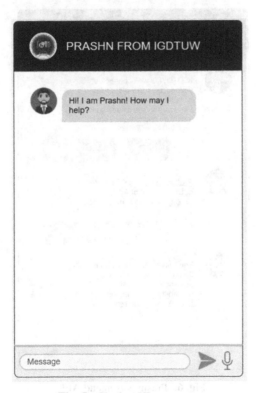

Fig. 5. Chatbot UI on startup

3.6 Voice Integrated API for Prashn

To make a chatbot a voice assistant, there are two essential components – Text to Speech and Speech to Text. Prashn uses the Speech Recognition module in python to record sound from client's microphone and recognize it using Google's Web Speech API. Users can click the mic button on the chatbot interface to trigger this functionality. The recognized text is then treated as a text message for intent prediction. The predicted response, whether generated through text message or speech recognition is spoken out using Web Speech API's Text to Speech function in JavaScript. The voice, language and pace can be configured in code to match with the personality of chatbot.

4   Result

Using 1D Convolution Neural Networks layer, we were able to create a reinforcement learning based voice assistant. It is capable of answering a variety of queries using Natural Language Processing asked through both speech and voice. The figure below shows an example of how Prashn resolves queries (Fig. 6).

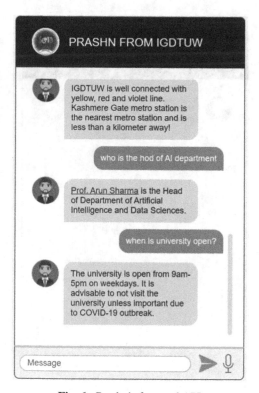

Fig. 6. Prashn's frontend API

5   Future Work

Chatbots have proven to be essential in various domains like healthcare, education, business etc. Prashn is a prototype of how voice assistants can help universities solve queries and provide information more effectively. It has been developed on a limited yet varied dataset for testing purpose.

Future work will include expanding the dataset to cover more domains and provide information more naturally and efficiently. Surveys to be conducted among university students to identify areas where voice assistants could be highly beneficial. Currently, the voice assistant responds to independent queries. Provision for continued conversation with contexts will make the conversation with user more natural flowing. Support for regional languages and dialects to be added to increase accessibility. Semantic sentence similarity using NLU models like BERT to also be explored to allow queries to be answered more efficiently. Methods of optimizing model by exploring various machine learning and deep learning techniques to be studied and implemented.

Improvements to be made in the UI to make it more responsive and user friendly while also focusing on aspects like data collection and privacy. An intuitive portal to add intents to the dataset to also be implemented to allow admins to update the chatbot frequently with updated information.

6 Conclusion

Chatbots are conversational agents that interact with user on a certain topic with inputs in natural language. A need of university voice assistant arises due to various reasons including outdated information and complex website structure [11]. It is observed that universities that implemented chatbots to solve queries had better reception from students as well as reduced burden on staff.

A voice assistant trained using deep learning is proposed and designed to be implemented on the university website to provide an efficient way of interacting with the users and provide solutions to their enquiries. The voice assistant is trained using a sequential model with one-dimensional convolution neural network. This model is chosen due to its better performance over recurrent neural network (RNN) based model in short-span environment [12]. The present work represents that the model used predicted the intents of a user query with 83.02% accuracy. It was then integrated into a text-text based chatbot frontend web application using flask. Further, the system was enhanced with pre-defined speech-speech APIs to make it more voice based interactive application. Future work includes expansion of domains, languages and dialects, optimization of model to improve efficiency and accuracy.

References

1. Csaky, R.: Deep Learning Based Chatbot Models (2019)
2. Petter Bae, B., Asbjørn, F.: Why do People use chatbots?, pp. 3–5 (2018)
3. Gambhir, P.: Review of Chatbot Design and Trends (2019)
4. Kumar, P., Sharma, M., Rawat, S., Choudhury, T.: Designing and developing a chatbot using machine learning, no. 1, pp. 87–91 ((2019))
5. Case Study: Georgia State University supports every student with personalized text messaging. https://mainstay.com/case-study/how-georgia-state-university-supports-every-student-with-personalized-text-messaging/

6. Ranoliya, B.R., Raghuwanshi, N., Singh, S.: Chatbot for university related FAQs. In: 2017 International Conference on Advances in Computing, Communications and Informatics (ICACCI), pp. 1525–1530. Springer, Heidelberg (2017)
7. Case Study: Voice Assistants for Universities. https://ipervox.com/voice-assistants-for-univer sities/
8. Building a Conversational Chatbot with NLTK and TensorFlow. https://heartbeat.comet.ml/building-a-conversational-chatbot-with-nltk-and-tensorflow-part-1f452ce1756e5
9. Wendland, A., Zenere, M., Niemann, J.: Introduction to text classification: impact of stemming and comparing TF-IDF and count vectorization as feature extraction technique. In: Yilmaz, M., Clarke, P., Messnarz, R., Reiner, M. (eds.) EuroSPI 2021. CCIS, vol. 1442, pp. 289–300. Springer, Cham (2021). https://doi.org/10.1007/978-3-030-85521-5_19
10. Deshpande, A., et al.: PTC Mogensen.pdf. XI (2017)
11. Lalwani, T., Bhalotia, S., Pal, A., Rathod, V., Bisen, S.: Implementation of a chatbot system using AI and NLP. Int. J. Innov. Res. Comput. Sci. Technol. (IJIRCST) **6**(3), 26–30 (2018)
12. Zhang, D., Wang, D.: Relation classification: CNN or RNN? In: Natural Language Understanding and Intelligent Applications, pp. 665–675, Springer International Publishing: Cham (2016). https://doi.org/10.1007/978-3-319-50496-4_60

Spectrogram Analysis and Text Conversion of Sound Signal for Query Generation to Give Input to Audio Input Device

Kavita Sharma(✉) and S. R. N. Reddy

Indira Gandhi Delhi Technical University for Women, Delhi 11006, India
{kavita004phd20,srnreddy}@igdtuw.ac.in

Abstract. The world is being reshaped by Natural Language Processing. Audio inputs are used in modern electronics. Different types of people supply input to the system in their native language. The system accepts the person's speech, processes it, and responds accordingly. Cooking is a huge problem for a variety of people, including the elderly, those who are confined to their beds, and those who have a specific sort of handicap, such as those who are unable to use their hands and require assistance at all times. To help these people reach their full potential, an audio input device for giving cooking instructions to a cooking system has been proposed in this paper. The gadget takes the user's spoken English language as input, converts it to text using deep learning algorithms, and generates instructions with the help of context-aware words extracted from the recorded audios to send the instruction to the cooking device. To analyses, the audio signal for user authentication is a challenging task due to gaps and pauses between spoken characters, and existing noise in the environment. As a result, the audio input device developed for kitchen systems must analyze the audio input signal to create a more secure environment for authenticated users. As a result, the objective of this paper is to analyze the audio input signal captured in real-time and process the accepted signal to convert into the text to generate instructions for a larger system. The sound signals captured in the real environment are analyzed with Mel spectrogram, MFCC spectrogram, and PRAAT software. The sound signal is processed with the help of a natural language toolkit to generate instructions.

Keywords: Mel-spectrogram · Audio signal · MFCC · Tokenization

1 Introduction

Processing of the sound signals received from the user has much popularity in the modern world as it fills the gap between machine understanding, learning, and human spoken language. It saves a lot of time for the user of the technology instead of giving commands to the machine with the help of written text in a particular machine-readable language. The advancement in speech technology has several challenges for the technology developer e.g.: recording of the speech spoken audio signals, analyzing then, removal of noise elements, and extracting the desired signal with maximum accuracy. Using machine

© Springer Nature Switzerland AG 2022
A. Dev et al. (Eds.): AIST 2021, CCIS 1546, pp. 171–181, 2022.
https://doi.org/10.1007/978-3-030-95711-7_15

learning and deep learning models, the ASR (Automatic Speech Recognizer) assists in recording audio speech signals and converting them to text. The display of various spectrograms aids in the study and classification of audio signals. This technology's implementation in the kitchen offers a lot of potential for increasing the efficiency of the cooking process. The study consists of attempting to synthesize a specific speaker's voice with a few lines to leverage a vast amount of labeled speech recorded via the audio input device and text data received after conversion of the recorded signal, from which labels are to be extracted to generate a query that is to be given to the culinary system. The most popular platform e.g.: Amazon Echo, Google Home, Cortona, Siri, etc. extracts the words from the recorded clips of the spoken audio in some language and text conversion. This extracted text is used for sending queries to the system working in the background and the user desired output is provided in the audio form again. A normal human being has no difficulty in operating a smart device using any input mode eg: text input, sign input, or audio input. However, a certain group of people, such as the elderly or those with a specific sort of impairment, face unique challenges when using text or sign input. With audio input, they feel at ease. People who are unfamiliar with technology, on the other hand, find auditory input to be comforting. As a result, the goal of this study is to take audio input from a variety of users.

The audio accepted by the user can be represented in different ways based on the application. The analysis of audio input is based on various parameters e.g.: spectral centroid, spectral shape, zero-crossing statistics, harmony, fundamental frequency and temporal envelop frequency, etc. For classification of the sound different representations are popular in literature. The magnitude representation of raw audio [2] is done with the help of Mel-scale and Mel Frequency Cepstral Coefficients. Mel spectrum [4, 6] is used to map characters using recurrent sequence to sequence feature prediction. The log-Mel spectrogram and MFCC characteristics help recognize Alzheimer's dementia and classify environmental sounds [7]. CycleGAN-VC2 (Cycle Consistent Adversarial Network Voice Conversion 2) [9] have mappings without using parallel corpus between source and destination speech. As a result, classifying the users' sounds is a vital duty for the system's security. As a result, the paper's major goal is to record user input to classify different audio inputs given by the user with the help of Mel-spectrogram and MFCC classification tools.

The remaining paper is organized as follows: The second section is a review of the literature on the tools used to classify audio signals. The suggested audio input device is described in Section three. The fourth section focuses on various audio signal formats. Section five contains the results and discussion of several audio signal representations, as well as the suggested model's potential reach. The overall paper is concluded in Section six.

2   Literature Survey

The audio signals are accepted for various types of applications to provide input based on the context of the application. When an audio signal is captured from the open environment, it has a different type of interference and noise data embedded with it. Thus, literature provides various methods for analysis and classification tasks of recorded audio data. Mel spectrogram and MFCC are the most popular signal classification tools of capturing the low-level shape of modulation spectra e.g.: Spectrograms [1] are used to generate audio using neural network single-channel STFT (Short-Time Fourier Transform), style transfer, The analysis of SNR (signal to noise ratio) [2] using the Mel-scale and Mel-Frequency Cepstral Coefficients spectrograms techniques increases recognition accuracy of an audio signal, spectrograms [3] are normalized into grayscale to extracts the block to extract features, character embedding [4] is mapped with Mel-scale spectrogram with the help recurrent sequence to sequence feature prediction. Mel spectrogram [5] extracts the appropriate hyperparameters of augmentation, parallel neural vocoder [6] integrate linear predictive synthesis filter in the model, the efficacy of log-Mel spectrogram and MFCC [7] are effective techniques of recognizing Alzheimer's dementia(AD), the environmental sound [8] classification is based on spectrogram to strain less informative and irrelevant frequencies from the signal, low dimensional features of an audio signal are defined by spectrograms [10] to capture the shape of modulation spectra, CycleGAN-VC3 [14] is enhanced version of CycleGAN-VC2, Acoustic Scene Classification [11, 12] gives scene's comprehensive with the help of spectrograms representation. Natural language toolkit [9, 13] is used for text mining to generate queries from the text extracted from the audio signal. Thus, in a nutshell, we can say that:

Spectrograms are the better tool for audio signal analysis, classification, and representation.

Natural language toolkit helps in text mining to extract the words from the text received from audio signal conversion.

3 Proposed Model: Audio Input Device

A typical guy can easily operate in the kitchen, but a person with a unique kind of impairment, such as someone who is unable to leave their home due to a health issue or is of advanced age, finds it difficult to perform everyday tasks without assistance. The kitchen is the most important place in the house, and people spend 8 to 10 h a day there preparing food. The smart kitchen is popular in this day when everything is going to be smart. Smart kitchens necessitate smart gadgets capable of controlling smart kitchen objects. Figure 1 depicts the proposed model in this paper, which is an audio input device. The audio input device is designed using a microcontroller and accepts audio signals from a human being for ASR (Automatic Speech Recognizer) The ASR recognizes the input signals and sends the input to the machine learning model where the audio signal is converted into text to extract the context-dependent features. When the system accepts the audio signal from the user, the signal is recorded as a wave file.

The wave file is recorded and given as input to the ASR system stored on the cloud. The designed device is a part of a system and resource-constrained device; thus, it stores only audio files and puts them through the same process. The remaining background programs are kept in the cloud and launched on the server as needed. When the user wishes to give the system instructions, he turns on the audio input device and begins speaking. The audio signal varies from user to user due to differences in pitch, phonemes, utterance level, spectrum, amplitude, and other factors. Sounds and noises make up the most basic audio data. Human speech is an example of this. Speech is more difficult to encode since it encodes spoken words. The first step in solving an audio classification problem is to listen to a sound sample and determine the class it belongs to from a list of available classes in the database.

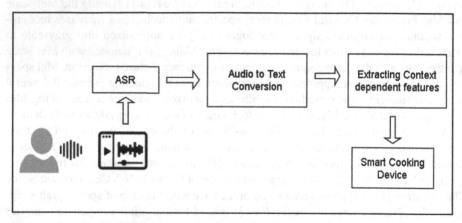

Fig. 1. Block diagram of audio input system working

The Speech-to-Text conversion training data is classified as follows:

Audio clips of spoken words (X) are input features.
Labels for the target (y): a text extracted from the transcript of the recorded audio of the user (Fig. 2).

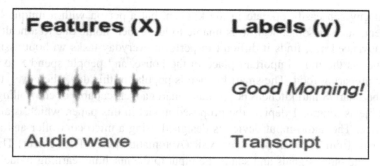

Fig. 2. Input and output of the device

Audio waves are used as input characteristics and text transcripts extracted from audio signals are used in analyzing and classifying the audio signal and target text for query generation in an automatic speech recognition system. The model is created to learn, interpret the audio input to make predictions based on text content extracted from the recorded audio clip and the extracted words and phrases. The audio data is then processed as seen in Fig. 3 and a Mel Spectrogram is generated to classify different signals. Classification of the sound signal by converting raw audio waves to Mel spectrogram images for extracting user sound signal and minimizing noise, deep learning popular Python library librosa is used here.

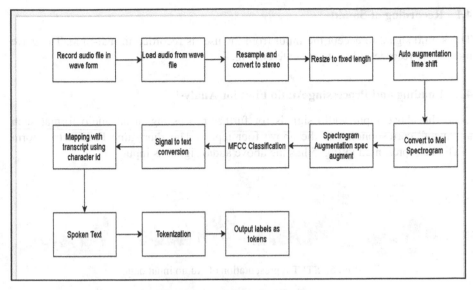

Fig. 3. Processing of audio data

4   Different Representations of Audio Signals

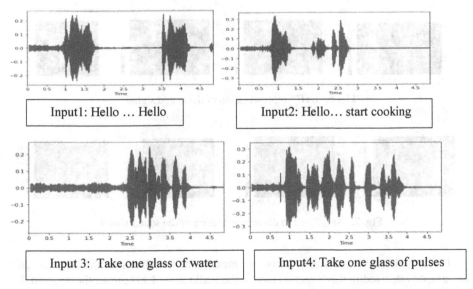

Fig. 4. Wave plotting of Audio sound signal for time

4.1 Recording of Sound

The sound signal to accept the input from the user is recorded in real-time. The wave plot of the recorded file is represented in Fig. 4.

4.2 Loading and Processing Audio Files for Analysis

Load the above input audio signals for further processing in an audio format such as ".wav" corresponding to the above four inputs. The short-time Fourier transform (STFT)is represented in Fig. 5 has the above audio signal as input.

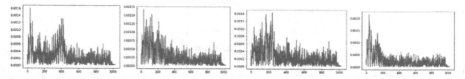

Fig. 5. STFT representation of Audio input data

The recorded wave audio data is sent to an array of 2D NumPy that contains an array of numbers for measurement of the amplitude and intensity of the sound signal at a specific movement of time.

Fig. 6. STFT representation of the sound signal

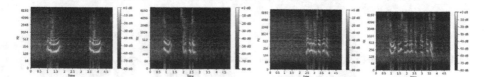

Fig. 7. Amplitude to dB representation of the sound signal

The sample rate reveals the number of measurements taken for consideration and the sample rate used in this paper to record the audio is 44.1 kHz thus, the array in the NumPy library has a single row of 44,100 values for each second of recorded audio. Mono and stereo are the two channels that are commonly used by audio signals. The recorded four audio uses two audio channels where the second channel has a similar sequence of amplitude numbers. Thus, the NumPy array has 3D with a depth of 2. As a result, the sample rate, channels, and duration are all converted to uniform dimensions (Fig. 6).

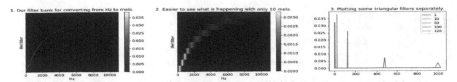

Fig. 8. Conversion of the sound signal in Mel and representation with 10 Mel of audio input1

Clips may be sampled at different speeds in real-time for different types of commands, or they may have a varying number of channels in separate audio files. As seen in Fig. 7, 8, 9 the clips will most likely have varying durations and dimensions.

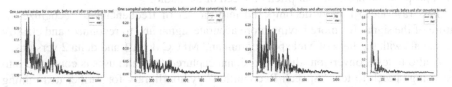

Fig. 9. Comprehensive analysis of original audio signal and Mel signal

The Mel Spectrogram has now been changed to MFCC (Mel Frequency Cepstral Coefficients) to extract only the most context-aware frequency coefficients corresponding to the human being's frequency ranges of talking to the surroundings. MFCCs provide a compressed form of the Mel Spectrogram (Fig. 10, 11).

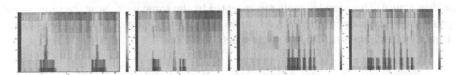

Fig. 10. Log Mel spectrogram representation of the sound signal

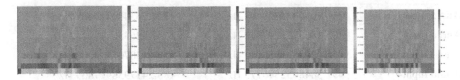

Fig. 11. MFCC representation of a sound signal with order 1

Data cleaning helps in standardizing the audio data dimensions as deep learning models need all inputs of similar size to process. As a result, the audio file is resampled into the same number of channels at the same sampling rate by padding the shorter sequences and truncating the longer sequences (Fig. 12).

Background noise is removed using a noise removal algorithm to improve audio quality. As a result, in Fig. 7, we get a better sound signal than in Fig. 4.

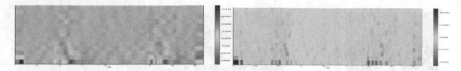

Fig. 12. Delta1 and Delta2 MFCC representation of the sound signal with order 2

By hyper-parameter and data augmentation, this stage improves the features of spectrograms for optimal performance. To extend the learning of the model to an accurate range of inputs, data augmentation techniques are used due to the diversity in the input data. It is done by randomly shifting the audio signal in the left or right direction by a small proportion based on user pitch or speed of the audio.

This raw audio is now decomposed into the set of frequencies to recognize the nature of the signal for more having more accurate signal and to recognize and classify the signals with the help of Mel spectrogram and MFCC delta 1 and delta 2 versions.

Audio to text conversion: the audio signal captured from the user is converted into text using speech to text "Speech Recognition" python library for further text mining process.

5   Results and Discussion

As we have analyzed from Fig. 4 to Fig. 12 with the help of code written in the python language and the sound signals are recorded manually with the help of code written in python. The sound signals contain the sentences used in an input device designed for the cooking device. The sound signals are accepted by the same user. Now the same sound signals are analyzed with the PRAAT audio analysis tool (Fig. 13) which provide the following measurements (Table 1) w.r.t spectrogram:

Table 1. Mean F1 and F2 of the audio signal in PRAAT audio analysis

Input	Mean F1	Mean F2
Audio Input1	430.2049424322493 Hz	1751.7334002196676 Hz
Audio Input2	405.8863713297039 Hz	1751.5263508130217 Hz
Audio Input3	476.0224521852952 Hz	1584.1387055004666 Hz
Audio Input4	491.3848052596775 Hz	1832.477938977869 Hz

We have analyzed the sound signals, having parameters shown in Table 2, with the help of Mel spectrogram, MFCC, and PRAAT tool representation which give a better representation than original sound and extract the sound features e.g.: pitch, intensity, pulses, etc. It also helps in the visualization of environmental noise embedded with the sound to clean the sound signal for further processing. After analyzing the audio signal is converted into text and processed with the nltk python library to extract the

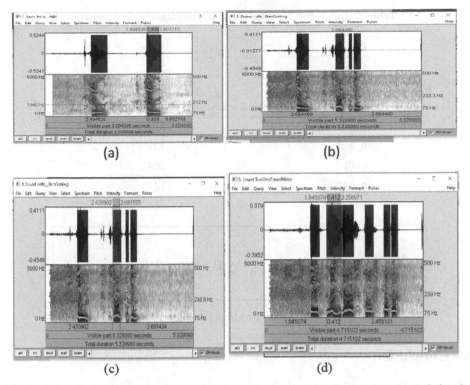

Fig. 13. Visualization of spectrogram, pitch, intensity, formants, and pulses w.r.t. sound signals in PRAAT software

context-aware text and generate instructions. The speech recognition library provides the following output corresponding to four audio inputs in Fig. 4.

After converting audio text into text, the tokenization process provides the following output (Figs. 14 and 15):

```
Converting audio transcripts into text ...
good morning
start cooking
Heaven glass of water
hello please have one cup of pulses
```

Fig. 14. Audio to text conversion of input data

Table 2. Different parameters used in audio signal representation

Property	Value
Channels	2
Rate of sampling	44100 Hz
Recording time of the audio waveform	5 s
Hop length	512
n_mel	10
n_fft	2048
n_mfcc	13

['hello', 'please', 'have', 'one', 'cup', 'of', 'pulses']

Fig. 15. Token generated from tokenization process

6 Conclusion

This paper has a novel framework for accepting the audio signal from the user using the microphone. The features of the audio signals are extracted for analysis with the help of a low-level spectrogram using python audio libraries and visualization tools. The same audio signals having sentences related to input to be provided to the cooking device are processed in PRAAT software and different features of the sound signals with environmental noise are analyzed. The audio signal is processed by a speech recognition library to convert the audio signal into text. The converted text is processed by the standard python library NLTK to generate the instruction for the larger system. In this paper, we have analyzed the audio signals to classify the inputs provided by the used and converted the audio signal into text, and tokenized the text. In future, the further analysis on audio input will be done to clean the sound signal and classify the sound signal to identify authenticated users to provide security to the authorized user and the more valid input signal to the text processing tool. In the future, the tokenized text will be used to generate instruction for the large system.

References

1. Wyse, L.: Audio spectrogram representations for processing with convolutional neural networks. arXiv preprint arXiv:1706.09559 (2017)
2. Papadimitriou, I., et al.: Audio-based event detection at different SNR settings using two-dimensional spectrogram magnitude representations. Electronics 9(10), 1593 (2020)
3. Dennis, J., Tran, H., Li, H.: Spectrogram image feature for sound event classification in mismatched conditions. IEEE Signal Process. Lett. 18(2), 130–133 (2011)

4. Shen, J., et al.: Natural TTS synthesis by conditioning wavenet on mel spectrogram predictions. In: 2018 IEEE International Conference on Acoustics, Speech and Signal Processing (ICASSP). IEEE (2018)
5. Hwang, Y., et al.: Mel-spectrogram augmentation for sequence-to-sequence voice conversion. arXiv preprint arXiv:2001.01401 (2020)
6. Juvela, L., et al.: GELP: GAN-Excited linear prediction for speech synthesis from mel-spectrogram. arXiv preprint arXiv:1904.03976 (2019)
7. Meghanani, A., Anoop, C.S., Ramakrishnan, A.G.: An exploration of log-mel spectrogram and MFCC features for Alzheimer's dementia recognition from spontaneous speech. In: 2021 IEEE Spoken Language Technology Workshop (SLT). IEEE (2021)
8. Khunarsal, P., Lursinsap, C., Raicharoen, T.: Very short time environmental sound classification based on spectrogram pattern matching. Inf. Sci. **243**, 57–74 (2013)
9. Jha, N.K.: An approach towards text to emoticon conversion and vice-versa using NLTK and WordNet. In: 2018 2nd International Conference on Data Science and Business Analytics (ICDSBA). IEEE (2018)
10. Kinnunen, T., Lee, K.A., Li, H.: Dimension reduction of the modulation spectrogram for speaker verification. In: Odyssey (2008)
11. Ngo, D., et al.: Sound context classification basing on join learning model and multi-spectrogram features. arXiv preprint arXiv:2005.12779 (2020)
12. Zheng, W., et al.: CNNs-based acoustic scene classification using multi-spectrogram fusion and label expansions. arXiv preprint arXiv:1809.01543 (2018)
13. Contreras, J.O., Hilles, S., Abubakar, Z.B.: Automated essay scoring with ontology based on text mining and nltk tools. In: 2018 International Conference on Smart Computing and Electronic Enterprise (ICSCEE). IEEE (2018)
14. Kaneko, T., et al.: CycleGAN-VC3: examining and improving CycleGAN-VCs for mel-spectrogram conversion. arXiv preprint arXiv:2010.11672 (2020)

A Contrastive View of Vowel Phoneme Assessment of Hindi, Indian English and American English Speakers

Pooja Gambhir[✉], Amita Dev, and S. S. Agrawal

Indira Gandhi Delhi Technical University for Women, Delhi, India
{pooja001phd19,vc}@igdtuw.ac.in

Abstract. Acoustic, Phonetic and accented variations play an important role in pronunciation assessment of different languages uttered by speakers. In this paper, we consider the pronunciation assessment of vowels of North Indian Hindi, Indian English and American English uttered by varying subjects. Indian English is a language spoken in the India as a second language. It is highly influenced by variety of Native Indian languages as well as usage, cultural, regional, social and educational background. It is observed that Indian speakers tends to speak English phonemes close to the articulation of their native language rather than that of the American English. This paper contributes towards the contrastive study of vowel triangles and the appearance of the closeness of vowel cardinal space (ɑ, i, u) of Hindi, Indian English and American English using distance formula.

Keywords: Vowels · Pronunciation · Hindi · Indian English · American English · Articulation

1 Introduction

India is linguistically rich and a diverse country belonging to several language families in which the most spoken language is Indo-Aryan languages and Dravidian languages. Hindi is an Indo-Aryan language in India and is one of the official standardized languages spoken by around 44% of total population of India as a first language mainly in Northern region where Uttar Pradesh have the highest proportion of Hindi speakers (91.3%) [1]. English is one of the two official languages of the Government of India, along with the Hindi language which is spoken by around 11.6% of Indian population (0.02% of Indians as their first language, 6.8% of Indians as second language and 3.8% of Indians as their third language) [2]. But, if we compare the percent of Indian speakers speaking Hindi and English, Hindi is still the most spoken language in India.

However, due to the cultural and jobs exposure there has been increase in percent of Indian people learning English as their second language which resembles more to the British English than American English although people who migrate to USA from India have rare difficulty in communicating with Americans. American English accent is rarely found with English speakers in India unless they have very frequent, fluent American accent or learnt it exceptionally (Table 1).

© Springer Nature Switzerland AG 2022
A. Dev et al. (Eds.): AIST 2021, CCIS 1546, pp. 182–194, 2022.
https://doi.org/10.1007/978-3-030-95711-7_16

Table 1. Distribution of population by speakers of Indian English [2]

Regions of India	Percentage of Indian English (as second language) spoken in different regions of India
Gujarat, J&K, MP, Jharkhand, Chhattisgarh, Bihar	0–2.4%
Rajasthan, UP, Orissa, Andhra Pradesh	2.4%–4.3%
Himachal Pradesh, West Bengal, Maharashtra, Telangana, Karnataka, Kerela, Tamil Nadu	4.3%–10.8%
Punjab, Haryana, Assam, Arunachal Pradesh, Sikkim	10.8%–21%
Delhi, Uttarakhand, Meghalaya, Goa	21%–44%

English is commonly used both for official and social communication from different regions of the country and is now mostly spoken by Indians of Northern and North-Eastern states than Southern Indian states. Notably, in Fig. 1 we observe that Assam, Uttarakhand including Delhi and Mumbai have relatively high proportion of English speakers. Generally, the pronunciation disparity between L1 (First language) and L2 (Second language) arises due to mismatch in their phonological peculiarities and from the unusual spelling-to-sound rules that contrast with the phonemic orthographic difference in Languages. Different L1 (Native language) interferences lead to distinct colorations between the variety of languages spoken. As the phonologies of English differs from that of Indian languages, it gives rise to specific regional varieties of spoken English. English as a second language pertains a quality of pronunciation inferences with the native language speakers of India in the style of speaking, their accents, different cultures and learning exposures which gives rise to an extensive study of measuring the similarity and differences in acoustic and segmental or suprasegmental variations between the L1(Native Indian)-L2(English) language. Since a large number of Hindi speakers learn English language for media communication, educational and technology purposes, the pronunciation of English by them remains largely influenced by the phonologies of their respective Hindi speaking style, Intonation, suprasegmental study, Consonants, Rhythms, Vocabulary and grammar and conventional English spelling. Researchers are majorly exploring the phonological and phonetic comparison of English with Indian language like IE phonology with native Indian languages, Gujarati & English L1 influence on English learning, English and Punjabi, linguistics of Hindi and Indian English speech sounds ([3–8]).

Given the findings of the previous research, the most prominent features of the Indian English vowel system for North Indian speakers are listed below: -

I.   Diphthongs /eɪ/, / əʊ/, /ʊə/ are realized as long monophthongs for the *PEAR* vowel /e_/ as /e:/, *GOAT* vowel /o_/ as /o:/ & /ɔ:/, *TOUR* vowel /u_/ as /u:/ respectively ([9][10])

II.   Lack of contrast between *BAIT* and *TRAP* vowels [11].

III.   The absence of quality contrast between *GOOSE* and *FOOT* vowels [9].

IV.   Similarity in pronunciation of silent vowel sounds such as in *BRIDGE* vowel → /brɪdʒ/.

V.   The lack of back mid *CAUGHT, LOT* vowel /ɔ/, /o/ respectively realized as /ɑ:/ [12].

VI.   North Indian speakers speaks English with addition of an extra 'a' and ending words with a rhyme such as: *singing* → *singinga, going* → *go-ingga.*

VII.   In words *Pale & Hole,* the diphthongs [eɪ] and [oʊ] respectively can be characterized and replaced by monophthong [e:] and [o:] [13]

VIII.   Many diphthongs are changed to long vowels such as *poor* → *pu:r, tour* → *tu:r etc.*[13]

IX.   Many North Indian speakers pronounce word hour →ha: (r), flower → fla: (r) instead of [aʊə(r)] and [flaʊə(r)] respectively [13]

Also, due to the persisting linguistic diversity on the subcontinent it is also possible that there may be more than one variety of Indian English which enhance the need to perform contrastive study among its spoken variety and different language dialects creating macaronic hybrid use of two languages, for example: Tanglish (Tamil + English), Gujalish (Gujarati + English), Hinglish (Hindi + English), Benglish (Bangla + English), Menglish (Marathi + English) etc. Further, such study helps researchers to analyse and design Speech acoustic models, phoneme recognition and synthesis systems for various multi-lingual speech variations such as categorization of phonemes for any language, phonetic segmentation using different models having prior study of phonology, Vowel recognition systems and many more [14-20]. This remains active research in the area of Speech acoustic and phonetic study.

2 Phonemic View of the Vowels of Hindi, Indian English and American English

In India, majority of English language learners exists outside their home territory and therefore language contact plays a vital role in development of phonological features of Indian English for example: Hindustani. India is a multilinguistic country with large number of native tongues spoken and thus a huge number of features may be shared by the speakers from a particular region as a result of the influence from their native tongue as first language. Therefore, it is important to take into consideration development effects of acoustic and phonetic features in the acquisition of second language. The elements making up the and distinguishing phones are the phonetic sound features characterized by relatively free air flow through the vocal tract, sonorants including vowels, semi-vowels, liquids and nasals which further results in the study of systematic features of sounds in the language.

Vowels are voiced phonemes that are produced without any appreciable constriction or blockage of air flow in the vocal tract. The vowels can be classified depending upon Lip rounding, Tongue position & Tongue Height. A distinctive characteristics of vowel trajectories for any language can be efficiently analyzed using Formant mean analysis considering the formant frequencies F1, F2... F_r ($r = 1, 2, 3...$). Vowels for any sound can be classified by three articulatory features: Shape (Rounded and Unrounded lips), length (Tense/lax) and position (front/central/back, high/mid/low). The open and close articulation for characterizing vowels is associated with low and high value of F1 formants respectively and the front and back articulation are associated with the low and high values of F2 respectively. The distinction be-tween rounded and unrounded vowels is represented by F3. The vertical position of tongue represents height of vowel whereas the horizontal position represents the back and front of the articulated vowel. From the formant mean analysis, F1 formant represents tongue height and F2 formant represents tongue position which helps analyze the vowel production of speech by the Speaker.

2.1 Related Review

In the recent past, research work has been carried towards phonetic peculiarities of Indian English with different structure of articulation by people but the study of Indian version of English is still needs progression. In general, the system of vowel sounds of Indian English is less different from standard English pronunciation with Indian native language accents such as Hindi [13]. For example, front vowel [a] is used instead of [ʌ] in many dialects. Disha and G. Bharadwaja investigated on formant mean analysis and formant space analysis of Indian English using PRAAT and observed significant variations in the accent from the first four formants individually for North Indian, South Indian, East Indian and West Indian English accent. The paper also plotted triangle for understanding the occurrence of vowel extremes in the accent [20]. R. Gargesh in his paper noticed that Indian English speakers' articulate words closer for the written spellings of words and not far distinctive from the articulation attained in American English [21]. For instance, English word FOOT is articulated with vowel /ʊ/ closer than vowel /u/ when spoken with Indian accent. Similarly for word CLOTH or THOUGHT vowel / ɔː/ > /o/ > /aː/, FLEECE vowel /iː/ > / ɪ/ etc.

2.2 Overview of Vowels of Hindi, Indian English and American English

Hindi: Hindustani language natively possesses a symmetrical ten-vowel system plus an English loanword /æː/ shown in Table 2. The vowels ɪ, ə, ʊ are short vowels, while ɛː, ɔː, iː, aː, uː, eː, oː are long vowels. Short vowels are represented as lax and tenseless whereas long vowels are represented as tense vowels.

Indian English: It is a syllabic-timed language due to the influence of L1 language and this circumstantiates IE to be a complex linguistic variety for analysis. D. K. Phull and G. Bharadwaja focused on vowel analysis of Indian English for four different regional accents of Indian English namely South, West, North, Eastern part of India [22]. Due to the diversity of accent variations and different dialects of speaking a language in India,

Table 2. Vowels of Hindi language

Long Vowels	Example words	Short Vowels	Example words
e:	रेलगाडी	ɪ	दिन
o:	मोदी	ə	अबतक
i:	भारतीय	ʊ	अनुसार
ɛ:	कैसे		
ɔ:	गौरतब		
a:	बारबार		
u:	रूप		

researchers have been working towards impact of L1 influence and accent variations on English. Indian English consists of a few vowels sounds as compared to its count in consonants. As of now, it has total seven long vowels and seven short vowels defined in Table 3.

Table 3. Vowels of Indian English

Long Vowels	Example words	Short Vowels	Example words
ɜ:	Firstly	ɪ	City
o:	Hope	ə	Perhaps
i:	Recently	ɒ	Officer
ɒ:	Always	ʊ	Could
a:	Asked	æ	Matter
e:	Always	ʌ	London
u:	Food	e	Friends

Especially as spoken by speaker with Hindi as a native language, the vowel phonemic system has similarities and dissimilarities and with that of English (often termed as Hindustani English) some of which is discussed in the below section. In Hinglish (Hindi + English), Hindi sounds, rhythms, pitch and intonation strongly interfere into English language.

Some of the distinguished features of Indian English and Hindi Vowels.

1) For most of the Indian English speakers, deletion of sound /r/ does not occur in any word position of speech as compared to that in American English where /r/ occurs before a vowel like /ɑːɹ/

SHARPEN → ʃɑːpən instead of ʃ ɑːɹ pən

2) Linguistic inference from Hindi in Indian English for words such as Pearl, Shirt, London shows replacement of vowel e with ɜ:/ ə:. Few examples are [23]

> e.g., CONSERVE → /kən'sɜ:rv/ or /kən'sə:rv/
> SHIRT → /ʃɜ:rt/ or /ʃə:rt/
> GIRL → /gɜ:rl/ or /gə:rl/

3) Epenthetic vowels / I, ə / often proceed the clusters /sp, st, sk / [6].

> e.g. SCHOOL → /Isku:l/ in Hindi & /sku:l/ in standard English
> SPOON → /Ispu:n/ in Hindi & /spu:n/ in Standard English
> STOOL → /Istu:l/ in /hindi & /stu:l/ in Standard English

4) The presence of full unreduced vowels in weak syllables instead of the schwa [12, 24].

American English: For most of the American English speakers, there are 15 vowel sounds (including 3 diphthongs: / aɪ, aʊ, ɔɪ/). The phonemic symbols for the vowels are shown in Table 4.

Table 4. Vowels of American English

Long Vowels	Ex. words	Short Vowels	Ex. words
aɪ /ī/	Tie	ɪ /ĭ/	Pit
oʊ /ō/	Blow	ɛ /ĕ/	Bed
i: /ē/	Bead	ɑ: /ŏ/	Bomb
ju /ū/	Few	æ /ă/	Glad
eɪ /ā/	Eight	ʌ /ŭ/	Bud
u: /oo/	Boot		
ʊ /oo/	Foot		
ɔ /aw/	Port		
aʊ /ow/	Plow		
ɔɪ /oi/	Boy		

Indian English and American English have spectrally phonetical distinct features. Many young Indians who read and listen to American English do not have trap-bath split of Received Pronunciation (RP-British English) affecting words such as last → /lɑːst/, class→/klɑːs/ and shows similarity towards Australian English. However completely split with standard Indian regional English. Some differences can be seen between two adjacent vowels which get replaced by single long monophthong followed by sound /r/. e.g. BEER → /Bir/, PEAR → /Per/ and some differences can be observed between the pair of /ɛ ~ æ/, /i: ~ ɪ/ and /u: ~ ʊ/.

Furthermore, among the distinctive features of vowel-sounds employed and observed between Hindi, Indian English and American English are:

1. Hindi and English /i/ are high, frontal, long and unrounded for '/kimat/' (COST) & 'BEAT'.
2. Hindi and English /i/ are high, frontal, long and unrounded for '/kimat/' (COST) & 'BEAT'.
3. Hindi and English /ə/ are high, front, tense, long and unrounded for कौन/kƏ/ (WHO) and CAUGHT.
4. Vowel /ɪ/ is high, front lax, short and unrounded for Hindi 'kitab' and English 'Sit'
5. Vowel /o/ is mid back, lax, short and rounded for Hindi '/kona/' (CORNER) and English 'COAT'
6. Vowel /ʌ/ is mid, back, lax and short for Hindi /kʌm/ (LESS) and English 'BUT'.
7. Vowel /u/ is high back, tense, rounded and long for Hindi /un/ (WOOL) & English 'BOOT'.
8. For most Indian English speakers, the 'PAUL' vowel /ɔ:/ is phonetically closer to /ʊ/, likewise 'PAID' vowel /e:/ is closer to /e:/ of रेल (RAIL) in Hindi.
9. The vowels produced in 'HAND' & 'LATE' have high level overlap with vowel of 'KIT' similar to vowels of Hindi.
10. The three vowels /ʊ/, /u/ and /o/ also shows closeness in the formant space. However, have contrastive space with vowels of American English
11. 'EAGLE' vowels /i/ and 'CITY' vowel /ɪ/ suggests close contrast. Likewise, 'FOOT', 'COULD' /ʊ/ and 'GOOSE', FOOD vowel /u/ and BATH /ɑ/ and STRUT /ʌ/ [25]
12. In Indian English, /e/ is replaced by either /æ/ or /ei/, /ɛ/ is replaced by /iə/ and /əu/ is replaced by /ɔ/.
13. For vowels, /ʌ/, /ə/ and /ɜ:/, IE has /ə/. Indians would pronounce bird as /bərd/ and cup as /kəp/.
14. /a/ as /e:/ (always) and never or rarely as /ə/ for instance the word ago as /e:gɒ/.
15. For female speakers, /ɜ:/ of AE 'GLAD', /ɛ:/of Hindi 'कैसे' and /æ/ of IE 'MATTER' are closely sinched

This paper presents a preliminary result of a phonetic analysis of vowel production of English spoken by Indian speakers as a second language, Hindi being their native language, through vowel triangle measurements and analysis based on formants space between ɑ, i, u, vowels of Hindi, Indian English and American English and concluded the paper with the following objectives.

1. To analyse the closeness of the articulated long vowel of Hindi, Indian English and American English through distance measurement.
2. To prove that Indian speakers tend to speak English phonemes close to the articulation of their Hindi native language rather than articulating it with American English.

3 Experiment Analysis

The present study investigated the similarities and differences in vowel sounds phonemic analysis using PRAAT tool with Hindi (native language), Indian English and American English language dataset. Formant analyses have been carried out in two stages: (i) Formant space analysis and (ii) Formant space distance measurement. Results from both the analysis is depicted below.

3.1 Dataset

For the present work, ten females and ten male's North Indian subjects from Delhi, India were selected for recording and collecting data of vowel sound utterances considering Hindi as their native language and English learnt during the school as second language. The data was recorded using PRAAT tool having mono channel and sampling rate of 16000 Hz. For American English, we considered the already available TIMIT database for ten female and ten male subjects with sample rate of 16000 Hz and 1-channel pcm.

3.2 Experiment Design and Result

The experiment design considered assessing the phonetic and pronunciation features of vowel sounds of Hindi, Indian English and American English Speakers' using PRAAT tool. In this work, formant values of the vowel sounds (F1 & F2 space) are extracted from the **spectrum** which are used as features for the vowel analysis. In the spectrum the vowels correspond to the lower frequency band indicated as dark bands through the **formants** which refers to the concentration of acoustic energy/peak around a particular frequency in the speech wave signal and corresponds to a resonance in the vocal tract. In case of speech the most information related to vowels is extracted and determined in the first four formants- F1, F2, F3, F4. The darker the band of formant on the spectrogram the stronger is the sound and prediction of the vowel sound spoken in that particular word selected. Using PRAAT, we have performed Vowel Triangle Analysis (VTA) to determine the utterances and pronunciation style of vowel sounds on the spectrogram of their speech waves. F1 and F2 formant values were extracted automatically at the midpoint of every vowel using formant tracking, inspected and a proper match corresponding to the vowel utterance was captured for all the respective subjects (10 Male & 10 Female speakers). We disseminated and predicted the formant space values between the vowel sounds / ɑ, i, u/ of Hindi, Indian English and American English to analyse and observe how close or far the vowel phonemes sounds are. Figure 1 & Fig. 2 represents the vowel triangle plot for these three language accents. The vowel triangle represents here the extremes of the formant space on the F1-F2 plane. The triangle considered 10 vowels responsible for the accent variation such as /i/, /ʌ/, /ɑ/, /el ɛ/, /u/, /ɪ/, /ʊ /, /o/, /ɔ/, /æ/. In this /ɑ/ represents high F1 nd low F2, /u/ represents both low F1 and F2 and /i/ represents low F1 and high F2. These vowel variations also emphasized on the difference on vowel positions from one another in different accents.

We significantly observed that Indian English and American English vowel sounds / ɑ, i, u/ pertains large formant space/gap as compared to that of Indian English and Hindi vowel sounds, both for male and female speakers which strongly indicates that the speaking phenomenon and vowel articulation of Hindi native speakers is closely related to that of Indian English language in accordance with the phonetic and phonemic style of vowel utterances unlike vowel sounds between Indian English an American English speaking which show distinguished formant space and articulation differences among the vowel utterances.

These accents of Hindi, Indian English and American English show variations in comparison with one another. Vowel /ɑ/ is raising and towards back in Indian English for both female and male subjects. Other vowels in Indian English are central and more towards front. The vowel /ʌ/ of Indian English, Hindi and American English accent have almost similar and close formant spaces.

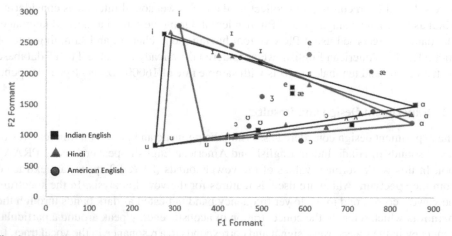

Fig. 1. VTA for Hindi, Indian English & American English Female speakers using formant's analysis

Second, the formant space between the vowel sounds "/ɑ, i, u/" was quantified to show the difference between two putative vowel categories using Euclidean distance measurement between i, ɑ, & u vowel sounds each of Hindi, Indian English and American English language for female and male speakers respectively. Euclidean distance is calculated on the basis of the formant values shown in Vowel triangle plot of vowel sounds "/ɑ, i, u/" Fig. 3 and Fig. 4 using following distance formula, along the formant dimensions of the vowel of each language to understand the closeness between the corresponding vowel occurrences depicted in Table 5(a) & 5(b) for female and male speakers respectively [25].

$$\text{Formant EuD} = \sqrt{\left[(y22 - y11)^2 + (x22 - x11)^2\right]} \qquad (1)$$

From the distance measurement, we observed that 'the vowel sounds (i, ɑ, u) of Indian English and American English Speakers voice have large vowel sounds formant space distance as compared to that of Indian English and Hindi language considering both female and male speakers. Exceptionally, we also observed that the above statements do not fall true for vowel "ɑ ~ ɑ" formant space between Indian English and American

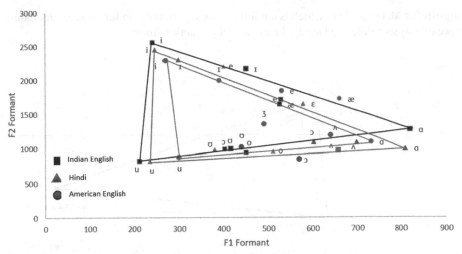

Fig. 2. VTA for Hindi, Indian English & American English Male speakers using formant's analysis

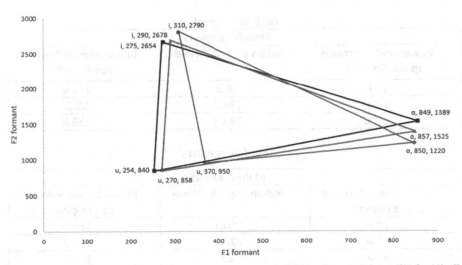

Fig. 3. Distance measurement of the Formant spaces between vowels sounds i, u and ɑ for Hindi, Indian English and American English male speakers

English for Male speakers which is a point of investigation in the future study including more examples related to Gender based vowel phonetics study.

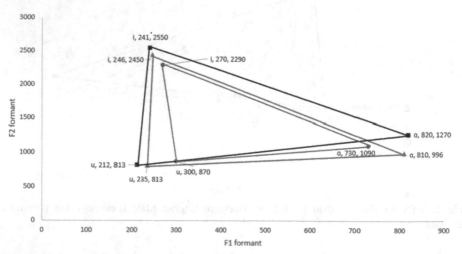

Fig. 4. Distance measurement of the Formant spaces between vowels sounds i, u and ɑ for Hindi, Indian English and American English male speakers

Table 5. Vowel sound formant space distance measurement of Hindi, Indian English and American English language for:

(a) Female speakers.

Female speakers		
Vowel sound formant space distance	Indian English ~ Hindi	Indian English ~ American English
i ~ i	28.3	140.4
ɑ ~ ɑ	136.2	305.08
u ~ u	24.08	159.8

(b) Male speakers

Male speakers		
Vowel sound formant space distance	Indian English - Hindi	Indian English – American English
i ~ i	100.1	261.6
ɑ ~ ɑ	274.1	201.2
u~ u	23	104.8

4 Conclusion

In this paper, the phonemic assessment of the articulated vowels of Hindi, Indian English and American English has been investigated using vowel triangle analysis, formant space analysis and Euclidean distance measurement between the formant space of the vowel categories to learn about the closeness between the vowel categories of each language. The outcome represents that the formant space for vowel ɑ, i:, u: of Indian English and American English vary significantly as compared to the formant frequencies of Indian English and Hindi language for both males and female Indian speakers. The objectives of the paper were achieved by the experiment conducted using PRAAT which also proved that Indian speakers speaks English phonemes close to the articulation of their native language consider Hindi in this experiment and carries distinguished formant space with American English. Further we will investigate more on the accent, consonants and intonations variations of Indian English with native Indian languages for males and female speakers.

Acknowledgement. We would like to thank Indira Gandhi Delhi Technical University (IGDTUW) for providing an opportunity to undertake and carry forward research program in the field of speech processing under the established Centre of Excellence in Artificial Intelligence (COE-AI) in IGDTUW.

References

1. Varghese, M.: A2A; 2016, India. https://www.quora.com/Which-Indian-state-speak-Hindimore-than-their-own-language. Accessed 25 July 2021
2. Rukmini, S.: In India who speaks English and Where? 2019, India. https://www.livemint.com/news/india/in-india-whospeaks-in-english-and-where1557814101428.html. Accessed 25 July 2021
3. Sirsa, H., Redford, M.A.: The effects of native language on Indian English sounds and timing patterns. J. Phon. **41**(6), 393–406 (2013)
4. Wiltshire, C.R., Harnsberger, J.D.: The influence of Gujarati and Tamil L1s on Indian English: a preliminary study. World Engl. **25**(1), 91–104 (2006)
5. Ona Masoko, S.T.: A synchronic analysis of Indian English (2017)
6. Chohan, M.N., García, M.I.M.: Phonemic Comparison of English and Punjabi. Int. J. Engl. Linguist. **9**(4), 347–357 (2019)
7. Mishra, S., Mishra, A.: Linguistic Interference from Hindi in Indian English. Int. J. Stud. Engl. Lang. Lit. **4**(1), 29–38 (2016)
8. Barman, B.: A contrastive analysis of English and Bangla phonemics. Dhaka Univ. J. Linguist. **2**(4), 19–42 (2009)
9. Wiltshire, C.R.: The "Indian English" of Tibeto-Burman language speakers. Engl. World-Wide **26**(3), 275–300 (2005)
10. Nihalani, P., Tongue, R.K., Hosali, P., Crowther, J.: *Indian and British English: A Handbook of Usage* and Pronunciation. Oxford University Press, Delhi (1979)
11. Sethi, J.: The vowel system in educated Panjabi-speakers' English. J. Int. Phon. Assoc. **10**(1–2), 64–73 (1980)
12. Bansal, R.K.: A phonetic analysis of English spoken by a group of well-educated speakers from Uttar-Pradesh. CIEFL Bull. (Hyderabad) **8**, 1–11 (1970)

13. Grolman, M.B., Biktagirova, Z.A., Kasimov, O.H.: Phonetic peculiarities of the English language in India. Int. J. Soc. Cult. Lang. **9**(1), 102–110 (2021)
14. Dev Amita Agrawal, S.S., Choudhary, D.R.: Hindi phoneme recognition using VQ, LVQ and TDNN techniques. In: Sixth International Workshop on Recent Trends in Speech Music and Allied Signal Processing. (IWSMSP-2001) 19–21 Dec 2001, National Physical Laboratory (NPL), Delhi (2021)
15. Dev, A., Agrawal, S.S., Choudhury, D.R.: Categorization of Hindi phonemes by neural networks. AI Soc. **17**(3), 375–382 (2003)
16. Balyan, A., Agrawal, S.S., Dev, A.: Automatic phonetic segmentation of Hindi speech using hidden Markov model. AI Soc. **27**(4), 543–549 (2012)
17. Archana Balyan, S.S., Agrawal, A.D.: A Hindi speech synthesizer using phoneme concatenation approach. Int. J. Graph. IMA Process. IFRSA J. **2**(1), 12–17 (2012)
18. Dev, A., Agrawal, S.S., Choudhary, D.R.: Comparison on the performance of Hindi phoneme recognition system using VQ, LVQ and TDNN techniques. J. Acousti. Soc. India Vellore. **29**, 344–352 (2001)
19. Bhatt, S., Dev, A., Jain, A.: Hindi speech vowel recognition using hidden Markov model. In: SLTU, pp. 201–204 (2018)
20. Dev, A., Amita Agrawal, S.S., Choudhary, D.R.: A limited vocabulary text dictation systems for Hindi speech. In: IEEE EIT 2001, 7–9 June 2001, Oakland University, Rochester, Michigan (2001)
21. Phull, D.K., Kumar, G.B.: Vowel analysis for Indian English. Procedia Comput. Sci. **93**(September), 533–538 (2016)
22. Gargesh, R.: Indian English : Phonology, no. January 2008 (2016)
23. Phull, D.K., Kumar, G.B.: Vowel analysis for Indian English. Procedia Comput. Sci. **93**, 533–538 (2016)
24. Masica, C.: The intelligibility of Indian English: measurements of the intelligibility of connected speech, and sentences and word material presented to listeners of different nationalities. Language **46**(3), 730–735 (1970). https://doi.org/10.2307/412321
25. Kalashnik, O., Fletcher, J.: An acoustic study of vowel contrasts in north Indian English. In: Proceedings of the 16th International Congress of Phonetic Sciences, pp. 953–956 (Aug 2007)
26. Nycz, J., Hall-Lew, L.: Best practices in measuring vowel merger. In: Proceedings of Meetings on Acoustics 166ASA, vol. 20, no. 1, p. 060008. Acoustical Society of America (Dec 2013)

Text-Based Analysis of COVID-19 Comments Using Natural Language Processing

Kanchan Naithani(✉), Y. P. Raiwani, and Rajeshwari Sissodia

Department of Computer Science and Engineering, HNB Garhwal University, Garhwal, Srinagar, Uttarakhand, India

Abstract. In dialectology, Natural Language Processing is the process of recognizing the various ontologies of words generated in human language. Various techniques are used for analyzing the corpus from naturally generated content by users on various platforms. The analysis of these textual contents collected during the COVID-19 has become a goldmine for marketing experts as well as for researchers, thus making social media comments available on various platforms like Facebook, Twitter, YouTube, etc., a popular area of applied artificial intelligence. Text-Based Analysis is measured as one of the exasperating responsibilities in Natural Language Processing (NLP). The chief objective of this paper is to work on a corpus that generates relevant information from web-based statements during COVID-19. The findings of the work may give useful insights to researchers working on Text analytics, and authorities concerning to current pandemic. To achieve this, NLP is discussed which extracts relevant information and comparatively computes the morphology on publicly available data thus concluding knowledge behind the corpus.

Keywords: NLP: Natural Language Processing · NLU: Natural Language Understanding · TBA: Text-Based Analysis · Knowledge Representation · WSD: Word Sense Disambiguation

1 Introduction

In the text-based analysis, corpus data characterize the "lexical", "syntactical", "semantic", and "positional" relationship with each other. The corpus vector is a relevant term related to Feature extraction emphasizing Ontologies that provide vital information regarding relations between the words [1].

The work done will provide an innovational pathway for the considerate indulgence of "Knowledge Extraction" from the corpus' perception. The conclusions will help in gaining insights into the most important topics discussed during the health and economic crisis based on the most frequent words used on Social Media Platforms. The hot topics deduced after the analysis of comments will help to know how well the people are handling their situations amidst the pandemic.

© Springer Nature Switzerland AG 2022
A. Dev et al. (Eds.): AIST 2021, CCIS 1546, pp. 195–209, 2022.
https://doi.org/10.1007/978-3-030-95711-7_17

2   Related Work

2.1   Recent Research Conducted on COVID19

In literature, quite a few procedures are presented to analyze ontologies that comprehend lexical relationships with the corpus and define how feature vectors are related with the individual words using words association [2–4]. Over the years, Natural Language Processing research has been done with English language orientation. The reason being, according to a survey, the total number of active users on various platforms use English, for expressing views on a global platform [8, 20].

Novel COVID -19 has created a mesh of digital data, where researchers and many help care centers are trying to understand the hot topics discussed by the public via various social media platforms. The most recent researches conducted by researchers for analyzing the web-based content after COVID-19's outburst are mentioned in Table 1. It was observed that while working with NLP, much of the statements present online show personal opinions in the majority and the research activities are performed on subjective datasets [19].

Table 1. Work done on Covid19 using NLP

Ref. no.	Researchers	Year	Work done & tools	Parameters	Outcome	Limitation
[8]	Güngör & Üsküdarli,	2019	"The effect of morphology in named entity recognition with sequence tagging"	Sequence tagging, Character-based embeddings, F1-measure	Augmenting word representations with morphological embeddings improves NER performance, which is further improved when combined with "character-based word representations"	Parameters chosen could have shown more clarity in context with the multiple languages used as the data set
[1]	Pittaras, Giannakopoulos, Papadakis and Karkaletsis	April. 2020	"Text classification with semantically enriched word Embeddings"	Semantic Frequency Vector, Accuracy, macro F1- score, TF-IDF normalized weights	The use of semantic information from resources such as "WordNet" significantly progresses the performance for classification	TF-IDF behavior observed in frequency based semantic vectors was not decent

(continued)

Table 1. (*continued*)

Ref. no.	Researchers	Year	Work done & tools	Parameters	Outcome	Limitation
[3]	Kusum Lata, Pardeep Singh, Kamlesh Dutta	Oct., 2020	"A comprehensive review on feature set used for anaphora resolution"	Anaphora Resolution Antecedent	The review presented an understanding of solving AR problems from the perspective of feature selection	Deeper level research work on positional relations of the features was absent
[4]	Klaifer Garcia & L. Berton	Dec., 2020	"Topic Detection and sentiment analysis in Twitter"	Precision and F1 Score	Mostly negative Polarity was observed in the LR and RF and Linear SVM	A more detailed analysis of the feelings was possible
[15]	Matteo Cinelli, Walter Quattrociocchi et al	Oct., 2020	"The COVID-19 social media infodemic"	stochastic gradient descent, word prediction vector, vocabulary size,	Intercept, coefficient, R^2 for various primary datasets were deduced for different datasets	Lexical and Semantic analysis could have been improved w.r.t. the information extracted

Limaye et al. studied some concerns regarding the misrepresentation of situations, information and even statistics on social media especially during a pandemic like COVID-19 and displayed them in a commentary article [12]. The largest social media in China, WeChat, was analyzed by Lu and Zhang to identify the trends referencing COVID-19 [13].

Research in the field of observing COVID -19 situation and its effect on people has created many influential topics, as shown in Fig. 1 that gained mass attention. An online survey conducted on online available social platforms like Facebook, YouTube, Twitter, Instagram, blogging sites and many official web discussing forums has shown that people concerned with the current epidemic have analyzed people's opinions in reference to these topics around the world including India to understand the lenient or harsh situations for them [13–15].

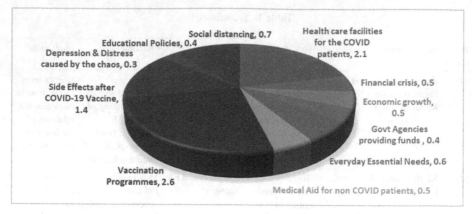

Fig. 1. Influential topics w.r.t. COVID-19 that gained mass attention [3, 4, 9–11, 14, 15]

3   Text-Based Analysis

NLP and Text Analysis techniques are generally practiced to recognize and extract information that is subjective in nature from a piece of text or corpus and this practice is known as Text-Based Analysis (TBA). It refers to the use of "computational linguistics" and "ontology-based analysis" to analytically categorize, extract, quantify, and study varying circumstances along with subjective information [5]. It is an evolving subject, which challenges the analysis and measurement of human language and transforms them into hard facts for enlightening the real, factual or cynical meaning behind the words [15, 21]. The pipeline for TBA can be achieved using Seven Basic steps as shown in Fig. 2:

a) **Identification of Language:** Different idiosyncrasies are present in multiple languages, that's why it is indeed a critical aspect to know what Language and what grammatical features we're dealing with. It involves predicting the natural language of the text by observing the features of the grammar that will be responsible for the other text analytics function. Approaches like Short Word Based Approach. Frequent Word-Based Approach and N-Gram Based Approach are used to Identify the Language of the corpus elements [6].

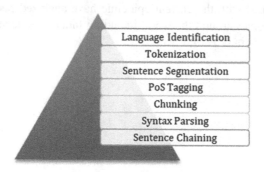

Fig. 2. Steps for TBA

b) **Tokenization:** After the language of the text is known, it can be broken up into Tokens, the basic entities of the connotation that are operated on, and this process of breaking down of the corpus into smaller unique entities is known as Tokenization. Tokens can be words, phonemes, punctuations, hyperlinks or any other smallest component of the grammar. For example, an English sentence made up of 5 words, may contain 5 tokens. Tokenization depends on the characteristics of a language, and each language has varied requirements for tokenization. For instance, in English, practices "white space" and "punctuation" are used for breaks, and could be tokenized without putting much effort. Most languages based on alphabets follow comparatively simple approaches to break the corpus. So, rules-based tokenization is prominently used for alphabetic Languages [6, 7].

c) **Sentence Segmentation:** Also known as Sentence Tokenization is the process of separating a sequence of written language into its component sentences. Once the tokens are identified, places where sentences end can be easily pointed. In order to run more complex text-based analytical functions such as syntax parsing, limits, where grammar ends in a sentence, must be known. In simpler terms, it breaks the paragraph into separate sentences [1, 19].

Example: Contemplate the COVID 19 comment Sample –

If you do not recommend it for 18 and under, how is it remotely safe for above 18-year-olds? Our makeup is not that different??? Thank god you came out and said not safe for 18 and under at least.

Sentence Segment produces the following result:

a) *"If you do not recommend it for 18 and under, how is it remotely safe for above 18-year-olds?"*
b) *"Our makeup is not that different???"*
c) *"Thank god you came out and said not safe for 18 and under at least."*

d) **PoS Tagging:** is the process of tagging every token collected from the corpus with its respective 'Part Of Speech'. PoS tagging helps in finding out how a word is used in a sentence for instance as – **nouns, pronouns, adjectives, verbs, adverbs, prepositions, conjunctions** or **interjections.**" It provides the fundamental step right before chunking to set the path for Word Sense Disambiguation (WSD) by properly identifying the part of speech of each for every token generated from the text-based corpus [8].

Example:
"Staying healthy and "social distancing" are mutually exclusive."
Output: -
[('staying', 'VBG'), ('healthy', 'JJ'), ('and', 'CC'), ('social, 'JJ'), ('distancing', 'NN'), ('are', 'VBP'), ('mutually', 'RB'), ('exclusive', 'JJ')].

e) **Chunking:** calls the PoS-tagged tokens for phrases. Chunking can be defined as the process of mining phrases from unstructured text. It is not responsible for the internal structure of the constituents, nor their usage in the leading sentence. It rather works on top of POS tagging by identifying those constituents in the form of a group of words like Noun Phrase, Verb Phrase, Prepositional phrase, etc. [8, 15].

Example:

The covid patient is lying in the ICU.

Chunking Output:

[The covid patient]_np [is lying]_vp [in the ICU]_pp

(*np* stands for "noun phrase," *vp* stands for "verb phrase," and *pp* stands for "prepositional phrase.")

f) **Syntax Parsing:** determines the structure of a sentence. In simpler terms, *Syntax Parsing* could be called *Sentence Diagramming* that acts as a preliminary step in processing any natural language features. It is considered as one of the most computationally-intensive steps while performing analysis on text-based content to gain insight into grammar and syntax. The Syntax tree for the above given example can be seen in Fig. 3.

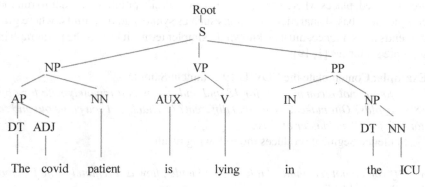

Fig. 3. Syntax parsing

g) **Sentence Chaining:** The concluding step in organizing the raw and amorphous text for further analysis at complex levels is called *sentence chaining*. It is the process to link individual but related sentences by the "strength of association" of the sentence w.r.t. the title of the content. The lexical chain helps in combining sentences, even if they are present apart from each other in a document. It detects the predominant topics for a machine and measures the overall context of the document. It also helps in observing where linkages are shown for ontological meaning to the comment thus providing morphological relations among words.

4   Natural Language Processing

Natural Language Processing (NLP) is categorized as a sub-domain of dialectology, computer science, knowledge engineering and artificial intelligence implicating fundamental relations between computers and humane dialects. Predominantly, it concentrated on organizing systems to process and analyze massive natural language data [18].

NLP makes use of Tokenization, Sentence breaking, Part of Speech tagging, Chunks of tokens and PoS tags. In machine learning (ML) jargon, these series of steps taken are called data pre-processing. The idea is to break down the natural language text into smaller and more manageable chunks. These can then be analyzed by ML algorithms to find relations, dependencies, and context among various chunks. NLP utilizes these fundamental functions in order to achieve its two components while taking ontologies and Knowledge Representation into consideration, i.e. Natural Language Understanding and Natural Language Generation.

4.1 Natural Language Understanding (NLU)

NLU aids the machine in understanding and analyzing the human language with the help of metadata extracted from content such as entities, keywords, relations, semantic and syntactic roles etc. [20]. It involves Mapping the given input into useful representation, Analyzing different aspects of the language, Interpreting Natural Language, Deriving Meaning, Identifying context and Deducing Insights. Word Sense Disambiguation (WSD), a function that is implemented via NLU makes sure that the machine is able to understand the two different senses of a word belonging to a glossary [21].

4.2 Natural Language Generation (NLG)

NLG helps in converting the machine formatted data into a representation that could be read by a human. It is achieved by three common steps i.e. planning of textual content, Planning of Sentence making, and finally Realization of the text that will be represented as a Natural Language [6].

It's important to note that in NLU, the process is to disambiguate the input sentence to produce a language that is known to the machine, whereas in NLG the process is about making decisions regarding the arrangement of representation into words known to humans [6, 21].

5 Data and Methodology

5.1 Data Collection

The data in the current research is collected manually and directly in real-time from three social media i.e., Facebook, Twitter and YouTube's official press conference. The data collection started in mid-July 2020 and continued extraction till mid-May 2021. An unstructured dataset of 60,365 text-based discussions from different posts and various concerning topics, was converted into structured data that included comments, tweets and replies related to the pandemic COVID -19 around the world.

5.2 Pre-processing of Data

Data were preprocessed using various basic steps except stemming or lemmatization in order to analyze the real word association, like applying stop word removal, punctuation removal, emoji removal, hyperlinks removal, numerical removal, eliminating extra white spaces and converting all upper cases to lower cases for achieving feature extraction by selecting most frequently used words.

5.3 Working of Proposed Analysis: Methodology

The stepwise process of the NLP for Novel TBA can be observed as follows:

Step 1. After preprocessing, tokens were generated for words as well as their respective PoS Tags for their respective hypernyms, in order to get maximum content discussed.

Step 2. It can be seen with the help of the following Table 2, that a Glossary is created and a gloss is tagged along the word for better understanding of context to accommodate easier search and lookup for further processing. Thus establishing basic parameters for WSD and understanding the real meaning and context of the comment.

Table 2. Sample Glossary for COVID19 Comments

Sample Words from Corpus	Word	Glossary
	COVID-19	G100 Series: G101Disease
	Bat	G200 Series: G201Mammal G202 An appliance used for hitting the ball in cricket G203 A wedge used for pottery
	Safe	G300 Series: G301 Protected from or not exposed to danger or risk G302 A strong fireproof cabinet with a complex lock, used for the storage valuables
	Passing	G400 Series: G401 Going past G402 The end of something G402 A person's death

Step 3. After that, the tokens are generated for words' distribution of the corpus on the basis of "is-a" relationship thus providing the concepts in the domain and also the relationships that hold between those concepts to observe the ontology behind the words used in some context.

Step 4. A Text bag is created, after extracting word definition corresponding to the Weighted Vector that will lead to a separate bag of features, 10 hot topics are generated on the basis of word usage and Ontology observed.

Step 5. These hot Topics are Labelled from S_1 to S_{10} depending upon the features classified with respect to the Weighted Vector in Lexicon, given by

$$\overline{V_w} = \sum_{i=1}^{10} S_i w_i. \tag{1}$$

– where S_i is the feature vector from the text bag and w_i is the average weight of the frequently used word.

Step 6. Evaluation of the maximum weighted overlapping between the context bag of words and the Si bag of Words is observed to chunk the sentences for respective Si's feature from the entire corpus.

Step 7. Corpus Analysis to achieve Word Sense Disambiguation through Proper Knowledge Representation is implemented.

Step 8. Finally results based on the novel TBA approach using NLP steps will deduce the interesting insights regarding COVID 19.

The entire process of how novel Text-Based Analysis was obtained via NLP steps that helped in further classification of the corpus into ten hot topics' categories is shown in the following Fig. 5, thus concluding their insights (Fig. 4).

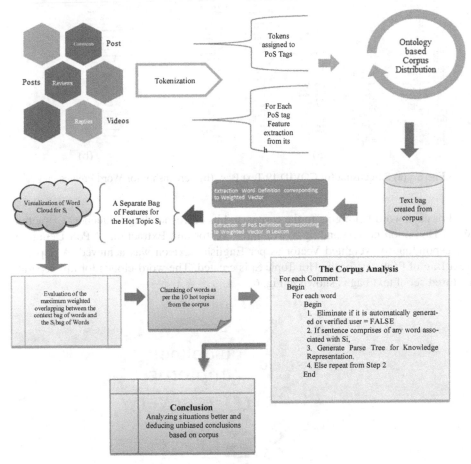

Fig. 4. Proposed analysis steps: methodology

6   Results and Discussions

The corpus analysis achieved in Sect. 5.3 using the novel TBA steps has displayed a decent approach to represent knowledge that is available on the social media platforms and resolving Word Sense Disambiguation. Since many comments, tweets and replies were irrelevant from the topic, a text bag, is created to eliminate those unnecessary comments, then observe the texts, that showed relevance to COVID-19 and are frequently used. The text Bag that was created after the ontology-based distribution as shown in Fig. 5(a) helped in collecting information for the words' usage that in turn helped in collecting the most frequently used words as shown in Fig. 5(b).

(a)   (b)

Fig. 5. (a) Screenshot for COVID 19 Text Bag. (b) Screenshot for Word Frequencies

For each word belonging to the corpus and its corresponding frequency, Extraction Word Definition corresponding to Weighted Vector and Extraction of PoS Definition corresponding to Weighted Vector as per English Lexicon was achieved. A Separate Text Bag of Features for the Hot Topic S_i is created. The word-clouds for this separate featured set of text bag is shown in Fig. 6.

Fig. 6. Visualization of Word Cloud for Si

After that, the selected Si text bag is explored as per the word definition corresponding to Weighted Vector V_w. A sample of COVID 19 with their meaning representation is present in Table 3. The correct form of the word is replaced with the tokens.

The metadata about the knowledge base is provided that is used for classifying and organizing the content into sub-categories. It is achieved using three basic entities: users, tags, and resources to focus on Sentence chaining that categorized the entire corpus into 10 main HOT Topics:

1. Following Social distancing
2. Distribution of Masks, Hand Sanitizer and food entities
3. Medical Conditions and Aid
4. Political Agendas during the crisis
5. Bed Availability
6. Oxygen Cylinders availability
7. Online Education Policies
8. Work from Home Routine
9. Financial Crisis
10. COVID Vaccination

In a similar way the entire corpus was classified into the previously mentioned ten Hot Topics with the observation being made that people are concerned about certain important factors affecting life and sciences during COVID19, that must be taken into consideration by authorities and researchers of the concerned field.

It was analyzed that the major problems faced during this crisis as shown in Fig. 7 were queries regarding Vaccine, for handling Finances during critical times and Medical Conditions not only for COVID patients but for patients suffering from other critical conditions as well, respectively. These are considered the most discussed topics over the social media platforms among the entire corpus from three platforms.

For the morphological understanding of the corpus and to observe the relation between topics for the Weighted Vectors, the top five most used words from the Si i.e. #deaths, #recovery, #Money, #work, #symptoms that have and were taken compared with all topics that were frequently used among these. The analysis of the features extracted from Si with respect to these weighted vectors is shown in Fig. 6.

The data relating to COVID-19 is mostly about sufferings, losses, the crisis faced by the public, guidelines levied by governing authorities and impact on the educational and working sector. The weighted vector score observed from Fig. 8, showed that for some families, it became very hard to even manage food two times a day and were completely dependent on the Distribution of food entities. It was extremely difficult to follow social distancing guidelines with family members staying under one roof even if one of them was diagnosed with the disease. Correspondingly, by observing the meaning representation as shown in Table 3 and weighted vector score w.r.t. work from home and online education policies people working on startup businesses and science researches had to suffer great loss, as their businesses, resources and researches that were ongoing for a long period of time faced serious consequences due to lack of regular monitoring and inconsistent interactions.

Table 3. The Sample meaning representation of comments from the corpus with their classification

Word	Sample Corpus	Meaning representation	Hot Topic Classification
profit	I can imagine the same people profiting off the human suffering of #COVID19	(parse output)	Financial Crisis
patients	The no. of COVID patients has started decreasing from the mid of September.	(parse output)	COVID Vaccination
guidelines	These are the guidelines one should always? èmember (?èmember is replaced with remember using Weighted Vector of the respective word in the Lexicon)	(parse output)	Following Social Distancing
symptoms	Common manifestations of COVID-19 are respiratory and can extend from mild symptoms to severe acute respiratory distress.	(parse output)	Medical condition and Aid

profit — Meaning representation:

```
++++Time                                    0.01 seconds (159.67 total)
Found 301 linkages (100 with no P.P. violations)
  Linkage 1, cost vector = (UNUSED=0 DIS=0 AND=0 LEN=18)

                                            +--------Jp---------+
                     +--------Os------+      +------DMu------+
+-Sp*i---I---+   +-IDBB+-Ds*y-----Mg----+-MVp--+  |   +-----AN-----+-Mp-
|     |      |   |    |   |     |       |     |  |  |  |           |
I.p can.v imagine.v the same people.s profiting.v off the human.n suffering.n

--+-Js-+
|   |
of COVID19

Constituent tree:

(S (NP I)
  (VP can
    (VP imagine
      (NP (NP the same people)
        (VP profiting
          (PP off
            (NP (NP the human suffering)
              (PP of
                (NP COVID19)))))))))
```

patients — Meaning representation:

```
++++Time                                    0.01 seconds (159.15 total)
Found 4 linkages (6 with no P.P. violations) at null count 4
  Linkage 1, cost vector = (UNUSED=4 DIS=9 AND=0 LEN=26)

                                      +---------------Xp----------------+
           +--------Wd-----------+                          +------+
           +------DG--------+    +-Ss--+---PP----+-Os--+-Mp-
LEFT-WALL the [no] [.] [of] COVID [patients] has.v started.v decreasing.g

--------------------------------+
----Mp-----------+
+----Jp---+      |
--+- -Ds-+  +-Js-+
|  |  |   |  |
from the mid.a of September .

Constituent tree:

(S (NP The no . of COVID)
  patients
  (VP has
    (VP started
      (NP (NP decreasing)
        (PP from
          (NP the mid)))
      (PP of
        (NP September))))
  .)
```

guidelines — Meaning representation:

```
++++Time                                    0.00 seconds (159.81 total)
Found 1 linkage (1 with no P.P. violations)
  Unique linkage, cost vector = (UNUSED=0 DIS=1 AND=0 LEN=13)

                       +------------Bp-----------+
           +---Dpt----+              +-----I-----+
+-Spx-+   +---Dmc---+--Rn----+-Ss---+       +---E----+
|     |   |     |       |    |      |       |        |
these are.v the guidelines.n one should.v always remember.v

Constituent tree:

(S (NP These)
  (VP are
    (NP (NP the guidelines)
      (SBAR (S (NP one)
        (VP should
          (VP (ADVP always)
            remember))))))))
```

symptoms — Meaning representation:

```
++++Time                                    0.00 seconds (161.53 total)
Found 2 linkages (2 with no P.P. violations)
  Linkage 1, cost vector = (UNUSED=0 DIS=0 AND=0 LEN=33)

+------A------+-----Mp----+-Js--+            +----Ss---+
common.s manifestations.n of COVID-19 are.v respiratory.a and can.v extend.v
from mild.a symptoms.n to severe.a acute.a respiratory.a distress.n

+------A------+-----Mp----+-Js--+            +----I----+-MV
common.s manifestations.n of COVID-19 are.v respiratory.a and can.v extend.v

   +---Mp---+          +-----A-----+
+-A-+  +--A--+ +--Js--+         +--A--+
|  |   |   |    |  |             |  |
from mild.a symptoms.n to severe.a acute.a respiratory.a distress.n

Constituent tree:

(S (NP (NP Common manifestations)
    (PP of
      (NP COVID-19)))
  (VP (VP are
      (ADJP respiratory))
    and
    (VP can
      (VP extend
        (PP from
          (NP mild symptoms))
        (PP to
          (NP severe acute respiratory distress))))))
```

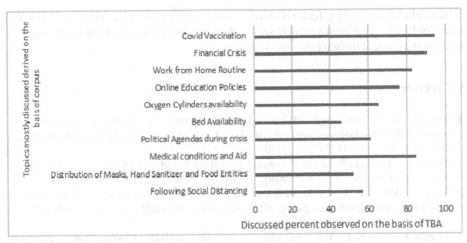

Fig. 7. Percentage analysis of hot topics discussed over the entire corpus

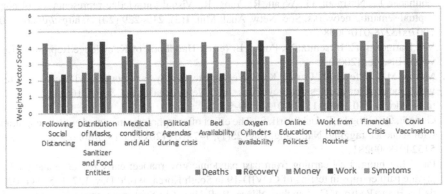

Fig. 8. Hot Topics w.r.t. Weighted Vectors of S_i

7 Conclusion and Future Work

The Novel TBA approach has provided crucial analysis steps to better understand the basic concepts of Natural Language Processing that were encountered during the initial level of data analysis. The implementation of Knowledge Representation as shown in Table 3 has revealed that the taxonomy of Constituent Tree could be parsed with the ontologies to get a better understanding of text analytics while trying to achieve text classification.

The corpus is constructed and categorized on the basis of most discussed topics derived from frequently used words of comments, tweets and replies on Facebook, Twitter and YouTube respectively with the help of R and Python packages. The collected data was converted to corpus and the ten hot topics that need attention were discussed.

The proposed work could make use of a more complex version for the morphological analysis of the corpus. Future research could use an investigative approach to find the

Lexical relations of varying features and their enactment on the sub-contexts and domains at deeper levels. Also, sentiments based on the knowledge extracted can be obtained to get even the cynical insights into the situation.

References

1. Pittaras, N., Giannakopoulos, G., Papadakis, G., Karkaletsis, V.: Text classification with semantically enriched word embeddings. Nat. Lang. Eng. **27**(4), 391–425 (2020). https://doi.org/10.1017/S1351324920000170
2. Nemes, L., Kiss, A.: Social media sentiment analysis based on COVID-19. J. Inf. Telecommun. **5**(1), 1–15 (2020). https://doi.org/10.1080/24751839.2020.1790793
3. Lata, K., Singh, P., Dutta, K.: A comprehensive review on feature set used for anaphora resolution. Artif. Intell. Rev. **54**(4), 2917–3006 (2020). https://doi.org/10.1007/s10462-020-09917-3
4. Garcia, K., Berton, L.: Topic detection and sentiment analysis in Twitter content related to COVID-19 from Brazil and the USA. Appl. Soft Comput. **101**, 107057 (2021). https://doi.org/10.1016/j.asoc.2020.107057
5. Zhuhadar, L., Nasraoui, O., Wyatt, R., Yang, R.: Visual knowledge representation of conceptual semantic networks. Soc. Netw. Anal. Min. **1**(3), 219–229 (2011). https://doi.org/10.1007/s13278-010-0008-2
6. Van Harmelen, F., Lifschitz, V., Porter, B. (eds.): Handbook of Knowledge Representation, vol. 1. Elsevier (2008)
7. Martin, M.K., Pfeffer, J., Carley, K.M.: Network text analysis of conceptual overlap in interviews, newspaper articles and keywords. Soc. Netw. Anal. Min. **3**(4), 1165–1177 (2013). https://doi.org/10.1007/s13278-013-0129-5
8. Güngör, O., Güngör, T., Üsküdarli, S.: The effect of morphology in named entity recognition with sequence tagging. Nat. Lang. Eng. **25**(1), 147–169 (2019). https://doi.org/10.1017/S1351324918000281
9. Park, J., Chung, E.: Learning from past pandemic governance: early response and public-private partnerships in testing of COVID-19 in South Korea. World Dev. **137**, 105198 (2021)
10. de las Heras-Pedrosa, C., Sánchez-Núñez, P., Peláez, J.I.: Sentiment Analysis and Emotion Understanding during the COVID-19 pandemic in Spain and its impact on digital ecosystems. Int. J. Environ. Res. Pub. Health **17**(15), 5542 (2020).https://doi.org/10.3390/ijerph17155542
11. Chen, Q., Min, C., Zhang, W., Wang, G., Ma, X., Evans, R.: Unpacking the black box: how to promote citizen engagement through government social media during the COVID-19 crisis. Comput. Hum. Behav. **110**, 106380 (2020). https://doi.org/10.1016/j.chb.2020.106380
12. Limaye, R.J., et al.: Building trust while influencing online COVID-19 content in the social media world. Lancet Digit. Health **2**(6), e277–e278 (2020). https://doi.org/10.1016/S2589-7500(20)30084-4
13. Yue, L., Zhang, L.: Social media WeChat infers the development trend of COVID-19. J. Infect. **81**(1), e82–e83 (2020). https://doi.org/10.1016/j.jinf.2020.03.050
14. Rajkumar, R.P.: COVID-19 and mental health: a review of the existing literature. Asian J. Psychiatry **52**, 102066 (2020). https://doi.org/10.1016/j.ajp.2020.102066
15. Cinelli, M., et al.: The COVID-19 social media infodemic. Sci. Rep. **10**(1), 16598 (2020). https://doi.org/10.1038/s41598-020-73510-5
16. Dias, G., Moraliyski, R., Cordeiro, J., et al.: Automatic discovery of word semantic relations using paraphrase alignment and distributional lexical semantics analysis. Nat. Lang. Eng. **16**(4), 439–467 (2010). https://doi.org/10.1017/S135132491000015X

17. Dornescu, I., Orăsan, C.: Densification: semantic document analysis using Wikipedia. Nat. Lang. Eng. **20**(4), 469–500 (2014). https://doi.org/10.1017/S1351324913000296
18. Akhtar, M.S., Ghosal, D., et al.: A multi-task ensemble framework for emotion, sentiment and intensity prediction, computation and language (2018). https://arxiv.org/abs/1808.01216
19. Malla, S.J., Alphonse, P.J.A.: COVID- 19 outbreak: an ensemble pre-trained deep learning model for detecting informative tweets. Appl. Soft Comput. **107**, 107495 (2021)
20. Macherey, K., Och, F.J., Ney, H.: Natural language understanding using statistical machine translation. In: 7th European Conference on Speech Communication and Technology (2001)
21. Russell, S.J.; Norvig, P.: Artificial Intelligence: A Modern Approach, p. 19. Prentice Hall (2003). ISBN 0-13-790395-2. http://aima.cs.berkeley.edu/

Indian Languages Requirements for String Search/comparison on Web

Prashant Verma[1](✉), Vijay Kumar[2], and Bharat Gupta[2]

[1] WSI, MeitY, New Delhi, India
[2] MeitY, New Delhi, India
{vkumar,bharatg}@meity.gov.in

Abstract. The document formats and protocols that based on character data is mainly prepared for the web. These protocols and formats can be access as resources that contain the various text files that cover syntactic content and natural language content in some structural markup language. In order to process these types of data, it requires various string based operations such as searching, indexing, sorting, regular expressions etc. These documents inspect the text variations of different types and preferences of the user for string processing on the web. For this purpose, W3C has developed two documents Character Model: String Matching and searching that act as building blocks related two these problems on the web and defining rules for string manipulation i.e. string matching and searching on the web. These documents also focus on the different types of text variations in which same orthographic text uses different character sequences and encodings. The rules defined in these documents act as a reference for the authors, developers etc. for consistent string manipulation on the web. The paper covers different types of text variations seen in Indian languages by taking Hindi as initial language and it is important that these types of variations should reflect in these documents for proper and consistent Indian languages string manipulations on the web.

Keywords: W3C · CSS · Unicode · Html · Head · Style · Body · Doctype

1 Introduction and Background

Unicode and ISO jointly defined the Universal character set for character Model. A web documents authored in the world writing system, languages, scripts to be exchanged, read and search through the successful character model. W3C Standard Document Character Model for the World Wide Web-String Matching gives specifications authors, content developers and software developers a general reference on string identity matching and searching on the World Wide Web. The goal of this document is to make web to process and transmit the text in a consistent, proper and clear way. The successful character model permits documents of web works on different writing systems, scripts, and languages on different platforms so that seamless information can be exchanged, read, and searched by the consumers on the web around the world [1].

A string-searching document of W3C covers string-searching operations on the Web in order to allow greater interoperability. String searching refers to matching of natural

© Springer Nature Switzerland AG 2022
A. Dev et al. (Eds.): AIST 2021, CCIS 1546, pp. 210–214, 2022.
https://doi.org/10.1007/978-3-030-95711-7_18

language through the "find" command in a Web browser [2]. It is possible to generate the same text with different character encodings. The Unicode allows this mechanism for the identical text. Normalization is the mechanism by Unicode that is usually perform while string search and comparisons. It converts the text to use all pre-composed and decomposed characters. The Unicode provides few chapters on the searching of the string. Out of which Unicode Collation Algorithm contains information on the searching [3].

2   Variations in User Inputs

2.1   Different Preferences by the Users

The Unicode Standard gives different alternatives to define text but requires that both text should be treated identical. In order to improve efficiency, it is recommended that an application will normalize text before performing string manipulation operations such as search, comparisons on the web. The different variations can occur while define Unicode text such that same character used different Unicode code points sequences [4]. This will cause unexpected results while searching and matching of string by the users as both string uses different code points. Additionally in Indian languages, the same text represents two orthographic representations with different encoding. The spelling variations lead to introduce the inappropriate searching results. The different users can use different spellings of the same text, as both spellings are in used. Some examples are shown below:

हिंदी/ɦĩdi/ &हिन्दी/ɦĩdi/ ,मंडी/mãɖi/ &मण्डी /mãɖi/,चम्पक /tʃə̃pək/ &चंपक /tʃə̃pək/

These types of spelling variation may occur in other Indian languages also.

2.2   Keyboard Representation

It is requires by the Unicode to store and interchanged the characters in the same logical order or we can say that order that user typed through the keyboards. It is not always true that in the different keyboard layouts, keystrokes and input characters are same and one to one. It is depends on the type of the keyboard layout. Some keyboards can produce numerous characters from a single key press and some keyboards use different keystrokes to produce one abstract character. It is the limitations of Indian languages that too many characters need to be fit in one single keyboard. This leads to input more complex Indian languages input methods and which makeover keystrokes sequence in character sequences [4].

The Unicode Standard needs that characters can be stored and interchanged in logical order, i.e. roughly corresponding to the order in which text is typed in via the keyboard or spoken. The main limitations of Indian languages is that a limited number of keys can fit on a keyboard. Some keyboards will generate multiple characters from a single key press. In Indian languages, too many characters to fit on a keyboard and must rely on more complex input methods, which transform keystroke sequences into character sequences. It might be occurs that different character sequences of the same text used by different users from the different keyboard and create issues in string identity matching.

3 Use-Cases

3.1 Text Variation in Syntactic Content Under HTML/CSS and Other Applications

The role of syntactic content in a document format and protocol is to represent the text that defines the structure of the document format and protocol. The different values used to define id, class name in markup languages and cascading style sheets are a part of syntactic content. In order to produce output as desired, we should ensure that the selectors and id or class name should be same. The below example represents id used with different character sequences.

In the above example, the id name defines in the HTML and CSS works on the same character sequences [5]. Gaps will be there if id name uses different character sequences. This is particularly occurs and leads an issue if markup language and the CSS are being handled or maintained by different persons.

Below examples shows the different character sequences as per Unicode Code Charts and different choices by the users on writing the characters as both forms can be written [6].

```
<!DOCTYPE html>
<html>
<head>
<style>
#हिंदी-शैली-ज़ांच{
  text-align: center;
  color: red;
}
</style>
</head>
<body>
<p id=" हिन्दी-शैली-ज़ांच">Text in red color</p>
<p>This paragraph is not affected by the style.</p>
</body>
</html>
```

हिंदी /ɦĩdi/ =0939+ 093F+0902+0926+0940

हिन्दी /ɦĩdi/=0939+ 093F+0928+094D+0926+0940

ज़ांच /zatʃ/ =095B+093E+0902+091A

ज़ांच /zatʃ/=091C+093C+093E+0902+091A

There are two types of variations are seen especially in Indian language i.e. spelling variations and different character sequences. The character sequences should be same in order to get the right results. Therefore, it is important that characters – to-characters should match so that proper string manipulation should be made on the web.

3.2 Implementation of Internationalized Domain Name and Email Addresses

For the benefit of large amount of users, it is required to internationalize the domain name and email addresses. In order to make this happen, there is a neccessity to deal with the various issues pertaining to Indian languages such as spelling and text input variations [7, 8]. The user does not have the knowledge of normalized form; user might be use different character sequences for domain name in Indian languages. So, it is required to implement different types of variations while searching and comparison of the strings so that the web document formats and protocols performed the right string-matching operation and user perceive the results.

3.3 Indian Language Search Operations on the Web

User can search natural language content by using find command on the web. Different Users might use different character sequences of the same text by performing find command. There should be some common mapping and implementation in order to satisfy the users need. There user might expect that typing one character will find the equivalent character in the same script such as in Devanagari script ल that represents DEVANAGARI LETTER LA and ळ that represents DEVANAGARI LETTER LLA etc.

The few examples are shown below:

आवाज़ /avaz/: 0906 + 0935 + 093E + 095B

आवाज़ /avaz/: 0906 + 0935 + 093E + 091C + 093C

फ़ाँसी /fãsi/: 095E + 093E +0901 + 0938 + 0908

फ़ाँसी /fãsi/: 092B + 093C + 093E + 0901 + 0938 + 0908

चम्पक /tʃə̃pək/ : 091A + 092E + 094D + 092A + 0915

चंपक /tʃə̃pək/ : 091A + 0902 + 092A + 0915

Additionally in Indian languages, some of the text represents two orthographic representations with different encodings. The spelling variations lead to introduce the inappropriate searching results. Some examples are shown below:

हिंदी /hĩdi/&हिन्दी /hĩdi/ ,मंडी /mə̃ɖi/&मण्डी /mə̃ɖi/ ,चम्पक /tʃə̃pək/ &चंपक /tʃə̃pək/,
ठंडा /tʰə̃ɖa/&ठण्डा /tʰə̃ɖa/, अम्वर /ə̃vər/&अंवर /ə̃vər/

4 Current Gaps and Requirements for Indian Languages

The above-defined W3C draft Standards specify the requirements while implementing string matching of syntactic content and search of natural language content by using matching rules. The following Indian language requirements need to introduce in the standards in order to perform proper string operations on the web:

1. Different kinds of character variations are not currently reflected in the Standards. Therefore there is a need to address these gaps for proper implementation and reference purpose. These variations have been discussed in the above sections.
2. Need to analysis variations with in the script such as equivalent form of character in the same script as discussed in above sub Sect. 3.3 and Singleton mapping such as ॐ[U + 0950 DEVANAGRI OM] & ॐ[U + 1F549 OM SYMBOL].
3. In addition, it is recommended that Indian languages characters need to be post processed through normalization defined by Unicode for comparison and searching on the web. This leads to the removal of various ambiguities occurs in Indian languages [9]. Unicode specifies the different normalized forms. such as NFD, NFC, NFKC etc. and discussed in Unicode technical report on Normalization forms [10]. It is recommended that NFC is best suitable normalize form for string manipulation on the web.

5 Conclusion

The paper discussed about the different variations in Hindi characters. The all-Indian languages requirements and variations for web search and comparison need to be reflected in the standards for reference and correct manipulation on the Web. The best way is to ensure that the characters should always be processed through normalization so that the user gets the consistent results. The different ways of text might cause unexpected results. Therefore, it is important for authors/developers to take care about the different requirements of Indian languages and for the correct implementation of syntactic and natural language content in the web documents. This paper can also be extended by the investigation of the different types of variations in other Indian languages apart from Hindi.

References

1. Character Model for the World Wide Web: String Matching (2021). https://www.w3.org/TR/charmod-norm/
2. W3C String Searching (2020). https://w3c.github.io/string-search/
3. UNICODE COLLATION ALGORITHM. https://www.unicode.org/reports/tr10/
4. Unicode Consortium. https://home.unicode.org/
5. Normalization in HTML and CSS. https://www.w3.org/International/questions/qa-html-css-normalization/
6. Unicode Devanagari Code Chart (2020). https://unicode.org/charts/PDF/U0900.pdf
7. Internationalization of Domain Names in Indian Languages 2015. https://www.researchgate.net/publication/277593254_Internationalization_of_Domain_Names_in_Indian_Languages, https://www.tandfonline.com/doi/abs/10.1080/03772063.2005.11416421
8. https://www.tandfonline.com/doi/abs/10.1080/03772063.2005.11416421
9. W3C Requirements for String Identity Matching and String Indexing. https://www.w3.org/TR/charreq/
10. Unicode Normalization Forms (2020). http://www.unicode.org/reports/tr15/

Dictionary Vectorized Hashing of Emotional Recognition of Text in Mutual Conversation

M. Shyamala Devi$^{(\boxtimes)}$, D. Manivannan, N. K. Manikandan, Ankita Budhia, Sagar Srivastava, and Manshi Rohella

Computer Science and Engineering, Vel Tech Rangarajan Dr. Sagunthala R&D Institute of Science and Technology, Chennai, Tamilnadu, India
shyamaladevim@veltech.edu.in

Abstract. Emotion detection is a subset of sentiment classification that interacts with emotion processing and analysis. The condition of just being emotional is frequently associated with making sensible qualitative stimulation of feelings or with environmental influence. With increase in the social media usage, people tend to have frequent conversation through several applications. Even police department tend to analyze the victim of any suicidal cases through the personal chat conversation. Machine learning could be used to analyze emotional detection of the person through text processing of their personal conversation. The text conversation dataset with 7480 conversations from KAGGLE warehouse and is used in the execution analysis to detect the emotional analysis. The text conversation dataset is preprocessed by removing the stop words. The tokens are extracted from the text using NGram method. The emotional labels are assigned for the tokens and the machine is trained to identify the emotions during testing. The emotional labels are converted into features to form corpus text for classifying the emotions in the conversation. The corpus is splitted to form training and testing dataset and is fitted to Dictionary Vectorizer, Feature Hashing, Count Vectorizer and Hash Vectorizer to extract the important features from the text conversation. The extracted features from the text conversation is the subjected to all the classifiers to analyze the performance of the emotion prediction. The scripting is written in Python and implemented with Spyder in Anaconda Navigator IDE, and the experimental results shows that the random forest classifier with dictionary vectorizer is exhibiting 99.8% of accuracy towards predicting the emotions from the personal conversations.

Keywords: Machine learning · Corpus · Vectorizer · Accuracy

1 Introduction

Emotions play a significant role in people's lives and make them who they really are. They provide relevant data to observers about our present condition and well-being. Businesses and individuals must be able to understand the key emotions expressed by people and use that as the basis for providing personalized recommendations to meet the individual requirements of the customers in order to provide effective services to

© Springer Nature Switzerland AG 2022
A. Dev et al. (Eds.): AIST 2021, CCIS 1546, pp. 215–223, 2022.
https://doi.org/10.1007/978-3-030-95711-7_19

customers. Emotion detection is a synergistic connection of emotions, also known as influences and innovation that derives its essential nature from applying emotion-defined technology to various areas and provide fine-grained outcome. Emotion recognition will play a promising position in the area of artificial intelligence, especially in the development of human–machine interfaces. It is the technique that identifies and analyzing the emotion of chat and text, i.e., people's mood swings can be easily accessed, and this process can be used in numerous social networking sites and enterprise applications.

2 Literature Review

The rise of Internet technology has pushed knowledge discovery and analysis to the forefront of business effectiveness. It enables service providers to provide customized services to their customers. Numerous research is being conducted in the field of text mining and analysis due to the ease of collecting information and the various services it provides. This article explores the concept of emotion detection from texts and identify the important approaches used by researchers in the study of text-based emotion detection systems [1]. The primary goal of sentiment classification for stock price forecasting is to identify customers' perceptions of products available. The purpose of this paper is to provide an overview and detailed comparison of various sentiment analysis approaches and methodologies with Sentiment Emotion Detection, as well as to discuss the shortcomings of conventional work and future directions for sentiment analysis methodologies on Sentiment Emotion Detection [2]. The person's feeling will be affirmed by making appropriate observational data such that by asking numerous questions until his or her scenario is correctly identified. Based on person responses, it attempts to refresh their mind if that person is in a terrible mood by supplying refreshments based on the persons character that were initially gathered. The proposed system functions as a preferred emotionally supportive network and will serve as a guide for the doctors conducting the analysis [3].

Understanding emotional responses at the fine-grained level of expressed feelings is critical for system improvement. Such critical observations cannot be acquired entirely through AI-based big data sentiment classification; thus, text-based emotion detection using AI in social networking sites big data has emerged as a promising area of Natural Language Processing investigation [4]. The majority of available research is based on binary categorizing text as favorable or unfavorable without examining the emotional responses that lead to that classification. However, the current regulations for in-depth evaluation of various content, combined with the uncertainty and multidimensional aspects of human views and feelings, have delivered such alternatives obsolete. Because of these requirements, current research focuses on explicitly stating emotions rather than just the sentiment conveyed in a given text [5, 6]. The ability to rapidly capture the overall public's sentiments regarding social gatherings, political movements, marketing strategies, and buying patterns has stimulated the interest of both the research community, for the exciting challenges and opportunities, and the business world, for the extraordinary consequences in marketing and financial market prediction. This has given rise to the emerging areas of computer vision and sentiment classification, which use human-computer interaction, information extraction, and multidimensional data processing to extract people's feelings from the vast amounts of internet community data

[6–8]. This survey examines theoretical frameworks that see emotional responses as manifestations, pictorial representations, cognitive evaluation outcomes, societal expectations, neurological circuitry products and goods, and emotional understandings of the basic feelings [9, 10]. Sentiment emotion detection could be used in a variety of fields, including emotion recognition, interpersonal behavior, data analysis, online learning, recommendation engines, and cognitive science [11, 12].

In personal communication, two levels have been identified: one transmits inappropriate messages that can be about anything or nothing, and the other communicates implicit messages about the speakers themselves. Both vocabulary and technologies have enabled significant efforts to comprehend the first, explicit channel, but the second is less well recognized. Recognizing the emotional responses of the other group is one of the most important tasks concerning the second, implicit channel. To accomplish this task, signal processing and decision - making techniques must be developed, while emotional and lingual assessments of emotion must be combined [13, 14]. SenticNet is a linguistic and beneficial source of information for concept-level sentiment classification that is open to the public. SenticNet 3 uses "flow of energy" to connect different parts of elongated popular and common information characterizations to one another, rather than graph mining and high dimensional reduction techniques. SenticNet 3 represents information with a representational opacity and models which is conceptual and impactful data affiliated with multi-word natural language expressions [15, 16]. Using binary neural network based classification model, a system for automatic sentiment detection was created. Because emotional responses appeared to be lexicalized continuously, we hypothesized that lexical and semantic characteristics could be a sufficient way of representing the data. Cross validation oversampling was used to determine the best evidences indicate for each of the emotional responses. To reduce linguistic variation, word recognition adjustment was performed on the input data [17, 18]. An expression classification model and a discriminator are included in the proposed multimedia emotion labelling approach. The expression classifier and discriminator are instructed concurrently in competition with one another [19].

3   Our Contributions

The overall architecture of the work is shown in Fig. 1. The following contributions are provided in this work.

- Firstly, the text conversation dataset with 7480 conversations from KAGGLE warehouse and is used in the execution analysis to detect emotional analysis.
- The text conversation dataset is preprocessed by removing the stop words. The tokens are extracted from the text using NGram method.
- The emotional labels are assigned for the tokens and the machine is trained to identify the emotions during testing.
- The emotional labels are converted into features to form corpus text for classifying the emotions in the conversation.
- The corpus is splitted to form training and testing dataset and is fitted to Dictionary Vectorizer, Feature Hashing, Count Vectorizer and Hash Vectorizer to extract the important features from the text conversation.

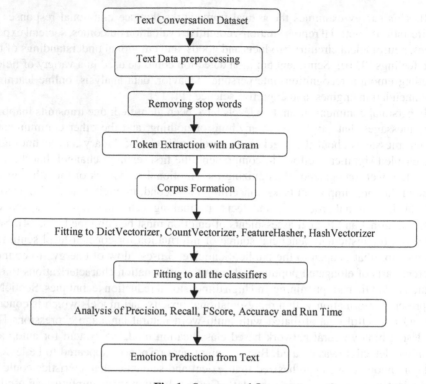

Text Conversation Dataset

↓

Text Data preprocessing

↓

Removing stop words

↓

Token Extraction with nGram

↓

Corpus Formation

↓

Fitting to DictVectorizer, CountVectorizer, FeatureHasher, HashVectorizer

↓

Fitting to all the classifiers

↓

Analysis of Precision, Recall, FScore, Accuracy and Run Time

↓

Emotion Prediction from Text

Fig. 1. System workflow

- The extracted features from the text conversation is the subjected to all the classifiers to analyze the performance of the emotion prediction.

4   Implementation Setup and Results

The Text conversation dataset with 7480 instances from KAGGLE repository is then subjected with the data preprocessing. The dataset information is shown in the Fig. 2. The stop words are removed from the text conversation dataset. The NGram method is used to extract the tokens from the text. During testing, the emotional labels are assigned to the tokens, and the machine is trained to recognize the emotions. The emotional labels are transformed into features, which are then used to generate corpus text for classifying the emotions in the conversation.

The corpus is splitted to form training and testing dataset and is fitted to Dictionary Vectorizer, Feature Hasher, Count Vectorizer and Hash Vectorized and its respective vectorized dataset is fitted to all the classifier for analyzing the performance of the emotion prediction and is shown in Table 1 – Table 4 and Fig. 3.

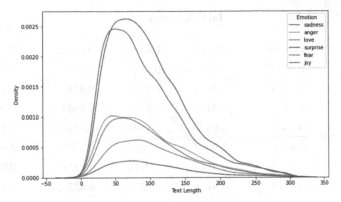

Fig. 2. Target Emotion Distribution in the dataset

Table 1. Classifier performance Indices with Dictionary Vectorizer.

Classifier	Precision	Rcall	FScore	Accuracy	RunTime
Logistic Reg	0.9067	0.9167	0.9067	0.9167	0.21
KNN	0.9367	0.9267	0.9247	0.9357	0.07
KSVM	0.9167	0.9117	0.9117	0.9147	1.26
GnaiveBayes	0.9433	0.9432	0.9432	0.9533	0.04
Dtree	0.9423	0.9443	0.9443	0.9435	0.06
Etree	0.9477	0.9337	0.9446	0.9567	0.08
RandomFor	0.9987	0.9987	0.9977	0.9987	0.10
Ridge	0.9667	0.9667	0.9667	0.9667	0.08
RCV	0.9117	0.9117	0.9117	0.9117	0.04
SGD	0.9273	0.9173	0.9273	0.9273	0.13
PAg	0.9121	0.9021	0.9121	0.9121	0.07
Bagg	0.9332	0.9232	0.9332	0.9332	0.11

Table 2. Classifier performance Indices with Feature Hasher.

Classifier	Precision	Rcall	FScore	Accuracy	RunTime
Logistic Reg	0.9117	0.9167	0.9167	0.9267	0.21
KNN	0.9227	0.9227	0.9237	0.9327	0.17
KSVM	0.9067	0.9117	0.9117	0.9147	1.16

(*continued*)

Table 2. (*continued*)

Classifier	Precision	Rcall	FScore	Accuracy	RunTime
GnaiveBayes	0.9433	0.9432	0.9432	0.9533	0.14
Dtree	0.9323	0.9343	0.9333	0.9335	0.16
Etree	0.9477	0.9437	0.9446	0.9567	0.08
RandomFor	0.9887	0.9887	0.9877	0.9887	0.12
Ridge	0.9667	0.9667	0.9667	0.9667	0.08
RCV	0.9117	0.9117	0.9117	0.9117	0.06
SGD	0.9273	0.9173	0.9273	0.9273	0.11
PAg	0.9021	0.9021	0.9121	0.9121	0.09
Bagg	0.9233	0.9233	0.9233	0.9232	0.14

Table 3. Classifier performance Indices with Count Vectorizer.

Classifier	Precision	Rcall	FScore	Accuracy	RunTime
Logistic Reg	0.9007	0.9007	0.9117	0.9017	0.20
KNN	0.9127	0.9127	0.9137	0.9127	0.07
KSVM	0.9067	0.9063	0.9066	0.9067	1.06
GnaiveBayes	0.9233	0.9232	0.9232	0.9333	0.13
Dtree	0.9323	0.9343	0.9333	0.9335	0.15
Etree	0.9477	0.9437	0.9446	0.9567	0.09
RandomFor	0.9787	0.9787	0.9777	0.9787	0.14
Ridge	0.9467	0.9447	0.9567	0.9567	0.09
RCV	0.9217	0.9127	0.9117	0.9117	0.16
SGD	0.9163	0.9166	0.9273	0.9273	0.12
PAg	0.9211	0.9111	0.9211	0.9221	0.08
Bagg	0.9003	0.9033	0.9033	0.9132	0.13

Table 4. Classifier performance Indices with Hash Vectorizer.

Classifier	Precision	Rcall	FScore	Accuracy	RunTime
Logistic Reg	0.9107	0.9107	0.9107	0.9017	0.18
KNN	0.9227	0.9217	0.9217	0.9217	0.07
KSVM	0.9167	0.9163	0.9166	0.9167	1.02

(*continued*)

Table 4. (*continued*)

Classifier	Precision	Rcall	FScore	Accuracy	RunTime
GnaiveBayes	0.9233	0.9232	0.9232	0.9333	0.12
Dtree	0.9223	0.9243	0.9233	0.9235	0.18
Etree	0.9477	0.9437	0.9446	0.9567	0.08
RandomFor	0.9687	0.9687	0.9677	0.9687	0.15
Ridge	0.9467	0.9447	0.9455	0.9555	0.06
RCV	0.9217	0.9127	0.9117	0.9117	0.12
SGD	0.9113	0.9116	0.9113	0.9273	0.13
PAg	0.9211	0.9111	0.9211	0.9221	0.09
Bagg	0.9003	0.9033	0.9033	0.9132	0.11

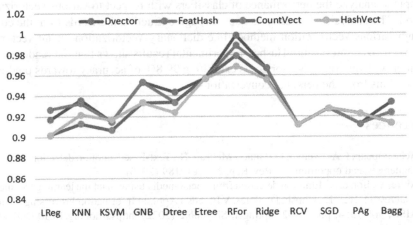

Fig. 3. Accuracy comparison of classifiers of vectorizers.

5 Mathematical Modelling and Analysis

The text conversation dataset is represented as follows in Eq. (1),

$$Text = \sum_{i=1}^{7480} \sum_{j-1}^{7480} \sum R_{ij} W_{ij} \tag{1}$$

Where 'R' represents the number of conversations in rows and 'W' represents the number of words in each rows. Each row in the text conversation can be represented by the Eq. (2).

$$RText = ((Adj|Noun) + |((Adj|Noun) * (Noun)?)(Adj|Noun) *)Noun \tag{2}$$

The number of tokens can be identified by the term frequency and is shown in Eq. (3),

$$Tokenterm = No_{term, Doc} TW_{Doc} \tag{3}$$

Where $No_{term,Doc}$ is the number of times the 'term' appears in the document 'Doc', and the TW_{Doc} is the total number of words in the document 'Doc'. The weight of the word in the row text is shown in Eq. (4).

$$\text{WeightWord} = \frac{No_{term,Doc}}{No_{term}} \tag{4}$$

The token extraction in the dataset is done by nGram method and is in Eq. (5).

$$Token(Word, key) = Token(key) \prod_{n=1}^{N} Token\left(\frac{Word}{Key}\right) \tag{5}$$

6 Conclusion

This paper explores the performance of classifying the emotion detection of the text. It attempts to analyze the performance of classifiers with respect to various vectorization method. The analysis of emotion is done through extracting the words form the corpus through various vectorization methods like dictionary vectorization, count vectorizer, Hash vectorizer and Feature Hasher. Experimental results shows that the random forest classifier with dictionary vectorizer is exhibiting 99.8% of accuracy towards predicting the emotions from the personal conversations.

References

1. Acheampong, F.A., Wenyu, C., Nunoo-Mensah, H.: Text-based emotion detection: advances, challenges, and opportunities. Rev. Rep. **2**(7), e12189 (2020)
2. Ahire, V., Borse, S.: Emotion detection from social media using machine learning techniques: a survey. In: Iyer, B., Ghosh, D., Balas, V.E. (eds.) Applied Information Processing Systems. AISC, vol. 1354, pp. 83–92. Springer, Singapore (2022). https://doi.org/10.1007/978-981-16-2008-9_8
3. Sekhar, C., Rao, M.S., Nayani, A.S.K., Bhattacharyya, D.: Emotion recognition through human conversation using machine learning techniques. In: Bhattacharyya, D., Thirupathi Rao, N. (eds.) Machine Intelligence and Soft Computing. AISC, vol. 1280, pp. 113–122. Springer, Singapore (2021). https://doi.org/10.1007/978-981-15-9516-5_10
4. Kusal, S., Patil, S., Kotecha, K., Aluvalu, R., Varadarajan, V.: AI based emotion detection for textual big data: techniques and contribution. Big Data Cogn. Comput. **5**(3), 43 (2021)
5. Krommyda, M., Rigos, A., Bouklas, K., Amditis, A.: Emotion detection in Twitter posts: a rule-based algorithm for annotated data acquisition. In: Proceedings of International Conference on Computational Science and Computational Intelligence, pp. 257–262 (2020)
6. Cambria, E.: Affective computing and sentiment analysis. IEEE Intell. Syst. **31**(2), 102–107 (2016)
7. Calvo, R., Mello, S.D.: Affect detection: an interdisciplinary review of models methods and their applications. IEEE Trans. Affect. Comput. **1**(1), 18–37 (2010)
8. Schuller, B.: Recognising realistic emotions and affect in speech: state of the art and lessons learnt from the first challenge. Speech Commun. **53**(9/10), 1062–1087 (2011)
9. Cowie, R., Douglas-Cowie, E., Tsapatsoulis, N., Votsis, G., Kollias, S.: Emotion recognition in human-computer interaction. IEEE Sig. Process. Mag. **18**, 32–80 (2001)

10. Cambria, E., Olsher, D., Rajagopal, D.: SenticNet 3: a common and common-sense knowledge base for cognition-driven sentiment analysis. In Proceedings of 28th AAAI Conference on Artificial Intelligence, pp. 1515–1521 (2014)

11. Desmet, B., Hoste, V.R.: Emotion detection in suicide notes. Exp. Syst Appl. **40**(16), 6351–6358 (2013)

12. Wang, S., Peng, G., Zheng, Z., Xu, Z.: Capturing emotion distribution for multimedia emotion tagging. IEEE Trans. Affect. Comput. **12**, 821–831 (2019)

13. Kraus, M.A., Drass, M.: Artificial intelligence for structural glass engineering applications - overview, case studies and future potentials. Glass Struct. Eng. **5**, 247–285 (2020)

14. Choi, S.H., Kim, H., Shin, K., Kim, H., Song, J.: Perceived color impression for spatially mixed colors. J. Disp. Technol. **10**(4), 282–287 (2018)

15. Dhaya, R.: Hybrid machine learning approach to detect the changes in SAR images for salvation of spectral constriction problem. J. Innov. Image Process. **3**(02), 118–130 (2021)

16. Hladnik, A., Poljicak, A.: Improving performance of content based image retrieval system with color features. Acta Graphica **27**, 7–12 (2017)

17. Conway, B.R., Eskew, R.T., Martin, P.R., Stockman, A.: A tour of contemporary color vision research. Vis. Res. **151**, 2–6 (2018)

18. Zarko, M., Robert, E., Matteo, T., Gegenfurtner, K.R.: Categorizing natural color distributions. Vis. Res. **151**, 18–30 (2018)

19. Messing, D.S., Van Beek, P., Errico, J.H.: The MPEG-7 colour structure descriptor: image description using colour and local spatial information. Image Process. **1**, 670–673 (2001)

Comparative Analysis of NLP Text Embedding Techniques with Neural Network Layered Architecture on Online Movie Reviews

Hemlata Goyal[⊠], Amar Sharma, Ranu Sewada, Devansh Arora, and Sunita Singhal

Manipal University Jaipur, Jaipur, India
hemlata.goyal@jaipur.manipal.edu

Abstract. In NLP world, there is a need to convert the text data into numerical form in a smart way of text embedding with the machine learning architecture. In this research, the comparative text embedding methods of Binary Term Frequency, Count Vector, Term Frequency - Inverse Document Frequency, and Word2Vec is used for converting text to meaningful representations of vectors, containing numerical values. In order to analyze the performance of the various text embedding techniques, Neural Network Layered Architecture is designed for movie review's polarity classification to include input layer, dense layers followed by the ReLU (Rectified Linear Unit) activation layers and Sigmoid activation function to make classifications on the basis of training–testing performance. Word2Vec text embedding scored the highest training and testing accuracy among all the text embedding techniques of Binary Term Frequency, Count Vector, Term Frequency - Inverse Document Frequency, and Word2Vec with 89.75% and 86.94% respectively with ± 1.0 *error* for the online movie reviews.

Keywords: Natural language processing · Text embedding · Count vector · Binary term frequency · TF-IDF · Word2Vec

1 Introduction

In NLP world, there is a need to convert the text data into numerical data in a smart way of vectorization or text embedding. Various methods have been used, either based on term frequency or the context (language modeling) to extract features from the text.

Text embedding is a basic technique in natural language processing in which syntactic and semantic features are taken from unlabeled text dataset [1]. This research aims to apply various techniques used for text embedding in NLP context and find out the best text embedding technique with the neural network layered architecture.

We can get different embedding for the same text document by applying various embedding approaches but for a specific, we don't know which approach will lead to producing the best results. Distributed vector representation of words-phrases and their compositionality results in a precisely syntactic-semantic word relationships in a large number [2, 3]. In this paper, we have done an in-depth analysis of different text embedding techniques on one specific task of polarity classification for the online movie reviews.

A. Dev et al. (Eds.): AIST 2021, CCIS 1546, pp. 224–231, 2022.
https://doi.org/10.1007/978-3-030-95711-7_20

Binary Term Frequency (BTF), Count Vector, Term Frequency – Inverse Document Frequency, Word2Vec embedding techniques have been used to derive vector representation of each online movie text review and applied on Neural Network architecture to compare the performance for each text embedding techniques in this research.

2 Literature Background

Text embedding is a basic technique in NLP in which syntactic and semantic features are taken from unlabeled text dataset. The aim of this research to apply various techniques used for text embedding in NLP context and find out the best text embedding technique with the neural network layered architecture. There are three major word embedding techniques namely, traditional, static and contextualized word embedding. The major consideration of word embedding is the incremental rate of scaling of dataset, data sparsity, position of word, and training speed of the dataset [4].

Machine learners can easily have used word embedding text after converting the freeform-text in healthcare [5], Question-answering system [6], Facebook, Twitter [7] are developed to use vector of various dimensionality on the basis of sentiment analysis and deep learning. Immense amount of efforts has already been put in sentiment analysis but there is much scope to deal the solution according to performance measure of word embedding technique and polarity of review (positive, negative or neutral) [8].

Binary Term Frequency (BTF), Count Vector, Term Frequency – Inverse Document Frequency, Word2Vec embedding techniques have been used to derive vector representation of each online movie text review and applied on Neural Network architecture to compare the performance for each text embedding techniques in this research.

Term Frequency (TF) is the ratio of each word token frequency and the word token sum of the document. In binary term frequency the relation of the term is 0,1 means in between two words. Count vector is also used for text vectorization in terms of document term matrix for a particular word occurs in the corpus [9, 10]. In tf-idf, words are weighted according to their significance. Capital letter, non-alphanumeric characters, special characters and not necessary punctuations are eliminated first. After it, we gathered terms that were similar [11, 12]. Word embedding methods are most popular and used in sentiment analysis for classification [13]. Word2Vec technique converts the words into meaningful vectors [14] with high accuracy.

Word embedding is used as feature input to Neural Network Layered Architecture to contextualize raw text data to get sentiment analysis of any text. Neural network consists with multiple layers (one input, many hidden layers, one output layer) network of neurons (weighted nodes) for classification and prediction, in which prediction accuracy is evaluated with the activation function (linear and nonlinear) [15].

The activation function is used to transform the summed weighted input received from the input layer node into the activation of the nodes in next layer. The **rectified linear activation function** (**ReLU**) is used in next 3 layers. ReLU is a piecewise linear default function which gives positive output for the input directly, otherwise zero [16].

Sigmoid function is a non-linear function, which is used to learn complex decision functions and separate the classes in nonlinear manner [17].

3   Methodology

3.1   About the Dataset

Dataset is taken in the raw form at the website link "https://www.kaggle.com/lakshmi25 npathi/imdb-dataset-of-50k-movie-reviews".

In this dataset, it contains 50,000 IMDB movie reviews and their corresponding polarity in terms of sentiment, is depicted in Table 1. In this a review is either of positive polarity or negative polarity.

Table 1. Dataset view

Review text	sentiment
One of the other reviewers has mentioned that after watching just 1 Oz episode you'll be hooked.	positive
A wonderful little production. The filming technique is very unassuming- very old-time-BBC fashion and gives a comforting, and sometimes discomforting, sense of realism to the entire piece.	positive
Basically there's a family where a little boy (Jake) thinks there's a zombie in his closet & his parents are fighting all the time.	negative

3.2   Data Preprocessing

Each of the review available in the dataset is processed as shown in Fig. 1.

Fig. 1. Methodology for filtration of reviews

Removing Duplications.   Data is downloaded in .csv format, analyzing and normalized the data to find duplicates entries there in the data and remove them to not waste time while training the model or our results don't get tampered.

Removal of Tags, Special Characters.   Tags and punctuations is not required in text review as it of no use to understand the emotion of the review and will just end up increasing the dimensionality of model thus increasing the latency.

Converting to Lowercase. Convert all the data to lowercase as during the training of the models it may consider same words as different as its case sensitive.

Removing of Stop Words. To remove stop words as it's not very important and removing them will help in bringing down the dimensionality of the model thus making it fast and better.

Stemming. Making similar words to their base word, removing the abbreviations used. At times these words will be treated differently even though they mean same such as "doesn't" and "does not" thus increasing dimensionality.

Word Embedding. After the pre-processing of text is done such as removal of duplicates, similar words, stop words, tags and so on we convert the words to vectors, model cannot work on words but only vectors. Here, Count vectorization is done with the CountVectorizer from Sklearn resulting in terms of document sparse matrix for a particular word occurs in the corpus.

Term Frequency (TF) is the ratio of each word token frequency and the word token sum of the document. In this paper, BTF is used which give the relation of the term 0,1 means in between two words. In tf-idf, words are weighted according to their significance. Capital letter, non-alphanumeric characters, special characters and not necessary punctuations are eliminated first. After it, we gathered terms that were similar. Tf-idf, mathematical formulation is shown in Eq. (1–3) that allots each words a specific value on basis of their repetitions in each news text.

$$tf(t, d) = \frac{f_d(t)}{\max_{w \in d} f_d(w)} \tag{1}$$

$$idf(t, D) = \ln\left(\frac{|D|}{|\{d \in D : t \in d\}|}\right) \tag{2}$$

$$tfidf(t, d, D) = tf(t, d).idf(t, D) \tag{3}$$

Afterwards, sklearn's TfidfVectorizer is used to convert the scanned text to tf-idf features, to construct a bag of terms, a count vector, and a tf-idf matrix.

Word2Vec technique converts the words into meaningful vectors with high accuracy. In this paper we have taken window size of 2 to make word pairs.

Binary Term Frequency (BTF), Count Vector, Term Frequency – Inverse Document Frequency, Word2Vec embedding techniques have been used and applied on the filtered reviews to get the vectorized representation. Neural Network machine learning architecture is used to compare the performance for each text embedding techniques in this research.

3.3 Neural Network Architecture

In order to analyze the performance of the various embedding techniques, one neural network is designed and depicted in Fig. 2.

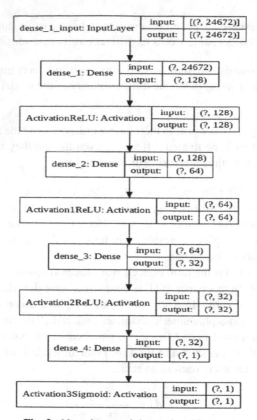

Fig. 2. Neural network layered architecture

Neural Network layered architecture as shown in Fig. 2, consisting of one input layer and four dense layers.

Each of the dense layer is followed by the ReLU (Rectified Linear Unit) activation layers except the last one. The last dense layer is Sigmoid activated to make classifications. Input is of shape (?, 24,672), here 24,672 are the numbers of terms in all the reviews after filtration.

In case of Word2Vec embedding 24,372 zeros are being padded in order to make the input dimension of size (?, 24,672).

The above states are obtained by considering randomly picked 20,000 out of total 50,000 IMDB movie reviews.

4   Results and Discussions

In this research paper, we have used the comparative text embedding methods of Binary Term Frequency, Count Vector, Term Frequency - Inverse Document Frequency, and Word2Vec for converting text to meaningful representations of vectors, containing numerical values and all the preprocessing steps (shown in Fig. 1) is applied on the online movie reviews dataset. In order to analyze the accuracy performance measure of the various text embedding techniques, Neural Network Layered Architecture is designed for movie review's polarity classification to include one input layer and four dense layers. Each of the dense layer is followed by the ReLU (Rectified Linear Unit) activation layers except the last one. The last dense layer is Sigmoid activated to make classifications on the basis of K-Fold-training and testing performance.

The accuracy obtained using different embedding techniques of Binary Term Frequency (BTF), Count Vector, Term Frequency – Inverse Document Frequency, Word2Vec embedding techniques for training–testing scored in percent of 76.44 -74.65, 78.46 – 77.84, 82.68 – 82.03, 89.75 – 86.94 respectively on movie review's classification with Neural Network Layered Architecture is shown in Table 2.

Table 2. Results of text embedding techniques on neural network layered architecture

Embedding technique	Accuracy on training set	Accuracy on testing set
Binary term frequency	76.44	74.65
Count vector	78.46	77.84
TF-IDF	82.68	82.03
Word2Vec	89.75	86.94

Word2Vec text embedding scored the highest training and testing accuracy among all the text embedding techniques of Binary Term Frequency, Count Vector, Term Frequency - Inverse Document Frequency, and Word2Vec with 89.75% and 86.94% respectively with ±1.0 *error* for the online movie reviews as shown in Fig. 3.

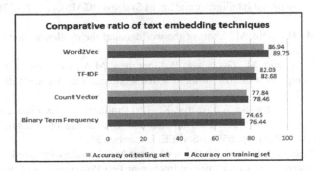

Fig. 3. Comparative performance measures of Neural Network Layered Architecture

5 Conclusion

In this research paper, we have used the comparative text embedding methods of Binary Term Frequency, Count Vector, Term Frequency - Inverse Document Frequency, and

Word2Vec for converting text to meaningful representations of vectors, containing numerical values. In order to analyze the performance of the various text embedding techniques, Neural Network Layered Architecture is designed for movie review's polarity classification to include one input layer and four dense layers. Each of the dense layer is followed by the ReLU (Rectified Linear Unit) activation layers except the last one. The last dense layer is Sigmoid activated to make classifications on the basis of training testing performance. Word2Vec text embedding scored the highest training and testing accuracy among all the text embedding techniques of Binary Term Frequency, Count Vector, Term Frequency - Inverse Document Frequency, and Word2Vec with 89.75% and 86.94% respectively with ± 1.0 *error* for the online movie reviews.

References

1. Li, Y., Yang, T.: Word embedding for understanding natural language: a survey. In: Guide to Big Data Applications, pp. 83–104. Springer, Cham (2018). https://doi.org/10.1007/978-3-319-53817-4_4
2. Mikolov, T., Sutskever, I., Chen, K., Corrado, G.S., Dean, J.: Distributed representations of words and phrases and their compositionality. In: Advances in Neural Information Processing Systems, pp. 3111–3119 (2013)
3. Musto, C., Semeraro, G., De Gemmis, M., Lops, P.: Word embedding techniques for content-based recommender systems: an empirical evaluation. In: Recsys posters
4. Wan, M., Gu, G., Qian, W., Ren, K., Chen, Q., Zhang, H., Maldague, X.: Total variation regularization term-based low-rank and sparse matrix representation model for infrared moving target tracking. Remote Sens. **10**(4), 510 (2018)
5. Khattak, F.K., Jeblee, S., Pou-Prom, C., Abdalla, M., Meaney, C., Rudzicz, F.: A survey of word embeddings for clinical text. J. Biomed. Inform. X, **4**, 100057 (2019)
6. Arora, R., Singh, P., Goyal, H., Singhal, S., Vijayvargiya, S.: Comparative question answering system based on natural language processing and machine learning. In: 2021 International Conference on Artificial Intelligence and Smart Systems (ICAIS), pp. 373–378. IEEE, March 2021
7. Kaplan, A.M., Haenlein, M.: Users of the world, unite! the challenges and opportunities of social media. Bus. Horiz. **53**(1), 59–68 (2010)
8. Ribeiro, F.N., Araújo, M., Gonçalves, P., Gonçalves, M.A., Benevenuto, F.: Sentibench-a benchmark comparison of state-of-the-practice sentiment analysis methods. EPJ Data Sci. **5**(1), 1–29 (2016)
9. Shahmirzadi, O., Lugowski, A., Younge, K.: Text similarity in vector space models: a comparative study. In: 2019 18th IEEE International Conference on Machine Learning and Applications (ICMLA), pp. 659–666. IEEE, December 2019
10. Lebret, R., Collobert, R.: Rehabilitation of count-based models for word vector representations. In: International Conference on Intelligent Text Processing and Computational Linguistics, pp. 417–429. Springer, Cham, April 2015. https://doi.org/10.1007/978-3-319-18111-0_31
11. Yun-tao, Z., Ling, G., Yong-cheng, W.: An improved TF-IDF approach for text classification. J. Zhejiang Univ.-Sci. A, **6**(1), 49–55 (2005)
12. Qaiser, S., Ali, R.: Text mining: use of TF-IDF to examine the relevance of words to documents. Int. J. Comput. Appl. **181**(1), 25–29 (2018)
13. Rezaeinia, S.M., Rahmani, R., Ghodsi, A., Veisi, H.: Sentiment analysis based on improved pre-trained word embeddings. Expert Syst. Appl. **117**, 139–147 (2019)

14. Stein, R.A., Jaques, P.A., Valiati, J.F.: An analysis of hierarchical text classification using word embeddings. Inf. Sci. **471**, 216–232 (2019)
15. Wang, Y., et al.: A comparison of word embeddings for the biomedical natural language processing. J. Biomed. Inform. **87**, 12–20 (2018)
16. Aggarwal, C.C.: Neural networks and deep learning, vol. 10, pp. 978–983. Springer (2018). https://doi.org/10.1007/978-3-319-94463-0
17. Buda, T.S., Caglayan, B., Assem, H.: DeepAD: a generic framework based on deep learning for time series anomaly detection. In: Pacific-Asia Conference on Knowledge Discovery and Data Mining, pp. 577–588. Springer, Cham, June 2018. https://doi.org/10.1007/978-3-319-93034-3_46

Current State of Speech Emotion Dataset-National and International Level

Surbhi Khurana[1]([✉]), Amita Dev[1], and Poonam Bansal[2]

[1] Indira Gandhi Delhi Technical University for Women, Delhi, India
{surbhi001phd20,vc}@igdtuw.ac.in
[2] Maharaja Surajmal Institute of Technology, GGSIPU, Delhi, India

Abstract. Research on emotion extraction from human speech is transitioning from a phase of exploratory study to one with the potential for significant applications, particularly in human–computer interaction. To achieve more accuracy while creating human-computer interaction, the computer system must be provided with good quality data that covers every aspect required for the interaction. The establishment of relevant databases is critical to progress in this area. This research will discuss the scope, naturalness, context, and descriptors of the dataset as the four primary challenges that must be taken care of while constructing databases for emotion embedded speech. Furthermore, the current state of the art is examined to get the status of available datasets for internally spoken languages like English, Dutch, French, and Chinese etc. and for Indian Spoken languages.

Keywords: Speech emotion recognition · Datasets · Context · Scope · Naturalness · International datasets · Indian datasets

1 Introduction

Human speech, par lingual, non verbal and facial expression are mainly the primary ways in which individuals communicate and connect with one another, with speech being the most effective way for exchanging information and thoughts. Speech is a multi-dimensional communication that includes language, speaker, emotion, and message. Understanding the effect of various emotions embedded in speech is critical as the presence of emotions makes communication more usual. If true emotion is included in a speech, human-robot contact can be improved, made more effective, and more natural. Finally, this aids in the artificial intelligence field.

Lie detection systems [1], audio/video retrieval [2], emotional bots , prioritization of customers calls, improvisation of medical tools, intelligent e-learning systems, language translation [3, 4], intelligent virtual games, smart cars, and categorization of voicemail are all examples of how emotion recognition can be utilised to impact human life. Emotion recognition from speech is a great study issue in the realm of voice processing because of these applications.

As demonstrated in Fig. 1, having a voice dataset is critical in the process of recognition emotions from speech. A lot of work has been done on dataset development at both

© Springer Nature Switzerland AG 2022
A. Dev et al. (Eds.): AIST 2021, CCIS 1546, pp. 232–243, 2022.
https://doi.org/10.1007/978-3-030-95711-7_21

the international and national levels. Speech corpora have been generated in a variety of languages, including Chinese, English, Italian, Japanese, Russian, and German. For official Indian languages such as Hindi, Telugu, Assamese, Gujarati, and Malayalam, there are just a few speech databases available. The idea of this swot is to summarize the emotional dataset requirement, as well as development challenges and a comparative analysis of the available dataset for SER systems.

It's crucial to understand the quality of the speech corpus that has been prepared, thus its analysis is on top priority [1]. Speech features are retrieved and analysed as detailed later. At the excitation source parameter, vocal tract structure, and linguistic levels, emotion-specific information is constantly present. Every emotion have its distinct impact on human speech, which can be noticed by evaluating numerous parameters/features such as MFCC [5], pitch, energy, and so on [2]. The structure of this paper is as follows: Sect. 1 states introduction, followed by Sect. 2 for the need of dataset, Sect. 3 describing the pillar for dataset, Sect. 4 for Dataset status at national and international level followed by Issues and then conclusion.

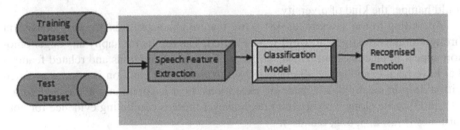

Fig. 1. Structure of SER model

2 Need of Dataset

As depicted in Fig. 1, it can be clearly noted that the emotion recognition from speech is dependent vastly on classification model, extracted speech features and moreover on the selection of good quality database. A sufficient emotional speech database is a requirement of any SER system. It is necessary to dig out speech features from the supplied dataset. Appropriate selection of features is critical since it conveys desired information and determines the system's overall efficiency.

In most cases, three types of features are taken from the database. 1) LP residual, glottal excitation signal, and other properties of the excitation source 2) Features of vocal tracks such as MFCC and LPCC 3) prosodic characteristics such as pitch and formants 4) Features combining above [6].

Extracted features are used to train various classifiers such as Gaussian mixture model and Hidden Markov model, Machine Learning and Deep Learning which will determine the unique mood. Choosing a classifier for process is usually dependent upon experimental outcome. Linear classifiers (Naive Bayes classifier) and nonlinear classifiers are the HMM, GMM, deep learning [7] based classifier.

3 Pillar of Dataset

Research based on speech embedded with emotion is transitioning from a phase of exploratory study to one with the potential for significant applications, particularly in human–computer interaction. When creating a database, four primary pillars must be considered: the scope, naturalness, context and the types of descriptors used. This section explains the above mentioned term along with its significance and related issues while creating a speech emotion recognition corpus.

3.1 Scope

Scope in database can be used to state the diversification of dataset. It includes the number of different speakers in a dataset, as well as the language spoken by the speaker, the speaker's native language, different type of emotional states, and the social/environmental setting. Moreover, not only on the language spoken it is also dependent upon the actor's gender, actor's age. Any attempt to generalize the scope of dataset could hamper the kind of diversity.

According to the assessment, [8] some feature characteristics are very consistent throughout the investigation, while others varied. The results for happy and anger emotion appear to be consistent. However, most of the other emotions and related features that have been examined at all contain discrepancies. Sad emotion is often associated with a drop in mean F0, but there are exceptions. Fear is commonly associated with a hike in F0 value along with speech rate, however there is conflicting evidence for both variables (Figs. 2, 3, 4, 5, 6 and 7).

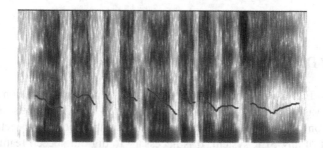

Fig. 2. F0 frequency for sad emotion-206.2 Hz

Some variances could simply be due to changes in process or misleading emotion categories, or among natural, elicitated and simulated data. Moreover, on the other hand, remaining parameters appear to reflect true changes in emotional vocal expression for eg- it varied for different speakers, from culture to culture, age to age, gender to gender and context to situation. Although there are few comparisons between languages and civilizations, they do reveal significant disparities.

Fig. 3. F0 frequency for fear emotion-269.5 Hz

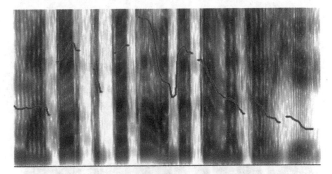

Fig. 4. F0 frequency for anger emotion-294.9 Hz

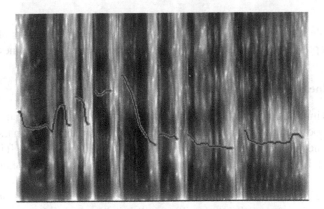

Fig. 5. F0 frequency for neutral emotion-214.6 Hz

Because speaking is primarily a cultural activity, signals of emotion embedded speech may be susceptible to cultural influences. Moreover, instead of expressing only basic emotions with maximum intensity, speech in everyday life tends to communicate intermediate emotional states. These observations show that the emotional breadth

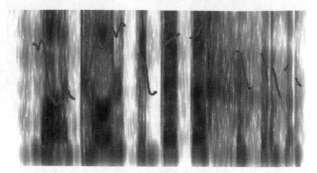

Fig. 6. F0 frequency for happy emotion-290.5 Hz

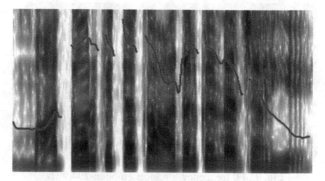

Fig. 7. F0 frequency for surprise emotion-308.8 Hz

of databases should be carefully considered. Because conventional lists of (non-basic) emotions comprise over a hundred words, the scope may need to be somewhat broad.

3.2 Naturalness

Having actors imitate emotional speech is the simplest approach to collect it. The problem with this method is that there is a surprising lack of emotional essence on the connection among performed data and spontaneous, ordinary emotional speech data. It is undeniably accurate that talented performers can produce speech that audiences can dependably categorize.

Acted speech audio is frequently not spoken instead actors read it only, and it is well known that read speech has specific qualities. Moreover, the traditional format is non-interactive, interpersonal consequences are yet not taken into account. Because the context is usually sparse, the spoken sentences do not show the vocal indicators of emotion development and how it fades over time, or how they are related to other parameter of signal.

Naturalness comes at a cost: a lack of control. Emotions are unpredictable, which makes collecting voice samples of speakers in a desired state, either elicited or spontaneous or natural, problematic. Recognizing the expressed emotion becomes a significant difficulty, especially if it is spontaneous. Some applications require data sets that are phonetically balanced, and its complex to envisage obtaining such balance with really natural speech. Bootstrapping, or using other pre verified content to direct is that is genuinely similar to nature, could be a long-term answer to such concerns.

3.3 Context

People use the context of words to establish the emotional meaning of voice qualities, according to direct evidence. As a result, datasets containing knowledge on the way vocal indicators connect to their surroundings are required if model wants to recognize or match human performance. There are three different sorts of contexts.

Semantic context: Emotionally charged words are more likely to appear in genuine emotional discourse. There is a clear possibility of content and vocal indicators interacting.

Structural context: Many indications of emotion, like as stress patterns and default intonation patterns, appear to be defined by syntactic structures. The hypothesis that emotion is signalled through differences in style that are conveyed in structural aspects of the spoken speech utterances is less well-known (length and duration of spoken phrases, total repetitions and gaps or interruptions in samples, etc).

Intermodal context: Humans transmit a great set of emotions over the phone demonstrates that the study based solely on voice is feasible. Speech, on the other hand, is frequently used as a supporting parameter to other sources of emotional information instead of as a standalone feature.

Descriptors and Accessibility.

Building a dataset necessitates the use of tools for describing the emotional and linguistic content of the material along with spoken speech samples on the other end.

Two difficulties stand out in terms of speech descriptors. To begin, coding must take into account the complete set of elements involved in vocal expressions of emotion, that includes supra segmental features like prosody, speech quality and non-linguistic features. Second, it must define the characteristics that are associated with emotion. The decision between continuous variables and categorical descriptors is crucial. The advantages of these different types have yet to be determined. Additional forms of labels (e.g. facial, age, gender, gestural) may be required if databases are multi-modal.

When a database is accessible to the entire speech community, it eliminates the need for duplication of effort, allows algorithms to be compared on the same data, and so on. Format and ethics are two major factors that influence availability.

The data files must be in a standardize and portable format. This is not only necessary for raw material coding formats (such as wav), but also to descriptor coding.

Moreover, copyright and ethical problems, particularly with innate data, are more fundamental. Natural emotional content is frequently highly personal, and speakers may oppose to its widespread dissemination. Radio, you tube, television, conversation shows, documentaries, and other programming, provide vast sources, but accessing them poses major copyright issues. It is evident that creating and characterizing datasets of the type that fit the needs we define is difficult.

4 Dataset Status at National and International Level

This section tries to summarise the current state of emotional speech datasets. Three of the pillars discussed above scope, naturalness and context are used to define different datasets. A generic name is used to identify a dataset. The scope of the project includes a variety of topics, emotions to examine, and the language used that indicate the cultural diversity of the dataset. Naturalness of the dataset is divided into three categories: simulated, elicitated, and natural; whether the content is scripted or not; and content structure (words, sentences or numbers). Elicitated refers to a range of strategies that produce results that fall somewhere between simulation and naturalness. Study also tries to look for any attempt to address the topic of emotional development and change through time, as well as whether the data is audio or multimodal i.e. audio–visual in nature.

Table 1 and Table 2 are used to summarise the status of dataset for International languages and Indic languages resp.

Table 1. Analysis of available speech emotion dataset for internationally spoken languages.

Identifier	Scope			Naturalness			Context
	Subject	Emotion	Spoken language	Dataset type	Scripted dataset	Linguistic structure	Modality
Danish emotional database [9]	4	Anger, Happiness, Neutral, Sadness, Surprise	Danish	Simulated	✔	2 words, 9 sentences and 2 passages	Audio
EMO-DB [10]	10	Anger, Boredom, Disgust, Fear, Happiness, Neutral, Sadness	German	Simulated	✔	500 Utterances	Audio
SAVEE	4	Anger, Boredom, Disgust, Fear, Happiness, Neutral, Surprise	English	Simulated	✔	480 Utterances	Audio-Video
RECOLA [11]	46	Arousal, Agreement, Dominance, Engagement, Performance, Rapport, Valence	French	Natural		3.8/2.9 h Of annotated audio visual/multimodal data	Audio-Visual
SAMAINE	150	Activation, Expectations, Power, Valence	English, Greek	Natural		959 Conversation	Audio

(continued)

Table 1. (*continued*)

Identifier	Scope			Naturalness			Context
	Subject	Emotion	Spoken language	Dataset type	Scripted dataset	Linguistic structure	Modality
eNTERFACE'05 [12]	42	Anger, Disgust, Fear, Happiness, Sadness, Surprise	English, Spanish, and French	Elicited	✔	English utterances-186, Spanish utterances-190, French utterances-175	Audio-Visual
IEMOCAP [13]	10	Anger, Frustration, Happiness, Neutral, Sadness	English	Elicited	✔	5 Sessions with conversation between male and female speaker	Audio-Visual
FAU AIBO [14]	51 German childrens and 30 English childrens	Anger, Boredom, Emphatic, Helpless, Joy, Motherese, Neutral, Reprimanding, Rest, Surprised, Touchy	English, German	Natural		51,393 words in German 5,822 words in English	Audio
BAUM speech dataset [15]	31	Anger, Boredom, Bothered, Contempt, Concentration, Disgust, Fear, Happiness, Interested, Surprise, Sadness, Thoughtful	Turkish	Acted and Natural		1184 Video clips	Audio-Visual
Chinese speech dataset [16]	8	Anger, Fear, Neutral, Happy, Sadness	Chinese	Simulated	✔	2400 Utterances	
Emotional speech database for corpus based synthesis [17]	2	Anger, Disgust, Fear, happiness, Sadness, Surprise, Neutral	Basque	Elicited	✔	702 Sentences per emotion	Audio
TV series ally McBeal [18]	6	Cold anger, Fear, Hot anger, Happy, Sadness, Neutral	English, German, Japanese	Simulated	✔	135 Utterances (45 utterances per language)	Audio–Visual

Table 2. Analysis of available speech emotion dataset for nationally spoken languages.

Identifier	Scope			Naturalness		Context	
	Subject	Emotion	Spoken language	Dataset type	Scripted dataset	Linguistic structure	Mode
IITKGP-SEHSC [19]	10	Anger, Disgust, Fear, Happy, Neutral, Sad, Sarcastic and surprise	Hindi	Simulated	✔	12000 (15 text prompts × 8 emotions × 10 speakers × 10 sessions)	Audio
Malayalam language speech emotional dataset [20]	16	Neutral, Happy, Sad and Anger	Malayalam	Acted	✔	20 sentences	Audio
SUST Bangla emotional speech corpus [21]	20	Anger, Disgust, Fear, Happiness, Neutral, Sadness and Surprise	Bangla	Acted	✔	7000 Utterances (20 speakers × 10 sentences × 5 repetitions × 7 emotions)	Audio
IIIT-H TEMD [22]	19 speakers (12 female and 7 male) Non Actors- 19 speakers (8 female and 11 male)	Anger, Happiness, Sadness, Neutral, and Surprise	Telugu	Natural-Drama speech	✔	5317 Annotated utterances	Audio
Gujarati speech emotional dataset [23]	9 (6 male and 3 Female)	Anger, Sadness, Surprise, Disgust, Fear, Happiness	Gujarati	Acted	✔	24 Different words	Audio
Emotional Hindi speech database [24]	28	Neutral, Happy, Anger, Sad, Sarcastic, Surprise	Hindi	Simulated	✔	6048 Utterances (28 speakers X6 emotions X12 statements X3 repetitions)	Audio

5 Issues

Database plays a vital role while working with any model based upon machine learning and deep learning algorithms. Model parameters like accuracy, precision are moreover, depends upon the quality of dataset used. However, if the model is used for detecting the presence of any specific emotion, the role of database increases drastically. Even not only upon the quality, model result will also vary on the speaker age group, gender of the speaker and the language along with their speaking style. However, during the database review following are the list of issue that researches have faced during database creation.

- The majority of the study on emotion embedded with speech is only supported by datasets instead of on databases. Term dataset are often refers to small compilations of content created to investigate a certain problem and sometime are not publicly available.
- Some of the speech dependent applications require data sets that are phonetically balanced [25], and hence it is challenging to envisage obtaining such balance with really natural speech.
- Naturalness in the database comes at a cost of lack of control. As, emotion is unpredictable, which makes collecting speech samples of actors in a desired state, problematic. Naturalness may interact with the need for proper labeling of emotional content. Acted content can be appropriately defined using category labels like sad, furious, glad, and so on.
- Some variances could simply be due to changes in process or misinterpretation of emotional grouping, or between real, elicitated or simulated data.
- Quality of database varies from speaker to speaker, their culture, speaker gender, age and context to situation, this diversity must be taken care of to reflect the true changes in emotional vocal expression.

6 Conclusion

The aim of the review is to understand the need and significance of dataset in determining emotions accurately using speaker speech samples. This paper emphasis on a comprehensive analysis of notably available speech emotion datasets for internationally spoken languages as well for nationally spoken Indic languages. The dataset used by SER systems must covers all the four aspects of scope, naturalness, context, and accessibility. However, there are still many issues that need to be solved while designing and developing SER dataset. Although much has been done to address the major challenges, there is still much more to be done. Various methods have been created, which address the issues that arise and point to future paths for the development of emotional databases.

References

1. Rao, K.S., Shashidhar, G.K.: Emotion Recognition using Speech Features. Springer, New York (2013). https://doi.org/10.1007/978-1-4614-5143-3
2. Rachman, F.H., Sarno, R., Fatichah, C.: Music emotion classification based on lyrics-audio using corpus based emotion. Int. J. Electr. Comput. Eng. (IJECE) **8**(3), 1720 (2018)
3. Kumari, R., Dev, A., Kumar, A.: An efficient adaptive artificial neural network based text to speech synthesizer for Hindi language. Multimedia Tools Appl. **80**(16), 24669–24695 (2021). https://doi.org/10.1007/s11042-021-10771-w
4. Bhatt, S., Jain, A., Dev, A.: Continuous speech recognition technologies—a review. In: Singh, M., Rafat, Y. (eds.) Recent Developments in Acoustics. LNME, pp. 85–94. Springer, Singapore (2021). https://doi.org/10.1007/978-981-15-5776-7_8
5. Swain, M., Routray, A., Kabisatpathy, P.: Databases, features and classifiers for speech emotion recognition: a review. Int. J. Speech Technol. **21**(1), 93–120 (2018). https://doi.org/10.1007/s10772-018-9491-z

6. Koolagudi, S.K.: Recognition of emotions from speech using excitation source features. Procedia Eng. **38**, 3409–3417 (2012)

7. Bhatt, S., Jain, A., Dev, A.: Feature extraction techniques with analysis of confusing words for speech recognition in the Hindi language. Wirel. Pers. Commun. **118**(4), 3303–3333 (2021). https://doi.org/10.1007/s11277-021-08181-0

8. Cowie, R., et al.: Emotion recognition in human–computer interaction. IEEE Signal Process. Mag. 18, 32–80 (2001)

9. Engberg, I.S., Hansen, A.V., Andersen, O., Dalsgaard, P.: Design, recording and verification of a Danish emotional speech database, pp. 1–4 (1997)

10. Burkhardt, F., Paeschke, A., Rolfes, M., Sendlmeier, W., Weiss, B.: A database of German emotional speech (2005)

11. Ringeval, F., Sonderegger, A., Sauer, J., Lalanne, D.: Introducing the RECOLA multimodal corpus of remote collaborative and affective interaction (2013)

12. Martin, O., Kotsia, I., Macq, B., Pitas, I.: The eNTERFACE' 05 audio-visual emotion database. In: IEEE Conference Publication, no. 1, pp. 2–9 (2019). https://ieeexplore.ieee.org/abstract/document/1623803

13. Busso, C., et al.: IEMOCAP: interactive emotional dyadic motion capture database. Lang. Resour. Eval. **42**(4), 335–359 (2008). https://doi.org/10.1007/s10579-008-9076-6

14. Batliner, A., et al.: You stupid tin box – children interacting with the AIBO robot: a cross-linguistic emotional speech corpus (2004)

15. Zhalehpour, S., Onder, O., Akhtar, Z., Erdem, C.E.: BAUM-1: a spontaneous audio-visual face database of affective and mental states. IEEE Trans. Affect. Comput. **8**(3), 300–313 (2017). https://doi.org/10.1109/TAFFC.2016.2553038

16. Zhang, S., Ching, P., Kong, F.: Automatic recognition of speech signal in Mandarin (2006)

17. Saratxaga, I., Navas, E., Hernáez, I., Luengo, I.: Designing and recording an emotional speech database for corpus based synthesis in Basque. In: Proceedings of the 5th International Conference on Language Resources and Evaluation, LREC 2006, pp. 2126–2129 (2006)

18. Braun, A., Katerbow, M.: Emotions in dubbed speech: an intercultural approach with respect to F0. In: 9th European Conference on Speech Communication and Technology, pp. 521–524 (2005). https://doi.org/10.21437/interspeech.2005-331

19. Koolagudi, S.G., Reddy, R., Yadav, J., Rao, K.S.: IITKGP-SEHSC : Hindi speech corpus for emotion analysis. In: 2011 International Conference on Devices and Communications, ICDeCom 2011 - Proceedings, pp. 1–5 (2011). https://doi.org/10.1109/ICDECOM.2011.5738540

20. Rajisha, T.M., Sunija, A.P., Riyas, K.S.: Performance analysis of Malayalam language speech emotion recognition system using ANN/SVM. Procedia Technol. **24**, 1097–1104 (2016). https://doi.org/10.1016/j.protcy.2016.05.242

21. Sultana, S., Rahman, M.S., Selim, M. R., Iqbal, M.Z.: SUST Bangla emotional speech corpus (SUBESCO): an audio-only emotional speech corpus for Bangla. PLoS One **16**(4) 1–27 (2021). https://doi.org/10.1371/journal.pone.0250173

22. Rambabu, B., Kumar, B.K., Gangamohan, P., Gangashetty, S.V.: IIIT-H TEMD semi-natural emotional speech database from professional actors and non-actors. In: LREC 2020 - 12th International Conference on Language Resources and Evaluation, Conference Proceedings, pp. 1538–1545, May 2020

23. Tank, V.P., Hadia, S.K.: Creation of speech corpus for emotion analysis in Gujarati language and its evaluation by various speech parameters. Int. J. Electr. Comput. Eng. **10**(5), 4752–4758 (2020). https://doi.org/10.11591/ijece.v10i5.pp4752-4758

24. Bansal, S., Dev, A.: Emotional Hindi speech database. In: 2013 International Conference Oriental COCOSDA Held Jointly with 2013 Conference on Asian Spoken Language Research and Evaluation, O-COCOSDA/CASLRE 2013, pp. 5–8 (2013). https://doi.org/10.1109/ICSDA.2013.6709867

25. Kumari, R., Dev, A., Kumar, A.: Automatic segmentation of Hindi speech into syllable-like units. Int. J. Adv. Comput. Sci. Appl. **11**(5), 400–406 (2020). https://doi.org/10.14569/IJACSA.2020.0110553

Context-Aware Emoji Prediction Using Deep Learning

Anushka Gupta[1]($\boxtimes$), Bhumika Bhatia[1], Diksha Chugh[1]($\boxtimes$),
Gadde Satya Sai Naga Himabindu[1], Divyashikha Sethia[1], Ekansh Agarwal[2],
Depanshu Sani[2], and Saurabh Garg[2]

[1] Delhi Technological University, Delhi 110042, India
divyashikha@dtu.ac.in
[2] Samsung Research Institute, Noida, India
{e.agarwal,d.sani,saurabh.garg}@samsung.com

Abstract. Emojis are a succinct and visual way to express feelings, emotions, and thoughts during text conversations. Owing to the increase in the use of social media, the usage of emojis has increased drastically. There are various techniques for automating emoji prediction, which use contextual information, temporal information, and user-based features. However, the problem of personalised and dynamic recommendations of emojis persists. This paper proposes personalised emoji recommendations using the time and location parameters. It presents a new annotated conversational dataset and investigates the impact of time and location for emoji prediction. The methodology comprises a hybrid model that uses neural networks and score-based metrics: semantic and cosine similarity. Our approach differs from existing studies and improves the accuracy of emoji prediction up to 73.32% using BERT.

Keywords: NLP · Emoji prediction · BERT

1 Introduction

The usage of emoticons or emojis has grown after the increasing usage in social media platforms and smart mobile devices. Their use becomes significant during the exchange of electronic messages as emojis can demonstrate or highlight a particular emotion. A vast population uses emojis in text messages daily. With the number of total emojis increasing to thousands, the task of emoji prediction has come to light in recent years. The motivation behind this paper is to aid users by recommending them the most appropriate emojis and providing them ease of access when using messaging platforms. It can provide more personalised recommendations based on the user's context, where context is the message's location, time, and content. Researchers find the task of emoji prediction not only essential but also challenging. Studies for emoji prediction mainly focus on using some text as input [3].Some researchers [1] use captions from social media for training. Although emoji usage is prevalent on social media platforms, it has become more relevant in messaging. They highlight emotions or sentiments and determine the

A. Dev et al. (Eds.): AIST 2021, CCIS 1546, pp. 244–254, 2022.
https://doi.org/10.1007/978-3-030-95711-7_22

tone of the message. Moreover, most papers focus on using text- based features that do not employ the user's time and location. User-specific features can provide more insights for personalised recommendations, as these affect a person's environment, which impacts emoji usage. The combination of the different parameters can help create a hybrid approach for emoji prediction. This paper presents a novel approach toward emoji prediction, with the following contributions:

- A dataset that contains conversational text messages and annotated values for time, location, and sentiment
- A novel method that uses time, location, and text together for emoji prediction
- A hybrid model that produces output using three different channels for emoji prediction

The rest of the paper comprises Sect. 2, which explains the related work, followed by a detailed description of the methodology in Sect. 3. Section 4 provides the results. Section 5 discusses the limitations of the work. Finally, in Sect. 6, we conclude the paper and state the future work.

2 Related Work

Prior studies have focused on extracting meaningful data from text inputs for emoji prediction. Some researchers, such as [4], explore the usage of labels for emoji prediction, wherein they assign a value to essential words in sentences through an attention mechanism. Bi-LSTM (Bidirectional Long Short-Term Memory), FastText, and Deepmoji models assign labels and weights to different parts of the text for estimating probabilities used for emoji prediction. Some studies use neural networks for emoji prediction on a Twitter dataset [12]. LSTM (Long Short-Term Memory) and CNN (Convolutional Neural Networks) outperform models in the comparative studies. Although these models provide promising results, there is a need for identifying more heuristic approaches.

For further advancement in emoji prediction, many papers explore more parameters to predict emoji, in addition to text. [5] focus on categorising emoji labels using text and image data to train semantic embeddings. The authors conduct a comparative study to compare predictions using only text input, visual data input, and its fusion. The results of this hybrid model indicate that multiple features and text can help in efficient emoji prediction.

Similarly, [1] combine visual and textual information for Instagram posts. The images uploaded in the posts give visual information, and the captions give textual information. Their results indicate that combining these two synergistic approaches in a single model improves the accuracy.

More features to predict emojis are presented by [2]. The authors conduct a study on the variation of emoji usage across different seasons. The paper uses a Twitter dataset with four subsets depending on the season at the time of posting. The four divisions are Spring, Summer, Autumn, and Winter. The LSTM model highlights the dependence of some emojis on the time of year. [11] propose a fusion of contextual and personal features. Contextual features from the text message and additional features such as user preference, gender, and current time give emoji predictions in a more personalised manner using a score-ranking matrix factorisation framework.

Some studies [10] focus on multi-turn dialogue systems for emoji prediction, and the dataset used is the Weibo2015 dialogues in Chinese. A novel model called H-LSTM (Hierarchical Long Short-Term Memory) is used to extract the meaning of sentences and then predict a suitable emoji for the reply. Hence, the authors demonstrate that predicting an emoji based on contextual information extracted from the messages gives better results. [9, 11] focus on predicting emojis influenced by user personality during message conversations. Test scenarios presented to users in a survey helped to get their preferences of emojis. The results show that personality features impact the emoji predicted.

Previous research work [12] uses datasets from online social media platforms for emoji use. However, it does not consider the conversational aspect in datasets and the usage dependency on the sentiment of message, exact word mapping, and semantic similarity. Emojis are more prevalent on messaging platforms, and to the best of our knowledge, no study has focused on using conversational data for emoji prediction. Hence, we propose an approach that addresses the conversational dataset issue. We use the time and location of text messages in predicting emojis as these impact the tone of the message. They help in emoji prediction by extracting the sentiment of the text message.

3 Methodology

3.1 Data Collection

This paper presents a novel dataset consisting of conversational text messages. Along with text messages, the dataset also includes the user's location and time because it impacts the context of the message. The model annotates data using 14 annotators from different backgrounds and regions to account for the variation in emoji usage from person to person. The model further determines the annotation for the location and time using the context of the conversation and the annotator's knowledge/perception of human nature and social presence.

3.2 Data Description

Every data instance is associated with one of the 15 sentiment classes. This work combines chat data from publicly available sources and manually annotates time, location, and sentiment values.

The time attribute in the dataset has the time for the text message in the 24-h notation. The location attribute contains one of the six generic classes.

– Home, Work, Trip, School/College, Frequently Visited Places, and Car. These locations were chosen as these broadly cover the most common places of visit.

Sentiment Classes: Furthermore, through these three input parameters, the model outputs one of 15 sentiment classes, which maps one relevant emoji as output. To determine the 15 sentiment classes, we have accounted for the prominent sentiments generally associated with messages and grouped 3–6 similar emojis associated with that sentiment class. The model groups similar emojis based on the following factors:

Table 1. Emojis and their corresponding sentiment classes.

Emojis	Sentiment Class
	Laughing
	Thinking
	Sad
	Shocked
	Hearts
	Sleepy
	Agree
	Gratitude
	Happy Party
	Relishing
	Amazed
	Angry
	Neutral-Skeptical
	Tease

- **Interchangeability:** They can be used in place of each other as they represent a similar semantic meaning
- **User preference:** A user may have their preference of emoji within a particular class for representation of a particular sentiment
- **Typical usage:** After analysing the most commonly used emojis, this work gathered the top 40 most frequently used emojis.

Table 1 illustrates the 15 sentiment classes and their associated emojis. Since the determination of the perfect emoji is subject to human annotation and each user's preference, grouping similar emojis into a sentiment class helps us determine the overall purpose or sentiment associated with a message.

3.3 Pre-processing

Standard Preprocessing: We use the three parameters: message, time, and location as our input. For the time attribute, we convert it to two-time intervals: Day and Night. Time instances between 6:00 and 18:00 come under the Day class, and the rest of the time intervals fall under the Night class. For textual data, which uses the message attribute, we make use of a standard preprocessing technique by applying the following techniques:

- Lowercasing
- Removed punctuation
- Lemmatisation
- Stopword Removal

Lemmatisation reduces the word to its base form while considering the context. We use the WordNet Lemmatizer, an extensive lexical database in English, trained on WordNet, which helps identify semantic correlations between words. The model also uses stopword removal to discard common English words or words that do not have significance.

Up Sampling: Due to the wide variety of conversations, some standard emojis have more usage than others. After analysing the dataset, some classes such as Sleepy, Relishing, and Party have comparatively less usage.

The model applies data augmentation on the message attribute from the Spacy module to increase the dataset size from around 7800 instances to approximately 12928 instances to balance the dataset. Data augmentation removes the bias due to the uneven distribution of target classes to increase the instances of certain classes with relatively very few data points. It further uses a synonym dictionary from the NLTK (Natural Language Toolkit) Spacy WordNet module to achieve this. The model replaces adjectives and verbs in the messages with synonyms to form different texts with similar contexts.

3.4 Model Architecture

This paper presents a novel method for emoji prediction using a hybrid algorithm by combining a deep learning model that uses the text, time, and location and two different algorithms which employ NLP-based techniques to map emojis to input text. The hybrid model consists of three channels, as shown in Fig. 1.

Cosine Similarity algorithm uses an emoji dictionary consisting of 1700 emojis along with their description. This algorithm takes the text message as input and tokenises the text to extract unique words. Then it computes the cosine similarity between words and names of the emojis. The cosine similarity value produced from the following equation measures the degree of similarity between the two.

$$cosinesimilarity(cos\theta) = (A.B)/|A||B| \tag{1}$$

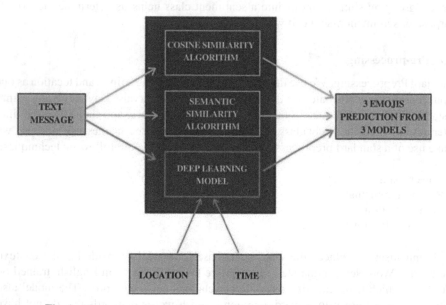

Fig. 1. Three channels used in the model architecture for Emoji Prediction

Here, A and B are the vector representations of the two texts – text message and names of emojis.

The cosine similarity metric maps the tokens from the input message with the tokens present in the name of an emoji in the emoji dictionary. The threshold value is set to 1 for emoji output to ensure that the word in the input message matches the emoji name in the dictionary. As shown in Table 2., the algorithm first cleans the text to remove stopwords for the message "The boy forgot luggage in the train." After the removal of stopwords, the text is "boy forgot luggage train." The algorithm then calculates similarity for every word and predicts an emoji.

This example correctly predicts the words 'train', 'boy', 'luggage' in the text message. However, for the word- 'forgot', the prediction is inaccurate. The emoji prediction depends on the similarity between the words in the text and the emoji description. Hence, the model sets the threshold as 1 and outputs emojis only when an exact mapping occurs.

Table 2. Emoji output for cosine similarity algorithm.

Word	Emoji	Cosine Similarity Score
Boy		1.00000
Frog		0.88388
Luggage		1.00000
Train		1.00000

Semantic Similarity algorithm maps emojis to sentences by estimating the similarity between the input text message and names of the emoji in the emoji dictionary that contains 1700 emojis by converting them into vectors and then evaluating the similarity between their vector representations. This value is between 0 and 1. The emoji corresponding to the emoji name with the highest similarity is the output for this channel. Both the Semantic Similarity algorithm and Cosine similarity algorithm use text message and NLP-based metrics for emoji prediction.

Deep Learning Model uses a supervised machine learning-based approach for emoji prediction. There are three parameters for training - text message, location, and time, along with 15 different sentiment classes, each corresponding to a set of emojis. Hence, this channel uses text messages, location, and time to predict one class out of the 15 classes.

Long Short-Term Memory (LSTM) [7] is a deep learning model that can process sequential data due to its architecture containing gates for the flow of information and a cell for remembering data points. This model is beneficial for NLP tasks as it can remember the sequence of data which is crucial for language-based models. For this study, we use LSTM Model for training an emoji classification model as LSTM can extract the context of the text message. Feasibility-wise, the use of both textual features and numerical features for classification is possible with the LSTM model.

Bidirectional Encoder Representation from Transformers (BERT) [6] is a pre- trained model based on the Transformer architecture [8] and trained for NLP tasks. This model is powerful for NLP tasks and has given remarkable results, especially for text classification. Unlike other word representations, it takes the context of the sentence into account while training, due to which it can get the semantic meaning of the sentence. We use the BERT-small model and fine-tune the hyperparameters for our task. We modify the architecture slightly to take both textual and numerical features (time and location) for emoji prediction.

To develop a model that predicts emoji based on text message, location, and time, we divide the input for the deep learning model into two types of input:

- *NLP Input:* This part contains the tokenised vector representations of the text message input.
- *Meta Input:* This contains the numerical data that comprises the one-hot encoded values of location and time.

The pre-trained small-bert-uncased model (4 layers, 512 Hidden layers, 8 activation) uses these two inputs, as shown in Fig. 2 for training. The model feeds the NLP input into an embedding layer, which it concatenates with the meta input. It then adds and finally applies a dropout of 0.1 followed by the Softmax activation function in the last layer for classification. The model has been trained for 20 epochs with an initial learning rate of 3e–5, using Adam optimizer. For the final output, the model predicts the top 2–3 emojis. It then combines the outputs from the Deep Learning Model (sentiment), Cosine Similarity, and the Sentiment Similarity for the prediction.

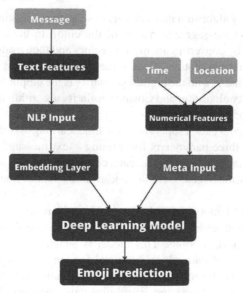

Fig. 2. Deep learning model architecture

4 Result

4.1 Quantitative Analysis

This section presents a comparative analysis to assess the results of the model from a quantitative perspective. Table 3.. presents the testing accuracy of BERT and LSTM models, using the parameters text message, time, and location. It shows that the pre-trained BERT Model gave the best results in comparison to LSTM.

Cosine and Semantic similarity algorithms are also applied, which are score- based approaches whose performance cannot be measured quantitatively for comparison due to their subjective nature. The purpose of including these two algorithms is to increase the usability of the model. Previous research work [9] lacks the incorporation of Semantic and Cosine similarity algorithms for emoji prediction, to the best of our knowledge.

Table 3. Testing accuracies of models for sentiment class.

Model	Text message	Text message, Time and location
BERT	72.99	73.32
LSTM	66.66	69.06

Although quantitative results for these algorithms are difficult to comprehend, we present their results in qualitative analysis.

4.2 Qualitative Analysis

To evaluate the performance of our work qualitatively, we consider various examples. For each input message, we output a combination of emojis from three channels. Each channel holds its significance, as a user may choose a sentiment- based emoji or an emoji representing a word in the message. We consider different situations corresponding to different times and locations and then analyse the emoji predictions for these instances as shown in Table 4. The sentences taken as examples are generic situations, and location and time values are chosen accordingly for each situation. As some emojis are time and location-specific, our usage of these features is novel for emoji prediction.

The results obtained for the LSTM model are relatively acceptable since the emojis predicted can be observed to be dependent on time and location. E.g., in this message, for the 'Night' location at 'Home,' a sleepy emoji is predicted, which is appropriate considering the user is likely to be sleepy at night if working at home. On the other hand, if the location is 'Work' and time is 'Day', then a thinking face emoji is predicted that indicates that the user is contemplating about work. However, from the table, it can be seen that predictions from the BERT model are not time and location-sensitive.

Hence, for the same message and different times and locations, the predictions are more satisfactory for the LSTM model. In addition to the LSTM and BERT model that uses the context, namely message, time, and location for emoji prediction, Cosine

Table 4. Examples of emoji prediction using three channels and impact of time and location on emoji prediction.

Text Message	Time	Location	LSTM Output	BERT Output	Semantic Similarity Output	Cosine Similarity Output
I have a lot of work	Night	Home	😔	😟	👍	-
I have a lot of work	Night	Work	😄	😟	👍	-
I have a lot of work	Day	Work	😣	😟	👍	-
I love your red dress	Night	Home	❤️	❤️	👗	-
I wanna have pizza	Night	Trip	🍕	🍕	🍕	-
Come fast an ambulance is needed	Day	Home	😟	😕	⏩	🚑
I would like to play basketball	Day	School/College	❤️	🙂	🏐	🏀

and Semantic algorithms compute using only the message attribute. While Semantic similarity gives good results, Cosine similarity predicts an emoji only when the Cosine similarity value is one. Hence, we observe an emoji prediction output for the Cosine similarity algorithm for messages with explicit mention of emoji names like 'ambulance' and 'basketball.'

From our observations, not every event can be correlated or dependent on a time and location. However, in most cases, it can aid in providing more suitable recommendations.

5 Limitations

The methods for emoji prediction presented in this paper use different parameters for which data is not publicly available. Hence, we developed the dataset by combining several conversational datasets and manually annotating the attribute's values: time, location, and sentiment class. The dataset posed a challenge due to manual annotation.

Due to the smaller dataset size, the number of emojis in each Sentiment class for the deep learning model is relatively small. There are over 3000 emojis, and this number keeps increasing as new emojis are developed and added to the existing dictionary. Although the two algorithms predict from a total of 1700 emojis, in comparison, our deep learning model predicts from a minimal list of emojis.

The accuracy for emoji prediction can be improved if the dataset size increases because NLP tasks require extensive data to yield good results. The distribution of Sentiment classes in the dataset is not uniform due to the small size and manual annotation, as shown in Fig. 3.

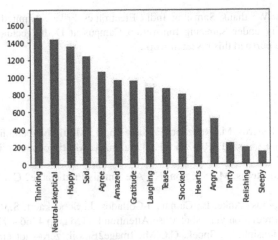

Fig. 3. Distribution of sentiment classes

This work comprises manual annotation of the dataset, and usage of emojis is very subjective; determining the most appropriate emoji class recommendation depends on the annotator's choice. It may lead to differences based on the annotator's culture, regional usage of emojis, and personal preference and understanding.

6   Conclusion and Future Work

There is a lack of extensive research focusing on conversational or chat-based data, which uses the attributes of time and location. Previous studies [5] in emoji prediction mainly focus on datasets taken from social media posts. This work presents a novel approach towards emoji prediction by using a conversational dataset. We develop our dataset and manually annotate the attributes in the dataset. It uses a novel model for emoji prediction that uses a hybrid approach by combining three different channels for emoji prediction.

The qualitative analysis shows that the emoji predictions using the three channels gave satisfactory results. The three emojis predicted for a particular text message, location, and time input choose emojis using the semantic similarity score, cosine similarity score, and the deep learning model. The quantitative results show that the pre-trained BERT deep learning model gave the best accuracy compared to the LSTM model.

There is much scope for improvement in the field of emoji prediction. We can combine different parameters for this task. We can use the Location attribute by creating a dictionary that maps location-specific keywords in the text message to the corresponding emojis. We can train the model on that dataset to get more location-specific emoji recommendations. Further expansion through a user-centric approach [9] can predict emojis by learning user preferences and predicting one emoji from the sentiment class based on the user's history and personal preference. Based on the scenario, different types of conversations can use different emojis in a Sentiment class, such as formal and informal conversations.

Acknowledgments. We thank Samsung India Electronics Private Limited for providing the Research Lab facility under Samsung Innovation Campus at Delhi Technological University (DTU), in which we pursued this research work.

References

1. Barbieri, F., Ballesteros, M., Ronzano, F., Saggion, H.: Multimodal emoji prediction (2018)
2. Barbieri, F., Ballesteros, M., Ronzano, F., Saggion, H.: Multimodal emoji prediction. CoRR abs/1803.02392 (2018)
3. Barbieri, F., Ballesteros, M., Saggion, H.: Are Emojis Predictable? CoRR abs/1702.07285 (2017)
4. Barbieri, F., Espinosa-Anke, L., Camacho-Collados, J., Schockaert, S., Saggion, H.: Interpretable Emoji Prediction via Label-Wise Attention LSTMs, pp 4766–4771 (2018)
5. Cappallo, S., Mensink, T., Snoek, C.G.M.: Image2Emoji: zero-shot emoji prediction for visual media. In: Proceedings of the 23rd ACM International Conference on Multimedia. Association for Computing Machinery, New York, pp 1311–1314 (2015)
6. Devlin, J., Chang, M-W., Lee, K., Toutanova, K.: BERT: Pre-training of Deep Bidirectional Transformers for Language Understanding. CoRR abs/1810.04805 (2018)
7. Hochreiter, S., Schmidhuber, J.: Long short-term memory. Neural Comput **9**, 1735–1780 (1997). https://doi.org/10.1162/neco.1997.9.8.1735
8. Vaswani, A., et al.: Attention is All you Need. ArXiv abs/1706.03762 (2017)
9. Völkel, S.T., Buschek, D., Pranjic, J., Hussmann, H.: Understanding emoji interpretation through user personality and message context. In: Proceedings of the 21st International Conference on Human-Computer Interaction with Mobile Devices and Services. Association for Computing Machinery, New York (2019)
10. Xie, R., Liu, Z., Yan, R., Sun, M.: Neural Emoji Recommendation in Dialogue Systems. CoRR abs/1612.04609 (2016)
11. Zhao, G., Liu, Z., Chao, Y., Qian, X.: CAPER: Context-Aware Personalized Emoji Recommendation. IEEE Trans. Knowl. Data Eng. 1 (2020). https://doi.org/10.1109/TKDE.2020.296 6971
12. Zhao, L., Zeng, C.: Using neural networks to predict emoji usage from twitter data (2017)

Development of ManiTo: A Manipuri Tonal Contrast Dataset

Thiyam Susma Devi$^{(\boxtimes)}$ and Pradip K. Das

Indian Institute of Technology Guwahati, North Guwahati, Assam, India
{thiyam.devi,pkdas}@iitg.ac.in

Abstract. Tone recognition plays a vital role in understanding speech for tonal languages. Integrating tonal information from a robust tone recognition system can improve the performance of Automatic Speech Recognition (ASR) for such languages. The tonal recognition approaches adopted so far have focused on Asian, African and Indo-European languages. In India, there are very few works on tonal languages, especially those spoken in its North-Eastern part, from which the Manipuri language is largely unexplored. This paper presents the development of a Tonal Contrast dataset for Manipuri, a low resource language. It also presents an initial analysis of the recorded data.

Keywords: Tonal contrast · Speech recognition · Low resource languages

1 Introduction

Humans use a system of communication called speech using a language, which consists of sounds, words and grammar. English, Hindi, French and most European languages' words comprise of a sequence of distinctive units known as phonemes. However, several languages in the world are tonal, as Yip [21] points out. Tonal languages use tones to determine the meaning of the speech units.

As these languages are spoken by limited people, many languages have become extinct. Here, technology plays a crucial role in stopping the extinction by providing the techniques of Natural Language Processing (NLP) and the Automatic Speech Recognition (ASR) for these languages of the world. ASR is also needed for fostering economic growth and prosperity. For more flexibility and to have human-machine interaction, ASR system for tonal languages is required. Several tone recognition techniques have been developed for various tonal languages [20] such as Mandarin, Thai, Vietnamese, Punjabi, Yoruba, etc. However, it is found that no work has been done on automatic tone recognition of the Manipuri tonal language.

1.1 Manipuri

Manipuri, also known as Meiteilon/Meiteiron, is one of the scheduled Indian Tibeto-Burman language spoken predominantly in Manipur, a northeastern state

A. Dev et al. (Eds.): AIST 2021, CCIS 1546, pp. 255–263, 2022.
https://doi.org/10.1007/978-3-030-95711-7_23

of India. Some people of Indian states, such as Assam, Mizoram and Tripura, and other countries like Bangladesh and Myanmar, also speak Manipuri. It is the official language of Manipur, which is spoken by over 1.5 million speakers. In Manipur, among 29 different ethnic groups, Manipuri is the only medium of communication [13]. Manipuri is a tonal language in which the tone distinguish the meaning of words. For speech recognition and pronunciation evaluation, the identification of tone in Manipuri is essential.

Manipuri has its own script, which is known as Meitei/Meetei Mayek script. The Meitei Mayek Script has 27 Mapung Mayek (main alphabets). There are 8 Lonsum Mayek (unreleased characters), 8 Cheitap Mayek (vowel signs), 3 Khudam Mayek (punctuation marks including diacritics) and Cheising Mayek for the numericals [3, 11].

1.2   Tones in Manipuri

Using pitch in a language to distinguish lexical or grammatical meaning is known as tone [2]. As mentioned before, Manipuri is a tone language [17]. It has a lexically significant, contrastive, but relative pitch on each syllable. There are two tones in Manipuri [6, 9, 11, 15, 19]:

1. A level tone: unmarked
2. A falling tone: marked by lum mayek, "."

Every syllable in Manipuri carries one of the two tones. The pitch (frequency) of level tone is lower than the pitch of the falling tone; thus, some authors (e.g., Chelliah 1997 [5]) have termed the level and falling tones low and high, respectively [19]. The level tone is unmarked while the falling tone marked as /`/ in English representation. Furthermore, the lum mayek or the falling tone mark, "." is represented in Manipuri script just after the syllable, which carries the falling tone.

2   Related Works

In the international scenario, intensive research is done in tonal language speech recognition in the last three decades. Peng et al. (2021) [14] proposed a Multi-Scale model that gathers the information at multiple resolutions capturing the attributes of tone variation. The experiment is performed on the dataset, Chinese National Hi-Tech Project 863. Their model achieve tone error rate (TER) of 10.5%. Hao et al. (2019) proposed a framework based on deep neural networks for Mandarin tone recognition. The model use both the prosodic and the articulatory features as the raw input data. A 5-layer-deep belief network is employed to generate high-level tone feature. The 863-data corpus is used for the experiment and achieved an average tone recognition rate of 83.03% accuracy. Nguyen et al. (2016) [16] investigated the effect of tone in the Vietnamese Large Vocabulary Continuous Speech Recognition System and built an acoustic model using the tonal feature. The experimental result obtained 19.25% improvement over the non-tonal phoneme system.

In India for the language Manipuri, Thoudam (1980) [15] doctoral thesis has devoted a chapter on Manipuri phonology. He suggested that there were only two distinctive tones in Manipuri, namely, falling tone and level tone. Mahabir (1982) [4] argued for two tones, falling and level in his master's thesis. Chelliah (1990) [18] studied the level ordered morphology and phonology in Manipuri and presented several phonological rules. Chelliah (1997) [5] explained the tone system in Manipuri. She presented a framework that correctly described that Manipuri exhibits a two-way tonal contrast, low tone and a default high tone. The fundamental frequency contours were used as the phonetic representations of the underlying tone pattern in the experiment. Meiraba (2014) [12] claimed that the tone bearing unit in Manipuri is the Rhyme of the syllable. The relative simplicity of the tone system of Manipuri is due to its rich consonantal inventory which can occur at the Coda position and that the realisation of tonal contrast can be affected by the Coda consonants.

3 Motivation

After exhaustive search it is found that there are limited tonal languages (Mizo, Punjabi, Singpho, Manipuri, etc.) in India and virtually no datasets are available for tonal analysis. It is also evident that there is a critical need to develop speech dataset of tonal contrast pairs to study the characteristic of the tonal variation leading to the understanding of distinct words for the language. This motivates us to develop a tonal contrast word pair for the Manipuri language and study the tone information present in it for developing robust ASR systems for Manipuri.

4 Creation of Tonal Contrast Word Pair Corpus

Fifty pairs of Manipuri tonal contrast words are collected from different sources [6,8,12,15,19]. The words are listed below in Fig. 2 with their respective meanings.

The data is collected from six people: three males and three females, age range of the speakers is from 21 to 45. All of them are native speakers, out of which three of them (two male and one female) are working in the Linguistic Department of Manipur University, Imphal and their recording is done in the Audio, Visual, Language and Phonetic Laboratory Complex of Manipur University. The remaining three native local speakers' recording is done in a quite office environment. A total of 50 tonal contrast words, five instances of each pair with some pause between the speech sounds, are recorded separately for each person. The steps of creating the dataset is shown in Fig. 1. The Cool Edit 2000 tool is used for recording the utterances. While recording, the following three parameters have been set in Cool Edit 2000.

Sampling Rate: It is the number of samples per second to be captured by the microphone into the system. Sampling rate is set to 44,100 Hz.

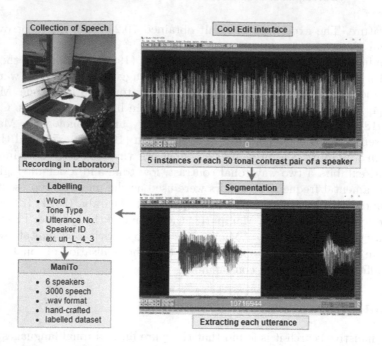

Fig. 1. Creation of ManiTo dataset.

Channel: Mono channel is selected. In mono, all audio signals are routed through a single audio channel.

Resolution: Each sample is represented using 16 bits.

4.1   Preprocessing

The recorded speech sounds are further analyzed and segmented manually, with about 1000 samples of silence at the beginning and end of each word and saved in a .wav format, where each wav file has been named by using word name, tone detail 'f' for falling and 'L' for level, instance number and speaker ID.

For example, un_f_2_1.wav

Word: un   Tone: falling   Instance: 2   Speaker ID: 1

The corpus, ManiTo consists of 3,000 hand-crafted labeled speech data of size 273 MB. The recordings are carefully double checked and stored.

5   Experimental Analysis

Praat [1] is a tool that can analyze, synthesize, and manipulate speech data. Praat version 6.1.51 is used for the experiment. From the developed dataset, the speech sample are analyzed using Praat. In tone analysis, features that reflect the pitch contour are lexically significant. The fundamental frequency, F0, acts as an indication for tone. For the preliminary study on ManiTo dataset, the

Sl. No.	Falling Tone	Meaning	Level Tone	Meaning
1	/ùn/	skin	/un/	ice, snow
2	/in/	push	/in/	follow
3	/tʰòŋ/	door	/tʰoŋ/	bridge
4	/mì/	man	/mi/	spider
5	/pùbə/	to borrow	/pubə/	to bring
6	/cà/	wax	/ca/	tea
7	/ì/	blood	/i/	thatch
8	/kʰòi/	navel	/kʰoi/	bee/fishing hook
9	/là/	wide basket	/la/	banana leaf
10	/sìŋ/	firewood	/siŋ/	ginger
11	/sə̀m/	hair	/səm/	basket
12	/mə̀ŋ/	dream	/məŋ/	grave
13	/kàŋ/	mosquito	/kaŋ/	manipuri game
14	/tìn/	worm	/tin/	saliva
15	/pì/	give	/pi/	tear
16	/kʰòŋ/	leg	/kʰoŋ/	canal
17	/kə̀nbə/	hard	/kənbə/	to protect
18	/tàbə/	to hear	/tabə/	to fall
19	/càbə/	eating	/cabə/	to hang around
20	/kə̀mbə/	killing	/kəmbə/	over ripen
21	/lèŋbə/	movement	/leŋbə/	making rows
22	/asə̀ŋbə/	to dye	/asəŋbə/	green
23	/kàbə/	to climb	/kabə/	burnt
24	/tòŋbə/	raised platform	/toŋbə/	riding
25	/tùmbə/	to sleep	/tumbə/	diluted
26	/lùbə/	clear	/lubə/	difficult
27	/sàbə/	to make	/sabə/	hot
28	/laùbə/	to shout	/laubə/	large hole
29	/kàwbə/	to kick	/kawbə/	to forget
30	/haìbə/	to say	/haibə/	to swing
31	/kə̀ubə/	short	/kəubə/	to call
32	/lòŋ/	spear	/loŋ/	fishing net
33	/pàbə/	thin	/pabə/	to read
34	/tùbə/	tailoring	/tubə/	fall
35	/sìbə/	to break down	/sibə/	death
36	/soìbə/	mistake	/soibə/	cut
37	/làbə/	roam	/labə/	male
38	/lànbə/	to cross	/lanbə/	wrong
39	/koìbə/	to travel	/koibə/	not shortcut
40	/lùmbə/	heavy	/lumbə/	warm
41	/sònbə/	weak	/sonbə/	to chant
42	/cʰənìŋ/	weight measuring unit	/cʰəniŋ/	lower abdomen
43	/sùbə/	wash	/subə/	hammering
44	/mùbə/	roast	/mubə/	black
45	/paìbə/	touch	/paibə/	fly
46	/pùŋ/	drum	/puŋ/	hour
47	/kə̀i/	granany	/kəi/	tiger
48	/hùi/	dog	/hui/	rivet
49	/là i/	flower	/ləi/	tongue
50	/pè/	grimace	/pe/	umbrella

Fig. 2. List of Manipuri tonal contrast word Pairs with their respective meanings.

pitch or F0 is extracted using Praat. Praat use the most accurate pitch analysis algorithm [7]. Figure 3 shows the analysis of falling tone "un" sound. The blue line is the pitch listing of the speech. Similarly, Fig. 4 shows the analysis of level tone "un" sound. From the two figures we can notice that the pitch of the level tone is lower than that of falling tone. Figure 5 shows the graph comparing the five utterances tonal contrast Pair1, "un" spoken by Speaker1. Figure 5a plots the pitch listing of falling tone, Fig. 5b plots the pitch listing of level tone, Fig. 5c is the normalisation of falling tone, Fig. 5d is the normalisation of level tone and Fig. 5e shows the comparison of average pitch listing of falling versus level tone. From the graph we can initially infer that the pitch of the falling tone is higher than that of level tone. Using parselmouth [10], a python library for the Praat software, mean F0, harmonics-to-noise-ratio(HNR), jitter, shimmer information are extracted and analysis is being conducted on this features to distinguish the tones accurately.

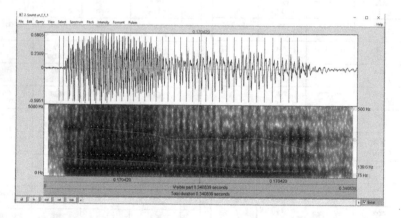

Fig. 3. Waveform and spectrogram with overlaid pitch contour of falling tone "un" sound.

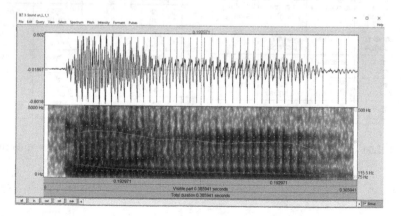

Fig. 4. Waveform and spectrogram with overlaid pitch contour of level tone "un" sound.

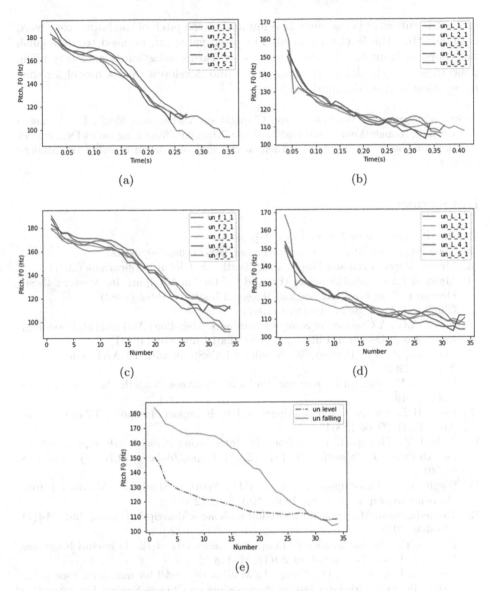

Fig. 5. Pitch contour of (a) "un" five utterances (falling tone) (b) "un" five utterances (level tone) (c) normalise pitch "un" (falling) (d) normalise pitch "un" (level) (e) average pitch comparison of level and falling tone.

6   Conclusion and Future Work

A speech dataset containing tonal contrast pair of the Manipuri language is being created. ManiTo containing 3,000 samples of Manipuri tonal contrast words is developed from data collected from 6 speakers. Fundamental analysis of the dataset is currently being done. It is found that the pitch of the falling tone word is higher than the level tone word. The pitch value can be used to distinguish the tones in Manipuri. Further analysis on feature selection is currently being done to accurately differentiate the tones and develop a robust model for tone recognition for the Manipuri language.

Acknowledgments. We thank Prof. Chungkham Yashawanta Singh, Dr. Yumnam Aboy Singh, Nameirakpam Amit and Laishram Niranjana from Linguistics Department of Manipur University, Imphal for their advice and support in creating the ManiTo dataset.

References

1. Praat. https://www.fon.hum.uva.nl/praat/
2. Tone linguistics. https://en.wikipedia.org/wiki/Tone_(linguistics)
3. Meetei Mayek Tamnaba Mapi Lairik, Textbook. Global Publications (2017)
4. Mahabir L.: A contribution to the study of tone in Manipuri. In: Master's thesis, Deccan College Postgraduate and Research Institute, Pune (1982)
5. Chelliah, S.L.: Tone in Manipuri (1997)
6. Khan, A.G.: A Contrastive Study of Manipuri (Meiteilon) And English Phonology. In: Thesis of Doctor of Philosophy, Guwahati University (1987)
7. Boersma, P., Van Heuven, V.: Speak and UnSpeak with PRAAT. Glot. Int. **5**, 341–347 (2001)
8. Singh, C.Y.: Manipuri Grammar, 2nd edn. Textbook, Rajesh Publications, New Delhi (2019)
9. Devi, H.S.: Loanwords in Manipuri and their impact. Linguist. Tibeto-Burman Area **27**(1), 29–60 (2004)
10. Jadoul, Y., Thompson, B., de Boer, B.: Introducing Parselmouth: a python interface to Praat. J. Phonetics **71**, 1–15 (2018). https://doi.org/10.1016/j.wocn.2018.07.001
11. Singh, L.S., Thaoroijam, K., Das, P.K.: Written Manipuri (Meiteiron) from phoneme to grapheme. Lang. India **7**(6), 2–22 (2007)
12. Takhellambam, M.: Tones in meiteilol: a phonetic description. Lang. India **14**(7), 440–460 (2014)
13. Haokip, P.: The languages of Manipur: a case study of the kuki-chin languages. Linguist. Tibeto-Burman Area **34**(1), 85–118 (2011)
14. Peng, L., Dai, W., Ke, D., Zhang, J.: Multi-scale model for mandarin tone recognition. In: 2021 12th International Symposium on Chinese Spoken Language Processing (ISCSLP), pp. 1–5 (2021). https://doi.org/10.1109/ISCSLP49672.2021.9362063
15. Thoudam, P.C.: A grammatical sketch of Meiteiron. In: Thesis of Doctor of Philosophy, Jawaharlal Nehru University, New Delhi (1980)
16. Nguyen, Q.B., Vub, T.T., Luong, C.M.: The effect of tone modeling in Vietnamese LVCSR system. In: Procedia Computer Science (2016)
17. Rev. W. Pettigrew: Manipuri (Meitei) Grammar with Illustrative Sentences. The Pioneer Press, Allahabad (1912)
18. Chelliah, S.L.: Level ordered morphology and phonology in Manipuri. Linguist. Tibeto-Burman Area **13**(2), 27–72 (1990)

19. Chelliah, S.L.: A Grammar of Meitei. Mouton de Gruyter, New York (1997), ISBN: 3110143216, 9783110143218
20. Singh, A., Kadyan, V.: Automatic speech recognition system for tonal languages: state-of-the-art survey. Arch. Comput. Methods Eng. **28** (2020). https://doi.org/10.1007/s11831-020-09414-4
21. Yip, M.: Tone. Cambridge Textbooks in Linguistics, Cambridge University Press, Cambridge (2002). https://books.google.co.in/books?id=KFv2lojXjpwC, ISBN: 9780521774451

Deep Neural Networks for Spoken Language Identification in Short Utterances

Shweta Sinha[1][(✉)] and S. S. Agrawal[2]

[1] Amity School of Engineering and Technology, Amity University Haryana, Gurugram, India
[2] KIIT College of Engineering, Gurugram, Haryana, India

Abstract. This work presents the elements of language identification (LID) in small segments created using short duration utterances. For low-resourced languages availability of data itself is a challenge. The paper tries to apply DNN for low resourced language. This paper presents a feed-forward deep neural network (FF-DNN) for language identification using acoustic features of short-time utterances. Two network topologies for DNN have been checked for their performance in LID task. The obtained findings of the experiments are compared to a well-established technique based on i-vector system. This i-vector system uses MFCC-SDC to represent speech feature that represent the acoustic characteristics and the back end is implemented using support vector machine (SVM) that serves as a classifier. These mechanisms were put in place to help with identification of Hindi and Punjabi, two widely spoken Indian languages. The speech utterances are divided into short segments of 5 s, 10 s, 20 s and 35-s duration. The system's efficiency is measured in EER (%) and for short time segments, a relative improvement of 3% is achieved by the DNN system, whereas the average error rate overall the utterances was decreased by 2% using DNN.

Keywords: LID · DNN · i-vectors · SVM · MFCC-SDC

1 Introduction

Language recognition or identification of speech utterances is a machine learning problem, and it deals with signal processing and pattern matching. The overall activity of automatic language identification aims to identify the belonginess of S spoken utterances to any language from the L language list. Only for past decade it is observed that the Indian Languages has gained the attention of researchers and technology has started playing roles for speech technology on a few of India's most important languages The knowledge has been utilized majorly in the domain of speaker identification [1, 2], speech recognition and speech synthesis. With the increase in global communication the demand for multi-lingual speech recognition has become a necessity and research is now focussed on automatic language identification (LID).

For a Speech recognition technology that works in multiple languages, the automatic language identification becomes an integral component to provide a quick response. The need for speech-to-speech language translation is in demand in several service sectors

© Springer Nature Switzerland AG 2022
A. Dev et al. (Eds.): AIST 2021, CCIS 1546, pp. 264–274, 2022.
https://doi.org/10.1007/978-3-030-95711-7_24

like travel, healthcare and hospitality etc. The translation system involving more than two languages requires an identifier for the languages at the early stage to identify the language of communication and then translation between the languages can be achieved. The demand for LID also prevails in forensic studies and call routing services. Although, at present the systems for automatic speech recognition [3], automatic speaker identification [4, 5], text to speech synthesis [6, 7] and automatic language identification [8] is available for commonly spoken languages of the developed countries, their need for a country with multiple languages spoken by the people inside the country boundary is essential. The major hurdle in extending these technologies to the languages of India are the availability of transcribed speech corpus along with standardization norms of the languages.

In this paper two techniques are discussed for LID applied on the Indian languages. Motivated by the performance of i-vector technology in LID for the languages like Mandarin and English [9] the i-vector has been exploited for Hindi and Punjabi. The use of i-vector front end features in conjunction with a sophisticated classification procedure that takes speaker and session variability into account has been emphasised in several research. The i-vector is a compact representation of a full utterance that is created using a factor analysis technique that maps the series of frames into a low-dimensional fixed-length vector space. Total variability space is the name for this low-dimensional space. The DNNs are relatively new for LID task. It's prominence in challenging machine learning applications and the performance in language-related tasks motivated the authors to use this technique for automatic LID [10].

Both these techniques are data-driven and a corpus for these languages has been created to configure the LID for short-term utterances to get acceptable performance in these two Indian languages. The quantity of data used for the experiment is equal for each of the two languages. The remainder of the paper is laid out as follows: Sect. 2 presents analysis of the speech features and techniques used to date. Section 3 presents different aspects of information contained in the language along with its processing by computer. This is followed by a description of the experimental setup used for language identification in Sect. 4. Section 5 discusses the results obtained by these experiments. The paper finishes with a conclusion and recommendations for future research. Section 6.

2 Background

Machine based LID is divided into two stages, the front end is in charge of the signal processing module in the first phase, which extracts speech features and performs a voice activity recognition task to remove non-speech segments from the sample. The speech features may include all auditory, prosodic, and phonetic characteristics [11] about the signal. The second phase of the LID deals with back-end modelling. The extracted feature vectors during the front-end processing are utilized to build models that represent language-specific fundamental characteristics of the input data.

LID systems were based on parallel phone recognition and language modelling [12]. These systems utilized the phonotactic content of the speech signal. Although these systems performed remarkably good, their heavy computational requirements became a hurdle in its use for building real-time applications. Other generative techniques utilized for LID task was Gaussian mixture models (GMM) [11], but they often lagged behind PPRLM approach in terms of performance. With the success of discriminative approaches i.e., the support vector machine (SVM) in a speaker recognition task, it was extended to LID task [13]. The use of DNN for LID tasks has been driven by recent trends in DNN [10, 14] and it has been observed that they surpass all performance statistics.

In the recent past, A few LID system innovations have made use of deep learning techniques. Lopez-Moreno et al. [14] used NIST LRE 2009 with a 5 million Google corpus to classify languages using feed-forward DNN (FF-DNN). They used acoustic-phonetic features and have achieved 43% improvements in Equal Error Rate. Richardson et al. [15] used FF-DNN with PLP features for classification of 6 language data from NIST 2009 LRE corpora. Montavon [16] used convolutional neural networks (CNN) for spoken language identification from VoxForge dataset. They compared shallow and deep CNN-TDNN architecture and indicates that the deep architecture outperforms shallow architecture by 5–10%.

3 Language Modelling and Processing

This section describes the probabilistic approach to modelling LID problem and highlights the information present inside the language structure which acts as cues at a different level. These cues guide in the selection of input features that are worked upon to identify the languages. Further, the process of identification is discussed in this section.

3.1 Probabilistic formulation of LID Problem

The mathematical foundation of LID is somewhat similar to speech pattern recognition. Bayes' probabilistic theory works behind all of these. This section presents a mathematical representation of the LID problem.

Let, $L = \{l1, l2, l3, \dots lm\}$ represent the set of languages. Let, $X = \{x1, x2, x3 \dots xn\}$ represent acoustic observations. The task is to identify the most likely language $l*$ out of all these languages in the set L., This can be represented using Bayes' theory as:

$$l* = arg \max_{l \in L} p(l|X) = arg \max_{l \in L} \frac{p(X|l).p(l)}{p(X)} = arg \max_{l \in L} p(X|l) \tag{1}$$

where, $p(l|X)$: Probability of l being observed when the observation sequence X is given $p(X)$: a priori probability associated with X.

The a priori $p(X)$ is constant for language classification decision and hence is negligible. Also, since all languages are equally probable, we can discard $p(l)$ and obtain a simplified equation as:

$$l* = arg \max_{l \in L} p(l|X) \tag{2}$$

The acoustic observations defining any language may be composite of acoustic information, a as sequence of m vectors $\{a1, a2 \dots am\}$, voicing information F0 as $f = \{f1, f2, f3\dots fm\}$, phonetic sequence $v*$ and segmentation sequence $s*$. the equation with the help of decomposed components can be written as:

$$l* = arg \max_{l \in L} p(l|v^*, s^*, a, f) = arg \max_{l \in L} p(v^*|l).p(a|v^*, s^*, l, f).p(s^*, f|v^*, l) \tag{3}$$

Here, (s^*, f) is the prosodic Information v^* represents phonemic information, $p(v^*|l)$ describes the probability of phone occurrence in the language; the phonotactic model. The probability $p(a|v^*, s^*, l, f)$ represents the acoustic model that in this case is language-dependent and also dependent on prosodic and phonemic information. The probability $p(s^*, f|v^*, l)$ is the prosodic model and is dependent on phonemic and language model.

3.2 Level of Information inside a Language

Language structure plays a very important role in identification. The characteristics of languages are controlled by its structure. The structure of any language is defined by the basic sound units in the phone inventory, the rules behind the syllable construction, the restriction that defines the combination to form syllables, morphemes or words of the language i.e., the phonotactic details. There can be a vast difference among the languages. For spoken language, the prosodic information is very essential. This information though dependent on speaker's characteristics have a major influence on recognition. The prosodic features include rhythm, stress and intonation of speech along with the pitch, formant frequency, and duration. With age and exposure, one's knowledge about languages increases and several cues can be identified to distinguish the languages. This information is embedded at different levels of language structure and works as cues for language identification. Figure 1 gives an overview of the level of information embedded inside a language structure.

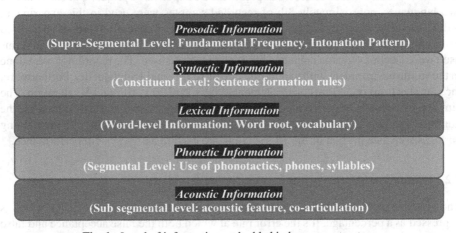

Fig. 1. Level of information embedded in language structure

3.3 Language Identification Process

The front-end receives the acoustic input, pre-process it and extracts the parameters that characterizes the features. The speech decoder is part of the language score block that creates a model based on the sound units and the language decoder scores a collection of languages L based on the sequence generated by the voice decoder. The last block at the back-end is the classifier that can be linear or non-linear. To make a final choice, they combine multiple scores (Fig. 2).

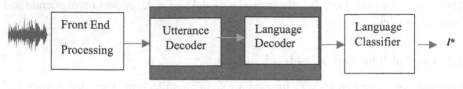

Fig. 2. Depiction of the LID system

4 Experimental Setup

Python programming language has been used for feature extraction and development of classification model.

4.1 Corpus used for LID

In this study, we used the Hindi and Punjabi languages for identifying purposes and the utterances used have been collected as part of the DIT sponsored project. For each of these two languages, approximately 3 h of recorded samples were used in this experiment. India's linguistic diversity is vast, and different languages frequently Words are borrowed from one another. The examples were meticulously documented, and the foreign terms used were labelled with the language in which they were used. The recordings were done in the studio environment with a sampling rate of 16 kHz and 16-bit quality. Furthermore, the samples from our corpus were segmented into 35 s, 20 s, 10 s and 5-s duration. The aim was to evaluate the performance for the short time utterances and also to increase the number of samples for training. The 35-s portion is utilized for training, The remaining parts, as well as a portion of the 35-s section, are used to assess system performance.

4.2 Evaluation Metrics

The system's performance is measured in terms of the equal error rate (EER), which is expressed as a percentage. It's the error rate at which both the false acceptance and false rejection rates are the same, i.e. Type I and Type II errors are the same. The identification test for each of the languages, is equivalent to the binary classification problem, hence the system's performance is the average of the two languages.

4.3 The i-vector Baseline System

The i-vector based system has been considered as a baseline system for LID task here and the performance of the DNN based LID systems is measured against this system.

The 13 MFCC coefficients are used to obtain shifted delta cepstral (SDC) features. These MFCC values were calculated using 20ms speech frames with a 10ms overlap and 24 Mel-scaled filter bands. For each of the two languages, variance and cepstral mean normalization are applied to the performance of these features. The SDC parameters are acquired by the use of numerous frames using 13–1-2–3 configuration [17]. These features are stacked with the MFCC features to obtain 52-dimension vector every 10 s. A single i-vector feature sequences are created from the utterance feature sequences.

The SDC features obtained for each small utterances are passed on to backend classifier. The backend classifier used here is the support vector machine with Radial Basis Function (RBF) kernel. The tuning of RBF kernel is done by obtaining the best (C,Y) pair value that can predict any unknown data. Here, the parameter C is used to penalise the training errors, and Y represents the kernel variance.

4.4   DNN based Language Identification

The deep neural network is a neural network composed of several layers. As opposed to conventional ANN there are several hidden layers in the DNN. These hidden layers make it suitable to handle more complex problems efficiently [18, 19]. FF-DNN is the simplest architecture where the network moves and operates in only one direction with no loopback. This network can be used for both classification and prediction. The most important feature of DNN is its support for the multi-level distributed representation of input data with no prior assumptions about the distribution of data. These advantages work as the motivating factor for using them for LID task.

Network Architecture. For LID we use dense FF-NN that is fully connected. For the activation function several options are available, and the most promising ones based on the literature has been taken into use. For the hidden layers the activation function is kept same throughout all the layers and at the output it has been changed. The system performance was tested with varying the network parameters and the activation function parameters several times. Finally the one with the best results were fixed and finalized. The activation function at hidden layers is the ReLU (Rectified Linear Units) function. The ReLU function receives input Xi and converts to output Y, that works as the next layer input as

$$y_i = ReLU(x_i) = max(0, x_i) \tag{4}$$

$$y_i = ReLU(x_i) = max(0, x_i) \tag{5}$$

The index of the units in the layer below is j, and the bias at unit i is b_i. Layer *Softmax* is employed as an activation function at the output, with the input Yi is mapped to the class likelihood p_i as:

$$p_i = \frac{exp(y_i)}{\sum_l exp(y_l)} \tag{6}$$

Cross entropy is used as a cost function for back-propagation in the training phase and is given as:

$$C = -\sum_i t_i log p_i \tag{7}$$

Where t_i is the target probability of the ith class.

Implementation. To implement LID using DNN, the inputs are the same as that of the i-vector baseline system that is 52-dimensional MFFCC-SDC data. To process further we combine 15 frames together by taking the current frame along with 7 frames each from the left and the right. This turns out to be $52*15 = 780$ features, that is the input layer uses 780 neurons. For the hidden layer, we have worked with two combinations, one having 3 hidden layers and the other with 6 hidden layers. After the input layer, the hidden layers (3H/6H) each with 1740 neurons are used. After that, the last layer using Softmax function is added and the number of neurons at this layer corresponds to the number of languages used. This is implemented as a closed set LID system, so no provision for out of set language is kept. The total number of free parameters that will be updated during training is W (includes weight and bias) is approximately 7.4 M/16.5 M in respective 3 and 6 hidden layer networks. The work is implemented using Python packages and MATLAB is used for speech pre processing and feature extraction.

The network training can be done in several modes. Here, the network is trained at the frame level keeping the learning rate fixed at 0.001 and Stochastic gradient descent in the asynchronous mode as the training algorithm. The DNN computes the class posterior probability for each of the frames and uses this knowledge while computing the probability for the next frame. The total score for any utterance is calculated by multiplying the class probability of all the frames of that utterance and averaging it.

$$S_l = \frac{1}{N} \sum_{i=1}^{N} log p(L_1|x_t, \theta) \tag{8}$$

Where, $p(L_l|x_t, \theta)$ represents the class probability of language l for the input utterance x_t at time t and θ represents the DNN parameters.

5   Evaluation and Results

The performance of both systems outlined above in the specified experimental setup is presented in this section. They are further compared and analysed. The first experiment is the baseline i-vector system and the second being a DNN system.

5.1   Results of the Baseline System

The backend classifier in the baseline system must fix the (C, Y) value [20]. The value of this pair is determined via cross-validation. The optimal value was determined after numerous cross validation rounds. for the given pair is obtained as 0.1 for C = 1. By varying the i-vector dimension. The system's efficiency is measured in EER % (Table 1) and the best performance is obtained for i-vector dimension = 400.

Table 1. Influence of differing i-vector dimensions for varying speech durations on system performance

Speech Utterance	5 Sec	10 Sec	20 Sec	35 Sec
Dimensions				
200	14.621	10.7	5.11	3.30
300	13.91	9.90	4.63	2.92
400	**13.21**	**9.42**	**4.30**	**2.79**
500	14.13	10.11	4.52	3.01
600	14.30	10.72	4.90	3.44

5.2 Results of DNN-LID System

Two variants of the DNN system was implemented to measure the impact of deep learning on LID. One with 3 hidden layers and the other with 6 hidden layers. These systems only the number of layers differs in these variants, with all other characteristics remaining the same. With the increase in the number of layers, the overall free parameters are increased but the additional layers may create fine layers of abstraction and find out better separability in high dimensions [21]. The input to both the systems were 52-dimension MFCC-SDC similar to the one used for i-vector extraction. In the DNN based system frame stacker is used to create the input for the network (discussed above). The system performance for both the structures was measured in terms of EER and have been presented in Table 2 for various speech duration.

Table 2. Influence of number of layers on the performance of DNN-based systems measured in EER (%)

	5 s	10 s	20 s	35 s
DNN_3H	10.21	6.10	4.23	3.02
DNN_6H	9.89	5.82	4.36	3.12

The performance of the two systems was found to be comparable with DNN system with 3 hidden layers (DNN_3H) giving an accuracy of 94.11% whereas, the system with 6 hidden layers (DNN_6H) gave the average accuracy as 94.20%.

5.3 Comparison of i-vector and DNN Systems

It has been observed that the i-vector LID system best performs for dimension 400, the RBF kernel parameters being (1,0.1). The performance of the three systems are compared in this section and is graphically represented in Fig. 3. The LID accuracy with the i-vector system is obtained as 92.5% and the DNN systems gave the accuracy of about 94%.

The EER in the comparison graph highlights that for small-time utterances DNN perform better than i-vector for LID. But, for the bigger utterances of 20 and 35 s, it is observed that the performance of all the three systems is comparable. This shows that DNN can better handle short-time speech as compared to i-vector. Also, the performance of two DNN-LIDs are approximately the same and increasing the parameters or, the layers do not impact much on the system performance.

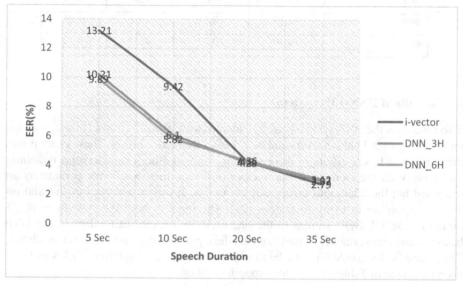

Fig. 3. Comparison of i-vector, DNN_3H and DNN_4H LID system in terms of EER (%)

5.4   Language Wise System Performance

In obtaining a further analysis of the LID approaches used in the present work the performance of each of the system were analysed separately for the three languages. Performance of all the speech segments in each of the three languages are presented in Fig. 4.

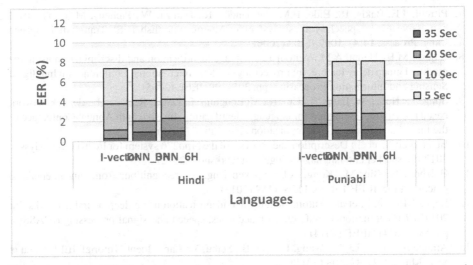

Fig. 4. i-vector and DNN systems performance comparison for each language for short speech segments

6   Conclusion and Future Work

The paper presents a probabilistic approach to LID. The capability of MFCC-SDC features have been explored to learn language-specific information from the speech signal and DNN is used to discriminate. The system performance is compared with the traditional i-vector-based LID systems with SVM as a backend classifier. It has been observed that even for short utterances DNNs can capture the discriminative features. The enhanced number of training data may influence the performance of DNN systems positively. It is further observed that DNN and i-vectors follow different optimization strategy and hence the fusion of these techniques can help capture their complementarity to further improve the system performance. Looking at the DNN system's potential, we feel DNN-LID can do a lot better, and we plan to explore different feature sets and network configurations in the future.

References

1. Bansal, P.: Amita dev and Shail Bala Jain, "Automatic speaker identification using Mel-frequency cepstral coefficients." Pb. Univ. Res. J (Sci.) **59**, 165–168 (2009)
2. Bansal, P., Dev, A., Shail Bala, J.: Automatic speaker identification using vector quantization. Asian J. Inf. Technol. **6**(9), 938–942 (2007)
3. Besacier, L., Barnard, E., Karpov, A., Schultz, T.: Automatic speech recognition for under-resourced languages: a survey. Speech Commun. **56**, 85–100 (2014)
4. Campbell, J.P.: Speaker recognition: a tutorial. Proc. IEEE **85**(9), 1437–1462 (1997)
5. Poonam, B., Amita, D., Shail, B.J.: Automatic speaker identification using vector quantization. Asian J. Inf. Technol. **6**(9) 938–942 (2007)
6. Kumari, R., Dev, A., Kumar, A.: An efficient adaptive artificial neural network based text to speech synthesizer for Hindi language. Multimedia Tools Appl. **80**(16), 24669–24695 (2021). https://doi.org/10.1007/s11042-021-10771-w

7. Pitrelli, J.F., Bakis, R., Eide, E.M., Fernandez, R., Hamza, W., Picheny, M.A.: The IBM expressive text-to-speech synthesis system for American English. IEEE Trans. Audio Speech Lang. Process. **14**(4), 1099–1108 (2006)

8. Rajesh, M.H., Hema, A.M.: Automatic language identification and discrimination using the modified group delay feature. In: Proceedings of 2005 International Conference on Intelligent Sensing and Information Processing, pp. 395–399. IEEE (2005)

9. Song, Y., Hong, X., Jiang, B., Cui, R., McLoughlin, I., Dai, L-R.: Deep bottleneck network based i-vector representation for language identification. In: Sixteenth Annual Conference of the International Speech Communication Association (2015)

10. Br¨ummer, N., et al.: Description and analysis of the brno276 system for lre2011. In: Odyssey 2012-the speaker and language recognition workshop (2012)

11. Haizhou, L., Bin, M., Kong, A.L.: Spoken language recognition: from fundamentals to practice. Proc. IEEE **101**(5), 1136–1159 (2013)

12. Lopez-Moreno, I., et al.: Automatic language identification using deep neural networks. In: 2014 IEEE international conference on acoustics, speech and signal processing (ICASSP), pp. 5337–5341. IEEE (2014)

13. Ambikairajah, E., Li, H., Wang, L., Yin, B., Sethu, V.: Lang. Ident. Tutorial. IEEE Circuits Syst. Mag. **11**(2), 82–108 (2011)

14. Zissman, M.A.: Comparison of four approaches to automatic language identification of telephone speech. IEEE Trans. Speech Audio Process. **4**(1), 31 (1996)

15. Torres-Carrasquillo, P.A., Singer, E., Kohler, M.A., Greene, R.J., Reynolds, D.A., Deller Jr, J.R.: Approaches to language identification using gaussian mixture models and shifted delta cepstral features. In: Seventh international conference on spoken language processing (2002)

16. Singer, E., Torres-Carrasquillo, P.A., Gleason, T.P., Campbell, W.M., Reynolds, D.A.: Acoustic, phonetic, and discriminative approaches to automatic language identification. In: Eighth European Conference on Speech Communication and Technology (2003)

17. Lopez-Moreno, I., Gonzalez-Dominguez, J., Martinez, D., Plchot, O., Gonzalez-Rodriguez, J., Moreno, P.J.: On the use of deep feedforward neural networks for automatic language identification. Comput. Speech Lang. **40**, 46–59 (2016)

18. Richardson, F., Reynolds, D., Dehak, N.: Deep neural network approaches to speaker and language recognition. IEEE Signal Process. Lett. **22**(10), 1671–1675 (2015)

19. Montavon, G.: Deep learning for spoken language identification. In: NIPS Workshop on Deep Learning for Speech Recognition and Related Applications, pp. 1–4. Whistler, Canada (2009)

20. Sinha, S., Jain, A., Agrawal, S.S.: Empirical analysis of linguistic and paralinguistic information for automatic dialect classification. Artif. Intell. Rev. **51**(4), 647–672 (2017). https://doi.org/10.1007/s10462-017-9573-3

21. Watanabe, S., Hori, T., Hershey, J.R.: Language independent end-to-end architecture for joint language identification and speech recognition. In: 2017 IEEE Automatic Speech Recognition and Understanding Workshop (ASRU), pp. 265–271. IEEE (2017)

AI Techniques

A Lightweight Deep Learning Approach for Diabetic Retinopathy Classification

Ruchika Bala[1]([⊠]), Arun Sharma[1], and Nidhi Goel[2]

[1] Department of Information and Technology,
Indira Gandhi Delhi Technical University for Women, Delhi, India
[2] Department of Electronics and Communication,
Indira Gandhi Delhi Technical University for Women, Delhi, India

Abstract. In the present time, chances of suffering from diabetes have drastically increased due to the genetic probability, lack of physical activities, high blood pressure and modern lifestyle related problems. Diabetic Retinopathy (DR) is an intense problem which affects blood vessels in the eye retina. Early detection of DR can avoid severe eye damage. Several machine-learning and deep-learning based techniques have been used for DR detection and classification. However, these techniques are complex, time consuming, and take millions of parameters in training and deploying the DR classifier. In this paper, a lightweight dual-branch based CNN architecture is proposed for DR classification. The proposed architecture involves 84,645 (0.084 M) parameters for training and deploying the model. APTOS dataset has been used for analysis.

Keywords: Diabetic retinopathy · Classification · Grading · Fundus images · Deep learning · Transfer learning · CNN · Convolutional Neural Network

1 Introduction

Diabetic Retinopathy (DR) is caused due to excess of sugar levels in people across the world. Early screening or detection helps in avoiding severe eye problems. This is especially important in rural areas where people are not aware about early diagnosis. Diabetes affects our eyes and causes various lesions. Figure 1 represents the lesions including microaneurysms (MA), heamorrhages (HR), hard exudates (yellow, white spots), soft exudates (cotton wool spots), etc. In accordance with the presence of these symptoms in the eye retina, severity level of DR is measured in different grades. DR is primarily categorized into two types as non-proliferative DR (NPDR) and proliferative DR (PDR). Based on the outcome of Early Treatment of Diabetic Retinopathy Study (ETDRS), DR is labelled as no DR, mild DR, moderate DR, severe DR, and PDR [1].

As per the WHO global report on diabetes (2016), by the age of 70, there have been 43% of deaths happened due to high blood sugar level [2]. Since, the number of patients is considerably more than the number of eye specialists, it is highly required to automate the process of screening.

A. Dev et al. (Eds.): AIST 2021, CCIS 1546, pp. 277–287, 2022.
https://doi.org/10.1007/978-3-030-95711-7_25

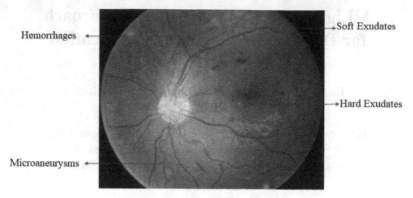

Fig. 1. Diabetic retinopathy lesions

Ophthalmologists perform scanning of various types of images like photographic retinal fundus images, Fluorescein Angiograms (FA), and Optical Coherence Tomography (OCT) to identify pathologies and their severity [3]. Analysis of FA and OCT for classification is tedious and not preferred for clinical investigation. Analysis of blood vessel patterns in the photographic retinal fundus images is the most recommended means in identifying DR pathologies and their severity level. Initially, various mathematical operations are performed to enhance contrast, smooth or sharpen edges, remove noise, resize, crop, etc. [4]. Separation of foreground pixels from the background pixels i.e. segmentation techniques are applied to extract features. The extracted features include shape, width, size, edges, color, tortuosity, ridges, bifurcation, etc. [5]. The extracted features are input to the model to categorize fundus images into DR severity scales.

Convolutional Neural Network (CNN) has been widely utilized for DR classification. Murugan et al. [6] has proposed CNN based model for feature extraction and classification to identify abnormal fundus images. Labhsetwar et al. [7] has implemented CLAHE with VGG [8] and ResNet [9] architectures on different datasets for DR classification. There is a trade-off between computational cost and the performance metrics. Either, these models give very high accuracy or involve very high computational cost.

This paper proposes a lightweight CNN model for DR classification. The proposed architecture uses two interconnected branches with each convolution layer employing 32 filter units having 3 × 3 kernel size. At the end, two dense layers are incorporated with the model to perform binary DR classification. Data augmentation and dropout are used to avoid overfitting and produce generalize results. Experiments have been performed on Kaggle APTOS dataset including 3662 images. Precise comparative analysis indicates that the computational cost of the proposed framework is very low in terms of a smaller number of parameters for training and deploying the network.

The next section discusses the state-of-the-art work in the diabetic retinopathy domain. Section 3 and 4 discusses the proposed architecture and experimental analysis respectively. The last section discloses the conclusion.

2 Related Work

Currently, widely used approaches for classification are based on machine-learning and deep-learning techniques [10–13]. Machine learning approaches are based on extracting features and feeding to the algorithms like SVM, KNN, ANN, fuzzy C means, decision tree, random forest, adaboost, etc. for DR classification [14].

Deep learning is gaining great interest in pattern recognition and computer vision. With the wide use of deep learning in industries, its use is highly recommended in medical imaging such as DR classification, cancer detection, MRI scanning, etc. In transfer-learning, a pre-trained model is used for other similar visual recognition problem domains to share knowledge.

Gulshan et al. [15] has proposed has proposed a deep CNN framework based on Inception-V3 model for detecting referable DR and DME. Two sets have been formed for validation based on EyePACS-1 and Messidor-2. These sets have been validated by 7 US based ophthalmologists and achieved 99% accuracy. Referral recommendations have been provided for future clinical testing. However, the framework used 22 million parameters for binary classification and need to be tested in real-time clinical testing.

Further, Agarwal et al. [16] proposed DR classification based on Inception-v3 architecture with combination of preprocessing operations. To increase the size of dataset, augmentation techniques are utilized. With pretrained weights of Inception-v3 architecture, accuracy of 69% and specificity of 94% have been obtained. Sahlsten et al. [17] has also proposed an architecture based on Inception-v3 having combination of five classifiers for DR classification. Initially, images have been pre-processed by cropping to a square shape having circular fundus area. Then, resize operation is performed on each of the cropped images. Further, the effect of resolution has been studied in terms of performance measures of the model. Dekhil et al. [18] implemented VGG model on APTOS dataset and obtained 77% accuracy.

Tymchenko et al. [19] has implemented ensemble of pre-trained model with regression, classification, and ordinal regression together. Ensemble of two EfficientNet models B4 and B5 with SE-ResNeXt50 has been developed for DR classification of fundus images. The method obtained 99.1% in both recall and specificity. Orlando et al. [20] proposed extraction of intensity and shape based hand-crafted features for DR classification based on random forest ensemble technique and LeNet convolution network. Sridhar et al. [21] has implemented binary and multi-class classification using ResNet modules based on adaboost and ANN through ensemble techniques.

Instead of directly using the pre-trained model, Kassani has modified the Xception model by incorporating auxiliary features extracted from intermediate convolutional layers [22]. Modified Xception has obtained better performance than the Xception network. Further, Gong et al. [23] developed DR classification by extracting feature distractor interference from CNN learning and used them in backpropagation to cover the loss. Four deep CNNs (ResNet50 [9], VGGNet [8], InceptionNet V4 [24], and EfficientNet-B0 [25]) are considered as base models. Shaban et al. [26] developed deep convolution neural network for DR classification and obtained 0.92 kappa score. Most of these models are based on millions of pretrained parameters, which make them computationally expensive.

The state-of-the-art techniques involve trade-off between time complexity and model performance by using complex architectures with millions of model parameters. To overcome these issues, the proposed work presents a lightweight architecture which makes it simple and provides good evaluation measures.

3   Material and Methods

3.1   Dataset Description

The Experimental analysis is performed on APTOS (Asia Pacific Tele-Ophthalmology Society) dataset obtained from Kaggle [27]. APTOS dataset includes 3662 fundus images. All images are guassian filtered and resized to a standard size of 224 × 224. These images are arranged in respective folders based on the severity level of DR. The distribution of these images as per the severity level is shown in Fig. 2. There are 1805 images with no symptoms of DR, 370 images with mild DR, 999 images with moderate DR, 193 images with severe DR, and 295 images with PDR.

Augmentation procedures are employed to remove the data imbalancing and increase the size of dataset. During data augmentation step, all pixels are rescaled to (0, 1) to avoid differences in pixel intensities and boost the training process. Rescaled images have undergone several geometrical transformations such as rotation, width-shift, height-shift, shear, zoom, etc. to bring diversity in the dataset.

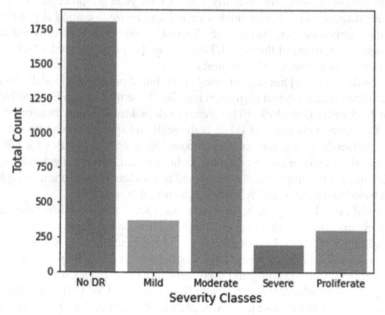

Fig. 2. Distribution of images

3.2   Proposed Architecture

DR classification is primarily based on identifying both lesions and their severity level. The proposed framework comprised of on-the-fly data augmentation followed by implementing a light-weight CNN model architecture to obtain pre-processed fundus images whereas the second step includes a light-weight CNN model architecture to output one of the multi-level DR classifications by extracting intrinsic features from the fundus images. Our model is significantly simpler than other techniques in term of number of parameters, and still achieves better results than those techniques. The broad-level block diagram of the proposed framework is shown in Fig. 3.

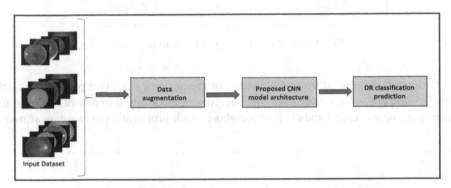

Fig. 3. Block diagram of proposed framework

The proposed Architecture performs DR screening of retinal fundus images. The proposed CNN architecture is a lightweight CNN-framework having two branches. The first branch includes a convolutional layer C11 followed by three blocks B11, B12, and B13, whereas the second branch consists of three blocks B21, B22, and B23. Each block in both branches consists of a convolutional layer followed by down-sampling using a max-pooling layer of size 2 × 2. Each convolutional layer uses 3 × 3 kernel size, and ReLU activation with 32 units. The structure of a block B is illustrated in Fig. 4.

Initially, pre-processed input images are given as input to the C11 layer of the first branch. Output of the C11 layer is fed to the block B11, output of the block B11 is fed to the block B12, and output of the block B12 is fed to the block B13. Further, concatenation of the output of the C11 layer and the pre-processed input images is given as input to the first block B21 of the second branch. Similarly, concatenation of output of the block B21 and the block B11 is fed to the block B22, and concatenation of output of the block B22 and the block B12 is fed to the block B23. Then output of the block B13 and the block B23 are merged together and flattened by feeding to global max pooling layer. At end, the output of convolution layer is fed to a dense layer of size 128 units, which is connected to an output dense layer of size 1 unit in the network to yield binary classification of DR. In DR screening, '0' label indicates no signs of DR in the fundus images and '1' indicates DR affected images. Both the branches are interconnected to extract different positional features of the fundus images, which is depicted in Fig. 5.

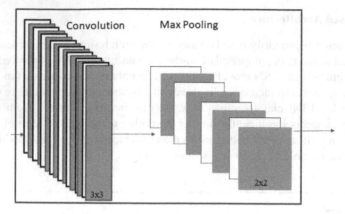

Fig. 4. Structure of blocks of CNN architecture

Dropout layer is used for regularization of the network [28]. Our proposed model uses 0.3 dropout, which means one in 3 neurons is randomly dropped or not used in training the network, and updating the weights in back-propagation to avoid overfitting.

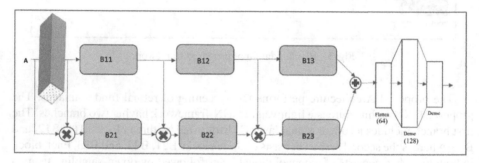

Fig. 5. Lightweight CNN model architecture.

3.3 Evaluation Metrics

In diabetic retinopathy, several retinal lesions are formed in the eye based on the severity of the DR stage. Since the lesions are of very small size, so small size kernels are consistently used to capture their presence. During the evaluation stage, the effectiveness of the proposed framework is measured by analyzing accuracy, sensitivity, specificity, recall, precision, and F1 score. The representation of these metrics is provided below.

$$Accuracy = \frac{TP + TN}{TP + FN + FP + TN} \tag{1}$$

$$Precision = \frac{TP}{TP + FP} \tag{2}$$

$$Recall = \frac{TP}{TP + FN} \tag{3}$$

$$Fscore = \frac{2 * Precision * Recall}{Precision + Recall} \tag{4}$$

where TP denotes true positive that is predicted output is positive when the actual label is positive. FP denotes false positive that is predicted output is positive when the actual label is negative. TN denotes true negative that is predicted output is negative when the actual label is negative. FN denotes false negative that is predicted output is negative when the actual label is true.

4   Experimental Analysis

During experimentation, dataset is randomly divided into 3 sets in the ratio of 80:10:10 for training, validation and testing respectively before commencing the training. During the training stage, different parameters are set like 5 as a batch-size, and 0.0001 as a learning rate (lr).

Table 1. Performance metrics of the proposed frameworks

Metric (in %)	Proposed work
Training accuracy	92.50
Training loss	0.1655
Validation accuracy	98.75
Validation loss	0.072
Testing accuracy	92.50
Testing loss	0.1639
Precision	64
Recall	80
F-1 Score	71

The performance metric values are obtained on APTOS dataset images of size 224 × 224 [19]. The proposed framework is analyzed in terms of training- validation accuracy and loss measures. Figure 6 shows accuracy plots of training and validation datasets for DR screening. The training-validation accuracy plot shows training accuracy score values with best accuracy score of 0.9250, and validation-accuracy score of 0.9875 for binary classification. The loss plot shows loss score value with least training loss value of 0.1655 and least validation-loss score of 0.072.

Table 1 summarizes the obtained performance metrics of the proposed framework on test dataset. The obtained values for binary classification indicate very good training and testing accuracy of 0.9250. The recall, precision, and F1-score are 0.80, 0.64 and 0.71 respectively.

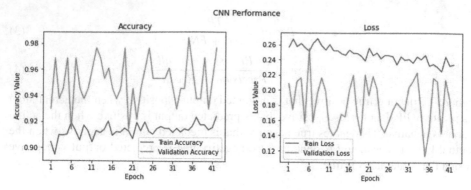

Fig. 6. Binary classification - Accuracy loss plots

5   Discussion

In this section, comparison of the proposed CNN architecture with some of the prior arts in the field of DR classification is presented. With respect to DR classification, the literature covering APTOS dataset for experimentation are selected for comparison in Table 2.

Agarwal et al. [16] proposed DR classification based on Inception-v3 architecture. At first, image segmentation is performed via combination of preprocessing operations. Augmentation techniques are utilized and Inception-v3 architecture is applied on the images to predict DR classification and obtains accuracy of 69% and specificity of 94%. The method of Agarwal et al. involves lot of preprocessing which makes their method more complex and tedious. Even though Inception-v3 uses a smaller number of parameters than other deep CNN architectures, but yet requires much more parameters than the proposed model. The present proposed model obtains accuracy of 92.50% with simple architecture and less computational complexity, which are the main attributes of our model.

Deep CNN architectures for binary and multi-class DR classification based on skip connections is implemented using ResNet model by Sridhar et al. [9, 21]. For binary classification, four ResNet models are built considering images having no signs of DR with each set of images selected from mild, moderate, severe and proliferate DR images. Output of these sub-models are combined together by Adaboost ensemble technique to predict final output. For multi-class classification, multiple ResNet models are built with all images together. The outputs are fed to the ANN for predicting the final grade. The entire architecture is based on ensemble techniques to boost the accuracy of the algorithm. Different sizes of filters such as 8×8, 16×16, and 32×32 and variable filter units such as 16, 64, 128, and 256 are used in different stages of the model. Based on these hyper-parameters, the overall number of parameters used in the model is roughly calculated as 0.13M. Binary classification architecture gives better results than multi-class classification. Use of large number of big filters, ResNet architecture, and application of ensemble techniques make the overall architecture complex and involves lot of parameters in training. However, the proposed method is a simple architecture, which uses 32 filters each of size 3x3 across the network and involves 0.084M parameters in total, which makes our approach simple and efficient.

Shaban et al. [26] proposed DR classification using deep convolution network having 18 CNN layers and 3 dense layers. They performed augmentation to remove data imbalancing. During training, 5-fold and 10-fold cross validation is performed with pre-trained weights of VGG. The method obtained 89% in validation accuracy and sensitivity, and 95% in specificity. The use of VGG pretrained weights contributes to 138 M parameters which makes the model heavy and complex.

Dekhil et al. [18] proposed a DR classifier based on transfer learning using VGG with preprocessing and obtained 77% accuracy score.

Overall, the precise comparison of various evaluation metrics of the proposed framework and prior arts is mentioned in Table 2.

Table 2. Comparative analysis.

Metric	Agarwal et al. [16]	Sridhar et al. [21]	Shaban et al. [26]	Dekhil et al. [18]	Proposed work
Accuracy	69	78.89	89	77	97.50
Precision	–	86	–	–	64
Recall	–	79	89	–	80
Specificity	94	–	95	–	–
F-1 score	–	79	–	–	71
Number of parameters	24M	0.013	138M	–	0.084M

6 Conclusion

Existing approaches of implementing DR classification are complex, time-consuming and require millions of parameters in training and deploying the model. In this paper, the proposed architecture presents a lightweight dual branch CNN framework for DR classification. The architecture involves two branches with each convolutional layer having 32 filters and 3x3 kernel. Both the branches are interconnected to extract different positional features. The proposed architecture is a lightweight model including 0.084 million parameters in training and deploying the network, which makes it simple and efficient. In future, research is required to confirm whether the proposed work can be applied in clinical settings. Research is also planned to train the proposed architecture further to improve the DR classification performance metrics.

References

1. Wilkinson, C., et al.: Proposed international clinical diabetic retinopathy and diabetic macular edema disease severity scales. Ophthalmology **110**(5), 1677–1682 (2003)

2. Kamm, J.: Global report on diabetes, Technical Report, World Health Organization 330 (2016)
3. Wu, L., Fernandez-Loaiza, P., Sauma, J.: Classification of diabetic retinopathy and diabetic macular edema. World J. Diabetes **4**(6), 290–294 (2013)
4. Memari, N., Ramli, A.R., Saripan, M.I.B., Syamsiah, M., Moghbel, M.: Retinal blood vessel segmentation by using matched filtering and fuzzy c-means clustering with integrated level set method for diabetic retinopathy335assessment. J. Med. Biol. Eng. **39**(5), 713–731 (2019)
5. Panchal, P., Bhojani, R., Panchal, T.: An algorithm for retinal feature ex-traction using hybrid approach. In: 7th International Conference on Communication, Computing and Virtualization (ICCCV), vol. 99, pp. 61–68, Mumbai, India, 26–27 February 2016
6. Murugan, R., Roy, P., Singh, U.: An abnormality detection of retinal fundus images by deep convolutional neural networks. Multimedia Tools Appl. **79**(33–34), 24949–24967 (2020). https://doi.org/10.1007/s11042-020-09217-6
7. Labhsetwar, S.R., Salvi, R.S., Kolte, P.A., Venkatesh, V.S., Baretto, A.M.: Predictive analysis of diabetic retinopathy with transfer learning, arXiv arXiv:2011.04052.35016 (2020)
8. Simonyan, K., Zisserman, A.: Very deep convolutional networks for largescale image recognition. In: 3rd International Conference on Learning Representations (ICLR), San Diego, CA, USA, 7–9 May 2015
9. He, K., Zhang, X., Ren, S., Sun, J.: Deep residual learning for image recognition. In: 2016 IEEE Conference on Computer Vision and Pattern Recognition (CVPR), pp. 770–778 (2016). https://doi.org/10.1109/CVPR.2016.90
10. Kaur, S., Goel, N.: A dilated convolutional approach for inflammatory lesion detection using multi-scale input feature fusion. In: 2020 IEEE Sixth International Conference on Multimedia Big Data (BigMM), pp. 386–393. IEEE (2020)
11. Kumari, R., Dev, A., Kumar, A.: An efficient adaptive artificial neural network based text to speech synthesizer for Hindi language. Multimedia Tools Appl. **80**(16), 24669–24695 (2021). https://doi.org/10.1007/s11042-021-10771-w
12. Jaiswal, G., Sharma, A., Yadav, S.K.: Critical insights into modern hyperspectral image applications through deep learning, Wiley Interdisc. Rev. Data Min. Knowl. Discovery **11**(6), e1426 (2021)
13. Carrera, E.V., Gonzalez, A., Carrera, R.: Automated detection of diabetic retinopathy using SVM. In: IEEE XXIV International Conference on Electronics, Electrical Engineering and Computing (INTERCON), Cuzco, Peru, 15–18 August 2017
14. Yu, S., Xiao, D., Kanagasingam, Y.: Machine learning based automatic neo- vascularization detection on optic disc region. IEEE J. Biomed Health In-365form **22**(3), 886–894 (2018). https://doi.org/10.1109/JBHI.2017.2710201
15. Gulshan, V., et al.: Development and validation of a deep learning algorithm for detection of diabetic retinopathy in retinal fundus photographs. JAMA **316**, 2402–2410 (2016)
16. Agarwal, R., Mahamuni, A., Gautam, N., Awachar, P., Sagar, P.: Detection of diabetic retinopathy using convolutional neural network. Int. J. Recent Technol. Eng. (IJRTE) **8**(4), 1957–1960 (2019)
17. Sahlsten, J., et al.: Deep learning fundus image analysis for diabetic retinopathy and macular edema grading. Tech. Rep. Sci. Rep. **9**(10750), 405 (2019). https://doi.org/10.1038/s41598-019-47181-w
18. Dekhil, O., Naglah, A., Shaban, M., Ghazal, M., Taher, F., Elbaz, A.: Deep learning based method for computer aided diagnosis of diabetic retinopathy. In: 2019 IEEE International Conference on Imaging Systems and Techniques (IST), pp. 1–4 (2019). https://doi.org/10.1109/IST48021.2019.9010333
19. Tymchenko, B., Marchenko, P., Spodarets, D.: Deep learning approach to diabetic retinopathy detection, arXiv arXiv:2003.02261 (2020)

20. Orlando, J.I., Prokofyeva, E., Del Fresno, M., Blaschko, M.B.: An ensemble deep learning based approach for red lesion detection in fundus images. Comput. Methods Program. Biomed. **153**, 115–127 (2018). https://doi.org/10.1016/j.cmpb.2017.10.017. Epub 2017 October 14 PMID: 29157445

21. Sridhar, S., Sanagavarapu, S.: Detection and prognosis evaluation of diabetic retinopathy using ensemble deep convolutional neural networks. In: IEEE International Electronics Symposium (IES), Surabaya, Indonesia, pp. 78–85, 29–30 September 2020. https://doi.org/10.1109/IES 50839.2020.9231789.420

22. Kassani, S.H., Kassani, P.H., Khazaeinezhad, R., Wesolowski, M.: Diabetic retinopathy classification using a modified Xception architecture. In: 9th IEEE International Symposium on Signal Processing and Information Technology, Ajman, United Arab Emirates, pp. 1–6, 10–12 December 2019. https://doi.org/10.1109/ISSPIT47144.2019.9001846.425

23. Gong, L., Ma, K., Zheng, Y.: Distractor-aware neuron intrinsic learning for generic 2D medical image classifications, In: Martel, A.L. et al. (ed.), Medical Image Computing and Computer Assisted Intervention – MICCAI 2020, Lecture Notes in Computational Science and Engineering, vol.12262, pp. 591–601. Springer, Cham (2020). https://doi.org/10.1007/978-3-030-59713-957.430

24. Szegedy, C., Ioffe, S., Vanhoucke, V., Alemi, A.: Inception-v4, inception-resnet and the impact of residual connections on learning. In: 2016 Computer Vision and Pattern Recognition, Las Vegas, Nevada, USA (2016)

25. Mingxing, T., Quoc, V. L.: Efficientnet: rethinking model scaling for convolutional neural networks. In: 2019 International Conference on Machine Learning, pp. 6105–6114 (2019)

26. Shaban, M., Ogur, Z., Mahmoud, A., Switala, A., Shalaby, A., Abu Khalifeh, H., et al.: A convolutional neural network for the screening and staging of diabetic retinopathy. PLoS ONE **15**(6), e0233514 (2020). https://doi.org/10.1371/journal.pone.0233514

27. Kaggle, APTOS dataset. https://www.kaggle.com/sovitrath/diabetic-retinopathy-224x224-gaussian-filtered

28. Srivastava, N., Hinton, G., Krizhevsky, A., Sutskever, I., Salakhutdi-nov, R.: Dropout: a simple way to prevent neural networks from overfitting. J. Mach. Learn. Res. **15**, 1929–1958 (2014)

Machine Hearing a Cognitive Service for Aiding Clinical Diagnosis

Arun Gopi[✉] and T. Sajini

CDAC, Thiruvananthapuram, Kerala, India

Abstract. Auscultation is being used for screening and monitoring respiratory diseases and is performed using a stethoscope. Auscultation the detection of abnormal respiratory sounds requires skilled medical professionals or clinical experts for diagnosis and an early diagnosis is always recommended for getting a higher probability of both curing and recovery. Respiratory disease being the most common with high morbidity the biggest challenge faced is the scarcity of clinical experts, non-availability of experts in rural and geographically challenged regions. Auscultation is an essential part of the physical examination, real-time and very informative, but based on the auditory perception of lung sounds. This requires the clinician considerable expertise and the perception variability may lead to misidentification of respiratory sounds. In this work, we are proposing an objective evaluation approach using deep learning techniques to address the limitations of the existing approach, a machine hearing technique to aid clinical decisions. In this work, breath sounds are used for analysis. The wheeze and crackles are the indicators of underlying ailments like namely Pneumonia, Bronchiectasis, Chronic Obstructive Pulmonary Disease (COPD), Upper Respiratory Tract Infection (URTI), Lower Respiratory Tract Infection (LRTI), Bronchiolitis, Asthma, and healthy. These sounds were analyzed for classifying the 8 categories of pulmonary diseases. CNN and RNN architectures were used for the classification of respiratory diseases. Features like Mel Frequency Cepstral Coefficients are extracted from the breath sounds. These coefficients were used as the feature for training the CNN and RNN architecture. Data Augmentation techniques like time stretching and shifting were applied to handle the imbalance in the data set. The CNN architecture gave a better accuracy of 0.89 and RNN with a slightly low of 0.833. The proposed approach proves to be a successful solution for the classification. The accuracy can be further improved with real-time data. In the future, this can be extended to develop a machine hearing as a decision support system for the clinical experts.

Keywords: Deeplearning · Pulmonary sound classification · Wheeze · Crackle · MFCC · Auscultation

1 Introduction

Chest Auscultation is one of the common approaches for the diagnosis for screening and monitoring respiratory diseases. This is usually done with a stethoscope, a noninvasive

© Springer Nature Switzerland AG 2022
A. Dev et al. (Eds.): AIST 2021, CCIS 1546, pp. 288–304, 2022.
https://doi.org/10.1007/978-3-030-95711-7_26

method in the detection of pulmonary diseases based upon abnormalities in respiratory sounds [1]. Skilled clinicians or medical professionals are required for the accurate diagnosis of these respiratory diseases.

Restrictive and Obstructive are the two types of pulmonary diseases. Restrictive are cases that cause difficulty in inspiration which are caused by the fibrosis of the chest wall and amyloidosis. The patients cannot fill the lungs. Whereas in obstructive the patients find difficulty in expiration which is caused by Asthma and Chronic Obstructive Pulmonary Disease (Emphysema i.e., loss of elastic quality, Chronic Chronitis). Different types of audio signals can be used for pulmonary disease analysis. This includes internal sounds like breath sound and vocal, sound by external stimuli through percussion [2]. In this work, the breath sounds are considered for the analysis. The breath sounds associated with pulmonary diseases which are considered in the diagnosis of respiratory diseases are normal, rhonchus, squeak, stridor, wheeze, crackle, bronchovesicular, friction rub, bronchial, absent, decreased, aggravation. The respiratory sounds embed invaluable information of the healthy condition of the heart concerning the respiratory disease conditions. In the case of Pulmonary diseases, an absence of normal breath sounds or signs of adventitious sounds can be an indicator [3]. This physiology decides different pathologies [4]. An inflammation affects breath, it results in specific patterns in frequency domain features and time-frequency domain features of breath sound.

Respiratory sounds include invaluable information concerning the physiologies and pathologies of lungs and airway obstruction. The distinction between normal and abnormal respiratory is critical for accurate clinical diagnosis. Often respiratory diseases are diagnosed in their later stages which reduces the chances of effective treatment. In all these cases an early diagnosis is always recommended which aids in curing the medical condition or even stalling the progression of the disease.

The main challenge in the clinical diagnosis of these diseases is the limited availability of medical experts for attending the patients. In countries like India where we have a diverse geographic area, the distribution of clinical experts is uneven. We face a lack of experts and facilities in rural and geographically challenged regions. The current doctor to patient ratio is less than the WHO-Prescribed norm (Recommends 1:1000 and currently this is 1:1456, as per budget 2020). Lung disease is the 3rd major cause of death in the world.

According to the World Health Organization (WHO), the five major respiratory diseases, namely chronic obstructive pulmonary disease (COPD), tuberculosis, acute, lower respiratory tract infection (LRTI), asthma, and lung cancer, cause the death of more than 3 million people. As per the medical reports, 75.6% and 20% of chronic respiratory diseases are caused by COPD and asthma, in India in 2016 and the cases in India increased from 28.1 million (27.0–29.2) in 1990 to 55.3 million (53.1–57.6) in 2016, an increase in prevalence from 3.3% (3.1–3.4) to 4.2% (4.0–4.4) [21]. Another challenge to be addressed is how reliable is the clinical screening or diagnosis? Whether the expert and excellent diagnoses are being done for the needy despite the regional and geographic limitations?

Auscultation is one of the methods used for the diagnosis of respiratory diseases. It noninvasively helps in the detection of pulmonary diseases based upon abnormalities in respiratory sounds and uses a stethoscope [1]. The lung sounds heard are the sound of the airflow in the lungs during the inspiration and expiration phases. These sounds are non-stationary and non-linear signals, hence making it difficult for physicians to recognize any abnormalities. Characteristics of lung sound for diagnosis of lung disorders are shown in Fig. 1.

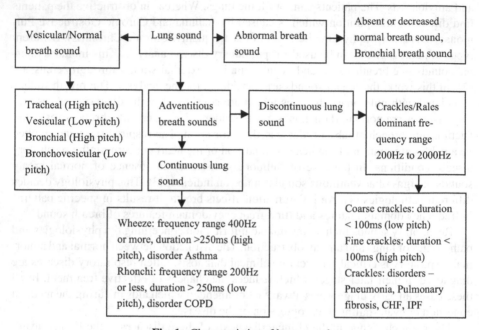

Fig. 1. Characteristics of lung sound

Physical structural changes in the pulmonary system cause changes in frequency components of the breath sounds [7]. These patterns are unique for different breath sounds, and may not be noticeable to human ears, and cause varied interpretation in diagnosis. These unique patterns may be identified by machine learning techniques, resulting in the development of automated diagnostic systems that can augment physicians.

The lung sounds are non-stationary; the spread of frequency associated with the artifact introduced by disease is strongly correlated with the nature of the abnormality [17]. Normal healthy lung sound power spectrum ranges up to 100 Hz and can be detected till 2000 Hz.

The Crackles and Wheezes pulmonary sounds have significant relevance in the diagnosis of respiratory diseases since these signals can indicate the healthy condition of the lungs. They are the indicators of underlying ailments like namely Pneumonia, Bronchiectasis, Chronic Obstructive Pulmonary Disease (COPD), Upper Respiratory Tract Infection (URTI), Lower Respiratory Tract Infection (LRTI), Bronchiolitis, Asthma, and healthy.

Crackles are short, explosive breath sounds that are caused by the rapid opening of abnormally closed airways. Wheezes are harmonic lung sounds caused by obstructed airways that vibrate as air passes through them [3]. The Crackles indicate pneumonia, pulmonary edema, bronchiectasis, and interstitial fibrosis. The wheezing sound can be an indicator of bronchial asthma, COPD, presence of a tumor or foreign body.

The frequency range of the lung wheeze sound is from 60 to 2000 Hz [15]. The frequency range of the crackle sounds falls within the same range of wheezing, with the major contribution being in the range of 60 Hz to 1,200 Hz [16]. There is a remarkable overlap of frequency ranges between categories. Thus, conventional sound pattern and frequency-based identification techniques fail to distinguish these categories. Figure 2 shows the distinctive characteristics of the audio signal with crackle, wheeze, and normal sounds.

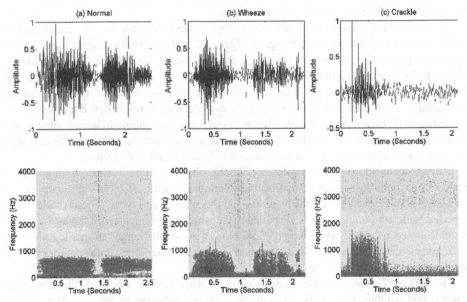

Fig. 2. Time-domain characteristics and spectrogram of (a) normal, (b) wheeze, and (c) crackle lung sound cycle [22].

The time domain characteristic of wheezes and crackles is shown in Fig. 2.

- Wheezes are sinusoidal signals in the range of 100 and 1000 Hz and duration less than 80 ms.
- Crackles, wave deflection duration typically less than 20 ms.

Change in the physiology of the lung is uniquely reflected in frequency components of the corresponding signals [7]. These crackles, wheezes, or a combination of both signifies the occurrence of conditions namely Pneumonia, Bronchiectasis, Chronic Obstructive Pulmonary Disease (COPD), Lower Respiratory Tract Infection (LRTI), Upper Respiratory Tract Infection (URTI), Bronchiolitis, or Asthma. The absence of the artifacts in-breath signifies a healthy respiratory system.

Change in the physiology of the lung is uniquely reflected in frequency components of the corresponding signals [7]. These crackles, wheezes, or a combination of both signifies the occurrence of conditions namely Pneumonia, Bronchiectasis, Chronic Obstructive Pulmonary Disease (COPD), Lower Respiratory Tract Infection (LRTI), Upper Respiratory Tract Infection (URTI), Bronchiolitis, or Asthma. The absence of the artifacts in-breath signifies a healthy respiratory system.

In this work, we propose a technology-based solution for the diagnosis of the healthy and seven distinct disease classes, namely Pneumonia, Bronchiectasis, COPD, URTI, LRTI, Bronchiolitis, and Asthma. The proposed solution can aid the medical practitioner in effective diagnosis of the respiratory disease without a miss and overcome the difficulties faced due to low hearing or performing diagnosis in a noisy environment. The advantage of using automated lung sound analysis is that this method is non-invasive, person independent, and less time-consuming.

Artificial Neural Network (ANN) based approaches can be used for the classification of the patterns of these complex signals. Deep Neural Networks (DNN) modeled on symptom-physical signs and objective tests can better facilitate diagnosing adult asthma, compared with classical machine learning, such as logistic analysis and SVM [8]. Deep Learning (DL) can help enhance the detection of respiratory diseases from auscultation sound data, given their well-recognized ability of learning complex non-linear functions from large, high-dimensional data. Recently deep learning methods have shown state-of-the-art performances in a wide range of domains, such as machine translation, image segmentation, emotional speech analysis, speech, and signal recognition.

In this scenario, we are trying to model the problem of classification of lung sounds based upon pathology with Convolutional Neural Networks (CNN) with deep layers and also with Recurrent Neural Network (RNN) with deep layers. These models can be used to detect patterns in Mel-Frequency Cepstral Coefficients (MFCC) as the audio signal feature to predict the disease class. One of these challenges in medical domain problems is the availability of data. In this work, we explored open data sets for proving the success of the proposed methods.

ICBHI 2017 publicly available database is employed during this work. Other notable lung sound databases available are namely, Marburg Respiratory Sounds (MARS) [9] which was compiled using Lung sound CDs which are commercially available for training doctors and nurses to understand lung sounds, R.A.L.E. repository which is a commercially available database [10], and European project CORSA which was developed aimed at standardizing the recording process of respiratory sounds [11].

Other notable lung sound databases available are namely, MARS [9] which was compiled using Lung sound CDs. MARS is commercially available for training doctors and nurses to understand lung sounds, R.A.L.E. repository [10]. The European project CORSA which was developed aimed at standardizing the recording process of respiratory sounds [11].

The main objective of this study includes understanding the respiratory sounds and their nature and the diagnosis using the subjective evaluation methods, analyzing the respiratory signals to identify relevant acoustic features for classification of the abnormal breath, designing and implementing a DL architecture for classification of the respiratory sounds and finally to recommend a successful model for supporting the clinician for diagnosis of respiratory diseases.

Deeplearning CNN and RNN architecture is applied to classify the signal into the 8 respiratory disease classes. The proposed solution gave an accuracy of 0.894 for the CNN based approach and an accuracy of 0.833 for RNN proving the success of the solution in the classification of respiratory diseases.

The proposed work reduces the diagnostic time and addresses the issue of the lack of medical experts for handling patients with respiratory diseases. The DL model forms an objective evaluation aids for the clinician by performing a pre-diagnosis and forms a solution for extending the clinical support for the rural population. The work can be extended to develop a decision support system for early detection and support for the clinical diagnosis of respiratory diseases.

2 Database

International Conference on Biomedical Health Informatics (**ICBHI**) 2017 publicly available benchmark dataset of lung auscultations [12] is used for the study. It is prepared by two independent research teams of Portugal and Greece.

ICBHI dataset has audio recordings sampled at different frequencies 4 kHz, 10 kHz, and 44.1 kHz, duration 5.5 h, ranging from 10s to 90 s, in 920 audio samples of 126 subjects from different anatomical positions with heterogeneous equipment [12]. The database contains audio signals captured from seven different chest locations: trachea, left and right anterior, left and right posterior, and left and right lateral. The samples are professionally annotated based on the patient's pathological condition, i.e. healthy and seven distinct disease classes, namely Pneumonia, Bronchiectasis, COPD, URTI, LRTI, Bronchiolitis, and Asthma and according to the presence of respiratory anomalies, i.e. crackles and wheezes in each respiratory cycle. Further details about the dataset and data collection methods can be found in [13].

3 Methodology

3.1 Experimental Overview

The proposed work is aimed at classification of breath sounds obtained by auscultation into the different classes using deeplearning architectures. CNN and RNN classification models were designed and both the models are compared using suitable performance matrices. The main processes involved are data collection and Analysis, augmentation and preprocessing, define network and train and evaluate. The block diagram of the process is shown in Fig. 3.

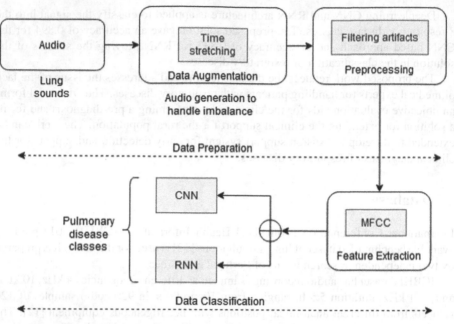

Fig. 3. Block diagram for automatic breath sound diagnosis model

3.2 Procedures

Data Collection and Analysis

The ICBHI dataset was analyzed to understand the distribution of 8 classes. Figure 4 shows the distribution of the dataset for each class. The dataset was unbalanced and the number of data representing COPD class was high. Imbalance data is one of the factors which affect the accuracy of the model in machine/deep learning approaches.

Data Preprocessing

Noise filtering is performed to remove the unwanted artifacts in the dataset. Heart sounds are one such, since the 8 classes are not determined by the heart sounds it is removed. The dominant frequency of heart sound is typically below 150 Hz, whereas the dominant frequency of lung sounds ranges between 150 Hz and 2500 Hz [14]. So, all audio signals are filtered with 6th order Butterworth bandpass filter to obtain 150 Hz to 2500 Hz frequency components.

Data Augmentation

The ICBHI 2017 dataset is highly imbalanced, with around 86% of the data belonging to COPD. The imbalanced dataset is a common problem faced by datasets in the medical domain [19]. A random stretch of 10% is performed to replenish the classes with low audio samples. For CNN classification the images must be of the same size. Since the

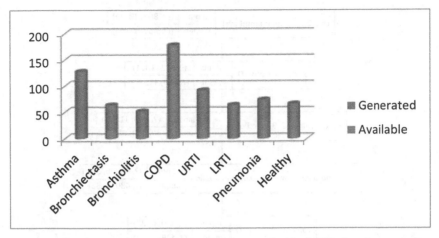

Fig. 4. The class distribution in the dataset (excess data in COPD class is removed)

audio samples in the dataset are of varied length, the extracted features are padded or stretched to ensure uniform length.

Data Feature
The diagnosis is normally performed based on the audio perception of the clinical expert. Mel-frequency Cepstral Coefficient (MFCC) is one of the commonly used features for lung sound classification [14]. The short-time Fourier transform (STFT) is computed using hamming windows which are commonly used since it reduces spectral leakage.

Logarithmic Transformation (LT) is applied to the obtained amplitude spectrum. LT mimics the way the human brain perceives the loudness of a sound. 13-dimensional feature vectors are generated using the 13 Discrete Cosine Transform (DCT) coefficients of log filterbank energies.

Classification
The classification of 8 classes of respiratory diseases was done using deep neural networks namely, CNN and RNN.

CNNs are a proven method for image classification. Recently there have been several works using CNN for medical images and classifying sounds using spectrogram images [20]. CNNs are invariant to shift or space, so the architecture is also called shift or space invariant artificial neural networks (SIANN). CNN's are composed of convolution, pooling, and fully connected layers. Depending on the complexity of the classification task multiple convolutional layers are added to the architecture. The hyperparameters and layers are adjusted for improving the accuracy of the classification model. Rectified Linear Unit (ReLU) and Softmax activations are used in the hidden and the final layer.

The input to the first convolutional layer is MFCC of size 862 × 13 for n audio signals. The details of CNN architecture are shown in Fig. 5. CNN is capable of capturing the unique patterns determining the classes but CNN fails to address the temporal dependencies.

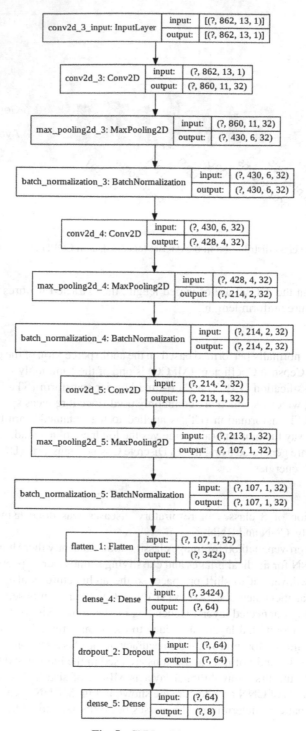

Fig. 5. CNN architecture

RNN helps in modeling sequence data where connections between nodes form a directed graph along a temporal sequence. RNN are neural networks that allow outputs from the previous layer or time to be used as input to the layer instance in current time while having hidden states. RNN can handle signals with variable length and shares weight across time.

LSTM is used since it gives more controllability and more accurate results, but it comes with more complexity and operating cost. LSTM has a memory unit (gated recurrent unit- GRU) and a forget gate.

The full architecture of the RNN classification model based, the many-to-one model is shown in Fig. 6.

MFCCs extracted from several frames of audio are provided as input to the initial layers of the classification model. MFCC's was extracted with a Fast Fourier Transform

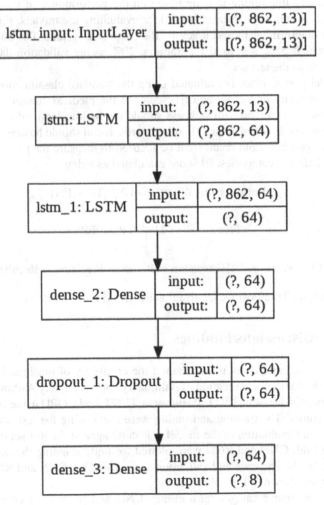

Fig. 6. RNN architecture

(FFT) window of size 2048 and hope length (number of audio frames between Short Time Fourier Transform columns) of size 512.13 number of coefficients were used. The architecture has two LSTM layers of dimensionality of 64 each at the initial stages. It is succeeded by a dense layer of dimension 64 with a dropout rate of 0.3. It uses ReLU as an activation function. Architecture ends with a dense layer of size 8, which corresponds to the number of categories and uses softmax as an activation function.

All development work was done in Python making use of important libraries like Librosa which helps to work with audio and perform analysis, Scikit-Learn, Tensorflow, and Numpy.

Evaluation of Developed Models

The data is used for training, validation, and testing, so it is split into three categories using automated techniques. The training sets are used for training the model and evaluation of the model and fine-tuning is done based on the performance of the model on the validation set. A validation dataset is used for evaluating the models. Finally, test sets are used for determining the accuracy of the proposed system. The dataset had 718 samples of which 55% was used for training, 20% as the validation dataset, and the remaining 25% as the test set.

The model performance is evaluated using the standard classification metrics like Accuracy, Sensitivity or Recall, and F1-Score. In the medical domain, false-negative need to be low i.e. a person with sickness should not be misclassified as healthy and a healthy person misclassified as sick. In other words, recall should be high. The F1-score that combines precision and recall shall be focused to measure the performance of the model upon different categories. F1Score calculated as below.

$$\text{Recall or sensitivity} = \text{TP} / (\text{TP} + \text{FN}) \tag{1}$$

$$\text{Precision} = \text{TP} / (\text{TP} + \text{FP}) \tag{2}$$

$$\text{F1} - \text{score} = 2 \times [(\text{Precision} \times \text{Recall}) / (\text{Precision} + \text{Recall})] \tag{3}$$

TP, FP, FN are True Positives, False Positives, and False Negatives respectively.

4   Results/Discussions/Findings

Experiments were carried out to understand the capability of machine learning using neural networks for the classification of pulmonary sounds namely Asthma, Bronchiectasis, Bronchiolitis, Healthy, LRTI, Pneumonia, URTI, and COPD using both CNN and RNN architectures. The training and tuning were done using the test sets and validation set. The final evaluation of the model was done against the test set data. Loss and Accuracy for both CNN and RNN were plotted for understanding the accuracy of the proposed approach. The train and validation accuracy of the CNN and RNN model for classification are shown in Figs. 7 and 8.

The loss and sparse categorical accuracy CNN and RNN is given in the Table 1 below.

Table 1. Comparison of training and validation for CNN and RNN, the Loss and Accuracy

Sl.No	Training set		Validation set	
	Loss	Accuracy	Loss	Accuracy
CNN	0.0868	0.9884	0.2803	0.9630
RNN	0.8166	0.6767	0.7421	0.7130

The parameters were tuned for improving the classification accuracy. CNN trained with a learning rate (α) 0.0001 and RNN with learning rate (α) 0.0001 gave the best results compared with a learning rate of 0.001.

The results show that the performance of CNN is better than RNN in capturing the pattern required for the classification of respiratory disease classes.

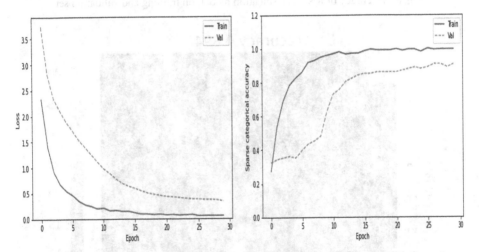

Fig. 7. Loss and accuracy of CNN classification model, on training and validation set.

The confusion matrix for the CNN and RNN classification is shown in Figs. 9 and 10 for visualizing the accuracy of both models in classifying the 7 classes of respiratory diseases.

CNN model gives a good F1-Score when compared with the RNN model for classification. The result of category asthma shall be discarded as the majority of data points in this category are augmented to handle imbalance. In the medical domain, data imbalance is a common challenge to be addressed. In the classification of respiratory diseases, F1-Score is more relevant than the accuracy for evaluating the performance of the model. For cases in which the data count is relatively low, a better interpretation is obtained by considering more than one metric. In real life, the classification accuracy of the classification category of a healthy person shall not be counted for the evaluation of performance, since the proposed work aims to identify the cases with the respiratory disease without a miss (Tables 2 and 3).

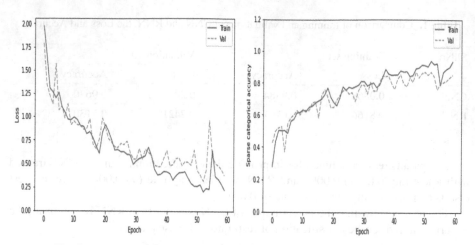

Fig. 8. Accuracy of RNN classification model, on training and validation set

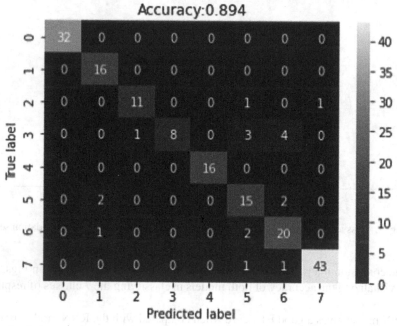

Fig. 9. Confusion matrix for CNN model on the test set.0–7 labels indicates classes asthma, bronchiectasis, bronchiolitis, healthy, IRTI, pneumonia, URTI and COPD

The experiment gave a good accuracy of 0.894 for the CNN model and 0.833 for the RNN based approach. The results prove that the ML based models can be used for aiding clinical diagnosis and can support the clinician by providing objective evaluation metrics. This will aid the clinician in closely observing the cases, hence avoiding the chances of missing critical cases of heart diseases.

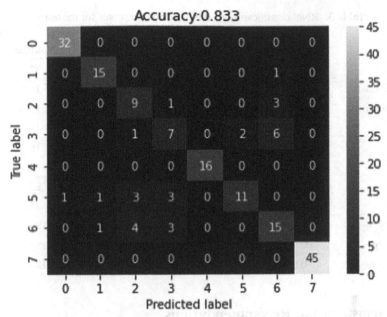

Fig. 10. Confusion matrix for (RNN) model on the test set.0–7 labels indicate classes asthma, bronchiectasis, bronchiolitis, healthy, IRTI, pneumonia, URTI, and COPD

Table 2. CNN classification model performance scores for the test set

	Precision	Recall	F1-Score	Support
Asthma	1	1	1	32
Bronchiectasis	0.84	1	0.91	16
Bronchiolitis	0.92	0.85	0.88	13
Healthy	1	0.5	0.67	16
LRTI	1	1	1	16
Pneumonia	0.68	0.79	0.73	19
URTI	0.74	0.87	0.8	23
COPD	0.98	0.96	0.97	45
Accuracy			0.89	180
Macro Avg	0.89	0.87	0.87	180
Weighted Avg	0.91	0.89	0.89	180

Table 3. RNN classification model performance scores for the test set

	Precision	Recall	F1-Score	Support
Asthma	0.97	1	0.98	32
Bronchiectasis	0.88	0.94	0.91	16
Bronchiolitis	0.53	0.69	0.6	13
Healthy	0.5	0.44	0.47	16
LRTI	1	1	1	16
Pneumonia	0.85	0.58	0.69	19
URTI	0.6	0.65	0.63	23
COPD	1	1	1	45
Accuracy			0.83	180
Macro avg	0.79	0.79	0.78	180
Weighted avg	0.84	0.83	0.83	180

5 Conclusions and Recommendations

In this work, we proposed a method for the automatic classification of lung sounds using a publically available ICBHI 2017 database. Automatic diagnosis of lung diseases is one of the most important issues in public health. Based on the database, a pipeline using signal processing techniques, data augmentation, and machine learning techniques were implemented to classify lung sounds. Only a few works have been done in the direct classification of lung sounds based upon pathology, however, major works are done for classification based upon physiology namely crackles and wheezes. In literature, traditional machine learning techniques are generally used for lung sound classification, although more recently, techniques based on deep learning are more prominent. The results of this work clearly show that it is possible to identify abnormal lung sounds without any labeling of the respiratory phases.

Experiments show that CNN and RNN models can be used in the classification of lung respiratory sound as an alternative for the traditional subjective approach of auscultation. The accuracy of CNN is better compared to the RNN model, but the classification result from both models shall be used for the objective scoring of the probability of respiratory diseases since the final decision will be taken by a clinical expert who will be aided by the objective scoring of the proposed approach.

Availability of data is one of the limiting factors in an accuracy improvement. Availability of amble data is crucial for successful experiments in the health domain. The padding of features for length normalization improved the performance of CNN significantly however RNN model performance was found to be seriously affected. Audio time-stretching for length normalization was found to give better results for both CNN and RNN models.

Despite its advantages, automated lung sound analysis has not yet been developed to a level that can be used in a clinical setting as a medical device. So, the development of real-time automated lung sound analysis is a major area of future research and the categories are limited to the availability of the dataset.

Together with future Work (next section), we believe that we could develop a diagnosis as a service Application Programming Interface (API) for use in mobile devices and medical equipment, bystander support systems.

6 Directions for Future Work

As an extension of this work, we focus on experimenting with real-time data. For achieving this goal we will be collecting real-time data by collaborating with medical departments. Currently, there is no publicly available dataset with sufficient data for every category which is crucial for this type of work. Due to the very sensitive nature of the respiratory signals, augmentation techniques in real data is very much preferred. Even though this is a challenge, data augmentation techniques using variational autoencoders can be used for this task [18].

At the architectural level mixing of alternative DL architectures, use of ensemble learning which is currently used in medical context problems shall be used and weighted output shall be used for making the final decision. Ensemble learning shall allow the use of both CNN and RNN models for diagnosis, thus the distinct pattern classification properties of these can be leveraged. In the future, we plan to develop an Application Programmable Interface (API) for recording the audio and saving it in a remote database as part of the Patient Health Record (PHR). This allows later analysis and diagnosis, saving of diagnosis results as part of PHR.

References

1. Rao, E.H., Royston, T.J., Kornblith, A., Roy, S.: Acoustic methods for pulmonary diagnosis. IEEE Rev. Biomed. Eng. **12**, 221–239 (2019) https://doi.org/10.1109/RBME.2018.2874353
2. Mansy, H.A., Royston, T.J., Balk, R.A., Sandler, R.H.: Pneumothorax detection using pulmonary acoustic transmission measurements. Med. Biol. Eng. Compu. **40**(5), 520–525 (2002). https://doi.org/10.1007/BF02345449
3. Laennec, R.T.H., Forbes, J.: A Treatise on the Diseases of the Chest,and on Mediate Auscultation. Samuel Wood and Sons, New York (1838). cited by 236
4. Basu, V., Rana, S.: Respiratory diseases recognition through respiratory sound with the help of deep neural network. In: 2020 4th International Conference on Computational Intelligence and Networks (CINE). IEEE (2020)
5. Colonna, J., et al.: Automatic classification of anuran sounds using convolutional neural networks. In: Proceedings of the Ninth International Conference on Computer Science & Software Engineering (2016)
6. Chamberlain, D., et al.: Application of semi-supervised deep learning to lung sound analysis. In: 2016 38th Annual International Conference of the IEEE Engineering in Medicine and Biology Society (EMBC). IEEE (2016)
7. Thorpe, W., et al.: Acoustic analysis of cough. In: The Seventh Australian and New Zealand Intelligent Information Systems Conference. IEEE (2001)
8. Tomita, K., Nagao, R., Touge, H., Ikeuchi, T., Sano, H., Yamasaki, A., Tohda, Y.: Deep learning facilitates the diagnosis of adult asthma. Allergology Int. **68**(4), 456–461 (2019). ISSN 1323-8930

9. Gross, V., Hadjileontiadis, L.J., Penzel, T., Koehler, U., Vogelmeier, C.: Multimedia database "Marburg Respiratory Sounds (MARS)", vol. 451, pp. 456–7 (2003)
10. RALE: A computer-assisted instructional package. Respir Care 35, p. 1006 (1990)
11. Sovijärvi, A.R.A., Vanderschoot, J., Earis, J.E.: Standardization of computerized respiratory sound analysis. Eur. Resp. Rev. **10**, 585 (2000)
12. ICBHI 2017 Challenge (2017). https://bhichallenge.med.auth.gr/
13. Rocha, B., et al.: A respiratory sound database for the development of automated classification. In: International Conference on Biomedical and Health Informatics, pp. 33–37. Springer (2017)
14. Palaniappan, R., Sundaraj, K., Uddin Ahamed, N.: Machine learning in lung sound analysis: a systematic review. Biocybernetics Biomed. Eng. **33**(3), 129–135 (2013)
15. Pasterkamp, H., Kraman, S.S., Wodicka, G.R.: Respiratory sounds: advances beyond the stethoscope. Am. J. Respiratory Critical Care Med. **156**(3), 974–987 (1997). Cited by 828
16. Abbas, A., Fahim, A.: An automated computerized auscultation and diagnostic system for pulmonary diseases. J. Med. Syst. **34**(6), 1149–1155 (2010)
17. Datta, S., et al.: Automated lung sound analysis for detecting pulmonary abnormalities. In: 2017 39th Annual International Conference of the Ieee Engineering in Medicine and Biology Society (Embc). IEEE (2017)
18. García-Ordás, M.T., et al.: Detecting respiratory pathologies using convolutional neural networks and variational autoencoders for unbalancing data. Sensors **20**(4), 1214 (2020)
19. Belarouci, S., Chikh, M.: Medical imbalanced data classification. Adv. Sci. Technol. Eng. Syst. J. **2**, 116–124 (2017). https://doi.org/10.25046/aj020316
20. Yadav, S.S., Jadhav, S.M.: Deep convolutional neural network based medical image classification for disease diagnosis. J. Big Data **6**, 113 (2019). https://doi.org/10.1186/s40537-019-0276-2
21. Healthdata Homepage. http://www.healthdata.org/research-article/burden-chronic-respiratory-diseases-and-their-heterogeneity-across-states-india. Accessed 10 Dec 2021
22. Sengupta, N., Sahidullah, Md., Saha, G.: Lung sound classification using cepstral-based statistical features. Comput. Biol. Med. **75** (2016). https://doi.org/10.1016/j.compbiomed.2016.05.013

Critical Insights on Cancer Detection Using Deep Learning

Harsimar Kandhari[1], Sagar Deep[1], Garima Jaiswal[2(⊠)], and Arun Sharma[2]

[1] Amity University, Noida, India
{harsimar.kandhari,Sagar.deep}@s.amity.edu
[2] Indira Gandhi Delhi Technical University for Women, Delhi, India
arunsharma@igdtuw.ac.in

Abstract. Cancer is grouped into many diseases that can originate in any organ of the human body. It is a type of tumor (cancerous), defined as the uncontrolled growth of damaged or abnormal cells. After originating, they spread to other parts of the body, causing tumors to grow there, too, called metastasis. Cancerous tumors are also known as malignant tumors. To prepare an effective treatment for cancer patients, it must be detected in the early phase. Machine learning and deep learning algorithms may assist in automating this task. One of the most commonly used deep learning techniques is Convolutional Neural Network (CNN). The present study reviews cancer detection using deep learning approaches by elaborating the datasets, results, limitations, and approaches.

Keywords: Deep learning · Cancer detection · Machine learning · Malignant tumors · CNN

1 Introduction

World over, cancer causes a large number of deaths. The American Cancer Society reports that, skin cancer caused 96480 deaths, lung cancer caused 142,670, breast cancer caused 42,260, prostate cancer caused 31620, and brain cancer caused 17760 deaths in 2019. Most cancers are diagnosed by analysing whole slide images of the tissue of the organ/part of the body under consideration. If done manually consumes a lot of time and effort (due to the confusing and complicated regional and cellular features of the slides). It is expected that experienced and expert pathologists do WSI analysis to reduce diagnosis errors and thus treatment. But such pathologists can't be afforded by every medical centre [1]. Thus, to help doctors make medical image interpretation more efficient, CAD systems were brought in early 1980s [2]. Nowadays we apply the concepts of deep learning, particularly CNN, LSTM, RNN, etc., to enhance image processing further.

The researchers utilized datasets from various institutes and organizations to train models and captured the parameters such as accuracy and AUC score of various models to compare their performance and determine the best one. The first CNN that showcased a better performance than the other modern advancements in object classification and

© Springer Nature Switzerland AG 2022
A. Dev et al. (Eds.): AIST 2021, CCIS 1546, pp. 305–317, 2022.
https://doi.org/10.1007/978-3-030-95711-7_27

detection was AlexNet, followed by VGG-16, GoogLeNet/Inception, and ResNets, each with its specific framework and qualities. They are differentiated by the number of convolutional layers, size of the kernels used for dimensionality reduction [3]. Other networks which may be employed for the same purpose are ANN and MLP. To find the most accurate model, all of these need to be applied to the same dataset under the same conditions [4, 5]. We also considered the Shallow-Deep CNN, which was built to derive "virtual" recombined images from LE images. In contrast, deep CNN extracted novel features to identify instances as benign or cancerous using ensemble models [6].

2 Related Work

With the evolution in this domain, the papers were extracted from various online databases like Springer, Elsevier, Wiley, IEEE, ACM Digital Library, etc. We analysed the approaches, results, datasets, and limitations of the methods implemented to cancer detection using deep learning approaches.

A data-agnostic method that becomes an expert at the task of automating the process of diagnostic reasoning, something that humans do with great proficiency and shows unprecedented advantages over previous work is proposed by [1]. It's a CAD technology improved with AI for applying it to diagnostic pathology that showcases predictions with visual explanation and natural language descriptions, which provides the pathologists intelligible information while undertaking a second review and conducting a visual assessment. The authors in [2] explain the basics of diagnosing cancer and elaborating the evaluation criteria. The 'how' behind machine learning in medical imaging was also provided (including segmentation of images, processing of both types i.e., preand post). The next part described GANs, CNNs, (DANs) deep encoders, which are some of the techniques in deep learning. The author portrays the successful compilation of the models applied to detect skin cancer, breast cancer, lung cancer, and brain cancer. To diagnose for breast cancer, deep CNNs were used on mammograms in [3]. Two differently sized mammogram databases (digitized) were used to assess the performance of the various networks. There exist 400 images in the first database and 1696 in the other one. There are two ways in which training was performed. First, the weights can be initialized with random values. Second, optimized weights from a network (by training that network on another dataset), and the network is fine-tuned for the current database.

ANNs, MLP, and CNN are used to detect malignant tumors in breasts to diagnose breast cancer in [4] based on their accuracy to find the best method for identifying the malignancies in breast cells. It was observed that CNN gives an accuracy that is slightly higher than that of MLP while diagnosing for breast cancer. The error was minimized by reducing the number of hidden layers in CNN and using artificial meta-plasticity in MLP. The authors in [5] proposed a Shallow Deep (SD) -CNN, which derived "virtual" recombined images from LE images. In contrast, deep CNN was incorporated to extract novel features from them to identify instances as benign or cancerous using ensemble models. To ensure that the proposed method was genuine, a deep-CNN was initially developed using a total of 49 cases of CEDM obtained from the Mayo Clinic. When LE imaging was used, an accuracy of 85% was obtained, and the AUC score was found to be 0.84, whereas 89% accuracy and 0.91 AUC score was obtained when both recombined imaging and LE were implemented. Then, the shallow-CNN was developed using the same cases (as used for the deep-CNN) to learn about mapping (nonlinear) from LE to recombined images. Next, the INbreast dataset was used as a source of 89 FFDM cases to generate "virtual" recombined images. When FFDM was used alone, an 84% and 0.87 of accuracy and AUC score were obtained, respectively, but SD-CNN further increased the accuracy to 0.90 and the AUC score to 0.92.

The authors in [6] used CT scan images(Mini-MIAS Dataset) as a dataset to detect breast cancer in early stages. By examining, CNN the system was trained to classify images between benign and malignant. Both image segmentation and image preprocessing were implemented. In the Tensorflow environment, the network gave an accuracy of 87.98% with 6 h of training time whereas in Matlab environment it gave an accuracy of 84.02% with 45 min of training time. The images were reduced to the size of 48x48 pixels. The techniques used in preprocessing phase were – Adaptive Histogram Equalization (contrast of an image is augmented.) and Image fusion (i.e., a technique of superimposing one image upon the second image.) Bhatia et al. [7] used CT scan images as datasets to detect lung cancer. UNet and ResNet models were explored, followed by feature feeding into several classifiers like XGboost and random forests. Pre-processing was carried by normalization and zero centering. CAD system based on CNN and feature fusion was used to detect breast cancer in [8]. In this study, CNN and unsupervised Extreme Learning Machine (ELM) clustering were used. The steps involved are breast image preprocessing, mass detection, feature extraction, training data generation, and classifier training. The various algorithms examined in image preprocessing were adaptive mean filter algorithm, contrast enhancement algorithm.

The authors in [9] used Stacked Denoising Autoencoders (SDAE). Different machine learning algorithms were explored to observe how compact features can be adequate for the classification task. Meaningful gene relationships were extracted using SDAE. The SDAE encoded features were fed to a shallow ANN and SVM model. Then the SDAE weights extracted from different layers were utilized to extract genes. An unsupervised feature learning approach for cancer detection was employed in [10] using a gene expression database. The authors used PCA to reduce the dimensionality of feature space. Ragab et al. [11] used a CAD system involving two segmentation approaches. One approach manually determined the region of interest (ROI), and the second used the threshold and region-based technique. A DCNN (AlexNet) with an SVM classifier was explored for feature extraction to obtain better accuracy. The datasets used were the digital database for screening mammography (DDSM) and the Curated Breast Imaging Subset of DDSM (CBIS-DDSM). In image processing, image enhancement was implemented using adaptive histogram equalization.

The authors in [12] used diffusion-weighted magnetic resonance imaging(DWI) as a dataset to detect prostate cancer. In this, an automated CNN-based pipeline was proposed for cancer detection. For processing, all the DWI images were normalized across a function followed by random forest to classify patients into groups with or without prostate cancer. For this research, ResNet was used as the base architecture. Mambou et al. [13] used a dataset of the rmogram images for the detection of breast cancer. The authors used DNN with an SVM classifier. In image pre-processing, the images were cropped to remove unwanted areas and from each image. For classification a variation of SVM called Linear Super Vector Classification (Linear SVC) is used.

Saric et al. [14] proposed an approach which was fully automated and based upon the concept of deep learning for detecting lung cancer in histopathological WSIs. The accuracy in patch classification and the AUC score were found to be higher in case of VGG16, which was compared withResNet50. From the results showcased, it was clear that CNN was capable of performing diagnosis for lung cancer with WSIs,but a lot more effort was still required to improve the categorization accuracy. The authors in [15] have simply proposed a method for optimum classification of images, a CNN trained and tested on a dataset of breast tissue samples' images taken from BreakHis database. These images were put in different classes(labelled malignant or benign) by experts.But the downside of the dataset was that the images contained redundant pixels that only added hindrance to the model's computation process, so they were processed with the OpenCV library. This was followed by feature extraction wherein, filters were used for feature learning and pooling was applied to reduce the images' size. Finally, the model was tested and found to give an accuracy of 99.86%.

Hu et al. [16] developed a methodology to for better diagnosis of breast cancer. The images used for training and validation were that of 927 lesions from 616 women, each one consisting of two sequences (DCE and T2w). A CNN was used to learn the features from these sequences and down the road, these features were used for SVM classifiers' training. It was concluded that the method used here can improve the diagnosis process for mpMRI by lowering the number of false positives and increasing the positive predictive value. The authors in [17] have presented a deep learning-based CAD system that analysed those whole slide images that have already been patch sampled and pre-processed using a patch-scoring algorithm and filters, respectively. A custom CNN used these patches as input, which generated a report showing malignant regions on a heatmap.

The authors in [20] aimed to help in the augmented csytoscopic bladder cancer detection by creating a deep learning algorithm. They utilized CystoNet which is a deep learning algorithm created using convolutional neural network for the purpose of augmented bladder cancer detection. 141 White light videos (which are used in the process of white light cystoscopy) from 100 patients undertaking the TURBT during the years 2016–2019 were taken as dataset for development of the algorithm. For the purpose of validation dataset, videos were taken from 54 more patients. From the videos, the needed frames were selected and the outlining of tumor was done by utilising LabelMe. The model displayed per frame sensitivity of 90.9% and specificity of 98.6% for the validation dataset. Image Classification was performed on Brain MRI images for the detection of cancer and its performance was compared with existing methods in [21]. Brain MRI images in DICOM format from RIDER database (containing images from 19 patients) were used as dataset. Images are then extracted from these DICOM files in the form of 2D arrays which are then flattened. DWA-DNN approach is used where the Deep Wavelet Autoencoder (DWA) is utilized the processing the images which are then classified using Deep Neural Network (DNN). It was noted that the proposed DWA-DNN model had a better average accuracy (93%) when compared to DNN (89%) and AE-DNN (91%).

Selvathi et al. [22] developed an automated system for breast cancer detection utilizing mammogram images. 322 digital films containing mammogram images of size 1024 x 1024 were used as dataset. Various image pre-processing techniques like Digitalization Noise Removal, Artifact Suppression and Background Separation were used on the images followed by the use of ROI segmentation using the Seeded Region Growing (SRG) technique. The proposed model employs three techniques for detection of breast cancer which are Convolutional Neural Network (CNN), Sparse Autoencoder (SAE) and Stacked Sparse Autoencoder (SSAE). The proposed model displayed an accuracy of 97% for CNN, 98.5% for SAE and 98.9% for SSAE. The authors in [23] developed an automated system for the accurate detection of liver cancer. 225 liver cancer CT scan images from imaging centre, IMS and SUM hospital were used as the dataset. The dataset contained images from three types of liver cancer- HEM, HCC and MET- with 75 samples from each type. 70% of dataset was used as training set and the rest was taken as testing set. Then watershed transform is applied on the dataset for obtaining smooth structure at the boundary. Then the Gaussian mixture model is applied next. In the proposed model a Deep Neural Network using Keras was utilized for classification. The model achieved an accuracy of 99.39% for training set and 98.38% for the testing set.

The most intricate part of skin cancer detection is differentiating between the harmless nevus and the malignant melanoma because it requires a considerable measure of expertise and resources. In order to make this process less demanding, Hosny et al. [24] have proposed a method which uses data augmentation and fine tuning, while applying transfer learning to (the DCNN) AlexNet, all while the classification layer is exchanged with a softmax layer, so that the lesion can be classified into, common nevus, atypical nevus and melanoma.

Asuntha et al. [25] used histogram equalization and adaptive bilateral filter for enhancing the contrast in the image and denoising it, respectively. The ABC segmentation approach is applied to segment the lung region. After that, eight features are used feature extraction, followed by feature selection with the help of Particle swarm Optimization algorithm. Deep learning is used to classify the lung disease and its severity. Daghrir et al. [26] trained a CNN model on 640 images for 10 epochs along with two other classifiers, namely, SVM and KNN. The CNN, SVM and KNN models gave accuracies of 85.5%, 71.8% and 57.3%, respectively. But, when the three were fused via the majority voting approach, the ameliorated performance came out to be 88.4%.

Elnakib et al. [27] has proposed a system that first enhances the contrast of the low dose CT images and then, the VGG19 architecture of deep learning is used for feature extraction. Afterwards, the genetic algorithm is used to select the most promising features. Finally, the SVM classifier is used to detect the lung nodules which come up with an accuracy of 96.25%. Ismael et al. [28] trained their model on a dataset of 3064 MRI images of brain tumor. Since the dataset was not large enough, many data augmentation techniques were employed to increase its size, such as, flipping, rotating, zooming etc. Moreover, the ResNet-50 model (CNN architecture) was trained on this dataset for classifying the type of brain tumors into three types. A major reason for its usage is that it provides the solution to vanishing gradients and degrading accuracies.

Song et al. [29] develop a clinically applicable system for the detection of gastric cancer. The proposed system makes use of the PLAGH dataset which is divided into six parts. It also makes use of multicentre dataset containing images from PUMCH and CHCAMS and Perkins Union Medical College. Image Pre-processing techniques like rotation, random flips, gaussian and motion blurs and colour jittering in brightness, contrast, saturation and hue are applied. The proposed system makes use of CNN Model of DeepLab V3 Architecture which follows a binary image segmentation approach. The proposed model achieves an average specificity of 80.6%.

Table 1. Comparative study on cancer detection using deep learning.

Reference ID	Approach	Preprocessing technique	Accuracy	Dataset	Results/Limitations
Zhang et al. [1]	s-net (tumor detection), Inception-v3 CNN (Cellular-level ROI characterization.), LSTM (to design a language model)	The dataset was highly accurate and without any noise. (as was verified several times by pathologists). Low-quality slides were removed	Mean accuracy of System = 94.6% Mean accuracy of Pathologists = 84.3% AUC score (for 100 test whole slides) = 97% AUC score (for 293 validation and test whole slides) = 95%	913 haematoxylinand eosin (H&E) stained whole slides from patients with bladder cancer, obtained from multiple medical sources	Its performance can be demonstrated for other types of cancer with further research It is desirable that the future models use contextual clinical information of the patients instead of just the pixel knowledge of WSIs for precision medicine
Munir et al. [2]	Architectures of CNN	Tree-structured nonlinear filtering (TSF), Directional and Tree-structured wavelet transform (DWT & TSWT)	Accuracy = 87.14%, Sensitivity = 0.77% Specificity = 0.93%	2D sliced images, 3D images, MR images from various sources	
Tsochatzidis et al. [3]	CNN	The format of images from CBIS-DDSM is changed to DICOM, and for each lesion, an updated segmentation for ROI is provided	Better performance is recorded when a pretrained network is fine-tuned and used instead of a network trained from scratch	400 mass ROIs extracted from the DDSM	Building (mammographic) datasets on a big scale assist the ongoing research in CAD diagnosis, digital mammography, and tomosynthesis

(*continued*)

Table 1. (*continued*)

Desai et al. [4]	ANN,MLP, and CNN	ROI extraction or extraction of that WSI region, which contains the tissue of the region of interest	CNN gives higher accuracy than MLP The accuracy for patch classification, as given by VGG16 = 97.9%	Image sets of mammograms	Stain normalization, more extensive training set and image augmentation can provide better performance in the future Networks can be trained from scratch, rather than using pre-trained weights (with magnet)
Gao et al. [5]	SD-CNN	Identifying a minimum-area bounding box around the tumor, max-min normalization, resizing	LE imaging Accuracy – 85% AUC – 0.84 LE and recombined imaging Accuracy - 89% AUC - 0.91	Institutional dataset from MayoClinic (InArizona) and a public dataset taken from INbreast	The patch sizes of both output and input images can be assessed for their effect on cancer diagnosis The clinical interpretations of the features generated by the trained ResNet will be helpful for physicians
Batra et al. [6]	Convolutional Neural Network		In TensorFlow environment, accuracy is 87.98% In MATLAB environment, accuracy is 84.02%	Mini-MIAS Dataset	A better CNN can be developed to reduce the tradeoff between accuracy and training time New feature extraction techniques can be used to obtain better results
Bhatia et al. [7]	Random Forests and XGBoost	Image fusion and Adaptive Histogram Equalization	It has accuracy of 84%	Lung Image Database Consortium image collection (LIDC-IDRI)	The efficiency of tree-based classifiers such as random forests and XGBoost are compared
Wang et al. [8]	CNN and unsupervised extreme learning machine (ELM) clustering is used		Using ELM, we get highest accuracy of 86.5% Using SVM, we get highest accuracy of 81.75%	Mammogram Dataset	Mass detection and Mass diagnosis are carried out by applying features extracted using CNN

(*continued*)

Table 1. (*continued*)

Danaee et al. [9]	Stacked Denoising Autoencoders (SDAE) and ANN	Normalization and zero centering	The highest accuracy is 98.26%	The Cancer Genome Atlas (TCGA) database	The extraction of DCGs needs to be improved A larger dataset is required
Fakoor et al. [10]	Unsupervised feature learning is used	PCA	The highest average classification accuracy is 93.33%	Gene Expression Dataset	Data which is obtained can be used in feature learning separately from their use to the final classification
Ragab et al. [11]	DCNN (AlexNet) along with SVM Classifier is used		SVM accuracy is 87.2%	Digital database for screening mammography and Curated Breast Imaging Subset of DDSM	The system proposed can also be used to detect other abnormalities in the breasts An intense convolutional network (VGG) and ResNet can also be used
Yoo et al. [12]	Random forests are used for classification	Adaptive Histogram Equalization	AUC of 0.87	Diffusion Weighted magnetic resonance Imaging (DWI) Dataset	A stack of 5 CNN's is used for better results Other architectures like 3D CNN and RNN can be used
Mambou et al. [13]	DNN is used with SVM classifier			Frontal thermogram images dataset from Research Data Base (DMR)	Infrared imaging can lead to a very accurate tumor detector A thermal sensitivity camera of 0.5 can be used
Saric et al. [14]	Two CNN architectures -VGG andResNet	Normalized across a function	Accuracy ResNet50 - 0.7205 VGG16 - 0.7541	Dataset was taken from "Automatic Cancer Detection and Classification in Whole slide Lung Histopathology"	By adding stain normalization, image augmentation, a training set of considerable size, and training the model from scratch rather than using weights that are pretrained (on ImageNet), the accuracy of classification can be increased

(*continued*)

Table 1. (*continued*)

Dabeer et al. [15]	CNN		Prediction accuracy = 99.86%	BreakHis dataset	Autoencoders can be used to compress the data. As they don't lose the prominent features thus of the image, they can regenerate up to 90% of the original image Multi-model fusion and Spectral imaging can be used to improve the method
Hu et al. [16]	CNN based mpMRI, CADx	Grayscale RGB conversion and image culture	AUC DCE = 0.85 AUC T2w = 0.78 AUCImageFusion = 0.85 AUCFeatureFusion = 0.87 AUCClassifierFusion = 0.86	MR scans of 927 different lesions on 616 different women	Validation can be performed on independent datasets to investigate the robustness of this method with respect to patient populations, imaging manufacturers, and facility protocols Other MRI sequences, such as diffusion-weighted imaging, can be used The performance can be improved by using a database of larger size
Lopez et al. [17]	PROMETEO (a custom CNN)		Accuracy - 99.98% F1 score - 99.98% AUC score - 0.999	Dataset was provided by Pathological Anatomy Unit of Virgen de Valme Hospital in Seville (Spain)	A "universal" and stable CAD software could be developed by using stain-normalized images because then; it would give better performance than the network which used non-stain-normalized images Larger datasets are required for better classification, and region-specific labels from pathologists were not available for external hospitals

(*continued*)

Table 1. (*continued*)

Shkolyar et al. [20]	Cystonet (a custom CNN)	ROI extraction	Per frame Sensitivity- 90.9% Per frame Specificity- 98.6%	White light videos from 100 patients undergoing TURBT	Cystonet may help in improving the availability and quality of cystoscopy
Mallick et al. [21]	DWA based DNN		Average Accuracy- 93%	Brain MRI images from RIDER database	The DNN could be combined with different autoencoders to get different results
Selvathi et al. [22]	CNN, SAE and SSAE	Compression techniques were used to remove the redundant pixels from the image	CNN Accuracy- 97% SAE Accuracy- 98.5% SSAE Accuracy- 98.9%	322 digital films containing mammogram images	This model can help in accurate and fast detection of cancerous lesion
Das et al. [23]	DNN using Keras		Training Accuracy- 99.39% Testing Accuracy- 98.38%	225 liver cancer images from IMS and SUM Hospital, India	Its main limitation is the volumetric size calculation of lesions
Khalid et al. [24]	AlexNet	Lesion segmentation was done. An ROI was cropped from the image around each lesion	Accuracy - 98.61% Sensitivity - 98.33% Specificity - 98.93% Precision 97.73%	ph2 dataset	A large number of labelled images is a prerequisite for this model to work properly The model was able to classify the images into three types successfully.
Asuntha et al. [25]	FPSOCNN		Accuracy – 94.97% Sensitivity -96.68% Specificity - 95.89%	Aarthi Scan Hospital dataset, LIDC dataset	The model quickly detected the locations where lung nodules were present
Daghrir et al. [26]	CNN, KVM, SVM	A type of colour normalization, Reinhard stain-normalization, was applied	Accuracies: CNN - 85.5% SVM - 71.8% KNN - 57.3% Ameliorated result – 88.4%	A public dataset from the ISIC archive, with more than 23000 images of melanoma	Further research could be carried out keeping the "ugly-duckling" concept as a base Moreover, semi-supervised learning could be considered in case enough labelled data is not available

(*continued*)

Table 1. (*continued*)

Elnakib et al. [27]	VGG19, SVM	Patch sampling using a	Accuracy - 96.25% Sensitivity- 97.5% Specificity- 95%	320 LDCT images from I-ELCAP	Several false positive and false negative cases were witnessed in the classification result of this model So, further research is required to improve the accuracy
Ismael et al. [28]	ResNet-50	novel filter process using a formula for patch scoring by Deron Eriksson	Accuracy - 99%	3064 T1-weighted contrast-enhanced MRI images	The present model is designed to classify only three types of brain tumors. It can be modified for a greater number of the types
Song et al. [29]	CNN Model of DeepLab V3 Architecture		Average Specificity- 80.6%	Dataset from PLAGH	The model shows the use of histopathological AI-aided systems in everyday scenarios

Table 1 depicts the specific pointers of the papers reviewed-preprocessing technique used, the results and limitations of the methods applied, the technical approaches taken, along with the performance parameters of the networks they presented, such as accuracy and AUC score. Table 1 clearly illustrates the best model for particular datasets along with desired outputs. For example, in the case of cancer detection, false negatives can be extremely dangerous as they mislead the patient into not seeking proper treatment or taking those steps that increase the livelihood of their survival. So, to find a network suiting this prerequisite, we have to vary the number of layers in the CNNs, types of filters, size of images, etc.

3 Conclusion and Future Scope

Cancer is a very harmful disease that can prove to be fatal if not detected on time. So, there is a dire need for efficient detection of cancer, which can be achieved by using CAD models, machine learning algorithms, and deep learning techniques. Manual detection of cancer is time-consuming and tedious, so that ML algorithms can give much better results. The images may be preprocessed, and the dataset can also be augmented using various techniques to improve the result further. Deep learning approaches are well known for achieving state-of-art results in many domains. These techniques may be examined to automate the cancer detection process.

References

1. Zhang, Z., et al.: Pathologist-level interpretable whole-slide cancer diagnosis with deep learning. Nature Mach. Intell. **1**(5), 236–245 (2019)
2. Munir, K., Elahi, H., Ayub, A., Frezza, F., Rizzi, A.: Cancer diagnosis using deep learning: a bibliographic review. Cancers **11**(9), 1235 (2019)
3. Tsochatzidis, L., Costaridou, L., Pratikakis, I.: Deep learning for breast cancer diagnosis from mammograms—a comparative study. J. Imaging. **5**(3), 37 (2019)
4. Jaiswal, G., Sharma, A., Yadav, S.K.: Critical insights into modern hyperspectral image applications through deep learning. Wiley Interdisciplinary Rev. Data Mining Knowl. Discovery **11**(6), e1426 (2021)
5. Jaiswal, G., Sharma, A., Yadav, S.K.: Analytical approach for predicting dropouts in higher education. Int. J. Inf. Commun. Technol. Educ. (IJICTE). **15**(3), 89–102 (2019)
6. Desai, M., Shah, M.: An anatomization on breast cancer detection and diagnosis employing multi-layer perceptron neural network (MLP) and Convolutional neural network (CNN). Clinical eHealth, 24 Nov 2020
7. Gao, F., et al.: SD-CNN: a shallow-deep CNN for improved breast cancer diagnosis. Comput. Med. Imaging Graph. **1**(70), 53–62 (2018)
8. Batra, K., Sekhar, S., Radha, R.: Breast cancer detection using CNN on mammogram images. In: Smys, S., Tavares, J.M.R.S., Balas, V.E., Iliyasu, A.M. (eds.) ICCVBIC 2019. AISC, vol. 1108, pp. 708–716. Springer, Cham (2020). https://doi.org/10.1007/978-3-030-37218-7_80
9. Bhatia, S., Sinha, Y., Goel, L.: Lung cancer detection: a deep learning approach. In: Soft Computing for Problem Solving 2019, pp. 699–705. Springer, Singapore (2019)
10. Wang, Z., et al.: Breast cancer detection using extreme learning machine based on feature fusion with CNN deep features. IEEE Access. **16**(7), 105146–105158 (2019)
11. Danaee, P., Ghaeini, R., Hendrix, D.A.: A deep learning approach for cancer detection and relevant gene identification. In: Pacific Symposium on Biocomputing, pp. 219–229 (2017)
12. Fakoor, R., Ladhak, F., Nazi, A., Huber, M.: Using deep learning to enhance cancer diagnosis and classification. In: Proceedings of the International Conference on Machine Learning 2013 June, vol. 28, pp. 3937–3949. ACM, New York (2013)
13. Ragab, D.A., Sharkas, M., Marshall, S., Ren, J.: Breast cancer detection using deep convolutional neural networks and support vector machines. PeerJ. **28**(7), e6201 (2019)
14. Yoo, S., Gujrathi, I., Haider, M.A., Khalvati, F.: Prostate cancer detection using deep convolutional neural networks. Sci. Rep. **9**(1), 1 (2019)
15. Mambou, S.J., Maresova, P., Krejcar, O., Selamat, A., Kuca, K.: Breast cancer detection using infrared thermal imaging and a deep learning model. Sensors. **18**(9), 2799 (2018)
16. Šarić, M., Russo, M., Stella, M., Sikora, M.: CNN-based method for lung cancer detection in whole slide histopathology images. In: 2019 4th International Conference on Smart and Sustainable Technologies (SpliTech), 18 June 2019, pp. 1–4. IEEE (2019)
17. Dabeer, S., Khan, M.M., Islam, S.: Cancer diagnosis in histopathological image: CNN based approach. Inform. Med. Unlocked **16**, 100231 (2019)
18. Hu, Q., Whitney, H.M., Giger, M.L.: A deep learning methodology for improved breast cancer diagnosis using multiparametric MRI. Sci. Rep. **10**(1), 1–1 (2020)
19. Duran-Lopez, L., Dominguez-Morales, J.P., Conde-Martin, A.F., Vicente-Diaz, S., Linares-Barranco, A.: PROMETEO: a CNN-based computer-aided diagnosis system for WSI prostate cancer detection. IEEE Access. **8**, 128613–128628 (2020)
20. Shkolyar, E., et al.: Augmented bladder tumor detection using deep learning. Eur. Urol. **76**(6), 714–718 (2019)
21. Mallick, P.K., Ryu, S.H., Satapathy, S.K., Mishra, S., Nguyen, G.N., Tiwari, P.: Brain MRI image classification for cancer detection using deep wavelet autoencoder-based deep neural network. IEEE Access. **15**(7), 46278–46287 (2019)

22. Selvathi, D., Aarthy Poornila, A.: Deep learning techniques for breast cancer detection using medical image analysis. In: Hemanth, J., Balas, V.E. (eds.) Biologically rationalized computing techniques for image processing applications. LNCVB, vol. 25, pp. 159–186. Springer, Cham (2018). https://doi.org/10.1007/978-3-319-61316-1_8

23. Das, A., Acharya, U.R., Panda, S.S., Sabut, S.: Deep learning based liver cancer detection using watershed transform and Gaussian mixture model techniques. Cognitive Syst. Res. 1(54), 165–175 (2019)

24. Hosny, K.M., Kassem, M.A., Foaud, M.M.: Skin cancer classification using deep learning and transfer learning. In: 2018 9th Cairo international biomedical engineering conference (CIBEC), 20 Dec 2018, pp. 90–93. IEEE (2018)

25. Asuntha, A., Srinivasan, A.: Deep learning for lung Cancer detection and classification. Multimed. Tools Appl. 79(11), 7731–7762 (2020)

26. Daghrir, J., Tlig, L., Bouchouicha, M., Sayadi, M.: Melanoma skin cancer detection using deep learning and classical machine learning techniques: a hybrid approach. In: 2020 5th International Conference on Advanced Technologies for Signal and Image Processing (ATSIP), 2 September 2020, pp. 1–5. IEEE (2020)

27. Elnakib, A., Amer, H.M., Abou-Chadi, F.E.: Early lung cancer detection using deep learning optimization

28. Ismael, S.A., Mohammed, A., Hefny, H.: An enhanced deep learning approach for brain cancer MRI images classification using residual networks. Artif. Intell. Med. 102, 101779 (2020)

29. Song, Z., et al.: Clinically applicable histopathological diagnosis system for gastric cancer detection using deep learning. Nature Commun. 11(1), 1–9 (2020)

OHF: An Ontology Based Framework for Healthcare

Shivani Dhiman[1(✉)], Anjali Thukral[2], and Punam Bedi[1]

[1] Department of Computer Science, University of Delhi, New Delhi, India
{shivani,pbedi}@cs.du.ac.in
[2] Keshav Mahavidyalaya, University of Delhi, New Delhi, India
athukral@keshav.du.ac.in

Abstract. Timely and holistic recommendations in disease diagnosis process may prove a great assistance to a medical practitioner. However, the amount of structured or unstructured data generated in medicinal domain are voluminous and thus imposes challenges. In order to make machines understand the data semantically and infer useful insights from patient's information, the data needs to be semantically represented in an ontology. Therefore, in this paper we explore various ontologies existing in the medicinal domain. The paper proposes an Ontology-Based Framework for Healthcare (OHF) using these existing ontologies, and also proposes Healthcare Ontology (HO) which is a semantic representation of knowledgebase of patients' healthcare information available in the form of Electronic Health Record (EHR). The OHF consisting of systematically generated and exhaustive ontologies may be utilized for predicting semantic inferences related to a patient's medical condition. A case study is being used to explain working of the framework in disease diagnosis.

Keywords: Electronic Health Record · Ontologies · Clinical diagnosis · Reasoning

1 Introduction

Artificial Intelligence (AI)-enabled Healthcare [1] is an upcoming specialized area of research which explores ways to provide better care to patients' well-being. Providing clinical decision support to a medical practitioner with accurate and timely recommendations in disease diagnosis is one of the important areas where AI based techniques can be leveraged. However, heterogeneity and lack of structure in the medicinal data pose challenges.

The volume of digital data has seen a very high surge since 1980s and is doubling every 40 months. Medicinal domain is one of the highest contributors [2, 3] to this volume. The medicinal data is highly heterogeneous and semi-structured (a combination of structured and unstructured data) in nature. There is a need to organize this data so that the knowledge present in it can be exploited in automating clinical tasks such as treatment recommendations, retrieving relevant medical information, disease diagnosis etc.

© Springer Nature Switzerland AG 2022
A. Dev et al. (Eds.): AIST 2021, CCIS 1546, pp. 318–328, 2022.
https://doi.org/10.1007/978-3-030-95711-7_28

Ontology, a knowledge representation technique, is an explicit specification of conceptualization [4] which allows modelling, analysis and reasoning upon a domain of interest. It is used to eliminate heterogeneity in medicinal terminologies and discover knowledge by empowering reasoning tools [5].

In diagnostic process, patient details are primary requirement which are present in the form of Electronic Health Record (EHR) [6]. EHR is used to collect patient records in a digital format. It stores structured, semi-structured and textual data electronically that ensures rapid access to patient information. However, the available EHR is in either relational or textual formats due to which it is not in sync with the existing medical vocabularies which are in the form of ontologies. This makes the semantic interpretation and reasoning difficult.

Therefore, this paper proposes an Ontology based framework (OHF) consisting of existing biomedical ontologies and another proposed Healthcare Ontology (HO). The OHF helps a medical practitioner at various steps of disease diagnosis process. It provides suggestions regarding symptoms of a patient and provides recommendations about missing investigations, which would help a practitioner to reach a better and precise diagnosis. Thereby, leading to an efficient diagnosis and thus a better healthcare.

The rest of the paper is organized into four sections. Section 2 describes the concept of ontology in AI. The proposed Healthcare Ontology and Ontologies based Framework for Healthcare comprising of HO and existing medicinal ontologies have been presented in Sect. 3. Section 4 demonstrates the working of proposed system for disease diagnosis with the help of a case study. Finally, Sect. 5 concludes the paper.

2 Ontology in Medicinal Domain

According to the earliest definition in philosophy, Ontology is known as science of being [7] which studies the nature and existence of beings. It forms a system of categories that gives a comprehensive classification of existing entities (nature and beings). The Knowledge representation and reasoning, a field of Artificial Intelligence (AI) uses ontology as one of the techniques to represent knowledge in a domain. It is defined as unambiguous description of conceptualization of a domain [8, 9] and thus forms a basis for development of intelligent systems.

The development of ontologies in clinical field started since 19th century. Some of the standard ontologies that are being extensively used in different medical applications are explained in this section. Table 1 lists name of ontologies in the medicinal domain, their time of inception (outset), developing and maintaining authority and a few important ontological concepts that exist in the respective ontologies. These ontologies are well established and are regularly updated. Their updated versions are being released by the maintaining authorities in a timely manner. Most researchers [10–12] have based their studies on these existing biomedical ontologies rather than designing ontology from scratch as these ontologies cover medicinal domain in depth.

Table 1. Existing ontologies in medicinal domain

S no	Ontology	Outset (year)	Maintained by organization	Concepts included in Ontology
1	International Classification of Disease[1] (ICD) [13]	1949	World Health Organization (WHO)	Diagnosis and procedure codes, morbidity details. Effective version in usage ICD-10, more than 55,000 different codes
2	Clinical Term Version or Read Codes (CTV) [14]	1986	UK Terminology Center, NHS	Clinical terms, drugs and appliances Last version CTV3, inactive now
3	Logical Observation Identifiers, Names, and Codes[2] (LOINC) [15, 16]	1994	Regenstrief Institute	Laboratory tests, microbiology test, clinical documents (e.g., reports)
4	Gene Ontology[3] (GO) [17]	1998	Gene Ontology Consortium, OBO Foundry	Molecular function, Cellular component, Biological Process. 44,085 GO terms, 7,931,218 annotations, 1,564,454 gene products and 4,743 species
5	Systematised Nomenclature of Medicine Clinical Terms[4] (SNOMED-CT) [18, 19]	1999	International Health Terminology Standards Development Organisation (IHTSDO)	Diagnosis, clinical findings, diagnostic procedures, observables, body structure, organisms, substances, pharmaceutical products, physical objects, physical forces, specimens. It has 352,567 concepts as on January 31, 2020
6	RxNorm[5] [20]	2002	Unified Medical Language System (UMLS)	Drug entities, defining elements of drug products, quantity factor, and qualitative distinction

(continued)

Table 1. (*continued*)

S no	Ontology	Outset (year)	Maintained by organization	Concepts included in Ontology
7	Disease Ontology[6] (DO) [21, 22]	2003	Institute for Genome Sciences (IGS), University of Maryland School of Medicine	Contains greater than 8043 Human Diseases
8	Foundational Model of Anatomy[7] (FMA) [23]	2003	Structural Informatics Group at the University of Washington	Source of biomedical informatics, phenotypic structure of human body
9	Symptom Ontology[8] (SYMP) [24]	2005	IGS, University of Maryland	Contains greater than 900 symptoms
10	RadLex[9] [25]	2006	Radiology Society of North America (RSNA)	More than 8000 pathologic and anatomic terms
11	Human Phenotype Ontology[10] (HPO) [26]	2007	Monarch Initiative, Global Alliance for Genomics and Health (GA4GH) strategic roadmap	Over 13,000 terms and more than 156,000 annotations related to hereditary diseases
12	Drug Ontology[11] (DrOn) [27]	2013	U.S. National Library of Medicine (NLM)	Drug Products, their ingredients, biological activity

[1] https://www.who.int/classifications/classification-of-diseases
[2] https://loinc.org/
[3] http://geneontology.org/
[4] https://www.snomed.org/
[5] https://www.nlm.nih.gov/research/umls/rxnorm/index.html
[6] https://disease-ontology.org/
[7] http://si.washington.edu/projects/fma
[8] http://purl.obolibrary.org/obo/symp.owl
[9] http://radlex.org/
[10] https://hpo.jax.org/app/
[11] http://purl.obolibrary.org/obo/dron.owl

Existing biomedical ontologies (discussed in Table 1) exploit various medicinal areas but in isolation. For example, Disease Ontology (DO) contains different diseases such as genetic disease, physical disorders, infectious disease etc. whereas LOINC focuses on clinical documents and laboratory observations. Similarly, Symptom Ontology comprises different disease symptoms including abdominal symptoms, cardiovascular system symptoms, digestive system symptoms etc., DrOn contains Drug codes by ingredients, Drug's mechanism of action, physiological effect of drugs etc.

Biomedical ontologies are used to represent (annotate) medicinal terminologies (such as procedures, medicine, drugs, laboratory observation, clinical documents etc.) using a coding system. This coding system provide a means for global sharing of clinical vocabulary and facilitate the exchange of medicinal vocabulary among various medical facilities.

The existing biomedical ontologies collectively form a medicinal knowledgebase that can be utilized to diagnose diseases in a patient and provide preventive healthcare. However, to do so, patient details including patients' history, various examination reports, findings, demographics, and other relevant information are also required to be captured in an ontology to have a semantic representation. This has been accomplished through the proposed Healthcare Ontology (HO), described in the next section. Foremost, the section details the proposed framework, OHF that integrates all ontologies so as to enable vocabulary exchange and semantic reasoning on the knowledgebase.

3 Proposed Ontology Based Framework for Healthcare

The proposed Ontology based Framework for Healthcare consists of Healthcare Ontology (defined later in the section) and four other existing ontologies as shown in Fig. 1. These ontologies are Disease Ontology (DO) for disease information, SYMP for human symptoms developed during the progression of disease, SNOMED-CT for laboratory observations and procedures and Demographics containing patient demographic information etc. A CDSS (Clinical Decision Support System) based application is used as a Graphical User Interface (GUI) interface between a healthcare staff (user) and the knowledgebase consisting of ontologies. The next section shows an experimental study on the OHF, based on a case study [28] to demonstrate the process of disease diagnosis and various recommendations generated during the process.

Healthcare Ontology: Patients' records consisting of their medical history, demographics, symptoms, findings, and examination reports etc. contained in EHR have been mapped to the proposed Healthcare Ontology (HO). Various rules and axioms have also

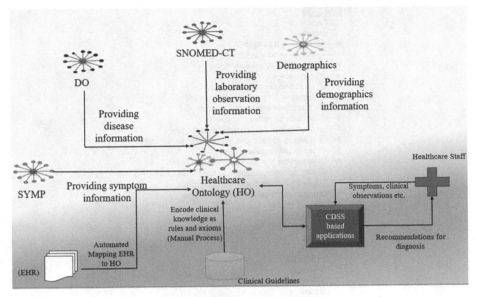

Fig. 1. OHF for clinical diagnosis

been added to the HO based on the clinical guidelines [29, 30]. The schema for HO has been defined using Resource Description Framework Schema (RDFS). A screenshot of the HO built in Protégé [31] is shown below in Fig. 2.

Disease Diagnosis Using HO and OHF: The proposed framework OHF containing HO provides recommendations during the process of disease diagnosis. The process is majorly divided into four stages as shown in Fig. 3.

Step 1: Foremost, chief complaints of the patient are fed-in by a medical practitioner using a GUI interface. These complaints are augmented in HO using the existing ontologies in the framework.

Step 2: It might happen that a patient does not report all its symptoms (complaints) during the first interaction with a medical practitioner. Therefore, in the second step of the disease diagnosis process, related and possible set of symptoms other than the primary symptoms are recommended. These recommendations are inferred by applying SWRL rules (Semantic Web Rule Language) [32] on the SYMP ontology. The set of symptoms that are recommended by the OHF, are further enquired from the patient and a manual confirmation is done by the practitioner. The confirmed set of symptoms are then augmented to the HO.

Step 3: A list of tests and investigations are recommended in the third step of disease diagnosis process. These recommendations can later be helpful to reach to the final diagnosis. The OHF applies SWRL rules on the SNOMED-CT ontology and DO to generate these recommendations. These recommendations are again analyzed by the practitioner before prescribing tests to the patient. The test results/ investigation reports of the patient are again augmented to the HO.

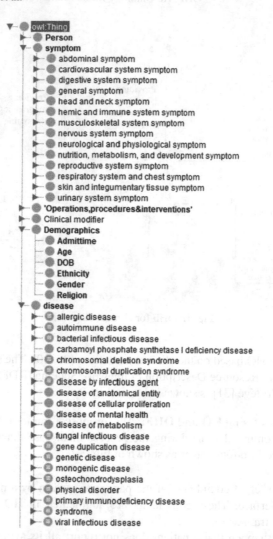

Fig. 2. Screenshot of healthcare ontology

| Get Chief Complaints | Recommend Data for Missing Symptoms | Recommend further tests and investigations, if needed | Plausisble Diagnosis Recommen dations |

Fig. 3. Disease diagnosis using HO and OHF

Step 4: A series of SWRL rules are applied on the disease ontology (DO) and HO in the last step to recommend plausible diagnosis.

An experimental study conducted on the proposed framework using HO and existing ontologies is presented in the next section.

4 Experimental Study

The authors in paper [28] presented a patients' case study of a *"73-year-old woman with progressive shortness of breath"*. The presentation of the patient in [28] was delineated as follows: *"A 73-year-old women was reported with severe dyspnea, harsh cough with clear sputum, weight loss, and has smoking history. Patient had history of hypothyroidism, gastroesophageal reflux disease, hypertension, and hyperlipidemia. No family history of lung disease. Patient worked as a landscape designer professionally. In physical examination, blood pressure, heart rate, respiratory rate, cardiac and lung auscultations were reported. Laboratory examination including blood count, hemoglobin, eosinophils, Arterial blood gas analysis, Pulmonary Function Test (PFT) were also noted."* A prototype system based on the proposed OHF was built to generate recommendations during the process of disease diagnosis. The above-mentioned case study is being used to describe a step by step working of the prototype based on HO and OHF.

Step 1: The patient came with the chief complaints of severe dyspnea and cough. These were fed-in by a medical practitioner using a GUI interface. These primary symptoms were augmented in HO using existing ontologies in the framework.

Step 2: The OHF recommended additional symptoms in order to have a more precise clinical examination. During the experimental study, the OHF recommended fatigue, cyanosis, fainting, excessive sweating, fever, and swelling (edema) in ankles, feet and legs as associated (related) symptoms. LHS of the following rule was applied on the SYMP ontology to produce a list (RHS) of symptoms related to the primary symptoms (complaints). After confirmation, these symptoms were augmented to the HO.

$$
\begin{array}{l}
Patient(?x) \wedge \\
hasPatientSymptom(?x, SevereDyspnea) \\
->
\end{array}
\quad
\begin{array}{l}
RecommendSymptom(Cyanosis, ?x) \wedge \\
RecommendSymptom(Fatique, ?x) \wedge \\
RecommendSymptom(Fainting, ?x) \wedge \\
RecommendSymptom(ExcessiveSweating, ?x), \wedge \\
RecommendSymptom(Orthopnea, ?x) \wedge \\
RecommendSymptom(Cough, ?x),
\end{array}
$$

Step 3: In the third phase, Pulmonary Function Tests (PFT), Diffusing capacity of lung (D_{LCO}), Arterial blood gas analysis (ABG), Chest Radiography, and Electrocardiography (ECG) were recommended for further investigations based on the patient's symptoms. These recommendations were provided to the practitioner, which were later prescribed to the patient for further investigations. The findings of these tests were augmented to HO. An example of one of the SWRL rules applied on SNOMED-CT to recommend tests/ investigations is shown below.

$$
\begin{array}{l}
Patient(?x) \wedge \\
hasPatientSymptom(?x, \\
SevereDyspnea) ->
\end{array}
\quad
\begin{array}{l}
RecommendTest(?x, PFT) \wedge RecommendTest(?x, \\
DLCO) \wedge RecommendTest(?x, ECG)
\end{array}
$$

Step 4: The OHF recommended Interstitial Lung Disease (ILD) as the plausible diagnosis in its last step. The patient in the case study was diagnosed with the same disease.

The ontological concepts that were referred from the existing ontologies during the systematic processing of disease diagnosis on the case study are summarized below in Table 2.

Table 2. Concepts referred from the existing medicinal Ontologies to augment HO with respect to the patient in the case study.

Symptoms (referred from SYMP ontology)	Acute Dyspnea; Cough with sputum, Fatigue; Weight loss; Chest pain; Orthopnea
Tests and Investigations (referred SNOMED-CT ontology and DO)	Cardiac auscultation findings: Heart sounds normal; Chest auscultation findings: Inspiratory crackles, Respiratory squeak; Systolic Blood Pressure (BP), Diastolic BP, Heart Rate, Respiratory Rate, Oxygen Saturation; Pulmonary Function Test (PFT), Respiratory Volume Findings: Forced Vital Capacity (FVC), Forced expiratory volume (FEV), Respiratory function findings: FEV1/FVC ratio; D_{LCO}
Disease Diagnosis (referred DO and HO)	Medical history: Hypertension; gastroesophageal reflux disease; familial hyperlipidemia; hypothyroidism Intermediate diagnosis (before tests reports): Respiratory system disease, Chronic obstructive pulmonary disease (COPD), Bronchiolitis, Chronic Heart Failure; Plausible Diagnosis (final recommendation by OFH): Interstitial lung disease (ILD)

5 Conclusion

An Ontology based Framework for Healthcare (OHF) has been presented in the paper. The OHF was designed to leverage medicinal knowledge from existing biomedical ontologies namely, SYMP (Symptom ontology), SNOMED-CT for laboratory observations and procedures, and DO (Disease ontology), to recommend plausible diagnosis for a patient with the reported primary symptoms or chief complaints. The paper also presented a Healthcare Ontology (HO) to contain health records of patients while using medicinal vocabulary from the existing ontologies. Preliminary patients' details in the HO were mapped from the Electronic Health Records (EHR). A set of SWRL rules were applied on the ontologies to augment HO and to generate recommendations during the process of disease diagnosis. An experimental study was carried out using a case study given in the paper "*73-Year-Old Woman with Progressive Shortness of Breath*".

The OHF was able to suggest symptoms in addition to those that were reported by the patient. It was also able to recommend missing/required tests and investigation reports. Based on the confirmed symptoms and results from the test reports, the OHF recommended a plausible diagnosis. In the experimental study, the OHF diagnosed Interstitial Lung Disease (ILD) for the patient under study, which was found similar to the diagnosis made in the case study. The OHF, thus can prove helpful to a medical practitioner by providing timely recommendations during the different stages of disease diagnosis. This can improvise and expedite the whole process of diagnosis leading to a better healthcare. Besides this, the OHF also semantically organises patients' health records which can be used further to recommend various preventive healthcare measures to a patient.

References

1. Reddy, S., Fox, J., Purohit, M.P.: Artificial intelligence-enabled healthcare delivery. J. R. Soc. Med. **112**, 22–28 (2019). https://doi.org/10.1177/0141076818815510
2. Hilbert, M., López, P.: The world's technological capacity to store, communicate, and compute information. Science **80**(332), 60–65 (2011). https://doi.org/10.1126/science.1200970
3. Car, J., Sheikh, A., Wicks, P., Williams, M.S.: Beyond the hype of big data and artificial intelligence: Building foundations for knowledge and wisdom. BMC Med. **17**, 1–5 (2019). https://doi.org/10.1186/s12916-019-1382-x
4. Gruber, T.R.: A translation approach to portable ontology specifications. Knowl. Acquis. **5**, 199–220 (1993). https://doi.org/10.1006/knac.1993.1008
5. Zeshan, F., Mohamad, R.: Medical ontology in the dynamic healthcare environment. Procedia Comput. Sci. **10**, 340–348 (2012). https://doi.org/10.1016/j.procs.2012.06.045
6. Mallappallil, M., Sabu, J., Gruessner, A., Salifu, M.: A review of big data and medical research. SAGE Open Med. **8**, 205031212093483 (2020). https://doi.org/10.1177/2050312120934839
7. Maedche, A.: Ontology — Definition & Overview. In: Ontology Learning for the Semantic Web. The Kluwer International Series in Engineering and Computer Science. 11–27. Springer, Boston (2002). https://doi.org/10.1007/978-1-4615-0925-7_2
8. Gruber, T.: Ontology (Computer Science) - definition in Encyclopedia of Database Systems (2009)
9. Bozsak, E., et al.: KAON — towards a large scale semantic web. In: Bauknecht, K., Tjoa, A.M., Quirchmayr, G. (eds.) EC-Web 2002. LNCS, vol. 2455, pp. 304–313. Springer, Heidelberg (2002). https://doi.org/10.1007/3-540-45705-4_32
10. Shen, Y., et al.: An ontology-driven clinical decision support system (IDDAP) for infectious disease diagnosis and antibiotic prescription. Artif. Intell. Med. **86**, 20–32 (2018). https://doi.org/10.1016/j.artmed.2018.01.003
11. Dissanayake, P.I., Colicchio, T.K., Cimino, J.J.: Using clinical reasoning ontologies to make smarter clinical decision support systems: a systematic review and data synthesis. J. Am. Med. Informatics Assoc. **27**, 159–174 (2020). https://doi.org/10.1093/jamia/ocz169
12. Zaman, S., Sarntivijai, S., Abernethy, D.R.: Use of biomedical ontologies for integration of biological knowledge for learning and prediction of adverse drug reactions. Gene Regul. Syst. Bio. **11** (2017). https://doi.org/10.1177/1177625017696075
13. Guralnick, L.: Manual of the international statistical classification of diseases, injuries, and causes of death. Am. J. Trop. Med. Hyg. **8**, 1–393 (1959). https://doi.org/10.4269/ajtmh.1959.8.83
14. Cowie, J.M., et al.: A review of Clinical Terms Version 3 (Read Codes) for speech and language record keeping. Int. J. Lang. Commun. Disord. **36** (2001). https://doi.org/10.1080/13682820150217608

15. Forrey, A.W., et al.: Logical Observation Identifier Names and Codes (LOINC) database: a public use set of codes and names for electronic reporting of clinical laboratory test results. Clin. Chem. **42**, 81–90 (1996). https://doi.org/10.1093/clinchem/42.1.81

16. McDonald, C.J., et al.: LOINC, a universal standard for identifying laboratory observations: A 5-year update. Clin. Chem. **49**, 624–633 (2003). https://doi.org/10.1373/49.4.624

17. Carbon, S., et al.: The gene ontology resource: enriching a gold mine. Nucleic Acids Res. **49**, 325–334 (2021). https://doi.org/10.1093/nar/gkaa1113

18. Stearns, M.Q., Price, C., Spackman, K.A., Wang, A.Y.: SNOMED clinical terms: overview of the development process and project status. In: Proceedings of the AMIA Symposium, pp. 662–666 (2001)

19. Gaudet-Blavignac, C., Foufi, V., Bjelogrlic, M., Lovis, C.: Use of the systematized nomenclature of medicine clinical terms (snomed ct) for processing free text in health care: Systematic scoping review (2021). https://doi.org/10.2196/24594

20. Bona, J.P., Brochhausen, M., Hogan, W.R.: Enhancing the drug ontology with semantically-rich representations of National Drug Codes and RxNorm unique concept identifiers. BMC Bioinform. **20**, 1–14 (2019). https://doi.org/10.1186/s12859-019-3192-8

21. Schriml, L.M., et al.: Disease ontology: a backbone for disease semantic integration. Nucleic Acids Res. **40**, 940–946 (2012). https://doi.org/10.1093/nar/gkr972

22. Schriml, L.M., et al.: Human Disease Ontology 2018 update: classification, content and workflow expansion. Nucleic Acids Res. **47**, 955–962 (2019). https://doi.org/10.1093/nar/gky1032

23. Rosse, C., Mejino, J.L.V.: A reference ontology for biomedical informatics: the foundational model of anatomy. J. Biomed. Inform. **36**, 478–500 (2003). https://doi.org/10.1016/j.jbi.2003.11.007

24. Kibbe, W.A., et al.: Disease Ontology 2015 update: an expanded and updated database of Human diseases for linking biomedical knowledge through disease data. Nucleic Acids Res. **43**, 1071–1078 (2015). https://doi.org/10.1093/nar/gku1011

25. Langlotz, C.P.: RadLex: a new method for indexing online educational materials (2006). https://doi.org/10.1148/rg.266065168

26. Robinson, P.N., Köhler, S., Bauer, S., Seelow, D., Horn, D., Mundlos, S.: The human phenotype ontology: a tool for annotating and analyzing human hereditary disease. Am. J. Hum. Genet. **83**, 610–615 (2008). https://doi.org/10.1016/j.ajhg.2008.09.017

27. Hanna, J., Joseph, E., Brochhausen, M., Hogan, W.R.: Building a drug ontology based on RxNorm and other sources. J. Biomed. Semantics. **4**, 1–9 (2013). https://doi.org/10.1186/2041-1480-4-44

28. Moss, J.E., Maniaci, M.J., Johnson, M.M.: 73-Year-old woman with progressive shortness of breath. Mayo Clin. Proc. **85**, 95–98 (2010). https://doi.org/10.4065/mcp.2008.0584

29. Global Initiative For Chronic Obstructive Pulmonary Disease Inc.: POCKET GUIDE TO COPD DIAGNOSIS, MANAGEMENT, AND PREVENTION A Guide for Health Care Professionals (2020)

30. Segal-Gidan, F., Cherry, D., Jones, R., Williams, B., Hewett, L., Chodosh, J.: Update 2008: Alzheimer Guideline. Alzheimer. 7 (2011)

31. Gennari, J.H., et al.: The evolution of Protégé: an environment for knowledge-based systems development. Int. J. Hum. Comput. Stud. **58**, 89–123 (2003). https://doi.org/10.1016/S1071-5819(02)00127-1

32. Horrocks, I., Patel-schneider, P.F., Boley, H., Tabet, S., Grosof, B., Dean, M.: SWRL: a semantic web rule language combining OWL and RuleML (2004)

Enhancing the Deep Learning-Based Breast Tumor Classification Using Multiple Imaging Modalities: A Conceptual Model

Namrata Singh[1(✉)], Meenakshi Srivastava[1], and Geetika Srivastava[2]

[1] Amity Institute of Information Technology, Amity University, Lucknow, India
msrivastava@lko.amity.edu
[2] Department of Physics & Electronics, Dr. Ram Manohar Lohia Avadh University,
Ayodhya, India

Abstract. Breast tumors' preliminary and unambiguous prognosis is critical for early detection and diagnosis. A specific study has established automated techniques that use only science imaging modalities to speculate on breast tumor development. Several types of research, however, have suggested rephrasing the current literature's breast tumor classifications. This study reviewed various imaging modalities for breast tumors and discussed breast tumor segmentation and classification using preprocessing, machine learning, and deep neural network techniques. This research aims to classify malignant and benign breast tumors using appropriate medical image modalities and advanced neural network techniques. It is critical to improving strategic decision analysis on various fronts, including imaging modalities, datasets, preprocessing techniques, deep neural network techniques, and performance metrics for classification. They used preprocessing techniques such as augmentation, scaling, and image normalization in the respective investigation to minimize the irregularities associated with medical imaging modalities. In addition, we discussed various architectures for deep neural networks. A convolutional neural network is frequently used to classify breast tumors based on medical images to create an efficient classification paradigm. It could be an existing network or one that has been developed from scratch. The accuracy, area-under-the-curves, precision, and F-measures metrics of the developed classification paradigm will be used to evaluate its performance.

Keywords: Classification of breast cancer · Deep learning · Medical imaging techniques · Convolutional neural network

1 Introduction

Initial and unambiguous prognoses are critical in establishing a favourable prognosis and the life expectancy of malignancy patients (World Health Organization) [1]. Breast tumors are categorized as benign or malignant. Though benign tumors are non-cancerous, malignant tumors are cancerous. Both malignant and benign tumors have additional subtypes that must be identified and diagnosed separately since each form has a unique prognosis and treatment strategy. Appropriate diagnosis defines a detailed definition within

© Springer Nature Switzerland AG 2022
A. Dev et al. (Eds.): AIST 2021, CCIS 1546, pp. 329–353, 2022.
https://doi.org/10.1007/978-3-030-95711-7_29

each subtype of breast tumor, referred to as breast tumor multi-classification. Clinical imaging modalities are preferred to alternative research methods for breast tumor diagnosis. Mammography, autopsy (US) imaging or sonograms, magnetic resonance (MRI), tomography (CT), even histopathology (HP) scans are all standard medical diagnostic modalities for breast cancer screening [2–4]. Clinical imaging is typically performed by a specialist radiologist, sinologist, or toxicologist in particular. A confident opinion is established where at least two pathologists concur on the clinical picture analysis; in some instances, a single pathologist expresses their opinion. Non-automated clinical picture analysis, on the other hand, poses difficulties [5, 6]. To begin, a healthcare centre often lacks more than one specialist pathologist, especially in developing countries. Second, pathologists find the method of picture analysis for the multi-class classification of breast tumors tedious and time-consuming. Finally, accurate breast tumor subcategory diagnosis is contingent upon a skilled pathologist's professionalism and domain knowledge. In this situation, it can result in a misdiagnosis, especially during the early stages. In healthcare, computerized clinical photos have ceded superiority to artificial intelligence using a CAD scheme for pattern recognition. By automating clinical picture processing, CAD applications assist radiologists, sinologists, and pathologists.

As a consequence of reducing false positive and negative prognoses, this strategy decreases dependence (non-automation), raises the diagnosis rate, and reduces gross drug spending [7]. Experts have promoted the use of clinical imaging modalities to classify breast tumors [8–12]. On the contrary, multiple studies have established the usage of Multimodal Artificial Neural Networks for breast tumor detection [13]. The state-of-the-art ANN strategies for breast picture multimodality analysis were shown. They explored different ANN forms for breast tumor diagnosis utilizing several imaging modalities, including mammography, ultrasound, MRI, and thermal imaging. Numerous clinical imaging modalities and ANN-based recognition algorithms for breast tumor classification have been investigated. They published a comparative study of clinical imaging techniques and the benefits and risks of clinical imaging modalities. The survey conducted an in-depth analysis of and selection from accepted sources to ensure the validity and nobility of selected research papers. Additionally, this report makes a strong case against DNN compliance on unorthodox, publicly accessible datasets. To summarise, this survey proposes remarkable creative clinical picture processing and analysis for prospective researchers interested in conducting clinical image analysis of breast tumors using DNNs [14–16] (Fig. 1).

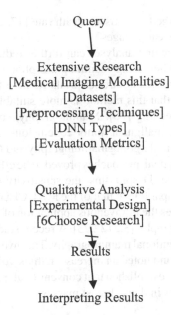

Query

Extensive Research
[Medical Imaging Modalities]
[Datasets]
[Preprocessing Techniques]
[DNN Types]
[Evaluation Metrics]

Qualitative Analysis
[Experimental Design]
[6Choose Research]

Results

Interpreting Results

Fig. 1. Research methodology

2 Literature Review

2.1 Survey Scope Identification

- Choose Medical imaging Determine the imaging modalities which would be used to diagnose the breast tumor.
- Identification of medical imaging datasets to enhance a classification system.
- Mention efficient preprocessing methods that can be used to stimulate classification outcomes.
- Define the ANN forms that would be used to distinguish images utilizing imaging modalities.
- Conclude the quality assessment metrics.

2.2 Efficient Techniques

2.2.1 Clinical Imaging Modalities

2.2.1.1 Mammogram

Mammography is the conventional method for detecting breast tumors using clinical imaging. It investigates using low-dose amplitude-X-rays. Malignant tumors and calcium collaterals appear brighter in the images. This classification can be used to differentiate DCIS from calcifications. Mammography is the standard method for detecting early-stage tumors in the breast before they become clinically significant. Mammography has resulted in a decrease in the mortality rate [16–18, 24]. Mammographic screening analyses have demonstrated unequivocally that detection and treatment of breast cancer at an early stage surmounts the tumor tissue death rate [17, 25]. However, it is difficult to detect a breast tumor in its early stages.

Nonetheless, further screening analyses can further reduce the mortality rate from breast cancer. Screening studies using mammogram photographs have been found to decrease mortality in randomized controlled trials relative to the placebo group [19–21]. It has been established that this method is more suitable for initial screening and can be used for routine screening [20]. Mammography, sonography, and MRI were used to exclude cases of rare malignant tumor conclusions [21]. DCIS was detected in 78.9% and 68.4% of patients undergoing mammography and MR MRI, respectively. The combination of all three analytical approaches proved to be effective in detecting invasive cancer and multifocal disease. Despite this, the sensitivity of the mammography and sonography mixture was comparable to that of the MRI. CEDM is a recent advancement in mammography that involves the intravenous application of an iodinated contrast agent in conjunction with mammography [3,2122,23]. A recent study evaluated the diagnostic benefits of CEDM over conventional mammography. The investigator discovered a rise in sensitivity from 0.43 to 0.62 and noted an increase in thick volumes. This is a potentially good advantage, as it has been established that conventional mammography is ineffective at detecting malignant tumors in dense breast masses.

2.2.1.2 Ultrasound

It is intended to classify breast tumors and is also used as a secondary method for evaluating the segment of a suspected lesion. The ultrasound transducer transmits high-frequency echo waves through the breast masses and detects the resulting sound waves. Waves with unique identifiers are used to illustrate two-dimensional photographs. In addition, continuous actual images may be collected by relocating the sensor to cover the breast. Ultrasound can be used in conjunction with mammography in clinical studies to assess evident and imperceptible tumor malformations. However, ultrasound screening leads to unsatisfactory false positive and false negative results [3, 26]. As a result, there is little evidence to support the use of ultrasound for breast tumor screening.

Person mammography abstains from identifying common malignancies in dense-breasted women. The symptomatic recognizes the significance of mammography with an AWBU for patients with dense breasts and an increased risk of breast cancer [27]. An analysis determined that 87% of AWBU-identified malignancies were detected in patients with thick breasts' 68% performance rate. As a consequence, AWBU culminated in a significant improvement in tumor identification when compared to mammography pictures. The author proposes that sonography can be performed indefinitely alongside mammography or other imaging modalities [28]. However, this person would be incapable of reliably detecting tumors. Additional studies promote the concurrent use of mammography and ultrasound. According to this study result, integrating screening ultrasound and mammography will find an extra 1.1 to 7.2 tumors in 1000 high-risk patients, considering the risk of an elevated false-positive rate [29]. According to relatively new studies examining the effectiveness of complete breast ultrasound using BI-RADS ultimate test parts in women with mammographically dim dense breast masses [30], ultrasound is advantageous for prominent breast evaluations. Ultrasound automation advancements include 3D ultrasound, which converts high-quality wave data to 3D perceptions [8, 28], automated ultrasound for an excellent dominant presence of the breast tumor [29], Doppler Ultrasound [31], and sono elastography [32].

2.2.1.3 Magnetic Resonance Imaging

The applicability of advanced state-of-the-art imaging modalities for the accurate description of personal breast tumors and their efficacy in limiting chemotherapeutic implications is discussed [11, 33]. MRI allows the study of vascular improvements correlated with neoangiogenesis [34]. It is widely used in research and is increasingly being used to analyze tumefaction input in response to approach. It is anticipated that novel adverse factors and advances in determination and scientific methods would promote MRI in investigating the vascular necessity of lesion germination and the outcomes of vascular-directed therapies. Breast magnetic resonance imaging (MRI) is a widely used clinical imaging modality to detect breast tumors [19, 35]. Early findings show that MRI will dramatically increase the outcome of screening particular at-risk patients.

Additionally, the output can be used to interpret the function of breast MRI in the initial diagnosis of breast tumors. Breast MRI output with 3 T electromagnets indicated that MRI would exhibit superior spatial and temporal interpretation and a higher signal-to-noise ratio [22, 36]. Thus, MRI is helpful for people who are at an increased risk of developing breast cancer. It offers beneficial image understanding, is sufficient for evaluating bulky masses, helps assess transposed breasts, allows for parallel assessment, and decides whether lumpectomy is the most effective solution. In addition, it has no harmful effects due to the absence of radiation [37]. However, MRI restrictions are insufficient for DCIS, can result in a high rate of false positives, are slower, more expensive, and may not detect all calcifications. Recently, a review was performed to assess the efficacy of mammography and MRI in eradicating breast cancers in high-risk individuals [3, 38]. The critics found no meaningful link and recommended that all screening modalities improve the gap in detecting early-stage malignant tumors.

2.2.1.4 Histopathologic Images

Histopathological imaging is used to collect mass specimens from rare breast regions using glass microscope slides. Slides are stained with hematoxylin and eosin and studied under a microscope by specialists to determine malignant masses [1]. Additionally, these stained slides are analyzed and digitally lit. Pathologists with expertise usually procure ROI patches from WSI to detect different benign or malignant subtypes that are not possible with grayscale photos. Apart from breast tumor diagnosis, biopsy imaging is a standard for various malignancy types, including liver, kidney, and bladder cancer [39]. As a result, several researchers have used histopathological photographs to precisely identify several classes [40–47]. As previously reported, histopathological imagery is useful for identifying specific subtypes of benign or malignant tumors. Automated detection of breast tumors using this picture has many advantages over mammograms and other imaging modalities. For instance, histopathological photos classify tumors into numerous subtypes rather than binary groups and monitor treatment outcomes [1, 2].

It may be shared online in order to receive a reliable report by every freely accessible specialist pathologist. Though HP photos are reliable for automatic classification, they do have a few drawbacks. Additionally, color contrast is high due to the staining method, lab regulations, and scanner brightness in HP image enhancement, making it difficult to properly train a multi-class DNN model. In comparison, WSI images allow the formulation of multiple ROIs necessary for DNN model training.

2.2.1.5 Positron Emission Tomography

PET is an atomic-resolution clinical imaging technique that generates three-dimensional photographs. It denotes a series of rays emitted by the radionuclide injection into the subject. Improved glucose metabolism in cancerous tumors is consistent with stable cells [3]. Therefore, PET photos show a difference between malignant and regular cells. In addition, it provides knowledge regarding the analytic strengths of the breast and masses. PET, on the other hand, is highly expensive and creates low-resolution pictures.

Additionally, the victim is subject to pollution susceptibility. PET has been used widely to predict drug determination in many cancers [48]. PET and SPECT all make use of radiolabeled isotopes [49]. Both provide a one-of-a-kind chance to investigate mammalian models of breast carcinoma while remaining true to human imaging. MRI and PET are comparable and helpful in monitoring the result and testing residual disease in patients with sectionally venerable breast cancer treated with neoadjuvant chemotherapy [50]. Their study concluded that the dual use of MRI and PET was beneficial and suggested enhancements over clinical breast exams. PET was more accurate at predicting diseased non-response, and the response measured with MRI was well correlated with a macroscopic pathological systematic response. SMM, SPECT, and PET may be adjunct imaging modalities to detect and stage breast tumors. They can not, however, fully replace invasive methods due to their insufficient sensitivity [3, 8, 51]. It is advantageous for assessing clear breast cancers in women with thick masses. Numerous catalysts and receptors have been developed with the aim of PET imaging breast cancer. Fluorodeoxyglucose is beneficial for diagnosing and staging persistent breast cancer.

2.2.1.6 Multimodalities

Apart from classifying malignant breast tumors using a single imaging modality, some researchers have chosen to train innumerable classification models employing two distinct imaging modalities: mammogram and MRI [1, 53]. Additionally, it was listed as normal, healthy, or cancerous utilizing several imaging modalities, including mammograms and ultrasound photos. Numerous imaging modalities for both the classification of malignant breast tumors are usually verified where the extensive cumulative databases are insufficient [54]. Additionally, a system educated on several data sets and using multiple modalities is highly reliable when identifying medical images. Finally, the classifier's implementation is unaffected by the photographs captured on various computers, the many imaging rules, and the circumstances of the supervising images. As a consequence, a standard of templates is reliable for use in real-world situations [55].

2.2.2   Datasets

This section discusses a detailed examination of well-known datasets that were used in numerous breast tumor classification considerations. Through studying the implementation of advanced classification paradigms, researchers may create new classification paradigms. Regardless of the database category conceptually, classification is done using grayscale or colored pictures. Grayscale photographs are used for mammograms, ultrasounds, and MRIs, while colored images are used for HPs.

Table 1. Clinically imaging modalities

Author's	Medical Imaging Modalities	Database(s)	Description	Application
Arefan et al., Carneiro et al., Dhungel et al., Duraisamy and Emperumal, Jaffar, Kumar et al., Qiu et al., Rouhi, Samala et al., Samala et al. and Sun et al	Mammograms	DDSM, BCDR, INbreast, Mini-MIAS,	There are three types of mammograms: screen-film mammograms (SFMs), digital mammograms (DMs), and digital breast tomography (DBT). While SFMs and DMs are two-dimensional grayscale medical images, DBT offers several frames of two-dimensional grayscale images resembling black-and-white video	Compared to HP, DM technology is a time-and cost-effective approach to capturing, storing and interpreting images

(continued)

Table 1. (*continued*)

Author's	Medical Imaging Modalities	Database(s)	Description	Application
Han et al., Nascimento et al. and Zhang et al	Ultrasound	BUSI, DDBUI, SNUH, OASBUD, ImageNet	Sonograms are another term for US images. Three distinct combinations of US images are used: simple 2D grayscale US images, US images with enhanced additive features from shear-wave elastography (SWE) color images, and US images with Nakagami colored images	In comparison to HP, it requires fewer skills and expert expertise to diagnose and classify images. To assist as a proper diagnosis, a multitude of computer-aided diagnostic (CAD) systems are available. In comparison to DM screening, DBT has a significantly better probability of screen-detected cancer. The Real-time images are captured. Thus, a breast lesion may be seen from various perspectives, lowering the incidence of false positives during widespread diagnosis availability of a very safe (noninvasive and radiation-free) technology. As a result, it was recommended for regular checkups of pregnant women

(*continued*)

Table 1. (*continued*)

Author's	Medical Imaging Modalities	Database(s)	Description	Application
Bakkouri and Afdel	Mammograms and ultrasound images	BCDR	Specific research classified breast cancer using a mix of two grayscale imaging modalities termed multimodality. Mg with MRI and US with CT are two of these combos	A model trained on multiple sites, multiple data sets, and multiple modalities is resilient when classifying real-world medical images
Araujo et al., Bardou et al., Nahid and Kong, Nahid et al., Spanhol et al	Histopathology images	BICBH, BreakHis	HP Images are colorful images saturated with H&E and classified into two categories: whole slide images (WSI) and image patches derived from WSI by any skilled pathologist	This imaging modality may be processed in two ways: whole slides or ROIs derived from WSI. Because images are colorful, they may detect a mix of different types of cancer rather than detecting malignancy only via grayscale imaging techniques. Overall, this results in a more favourable prognosis and earlier treatment. Breast tissues may be discussed in detail. HP images offer more reliable diagnoses than other imaging modalities. Multiple ROI images may be generated from WSI, reducing the risk of lacking cancer tissue identification, particularly early, and minimizing the FN rate. Images may be communicated electronically to get expert advice, particularly in uncertain situations when two distinct cancer types are challenging to identify. It can be archived for analysis purposes or reference

Additionally, most studies used binary classification, while others focused on multi-class issues in breast tumor classification. In comparison, extraordinary inquiries classified breast density into three categories: poor, large, and medium. Contrary to assumptions, the plurality of considerations utilized binary grouping and others obtained more desirable results when deciding multi-class problems. [58, 60].

Table 1 demonstrates that the average number of inquiries exceeds 27 since various investigations used different datasets for accuracy. As a result, they are quantified in different groups. According to our research, the various widely used and factual mammography databases are DDSM, ultrasound is BCDR, and high-resolution imaging is broken. These databases include various clinical photos of patients, which are required to train robust classification paradigms. It is astounding that no freely available databases have been used for clinical imaging modalities such as CT, MRI, or PET. As a result, publicly accessible databases can include insufficient clinical images to train classification paradigms [31, 43, 56–65, 68–74].

Numerous researchers used the datasets to identify breast tumors of various forms, as described in the various research paper such as BCDR, CBIS-DDSM, DDSM, INBreast, MIAS, mini-MIAS, UCI, BICBH, Break His, Bordet Radcliffe NUH dataset GSE45255.GPL96, Erasmus Medical Center (EMC) dataset 1 - GSE2034.GPL96; Europe and Cleveland (EMCT) dataset - GSE12093.GPL96, Guy's hospital dataset (GUYT2) GSE9195.GPL570.fCEL, Johannes Gutenberg University (MAINZ) dataset - GSE11121.GPL96, Karolinska (STO) dataset - + GPL97, Memorial Sloan-Kettering Cancer Center (MSKCC) dataset GSE2603.GPL96_Clinical samples, Nagalla 2013 reconstituted public dataset, Guys hospital (GUYT) dataset GSE6532.GPL570, John Radcliff Hospital (OXFU, OXFT) dataset GSE6532.GPL96 + GPL97, TRANSBIG (TBIG) dataset -GSE7390.GPL96, University of California San Francisco (YAU) dataset - GSE7378.GPL4685, Uppsala and Singapore dataset -GSE4922.GPL96 + GPL97 [5, 65, 74] (Table 2).

2.2.3 Preprocessing

2.2.3.1 Noise Removal

The authors chose a one-parameter square-root noise model to develop an adaptive VST capable of stabilizing the noise variance to a unitary standard deviation. It is important to emphasize that this noise model does not consider the noise power spectral density. Additionally, since the VST is a pointwise transmutation, much of the spatial correlation is preserved throughout the noise [66, 67]. Thus, it seems as if associated noise has a little detrimental effect on the approach's effectiveness. On three medical image datasets, they evaluated the adaptive VST to a previously published VST [68]. Due to the adjusted anode materials used, the scatter plots of noise levels before variance stabilization reveal two clusters in the Hologic and GE datasets. To be precise, rhodium was used in place of molybdenum to account for breast masses in 15% and 51% of images, respectively, for Hologic and GE. Despite this, the adaptive VST was effective at noise stabilization (PMSE 1%).

In contrast, the set-up transform did not incorporate the varying noise levels indicated by the PMSE's high standard deviations. Additionally, it can be examined by inspecting

Table 2. Datasets

Database	Link	Author
BCDR	https://bcdr.ceta-ciemat.es/information/about	Moura and López
CBIS-DDSM	https://wiki.cancerimagingarchive.net/display/Public/CBIS-DDSM	Clark et al.
DDSM	http://marathon.csee.usf.edu/Mammography/Database.html	Chris Rose et al.
INBreast	http://medicalresearch.inescporto.pt/breastresearch/index.php/Get_INbreast_Database	Moreira et al.
MIAS	https://www.repository.cam.ac.uk/handle/1810/250394	Suckling et al.
mini-MIAS	http://peipa.essex.ac.uk/info/mias.html	Suckling et al.
UCI	https://archive.ics.uci.edu/ml/datasets/Breast%2bCancer%2bWisconsin%2b%2528Original%2529	Dua et al.
BICBH	https://rdm.inesctec.pt/dataset/nis-2017-003	Araújo et al.
BreakHis	https://web.inf.ufpr.br/vri/databases/breast-cancer-histopathological-database-breakhis/	Spanhol et al.
BUSI	https://scholar.cu.edu.eg/?q=afahmy/pages/dataset	Dhabyani et al.
DDBUI	https://www.atlantis-press.com/proceedings/jcis2008/1735	Tian et al
OASBUD	http://bluebox.ippt.gov.pl/~hpiotrzk/	Piotrzkowska et al.
ImageNet	https://image-net.org/	Deng et al

scatter plots of noise levels following variance stabilization. Surprisingly, the fixed VST has two noiseless clusters. On the other side, the adaptive VST is primarily consisting of a single cluster. This was a likely outcome, as the fixed VST was invented to rescale the noise to a level determined by the characteristics of the input image [68, 69]. The two VSTs were used to preprocess four MC detectors that anticipate various training approaches and image characteristics. MC detection execution with the adaptive VST was significantly more unusual than without variance stabilization in all test cases. The mean sensitivity changes were necessary, especially for detectors where noise significantly affects the input pixel intensities. Cascade is focused on Haar-like peculiarities expressly developed for MC detection. Appropriately, CNN senses and removes low-level features from the initial layers automatically. They conclude that reducing the noise variation in the input data was beneficial for the layers that extracted contrast and spatial details from the 11 mm picture patches. As a result, this persuaded us that the successive layers' training task, which results in more complicated features, merits further investigation, e.g., through checking alternative CNN architectures.

Additionally, results for MC identification with the adaptive VST are statistically substantially more eminent than with the set VST. This means that the MC analyzer can provide the same noise level for all images and even do variance stabilization. Finally, the most significant advancement has been made with SVM, which is vulnerable to data anomalies due to its training with function vectors derived instantly from the patch [4, 69, 70].

2.2.3.2 Artefact Removal

Clinical photographs are de-artefacts to delete any non-relevant domains from the original file. Unique clinical imaging modalities inhabited numerous objects such as marks, salaries, invisible markers, white strips, boundaries, thorax, lungs, chest wall, and pectoral muscle. It can be eradicated before the creation of a malignant tumor classification scheme. Numerous studies [1, 43, 71–73] established that preprocessing methods are irrelevant to the domain since they do not use the whole clinical picture but only (tumor image) ROIs for classification. Despite this, Arefan et al. [71] derived non-relevant domains from mammograms on two levels: constructing binary images generated by pixel thresholding to classify related regions and extracting small segregated areas.

Examined ultrasound photos acquired after extracting the abdominal segment by inspecting the rib cage tip. Additionally, Sert et al. [73] eliminated white bands found at mammogram edges by thresholding the amplitude equivalent. Consequently, the ROI is isolated from the expected clinical picture before multi-classification of the oily, glandular, or thick breast is done [2, 72].

2.2.3.3 Normalization & Enhancement

Associating color and light requirements affects medical image retrieval and digitization. As a result, several color and light conditions have an impact on all pixel values. Researchers employed a range of techniques that can be narrowly grouped into two categories: global or local picture normalization and enhancement techniques to resolve these problems. Global image normalization and enhancement techniques, such as histogram, mean, and median contrast/intensity normalization, execute the same process on all pixels in an image. By comparison, local picture normalization and enhancement strategies work on any pixel independent of its contrast or intensity concerning its neighbours. It employs techniques for enhancing picture features before serving them to some DNN for classification. DNNs typically work better with normalized and decor-related input images, as these properties aid in gradient-based optimization and learning. Several factors manipulated global contrast normalization by using mean filters to overcome the multi-class classification problem. We removed the speckle noise and blurring effect in ultrasound pictures using Wiener and mean-variance and spatial correlations.

Additionally, the researcher used a mean filter and wavelet shrinkage to reduce the impulse noise commonly seen in Ultrasound pictures. Further, picture local contrast was enhanced using contrast limited adaptive histogram equalization (CLAHE). Some use a combination of the bilateral filter and log transformation [1, 2, 10, 74].

2.2.3.4 Stain Normalization

HP biopsy photos are developed in DP laboratories using various additives, stains, lighting effects, and scanners. As a result, it is possible to obtain irregularities in histopathological photographs. In addition, certain determinators can create significant differences in patient records, including though images are produced in the laboratory. Eliminating these irregularities, early studies relied on RGB histogram specification; some researchers used satin normalization or removal strategies before classifying [75, 76]. For instance, the author used Retinex to generate a non-linear transformation to normalize illumination, confirming a method for performing non-linear mapping-based stain normalization [76]. Additionally, stain normalization methods and mean standard deviation procedures correlate RGB channels with the testimonial image [74].

2.2.3.5 Roi

An initial breast image may comprise many benign and malignant masses, and discrimination of these regions is named ROI extraction. ROI extraction has two crucial advantages. First, it multiplies the training and testing images needed for classification, encouraging DNNs to learn only benign and malignant regions, somewhat irrelevant ones. Second, as specified in several investigations, obtained ROIs from the initial image before the classification. For example, I received ROI from 3D Mammogram DBT images. Likewise, the author cropped the ROI of benign and malignant tissues before the classification [74].

2.2.4 Artificial Neural Network

An ANN can perform various real-world training datasets, including vectorized data and emails containing medical images. Numerous ANNs are enhanced to prepare a variety of data types. For example, researchers used two forms of ANNs to distinguish medical images: SNNs and DNNs. In addition, several researchers have used DNNs for classification.

2.2.4.1 Shallow Neural Network

A single artificial neural network (ANN) is a mathematical function that simulates the process of a biological neuron. SNNs have only one hidden layer. An ANN's primary configuration is the artificial neuron connected with a cell, node, or secret unit. The yield of an ANN is shown by the attachment weights that enhance the effect of an input. Any transfer function may be used to emulate the non-linear properties of a single neuron. Later, when using an enhancement mechanism, neuron impulses are anticipated [20, 74, 78].

2.2.4.2 Multi-layer Neural Network

A DNN of the ML-NN form contains three layers: input, secret, and output. It does, though, train and customizes to produce the desired outcomes. Configuring a machine learning neural network entails initializing and modifying the training datasets, such as initializing weights by producing prior domain knowledge before initiating the training law. For instance, increasing the number of hidden layers will improve generalization efficiency[74].

2.2.4.3 Deep Belief Networks

The researcher will use guided learning to prepare DBNs for classification. Withstanding this, one analysis explicitly used the advantages of DBN for the same reason. They classified breast ultrasound-based SWE-coloured images using a two-layered DBN composed of PGBM and RBM. PGBM is a word that refers to a method that is used to differentiate between acceptable and incorrect characteristics. Additionally, RBM was used to satisfy relevant traits to assess the association between the related features. Through using RBM-derived functions, SVM was used to evaluate benign or malignant conditions. The primary advantage of using a DBN for model classification is that it is often trained layer by layer, allowing for immediate optimization of each layer for improved feature generalization. The final layers and the final secret layer may be educated unsupervised or monitored [74].

2.2.4.4 Stacked Denoising Autoencoder

The author concluded that the output of the SDAE-based model is comparable to that of every other kind of DNN model. It is vital to have noise-reducing capabilities, mainly because real medical photos often involve noise from unconventional references. Thus, automated noise suppression for medical photographs promotes the acquisition of additional critical functionality. Additionally, layer-by-layer training makes it easier to optimize and standardize training datasets. Although the primary advantage is that SDAE is non-toxic, it may have certain drawbacks. SDAE, for example, performs insufficiently on low-dimensional data within dimensions. Data of several sizes, such as diagnostic images [74].

2.2.4.5 Principal Component Analysis Network

Pets are easier to plan, run, and practice than other deep learning networks that handle various high-dimensional data forms. It is adaptable due to binary hashing and block diagrams, allowing scientific analysis and confirming its efficacy. Additionally, it has a wide receptive area for obtaining the total remarks of artefacts in a picture and studying invariance[74].

2.2.4.6 Convolutional Neural Network

CNN has a track record of accurately classifying pathological images, earning the confidence of researchers. It usually consists of multiple layers, including an input layer, convolutional layers, ultimately linked layers, and an output layer that uses softmax to estimate mark probabilities. Convolutional layers gain high-level features successfully, while FC layers acquire pixel-level features. Apart from the main layers, some other layers contribute to the network's reliability. For example, a steadily decreased spatial representation to minimize the number of datasets, and network computing may be used after convolution layers. Following the FC layer, a dropout layer is usually used to mitigate network overfitting. Nonetheless, teaching is controlled using back-propagation, and pre-trained models are trained on real pictures. Two strategies for implementing TL for BrC classification were verified by researchers[74].

Types of ANN

Interpretations for using different ANN types to discern images acquired from various imaging modalities [74].

- SNN

  - Limited scale networks
  - Efficient to establish, train, and enhance the activation functions
  - significantly increases generalization efficiency.
  - It needs minimal preparation time, computing capacity, and processing to contain weight.

- **ML-NN**

  - It integrates several of the strengths of SNN with the added benefit of increased concealed layers, which aids in classification efficiency.
  - Data with a high dimension could be used to improve functionality extraction.

- **DBN**

  - This reliable, greedy learning procedure may be proceeded by or merged with appropriate learning procedures that perfect all of the weights to enhance the network's generative or discriminative efficiency.
  - It can be used to analyze high-dimensional data with correlated features.

- **SADE**

  - Automated binarization of multidimensional data improves the accuracy of classification models when used in collaboration with actual clinical images.
  - Will sense cross-entropy, which the learning algorithm for the model, such as back-propagation, aims to counteract.

- **PCA-Net**

  - Due to its wide receptive area can extract global insights about the artefacts in a picture and capture higher-level semantic content.
  - The planet is resilient for scientific analysis and evidence of its efficacy due to its binary hashing and block histogram.

- **CNN(De novo)**

  - CNN (UDM): It is possible to build customized deep CNN versions.
  - A model can be generated based on the type and volume of images.
  - CNN (CDM): Consists of the same qualities as CNN (UM)
  - Additionally, the model may be helpful even when the number of target images is limited when solving multi-class classification problems.
  - CNN (COM): It is possible to build detailed deep CNN designs.
  - Learning, assessment, and analysis were carried out with many artefacts with the same modality. Typically, optimal efficiency could be seen.
  - The source images, typical images from a complete dataset, are insufficient for learning. This method is preferred since it enables the usage of all target images only for experimental purposes.

- **CNN(pre-trained)**

  - Deep CNN classifiers are based efficiently and accurately with fewer tools than de novo models. Even though the reference data is smaller in scale, they can achieve good outcomes, such as HP classification images.

- In comparison to FTM-LL, CNN (FTM-ARL) can learn more structured and accurate weights from limited quantities of data set such as classification images.

Constraints for using different ANN types to discern images acquired from various imaging modalities [74].

- **SNN**

  - may not demonstrate a high level of efficiency when dealing with multidimensional data.
  - Performance is entirely dependent on the features and functions of the ANN.
  - Predictions are difficult to speculate.

- **ML-NN**

  - It will include several of the drawbacks of SNN. However, a more significant number of concealed layers requires further data to achieve a higher level of classification efficiency.

- **DBN**

  - Incapable of tracking the failure during the log probability computation.

- **SADE**

  - Dimensionality reduction works best on high-dimensional data than on low-dimensional data due to the increased constraints usually located among higher dimensions, such as the classification of medical images.

- **PCA-Net**

  - Simple hashing can not provide sufficient details to map the functions. As a result, it has an impact on the actual results.
  - When data contains a large number of insignificant facts, this is preferred.

- **CNN(De novo)**

  - CNN (UDM): a typically challenging model to learn with a limited dataset of pixels to solve a classification query.
  - Designing and enhancing a deep network with accurate data requires a high level of knowledge. May need a significant amount of time and resources to achieve the best outcomes.
  - CNN (CDM): Learning the model twice would take longer and could entail additional funding.
  - It is difficult to refine model testing using statistical parameters from disparate contexts, such as ImageNet and BreakHis.

- Requires a sufficient number of cases divided proportionally throughout CNN (COM): Medical data captured from distinct locations is often acquired using disparate image acquisition protocols. As a practice, additional and meticulously applied to preprocess methodologies are needed to obtain a consistent classifier.

- **CNN(pre-trained)**

  - If the reference dataset is limited, the findings can be unreliable.
  - Additionally, retraining involves class-wise equilibrium data to generate impartial outcomes, typically not available in actual medical images.
  - The limitations are identical to CNN (FTM-LL), except CNN (FTM-ARL): As new layers are introduced and learned from scratch, the learning rate may increase.
  - Enhancing newly added layers requires caution to achieve optimal performance.

2.2.5 Evaluation Parameters

1. **Confusion matrix:** This specific tabular arrangement allows for the simulation of an algorithm's representation. Each column in the uncertainty matrix represents the expected class, while each row represents the actual class or vice versa.
2. **Accuracy:** This measure shows how many of the cumulative instances are classified correctly. It merely indicates how correctly regular patients estimate and how accurately cancerous patients diagnose [1, 13, 74].

$$Ac = (TP + TN)/(TP + TN + FP + FN)$$

3. **Misclassification rate:** This is the proportion of incorrect classifications to total participants [1, 74].

$$Mr = (FP + FN)/Total$$

4. **Sensitivity:** This formation shows the proportion of confident instances that predict correctly. It indicates the degree to which breast cancer patients accurately estimate gross cancerous patients. As a result, it should be set as large as possible. The term "Low Sensitivity" refers to many cancer cases being misdiagnosed and may receive routine treatment. As a result, sensitivity plays a critical role in clinical picture diagnosis [12, 16, 17, 74].

$$a. \quad Sn = TP/(TP + FN)$$

5. **Specificity:** This formation indicates the proportion of overall pessimistic forecasts that are correct. It shows how much of the typical cancer patient's prognosis is correct. It should be as high as practicable but less critical than clinical picture diagnosis exposure [1, 12, 74].

$$a. \quad Sp = TN/(TN + FP)$$

6. **Precision:** This formation illustrates the proportion of optimistic forecasts that are correct. It simply indicates how much breast cancer tumor prediction is accurate. For clinical picture detection, specificity and accuracy should be strong to prevent misdiagnosis of cancerous patients [11, 74].

$$Pr = TP/(TP + FP)$$

7. **F measure:** By emphasizing more pain over severe ideals, this formation represents both Sn and Pr's concurrent effect harmonically. It contrasts two miniatures with a high Sn content but a low Pr content and one with a low Sn content but a high Pr content [11, 74]. (Table 3)

$$F\,Measure = 1 + b2\,(Pr \times Sn)/b2 \times Pr + Sn$$

Table 3. Evaluation parameters

Measures	Equations
Accuracy (Ac)	Ac = (TP + TN)/(TP + TN + FP + FN)
Sensitivity (Sn) or Recall (Rc)	Sn = TP/(TP + FN)
Specificity (Sp)	Sp = TN/(TN + FP)
Precision (Pr)	Pr = TP/(TP + FP)
FMeasure	F Measure = $(1 + \beta2)$ (Pr × Sn)/($\beta2$ × Pr + Sn)
AUCROC	AUC = Σ i Ri (Ip) − Ip(Ip + 1)/2/Ip + In

3   Conceptual Model

The proposed architecture can be easily understood with the help of a flow chart (Fig. 3).

3.1   Information Abstraction

Researchers can use multiple clinical imaging modalities instead of a single clinical image as predominant contributions to clinical image analysis. The imaging methodology's determination for a focused clinical examination requires clinical bits of knowledge explicit to organs under investigation to achieve knowledge about the anatomical design in the breast. The preprocessing procedures may have dramatic beneficial outcomes on the nature of highlight extraction and the aftereffects of image investigation. Preprocessing improves the clinical image information that smothers undesirable bends or upgrades some image highlights significant for additional processing. It is analytically outrageous to mapping the comprehensive clinical images to label masks. Downsampling the idea is also inefficacious, as many architectures of consideration manifest at

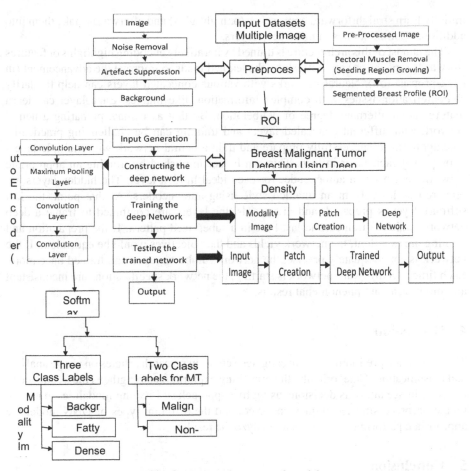

Fig. 2. Proposed conceptual model

an admirable scale. So, an impermeable resemblance must be insight for patches from the image. Imaging modalities experience digitization commotions, like straight lines. Radiopaque antiquities, for example, wedges and names, are likewise present in the images. The presence of pectoral muscle in image predispositions recognition methods suggests eliminating the Pectoral muscle during clinical manifestation preprocessing. Extraction of the breast lesion profile region and the pectoral muscle is a fundamental preprocessing step, while CAD helped recognition. It permits the investigation for irregularities to be restricted to the malignant tissue locale without excessive impact from the image's foundation. Region of Interest is a chosen subset of tests inside a dataset distinguished for a specific reason. An ROI is a segment of an image that must be filtered to implement out some other procedure. ROI can be characterized by applying a binary mask; a new image is identical to the image to be processed. Deep non-linear frameworks have been demonstrated to generate viable descriptors in feature acknowledgement and localization in characteristic images. Motivated by the human mind, these frameworks initially learn straightforward approaches (or highlights) and afterwards make them into additional Complex ones in more deep layers.

The utmost of this architecture is trained by iteratively encoding highlights or features (forward propagation) and refreshing the learned loads to improve the advancement (in back-propagation). Neural networks with various concealed layers can help to clarify characterization issues with complex information, like images. Each layer can learn features at an alternate degree of deliberation. Be that as it may, preparing a neural network with different concealed layers and training can be challenging practically. One approach to successfully prepare and train a neural network with multiple layers is preparing each layer in turn. This can be accomplished by training an appropriate network known as an autoencoder for each ideal hidden layer. The hidden layers are prepared exclusively in an unaided style using autoencoders. At that point, the last softmax layer is prepared, and afterwards, the layers are combined to frame a deep network, which is trained one last time in a supervised pattern. If the preparation and training are excellent, the network yields and the objectives would be equivalent. If the network is not adequately precise, the network can be engaged and trained once more. Each time a feedforward network is starting, the network specifications are inconsistent and might generate phenomenal results.

4 Discussion

This evaluation predominantly investigated scholarly research articles on image analysis and classification. Categorically, the prevailing exploration strengthens the assurance to improve image analysis decisions using five approaches: imaging modalities, datasets, image preprocessing techniques endorsed, and the different types of DNN model the appropriate performance metrics to analyze the results.

5 Conclusion

This analysis will assist the novice in classifying the breast tumor using a deep neural network. This research aims to design and assess breast tumor classification architecture. It includes selecting the preferred medical image from various imaging modalities, appropriate datasets, image processing techniques, DNN techniques, and evaluation metrics practices. Thus, the comparisons of different image modalities such as mammography, MRI, ultrasound, PET, and CT should be analyzed to provide various lesion attributes to enhance the classification results. Public datasets comprise a similar patient's multimodality images and some other message or clue, for instance, DNA sequence. Such a type of dataset can help reduce frequent pattern growth using automated systems. Numerous public and private datasets of breast cancer are available. The private datasets are small in size comparatively. The public datasets are readily available in the public domain, and it contains multimodalities images of similar patients alongside some other information such as DNA sequence, etc. According to the observation, most investigators have been chosen the public datasets over the private datasets. Pre-processing was essentially approved to eliminate image paradoxes before encouraging the classification model. However, it should follow attentively to prevent critical data. This review identified different characteristics of DNN architecture to classify breast tumors. This analysis explains distinct new state-of-the-art challenges that require comprehensive accomplishment to enhance classification architecture.

References

1. World Health Organization (2018) Cancer. http://www.who.int/en/news-room/fact-sheets/det ail/cancer. Accessed 20 Sept 2018
2. Beutel, J., Kundel, H.L., Van Metter, R.L.: Handbook of Medical Imaging, vol. 1. SPIE Press, Bellingham (2000)
3. Goceri, E.: Advances in digital pathology. Paper presented at the international conference on applied analysis and mathematical modelling. Istanbul, Turkey (2017)
4. Kasban, H., El-Bendary, M., Salama, D.: A comparative study of medical imaging techniques. Int J. Inf. Sci. Intell. Syst. **4**, 37–58 (2015)
5. Gurcan, M.N., Boucheron, L.E., Can, A., et al.: Histopathological image analysis: a review. IEEE Rev. Biomed. Eng. **2**, 147–171 (2009). https://doi.org/10.1109/rbme.2009.2034865
6. Sophie Softley Pierce, P.M., Breast Cancer Care: Three-quarters of NHS Trusts and Health Boards say 'not enough' care for incurable breast cancer patients (2017)
7. Goceri E, Songul C (2018) Biomedical information technology: image-based computer-aided diagnosis systems. Paper presented at the international conference on advanced technologies. Antalya, Turkey
8. Chen, J.M., Li, Y., Xu, J., Gong, L., Wang, L.W., Liu, W.L., Liu, J.: Computer-aided prognosis on breast cancer with hematoxylin and eosin histopathology images: a review. Tumor Biol. **39**(3), 12 (2017). https://doi.org/10.1177/1010428317694550
9. Goceri, E., Goceri, N.: Deep learning in medical image analysis: recent advances and future trends. Paper presented at the international conferences computer graphics, visualization, computer vision, and image processing. Istanbul, Turkey (2017)
10. Jalalian, A., Mashohor, S., Mahmud, R., Karasfi, B., Saripan, M.I.B., Ramli, A.R.B.: Foundation and methodologies in computer-aided diagnosis systems for breast cancer detection. Exclusive J **16**, 113–137 (2017). https://doi.org/10.17179/excli201-701
11. Lee, H., Chen, Y.-P.P.: Image-based computer-aided diagnosis system for cancer detection. Expert Syst. Appl. **42**(12), 5356–5365 (2015). https://doi.org/10.1016/j.eswa.2015.02.005
12. Litjens, G., Kooi, T., Bejnordi, B.E., Setio, A.A.A., Ciompi, F., Ghafoorian, M., et al.: A survey on deep learning in medical image analysis. Med. Image Anal. **42**, 60–88 (2017). https://doi.org/10.1016/j.media.2017.07.005
13. Mehdy, M.M., Ng, P.Y., Shair, E.F., Saleh, N.I.M., Gomes, C.: Artificial neural networks in image processing for early detection of breast cancer. Comput. Math. Methods Med. (2017). https://doi.org/10.1155/2017/2610628
14. Nahid, A.A., Kong, Y.: Involvement of machine learning for breast cancer image classification: a survey. Comput. Math. Methods Med. (2017). https://doi.org/10.1155/2017/3781951
15. Sathish, D., Kamath, S., Rajagopal, K.V., Prasad, K.: Medical imaging techniques and computer-aided diagnostic approaches for detecting breast cancer, emphasizing thermography—a review. Int. J. Med. Eng. Inf. **8**(3), 275–299 (2016). https://doi.org/10.1504/IJMEI.2016.077446
16. Yassin, N.I.R., Omran, S., El Houby, E.M.F., Allam, H.: Machine learning techniques for breast cancer computer-aided diagnosis using different image modalities: a systematic review. Comput. Methods Programs Biomed. **156**, 25–45 (2018). https://doi.org/10.1016/j.cmpb.2017.12.012

17. Kerlikowske, K., Grady, D., Rubin, S.M., Sandrock, C., Ernster, V.L.: Efficacy of screening mammography. A meta-analysis. JAMA **273**(2), 149–154 (1995). PMID: 7799496
18. Nyström, L., Andersson, I., Bjurstam, N., Frisell, J., Nordenskjöld, B., Rutqvist, L.E.: Long-term effects of mammography screening: updated overview of the Swedish randomised trials. Lancet **359**(9310), 909–919 (2002). https://doi.org/10.1016/S0140-6736(02)08020-0.Err atum.In:Lancet2002Aug31;360(9334):724. PMID: 11918907
19. Kopans, D.B.: Beyond randomized controlled trials: organized mammographic screening substantially reduces breast carcinoma mortality. Cancer **94**(2), 580-1 (2002); author reply 581–3. https://doi.org/10.1002/cncr.10220. PMID: 11900247
20. Kopans, D.B.: Sonography should not be used for breast cancer screening until its efficacy has been proven scientifically. AJR Am. J. Roentgenol. **182**(2), 489–491 (2004). https://doi.org/10.2214/ajr.182.2.1820489. PMID: 14736687
21. Tabar, L., Yen, M.F., Vitak, B., Chen, H.H., Smith, R.A., Duffy, S.W.: Mammography service screening and mortality in breast cancer patients: 20-year follow-up before and after the introduction of screening. Lancet **361**(9367), 1405–1410 (2003). https://doi.org/10.1016/S0140-6736(03)13143-1. PMID: 12727392
22. Malur, S., Wurdinger, S., Moritz, A., Michels, W., Schneider, A.: Comparison of written reports of mammography, sonography, and magnetic resonance mammography for preoperative evaluation of breast lesions, emphasizing magnetic resonance mammography. Breast Cancer Res. **3**, 55–60 (2001)
23. Williams, M.B., Judy, P.G., Gong, Z., Graham, A.E., Majewski, S., Gunn, S.: Scanner for integrated X-Ray breast tomosynthesis and molecular breast imaging tomosynthesis. In: Martí, J., Oliver, A., Freixenet, J., Martí, R. (eds.) IWDM 2010. LNCS, vol. 6136, pp. 444–451. Springer, Heidelberg (2010). https://doi.org/10.1007/978-3-642-13666-5_60
24. Domain, C., Balleyguier, C., Adler, G., Garbay, J.R., Delaloge, S.: Contrast-enhanced digital mammography. Eur. J. Radiol. **69**(1), 34–42 (2009). https://doi.org/10.1016/j.ejrad.2008.07.035. Epub 2008 Sep 13. PMID: 18790584
25. Diekmann, F., Freyer, M., Diekmann, S., Fallenberg, E.M., Fischer, T., Bick, U., Pöllinger, A.: Evaluation of contrast-enhanced digital mammography. Eur J Radiol. **78**(1), 112-21 (2011). https://doi.org/10.1016/j.ejrad.2009.10.002. Epub 2009 Nov 19. PMID: 19931350
26. The, W., Wilson, A.R.: The role of ultrasound in breast cancer screening. A consensus statement by the European Group for Breast Cancer Screening. Eur. J. Cancer **34**(4), 449–450 (1998). https://doi.org/10.1016/s0959-8049(97)10066-1. PMID: 9713292
27. Kelly, K.M., Dean, J., Comulada, W.S., Lee, S.J.: Breast cancer detection using automated whole breast ultrasound and mammography in radiographically dense breasts. Eur. Radiol. **20**(3), 734–42 (2010). https://doi.org/10.1007/s00330-009-1588-y. Epub 2009 Sep 2. PMID: 19727744; PMCID: PMC2822222
28. Berg, W.A., et al.: ACRIN 6666 Investigators. Combined screening with ultrasound and mammography vs mammography alone in women at elevated risk of breast cancer. JAMA. **299**(18), 2151–63 (2008). https://doi.org/10.1001/jama.299.18.2151. Erratum in: JAMA. 2010 Apr 21;303(15):1482. PMID: 18477782; PMCID: PMC2718688
29. Youk, J.H., Kim, E.K., Kim, M.J., Kwak, J.Y., Son, E.J.: Performance of hand-held whole-breast ultrasound based on BI-RADS in women with mammographically negative dense breasts. Eur Radiol. **21**(4), 667–675 (2011). https://doi.org/10.1007/s00330-010-1955-8. Epub 2010 Sep 19. PMID: 20853108
30. Sree, S.V., Ng, E.Y., Acharya, R.U., Faust, O.: Breast imaging: a survey. World J. Clin. Oncol. **2**(4), 171–178 (2011). https://doi.org/10.5306/wjco.v2.i4.171.PMID:21611093; PMCID:PMC3100484
31. Kook, S.H., Park, H.W., Lee, Y.R., Lee, Y.U., Pae, W.K., Park, Y.L.: Evaluation of solid breast lesions with power Doppler sonography. J. Clin. Ultrasound. **27**, 231–237 (1999)

32. Scaperrotta, G., et al.: Role of sonoelastography in non-palpable breast lesions. Eur Radiol. **18**, 2381–2389 (2008)
33. Basildon, J.P.: Current and future technologies for breast cancer imaging. Breast Cancer Res. **3**(1), 14–16 (2001). https://doi.org/10.1186/bcr264.PMID:11300100;PMCID:PMC138671
34. Leach, M.O.: Breast imaging technology application of magnetic resonance imaging to angiogenesis in breast cancer. Breast Cancer Res. **3**, 22 (2000). https://doi.org/10.1186/bcr266
35. Schnall, M.D.: Application of magnetic resonance imaging to early detection of breast cancer. Breast Cancer Res. **3**(1), 17–21 (2001). https://doi.org/10.1186/bcr265.PMID:11300101; PMCID:PMC138672
36. Lehman, C.D., Schnall, M.D.: Imaging in breast cancer: magnetic resonance imaging. Breast Cancer Res. **7**(5), 215–219 (2005). https://doi.org/10.1186/bcr1309. Epub 2005 Aug 5. PMID: 16168141; PMCID: PMC1242161
37. Stephan, P.: In: Hayat, M.A., (ed.) Lung and breast carcinomas. Elsevier; 2010. Mammography and Breast MRIs. http://breastcancer.about.com/od/mammograms/a/mammo_vs_mri_2. htm
38. Lee, J.M., Halpern, E.F., Rafferty, E.A., Gazelle, G.S.: Evaluating the correlation between film mammography and MRI for screening women with increased breast cancer risk. Acad. Radiol. **16**, 1323–1328 (2009)
39. Rubin, R., Strayer, D.S., Rubin, E.: Rubin's Pathology: Clinicopathologic Foundations of Medicine. Lippincott Williams & Wilkins, Philadelphia (2008)
40. Abdullah-Al, N., Bin, A.F., Kong, Y.N. IEEE: Histopathological breast-image classification with image enhancement by convolutional neural network. Paper presented at the 2017 20th International conference of computer and information technology, New York (2017)
41. Araujo, T., Aresta, G., Castro, E., Rouco, J., Aguiar, P., Eloy, C., et al.: Classification of breast cancer histology images using convolutional neural networks. PLoS ONE **12**(6), 14 (2017). https://doi.org/10.1371/journal.pone.0177544
42. Bardou, D., Zhang, K., Ahmad, S.M.: Classification of breast cancer based on histology images using convolutional neural networks. IEEE Access (2018). https://doi.org/10.1109/access.2018.2831280
43. Bayramoglu, N., Kannala, J., Heikkila, J.: Deep learning for magnification independent breast cancer histopathology image classification. Paper presented at the Proceedings—international conference on pattern recognition (2017)
44. Cao, J., Qin, Z., Jin, J., Chen, J., Wan, T.: An automatic breast cancer grading method in histopathological images based on pixel-, object-, and semantic-level features. Paper presented at the 2016 IEEE 13th international symposium on biomedical imaging (ISBI) (2016)
45. Chang, J., Yu, J., Han, T., Chang, H., Park, E.: A method for classifying medical images using transfer learning: a pilot study on breast cancer histopathology. Paper presented at the 2017 IEEE 19th international conference on e-health networking, applications, and services (Healthcom) (2017)
46. Gandomkar, Z., Brennan, P.C., Mello-Thoms, C.: MuDeRN: multi-category classification of breast histopathological image using deep residual networks. Artif Intell Med. (2018). https://doi.org/10.1016/j.artmed.2018.04.005
47. Murtaza, G., Shuib, L., Mujtaba, G., Raza, G.: Breast cancer multi-classification through a deep neural network and hierarchical classification approach. Multimed. Tools Appl. (2019). https://doi.org/10.1007/s11042-019-7525-4
48. Fass, L.: Imaging and cancer: a review. Mol Oncol. **2**(2), 115–52 (2008). https://doi.org/10.1016/j.molonc.2008.04.001. Epub 2008 May 10. PMID: 19383333; PMCID: PMC5527766
49. Berger, F., Gambhir, S.S.: Recent advances in imaging endogenous or transferred gene expression utilizing radionuclide technologies in living subjects: applications to breast cancer. Breast Cancer Res. **3**(1), 28–35 (2001). https://doi.org/10.1186/bcr267. Epub 2000 Dec 11. PMID: 11250742; PMCID: PMC139436

50. Chen, X., et al.: Combined MRI and PET scans to monitor response and assess residual disease for locally advanced breast cancer treated with neoadjuvant chemotherapy. Acad. Radiol. **11**, 1115–1124 (2004)
51. Bénard, F., Turcotte, E.: Imaging in breast cancer: single-photon computed tomography and positron-emission tomography. Breast Cancer Res. **7**(4), 153–62 (2005). https://doi.org/10.1186/bcr1201. Epub 2005 May 12. PMID: 15987467; PMCID: PMC1175073
52. Schilling, K., Narayanan, D., Kalinyak, J.E.: Effect of breast density, menopausal status, and hormone use in high-resolution positron emission mammography. Radiol. Soc. North Am., VB31–04 (2008)
53. Hadad, O., Bakalo, R., Ben-Ari, R., Hashoul, S., Amit, G.: Classification of breast lesions using cross-modal deep learning. Paper presented at the proceedings—international symposium on biomedical imaging (2017)
54. Khan, M.H.M.: Automated breast cancer diagnosis using artificial neural network (ANN). Paper presented at the 2017 3rd Iranian conference on signal processing and intelligent systems, New York (2017)
55. Ramadan, S.Z.: Methods Used in Computer-Aided Diagnosis for Breast Cancer Detection Using Mammograms: A Review, Volume 2020 |Article ID 9162464 | https://doi.org/10.1155/2020/9162464
56. Moura, D.C., Guevara López, M.A.: An evaluation of image descriptors combined with clinical data for breast cancer diagnosis. Int J Comput Assist Radiol Surg. **8**(4), 561–574 (2013). https://doi.org/10.1007/s11548-013-0838-2. Epub 2013 Apr 13. PMID: 23580025
57. Clark, K., et al.: The Cancer Imaging Archive (TCIA): maintaining and operating a public information repository. J. Digit. Imaging **26**(6), 1045–1057 (2013). https://doi.org/10.1007/s10278-013-9622-7.PMID:23884657;PMCID:PMC3824915
58. Lee, R.S., Gimenez, F., Hoogi, A., Miyake, K.K., Gorovoy, M., Rubin, D.L.: A curated mammography data set for use in computer-aided detection and diagnosis research. Sci. Data **4**, 170177 (2017). https://doi.org/10.1038/sdata.2017.177. PMID: 29257132; PMCID: PMC5735920
59. Chris Rose, D.T., Williams, A., Wolstencroft, K., Taylor, C.: DDSM: digital database for screening mammography (2006). http://marathon.csee.usf.edu/Mammography/Database.html. Accessed 26 Aug 2018
60. Moreira, I.C., Amaral, I., Domingues, I., Cardoso, A., Cardoso, M.J., Cardoso, J.S.: In breast: toward a full-field digital mammographic database. Acad. Radiol. **19**(2), 236–248 (2012)
61. Suckling, J., Parker, J., Dance, D., Astley, S., Hutt, I., Boggis, C., et al.: Mammographic Image Analysis Society (MIAS) database v1, p. 21 (2015)
62. Dua, D.: KT UCI machine learning repository. The University of California, School of Information and Computer Science, Irvine (2017). http://archive.ics.uci.edu/ml
63. Araújo, T., Aresta, G., Castro, E., Rouco, J., Aguiar, P., Eloy, C., et al.: Classification of breast cancer histology images using convolutional neural networks. PLoS ONE **12**(6), e0177544 (2017)
64. Spaniel, F.A., Oliveira, L.S., Petitjean, C., Heutte, L.: A dataset for breast cancer histopathological image classification. IEEE Trans. Biomed. Eng. **63**(7), 1455–1462 (2016)
65. Roelands, J., et al.: A collection of annotated and harmonized human breast cancer transcriptome datasets, including immunologic classification. In: F1000Res, March 2017 20;6:296. https://doi.org/10.12688/f1000research.10960.2. PMID: 29527288; PMCID: PMC5820610
66. Bria, C.M., Mordang, J.-J., Karssemeijer, N., Molinara, M., Tortorella, F.: LUT-QNE: look-up-table quantum noise equalization in digital mammograms. In: International Workshop on Digital Mammography, pp. 27–34. Springer (2016)
67. Borges, L.R., Guerrero, I., Bakic, P.R., Foi, A., Maidment, A.D.A., Vieira, M.A.C.: Method for simulating dose reduction in digital breast tomosynthesis. IEEE Trans. Med. Imaging **36**(11), 2331–2342 (2017)

68. Azzari, L., Foi, A.: Variance stabilization in Poisson image deblurring. In: Proceedings of 2017 IEEE International Symposium Biomedical Imaging (ISBI), Melbourne, Australia (2017)
69. Tromans, C.E., Cocker, M.R., Brady, M.: Quantification and normalization of x-ray mammograms. Phys. Med. Biol. **57**(20), 6519 (2012)
70. Bria, A., et al.: Improving the automated detection of calcifications using adaptive variance stabilization. IEEE Trans. Med. Imaging **37**(8), 1857–1864 (2018). https://doi.org/10.1109/TMI.2018.2814058
71. Arefan, D., Talebpour, A., Ahmadinejhad, N., Asl, A.K.: Automatic breast density classification using neural network. J. Instrum. (2015). https://doi.org/10.1088/1748-0221/10/12/t12002
72. Bevilacqua, V., Brunetti, A., Triggiani, M., Magaletti, D., Telegrafo, M., Moschetta, M.: An optimized feedforward artificial neural network topology to support radiologists in breast lesions classification. Paper presented at the GECCO 2016 companion—proceedings of the 2016 genetic and evolutionary computation conference (2016)
73. Sert, E., Ertekin, S., Halici, U.: Ensemble of convolutional neural networks for classification of breast microcalcification from mammograms. Paper presented at the Proceedings of the annual international conference of the IEEE engineering in medicine and biology society, EMBS (2017)
74. Murtaza, G., et al.: Deep learning-based breast cancer classification through medical imaging modalities: state of the art and research challenges. Artif. Intell. Rev. **53**(3), 1655–1720 (2019). https://doi.org/10.1007/s10462-019-09716-5
75. Reinhard, E., Adhikhmin, M., Gooch, B., Shirley, P.: Color transfer between images. IEEE Comput. Graphics Appl. **21**(5), 34–41 (2001)
76. Macenko, M., Niethammer, M., Marron, J.S., Borland, D., Woosley, J.T., Guan, X., et al.: A method for normalizing histology slides for quantitative analysis. Paper presented at the IEEE international symposium on biomedical imaging: from nano to macro, 2009. ISBI 2009 (2009)
77. Khan, A.M., Rajpoot, N., Treanor, D., Magee, D.: A non-linear mapping approach to stain normalization in digital histopathology images using image-specific color deconvolution. IEEE Trans. Biomed. Eng. **61**(6), 1729–1738 (2014)
78. Lopez-Martin, M., Carro, B., Sanchez-Esguevillas, A., Lloret, J.: Shallow neural network with kernel approximation for prediction problems in highly demanding data networks. https://www.researchgate.net/publication/330712973_Shallow_neural_network_with_kernel_approximation_for_prediction_problems_in_highly_demanding_data_networks

EEG Based Stress Classification in Response to Stress Stimulus

Nishtha Phutela[1]($\boxtimes$), Devanjali Relan[1], Goldie Gabrani[2],
and Ponnurangam Kumaraguru[3]

[1] Computer Science and Engineering Department, BML Munjal University, Gurugram,
Haryana, India
{nishtha.phutela,devanjali.relan}@bmu.edu.in
[2] College of Engineering, Vivekananda Institute of Professional Studies, Pitampura,
New Delhi, India
[3] Computer Science Department, IIIT Hyderabad, Gachibowli, Hyderabad, India
pk.guru@iiit.ac.in

Abstract. Stress, either physical or mental, is experienced by almost every person at some point in his lifetime. Stress is one of the leading causes of various diseases and burdens society globally. Stress badly affects an individual's well-being. Thus, stress-related study is an emerging field, and in the past decade, a lot of attention has been given to the detection and classification of stress. The estimation of stress in the individual helps in stress management before it invades the human mind and body. In this paper, we proposed a system for the detection and classification of stress. We compared the various machine learning algorithms for stress classification using EEG signal recordings. Interaxon Muse device having four dry electrodes has been used for data collection. We have collected the EEG data from 20 subjects. The stress was induced in these volunteers by showing stressful videos to them, and the EEG signal was then acquired. The frequency-domain features such as absolute band powers were extracted from EEG signals. The data were then classified into stress and non-stressed using different machine learning methods - Random Forest, Support Vector Machine, Logistic Regression, Naive Bayes, K-Nearest Neighbors, and Gradient Boosting. We performed 10-fold cross-validation, and the average classification accuracy of 95.65% was obtained using the gradient boosting method.

Keywords: Stress classification · Machine learning · MUSE headband · EEG signal

1 Introduction

Stress is one of the most common problems in the western world and is increasing in the middle-class population in India due to the adoption of the western lifestyle. In today's world, work and occupation-related stress are increasing day by day. Moreover, the job that demands to multitask is another major cause of stress [1]. According to the American Institute of Stress, around 73–77% population experience stress that affects

© Springer Nature Switzerland AG 2022
A. Dev et al. (Eds.): AIST 2021, CCIS 1546, pp. 354–362, 2022.
https://doi.org/10.1007/978-3-030-95711-7_30

not only the physical health but also the mental wellbeing. Further, around 48% of people are suffering from sleep disorder due to stress [2]. Recent survey on LinkedIn's showed that 40% of working Indian professionals experience increased stress or anxiety. The survey also showed that 36% of them feel that stress is adversely impacting their work-life balance [3].

According to WHO, by the year 2030, mental illnesses result in various diseases globally. Globally, approximately 15.5% population are affected by mental illnesses and these statistics are rising exponentially. Stress is also a type of mental illness that can badly affect an individual's health. Traditionally, stress was analyzed only by medical personnel without the use of any technology. Medical staff trained in mental health used to perform psychotherapies which involved face to face interaction with the people facing mental health concerns. Advances in computing technology have created opportunities for close collaboration between computer engineers and medical practitioners studying mental health. With the plethora of sensing devices now being available, emerging technologies like Big Data Analytics (BDA), Human–Computer Interaction (HCI), Machine Learning (ML), Artificial Intelligence (AI) and Internet of Things (IOT) have started to emerge as technologies with capabilities to develop applications that help people with their stress-related mental health problems [4–6]. These technologies have become an umbrella to offer new opportunities for screening and predicting stress-related mental health problems. Coupled with the power of data science, these can transform the way technology can be used to identify and treat people who have stress-related mental illnesses. A persistence of long term or short-term stress effect the individual neurology and thus results in depression [7–10]. Moreover, stress-related disorders such as cardiovascular disease, anxiety and depression are also rising in today's busy world [11]. Thus, to prevent the onset of depression it is important that stress symptoms can be detected timely.

In order to detect stress and initiate stress management treatment it is vital to have reliable tools to measure physiological stress in response to stimulus [12]. Stress can be quantified using different features and biomarkers extracted from electroencephalography (EEG) and electrocardiography (ECG) signals [13]. EEG is one of the most common, widely, and non-invasive modality to record signal in order to study brain function [14–18]. Each frequency band of EEG signals (delta, theta, alpha, beta, and gamma) can be used to extract the distinguishing feature to classify different brain states [17, 19–21].

2 Related Work

For stress management, it is vital to detect the stress level timely, which reduces the risk of adverse health consequences. The accuracy of the designed methods relies on various factors such as sensors that can measure physiological signals, quality of signal and the machine learning model. Different authors made multiple attempts to classify stress. Different datasets, stress induction methods, EEG headbands with varying channels, machine learning models etc. were used to classify stress into various categories.

In one of the studies, the authors related stress with the circumplex model of affect. This model characterizes several emotions in the domain of arousal and valence [22]. The authors used the DEAP dataset, containing 32-channel EEG data, for the detection of stress. They extracted time-based, spectral features from complex non-linear EEG signals. They found that stressed state is associated with reduced asymmetry as compared to non-stressed state. Using coherence analysis, they also found that during the stressed state the activity in the right side of the brain is more than the left.

In another study, the authors induced stress into the subject using Stroop and memory test [1]. They used 14 channel EEG device to acquire the data. Band power features were extracted from the EEG signals. These features were used to classify stress type from relaxed condition using Support Vector Machines (SVM). The authors obtained an accuracy of 77.53% in this three-level classification of stress. The subjects provided the ground truth in 3-item questionnaire presented after each task.

In another paper [17], the authors performed 2 and 3 class stress classification using EEG signals. They used a MUSE headband containing four electrodes for the acquisition of the EEG signal. Frequency domain features were extracted from the Fast Fourier Transformed (FFT) EEG signal. The stress was induced using audio tracks and State Trait Anxiety Inventory (STAI) was used to assess subject's self-reported stress. They performed classification using various machine learning methods and achieved the best classification accuracy of 98.7% and 95.6%, for 2 and 3 classes respectively, was achieved using Logistic Regression.

In another study, the authors used Stroop color-word Test (SCWT) to induce the stress and used a combination of power-based features, fractal dimension (FD) and statistical features for the inter-subject classification [23]. The features were extracted from 14 electrode EEG headbands. The stress level was classified using k nearest neighbors (k-NN) and support vector machine. Finally, the fivefold cross-validation was performed to validate the model. It was found that SVM outperformed k-NN when a combination of statistical and FD features was used. Three levels stress classification achieved an average accuracy of 75.22% whereas, two levels stress classification resulted in an accuracy of 85.17% using SVM.

The system proposed by authors for stress classification extracted various features such as correlation, rational asymmetry, power spectral density, differential asymmetry, and power spectrum from different EEG frequency bands [24]. They compared the SVM (with polynomial kernel function), MLP (4 hidden layers) and Naïve Bayes for stress classification. Their system achieved the best accuracy of 92.8% (2 class) and 64.28% (3 class) using MLP.

In another paper, system was proposed to classify different mental states - relaxing, neutral and concentrating [25]. They tested a various features selection algorithms and classifier. They compared the performance of the proposed system in terms of accuracy and number of features used. They perform 10-fold cross validation to validate the accuracy of the designed model. They summarized optimal 44 features, from a set of 2100 features, required for the stress classification. Their designed system resulted in overall accuracy of 87% with Random Forest Classifier.

In [26], the frequency domain features were extracted from EEG recordings. They found support vector machine as the best classifier, among all the tested classifiers, to classify human stress when used with alpha asymmetry as one of the features. They found that alpha asymmetry can be regarded as one of the potential biomarkers for stress classification, when labels are assigned using expert evaluation.

The authors in [27] utilized frequency-based features to classify four types of negative emotions using 4 channel EEG signals. They used movie clips as emotion elicitation material. They tried multiple machine learning algorithms and found that Long Short-Term Memory (LSTM) can achieve the best accuracy of 92.84% by using 10-fold cross validation.

Various authors proposed different systems to classify stress. However, we found no studies to see the impact of COVID news and videos on human stress levels. We examine the effect of videos related to COVID on the human mental state using EEG signals on healthy participants. Four groups of features (five PSD features for each of the four electrode positions) are extracted from EEG signals acquired using MUSE headband. These features were then used to classify data into stress and non-stress using six different classifiers - Logistic Regression, Random Forest, Naive Bayes, Support Vector Machine, K-Nearest Neighbors and Gradient Boosting methods. The major contributions of the paper are:

1. A 4-channel EEG dataset containing the brain activity of 20 subjects while watching stressful covid video.
2. To perform stress classification from various classifiers using four groups of frequency domain features.

The paper is structured as follows: Sect. 3 explains the detailed methodology. Experimental results obtained for stress classification are presented in Sect. 4. The limitations of the current work and the possible ways to address these in the future are written in Sect. 5.

3 Methodology

Various steps involved in the proposed system for stress classification using EEG signals consists of inducing stress, EEG data acquisition, pre-processing, feature extraction, and classification. The subsequent section describes each step for stress classification using EEG signals.

3.1 EEG Data Acquisition

Device Description: The EEG signal of subjects was acquired using a four channel MUSE EEG headband in response to stimulus. The MUSE headband is an off-the shelf non-clinical device for capturing the brain signals (see Fig. 1a). This device contains 4 sensors: TP9, AF7, AF8 and TP10. These sensors are in turn dry electrodes that have been placed according to the 10–20 system of electrode placement (Fig. 1b). The device produces raw as well as pre-processed FFT signals. These signals can be transferred over Bluetooth from the device to an android application called MUSE monitor. This application can store the signals in csv format and transfer to the laptop for further processing.

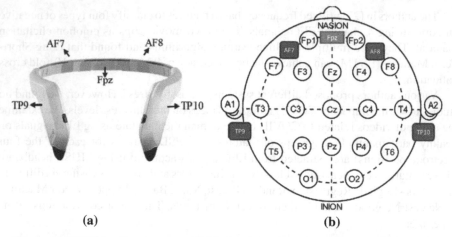

Fig. 1. (a) MUSE headband to record EEG signal (b) Electrode positioning on head scalp

Stimuli: To induce the emotion of stress, we chose two kind of video content: a) Stressful video content and b) Relaxing video content. The stressful videos were those containing covid related news showing the number of increasing covid cases and deaths and the severity of the disease. The relaxing videos had comedy scenes that would relax the subject. Each video was of a duration of 3 min. A gap of 2 min was given between each video clip to avoid the interference of stressed feeling on non-stressed feeling and vice versa. This stimulus is chosen to target two classes of stress: stressed and non-stressed.

Subjects: A total of 20 healthy subjects, in the age group of 18–30 years, (both males and females) voluntarily participated in this study. The data from 2 subjects were dropped because two sensors got disconnected in the middle of the experiment. Therefore, we performed analysis on the EEG data of 18 subjects. The procedure and protocol were explained thoroughly, and consent form was taken from each of the participants. The experiment was conducted according to the principle of Helsinki. After watching each clip, a self-assessment form was filled by the subjects to rate their experience about the video shown on a five-point scale (0-Non stressful at all, 5-lot stressful). A rating of greater than 3 was regarded as stressful. The labels provided by them was considered as ground truth. Since stress also depends on the perception of an individual, these self-reported labels were compared with the labels that we had set for the videos. If the labels did not match, we dropped the data of the subject from our analysis. But the self-reported labels of all the subjects matched with the pre-rated labels. This served as validation for ground truth.

3.2 Data Pre-Processing and Feature Extraction

Recorded EEG data often contains noise and artefacts. Thus, signal pre-processing plays an important role to remove noise to improve signal to noise (SNR) ratio. The MUSE headband gives the pre-processed Fast Fourier Transform signals. The built-in pre-processing system of MUSE headband was used to remove the noise from the

EEG signals. It applies a notch frequency of 50 Hz. Butterworth's fourth order filter with different cut-off frequencies are used inside MUSE to remove undesirable frequency signals to extract the five frequency bands of interest \cite{teo2018eeg}. The pre-processed data in the frequency domain are categorized in the following frequency ranges: delta (0.5–4 Hz), theta (4–8 Hz), alpha (8–13 Hz), beta (13–32 Hz) and gamma (32–100 Hz). Each of these signals corresponds to the four electrode positions. Thus, the pre-processed dataset contains 20 features (five features from each of the four sensor positions). Figure 2 shows the raw data visualized using Mind Monitor android application. Each of the features derived through FFT are discrete frequency values on a log scale.

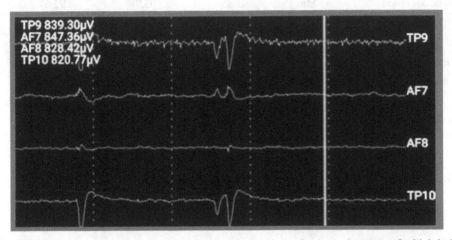

Fig. 2. Raw EEG values show each sensor raw data in microvolts (μv), the range of which is 0- ~ 1682

3.3 Classifiers

To classify the EEG recording into stress and non-stress categories, different classification algorithms were used and compared. We used Random Forest, Support Vector Machine, Logistic Regression, Naive Bayes, K-Nearest Neighbors and Gradient Boosting methods for stress classification. The performance of the classification algorithms was assessed using a 10-fold cross validation method. During the validation process using 10-fold cross validation method, first the data was divided into 10 equal parts and out of which one part was used to test the data and remaining data was used to train the model.

This process was repeated, and each iteration yield different performance parameters. Thus, minimum, maximum, and standard deviation was evaluated and presented in Table 1.

Table 1. Table summarizing the results obtained for stress classification using different classifiers

Algorithm		Accuracy	Precision	AUC
Logistic regression	Min	77.43	85.76	83.4
	Max	83.4	96.82	91.56
	Avg.	82.26	87.33	85.75
SVM	Min	78.88	87.2	91.5
	Max	88.52	95.17	95.6
	Avg.	85.46	92.26	93.89
Random Forest	Min	92.85	93.78	92.67
	Max	96.86	97.67	97.29
	Avg.	94.68	95.55	96.77
Naive Bayes	Min	76.23	86.26	89.26
	Max	82.45	91.89	92.57
	Avg.	81.99	84.78	87.64
K-NN	Min	82.22	86.59	87.20
	Max	88.43	89.21	90.5
	Avg.	85.91	88.51	89.28
Gradient Boosting	Min	94.43	94.6	93.65
	Max	97.78	98.29	98.89
	Avg.	95.65	96.54	96.72

4 Result

In this work, the task of stress classification while watching COVID news has been accomplished. Table 1 shows the results obtained from stress classification using various algorithms. The performance metrics - Accuracy, Precision and Area under the ROC curve (AUC) have been used to compare the results. This table also shows the statistical measure such as: minimum (Min.), maximum (Max.) and average (Avg.) of performance metrics. For example, the metrics - Min. and Max - denote the minimum and maximum accuracy obtained at a particular fold in 10-fold cross-validation; Avg. denotes the average accuracy obtained from all folds. Results show that the Gradient Boosting algorithm outperformed all other algorithms with an average accuracy of 95.65% as shown in Table 1. Moreover, the precision obtained with Gradient boosting is high, and it shows the robustness of the proposed system. High precision shows the percentage of correctly classified instances among the ones classified as stress groups. Stress classification system proposed by different authors used 32 channel EEG acquisition device [22, 28] and uses different features or feature selection methods [17, 23]. We have proposed a simple system that uses direct features provided by a 4-channel EEG system for stress classification.

5   Conclusion

In this work, we have presented EEG signals-based stress classification using various machine learning models. In our study, the Gradient Boosting classifier obtains the highest accuracy. Furthermore, various studies used the 4 channels Interaxon Muse for stress classification [17, 18, 24–26] which is the same as used in this study. We achieved either comparable or better accuracy compared to their studies. Moreover, our system outperforms as compared to the approach proposed in [1, 23] for stress detection. But at the same time, it is essential to note that direct comparison is not possible because of the difference in the type of stimulus used, the number of participants, the feature selection techniques and classifiers used in all the studies.

Various studies induce stress in the participants using multitasking activities (such as Stroop and a memory test) [1, 29]. In contrast, we used COVID videos to induce stress in the participants during the 2nd wave of the pandemic. Furthermore, to reduce the bias of having an already stressed subject in our study, we selected the participants who did not have any causality in their family or immediate family. From the result obtained, we can conclude that the impact of our stress stimulus (covid news and videos) was so much that we could differentiate between stressed and non-stressed states with high accuracy.

References

1. Smitha, K., Xin, N.Y., Lian, S.S., Robinson, N.: Classifying subjective emotional stress response evoked by multitasking using EEG. In: 2017 IEEE International Conference on Systems, Man, and Cybernetics (SMC), pp. 3036–3041 (2017). https://doi.org/10.1109/SMC.2017.8123091
2. Patterson, E.: Stress facts and statistics. https://www.therecoveryvillage.com/mental-health/stress/related/stress-statistics/
3. Khetarpal, S.: Rising stress levels of India inc: overwork, financial woes, remote work take toll on mental health. https://www.businesstoday.in/current/economy-politics/rising-stress-levels-of-india-inc-overwork-financial-woes-remote-work-take-toll-on-mental-health/story/419099.html
4. Boukhechba, M., Daros, A.R., Fua, K., Chow, P.I., Teachman, B.A., Barnes, L.E.: Demonicsalmon: monitoring mental health and social interactions of college students using smartphones. Smart Health 9, 192–203 (2018)
5. Cásić, K., Popović, S., S˘arlija, M., Kesedžić, I., Jovanovic, T.: Artificial intelligence in prediction of mental health disorders induced by the covid-19 pandemic among health care workers. Croatian Med. J. 61(3), 279 (2020)
6. Liang, Y., Zheng, X., Zeng, D.D.: A survey on big data-driven digital phenotyping of mental health. Inf. Fusion 52, 290–307 (2019)
7. Heim, C., Nemeroff, C.B.: Neurobiology of early life stress: clinical studies. In: Seminars in Clinical Neuropsychiatry. vol. 7, pp. 147–159 (2002)
8. McGonagle, K.A., Kessler, R.C.: Chronic stress, acute stress, and depressive symptoms. Am. J. Community Psychol. 18(5), 681–706 (1990)
9. Cohen, S., Janicki-Deverts, D., Miller, G.E.: Psychological stress and disease. Jama 298(14), 1685–1687 (2007)
10. Steptoe, A., Kivimäki, M.: Stress and cardiovascular disease. Nature Rev. Cardiol. 9(6), 360–370 (2012)

11. Schneiderman, N., Ironson, G., Siegel, S.D.: Stress and health: psychological, behavioral, and biological determinants. Annual review of clinical psychology 1 (2005)
12. Jaiswal, M., Bara, C.P., Luo, Y., Burzo, M., Mihalcea, R., Provost, E.M.: Muse: a multimodal dataset of stressed emotion. In: Proceedings of the 12th Language Resources and Evaluation Conference, pp. 1499–1510 (2020)
13. Zheng, R., Yamabe, S., Nakano, K., Suda, Y.: Biosignal analysis to assess mental stress in automatic driving of trucks: palmar perspiration and masseter electromyography. Sensors 15(3), 5136–5150 (2015)
14. Mehreen, A., Anwar, S.M., Haseeb, M., Majid, M., Ullah, M.O.: A hybrid scheme for drowsiness detection using wearable sensors. IEEE Sens. J. 19(13), 5119–5126 (2019)
15. Raheel, A., Anwar, S.M., Majid, M.: Emotion recognition in response to traditional and tactile enhanced multimedia using electroencephalography. Multimed. Tools Appl. 78(10), 13971–13985 (2019)
16. Umar Saeed, S.M., Anwar, S.M., Majid, M., Awais, M., Alnowami, M.: Selection of neural oscillatory features for human stress classification with single channel EEG headset. BioMed research international 2018 (2018)
17. Asif, A., Majid, M., Anwar, S.M.: Human stress classification using EEG signals in response to music tracks. Comput. Biol. Med. 107, 182–196 (2019)
18. Anwar, S.M., Saeed, S.M.U., Majid, M., Usman, S., Mehmood, C.A., Liu, W.: A game player expertise level classification system using electroencephalography (EEG). Appl. Sci. 8(1), 18 (2018)
19. Sanei, S., Chambers, J.A.: EEG Signal Processing. Wiley, Hoboken (2013)
20. Al-Shargie, F., Tang, T.B., Badruddin, N., Kiguchi, M.: Towards multilevel mental stress assessment using SVM with ECOC: an eeg approach. Med. Biol. Eng. Comput. 56(1), 125–136 (2018)
21. Arpaia, P., Moccaldi, N., Prevete, R., Sannino, I., Tedesco, A.: A wearable EEG instrument for real-time frontal asymmetry monitoring in worker stress analysis. IEEE Trans. Instrum. Meas. 69(10), 8335–8343 (2020). https://doi.org/10.1109/TIM.2020.2988744
22. Giannakakis, G., Grigoriadis, D., Tsiknakis, M.: Detection of Stress/anxiety State from EEG Features During Video Watching (2015). https://doi.org/10.1109/EMBC.2015.7319767
23. Hou, X., Liu, Y., Sourina, O., Tan, Y. R. E., Wang, L., Mueller-Wittig, W.: EEG based stress monitoring. In: Proceedings - 2015 IEEE International Conference on Systems, Man, and Cybernetics, SMC 2015, pp. 3110–3115 (2016). https://doi.org/10.1109/SMC.2015.540
24. Arsalan, A., Majid, M., Butt, A.R., Anwar, S.M.: Classification of perceived mental stress using a commercially available EEG headband. IEEE J. Biomed. Health Inform. 23(6), 2257–2264 (2019). https://doi.org/10.1109/JBHI.2019.2926407
25. Bird, J.J., Manso, L.J., Ribeiro, E.P., Ek´art, A., Faria, D.R.: A study on mental state classification using EEG-based brain-machine interface. In: 2018 International Conference on Intelligent Systems (IS), pp. 795–800. IEEE (2018)
26. Saeed, S.M.U., Anwar, S.M., Khalid, H., Majid, M., Bagci, U.: Eeg based classification of long-term stress using psychological labeling. Sensors 20(7), 1886 (2020)
27. Acharya, D., Goel, S., Bhardwaj, H., Sakalle, A., Bhardwaj, A.: A long short term memory deep learning network for the classification of negative emotions using EEG signals. In: 2020 International Joint Conference on Neural Networks (IJCNN), pp. 1–8. IEEE (2020)
28. Koelstra, S., Muhl, C., Soleymani, M., Lee, J.S., Yazdani, A., Ebrahimi, T., Pun, T., Nijholt, A., Patras, I.: Deap: a database for emotion analysis; using physiological signals. IEEE Trans. Affect. Comput. 3(1), 18–31 (2011)
29. Ehrhardt, N.M., Fietz, J., Kopf-Beck, J., Kappelmann, N., Brem, A.K.: Separating EEG correlates of stress: cognitive effort, time pressure, and social-evaluative threat. Eur. J. Neurosci. 2021, 1–10 (2021)

Latest Trends in Gait Analysis Using Deep Learning Techniques: A Systematic Review

Dimple Sethi[1]([✉]), Chandra Prakash[2], and Sourabh Bharti[1]

[1] Indira Gandhi Delhi Technical University, Delhi, India
sourabhbharti@igdtuw.ac.in
[2] National Institute of Technology, Delhi, India
cprakash@nitdelhi.ac.in

Abstract. Marker-less analysis of human gait has made considerable progress in recent years. However, developing a gait analysis system capable of extracting reliable and precise kinematic data in a standard and unobtrusive manner remains an open challenge. This narrative review considers the transformation of methods for extracting gait extremity information from videos or images, perceived how analysis methods have improved from arduous manual procedures to semi-objective and objective marker-based systems and then marker-less systems. The gait analysis systems widely used restrict the analysis process with the use of markers, inhibited environmental conditions, and long processing duration. Such limitations can impede the use of a gait analysis system in multiple applications. Advancement in marker-less pose estimation and Q-learning-based techniques are opening the possibility of adopting productive methods for estimating precise poses of humans and information of movement from video frames. Vision-Based gait analysis techniques are capable of providing a cost-effective, unobtrusive solution for estimation of stick images and thus the analysis of the gait. This work provides a comprehensive review of marker-less computer vision and deep neural network-based gait analysis, parameters, design specifications, and the latest trends. This survey provides a birds-eye view of the domain. This review aims to introduce the latest trends in gait analysis using computer vision methods thus provide a single platform to learn various marker-less methods for the analysis of the gait that is likely to have a future impact in bio-mechanics while considering the challenges with accuracy and robustness that are yet to be addressed.

Keywords: Human Gait analysis · Marker-less techniques · Pose estimation · Stick images · Abnormality detection

1 Introduction

Gait can be defined as the coordinated action of the brain, nerves, and muscles which results in the translatory progression of the whole human body. Human

© Springer Nature Switzerland AG 2022
A. Dev et al. (Eds.): AIST 2021, CCIS 1546, pp. 363–375, 2022.
https://doi.org/10.1007/978-3-030-95711-7_31

gait is a bipedal gait in which both the legs perform their functions alternatively. Analysis of gait provides us vital information about the health of an individual. The pattern generated by the analysis is used for the diagnosis of diseases, sports, rehabilitation, biometrics. Dysfunction of gait or aberration in these patterns may arise from injury. Marker-based and Marker-less approaches are used by rehabilitation centers for the analysis of gait variables. Also, the analysis will help in estimating the effectiveness of a particular drug. Variables that can be estimated for analysis of gait are phases (swing phase and stance phase), step length and width, stride length, cadence etc. The gait cycle initiates when a foot contacts the ground and ends when same foot contacts the ground again. Each gait cycle begins with initial contact of stance phase followed by swing phase until the cycle ends with the limb's next initial contact as shown in Fig. 1. 60% of the gait cycle comprises of stance phase and 40% of swing phase. Four periods of the stance phase are: loading response, midstance, terminal stance, and pre-swing. Three periods of swing phase are: initial swing, midswing, and terminal swing. Important terminology related to gait are defined in Table 1. A scaling system was used in early times for the estimation of gait variables and thus analysis. Experts ask the subject to walk for a defined interval of time on a defined area. The way the person walks was observed by the expert and thus analysis is done. The observation method used was dependent on the expert's understanding, so it was not so reliable. With the advancement in technology, new methods were introduced that make use of sensors for the analysis of the gait. The results of the sensor-based analysis are used as benchmarks. The results provided by sensor-based methods were much reliable and efficient. Also, the error rate was reduced. But the use of sensors was an expensive task, sensors also hinder the real gait of the person. Nowadays, computer vision-based technologies are used to overcome the limitations of sensor-based technologies. Researchers are working on various technologies like Pose Estimation, Deep Learning, Q-Learning methods to analyze the gait and to get a reliable, efficient, and low-cost method for extraction and analysis of gait patterns. This review paper aims to provide insights into the marker-less gait analysis techniques. Innovative marker-less techniques can be applied in various domains and provide promising solutions. Collaborative work is required between bio-mechanic researchers and computer vision experts to develop more accurate.

This paper is divided into four sections: Sect. 1 includes the introduction to the gait analysis and use of marker-less techniques for analysis, gait terminologies and gait parameters. Section 2 includes a Gait Analysis Techniques. Section 3 includes latest trends in gait analysis followed by a conclusion in Sect. 4.

2   Gait Analysis Techniques

In recent years, many research works were proposed to relate the gait pattern of individual with the mental and physical health. The variation in the gait patterns makes it important biological information to support the clinical analysis. Weakened body parts are accurately recognized in the gait patterns, which

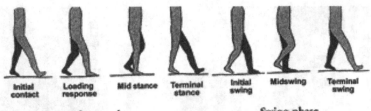

Fig. 1. Gait cycle [11]

Table 1. Basic gait terminology

Terminology	Description
Heel strike	Defined as the initial contact point made with the ground
Loading response	Stance period double support
Mid-stance	Time when the leg removes from the ground till the weight is back on foot
Terminal stance	Time when the foot leaves the ground, marks the top of stance phase and start of swing part
Pre-swing	Foot is pushed and elevated off the bottom
Toe off	Terminal contact is made with the front of the feet
Mid-swing	Time when swinging foot surpasses foot in stance phase
Terminal-swing	Last extension of shank occurs, the leg is aligned for starting foot contact to start out the new cycle

on early detection may prevent bigger health issues such as muscular-skeletal problems, cardiovascular issues and mental health issues [12]. Figure 3 shows the use of Marker-Based Analysis. The gold standard system for gait analysis was carried out by using opto-photogrametric system which involved the use of retro-reflective markers fixed onto the human body to extract the gait patterns. Even though the marker-based gait analysis provided accurate gait measures, it is carried out in big laboratories and it is highly expensive [27]. To overcome the limitations of the traditional marker-based gait analysis, many alternative methods using wearable sensors such as wrist sensors, shoe sensors etc., were introduced but the performance of these invasive methods was not satisfactory when compared to the gold standard system. Human Gait analysis approaches can be categorized into four categories:

– Computer Vision Based
– Sensor Based
– Equipment Based
– Combined

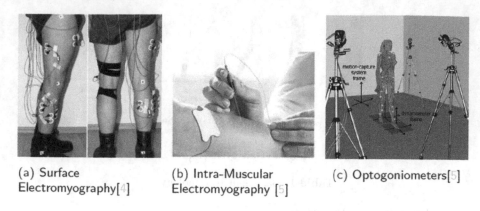

(a) Surface
Electromyography[4]

(b) Intra-Muscular
Electromyography [5]

(c) Optogoniometers[5]

Fig. 2. Marker-based analysis

In the case of the vision-based approach, gait parameters can be extracted with the help of markers or without markers. The markers are attached to the body of the subject, these can be active markers or passive markers. With active markers, the extraction is done using the LEDs which results in high-efficiency results but there are limitations of using such markers as proper lab setup is required, also it hinders the real gait of the subject. Another technique is the marker-less approach, in which no markers are attached to the body of a human, only the video is recorded and with the help of various image processing techniques, pose estimation techniques, and deep neural network techniques, the analysis is done as shown in Fig. 2. The advancement of technology over decades has resulted in development of marker-less gait analysis systems which are low

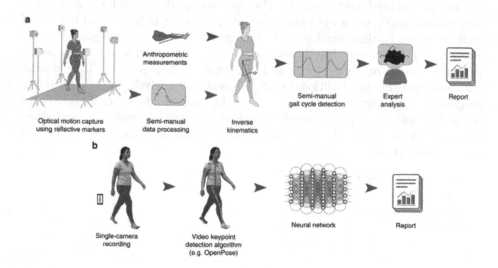

Fig. 3. Gait analysis using neural networks [16]

cost and non-invasive as discussed in Table 3 and Table 4. The marker-less gait analysis system can be carried out by using depth sensors such as kinect V2 and RGB-D camera for pose estimation based on 2D and 3D inputs [11,20]. The marker-less system was classified into two types namely model based approach and model free approach. The main difference of these two types is that, in the model free approach the skeletal joints are obtained based on the pre-defined anatomy of human body whereas the model based approaches estimate the skeletal joints by pose estimation algorithms. Some research works concluded that the skeletal joints obtained from the model free approaches had latency and are not sufficient for clinical gait analysis [14]. The existing model based approaches used 2D camera for motion capturing and Deep Convolutional Neural Network (DCNN) for joints extraction to carry out the gait analysis. To increase the efficiency of the marker-less gait analysis and to use it for clinical purposes, RGB-D cameras were introduced which will collect both the RGB image and depth image for each frame. Pose estimation is an area that has gained much popularity in recent years. Monocular images and videos are used in pose estimation. Opensource libraries like OpenPose, MxNet, toolkits like GluonCv are used for the detection of key points. Models like VGG-16, VGG-19, ResNet, RCNN can be used for the detection of human poses and thus, detection of various key points. However, these approaches are not fully explored for the lower limb section for gait analysis. The entire process of walking can be pertinently described using the gait phases and facilitate a better understanding of mechanisms of periodic walking [8].

Above discussed are the techniques that can be used for the analysis of gait. Vision-based gait analysis techniques are adopted in everyday life for accurate analysis of motion during training, rehabilitation, diagnostic purpose or biometrics. However, the accuracy and validity may vary according to the different scenarios. More research work is required to ensure validity and accuracy under different environmental conditions.

3   Latest Trends in Gait Analysis

Table 2 shows the existing literature survey on existing techniques for clinical gait analysis. Few review papers are available that can provide a good insight into marker-less gait analysis techniques. Most of the review papers written in the gait analysis domain are focused on marker-based approaches. In [7] authors reviewed the evolution of computer vision techniques for the analysis of the gait. The major application areas covered under this survey include sports and rehabilitation centers. Authors have covered the historical progression in gait analysis using computer vision techniques, they have covered Manual Digitisation techniques, Automated marker-based systems, Marker-less motion analysis systems, Image processing techniques. Our paper contributes towards the latest methods that include pose estimation for the analysis of the gait. In [15] authors proposed a classification method based on Gated Recurrent Unit (GRU) classifier and 3D skeleton joint data. Six Kinect-v2 depth sensors were deployed to acquire the depth images. The Microsoft SDK was used to process the depth information and provide the skeleton joint data. The guidelines for the pathological gaits were determined and 10 subjects were used for the data acquisition process. The joints were grouped to train the GRU with the most relevant joint group and eliminate the irrelevant joints for each gait classification. The proposed method classified the gaits into six classes such as normal gait, antalgic gait, stiff-legged gait, lurching gait, steppage gait, and Trendelenburg gait. The leave-one-subject-out validation method was used to estimate the accuracy of the proposed method. The result showed that the proposed system achieved better classification accuracy.

Problems Identified: Only depth images are considered as input which is not sufficient for gait analysis, lack of depth image smoothing causes the presence of noise in depth images which will further affect the accuracy of gait analysis.

Proposed Solution: Both RGB images and depth images with respect to a specific frame are considered and the latent noise levels can be filtered.

In [12] authors proposed a gender classification model based on gait analysis. Two Kinect v2 depth sensors were used to acquire the input depth images. The Microsoft SDK was used to process the depth information and provide the skeleton joint data. 81 participants were used for the data acquisition process. The factors such as gait cycle, principle frequency, central tendency and dispersion, spatial variables, and center of mass were calculated. The significant features were extracted from the factors and these features were fed into the support vector machine (SVM) classifier. The proposed method was able to classify the gender-based gait analysis with better accuracy.

Problems Identified: The proposed method uses support vector machine for classification which will require large training time and small calibrations cannot be performed since the final model is not easy to see which will increase the time consumption.

Proposed Solution: In order to reduce the time consumption the Deep network should be used which requires minimal training time.

In [20] authors proposed a method for gait analysis to classify the normal and abnormal gaits based on human pose estimation. The video recorded from a 2D camera was given as the input. The human pose estimation was carried out by a part-affinity field approach in a Convolutional Neural Network (CNN). The 2D skeleton joints were used to train the CNN classifier. The collected data were segregated into five classes' normal, abnormal toe (right and left), abnormal foot (right and left) for proper training. 80% of the data-set was used for training and the remaining 20% was used for testing. The proposed method was tested and the result showed that it had more accuracy in classifying the abnormal gaits.

Problems Identified: The evaluation of gait parameters in 2D space impedes objective clinical evaluation; therefore the joints estimated will contain more redundancy. This will further affect the accuracy of the classification.

Proposed Solution: Both RGB images and depth images with respect to a specific frame are considered and the latent noise levels can be filtered.

In [13] authors proposed a gait analysis method to classify the abnormal gait. In this method, the depth images along with the respective RGB image was taken as the input. The depth image was pre-processed by using a bilateral filter and the pose estimation was done by part affinity approach in a Deep Convolutional Neural Network. A 6D camera was used to track the surrounding in three dimensions. The 3D lower limb skeleton was fused with the 3D canonical coordinate system using the Simultaneous Localization And Mapping (SLAM) algorithm. Sixteen subjects were used in the data acquisition process. The joint angle features were extracted from the 3D lower limb skeleton. The statistical features such as step length, gait cycle time, gait symmetry measure were trained in an SVM classifier, and the temporal features such as joint angles were trained in the Bi-LSTM classifier. The proposed method was tested and validated using the leave one subject out protocol; the result showed that the proposed method is efficient in classifying the abnormal gaits.

Problems Identified: Support vector machine is used in this method to classify the gait based on quantitative features but SVM requires large training time, since the final model is not easy to even small calibrations cannot be performed.

Proposed Solution: In order to reduce the time consumption the and increase the accuracy we use Deep network which requires minimal time for training.

In [17] authors proposed a 3D abnormal gait analysis based Virtual Sample Generation to classify abnormal gaits. The 3D body model was obtained from the depth information and the point cloud data. The model was structured based on the parameters such as height weight, age, gender, and skeletal joints. The symmetrical virtual samples were generated based on the Extremely Learning Machine model to predict the symmetrical data of abnormal gait. The conditional adversarial network was used to train the model for generating information according to both label and perturbation. The generated body model was evaluated in gait analysis and it showed better performance in classifying abnormal gait.

Problems Identified: The proposed model will classify the abnormal gait only based on pre-defined actions, even the normal gait of the person's action which are not defined by the model will be classified as abnormal and thereby reducing the accuracy of the model.

Proposed Solution: All the significant parameters required to perform gait analysis are considered and the classification of gaits based on the features is carried out.

[3] uses sensors accelerometer and gyros to estimate knee and hip angle. They proposed an algorithm, to reduce the cost applied in the standard gait analysis devices. The algorithm uses accelerometers gyroscopes and mathematics manipulation using kinetic relation to estimate joint angle. They focused more on reducing the integral error, which arises because of gyros drift. They used complementary filter methods to compare and validate their results.

Table 2. Literature survey of clinical gait analysis

Year	Objective of the study	Parameters of Gait	Semi subjective analysis	Objective analysis	Machine learning techniques	Pose estimation techniques	Performance measures	Gait abnormalities
2019 [23]	Three systems were used to analyze gait patterns, a pressure sensitive walkway system (GAITRite-System, GS) as gold standard, Motognosis Labs Software using a Microsoft Kinect Sensor (MKS), and a smartphone camera-based application (SCA)	✓	X	✓	X	X	✓	X
2019 [24]	Compared and analysed 2-min test walk and the 6MWT in healthy young and older adults with respect to gait performance and gait differences. Both demonstrate similar results for gait assessment	✓	✓	✓	X	X	X	X
2019 [19]	In-shoe plantar measurement propose an efficient future research work as well as an equipment to analyze gait data	✓	X	✓	✓	X	X	X
2020 [4]	Computer vision algorithm is proposed for detection of gait activities	✓	X	✓	✓	X	✓	X
2020 [1]	Analysis of methods worked on age and gender estimation by using sensors. Concluded that deep learning-based solutions are in the lead	X	X	✓	✓	X	X	X
2020 [22]	The trends in analysing gait using wearable sensors and ML are comprehensively reviewed	X	X	✓	✓	X	X	X
2020 [21]	With the use of pose estimation and CNN classification of normal and abnormal gait is done, the accuracy achieved is 97.3%	X	X	X	✓	✓	X	✓

[26] proposed a method in which they use low cut high pass filters applied on the shank and inclination angle signals, to derive knee angle from angular velocities. As the method uses high pass filtering, the low pass signals were lost, and hence the method is not suitable for real-time data. They estimated the knee angle, but without the use of integration, to avoid integration error drift. The method was based on the data obtained from accelerometers. They estimated the angles by comparing the signals obtained from sensors mounted on the leg. [19] identified joint angles and absolute angles of each segment using bandpass filtering. Absolute segment angles are determined using the difference between signals of two accelerometers and joint angle is calculating by the neighboring segment's absolute segment angles. The filtering method used by them is the same as that of the filtering method used in the navigation system. Butterworth filtering method is used to minimize offset drift. If the patient is suffering from a high level of disease then this system was not acceptable as this method doesn't provide accurate results in case of slow gait. Another real-time method was proposed where tri-axial accelerometers are used. Along with this auto, correction methods were used to evaluate the characteristics of the gait for a repeated period. [18] proposed a method for estimating key points without the use of sensors. With the help of regression-based, Deep Neural Networks

Table 3. Gait analysis using machine learning techniques.

ML technique	Approach	Application	DataSet and domain
Clustering and Principle Component Analysis	Vision Based	Clinical Analysis	Cluster analysis and PCA for classification in 113 healthy subjects
SVM-Multi-class Support Vector Machine	Vision Based	Geriatric Care	Dataset: UCF-Sports; Activity Recognition
Support Vector Machine	Hybrid	Normal Gait Analysis	14 healthy and 13 unhealthy patients with Patellofemoral pain; automatic recognition
Fuzzy	Hybrid	Gait Analysis	With kinematic parameters estimation of muscle activity.Prediction
Gaussian process regression	Vision Based	Normal Gait Analysis	12 kinematic parameters estimated using prediction model; 50 healthy males and 63 healthy females
Support Vector Machine	Vision Based	Geriatric Care	In 60 persons difference was identified in the lower limbs
SVM-linear kernel and RBF kernel	Hybrid	Clinical Gait Analysis	Lower muscular fatigue in 17 young subjects
Supervised and unsupervised features + PCA	Sensor Based	Geatric Care	DAPHNet dataset; Freezing of Gait-detection and Prediction
Deep Learning-Convolutional Networks	Hybrid	Activity Recognition	Actitracker, Skoda, and Opportunity
NN-SOM	Hybrid	Activity Recognition	Emotion recognition on 22 subjects using gait patterns
Hidden Markov Model	Sensor Based	Activity Recognition	20 activity by 20 subjects
Neural Network-modified Clockwork RNNs	Surveillance	Sensor Based	Google data from abacus project
KPCA Genetic Algorithm	Surveillance	Vision Based	CASIA Dataset

Table 4. Existing marker-less techniques for gait analysis

Citation	Objective	Approach	Dataset	Results
[9] 2008	A method that estimates the orientation of limbs independent of the view and helps in the correct inclination of limbs	Gait Reconstruction algorithm used for normalization and correction of inclination of limbs	Total video sequences = 200 Number of Subjects = 3	For Azimuth = 0° and Elevation = 0° RMS = 0.995 MCC ALPHA = 0.974 BETA = 0.972 For Azimuth = 20° and Elevation = 0° RMS = 1.441 MCC ALPHA = 0.982 BETA = 0.960
[8] 2009	2D gait analysis without markers for a clinical application that will analyze the video frames and extracts the kinematic information	Silhouette-based approach used	Synthetic video sequences of humanoid; resolution 500 × 490 pixels with 30 frames per second	Angle's errors with different spatial resolution. Image resolution/mean height = 500 × 490/20 me (deg) = 2.04 σe (deg) = 2.12 Processing time (s/frame) = 1.44 Image resolution/mean height = 250 × 245/100 me (deg) = 2.80 σe (deg) = 2.15 Processing time (s/frame) = 0.97
[29] 2011	Recognition and classification of Gait Motion	Detection of the human, Body points and joint angles are used for the extraction of gait figures and classification	16 females and 84 males, total 100 subjects with seven image sequences each	Classification rates of 97% CCR for 30 subjects and 84% CCR for 100 subjects
[28] 2014	Determination of segmental movement using marker-less approach	Kinematic and temporal parameter estimation using image flow analysis. CMUs 3D motion capture databases for estimation of lower limns kinematics. Ensemble Kalman Filtering is used for marker-less gait analysis	5 video sequences with different cloth and shoes. Saggital plane with 60fps and resolution 640 × 480 per frame is used	Average upper leg error = 4.18° Average lower leg error = 2.28° Average foot error = 6.14° Average left side Error = 3.84° Average right side Error = 4.56°
[2] 2014	To check the feasibility of kinect in Marker-less gait analysis	Use of Microsoft's Kinect XBOX	With kinect system 5 selected joints were tracked on both marker-based and marker-less system	Correlation coefficient of 90.16% between the Kinect camera's Marker-based and Marker-less systems
[6] 2015	Analysis of kinematic data is performed on the lower limb using a 2D marker-less approach	A multi-segmental model is used for the lower limb	10 Subjects in white garments of the age group between 30–36 were taken	Differences between the joint kinematics estimates ranged from 3.9 deg to 6.1 deg for the hip, from 2.7 deg to 4.4 deg for the knee, and from 3.0 deg to 4.7 deg for the ankle
[10] 2018	Tracking of joints using a single RGB camera using computer vision algorithms	OpenPose for pose. For Foot orientation: GrabCut algorithm is applied. Sparse Dictionary Learning is used for parameter reduction	4 healthy subjects(3 Males and 1 Female)	Frame Error < 5° Estimation of dorsiflexion angle is more accurate than the estimation of inversion angle

they identified body joints. This proposed method results in high precision estimates. The key point values obtained with this method can be used for the identification of knee angles. The method is very simple but provides précised results as they have cascading of DNN-based predictors. [25] proposed a method that estimates key points with the help of heatmaps instead of direct regression approach. Heatmaps are generated, when an image is passed through multiple resolutions, and features are extracted at the same time. Instead of continuous regression, the output generated is in the form of a discrete heatmap. But this method lack structure modeling. [5] uses the concept of iterative error feedback method, in which the error in the current stage is predicted and is resolved in the later stages. The model can be called a self-correcting model, as instead of directly generating the output, it will iterate over and over, until the errors are not properly resolved.

A comprehensive review of articles on marker-less gait analysis published in reputed journals and conferences has been presented. Even though the current techniques are providing accurate results but still the system is not capable enough to generate the actual gait patterns. The existing methods make use of fixed viewpoints and mainly worked in 2 Dimension space. There is an urgent need to work in 3 Dimensional space to generate the actual gait pattern.

4   Conclusion

In this paper, we have reviewed, discussed, and summarized various marker-less approaches for the analysis of the gait. Other existing surveys are covering aspects of gait analysis using marker-based or sensor-based technologies. Not much review is done on marker-less technologies which is the need of time. Researchers need such review papers in order to work in this domain and come out with some promising automatic motion analysis systems. Marker-less gait analysis has gained much popularity in the gait domain as it can provide a cost-effective accurate way of analysis. Various Machine Learning, Deep Learning, Computer Vision techniques are discussed in this paper, which will help in the extraction of important features like spatiotemporal, kinetic, and kinematic features and thus identification of gait abnormalities. The subjective method of gait analysis was based on expert observation-only which lacks reliability, specificity, sensitivity, and validity whereas the approaches discussed in the paper make the analysis process simpler and also deals with the dynamic adaptability of gait and provides a cost-effective and reliable method for the analysis of the gait.

In the coming years, real-time applications of gait analysis can be designed which help in the routine diagnostic of the patient's gait. Researchers from biomechanics field and computer vision experts need to work together to make the analysis process simpler and also deals with the dynamic adaptability of gait that provides a cost-effective and reliable method for the analysis of the gait. In sports, rehabilitation, biometrics analysis of gait has become one of the most promising research domains. So exhaustive research is required in this field, so the future interactive systems will be used to monitor, analyze and provide feedback on a person's gait to improve the quality of life.

References

1. Ahad, M.A.R., et al.: Wearable sensor-based gait analysis for age and gender estimation. Sensors **20**(8) (2020). https://www.mdpi.com/1424-8220/20/8/2424
2. Alnowami, M., Khan, A., Morfeq, A.H., Alothmany, N., Hafez, E.A.: Feasibility study of markerless gait tracking using kinect. Life Sci. J. **11**(7), 514–523 (2014)
3. Alonge, F., Cucco, E., D'Ippolito, F., Pulizzotto, A.: The use of accelerometers and gyroscopes to estimate hip and knee angles on gait analysis. Sensors **14**(5), 8430–8446 (2014)
4. André, J., et al.: Markerless gait analysis vision system for real-time gait monitoring. In: 2020 IEEE International Conference on Autonomous Robot Systems and Competitions (ICARSC), pp. 269–274 (2020). https://doi.org/10.1109/ICARSC49921.2020.9096121
5. Carreira, J., Agrawal, P., Fragkiadaki, K., Malik, J.: Human pose estimation with iterative error feedback. In: Proceedings of the IEEE Conference on Computer Vision and Pattern Recognition, pp. 4733–4742 (2016)
6. Castelli, A., Paolini, G., Cereatti, A., Della Croce, U.: A 2D markerless gait analysis methodology: validation on healthy subjects. Comput. Math. Methods Med. **2015** (2015)
7. Colyer, S.L., Evans, M., Cosker, D.P., Salo, A.I.: A review of the evolution of vision-based motion analysis and the integration of advanced computer vision methods towards developing a markerless system. Sports Med.-Open **4**(1), 1–15 (2018)
8. Goffredo, M., Carter, J.N., Nixon, M.S.: 2D markerless gait analysis. In: Vander Sloten, J., Verdonck, P., Nyssen, M., Haueisen, J. (eds.) 4th European Conference of the International Federation for Medical and Biological Engineering. IFMBE, vol. 22, pp. 67–71. Springer, Heidelberg (2009). https://doi.org/10.1007/978-3-540-89208-3_18
9. Goffredo, M., Seely, R.D., Carter, J.N., Nixon, M.S.: Markerless view independent gait analysis with self-camera calibration. In: 2008 8th IEEE International Conference on Automatic Face Gesture Recognition, pp. 1–6 (2008). https://doi.org/10.1109/AFGR.2008.4813366
10. Gu, X., Deligianni, F., Lo, B., Chen, W., Yang, G.: Markerless gait analysis based on a single RGB camera. In: 2018 IEEE 15th International Conference on Wearable and Implantable Body Sensor Networks (BSN), pp. 42–45 (2018). https://doi.org/10.1109/BSN.2018.8329654
11. Gu, X., Deligianni, F., Lo, B., Chen, W., Yang, G.Z.: Markerless gait analysis based on a single RGB camera. In: 2018 IEEE 15th International Conference on Wearable and Implantable Body Sensor Networks (BSN), pp. 42–45. IEEE (2018)
12. Guffanti, D., Brunete, A., Hernando, M.: Non-invasive multi-camera gait analysis system and its application to gender classification. IEEE Access **8**, 95734–95746 (2020)
13. Guo, Y., Deligianni, F., Gu, X., Yang, G.Z.: 3-D canonical pose estimation and abnormal gait recognition with a single RGB-D camera. IEEE Robot. Autom. Lett. **4**(4), 3617–3624 (2019)
14. Huynh-The, T., Hua, C.H., Tu, N.A., Kim, D.S.: Learning 3D spatiotemporal gait feature by convolutional network for person identification. Neurocomputing **397**, 192–202 (2020)
15. Jun, K., Lee, Y., Lee, S., Lee, D.W., Kim, M.S.: Pathological gait classification using Kinect v2 and gated recurrent neural networks. IEEE Access **8**, 139881–139891 (2020)

16. Kidziński, Ł, Yang, B., Hicks, J.L., Rajagopal, A., Delp, S.L., Schwartz, M.H.: Deep neural networks enable quantitative movement analysis using single-camera videos. Nat. Commun. **11**(1), 1–10 (2020)

17. Luo, J., Tjahjadi, T.: Multi-set canonical correlation analysis for 3D abnormal gait behaviour recognition based on virtual sample generation. IEEE Access **8**, 32485–32501 (2020)

18. Papandreou, G., et al.: Towards accurate multi-person pose estimation in the wild. In: Proceedings of the IEEE Conference on Computer Vision and Pattern Recognition, pp. 4903–4911 (2017)

19. Ramirez-Bautista, J.A., Huerta-Ruelas, J.A., Chaparro-Cárdenas, S.L., Hernández-Zavala, A.: A review in detection and monitoring gait disorders using in-shoe plantar measurement systems. IEEE Rev. Biomed. Eng. **10**, 299–309 (2017). https://doi.org/10.1109/RBME.2017.2747402

20. Rohan, A., Rabah, M., Hosny, T., Kim, S.H.: Human pose estimation-based real-time gait analysis using convolutional neural network. IEEE Access **8**, 191542–191550 (2020)

21. Rohan, A., Rabah, M., Hosny, T., Kim, S.H.: Human pose estimation-based real-time gait analysis using convolutional neural network. IEEE Access **8**, 191542–191550 (2020). https://doi.org/10.1109/ACCESS.2020.3030086

22. Saboor, A., et al.: Latest research trends in gait analysis using wearable sensors and machine learning: a systematic review. IEEE Access **8**, 167830–167864 (2020). https://doi.org/10.1109/ACCESS.2020.3022818

23. Steinert, A., Sattler, I., Otte, K., Röhling, H., Mansow-Model, S., Müller-Werdan, U.: Using new camera-based technologies for gait analysis in older adults in comparison to the established GAITRite system. Sensors **20**(1) (2020). https://doi.org/10.3390/s20010125. https://www.mdpi.com/1424-8220/20/1/125

24. Swanson, C.W., Haigh, Z.J., Fling, B.W.: Two-minute walk tests demonstrate similar age-related gait differences as a six-minute walk test. Gait Posture **69**, 36–39 (2019)

25. Tompson, J.J.R.: Localization of humans in images using convolutional networks. Ph.D. thesis, New York University (2015)

26. Tong, K., Granat, M.H.: A practical gait analysis system using gyroscopes. Med. Eng. Phys. **21**(2), 87–94 (1999)

27. Vilas-Boas, M.d.C., et al.: Validation of a single RGB-D camera for gait assessment of polyneuropathy patients. Sensors **19**(22), 4929 (2019)

28. Vishnoi, N., Mitra, A., Duric, Z., Gerber, N.L.: Motion based markerless gait analysis using standard events of gait and ensemble Kalman filtering. In: 2014 36th Annual International Conference of the IEEE Engineering in Medicine and Biology Society, pp. 2512–2516 (2014). https://doi.org/10.1109/EMBC.2014.6944133

29. Yoo, J.H., Nixon, M.S.: Automated markerless analysis of human gait motion for recognition and classification. ETRI J. **33**(2), 259–266 (2011)

Detection of Skin Lesion Disease Using Deep Learning Algorithm

Sumit Bhardwaj[✉], Ayush Somani, and Khushi Gupta

ECE Department, ASET, Amity University, Noida, India

Abstract. Skin lesions are a part of the skin that has an unusual development or appearance contrasted with the skin around it. They may be something you are born with or something you acquire over your lifetime. They can be classified into two types: benign (non-cancerous) or malignant (cancerous). Some studies have been conducted on the computerised detection of malignancy in images. However, due to various problematic aspects such as reflections of light from the skin's surface, the difference of colour lighting, and varying forms and sizes of the lesions, analysing these images is extremely difficult. As a result, evidence-based automatic skin cancer detection can help pathologists improve their accuracy and competency in the primitive stages of ailment. Our proposed method is to detect the early onset of skin lesions using python as a tool to detect benign (non-cancerous) or severe (cancerous) lesions using a machine learning approach. The dataset consists of nine different classes of skin lesion diseases: Melanoma (MEL), Melanocytic nevus (NV), Basal cell carcinoma (BCC), Actinic keratosis (AK), Benign keratosis (BKL), Dermatofibroma (DF), Vascular lesion (VASC), Squamous cell carcinoma (SCC), None of the above (UNK). In our proposed work, a DCNN model is created for classifying cancerous and non-cancerous skin lesions. We use techniques such as filtering, feature extraction for better categorization which will enhance the final analysis value. From our proposed model we have achieved a training accuracy of 90.7%.

Keywords: Skin lesions · Deep convolutional neural network · Benign · Malignant

1 Introduction

The largest organ of our body is skin. It serves as a protecting defence in opposition to heat, light, injury, and infection [1]. Skin is presented to the external climate along these lines the likelihood of sickness and disease to it is more, subsequently, we need to give more noteworthy thoughtfulness regarding skin The patch on the human body which is affected is known as lesion area. These are quite frequent and can occur as a result of localised skin injury such as sunburns or dermatitis [2]. Other factors include infections, diabetes, and autoimmune or genetic diseases, which are typical symptoms of underlying disorders. The reasons for skin lesions are injury, maturing, irresistible illnesses, sensitivities, and little infections of the skin or hair follicles. Constant sicknesses, for example, diabetes or immune system problems can cause skin injuries. Skin

© Springer Nature Switzerland AG 2022
A. Dev et al. (Eds.): AIST 2021, CCIS 1546, pp. 376–384, 2022.
https://doi.org/10.1007/978-3-030-95711-7_32

malignancy or precancerous changes additionally show up as skin lesions. Although the majority of skin lesions are benign and innocuous, a small percentage of them are malignant or premalignant, meaning they have the potential to become cancerous, which is deadly. Nowadays, computer-assisted diagnosis is more common in the medical profession. For an unskilled dermatologist, early identification of skin illness is more difficult. Computer-Aided Diagnosis Systems is becoming a vital topic of a clinical study by combining digital image processing for cancer diagnosis. Machine learning algorithms play a significant role in the automation of numerous procedures in the medical profession. Dermoscopy has been shown to reduce diagnostic accuracy in the hands of inexperienced practitioners. We observed that the majority of studies focus on only three diseases: melanoma, nevus, and seborrheic keratosis. However, several other disorders are as important in the medical profession [3]. As a result, we take into account certain additional illnesses, such as BCC, AK, DF, VASC, SCC as well as the illnesses listed before The features extraction, which is utilised to characterise the lesion areas, is an essential element of the suggested model. Another item to note is the learning methods; many different classifiers are utilised, however, we obtained our findings using the CNN classifier. The remaining work is organised as follows: it discusses the dataset, the suggested model, the experiments, the findings, and the conclusions.

2 Literature Review

Md Shahin Ali et al. (2021) shows how a DCNN model may be used to classify skin cancer. AlexNet, VGG-16, MobileNet, and other transfer learning methods are compared to the DCNN model. On the HAM10000 data, the model achieved the highest training and testing accuracy of 93.16% and 91.93%, respectively [4]. M. F. Rasul et al. (2020) describe how SegNet and BCDU-Net have better performance than U-Net in detecting melanoma patterns on dermoscopic pictures, both of which had an accuracy of above 90% [2]. Marwan Ali Albahar (2019) created a prediction model which classifies cancerous and non-cancerous skin lesion disease based on a revolutionary regularizer method. The training and test stage, we explored the classification performances with an accuracy of over 85% [5]. Balazs Harangi (2018) built a DCNN model to enhance their individual accuracy focussed on classifying dermoscopic pictures by computerized MEL detection model by study of skin lesion images with an accuracy of over 80% using EfficientNet-B6 [6]. Aya Abu Ali et al. (2017) proposed a model using CNN to categorise MEL pictures into cancerous and non- cancerous ones. The proposed technique uses the LightNet deep learning framework. The LightNet's convolutional neural network architecture has been updated to operate with ISBI skin challenge data set. Melanoma classification is accomplished with an accuracy of 81.6% without the need of lesion segmentation or sophisticated picture pre-processing [1]. SVM and k-NN classifiers, as well as their fusion, are used to classify extracted features with an accuracy of 46.71% and 34% of F-measure for different classifiers, respectively, and 61% of F-measure [7]. Proposal of an updated model that uses an unique regularize approach to classify skin lesions as benign or malignant. The suggested model was 97.49% accurate on average. The AUCs for NV vs MEL, SK vs BCC, SK vs MEL, and SL vs MEL, respectively, are 0.77, 0.93, 0.85, and 0.86 [8]. The collected characteristics are stratified using a deep learning technique called a CNN classifier. An accuracy of 89.5% was obtained, with a training accuracy of 93.7% [3].

3 Methodology

The next phases and the flowchart of our methodology are described in this section as shown in Fig. 1. For the purpose of different skin lesion diseases classification, we are using DCNN and transfer learning algorithm in our proposed model for obtaining the required results.

3.1 Dataset Description

The dataset consists of nine distinct classes of skin lesion diseases: BCC, MEL, DF, NV, SCC, BKL, AK, VASC, UNK. Figure 2 shows samples from the dataset. The used dataset consists of 25,331 images. We are using these images as our training data. The numbers of images in each class can be inferred from Table 1 below:

3.2 Data Preparation

To develop an effective model, we change raw data into a more appropriate form via data preparation. Our data collection includes sets of pictures comparing comparable lesions from different angles or photographs of the same lesions on the same subject. Some hazy and far-away pictures were deleted from the dataset, but they were still utilised in training. Feature extraction, data transformations, dimension reduction, and other variables in data preparation help to prepare the data for training.

3.3 Data Pre-processing

It is the most important step for preparing primary data for use by a ML model. The primary goal of this step is to improve the quality of the initial medical pictures with the help of eliminating clamours and artefacts [4]. In addition, we used data reduction, data normalisation, feature extraction, and ultimately, we transformed the label string data into numerical information.

3.4 Data Reduction

In this procedure, we decrease some pictures from the initial dataset into smaller parts in an imaging dataset. Because there are pictures with clamour, lesser contrast and images with mole alongside the lesion area, getting the best rate of classification from the whole data is a huge problem [6]. We manually deduced various pictures that match these properties in our suggested DCNN model.

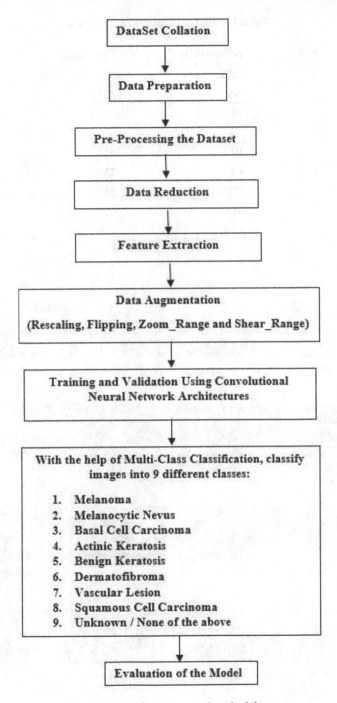

Fig. 1. Steps of our proposed methodology

Table 1. Number of images in each class

S. no.	Name of class	No. of images
1	MEL	4522
2	NV	12877
3	BCC	3323
4	AK	867
5	BKL	2624
6	DF	239
7	VASC	252
8	SCC	627
9	UNK	0

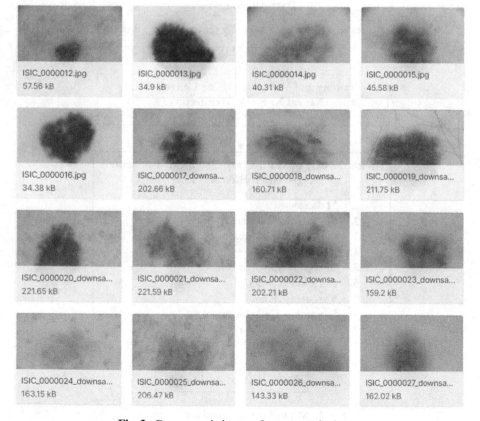

Fig. 2. Dermoscopic images from a sample dataset

3.5 Feature Extraction

Feature extraction is a method used in image processing to break down large images into smaller groups. In this study, we withdraw a significant number of characteristics that aid in the identification and recognition of patterns across a vast number of datasets Furthermore, it chooses and add up variables to pull out characteristics which reduces the amount of resource while preserving the original data's information.

3.6 Data Augmentation

It is a method for artificially increment of the quantity of data by incorporating slightly modified copies into the current training data without actually gathering new data. This can be done by data warping, the training dataset size may be artificially increased, or the model can be protected from overfitting at the source. To avoid over-fitting, we used principal component analysis to augment our dataset by various augmentation settings like rotation, mirroring, and colour-shifting.

3.7 CNN Architecture and Training

The CNN architecture consists of nine layers, having equal distribution among convolutional types, fully connected types and pooling layers and kernel size for the first convolutional layer (CL) is 3 with "relu" activation and unit as 32. The input shape for the first layer is 256 * 256 * 3. This layer is then connected to a pooling layer which uses the function called Max Pooling and the size of this function is 2 * 2. The final output of pooling layer is transferred to the next convolutional layer which has all the same parameters as of the first convolutional layer except for the input size and this layer is further connected with the MaxPooling layer which also has the same parameters as described before. The value of the unit got increased by the factor two i.e., 64 and rest all parameters are same in convolutional layer as well as for MaxPooling layer. The output obtained is then flattened and provided to a FCL which has units as 128 and "relu" activation, this output is then provided to a next FCL which has the same activation but with unit reduced to 64 and this layer is then connected to final FCL of our CNN model which get reduced to 9 units as we have 9 different classes of disease present in our dataset.

The CNN model is then compiled using optimizer as "adam", loss as "categorical_crossentropy" and matrics as "['accuracy']" (Fig. 3).

4 Result

The system was put to the test by giving it pictures from the database. At the most basic level, the system distinguishes between cancers that spread (malignant) and cancers that do not spread (benign). In both situations, the model predicts whether the input picture is benign or malignant. From our proposed model we have achieved a training accuracy of 90.7% (Figs. 4 and 5).

A simple mechanism was also created on google colab, in which we can upload any skin lesion image, the image will undergo pre-processing and be put to the test in real-time. After that, it classifies and shows the resultant disease as in the title axis (Fig. 6).

```
Layer (type)                      Output Shape             Param #
=================================================================
conv2d (Conv2D)                   (None, 254, 254, 32)     896

max_pooling2d (MaxPooling2D)      (None, 127, 127, 32)     0

conv2d_1 (Conv2D)                 (None, 125, 125, 32)     9248

max_pooling2d_1 (MaxPooling2      (None, 62, 62, 32)       0

conv2d_2 (Conv2D)                 (None, 60, 60, 64)       18496

max_pooling2d_2 (MaxPooling2      (None, 30, 30, 64)       0

flatten (Flatten)                 (None, 57600)            0

dense (Dense)                     (None, 128)              7372928

dense_1 (Dense)                   (None, 64)               8256

dense_2 (Dense)                   (None, 9)                585
=================================================================
Total params: 7,410,409
Trainable params: 7,410,409
Non-trainable params: 0
```

Fig. 3. CNN architecture

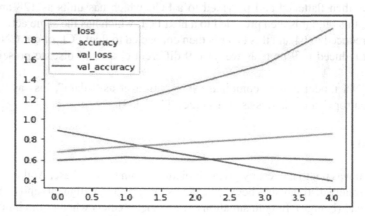

Fig. 4. Performance curve based on accuracy and loss

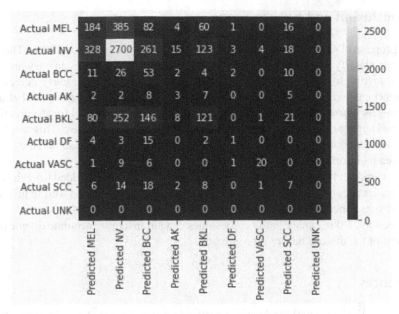

Fig. 5. Confusion matrix of skin lesion classifier

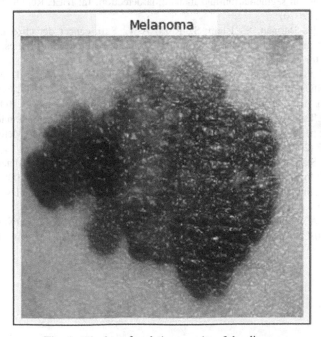

Fig. 6. Display of real-time results of the disease

5   Conclusion and Future Scope

In our proposed DCNN model the accuracy achieved by us was above 90%. The CNN model can classify 9 distinct types of skin lesion disease. It provides an easy and faster way for anyone to detect skin lesion disease with good accuracy. Early detection of skin cancer can aid in a more accurate diagnosis and treatment of the disease before the situation gets worse. We are planning to extend our proposed model for the creation of an android app that can be used by anyone to detect skin lesion disease. This would help many people who are not aware by early detection of these diseases so that they can get better treatment on time.

This work can be further continued, and more images could be added to each class to obtain higher accuracy and we can add many more disease classes as well in this model to improve its functionality and public usage.

Detection of skin cancer in the early stages can aid in a more accurate diagnosis and treatment of the disease before it progresses.

References

1. Ali, A.A., Al-Marzouqi, H.: Melanoma detection using regular convolutional neural networks. In: International Conference on Electrical and Computing Technologies and Applications (ICECTA) (2017)
2. Rasul, Md.F., Dey, N.K., Hashem, M.M.A.: A comparative study of neural network architectures for lesion segmentation and melanoma detection. In: IEEE Region 10 Symposium (TENSYMP) (2020)
3. Hasan, M., das Barman, S., Islam, S., Reza, A.W.: Skin cancer detection using convolutional neural network. In: ACM International Conference Proceeding Series, pp. 254–258. Association for Computing Machinery (2019)
4. Ali, M.S., Miah, M.S., Haque, J., Rahman, M.M., Islam, M.K.: An enhanced technique of skin cancer classification using deep convolutional neural network with transfer learning models. Mach. Learn. Appl. **5**, 100036 (2021). https://doi.org/10.1016/j.mlwa.2021.100036
5. Mahbod, A., Tschandl, P., Langs, G., Ecker, R., Ellinger, I.: The effects of skin lesion segmentation on the performance of dermatoscopic image classification. Comput. Methods Programs Biomed. **197** (2020). https://doi.org/10.1016/j.cmpb.2020.105725
6. Harangi, B.: Skin lesion classification with ensembles of deep convolutional neural networks. J. Biomed. Inform. **86**, 25–32 (2018). https://doi.org/10.1016/j.jbi.2018.08.006
7. Sumithra, R., Suhil, M., Guru, D.S.: Segmentation and classification of skin lesions for disease diagnosis. Procedia Comput. Sci. **45**, 76–85 (2015)
8. Albahar, M.A.: Skin lesion classification using convolutional neural network with novel regularizer. IEEE Access **7**, 38306–38313 (2019). https://doi.org/10.1109/ACCESS.2019

Applying XGBoost Machine Learning Model to Succor Astronomers Detect Exoplanets in Distant Galaxies

Nidhi Agarwal[1,4](✉) ⓘ, Amita Jain[2] ⓘ, Ayush Gupta[3], and Devendra Kumar Tayal[4] ⓘ

[1] Kiet Group of Institutions, Ghaziabad, India
nidhi.agarwal@kiet.edu
[2] NSUT Delhi, Delhi, India
[3] University of Turku, Turku, Finland
ayush.a.gupta@utu.fi
[4] IGDTUW, Delhi, India
chiefproctor@igdtuw.ac.in
https://www.kiet.edu, https://www.aiactr.ac.in,
https://www.utu.fi, https://www.igdtuw.ac.in

Abstract. The time when TRAPPIST-1 news became official on 22.02.2017, detection of planets beyond Milky Way Galaxy or planets orbiting around their own sun-like stars became one of the burning topics unlike prior times. There are seven famous exoplanets in TRAPPIST-1 system which are just forty light-years distant, and are available to be explored by our planets and other spacial telescopes. But several thousand other exoplanets are known to astronomers whose habitability is misleading as there is no evidence about contrasting effects take place between these bright stars and their suspected exoplanets. Since majority of the exoplanets are found using transit principle method, so in this research paper a new tool using XG Boost supervised Machine Learning Model is proposed to detect their presence. The results show that the prediction accuracy, precision and F1-score of this model is very high as compared to the other methods used in literature till now. This work is novel as till now no research work implements XGBoost based model of Machine Learning with highly accurate predictive power. None of the previous work has taken care of all the steps of data pre-processing and handling imbalanced data.

Keywords: Exoplanets · Machine Learning · Transit principle · XG boost model · Supervised machine learning · SMOTE

1 Introduction

There are deep Physical and mathematical theories on exploring exoplanets in the space. There are billions of galaxies in the universe. These galaxies have millions of stars. One such galaxy is the Milky-way galaxy in which our solar system exists. The solar system has a star called Sun which has its own light. In astronomy, a star is a heavenly body

© Springer Nature Switzerland AG 2022
A. Dev et al. (Eds.): AIST 2021, CCIS 1546, pp. 385–404, 2022.
https://doi.org/10.1007/978-3-030-95711-7_33

which has its own light. There are 8 planets in our solar system orbiting around the Sun. Similar to this, in some other galaxy there would be a star and probably a planet would be revolving around that star. Whenever a planet, while orbiting its star, comes in between the telescope and the star, the brightness of the star recorded by the telescope is lower whereas when the planet goes behind the star, the brightness of the light recorded by the telescope is higher. This method of detecting exoplanets in far-distant galaxies through the brightness of the light emitted by a star is called the Transit Method. This is how NASA finds a planet beyond our solar system [1, 2].

The novel work in this paper applies one of the supervised ML algorithms XG-Boost to predict the presence of exoplanets with very high accuracy and other predictive parameters. This tool will help astronomers to detect the presence of exoplanets accurately and with high precision. The paper is divided into 6 sections. Section 1 introduces the method used by NASA for the detection of exoplanets and need for accurate prediction, Sect. 2 enumerates the work done in this area till now, Sect. 3 discusses the proposed methodology with all implementation details, Sect. 4 shows the results, Sect. 5 compares our work with prior work and finally Sect. 6 concludes the paper.

2 Work Done Till Date

The contribution of Machine Learning (ML) is quite deep seated in the field of astronomy also. There is always an urge to detect the existence of exoplanets with high predictive accuracy and precision power. Researchers have made a lot many efforts in the recent past by adopting various algorithms based on ML. Many researchers have even implemented more than one ML models, but none of the models have been able to exhibit predictive accuracies equivalent to our model or if they were, there have been many pitfalls in the proper implementation of models.

The first work to implement ML in this problem area to automate the work of exoplanet detection was done by developing tool kit ASTROMLSKIT. Various ML algorithms like KNN, SVM, LDA, Naïve Bayes, Decision Tree, Random Forest. Naïve Bayes gave maximum accuracy of 98.86% [3].

ML was used to create a regression model using 6 algorithms CART, RF, SVM, LR, FFNN and Naïve Bayes with CART giving highest accuracy of 99.89%, but there were a lot many shortcomings as discussed in Table 1 [4].

Gradient Boosted Regression Trees were used for the first time showing 100% accuracy. But the dataset was small, highly imbalanced and did not include k-fold validation test [5].

An automated software Exoplanet was developed which was quite similar to ASTROMLSKIT developed in [3], but with many more capabilities. It allowed users to select ML model of their choice, but had certain limitations as revealed in Table 1 [6].

Algorithms SVM, LDA, KNN, DT, RF were applied to obtain highest accuracy of 97.84% with SVM, but the data was highly imbalanced [7].

The role of hybrid model using DT, SVM, RF, ANN, KNN was highlighted without much implementation details. The two underlying problems which they faced with hybrid model were - how to deal with missing data and how to pre-process the data [8].

The problem of imbalanced data was tried to overcome by applying SMOTE analysis. It was also highlighted that accuracy was not the only criteria to measure the predictive power of an algorithm, rather precision, recall and f1-score should also be compared. Random Forest was able to obtain f1-score of 90% with balanced data using SMOTE [9].

Various other techniques were used for the detection of exoplanets instead of ML [10, 11]. Author has considered the emission of low frequency radiations or radio signals from magnetized exoplanets. However, not a single detection was found. The main reasons for this absence of radio signals of exoplanets might be due to restricted sensitivity of the instruments, observational frequency and ionospheric distractions. Also, the RFI situational values were also ignored by the researchers [10]. In further work [11], Bentum has suggested the deployment of a space-based observatory to overcome the problems of ionospheric cut-off and high man-made noise. But he only proposed the algorithm, which still needed to be implemented on real time data.

ML was used to investigate the possibility using training data sets to standardize periodograms in order to improve the control of the resulting false alarm rate. Researchers concluded that when standardization is performed with a simple averaged periodogram as a noise, then PSD estimated these tests as CFAR. But a big limitation of this study was the case for huge sizes of training data sets for periodicity analysis, the time series was not correlated to orthogonal exponentials [12].

The importance of fuzzy inference systems was revealed for exoplanet detection in another study [13]. The time series data was used to plot flux values against time domain by exploiting various properties of time curve, principal component analysis, time wraps at dynamic time. The work significantly generated lesser number of false positive values, but it concentrated mainly on various descriptive statistics factors of real time data, which are not sufficient to draw predictions. Accuracy, specificity, precision, F1-score play major role for most significant predictions. Error rate is dropped significantly in the work to 0.29 and maximum accuracy achieved is only 81% and that too after multiple runs [13]. Table 1 summarizes all the significant work done in literature till now.

Table 1. Models for detection of exoplanets

Work	ML algorithms used/Software Developed	Accuracy achieved	Achievers & highlights	Shortcomings
Saha et al. [3]	RF, NB, DT, SVM, KNN, LDA	98.86%	NB achieves highest accuracy	Smaller dataset, No K-fold validation
Hora et al. [4]	RF, NB, SVM, CART, LR, FFNN	99.89%	CART achieves highest accuracy	Highly imbalanced dataset, No K-fold validation

(continued)

Table 1. (*continued*)

Work	ML algorithms used/Software Developed	Accuracy achieved	Achievers & highlights	Shortcomings
Xin et al. [5]	Gradient Boosted	100%	NB achieves highest accuracy	Lesser samples available, No post-processing of data, No K-fold validation
Basak et al. [6]	"Exoplanet" automated s/w developed	–	–	How to deal with missing data, No pre-processing of data
Agrawal et al. [7]	RF, DT, SVM, KNN, LDA	97.84%	SVM achieves highest accuracy,10-fold validation done	Imbalanced data
Maxwell et al. [8]	RF, DT, SVM, KNN, ANN	–	RF, Boosted DT, SVM achieve higher accuracy than simple DT, KNN	No implementation details, smaller training size dataset
Singh et al. [9]	RF, DT, KNN, K-means, LR, NB	Accuracy not the only criteria, rather precision, recall and f1-score are also important	RF achieves highest f1-score of 90%, SMOTE applied successfully to balance the dataset	Time efficiency and cost effectiveness to be improved
Bentum [10]	Emission of low frequency radiations or radio signals from magnetized exoplanets is considered	–	Not a single detection was found	Restricted sensitivity of instruments, observational frequency and ionospheric distractions, RFI situational values were ignored

(*continued*)

Table 1. (*continued*)

Work	ML algorithms used/Software Developed	Accuracy achieved	Achievers & highlights	Shortcomings
Bentum [11]	Suggested the deployment of a space-based observatory to overcome the problems of ionospheric cut-off and high man-made noise in [10]	–	Only proposed the algorithm	Algorithm not implemented on real time data
Sulis et al. [12]	Asymptotic analysis of the periodograms statistics after standardization involving unknown number of sinusoids with unknown parameters in partially unknown colored noise	It's a feasibility study	It's feasible to detect exoplanets based on real time series data using Fourier transformations, but for large data sets only	Unable to cover all sizes of datasets. No ML algorithm implemented
Asif et al. [13]	Combination of descriptive statistics, PCAs and DTWs used	81%	DTWs inclusion elevated accuracy and reduced error to 0.29 value	Results based majorly on descriptive statistics, other important prediction attributes missing
Jagtap et al. [14]	Deep Learning models architecture ASTRONET suggested	–	No empirical data available, just a suggestive work	No experimental setup

The adoption of deep learning algorithms and a novel architecture called ASTRONET were proposed to detect exoplanet presence based on various exoplanetary parameters like gravity, mass, radius, eccentricity. A big disadvantage with this work is the absence of experimental setup and empirical values. It's only a suggestive work with no empirical data [14].

3 Proposed Methodology with Implementation Details

The dataset used in this research work is taken from National Aeronautics and Space Administration [1]. The dataset contains flux values for various stars expected to be orbiting around by various exoplanets, whose presence is being predicted in this research work. The csv file data is imported to the pandas Data frame using Python. The data frame is further divided into two DataFrames-training DataFrame and test DataFrame. The training dataset has 5087 rows and 3198 columns. Each row denotes a star. A LABEL column is present in both the DataFrames which tells the label or the classification of the star, i.e., whether it has at least one planet orbiting around it or not. The remaining 3197 columns, i.e., the columns from FLUX.1 to FLUX.3197 contain the brightness levels for each star. A brightness level is a floating-point value which could be either positive, negative or zero. Similarly, test DataFrame contains 570 rows and 3198 columns. Rows indicating FLUX values for 570 stars, ranging from FLUX.1 to FLUX.569 and one LABEL column to categorize the stars. This data in the form of CSV file, is imported to Pandas Data frame, which is then preprocessed to check for various missing values and imbalanced data. The data is then handled by normalizing it and applying SMOTE (Synthetic Minority Over-Sampling Technique). This is followed by developing Scatter and Line plots to check for the presence of exoplanets. It follows deploying the model and its further evaluation on the basis of various parameters discussed in the forthcoming sections (Fig. 1).

3.1 Loading the CSV File

Generally, data is stored in different files such as text (txt format) file, comma-separated value (csv format) file, tab-separated value (tsv format) file etc. One can read the contents of these files through Python. A comma-separated value (csv) file is used most commonly to store data. To load or read the contents of a csv file, one can use the read_csv() function in Pandas. The data is read in the form of a two-dimensional array called a Pandas Data Frame.

3.2 Obtaining Separate Training and Test DataFrames

Now create machine learning models using the training dataset to train the computer so that it can be trained from that dataset. It can make predictions based on what it has learnt. While learning, the computer tries to find a pattern in the data, how one information affects another, which information is the most critical one, etc. The test dataset is used to test the accuracy of the model that you have built. The higher the accuracy, the higher is the prediction capability of the machine. After creating the DataFrames one can use the "shape" keyboard to find out the number of rows and columns that exist in a DataFrame.

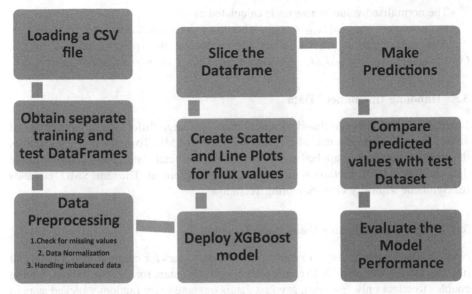

Fig. 1. Proposed methodology

3.3 Check for the Missing Values

In most of the cases, one does not get complete datasets. They either have some values missing from the rows and columns or they do not have standardized values. For example: If there is a date column in a dataset, then there is a huge chance that some of the dates are entered in the DD-MM-YYYY format, some in the MM-DD-YYYY format and so on. So, before going ahead with the analysis, it is a good idea to check whether the dataset has any missing values. If some data value is missing, then the best way to deal with it is to replace it with the median value of its column.

3.4 Data Normalization

After creating a DataFrame and inspecting data for the missing values, it needs to be normalized. Data normalization is a process of standardizing data. It brings every single data-point on a uniform scale. Both the training and test DataFrames contain highly varying FLUX values. The machine learning models are quite sensitive to the scale of data. They give more importance to the larger values while learning the properties of data. Hence, it becomes crucial for researchers to remove this bias by bringing down all the data-points on the same scale. There are various methods of data normalization, out of them the mean normalization method is used in this paper. It is described as under:

Consider a series of numbers having the values $x_1, x_2, x_3,,x_N$ where $N =$ total count for values of a series. Let.

x_{mean} denote the mean (or average) value of a series

x_{min} denote the minimum value in a series and

x_{max} denote the maximum value in a series

The normalised value in a series is calculated as

$x_{norm} = (x_p - x_{mean})/(x_{max} - x_{min})$ where $x_p = x_1, x_2, x_3, ..., x_N$.

After normalisation, the new values in the series will be $(x_1 - x_{mean})/(x_{max} - x_{min})$, $(x_2 - x_{mean})/(x_{max} - x_{min})$, $(x_3 - x_{mean})/(x_{max} - x_{min})...(x_N - x_{mean})/(x_{max} - x_{min})$.

3.5 Handling Imbalanced Data

Imbalanced data refers to that data where there is a large difference in the number of values for various classes in classification algorithms of ML. To deal with such scenario, the SMOTE method is applied to synthesize the artificial data points in the training dataset. The SMOTE method is the easiest one to implement. The term SMOTE stands for Synthetic Minority Over-Sampling Technique.

3.6 Slicing a Data Frame Using iloc() Function

Now the DataFrame is sliced to choose few arbitrary stars for creating scatter plots and line plots as it is not possible to create plots for all 5087 stars for training dataset. Slicing enables to select only few stars, say first 3stars or some other randomly picked stars in between the DataFrame for evaluation purpose which can always be extended for rest of the stars in the training DataFrame. For each of these stars, a Pandas series will be created which contains the brightness levels starting from first star flux value to the last star flux value i.e., from FLUX.1 to FLUX.3197.

3.7 Create Scatter Plots and Line Plots for Flux Values

One first needs to import a Python module named matplotlib.pyplot with plt as an alias. This module is exclusively designed for creating graphs such as bar graphs, histogram, line plot, scatter plot etc. Effectively, 3 Pandas series are created for first three stars. These scatter plots and line plots visualize the fluctuations in the brightness levels (or flux values) of the light emitted by the stars. If there is a periodic dip in the brightness levels, then one can say that the star has at least one planet. If there is no clear periodic dip in the brightness levels, then one could say that the star has no planet. In the datasets, such stars are labelled as 1.

3.8 Deploy XGBoost Prediction Model

The machine learns to recognize the flux values of stars having a planet on its own. When a new dataset containing only the flux values of a star is shown to the machine, it tells whether the star is having a planet or not having a planet. There are many machine learning models or algorithms to do this kind of prediction. In this paper, XGBoost Classifer model is used to classify whether a star has a planet or not. The stars which have at least one planet are labelled as 2 while the stars not having a planet are labelled as 1. To deploy the XGBoost Classifier model, one first has to import the xgboost library with xg as an alias. Then, use the XGBClassifier() function to initiate the model. Then, call the fit() function for respective NumPy arrays as input to deploy the model. Finally, call the predict() function with the test data in the form of NumPy array as an input to get the predicted values. The XGBoost Classifier is a computationally heavy model. It requires a very high RAM, CPU and GPU to run. It takes some time to learn the feature variables through the training data and then make predictions on the test data. Hence, its usage is preferred only if other lightweight (requiring less RAM, CPU and GPU) prediction models don't give much satisfactory results. As is evident from all the previous work carried out in this area, none of the researchers have taken care of all the data preprocessing steps or other parameters. This resulted in unsatisfactory values for various parameters.

3.9 Make Predictions for Training Dataset

The fit() function of the XGBoost Classifier model is used to fit the model and it takes two inputs. The first input is the collection of feature variables. The features are those variables which describe the features or properties of an entity. In this case, the FLUX.1 to FLUX.3197 are feature variables. Hence, the values stored in these columns are the features of a star in exoplanets dataset. The second input is the target variable. The variable which needs to be predicted is called a target variable. In this case, the LABEL is the target variable because the prediction model needs to predict which star belongs to which class or label in the test dataset. Hence, the values stored in the LABEL column are the target values. So, one needs to extract the target variable and the feature variables separately from the training dataset.

3.10 Comparison and Evaluation of the Model Performance

Various performance metrics play a crucial role to evaluate the performance of the model, especially while dealing with imbalanced data which is being balanced using SMOTE, an oversampling technique. The confusion matrix, precision, recall, and f1 score give better generalization of prediction results as compared to accuracy. A confusion matrix is a matrix of size 2×2 for binary classification with actual values on one axis and predicted values on another axis (Table 2).

Table 2. Confusion Matrix with parametric details

		Actual label values	
	Total values	Positive condition	Negative condition
Predicted label values	Predicted labels match	TP (*Correctly identified that labels match*)	FP (*Incorrectly identified that labels match*)
	Predicted labels don't match	FN (*Incorrectly identified that labels don't match*)	TN (*Correctly identified that labels don't match*)
	$Precision = \frac{TP}{TP+FP}$	$Recall\ or\ Sensitivity\ \frac{TP}{TP+FN}$	$f1-score = 2 * \frac{Precision*Recall}{Precision+Recall}$

The Confusion Matrix is constructed on the basis of the terms: true positive, true negative, false negative, and false positive. The meanings of these terms are represented in Table 1 as well as under.

True Positive (TP) — The model correctly predicts the positive class (prediction and actual both are positive).

True Negative (TN) — The model correctly predicts the negative class (prediction and actual both are negative).

False Positive (FP) — The model gives the wrong prediction of the negative class (predicted-positive, actual-negative).

False Negative (FN) — model wrongly predicts the positive class (predicted-negative, actual-positive).

On the basis of above metrics, other parametric values are calculated like Precision, Recall, *f1*-score which are also important measures to check the suitability of a prediction model in addition to accuracy. Confusion matrix, precision, recall, and *f1* score provide better insights into the prediction as compared to accuracy performance metrics.

Precision
It depicts "Out of all the positive predicted, what percentage is truly positive". The precision value lies between 0 and 1. A good prediction model provides a very large number of true positive (TP) values and a very low number of true negative values. Now, based on the TP and FP values, we define Precision. It is the ratio of the TP values to the sum of TP and FP values, i.e.,

$$Precision = \frac{TP}{TP + FP}$$

Recall/Sensitivity
Based on the TP and FN values, we define another parameter called recall. It is the ratio of the TP values to the sum of TP and FN values, i.e., it depicts that out of the total positive, what percentage are predicted positive.

$$Recall = \frac{TP}{TP + FN}$$

Imagine if the prediction model labels every star as 2, i.e., every star has a planet. Then, the number of TP values will be the maximum, i.e., 5 but the number of FP values will also be maximum, i.e., 565. In such a case, the precision value would be $Precision = \frac{5}{5+565} = 0.008$ which is a very low value.

Also, the model will give 0 FN values. Then, the recall value would be $Recall = \frac{TP}{TP + FN} = 1$.

So, even though the recall value would be equal to 1, the precision value would be close to 0. Hence, this would be a bad prediction model. Evidently, there is a trade-off. If the recall value is high, then the precision value will be low and vice-versa. Hence, there is an urge to find an optimum point where both, the precision and the recall values are acceptable.

The F1-Score
To find an optimum point where both, the precision and recall values, are high, another parameter called *f1*-score is calculated. It is a harmonic mean of the precision and recall values, i.e.,

$$f1 - score = 2 * \frac{Precision * Recall}{Precision + Recall}$$

It takes both false positives and false negatives into account. Therefore, it performs well on an imbalanced dataset. *f1*-score gives the same weightage to recall and precision.

Accuracy
It measures the fraction of correctly predicted values to the total number of values against which predictions are made. It refers to the correct rate of predictions. For a particular dataset, accuracy is quantity of correct or precise predictive count over total count for samples of complete data set.

$$Accuracy = \frac{TP + TN}{TP + FP + TN + FN}$$

4 Experimental Results

The Kepler space telescope dataset is used to create a Pandas DataFrame in order to find out which stars beyond our solar system have a planet. The dataset for training the model containing 3198 columns with various column names is depicted Fig. 2. The FLUX values ranging from FLUX.1 TO FLUX. 3198 from column 2 to column 3198 are feature variables, used to train the model. The first column named as LABEL column is target variable, which is used to categorize stars as having or not having exoplanets. It takes values as LABEL1 and LABEL2. LABEL1 represents the stars having no exoplanet

```
Index(['LABEL', 'FLUX.1', 'FLUX.2', 'FLUX.3', 'FLUX.4', 'FLUX.5', 'FLUX.6',
       'FLUX.7', 'FLUX.8', 'FLUX.9',
       ...
       'FLUX.3188', 'FLUX.3189', 'FLUX.3190', 'FLUX.3191', 'FLUX.3192',
       'FLUX.3193', 'FLUX.3194', 'FLUX.3195', 'FLUX.3196', 'FLUX.3197'],
      dtype='object', length=3198)
```

Fig. 2. Columns in training and testing DataFrame

and LABEL2 represents the stars having at least one exoplanet. Same columns exist in the test DataFrame also with same meaning, just the difference lies in the number of rows, which is 570 in case of test dataset as compared to 5087 in case of training dataset.

Top 5 rows of training and testing DataFrames are represented by Fig. 3. Both contain FLUX values for stars from star_0 to star_4 depicted by rows 1 to 5. Complete training DataFrame is depicted in Fig. 4.

```
   LABEL    FLUX.1     FLUX.2     FLUX.3   ...  FLUX.3194  FLUX.3195  FLUX.3196  FLUX.3197
0      2     93.85      83.81      20.10   ...      39.32      61.42       5.08     -39.54
1      2    -38.88     -33.83     -58.54   ...     -11.70       6.46      16.00      19.93
2      2    532.64     535.92     513.73   ...     -11.80     -28.91     -70.02     -96.67
3      2    326.52     347.39     302.35   ...      -8.77     -17.31     -17.35      13.98
4      2  -1107.21   -1112.59   -1118.95   ...    -399.71    -384.65    -411.79    -510.54

[5 rows x 3198 columns]
   LABEL    FLUX.1     FLUX.2     FLUX.3   ...  FLUX.3194  FLUX.3195  FLUX.3196  FLUX.3197
0      2    119.88     100.21      86.46   ...      31.93      35.78     269.43      57.72
1      2   5736.59    5699.98    5717.16   ...   -2265.98   -2366.19   -2294.86   -2034.72
2      2    844.48     817.49     770.07   ...     -95.23    -162.68     -36.79      30.63
3      2   -826.00    -827.31    -846.12   ...      20.25    -120.81    -257.56    -215.41
4      2    -39.57     -15.88      -9.16   ...     -81.46     -61.98     -69.34     -17.84

[5 rows x 3198 columns]
```

Fig. 3. Screenshots of top 5 rows (star_0 to star_4) of training and testing DataFrame

```
        LABEL  FLUX.1  FLUX.2  FLUX.3  ...  FLUX.3194  FLUX.3195  FLUX.3196  FLUX.3197
0       False   False   False   False  ...      False      False      False      False
1       False   False   False   False  ...      False      False      False      False
2       False   False   False   False  ...      False      False      False      False
3       False   False   False   False  ...      False      False      False      False
4       False   False   False   False  ...      False      False      False      False
...       ...     ...     ...     ...  ...        ...        ...        ...        ...
5082    False   False   False   False  ...      False      False      False      False
5083    False   False   False   False  ...      False      False      False      False
5084    False   False   False   False  ...      False      False      False      False
5085    False   False   False   False  ...      False      False      False      False
5086    False   False   False   False  ...      False      False      False      False

[5087 rows x 3198 columns]
```

Fig. 4. Screenshot of training DataFrame

The scatter plots and line plots for first three stars in the DataFrame i.e. star_0, star_1 and star_2 are depicted in Fig. 5, 6, 7, 8, 9 and Fig. 10.

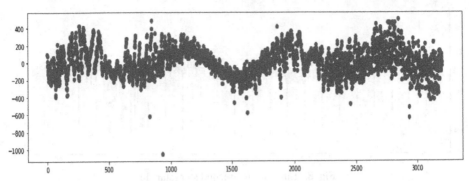

Fig. 5. Scatter plot for first star (star_0)

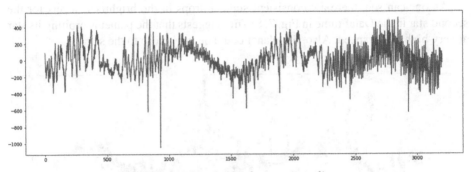

Fig. 6. Line plot for first star (star_0)

As one can see from the scatter plot of star_0 (Fig. 5), there is a periodic downward peak in the brightness level recorded by the Kepler telescope for this star. This suggests that the first star in the DataFrame has at least one planet. The line plot of Fig. 6 also confirms the periodic downward-peaks in the FLUX values. It concludes that star_0 has at least one exoplanet.

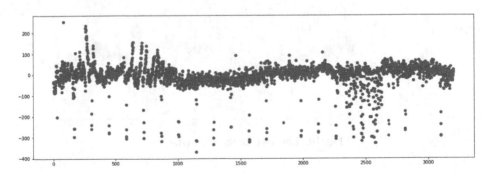

Fig. 7. Scatter plot for second star (star_1)

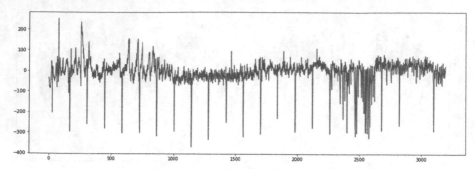

Fig. 8. Line plot for second star (star_1)

As one can see, there are consistent sudden drops in the brightness levels for the second star in the DataFrame in Fig. 7, 8. This suggests that the planet is orbiting its star at very high radial speed. Also, the planet could be very close to the star.

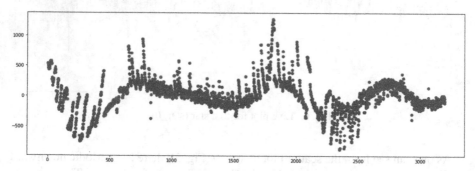

Fig. 9. Scatter plot for third star (star_2)

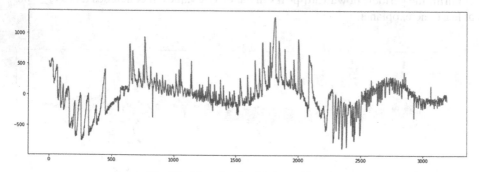

Fig. 10. Line plot for third star (star_2)

From Fig. 9 also one can spot a clear repetitive downward-peaks which confirms that the third star has at least one planet. The line plot from Fig. 10 also confirms the repetitive downward-peak pattern.

	LABEL	FLUX.1	...	FLUX.3196	FLUX.3197
count	5087.000000	5.087000e+03	...	5087.000000	5087.000000
mean	1.007273	1.445054e+02	...	-440.239100	-300.536399
std	0.084982	2.150669e+04	...	16273.406292	14459.795577
min	1.000000	-2.278563e+05	...	-700992.000000	-643170.000000
25%	1.000000	-4.234000e+01	...	-21.135000	-19.820000
50%	1.000000	-7.100000e-01	...	0.900000	1.430000
75%	1.000000	4.825500e+01	...	19.465000	20.280000
max	2.000000	1.439240e+06	...	207590.000000	211302.000000

[8 rows x 3198 columns]

Fig. 11. Descriptive statistics for training dataset

The descriptive statistics from Fig. 11 reveals the 8 major statistical values important to represent the dataset numerically. It represents the "count" - the number of rows in the dataset, "mean" - mean of column values, "std" -standard deviation of the column values, "min", "max" as minimum and maximum of column values, 25% 50% 75% as first, second and third quartile values.

	FLUX.1	FLUX.2	FLUX.3	...	FLUX.3195	FLUX.3196	FLUX.3197
0	0.053834	0.047391	0.006510	...	0.033024	-0.003127	-0.031759
1	-0.050411	-0.042317	-0.081922	...	0.022260	0.037550	0.043849
2	0.243983	0.245509	0.235186	...	-0.017259	-0.036384	-0.048782
3	0.518501	0.551177	0.480659	...	-0.019827	-0.019889	0.029163
4	-0.399904	-0.401872	-0.404199	...	-0.135528	-0.145458	-0.181590
...	...	...	...	...	...	...	...
5082	-0.191318	-0.193261	-0.167219	...	-0.054037	-0.016964	0.012450
5083	0.419089	0.376920	0.384402	...	0.039222	-0.023097	0.011590
5084	0.132006	0.134256	0.126314	...	0.041723	0.037159	0.037335
5085	0.005570	0.002376	-0.007557	...	-0.028346	-0.013317	-0.006191
5086	0.219815	0.208122	0.199000	...	-0.015145	-0.013327	0.015635

[5087 rows x 3197 columns]

Fig. 12. Normalized testing DataFrame

The mean normalization is applied on training dataset and the complete Normalized DataFrame is depicted in Fig. 12.

The normalized data is then balanced using the SMOTE analysis and Figs. 13, 14 and 15 depicts the line plots created using pandas data series for 6 arbitrary stars i.e., star_34 to star_39. The data from both pictorial and numerical representation seems to be highly balanced, thus enumerating the importance of deploying model using XGBoost approach in this work. The same thing can be confirmed by testing the model against test dataset, whose results are shown in following figures.

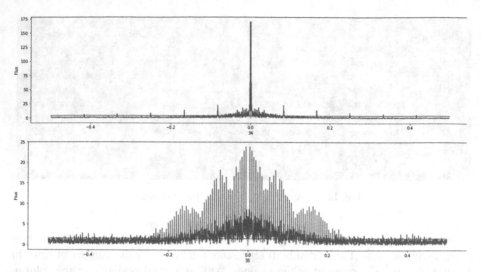

Fig. 13. Line plots for normalized, balanced (using SMOTE) pandas series for star_34, star_35

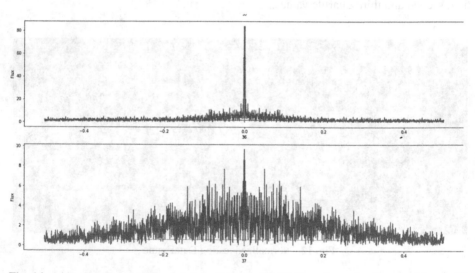

Fig. 14. Line plots for normalized, balanced (using SMOTE) pandas series for star_36, star_37

Finally, the Confusion Matrix and Classification Reports are obtained using our proposed model as shown in Fig. 16. The various values obtained are as under:

TP = 565, FP = 0, FN = 1, TN = 4

Which are fairly good values as compared to the other work done in literature till now, as all the steps taken to process the data, to balance the data and to first sort then deal with the missing data values are taken care of in this novel research work. Also, this prediction model is being used for exoplanet detection for the first time. As one can see, the value in the second row and the second column is greater than 0. Hence, the XGBoost Classifier

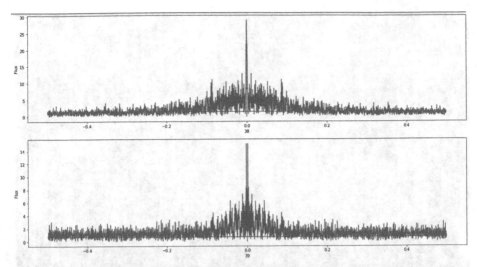

Fig. 15. Line plots for normalized, balanced (using SMOTE) pandas series for star_38, star_39

```
[[565   0]
 [  1   4]]
**********************************************************************
                   precision    recall   f1-score   support

              1       1.00       1.00       1.00       565
              2       1.00       0.80       0.89         5

       accuracy                             1.00       570
      macro avg       1.00       0.90       0.94       570
   weighted avg       1.00       1.00       1.00       570
```

Fig. 16. Confusion matrix and classification report using XGBoost prediction model

prediction model has successfully detected few stars belonging to class 2. However, it has also classified few stars as 1 which should also have been classified as 2 as shown in Fig. 17.

Nonetheless, this is a great achievement because out of 570 stars in the test dataset, only 5 of them have a planet. And detecting them is like finding a needle in a haystack. So, we are able to find out at least 3. Now, let's compute the precision, recall and f1-scores to test the efficacy of the XGBoost Classifier model. If the f1-score value is greater than 0.5, then we have a good classification model. Below ones are average values for both star labels. Other parametric values are yielding the following values:

Precision = 1.00, Recall = 0.90, f1-score = 0.94, accuracy = 100%

```
array([2, 2, 2, 1, 2, 1, 1, 1, 1, 1, 1, 1, 1, 1, 1, 1, 1, 1, 1, 1, 1, 1,
       1, 1, 1, 1, 1, 1, 1, 1, 1, 1, 1, 1, 1, 1, 1, 1, 1, 1, 1, 1, 1, 1,
       1, 1, 1, 1, 1, 1, 1, 1, 1, 1, 1, 1, 1, 1, 1, 1, 1, 1, 1, 1, 1, 1,
       1, 1, 1, 1, 1, 1, 1, 1, 1, 1, 1, 1, 1, 1, 1, 1, 1, 1, 1, 1, 1, 1,
       1, 1, 1, 1, 1, 1, 1, 1, 1, 1, 1, 1, 1, 1, 1, 1, 1, 1, 1, 1, 1, 1,
       1, 1, 1, 1, 1, 1, 1, 1, 1, 1, 1, 1, 1, 1, 1, 1, 1, 1, 1, 1, 1, 1,
       1, 1, 1, 1, 1, 1, 1, 1, 1, 1, 1, 1, 1, 1, 1, 1, 1, 1, 1, 1, 1, 1,
       1, 1, 1, 1, 1, 1, 1, 1, 1, 1, 1, 1, 1, 1, 1, 1, 1, 1, 1, 1, 1, 1,
       1, 1, 1, 1, 1, 1, 1, 1, 1, 1, 1, 1, 1, 1, 1, 1, 1, 1, 1, 1, 1, 1,
       1, 1, 1, 1, 1, 1, 1, 1, 1, 1, 1, 1, 1, 1, 1, 1, 1, 1, 1, 1, 1, 1,
       1, 1, 1, 1, 1, 1, 1, 1, 1, 1, 1, 1, 1, 1, 1, 1, 1, 1, 1, 1, 1, 1,
       1, 1, 1, 1, 1, 1, 1, 1, 1, 1, 1, 1, 1, 1, 1, 1, 1, 1, 1, 1, 1, 1,
       1, 1, 1, 1, 1, 1, 1, 1, 1, 1, 1, 1, 1, 1, 1, 1, 1, 1, 1, 1, 1, 1,
       1, 1, 1, 1, 1, 1, 1, 1, 1, 1, 1, 1, 1, 1, 1, 1, 1, 1, 1, 1, 1, 1,
       1, 1, 1, 1, 1, 1, 1, 1, 1, 1, 1, 1, 1, 1, 1, 1, 1, 1, 1, 1, 1, 1,
       1, 1, 1, 1, 1, 1, 1, 1, 1, 1, 1, 1, 1, 1, 1, 1, 1, 1, 1, 1, 1, 1,
       1, 1, 1, 1, 1, 1, 1, 1, 1, 1, 1, 1, 1, 1, 1, 1, 1, 1, 1, 1, 1, 1,
       1, 1, 1, 1, 1, 1, 1, 1, 1, 1, 1, 1, 1, 1, 1, 1, 1, 1, 1, 1, 1, 1,
       1, 1, 1, 1, 1, 1, 1, 1, 1, 1, 1, 1, 1, 1, 1, 1, 1, 1, 1, 1, 1, 1,
       1, 1, 1, 1, 1, 1, 1, 1, 1, 1, 1, 1, 1, 1, 1, 1, 1, 1, 1, 1, 1, 1,
       1, 1, 1, 1, 1, 1, 1, 1, 1, 1, 1, 1, 1, 1, 1, 1, 1, 1, 1, 1, 1, 1,
       1, 1, 1, 1, 1, 1, 1, 1, 1, 1, 1, 1, 1, 1, 1, 1, 1, 1, 1, 1, 1, 1,
       1, 1, 1, 1, 1, 1, 1, 1, 1, 1, 1, 1, 1, 1, 1, 1, 1, 1, 1, 1, 1])
```

Fig. 17. Label values compared against testing dataset for XGBoost

5 Comparison with Other Approaches

If the proposed model undergoes prediction using Random Forest Classifier method, Logistic Regression and Naïve Bayes then the Confusion matrix and Classification report in Fig. 18 depicting parametric values for Random Forest are *TP = 565, FP = 0, FN = 5, TN = 0.*

Precision = 0.50, Recall = 0.50, f1-score = 0.50, accuracy = 90%

```
[[565   0]
 [  5   0]]
*****************************************************************
              precision    recall  f1-score   support

           1       0.99      1.00      1.00       565
           2       0.00      0.00      0.00         5

    accuracy                           0.99       570
   macro avg       0.50      0.50      0.50       570
weighted avg       0.98      0.99      0.99       570
```

Fig. 18. Confusion matrix and classification report using random forest prediction model

Which are comparatively quite lesser values as compared to our model. The comparative bar graph for all the above said models and our proposed model for the 4 parameters is shown in Fig. 19.

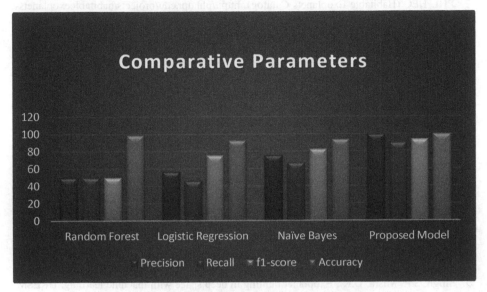

Fig. 19. Comparison of parameters for random forest and proposed model

6 Conclusion and Future Work

In this paper, a novel model is proposed to detect the presence of exoplanets beyond Milky way galaxy using XGBoost supervised machine learning algorithm. All the constraints like data preprocessing, data cleaning, data balancing is taken care of while developing the model. The empirical values for parameters such as precision, recall, f1-score and accuracy give highly strong predictive power results as compared to the work done previously. In the future, a hybrid model can be used having a combination of various machine learning and deep learning algorithms. Optimization techniques can further be applied to deal with time and efficiency issues of robust ensemble model.

References

1. National Aeronautics and Space Administration: Kepler and K2. https://www.nasa.gov/mission_pages/kepler/main/index.htm
2. PHL HEC (Habitable Exoplanets Catalog). http://phl.upr.edu/projects/habitableexoplanets-catalog/data/database
3. Saha, S., Bora, K., Agrawal, S., Routh, S., Narasimhamurthy, A.: ASTROMLSKIT: a new statistical machine learning toolkit: a platform for data analytics in astronomy (2015). 1504.07865
4. Hora, K.: Classifying exoplanets as potentially habitable using machine learning. In: Saini, A.K., Nayak, A.K., Vyas, R.K. (eds.) ICT Based Innovations. AISC, vol. 653, pp. 203–212. Springer, Singapore (2018). https://doi.org/10.1007/978-981-10-6602-3_20
5. Kok, M., Velazco J., Bentum, M.: CubeSat array for detection of RF emissions from exoplanets using inter-satellite optical communicators. In: IEEE Aerospace Conference, pp. 1–12 (2020). https://doi.org/10.1109/AERO47225.2020.9172296
6. Saha, S., et al.: Theoretical validation of potential habitability via analytical and boosted tree methods: an optimistic study on recently discovered exoplanets. Astron. Comput. **23**, 141–150 (2018)
7. Cheriton, R.: Towards integrated astrophotonic instruments for exoplanet biosignature detection. In: Conference on Lasers and Electro-Optics Pacific Rim (CLEO-PR), pp. 1–20 (2020). https://doi.org/10.1364/CLEOPR.2020.C6G_2
8. Maxwell, A.E., Warner, T.A., Fang, F.: Implementation of machine learning classification in remote sensing: an applied review. Int. J. Remote Sens. **39**(9), 2784–2817 (2018)
9. Singh, S.P., Misra, D.K.: Exoplanet hunting in deep space with machine learning. IJRESM **3**(9), 187–192 (2020)
10. Bentum, M.J.: The search for exoplanets using ultra-long wavelength radio astronomy. In: IEEE Aerospace Conference, pp. 1–7 (2017). https://doi.org/10.1109/AERO.2017.7943778
11. Bentum, M.J.: Algorithms for direct radio detections of exoplanets in the neighbourhood of radiating host stars. In: IEEE Aerospace Conference, pp. 1–7 (2018). https://doi.org/10.1109/AERO.2018.8396590
12. Sulis, S., Mary, D., Bigot, L.: A study of periodograms standardized using training datasets and application to exoplanet detection. IEEE Trans. Signal Process. **65**(8), 2136–2150 (2017). https://doi.org/10.1109/TSP.2017.2652391
13. Amin, R., et al.: Detection of exoplanet systems in Kepler light curves using adaptive neuro-fuzzy system. In: International Conference on Intelligent Systems IS, pp. 66–72. IEEE (2018)
14. Jagtap, R., Inamdar, U., Dere, S., Fatima, M., Shardoor, N.: Habitability of exoplanets using deep learning. In: IEEE International IOT, Electronics and Mechatronics Conferencence (2021)

PSRE Self-assessment Approach for Predicting the Educators' Performance Using Classification Techniques

Sapna Arora[1](✉), Manisha Agarwal[1], Shweta Mongia[2], and Ruchi Kawatra[3]

[1] Banasthali Vidyapith, P.O. Banasthali Vidyapith, Tonk 304022, Rajasthan, India
[2] University of Petroleum and Energy Studies, Dehradun, Uttarakhand, India
[3] Chitkara University Institute of Engineering and Technology, Chitkara University, Rajpura, Punjab, India

Abstract. With the growing interest in and significance of Educational Data Mining to educators' performance, there is a vital need to comprehend the full scope of job performance that can substantially impact teaching quality. However, a few educational institutions are attempting to improve educator effectiveness to improve student outcomes. Furthermore, for reasons of confidentiality, most institutions do not share their data. As a result, an assessment of a self-assessment strategy is required to improve educators' performance. With four input parameters and five classifiers (Logistics Regression, Naive Bayes, K-nearest Neighbor, Support Vector Machine- Linear, and Radial Basis Function), the proposed PSRE (Professional, Social, Research, and Emotional behavior) self-assessment approach is modeled to predict the overall performance of educators working in various Higher Educational Institutions. Overall, K-nearest neighbor has a high accuracy of 95.43%, which may help determine educators' progress and assist them in reaching new professional heights.

Keywords: Behavior · Classification · Educational Data Mining · Job performance · Quality teaching · Self-assessment

1 Introduction

The notion of accomplishment, which emerged during the computer science era, represents several challenges [1] to educational organizations, including quality-based education, staff development, work attitude, and improved results, among others. Quality-based education in all its comprehensiveness necessitates developing the values for the entities- students and educators which support the education sector in HEI (Higher Educational Institutions). For a long time, higher education institutions have started to focus on their internal academic challenges rather than the major organizational entities [2]. One of such entities is educators, which is a vigorous force behind the success of such quality-based education. Most of the pedagogical organizations are often perturbed for achieving better results for students, without emphasizing the overall development of educator-related aspects. In prior studies, it has been found that most of the researchers

© Springer Nature Switzerland AG 2022
A. Dev et al. (Eds.): AIST 2021, CCIS 1546, pp. 405–423, 2022.
https://doi.org/10.1007/978-3-030-95711-7_34

have emphasized some factors associated with personal, professional [3], research, or student feedback [4] to analyze the performance of educators, but not all at the same time. The novelty of the proposed work is to work with comprehensive job performance, accompanying professional, social, research, and emotional parameters simultaneously judged by educators itself which could positively impact the educator performance, which in turn be beneficial for the organization's success. Organizations can provide relevant training to boost the effectiveness of educators. A decent training provided by the employer is an excellent effort that provides educators with the opportunity to learn a wide range of skills. The education sector should become more upgraded, innovative and techno-savvy, to meet the competitive needs of today's educational system. To bring the education sector up to global standards, there is always a demand for talented and skilled educators who are strong not only professionally but also on other levels like research, social, and emotional.

EDM (Educational Data Mining) has become one of the disciplines that have attracted the interest of many research scholars and data scientists in data mining and obtaining meaningful patterns from educational data through Knowledge Discovery. EDM is concerned with establishing ways to study the unique sorts of data found in educational contexts and better understand the connected entities such as students and faculty and the environments in which they learn. EDM enables you to perform tasks such as discovering new knowledge based on academic usage statistics, assisting in the evaluation of educational frameworks, and possibly improving some aspects of the teaching and learning quality, and laying the foundation for the future by setting the stage for a more efficient educational process [5]. However, EDM employs a variety of users [6] including students, instructors, course makers, and administrators, but the authors recognize the role of the backbone i.e., educators in ensuring students' accomplishment. Most organizations evaluate educators' work performance based on student evaluation [7] and achievements, one of the oldest and most widely used EDM applications, and various methodologies and models have been used.

Pedagogical knowledge discovery and learning analytics research entail addressing more complex issues regarding what a student, instructor, or institution understands as well as how the information relates to improved performance. Learning analytics integrates data from a wide variety of sources (for example, learning and teaching behavior, academic success), quantitative models, and pattern classification to impact reforms in how individuals perceive, teachers teach, students learn, and higher education institutions design coursework [8]. Data available with the institutions will be more useful when working towards the improvement of student and educator performance. To fetch out the hidden knowledge from numerous amounts of educational data is acknowledged as EDM. An approach towards fetching valuable data related to educators from educational data disseminated worldwide gives a facet towards the organization's success. Khalifa [9] states that "Educators must continually improve themselves through seminars and other professional development programs that help them enhance their own teaching skills in order for them to become effective and efficient educators". These endeavors can be extended with machine learning through a self-assessment approach to the prediction of educator performance, which will not only give educators an idea of where they are lacking but will also be useful to educational institutions in determining where they can improve job satisfaction for educators by giving relevant training and thus improve academic and organization performance. EDM administers emerging techniques, investigates the educational data, and employs Data Mining scaffolding to handle conditions like recruitment, appraisal assessment, and performance improvement through self-assessment criteria. EDM employs a variety of machine learning techniques, including KNN (K-Nearest Neighbor), NB (Naive Bayes), DT (Decision Trees), SVM (Support Vector Machine, LR (Logistics Regression), and others. The proposed research lines up the assessment of educators in a comprehensive manner. In this similitude, the contributions of the research are-

1. Collection of educators' parameter instances from different parts of India.
2. Employing data mining classification models such as Logistics Regression, K-nearest neighbor, Naive Bayes, SVM-Linear, and RBF (Radial Function Basis) to determine an educator's overall job performance via self-assessment.
3. Predict the comprehensive job performance of educators by collecting the parameters associated with professional, research, social, and emotional levels.
4. Correlating the relationship between four different parameters-PSRE.

The sections of the research study are structured in a coherent fashion. Section 2 explores the related research work done on the prediction of educators' performance based on different parameters. Section 3 enumerates the tools and techniques used. Section 4 reveals the methodology used. In Sect. 5, a demonstration of the designated work has been given. Section 6 highlights the results and discussions of the stated work. Section 7 concludes with the work and shows the future preview.

2 Literature Review

The proposed study examines the job performance of educators as a model that should be implemented in higher education institutions. Romero and Ventura [10] conducted a comprehensive review that spanned the years 1995 to 2005. They evaluated the applications of EDM and the users, orientation, and current trends in EDM. They claim that educational systems have different characteristics that necessitate a unique solution to the mining issue. As a result, to tackle the challenges that are particular to the educational sector, certain specific data mining techniques are necessary. For the effective prediction of the performance of the related entities, prediction models that integrate all social, personal, professional, and other environmental factors are required, according to another study by Bhardwaj and Pal [11]. As a result, using a four-tier self-assessment approach to attain excellence, the focus here is on quality education via parameters associated with the entity and organizational performance. This study is an approach to organizational stimulation for employees in the form of policies and special training. The notion of job performance was recounted by different researchers [12–14] which was affixed with limited parameters like professional, training, research, or based on emotional intelligence. The PSRE approach employed in this study attempted to bring these parameters together under one framework to obtain a precise result for overall job performance. The application of data mining techniques with an educational domain could give a new facet to education. From Table 1, a glimpse of previous research could easily be retrieved.

Table 1. A comparative review of research studies

Objective	Algorithm	Dataset and parameters	Research gaps
Performance assessment of university lecturer [15]	K-Medoids, k-means	A total of 25 people was sampled from two study programmes at Universitas Muhammadiyah Kalimantan Teaching aspect, research aspect, and community service	Limited set of parameters, Small sample size
Two-layer classifier system for evaluating and predicting performance [16]	ID3, C4.5, and Multilayer Perceptron (MLP)	Case study data from a Nigerian University Professional qualification, status of the appointment, Work experience, Rank, latest and highest qualification	Inclusion of more parameters like student feed-back, emotional behavior, job satisfaction, etc. is desirable
Correlation between teaching performance and emotional intelligence [17]	T-test Levene's Test	A sample of 160 English student-teachers who are registered with Hodeida University's Faculty of Education General Mood, Positive impression, Inter and Intrapersonal factors, supervision, Stress, Adaptability	Analysis of aspects such as exercise activities and sleep time could make the research more effective
Predicted the research performance based on c-index and h-index publications [18]	Logistic Regression, Decision Tree ANN, SVM	Institute Research Management and Innovation contributed a dataset of 861 academicians Professional factors like experience, position, division, citation, article	Small sample size, Need to encompass more research features, Interrelation between research and teaching score is missing

(continued)

Table 1. (*continued*)

Objective	Algorithm	Dataset and parameters	Research gaps
Evaluation of student-based opinion mining work to evaluate the faculty's teaching performance [19]	LSTM	Data set generated from Sukkur IBA University students' remarks during the previous five years and the regular SemEval-2014 data set with a stratum of 45 individuals	Furtherance could be finer by encompassing emotional parameters
A theoretical model to show the correlation of emotional behavior and work performance [20]	N.A.	Interpersonal and intrapersonal ability, Stress management, Adaptability, Mood	The algorithm's implications and adequate data organization could lead to a recommended outcome
Association between the repercussion of teaching experience on the performance of students [21]	Cronbach's alpha coefficient	Data Sizes of 300 students and teachers were randomly worn from 150 secondary schools of three senatorial zones of Benue State, Nigeria. Professional factors	Limited parameters associated with academic performance are considered
Model for evaluation and prediction of the teacher's performance [22]	C4.5 ID3 MLP	Data from a case study conducted at a Nigerian university in the country's south west Professional factors	Only professional parameters are appraised
Analyzing the emotional intelligence in the field of the effective job performance of educationists [23]	N.A.	Dataset was collected from 212 Malaysian teachers from six secondary schools in Kedah via a questionnaire survey EI dimensions, Job performance, and demographic results	Results could be more potent in the case of a large size dataset

(*continued*)

Table 1. (*continued*)

Objective	Algorithm	Dataset and parameters	Research gaps
Model to evaluate teacher's performance using machine learning [24]	DT, KNN, Naive Bayes	Data was obtained from 813 instructors in Gaza City's Ministry of Education and Higher Education via a questionnaire Professional parameters and Training details	With the addition of research strands, the research could be much more productive

3 Tools and Techniques Used

An extensive questionnaire-based survey was done from 1578 personnel working on different ranks at various institutions, employing google forms and hardcopy distribution, to orient us to the current issues and exercises linked to the primary use of individual data. The reliability of the dataset achieved an acceptable value of 0.74004 through Cronbach Alpha Technique [25]. The survey covers four main aspects i.e., Professional, Social, Research, and Emotional (PSRE). Through the course of our research, a broad collection of questions using five-point Likert response scales [26] were developed to support the understanding of qualitative data from different educators at professional, social, research, and emotional traits with 3, 4, 6, and 14 traits respectively, as shown in Fig. 2. The scores at four different levels, i.e., PSRE, were evaluated using the collected data via google forms and manual responses. Google sheets were employed for proper speculating. To achieve meticulous outcomes, a realistic strategy was adopted. Logistics Regression [27, 28], Naive Bayes, SVM-RBF, SVM-linear, and KNN were the five classification techniques [29] used to assess the data. The models were implemented in python in the Jupyter notebook.

4 Methodology

Examining and elucidating a large amount of data without the use of tools [30–32] is a challenging undertaking for humans, especially in the case of organizations. Different tools, such as observation-based, mathematical, review-based, statistical, and so on, are used to examine data in predictive or descriptive research. EDM is an excellent method for uncovering facts buried in large volumes of data, and its supervised learning techniques aid in the prediction of values and the achievement of better results. The comprehensive job performance of an educator is predicted using predictive modeling in this study. These predictive models follow a chronology to fetch out useful data, as shown in Fig. 1.

4.1 Domain Recognition

To evaluate the overall performance of educators, it is necessary to recognize the parameters accompanying the parameters at different levels i.e., professional, social, research, and emotional. On these grounds, a contemplation of different parameters suggested by experienced people and former researchers is taken to evaluate each level effectively. These experienced personnel helped in clustering parameters for each level.

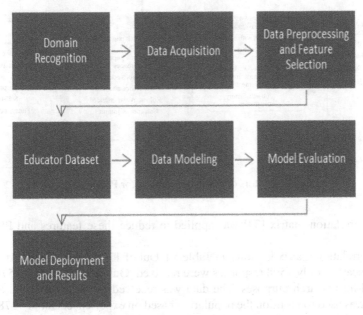

Fig. 1. Research methodology

4.2 Domain Acquisition

The recognition of parameter categories aided us in obtaining data and performing score analysis. After agreeing on the specifications, the next step was to collect data from a variety of educators who were working in different organizations. At each tier, the responses were scored differently. The responses received at different tiers evaluated a different score. Some of the major parameters on each tier are shown in Fig. 2. Moreover, the raw data with missing details needs to be preprocessed.

4.3 Data Preparation and Feature Selection

A questionnaire was designed based on Fig. 2 and distributed among 1700 educators. Moreover, the hard copy of the questionnaire was also distributed to access PSRE Score, which played a pivotal role in the overall assessment. Initially, the dataset consisted of five main attributes - Personal, Professional, Social, Research, and Emotional Score.

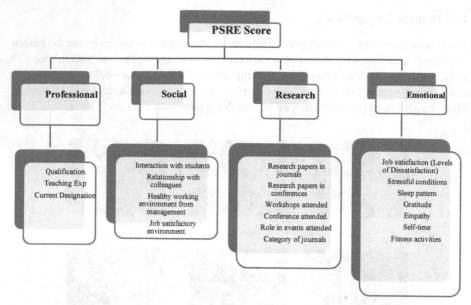

Fig. 2. Factors of evaluation criteria for PSRE score.

Pearson Correlation matrix [33] was applied to reduce these features and PSRE was selected.

The correlation matrix is shown in Table VI. Out of 1700 questionnaires distributed among educators, only 1598 responses were received. Out of 1598 entries, 1578 entries were used for research purposes. The data was received in the excel sheet. Stratified sampling was used to partition the population based on experience. Out of 1578 entries, 447, 709, and 422 entries inhabited in the 'Excellent', 'Good' and 'Need improvement' category of performance status., as shown in Fig. 3.

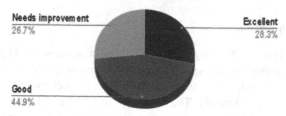

Fig. 3. Categorization of sampled data based on educator performance

4.4 Data Modeling

In EDM, data modeling refers to the process of teaching a machine-learning algorithm to predict the usefulness of features and modify it based on the input data. The model is included in this study to predict future outcomes based on self-evaluation. The predictive analysis is carried out using Logistic Regression, Naive Bayes, KNN, SVM-RBF, and SVM-linear classifier models.

Logistic Regression

Logistic regression [34] is a prominent and widely used classification approach in predictive analytics. Logistic regression, which estimates the likelihood of an event occurring, describes the relationship between the dependent variable (Y) and the independent variable (X), also known as determinants or predictors. Logistic regression is a popular supervised machine learning approach that uses the sigmoid function to address binary and multiclass classification problems. The educator dataset is divided into three categories: Excellent, Good, and Need improvement. The findings of LR, as shown in Table 4, reveal an accuracy percentage of 84.60%.

Naïve Bayes

Naive Bayes [35] is a well-known conditional probabilistic method that analyses outcomes using Bayes' formula. Given our prior knowledge, Bayes' Theorem allows us to determine the likelihood of a piece of data belonging to a given class. Equation 1 illustrates Bayes' Theorem.:

$$A(data) = \frac{A(category) * A(category)}{A(data)} \tag{1}$$

The probability of category given the actual data is A(category|data).
The probability of data belonging to a category is A(data|category).

KNN

KNN [36] is a supervised algorithm that perceives the most likely target category based on trait similarity. It is based on how closely one point's traits match those of the nearest points in the training set of data. To analyze the precise results in an educational dataset, it is possible to assess features on four levels, i.e., PSRE with neighbor size5 and distance metric as Minkowski.

SVM

SVM [37] is a sophisticated supervised algorithm that supports both classification and regression approaches and works with huge quantities of data. The proposed approach uses an SVM-Linear and SVM-RBF core to predict overall job performance.

4.5 Model Evaluation

The entire dataset is split into two parts: training and testing. The author divided the data into a 70:30 ratio in the Jupyter notebook, with 1052 entries as the training set and 526 entries as the testing set. The study's purpose is to create a model that can be used to evaluate total job performance using four major independent parameters: professional, social, research, and emotional. To investigate the impacts of numerous independent factors on performance status, several parameters were considered. After the algorithm has been trained on the train data, it must be evaluated on the test dataset.

4.6 Model Deployment and Results

The model deployment phase applies previously acquired knowledge to fresh input and generates actions. The process of deploying the models into the building phase to accomplish the output is referred to as model deployment in EDM. In our approach, four independent parameters PSRE and a target variable i.e., Performance is targeted with three different values i.e., Excellent, Good, and Need improvement. Among 1578 records the target Class contains three values such as 0(for excellent), 1 (for good), and 2 (for need improvement). To predict the performance, different metrics are used such as confusion matrix, accuracy, Kappa score, root mean square error, precision, recall, and F1 score.

Confusion Matrix

A Confusion Matrix is an embossed matrix used to illustrate a model's performance. The confusion matrix is extensively used in machine learning for supervised classification and assessing the performance of classification models. Rows and columns make up the squared layout of a confusion matrix, with rows reflecting the instances' actual classes and columns representing the predicted classes [38]. As illustrated in Fig. 4, the proposed approach uses a confusion matrix and heatmap generated in a jupyter notebook to represent three output classes: Excellent, Good, and Need improvement.

```
[[135  11   1]
 [ 15 170  27]
 [  1  24 142]]
```

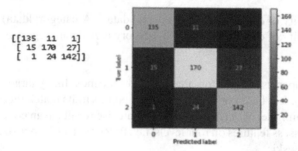

Fig. 4. Confusion matrix with heatmap with Naive Bayes Classifier (using jupyter notebook).

Accuracy

The ratio of the number of correct predictions (total number of true positives and true negatives) to the total input sample size, which includes True positives, True Negatives, False positives, and False negatives, is known as accuracy [39]. The highest level of accuracy attained with the educator dataset is 95.43.

Kappa Score

Kappa score [40] is a statistic used to examine interrater reliability. Kappa values of 0.8 or higher indicate good agreement; zero or below indicates no correlation. In Table 2, an illustration of true and predicted labels is given for the kappa value assessment of the Naïve Bayes classifier. Kappa Value is shown in Eq. 2.

$$Cohen's\ Kappa\ Value = (N \sum_{i=1}^{m} DVA - \sum_{i=1}^{m} TCo * TPr)/(N^2 - \sum_{i=1}^{m} TCo * TPr) \qquad (2)$$

Where DVA = Diagonal Values, TCo = Total Corrected values, TPr = Total Predicted values, N = Number of Patterns

$$526 \sum (135 + 170 + 142) - \sum (147 * 151 + 212 * 205 + 167 * 170)/526^2$$
$$- \sum (147 * 151 + 212 * 205 + 167 * 170) = 0.77$$

Table 2. Detailed values of Naive Bayes algorithm for Kappa value assessment

		Predicted labels			
		Excellent	Good	Need improvement	Total
True labels	Excellent	135	11	1	147
	Good	15	170	27	212
	Need improvement	1	24	142	167
	Total	151	205	170	526(N)

Precision Recall and F1-Score

The precision and recall [41–43] value of an algorithm is two well-known criteria for evaluating performance. The ratio of true positives to total positives, or true positives to false positives, is known as precision (ref Eq. 3). Recall, on the other hand, is a sample of true positives from a larger set of true positives and false negatives (ref Eq. 4). The F1-score is the weighted average of the previous two measurements (ref Eq. 5).

$$Precision = \frac{A}{A + B} \tag{3}$$

$$Recall = \frac{A}{A + D} \tag{4}$$

$$F1\ Score = 2 * \frac{P * R}{P + R} \tag{5}$$

Where,

A = True Positives, B = False Positives, C = True Negatives, D = False Negatives, P = Precision, R = Recall.

5 Simulated Work

The concept of comprehensive teaching job performance used in the proposed approach is based on different parameters. In the proposed approach, four main independent parameters i.e., PSRE are used. However, different particulars are collected from each educator to get into the details. These particulars are described in Table 3 which helped in prediction.

Table 3. Parameters used in the research approach.

Parameter name	Explanation	Values	Factors attained
Name	Name of educator	Nominal	–
University	Name of University	Nominal	–
Age	22 to 70	Numeric	–
Gender	Male, Female, Transgender	Nominal	–
Marital status	Married, Single, Separated, Divorced	Nominal	–
Dependents	0,1, 2…	Ordinal	–
Domain of Working	IT, mgmt., health, education, commerce, art	Nominal	–
Professional Score	Calculated from factors attained	Ordinal	Teaching experience, current designation, and qualification
Social Score	Calculated from factors attained	Ordinal	interaction with students, relationship with colleagues, a healthy working environment from management, Job satisfactory environment
Research Score	Calculated from factors attained	Ordinal	Research papers in c and h index journals, workshops attended, part of the conference, number of research papers in conferences, research papers in journals
Emotional Score	Calculated from factors attained	Ordinal	Stressful time, impulsive power, emotional decisions, empathy, social media apps, sleep pattern, fitness activity, mealtime, self-time, problem-solving approaches, self-regard, NGO or social cause work, body pain, morning consciousness
Performance status	Excellent, Good, Need improvement	Categorical	Target Variable-informed/predicted

6   Results and Discussion

Based on the study's findings, the data was divided into a 70:30 ratio for the training and testing phases. Exorbitant accuracy with the lowest error rates is utilized to find the optimal predictive models, as illustrated in Fig. 5.

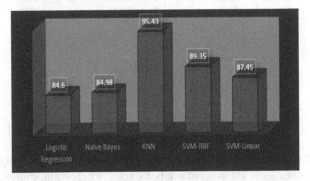

Fig. 5. Accuracy report bar chart of classifiers on educator's dataset

The confusion matrix, accuracy, kappa scores, and error rates MAE (Mean Absolute Error), MSE (Mean Squared Error), and RMSE (Root Mean Squared Error) are all shown in Table 4.

Table 4. Tabular representation of results

Algorithm			Predicted			Accuracy (in %)	Kappa Score	MAE MSE RMSE
			0	1	2			
LR	Actual	0	131	16	0	84.60	0.764	0.155
		1	9	182	21			0.159
		2	1	34	132			0.399
NB		0	135	11	1	84.98	0.772	0.153
		1	15	170	27			0.161
		2	1	24	142			0.401
KNN		0	144	2	1	95.43	0.930	0.049
		1	0	212	0			0.057
		2	1	20	146			0.238

(*continued*)

Table 4. (*continued*)

Algorithm			Predicted			Accuracy (in %)	Kappa Score	MAE MSE RMSE
			0	1	2			
SVM-RBF		0	142	3	2	89.35	0.839	0.112
		1	16	176	20			0.123
		2	1	14	152			0.351
SVM-Linear		0	133	13	1	87.45	0.809	0.129
		1	9	181	22			0.136
		2	1	20	146			0.369

To assess the recital values concerning Performance, the reckoning of precision, recall, and F1-score with classifier models Logistic Regression, Naive Bayes, KNN, SVM-RBF, and SVM-linear are introduced in Table 5. In the light of the results shown, it is resolutely believed through legend plots that KNN can assist educators to evaluate their overall performance.

The correlation matrix generated, as shown in Table 6 revealed a strong association between professional and research behavior, with a value of 0.6041. The research has found that emotional score is one of the criteria which can make a significant effect, bearing a moderate value of 0.5393 and 0.5699 with professional and research behavior.

However, the social score has the least impact on the emotional, professional, and research behavior, appearing with values of 0.1846, 0.1228, and 0.0902, respectively. Heatmap of correlation matrix generated from Table 6 is shown in Fig. 6.

As a culminating analysis towards accuracy and error metrics on the dataset was better in KNN. Moreover, overall job performance, emotional, professional, and research behavior toiled a paramount role.

Table 5. Precision, Recall, F1 Score through legend plots of classifier used in PSRE.

LR	Precision	Recall	F1-Score	Legend Plot
0	0.93	0.89	0.91	
1	0.78	0.86	0.82	
2	0.86	0.79	0.83	

NB	Precision	Recall	F1-Score	
0	0.89	0.92	0.91	
1	0.83	0.80	0.82	
2	0.84	0.85	0.84	

KNN	Precision	Recall	F1-Score	
0	0.99	0.98	0.99	
1	0.91	1.00	0.95	
2	0.99	0.87	0.93	

SVM-RBF	Precision	Recall	F1-Score	
0	0.89	0.97	0.93	
1	0.91	0.83	0.87	
2	0.87	0.91	0.89	

SVM-Linear	Precision	Recall	F1-Score	
0	0.93	0.90	0.92	
1	0.85	0.85	0.85	
2	0.86	0.87	0.87	

Table 6. Correlation matrix between features

	Personal	Emotional	Social	Professional	Research
Personal	1.0000	−0.0363	−0.0834	−0.3404	−0.2082
Emotional	−0.0363	1.0000	0.1846	0.5393	0.5699
Social	−0.0834	0.1846	1.0000	0.1228	0.0902
Professional	−0.3404	0.5393	0.1228	1.0000	0.6041
Research	−0.2082	0.5699	0.0902	0.6041	1.0000

	Personal	Emotional	Social	Professional	Research
Personal	1.0000	-0.0363	-0.0834	-0.3404	-0.2082
Emotional	-0.0363	1.0000	0.1846	0.5393	0.5699
Social	-0.0834	0.1846	1.0000	0.1228	0.0902
Professional	-0.3404	0.5393	0.1228	1.0000	0.6041
Research	-0.2082	0.5699	0.0902	0.6041	1.0000

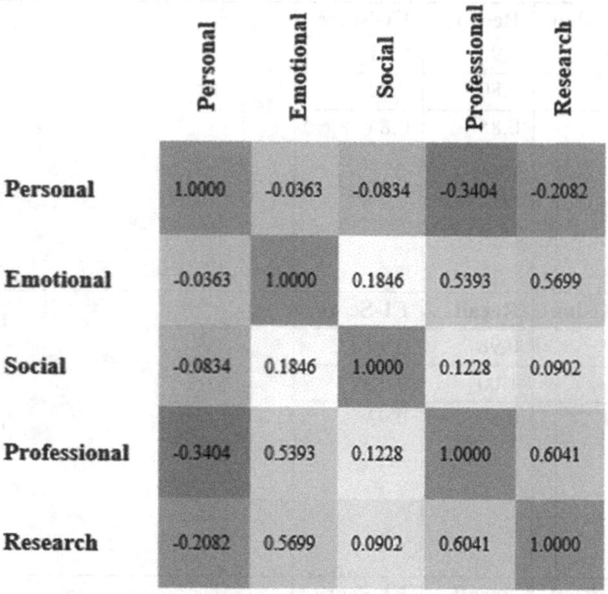

Fig. 6. Heatmap of Pearson correlation matrix between all features of the educators' dataset

7 Conclusion

This research offers useful insights on how to enhance job performance at various levels of an educator. It has provided educators a new outlook on themselves by using the PSRE model to break down work-related behavior into several tiers, which was previously limited. For the prediction of the overall job performance of educators, logistic regression, Naive Bayes, KNN, SVM-RBF, and SVM-linear are used with the 1578 educator's datasets. KNN with Minkowski data metric is found to be the best prediction model with an accuracy of 95.43% among 84.60%, 84.98%, 89.35%, and 87.45% with Logistic Regression, Naive Bayes, SVM-RBF, and SVM-linear respectively. The error metrics obtained in the case of KNN possess 0.049, 0.057 and 0.238 as MAE, MSE, and RMSE scores. The study has some limitations, such as the inclusion of only the educator's point of view and a limited dataset. Another issue is the lack of consideration for long-term impacts. Following up with educators to see how PSRE model implementation in the form of self-assessment affects their job performance across many areas (e.g., teaching performance, social interaction, emotional competence) for both instantaneous and long-term consequences is a recommendation for future research. This type of research is essential to discover more effective aspects that might play a crucial role in delivering best practices in teaching.

However, for institutional purposes, this model could be used to achieve pragmatic benefits like a better relationship between educators and organization, a happier workplace, more dedicated personnel, etc. by embracing the nuances where the educators are lacking and can work on it by providing appropriate training. For prospects, it is recommended to work with algorithms like ANN, LSTM, etc. to validate the uncovered facts associated with data.

References

1. Shin, J.C., Harman, G.: New challenges for higher education: global and Asia-Pacific perspectives. Asia Pacific Educ. Rev. **10**, 1–13 (2009)
2. Arora, S., Agarwal, M., Kawatra, R.: Prediction of educationist's performance using regression model. In: 7th International Conference on Computing for Sustainable Global Development (INDIACom), New Delhi, pp. 88–93. IEEE (2020). https://doi.org/10.23919/INDIAC om49435.2020.9083708
3. Pal, A.K., Pal, S.: Evaluation of teacher's performance: a data mining approach. Int. J. Comput. Sci. Mob. Comput. **2**(12), 359–369 (2013)
4. Maitra, S., Madan, S., Kandwal, R., Mahajan, P.: Mining authentic student feedback for faculty using Naive Bayes classifier. Procedia Comput. Sci. **132**, 1171–1183 (2018)
5. Romero, C., Venture, S., Bra, P.: Knowledge discovery with genetic programming for providing feedback to courseware authors. User Model. User-Adap. Inter. **14**(5), 425–464 (2004)
6. Romero, C., Ventura, S.: IEEE Trans. Syst. Man Cybern.-Part C Appl. Rev. **40**(6), 601–618 (2010)
7. Agaoglu, M.: Predicting instructor performance using data mining techniques in higher education. IEEE Access **4**, 2379–2387 (2016). https://doi.org/10.1109/ACCESS.2016.256 8756
8. Sonderlund, A.L., Hughes, E., Smith, J.: The efficacy of learning analytics interventions in higher education: a systematic review. Br. J. Educ. Technol. 1–25 (2018). https://doi.org/10. 1111/bjet.12720
9. Khalifa, H., Garcia, R.: The state of social media in Saudi Arabia's higher education. Int. J. Technol. Educ. Market. **3**(1), 65–76 (2013)
10. Romero, C., Ventura, S.: Educational data mining: a survey from 1995 to 2005. Expert Syst. Appl. **33**(1), 135–146 (2007). https://doi.org/10.1016/j.eswa.2006.04.005
11. Bhardwaj, B.K., Pal, S.: Data mining: a prediction for performance improvement using classification. Int. J. Comput. Sci. Inf. Secur. (IJCSIS) **9**(4), 136–140 (2011)
12. Arora, S., Agarwal, M., Mongia, S.: Comparative analysis of educational job performance parameters for organizational success: a review. In: Dave, M., Garg, R., Dua, M., Hussien, J. (eds.) Proceedings of the International Conference on Paradigms of Computing, Communication and Data Sciences. AIS, pp. 105–121. Springer, Singapore (2021). https://doi.org/10. 1007/978-981-15-7533-4_9

13. Rapisarda, B.A.: THE impact of emotional intelligence on work team cohesiveness and performance. Int. J. Organ. Anal. **10**(4), 363–379 (2002). https://doi.org/10.1108/eb028958

14. Arora, S., Kawatra, R., Agarwal, M.: PSE assessment based e-learning: novel approach towards enhancing educationist performance. In: New Paradigm in eLearning Technologies. EPFRA (2020)

15. Milkhatun, Rizal, A.F., Asthiningsih, N., Latipah, A.J.: Performance assessment of university lecturers: a data mining approach. Khazanah Informatika **6**(2), 73–81 (2020)

16. Asanbe, M.O., Olagunju, M.P.: Data mining technique as a tool for instructors' performance evaluation in higher educational institutions. Villanova J. Sci. Technol. Manag. **1**(1), 1–13 (2019)

17. Ayash Ezzi, N.A.: Teaching performance in relation to emotional intelligence among English student-teachers in the teacher-education program in Hodeidah, Yemen. Am. J. Educ. Learn. **4**(1), 12–28 (2019)

18. Ramli, N.A., Noor, N.H., Khairi, S.: Prediction of research performance by academicians in a local university using a data mining approach. AIP Conf. Proc. (2019). https://doi.org/10.1063/1.5121100

19. Sindhu, I., Daudpota, S., Badar, K., Bakhtyar, M., Baber, J., Nurunnabi, M.: Aspect-based opinion mining on student's feedback for faculty teaching performance evaluation. IEEE Access **4**, 108729–108741 (2019). https://doi.org/10.1109/ACCESS.2019.2928872

20. Kaur, J., Sharma, A.: Emotional intelligence and work performance. Int. J. Recent Technol. Eng. (IJRTE) **8**(2S3), 1658–1664 (2019)

21. Egwu, A.O., Adadu, C.A., Ojo, J., Anaboifo, M.A.: Teachers' teaching experience and students' academic performance in Science, Technology, Engineering and Mathematics (STEM) programs in secondary schools in Benue State Nigeria. World Educ. Forum **9**(1), 1–17 (2017)

22. Asanbe, M.O., Osofisan, A.O., William, W.F.: Teachers' performance evaluation in higher educational institution using data mining technique. Int. J. Appl. Inf. Syst. **10**(7), 10–15 (2016)

23. Mohamad, M., Jais, J.: Emotional intelligence and job performance: a study among Malaysian teachers. Procedia Comput. Sci. **35**, 674–682 (2016). https://doi.org/10.1016/S2212-5671(16)00083-6

24. Hemaid, R.K., Halees, A.M.: Improving teacher performance using data mining. Int. J. Adv. Res. Comput. Commun. Eng. **4**(2), 407–412 (2015)

25. Taber, K.S.: The use of Cronbach's Alpha when developing and reporting research instruments in science education. Res. Sci. Educ. **48**(6), 1273–1296 (2016). https://doi.org/10.1007/s11165-016-9602-2

26. Joshi, A., Kale, S., Chandel, S., Pal, D.K.: Likert scale: explored and explained. Curr. J. Appl. Sci. Technol. **7**(4), 396–403 (2015). https://doi.org/10.9734/BJAST/2015/14975

27. Surendheran, R., Ravi, M.: Application of logistic regression model to determine academic performance of MBA students of department of management studies, NIT Tiruchirappalli. Int. J. Manag. Bus. Stud. **7**(2), 45–49 (2017)

28. Niu, L.: A review of the application of logistic regression in educational research: common issues, implications, and suggestions. Educ. Rev. 1–27 (2018). https://doi.org/10.1080/00131911.2018.1483892

29. Jalota, C., Agrawal, R.: Analysis of educational data mining using classification. In: International Conference on Machine Learning, Big Data, Cloud and Parallel Computing (COMITCon) (2019)

30. Arora, S., Agarwal, M.: Empowerment through big data: issues and challenges. Int. J. Sci. Res. Comput. Sci. Eng. Inf. Technol. **3**(5), 423–431 (2018)

31. Arora, S., Kawatra, R.: Analysis & designing of three tier web spidering. In: Emerging Trends in IT, pp. 137–147. Kunal Books (2011)

32. Kawatra, R., Arora, S.: An effective approach towards encryption of limited data. IITM J. Manag. IT **7**(1), 32–36 (2016)

33. Goswami, S., Chakrabarti, A.: Feature selection: a practitioner view. I.J. Inf. Technol. Comput. Sci. **11**, 66–77 (2014)
34. Wright, R.: Reading and understanding multivariate statistics. In: Logistic Regression, pp. 217–244. American Psychological Association (1995)
35. Valle, M., Varas, S., Ruz, A.G.: Job performance prediction in a call center using a naive Bayes classifier. Expert Syst. Appl. **39**(11), 9939–9945 (2012)
36. Hu, Q., Yu, D., Xie, Z.: Neighborhood classifiers. Expert Syst. Appl. **34**(2), 866–876 (2008). https://doi.org/10.1016/j.eswa.2006.10.043
37. Suthaharan, S.: Support vector machine. In: Machine Learning Models and Algorithms for Big Data Classification. ISIS, vol. 36, pp. 207–235. Springer, Boston, MA (2016). https://doi.org/10.1007/978-1-4899-7641-3_9
38. Hasnain, M., Pasha, M., Ghani, I., Alzahrani, M., Budiarto, R.: Evaluating trust prediction and confusion matrix measures for web services ranking. IEEE Access **8** (2020). https://doi.org/10.1109/access.2020.2994222
39. Sokolova, M., Lapalme, G.: A systematic analysis of performance measures for classification tasks. Inf. Process. Manag. **45**(4), 427–437 (2009)
40. Tallón-Ballesteros, A., Riquelme, J.: Data mining methods applied to a digital forensics task for supervised machine learning. In: Muda, A.K., Choo, Y.-H., Abraham, A., Srihari, S.N. (eds.) Computational Intelligence in Digital Forensics: Forensic Investigation and Applications. SCI, vol. 555, pp. 413–428. Springer, Cham (2014). https://doi.org/10.1007/978-3-319-05885-6_17
41. Daud, A., Aljohani, N.R., Abbasi, R.A., Lytras, M.D., Abbas, F., Alowibdi, J.S.: Predicting student performance using advanced learning analytics. In: Proceedings of the 26th International Conference on World Wide Web Companion (2017)
42. Arora, S.: A novel approach to notarize multiple datasets for medical services. Imperial J. Interdiscip. Res. **2**(7), 325–328 (2016)
43. Kawatra, R., Arora, S., Kaur, A.: Application of fast Fourier transformation on image processing software. Int. J. Artif. Intell. Knowl. Discov. (IJAIKD) **1**(1), 33–37 (2011)

Comparative Analysis of Traditional and Optimization Algorithms for Feature Selection

Sakshi Singhal[(✉)], Richa Sharma, Nishita Malhotra, and Nisha Rathee

Indira Gandhi Delhi Technical University for Women, Delhi, India
sakshi043mca20@igdtuw.ac.in

Abstract. Machine learning enables the automation of the system to generate results without direct assistance from the environment once the machine is trained for all possible scenarios. This is achieved by a series of processes such as collecting relevant data in raw format, exploratory data analysis, selection and implementation of required models, evaluation of those models, and so forth. The initial stage of the entire pipeline involves the necessary task of feature selection. The feature selection process includes extracting more informative features from the pool of input attributes to enhance the predictions made by machine learning models. The proposed approach focuses on the traditional feature selection algorithms and bio-inspired modified Ant Colony Optimization (ACO) algorithm to remove redundant and irrelevant features. In addition, the proposed methodology provides a comparative analysis of their performances. The results show that the modified ACO computed fewer error percentages in the Linear Regression Model of the dataset. In contrast, the traditional methods used outperformed the modified ACO in the SVR model.

Keywords: Feature selection · ACO · Linear Regression · SVM · SVR

1 Introduction

Machine Learning [1] is a domain of artificial intelligence that operates on the principle of educating the machine to behave in a specific mode when a given input is provided. It makes the machine self-driven in the trained circumstances and promotes minimal user intervention in its functionality. This requires appropriate processing of data before it is fed to the machine as input. It generates the required output based on the machine learning methodology used in building the model in the succeeding stages. These data inputs hold independent values and are referred to as features, whereas output has values dependent on the behavior of these features. Therefore, it becomes crucial to extract the features that impact determining output values and remove the relatively irrelevant ones. Feature Selection [2] chooses the most significant set of features out of all the features present in the dataset. All the possible sets of features are taken into account, and the output is the set of attributes with the highest impact on the prediction variable. Feature selection plays a vital role in improving the results as the errors are

© Springer Nature Switzerland AG 2022
A. Dev et al. (Eds.): AIST 2021, CCIS 1546, pp. 424–431, 2022.
https://doi.org/10.1007/978-3-030-95711-7_35

reduced to a minimum by not considering the least effective features. It also ensures that cost-effectiveness in time required and memory consumption and other factors like the machine learning model's performance are reformed desirably. Feature Selection can be made using various traditional methods.

Some of these techniques are Correlation Statistics, Mutual Information Statistics, Chi-Square Test, and many more. These methods are broadly classified as Filter methods, Wrapper based methods, and Embedded Methods. Correlation Statistics is a traditional method used for feature selection that depends on how two variables change together. Apart from these traditional methods, we can also use optimization techniques for feature selection to obtain the desired results. Optimization algorithms like Ant Colony Optimization, Firefly, Intelligent Water Drops and others can help us achieve the same. Ant Colony Optimization [3] is an algorithm based on ants' ability to find the shortest route by depositing pheromones. The proposed approach discussed in this paper has made a comparative analysis between the traditional and optimized feature selection methods.

2 Related Work

Feature selection is an integral part of preprocessing the data. Still, it is often not given adequate consideration, which can contribute to failing machine learning models hereafter. On the other hand, there has been sufficient work to show the improvised credibility and reliability of models after practicing feature extraction. Moreover, the following research and experiments performed have brought optimization algorithms into the picture in recent years. There exist multiple techniques for this purpose that are worked upon following the application. Xue *et al.* [4] examine two PSO-based multi-objective feature selection algorithms and compares their results with other conventional feature algorithms where the PSO-based algorithm outperforms the conventional ones in classification. Here, the first algorithm utilizes nondominated sorting of PSO, whereas the second algorithm uses aspects of mutation, crowding, and PSO dominance for feature selection issues. Liu *et al.* [5] proposed a hybrid solution using Particle Swarm Optimization with Support Vector Machines and F-score method, which gives higher accuracy achieving feature subsets. It aims to develop a more generic mechanism for both feature selection and kernel parameter optimization simultaneously. Ghaemi and Feizi-Derakhshi [6] adopt the Forest Optimization Algorithm for selecting informative features, which increases the accuracies of classifiers in the real-world datasets. Moradi and Rostami [7] applied ant colony optimization using a filter-based feature selection method and generated feature subsets from graph clustering of modified ant colonies. Later, this methodology was compared to other Wrapper and filter-based methods on multiple classification problems where the former gave better predictions than the latter.

3 Methodology

The approach used to resolve the stated problem statement involves exploring the various aspects of the datasets chosen and performing data exploration. Data exploration and visualization is done for feature selection. Conventional methods (Correlation Statistics,

Mutual Information Statistics, and Chi-Square Testing) and optimization algorithm (Ant Colony Optimization) have been used to obtain the most significant features out of all the available features. LR and SVR models were built for the subset of features. Finally, the error metrics were computed and evaluated for all the different techniques. The flowchart given in Fig. 1 provides the pictorial representation of the proposed approach.

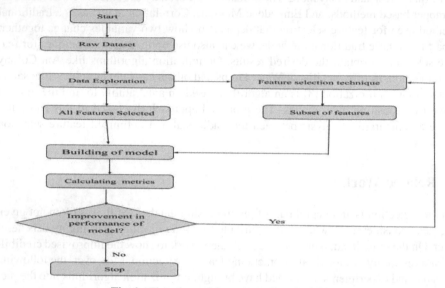

Fig. 1. Flowchart of the proposed methodology

3.1 Data Collection

The proposed methodology has been implemented using two datasets. Both datasets have been obtained from Kaggle, an online community for budding data scientists and machine learning practitioners. The first dataset [12] is a student dataset with 395 instances and 33 attributes. It contains the personal and school-related information of the students enrolled in math courses. The attribute G3 in the dataset is treated as a target variable dependent on the rest of the input variables. The second dataset [13] contains the information of people with 2938 instances and 22 attributes. The life expectancy has been calculated using the other attributes present.

3.2 Data Exploration and Visualization

It elaborates on the raw dataset described in the previous section by studying the independent behavior of the attributes and their dependencies on one another. It also updates the values of these attributes, if required for the later stages. Here, the nature of values is determined using different inspection mechanisms and then modified according to the required application. It includes checks for NAN/null values present in any column, duplicate entries, detecting certain outliers, etc., and dealing with them by removing them from the data frame to avoid any ambiguity in future analysis Feature Selection

3.3 Feature Selection

The term feature selection is defined as reducing the input variables involved in the predictive analysis of the target variable. This is considered an integral part data preprocessing phase as it reduces the computational cost of building the model and increases the model's efficiency to a greater extent. The following are some of the methods used for this purpose:

1. **Filter Method**
   Here, the technique usually selects features highly related to the target variable based on different statistical measures without any predetermined learning model.
2. **Wrapper Method**
   This approach searches for the best-performing feature subsets based on the predetermined learning model results.
3. **Hybrid Method**
   This technique combines both filter and wrapper methods where it attempts to overcome their shortcomings.

Various techniques fall under one of the particular method categories mentioned above. The type of technique used depends on the kind of data present in the independent variables of the given dataset, i.e., numeric or categorical.

3.3.1 Correlation Statistics

Correlation [14] is a process of simultaneous changes that occur in two variables, according to their dependency on each other. Pearson's coefficient is one of the most popular correlation measures that use the covariance of two variables for analyzing their linear relationship. Mutual Information Statistics. Mutual information [15] provides computational measures to study the dependencies that reside along with different variables.

3.3.2 Chi-Square Test

Chi-Square Test [16] is a helpful method used for feature selection. The testing of relationships between each feature helps to choose highly dependent features.

3.3.3 Ant Colony Optimization

ACO [17] is an optimization algorithm based on ants' ability to find the shortest route by depositing pheromones. Since this chemical fades away with time, the most traveled path is the pheromone-rich path used by each ant. Ants can smell the pheromone and follow the path. The probability of ants choosing the way increases with the increasing amount of pheromone. The movement of ants increases the likelihood of choosing that particular path [25].

3.4 Building a Model

After the decision of relevant features is taken depending on the methods mentioned above, data training needs to be done to make the machine learn. This phase is entitled to creating a model so that the machine can predict the value of the target variable in the future with precision and accuracy. The algorithms explained below are defined to indicate the value of the predictor variable in a regression scenario, where this variable has continuous and actual values.

3.4.1 Linear Regression

The relationship between an independent variable and a dependent variable can be found using Linear Regression [18]. It builds the best fit line so that maximum data points, i.e., target variable values, lie on that particular straight line or these data points are closest to the bar itself.

3.4.2 Support Vector Regressor

SVR [19] uses similar principles as SVM, designed explicitly for regression problems. The idea is to find the best fit hyperplane within the decision boundaries. Hyperplane has the maximum points present within the decision boundaries. Decision boundary 1 is +a distance from the hyperplane, and decision boundary 2 is –a from the hyperplane.

4 Model Evaluation and Results

It's crucial to analyze the model's performance built in the above section to understand whether it is functioning in the desired way. Here, the actual values of the target variable are compared with its predicted values and infer their error rates. The metrics used for this purpose are given in the subsequent subsections. Mean absolute error [20], Mean Squared Error [21], and Root Mean Squared Error have been used for model evaluation. The subsections below provide elaborated error computations in all the cases.

Table 1. Comparison of error metrics for SVR and linear regression models.

Method name	MAE		MSE		RMSE		K-fold cross validation (absolute average)	
	D1	D2	D1	D2	D1	D2	D1	D1
CR- SVR	1.24	2.6	4.57	13.90	3.72	3.72	2.12	3.46
CR-Linear Regression	1.3	2.92	4.43	14.50	2.10	3.80	1.96	3.70
MI-SVR	1.25	3.76	4.34	12.31	2.08	3.50	2.06	3.35
MI- Linear Regression	1.34	2.82	4.49	13.78	2.11	3.71	1.93	3.64
Chi-S- SVR	1.26	2.41	4.32	14.38	2.0791	3.79	2.1	3.53
Chi-S- Linear Regression	1.32	3.01	4.20	15.68	2.05	3.96	1.91	4.077
ACO-SVR	1.25	2.27	4.58	10.20	2.14	3.19	2.0	3.32
Regression	1.39	2.9	4.20	12.96	2.05	3.86	1.91	3.16

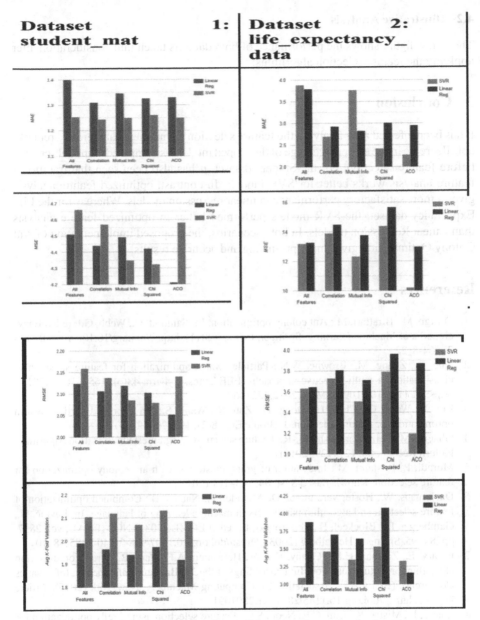

Fig. 2. Performance comparisons of datasets using evaluation metrics

4.1 Error Metrics

The following tables show the performance of both datasets, Dataset 1: D1 and Data set 2: D2 taken into consideration after applying the feature selection algorithms:

4.2 Illustrative Analysis

The below figure shows the performance of both datasets taken into consideration after applying the feature selection algorithms:

5 Conclusion

It has been inferred after applying the feature selection techniques that there is a remarkable decrease in the error percentage of developed models as compared to models created before feature selection. For the Student dataset, it has also been seen that traditional feature analysis works better for SVR models. In contrast, optimized feature analysis gives a more satisfactory performance in linear regression models. Whereas for the Life Expectancy dataset, the SVR models performed better in optimized feature analysis than Linear Regression models. In both scenarios, the proposed implementation of Ant Colony Optimization gives more promising and accurate results.

References

1. Dorigo, M., Birattari, M.: Ant colony optimization. In: Sammut, C., Webb, G.I. (eds.) Encyclopedia of Machine Learning. Springer, Boston (2011). https://doi.org/10.1007/978-0-387-30164-8_22
2. Xue, B., Zhang, M., Browne, W.N.: Particle swarm optimization for feature selection in classification: a multi-objective approach. IEEE Trans. Cybern. **43**(6), 1656–1671 (2013). https://doi.org/10.1109/TSMCB.2012.2227469
3. Liu, Y., Wang, G., Chen, H., Dong, H., Zhu, X., Wang, S.: An improved particle swarm optimization for feature selection. J. Bionic Eng. **8**(2), 191–200 (2011)
4. Ghaemi, M., Feizi-Derakhshi, M.-R.: Feature selection using Forest Optimization Algorithm. Pattern Recogn. **60**, 121–129 (2016)
5. Moradi, P., Rostami, M.: Integration of graph clustering with ant colony optimization for feature selection. Knowl.-Based Syst. **84**, 144–161 (2015)
6. Daelemans, W., Hoste, Véronique., De Meulder, F., Naudts, B.: Combined optimization of feature selection and algorithm parameters in machine learning of language. In: Lavrač, N., Gamberger, D., Blockeel, H., Todorovski, L. (eds.) ECML 2003. LNCS (LNAI), vol. 2837, pp. 84–95. Springer, Heidelberg (2003). https://doi.org/10.1007/978-3-540-39857-8_10
7. Emary, E., Zawbaa, H.M., Ghany, K.K.A., Hassanien, A.E., Parv, B.: Firefly optimization algorithm for feature selection. In: Proceedings of the 7th Balkan Conference on Informatics Conference (BCI 2015). Association for Computing Machinery, New York (2015). Article 26, 1–7. https://doi.org/10.1145/2801081.2801091
8. Zhang, L., Mistry, K., Lim, C.P., Neoh, S.C.: Feature selection using firefly optimization for classification and regression models. Decis. Support Syst. **106** (2018)
9. Yan, Z., Yuan, C.: Ant colony optimization for feature selection in face recognition. In: Zhang, D., Jain, A.K. (eds.) ICBA 2004. LNCS, vol. 3072, pp. 221–226. Springer, Heidelberg (2004). https://doi.org/10.1007/978-3-540-25948-0_31
10. https://www.kaggle.com/uciml/student-alcohol-consumption
11. https://www.google.com/url?q=https://www.kaggle.com/kumarajarshi/life-expectanc ywho&sa=D&source=hangouts&usg=1623059761384000&usg=AFQjCNFet3_t0XG6MX cGx2-gPY7mXgX9wQ

12. Pearson's correlation coefficient. In: Kirch, W. (eds.) Encyclopedia of Public Health. Springer, Dordrecht (2008). https://doi.org/10.1007/978-1-4020-5614-7_2569
13. Ross, B.C.: Mutual information between discrete and continuous data sets. PLoS ONE **9**(2), e87357 (2014). https://doi.org/10.1371/journal.pone.0087357
14. McHugh, M.L.: The chi-square test of independence. Biochem. Med. (Zagreb) **23**(2), 143–149 (2013). https://doi.org/10.11613/bm.2013.018
15. Dorigo, M.: Ant colony optimization. Scholarpedia **2**(3), 1461 (2007). revision #90969
16. Obson, J.D.: Multiple linear regression. In: Applied Multivariate Data Analysis. STS. Springer, New York (1991). https://doi.org/10.1007/978-1-4612-0955-3_4
17. Basak, D., Pal, S., Patranabis, D.: Support vector regression. Neural Inf. Process. – Lett. Rev. **11** (2007)
18. Mean absolute error. In: Sammut, C., Webb, G.I. (eds.) Encyclopedia of Machine Learning and Data Mining. Springer, Boston (2017). https://doi.org/10.1007/978-1-4899-7687-1_953
19. Mean squared error. In: Sammut, C., Webb, G.I. (eds.) Encyclopedia of Machine Learning. Springer, Boston (2011). https://doi.org/10.1007/978-0-387-30164-8_528
20. Shekhar, S., Xiong, H.: Root-mean-square error. In: Shekhar, S., Xiong, H. (eds.) Encyclopedia of GIS. Springer, Boston (2008). https://doi.org/10.1007/978-0-387-35973-1_1142
21. Refaeilzadeh, P., Tang, L., Liu, H.: Cross-validation. In: Liu, L., Özsu, M.T. (eds.) Encyclopedia of Database Systems. Springer, Boston (2009). https://doi.org/10.1007/978-0-387-39940-9_565
22. Rathee, N., Joshi, N., Kaur, J.: Sentiment analysis using machine learning techniques on Python. In: 2018 Second International conference on Intelligent Computing and Control Systems (ICICCS), pp. 779–785 (2018). https://doi.org/10.1109/ICCONS.2018.8663224
23. Kumar, V., Rathee, N.: Knowledge discovery from database using an integration of clustering and classification. Int. J. Adv. Comput. Sci. Appl. (IJACSA) **2**(3) (2011)
24. Ankita, N.S.: Improved link prediction using PCA. Int. J. Anal. Appl. **17**(4), 578–585 (2019)
25. Rathee, N., Chhillar, R.S.: Generation and optimization of test paths using modified ACO. Int. J. Control Theory Appl. (2017)

Session Based Recommendations using CNN-LSTM with Fuzzy Time Series

Punam Bedi[1], Purnima Khurana[1(✉)], and Ravish Sharma[2]

[1] Department of Computer Science, University of Delhi, Delhi, India
pbedi@cs.du.ac.in, pk0403@gmail.com
[2] P.G.D.A.V. College, University of Delhi, Delhi, India
ravish.sharma@pgdav.du.ac.in

Abstract. Session based Recommender systems consider change in preferences by focusing on user's short term interests that may change over a period of time. This paper proposes FS-CNN-LSTM-SR, a hybrid technique that uses CNN (Convolutional Neural Networks) and LSTM (Long Short Term Memory) deep learning techniques with fuzzy time series to recommend products to user based on his activities performed in a session. The advantage of our proposed method is that it combines the benefits of both CNN and LSTM. CNNs are capable of extracting complex local features and LSTM learn long term dependencies from sequential session data. The performance of FS-CNN-LSTM-SR is evaluated on YOOCHOOSE dataset from RecSys Challenge 2015 and is compared with three variations viz. LSTM-SR, CNN-LSTM-SR and FS-LSTM-SR. We observed that our proposed approach performed better than other three variations. The proposed technique is applicable on any E-commerce dataset where user purchasing choices need to be predicted.

Keywords: Session based recommender system · Deep learning · Fuzzy Time Series

1 Introduction

Recommender Systems are a boon in this era of huge data as they help users to make decisions from large number of available choices. Items, songs, people, places and even search results can be recommended to users. These systems provide personalized suggestions to the users which not only help users to take right decisions but also help the provider to retain their customers or users of the system [12, 19].

Traditional recommendation techniques such as Collaborative Filtering and Content based approach emphasize on long-term user preferences which are static in nature. A special class of recommender systems known as Sequential recommender systems recommends items to users considering sequential dependencies for the interactions between users and items. Most of the recommendation approaches do not take into consideration short term interest drifts and ignore user's preference shift through the time. Session-based Recommender systems are a category of recommender systems

© Springer Nature Switzerland AG 2022
A. Dev et al. (Eds.): AIST 2021, CCIS 1546, pp. 432–446, 2022.
https://doi.org/10.1007/978-3-030-95711-7_36

which take into account change in user preferences over the time by determining user's choices from their short term interests. These systems consider sequential interactions and also take into account user interest drifts from time to time.

Various recommendation techniques such as model based, machine learning and deep learning have evolved over the years [24]. Deep learning models are capable of handling non-linear user interactions which can be useful to determine the complex relationships between users and item interactions. The major advantage of deep learning is automatic feature extraction which reduces the manual efforts [9]. CNN (Convolutional Neural Network) is a deep neural network technique which assigns weights and biases to different aspects of input and determines important features. It is less prone to noisy data and is capable of learning crucial features independent from time [26]. RNN (Recurrent Neural Network) is the most suitable deep learning technique for session based recommender systems as it considers sequence of events within a session and is well suited when we want to predict future behavior based on the past logs or activities [3, 5, 16]. RNN suffers from vanishing gradient problem that occurs when the gradient becomes so small that there is no parameter update and the model cease to learn. LSTM (Long Short Term Memory), a variation of RNN, is the more advanced technique which maintains information in memory blocks and overcomes the vanishing gradient problem of RNN [7]. Fuzzy logic helps to deal with inconsistencies in a situation by considering an intermediate value rather than absolute true (1) or absolute false (0). It can be used with neural networks to refine the weights and help to better predict in uncertain situations. Also, fuzzy sets are used for modeling and predicting time series to obtain fuzzy time series.

Highlights of this paper:

- A hybrid technique combining the capabilities of fuzzy logic and deep learning has been utilized for generating Session based recommendations.
- A Convolutional layer is used for learning time independent important local features from input data.
- LSTM has been utilized for remembering sequence of events and providing recommendations based on user's preferences of the current session. It has been used to extract time series features.
- Various features of input data have been fuzzified to obtain fuzzy time series.
- Click patterns of users along with purchase patterns have been utilized for generating recommendations.
- The proposed technique is multivariate and generates a final list of items to be recommended to the user based on the class of predicted items, their co-occurring items as well as popularity of items.

The organization of this paper is as follows. Section 2 reviews the related work in this area. The proposed approach is explained in Sect. 3 and is subsequently evaluated and compared with three variations viz. LSTM-SR, CNN-LSTM-SR and FS-LSTM-SR in Sect. 4. Finally, Sect. 5 concludes this work.

2 Related Work

In this section, review of literature related to session based recommender systems and motivation for our work is presented.

Deep learning techniques provide better prediction results as they consider sequence of user's actions, automate feature extraction and extrapolate patterns [4]. Various deep learning techniques such as Recurrent Neural Networks (RNN) and Convolutional Neural Networks (CNN) have been used for development of social recommender systems [14] and session based recommendations. Session based recommendation has been utilized in various domains including music, e-commerce websites, travel destinations and hotels [6, 8, 13]. Researchers have argued that by modeling the whole session, more accurate recommendations can be provided and proposed an RNN-based approach for session-based recommendations [6]. RNN is used for time series data analysis and it takes into consideration sequential dependencies in the input data. LSTM, a variation of RNN, maintains information in the form of memory blocks and thus solves the problem of vanishing gradient that occurs in RNN [7]. LSTM is also capable of remembering longer sequences and is generally operated for text manipulation tasks where larger input needs to be remembered. So, many researchers have utilized them in a variety of domains including machine reading, financial market prediction, traffic speed prediction, trajectory prediction and even session based recommendations [2, 3, 10–12]. Srilakshmi et al. have applied LSTM on E-commerce datasets and the items are embedded using Graph based Embedding Technique [22] whereas Hidasi utilized GRU for session recommendations in E-commerce domain [6].

One or more deep learning techniques are often combined by researchers to exploit the advantages of every technique. CNN layers and LSTM layers can be cascaded one after another for sequential time series data. The convolutional layers are used for learning internal representation of time series data i.e. local features of the input data and the learned features are further fed into LSTM layer for identifying sequential dependencies and then making final predictions. Zhang et al. has also combined RNN and CNN for session based recommendation on E-commerce dataset [25]. Gabreil et al. has utilized both LSTM and CNN for session recommendation on news data [21]. We have implemented LSTM, CNN and combination of LSTM, CNN on YooChoose Dataset which is an Ecommerce dataset from RecSys Challenge 2015.

Uncertainty in user's behavior can be very well handled using fuzzy logic. Some features like amount of time spent on a product before it was bought, day of the week or month when the product was bought may not have crisp values. Such features account for uncertainty in user's behavior which can be handled by mapping their values to fuzzy values. Conventional time series has crisp values but cannot handle uncertain situations. Fuzzy time series works on the principle of fuzzy logic but the data is organized in the form of time series. Researchers have used deep learning techniques to model fuzzy Logical Relationships [15] and combined fuzzy time series with CNN for short-term load forecasting [17]. Wang, *et al.* has combined attention mechanism- a deep learning technique with fuzzy logic to create a fuzzy neural network for session based recommendation [23]. But, to the best of our knowledge no evidence has been found for utilization of both LSTM and CNN with fuzzy logic for session recommendations.

In this paper, we have proposed a hybrid technique which combines fuzzy time series and multivariate CNN-LSTM considering both numerical and categorical features for session based recommendations. Fuzzy logic deals with handling uncertainty in user's preferences, Convolutional layer for extracting deep and important features and multivariate LSTM learns patterns from both non-fuzzy and fuzzy features and also sequential dependencies from input data. LSTM alone takes longer time to train but when combined with CNN the number of epochs required to train the model are reduced. We have chosen LSTM over Recurrent Neural Networks (RNN) and Attention Mechanism due to its ability to handle sequential data with longer sequence. RNN suffer from vanishing gradient problem and even, the efficiency of attention mechanism for longer sequences is greatly reduced as more weight parameters add to training time.

3   Proposed FS-CNN-LSTM-SR (Fuzzy Time Series-CNN-LSTM-Session Based Recommendations)

A hybrid technique FS-CNN-LSTM-SR (Fuzzy Time Series-CNN-LSTM-Session Based Recommendations) is proposed that combines Convolutional layer of CNN and LSTM with fuzzy logic for session based recommendations.

The approach works in two phases viz. Preprocessing phase and Recommendation phase. The architecture of our proposed technique is shown in Fig. 1 below. Preprocessing phase is required to clean the data and transform it to be correctly processed by the proposed technique. This step includes filling missing values, retrieving required fields from data, extracting new features, converting original time series data into fuzzy time series, data normalization and padding. In Recommendation phase, data is prepared in a format to be worked upon by CNN-LSTM, prediction of user purchasing behavior is made and finally a list of items is recommended to user.

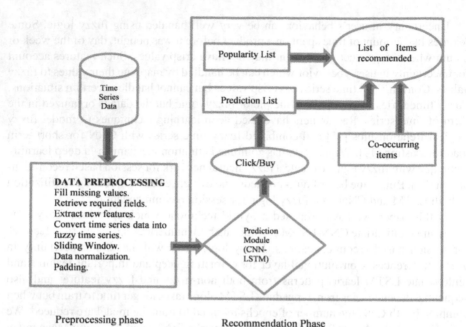

Fig. 1. Architecture of FS-CNN-LSTM-SR

3.1 Preprocessing Phase

The data has been preprocessed to be operated upon by proposed FS-CNN-LSTM-SR technique. The preprocessing steps are as follows:

Preprocessing

- Retrieve m attributes $\{x_1, x_2, \ldots, x_{.m}\}$ from input data files.
- Create a single file by merging different files on session id.
- Sort every session on the basis of timestamp (t, t+1, … , t+n) to obtain sequential records in a session.
- Derive new domain specific features such that attribute set expands to $\{x_1, x_2, \ldots, x_m, x_{m+1}, x_{m+2}, \ldots, x_{m+n}\}$.
- Convert Time Series data into Fuzzy Time Series data $\{fx_1, fx_2, \ldots, fx_m, fx_{m+1}, fx_{m+2}, \ldots, fx_{m+n}\}$.

Steps to Convert Input Time Series Data Into Fuzzy Time Series Data

- Define Universe of Discourse (UoD) for every input attribute x_i that needs to be mapped to fuzzy sets. x_i can be numerical or categorical.

- Partition UoD for every individual attribute into several overlapping intervals. The membership function can be Triangular, Gaussian or Trapezium. The number of partitions is different for individual attribute depending on the domain size of attribute.
- Convert Numerical values of each input feature x_i at timestamp 't', denoted by $x_i(t)$ into fuzzy values $fx_i(t)$ which results into a fuzzy time series.
- **Normalization:** Normalize all the attribute values between range 0 and 1. This step is performed so that no attribute has more impact on prediction due to its higher values.
- **Sliding Window:** Convert fuzzy time series data into a supervised learning problem such that the data of two previous timestamps '$t-2$' and '$t-1$' can be considered to predict user purchasing choice for the current time stamp 't'.
- **Data Padding:** Each session is appended with some rows so that all the sessions are same in length. The padded value is a value different from values not in any instance of the data (say -1).

3.2 Recommendation Phase

The preprocessed data is converted into a format so that it is further processed by CNN-LSTM model for prediction. The Recommendation Phase comprises of two modules viz. Prediction module and Recommendation module. Prediction module is used to predict the items which can become eligible for recommendation and Recommendation module determines the actual set of items to be recommended to user. Pred_List_User is the list of items maintained by prediction phase and Rec_List_User is the list of items to be recommended to user that is maintained by recommendation phase.

The items which are predicted in '*buy*' category by the prediction module and were not earlier bought by user are eligible for recommendation and stored in *Pred_List_user* for every user. The maximum prediction probability is a deciding factor to determine whether the user clicked (0) or bought (1) the product. The possible choices of prediction are shown below in Table 1.

Table 1. Actual and predicted values of item purchase status - Click/Buy

Actual	Predicted	Action
Click	Buy	Eligible for recommendation
Click	Click	Model learnt correctly
Buy	Click	Ignore
Buy	Buy	Model learnt correctly

The algorithm for the proposed technique is explained below. The algorithm is applicable for any E-Commerce dataset where user's purchasing behavior needs to be determined.

Algorithm

1. // Preprocessed data(obtained from section 3.1) is converted into a format to be operated upon by CNN-LSTM model in steps 2 to 5

2. $No\_of\_input\_instances$, $No\_of\_inp\_timestamps$, $No\_of\_features \leftarrow$ $Reshape(Preprocessed\_Data)$ // the shape requirement is for CNN-LSTM

3. Num_data, $Categorical\_data \leftarrow Split(Reshaped\_Data)$

4. $Processed\_cat\_data \leftarrow Embedding\_Layer(Categorical\_data)$ // to deal with high dimensionality

5. $Final\_processed\_data \leftarrow Data\_masking(Num\_data + Processed\_cat\_data)$ //to ignore padded values during training

6. // Steps 7 to 9 computes prediction of class(Click/Buy)

7. $z \leftarrow Conv\_layer, LSTM,\ Activation, Dropout(Final\_processed\_data)$ //combines three sets of four consecutively connected layers (Convolution, LSTM, Activation, Dropout)

8. $\sigma(z_i) = \frac{e^{z_i}}{\sum_{j=1}^{k} e^{z_j}}$ // Softmax Activation function where z_i is the input vector, z_j is the output vector and k is the number of classes.

9. $Click\ or\ Buy \leftarrow Predict(Activation\_layer)$ // Predicts that the item would be either clicked or bought

10. Create $Pred\_List\_User$ //Pred_List_User consists of those items which are predicted in buy category but not bought by user earlier.

11. Create $PopL_C$ // List of Items sorted in decreasing order of popularity grouped by Item Category

12. Create $GPopL$ // Global Popularity List

13. Create Rec_List_user // Ranked Item Recommendation List of n items

14. M $\leftarrow$ Length($Pred\_List\_User$)

15. IF M=n then

16. $Rec\_list\_user \leftarrow Pred\_list\_user$

17. ELSE IF M>n then

18.   Top_n $\leftarrow$ I$_1$, I$_2$,......, I$_n$ // Retrieve Top-n items from Pred_list_user

19.   Rec_list_user$\leftarrow$ Top_n

20. ELSE IF M<n then

21.   M_items$\leftarrow$Pred_List_user

22.   Rem_items$\leftarrow$ PI$_1$,PI$_2$,......PI$_{n-M}$ //Retreive top n-M items from PopL$_C$

23.   Rec_list_user$\leftarrow$ M_items+Rem_items

24. ELSE IF M=0 then

25.   Top_n $\leftarrow$ GI$_1$, GI$_2$,....., GI$_n$ // Retrieve top-n items from GPopL

26.   Rec_list_user $\leftarrow$ Top_n

27. ENDIF

28. Recommend Rec_list_user //This list consists of n-items

4 Experimental Study

The proposed hybrid technique FS-CNN-LSTM-SR has been implemented in Python using Keras Framework. Keras is a deep neural-networks API developed on top of Tensorflow or Theano, the open source libraries for extensive numerical computation. The input time series data has been converted into fuzzy time series using python pyFTS library which provides various methods of partitioning and membership functions [20].

4.1 Dataset

YOOCHOOSE dataset - It is an e-commerce dataset obtained from RecSys Challenge 2015 which consists of multiple independent temporal sequences in the form of sessions and here one session pertains to one user [1].

Number of unique sessions in the original data is 9249729 and total number of records is 34154697. The number of sessions of length one and length two are 1259711 and 3558087 respectively. These sessions have been filtered out by sliding window. The sessions left to be evaluated by our proposed technique are 4431931 with 14778812 records. Number of unique categories and number of unique items are 340 and 52739 respectively.

4.2 Evaluation Metrics

Precision, Recall and F1-measure [18] evaluation metrics have been utilized to evaluate the efficacy of the prediction module in recommendation phase of our proposed technique.

Precision, Recall and F1-measure for class 'Buy' are defined in Eqs. (1), (2) and (3). In the similar manner, Precision, Recall and F1-measure for another class 'Click' can be defined. The weighted average F1-score is defined below in Eq. (4). Let Act_{Buy}, $Pred_{Buy}$ denotes Actual Buy instances and Predicted Buy instances respectively.

$$Precision_{Buy} = \frac{Total \text{ \# } of \text{ } Act_{Buy} \text{ } predicted \text{ } as \text{ } buy}{Total \text{ \# } of \text{ } Pred_{Buy}} \tag{1}$$

$$Recall_{Buy} = \frac{Total \text{ \# } of \text{ } Act\_Buy \text{ } predicted \text{ } as \text{ } buy}{Total \text{ \# } of \text{ } Act_{Buy}} \tag{2}$$

$$F_{1Buy} = \frac{2 \times Precision_{Buy} \times Recall_{Buy}}{Precision_{Buy} + Recall_{Buy}} \tag{3}$$

$$Weighted_{avg}(F1) = \frac{Total \text{ \# } of \text{ } Act_{Buy} \times F_{1Buy} + Total \text{ \# } of \text{ } Act_{Click} \times F_{1Click}}{Total \text{ } instances} \tag{4}$$

Another evaluation criteria for determining the performance of a classifier is AUC-ROC i.e. Area under the Receiver Operating Characteristic curve. ROC curve depicts performance of classifier on minority or positive class. AUC summarizes an ROC curve and it is used to measure the distinguishing capability of classifier. It is computed by considering the true outcomes for both the classes (click, buy) from the test set and the probabilities predicted for the buy class (minority class). The AUC value lies between 0.0 and 1.0. More the AUC value better is the performance of classifier [27].

The performance of a recommender system is determined based on the rank of the predicted items and it has been evaluated using metrics Recall@K and MRR@K for our technique. We have taken 'K' as 20. Recall@20 is the proportion of cases in which the predicted item lies in top-20 items. MRR@20 (Mean Reciprocal Rank) is defined as the mean of the reciprocal ranks of the predicted items and takes into consideration actual rank of the items. The reciprocal rank of the items with rank greater than 20 has been considered to be zero. Recall@20 and MRR@20 are shown in Eqs. (5) and (6) below where 'T' is the total number of predicted items. All the predicted items are relevant for recommendation.

$$Recall@20 = \frac{\#\ of\ items\ recommended\ @20\ that\ are\ relevant}{Total\ \#\ of\ relevant\ items} \tag{5}$$

$$MRR@20 = (1/T)\sum_{n=1}^{T}\left(\frac{1}{rank(n)}\right) \tag{6}$$

4.3 Prediction

The prediction module was tested on three membership functions for fuzzy partitioning viz. Triangular, Trapezium and Gaussian membership functions as depicted in Fig. 2. Weighted-Average F1-score was calculated for each of the membership functions and trapezium membership outperformed the other two membership functions. For each interaction of every session, the prediction module predicts whether the item will be clicked or bought.

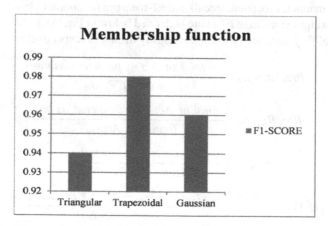

Fig. 2. F1-score for membership functions (Triangular, Trapezoidal, Gaussian)

We implemented four variations to generate top-K session recommendations and it has been observed that our proposed technique outperformed all other variations. Four variations are as follows:

a) LSTM-SR: The traditional LSTM was operated on original time series data.
b) CNN-LSTM-SR: Conv1D layer of Convolutional Neural Network was combined with LSTM in order to use the capabilities of both the models on original time series data.
c) FS-LSTM-SR: The traditional LSTM was operated on fuzzy time series data consisting of both fuzzy and non-fuzzy features.
d) FS-CNN-LSTM-SR: In this variation, CNN and LSTM models were combined and operated on fuzzy time series data consisting of both fuzzy and non-fuzzy features.

In literature, LSTM and CNN-LSTM have been utilized in various domains including Ecommerce, News, Music for session recommendations. We have implemented these existing techniques on YooChoose dataset and Keras Embedding layer has been utilized for embedding purpose. It was observed that fuzzy time series enhances the prediction accuracy when applied with LSTM in FS-LSTM-SR and CNN-LSTM in FS-CNN-LSTM-SR technique for both the categories: Click and Buy as shown in Table 2.

Table 2. Comparison of LSTM-SR, FS-LSTM-SR, CNN-LSTM-SR and FS-CNN-LSTM-SR for session based recommendations

Evaluation metric	LSTM-SR	FS-LSTM-SR	CNN-LSTM-SR	FS-CNN-LSTM-SR
Precision (CLICK)	0.86	0.90	0.88	0.91
Recall (CLICK)	0.95	0.93	0.96	0.92
Precision (BUY)	0.85	0.91	0.87	0.93
Recall (BUY)	0.68	0.72	0.65	0.75

Each categorical variable was dealt with separately and has been first encoded using label encoder and then embedding layer before fitting and evaluating. Embedding expects the categories to be ordinal encoded, but no relationship between categories is assumed. Embedding dimension of each categorical attribute has been chosen empirically as per the size of each attribute as shown in Table 3.

Table 3. Embedding dimension for individual attributes

Categorical attribute	Embedding size
ItemId	500
Category	50
Weekday	5
Time_of_the_day	5

Data has been reshaped to feed into CNN-LSTM since LSTM expects three dimensional inputs [samples, timestamps, features]. Three CNN-LSTM layers have been stacked to improve the performance of our proposed hybrid technique.

These variations have been tested on chunks of various sizes. For every chunk, 80% of the data has been selected for training and remaining 20% for testing. With the increase in data, the technique learnt to predict well. The weighted average F1-score for sessions of different sizes is shown below in Fig. 3. The x-axis represents session size and y-axis corresponds to F1-score. The graph shows that the weighted average F1-score improves as the data size increases since the model has more data to learn upon and FS-CNN-LSTM-SR technique outperformed all the techniques.

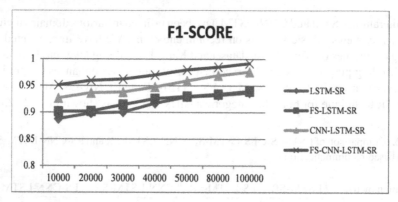

Fig. 3. F1-score for different number of sessions

Items are recommended based on the prediction results. The items in the *Rec_list_user* are the relevant top-n items to be considered by the user.

4.4 Hyperparameter Tuning

There are multiple hyperparameters which have been tuned to improve the performance of our proposed technique. With increase in number of epochs, the validation loss keeps on decreasing and it converges to a value for 100 epochs. It's value is minimum for the proposed technique FS-CNN-LSTM-SR and is shown below in Fig. 4. The x-axis represents number of epochs and y-axis represents validation loss using categorical cross entropy for our multi-class classification problem (Click (0), Buy (1), Padded value (-1)). The third category padded value (-1) does not interfere with the original categories and learning of the model is not affected at all.

The ROC-AUC curve for the minority class (i.e. buy class) is shown below in Fig. 5. The classifier was made to run on 100000 sessions for 100 epochs. The Area under the curve value is 0.94 which means that the prediction module is 94% capable of distinguishing between majority class (click) and minority class (buy).

Keras tuner has been used for hyper-parameter tuning in which optimum set of parameters determined were learning rate = 0.01, number of neurons = 16, activation function *'relu'* for the intermediate layers and 32 filters of size 2 for CONV1D layer. Dense, CNN-LSTM and Dropout layers have been used for processing input data. Dense layer is a deeply connected neural network layer. CNN layer is used to extract time independent important features which are further processed by LSTM Layer. LSTM

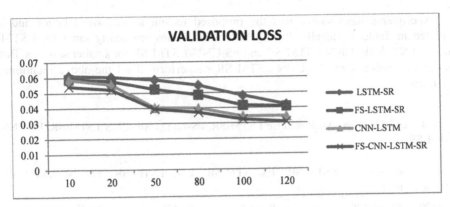

Fig. 4. Validation loss for different epochs

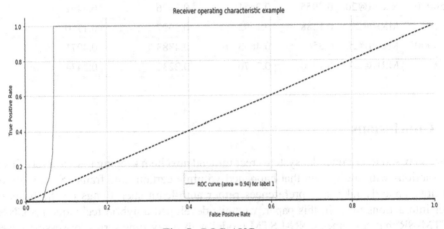

Fig. 5. ROC-AUC curve

layer is used to process sequential time series data. To prevent overfitting, dropout layer is used after every stacked LSTM layer. Categorical cross entropy and Softmax activation functions were used at the last layer. Random search in *Keras tuner* is utilized which does not search exhaustively and thus provide required set of parameters in lesser time and comparatively requires less computation power.

4.5 Recommendation

Items are recommended based on the prediction results. The items in the *Rec_list_user* are the relevant top-n items to be considered by the user. Session based recommender systems are evaluated using different metrics including Precision, Recall and MRR (Mean Reciprocal Rank). We have used Recall@20 and MRR@20 for evaluation of our proposed approach [13]. Recall@20 determines the proportion of relevant items in top-20 items and MRR@20 considers the reciprocal rank of the relevant items with rank less than 20.

Experiments have shown that the proposed technique performed better and is depicted in Table 4. Recall@20 and MRR@20 values are nearly same for LSTM-SR, FS-LSTM-SR, CNN-LSTM-SR and FS-CNN-LSTM-SR for smaller sessions. But, for larger session sizes FS-CNN-LSTM-SR outperformed all the above mentioned techniques.

Table 4. Recall@20 and MRR@20 for LSTM-SR, FS-LSTM-SR, CNN-LSTM-SR, FS-CNN-LSTM-SR

# of sessions	Evaluation metric	LSTM-SR	FS-LSTM-SR	CNN-LSTM-SR	FS-CNN-LSTM-SR
10000	Recall@20	0.1484	0.1469	0.1470	0.1471
	MRR@20	0.0961	0.0843	0.0922	0.0890
50000	Recall@20	0.2955	0.3451	0.3476	0.3492
	MRR@20	0.1288	0.1692	0.1697	0.1710
100000	Recall@20	0.3562	0.4633	0.4883	0.4971
	MRR@20	0.1720	0.2176	0.2232	0.2474

5 Conclusions

Session based Recommender systems recommend next item keeping in view a set of user interactions with the system that happened within a certain time frame. Such systems do not explicitly take user preferences rather auto-learn such things on the basis of user interactions only. In this paper, we have developed a hybrid technique FS-CNN-LSTM-SR that combines CNN-LSTM model with fuzzy-time series for session based recommendations. The input time series data has been converted into fuzzy time series by converting crisp sets of input attributes to fuzzy attributes. The fuzzy time series is then worked upon by CNN-LSTM. The technique considers predicted items, co-occurring items and popular items in creation of final set of recommended list for every user. The experimental results demonstrate that proposed hybrid technique provides better prediction results as compared to LSTM-SR, FS-LSTM-SR and CNN-LSTM-SR techniques. The proposed technique FS-CNN-LSTM-SR outperforms all the above techniques for larger chunks of input data selected from YOOCHOOSE dataset-RecSys challenge 2015.

References

1. Ben-Shimon, D., et al.: Recsys challenge 2015 and the YOOCHOOSE dataset. In: Proceedings of the 9th ACM Conference on Recommender Systems, pp. 357–358 (2015)
2. Cheng, J., et al.: Long short-term memory-networks for machine reading. arXiv Preprint arXiv:1601.06733 (2016)
3. Fischer, T., Krauss, C.: Deep learning with long short-term memory networks for financial market predictions. Eur. J. Oper. Res. **270**(2), 654–669 (2018)
4. Goodfellow, I. et al.: Deep Learning. MIT Press (2016)
5. Gregor, K., et al.: DRAW: a recurrent neural network for image generation. In: International Conference on Machine Learning, pp. 1462–1471 (2015)
6. Hidasi, B., et al.: Session-based recommendations with recurrent neural networks. arXiv Preprint arXiv:1511.06939 (2015)
7. Hochreiter, S.: The vanishing gradient problem during learning recurrent neural nets and problem solutions. Int. J. Uncertain. Fuzziness Knowl. Based Syst. **6**(02), 107–116 (1998)
8. Kouki, P., et al.: From the lab to production: a case study of session-based recommendations in the home-improvement domain. In: 14th ACM conference on Recommender Systems, pp. 140–149 (2020)
9. LeCun, Y., et al.: Deep learning. Nature **521**(7553), 436–444 (2015)
10. Lenz, D., Schulze, C., Guckert, M.: Real-time session-based recommendations using LSTM with neural embeddings. In: Kůrková, V., Manolopoulos, Y., Hammer, B., Iliadis, L., Maglogiannis, I. (eds.) ICANN 2018. LNCS, vol. 11140, pp. 337–348. Springer, Cham (2018). https://doi.org/10.1007/978-3-030-01421-6_33
11. Li, M., et al.: Predicting future locations of moving objects with deep fuzzy-LSTM networks. Transp. A Transp. Sci. **16**(1), 119–136 (2020)
12. Lu, J., et al.: Recommender system application developments: a survey. Decis. Support Syst. **74**, 12–32 (2015)
13. Ludewig, M., Jannach, D.: Evaluation of session-based recommendation algorithms. User Model. User-Adap. Inter. **28**(4–5), 331–390 (2018)
14. Nisha, C.C., Mohan, A.: A social recommender system using deep architecture and network embedding. Appl. Intell. **49**(5), 1937–1953 (2019)
15. Panigrahi, S., Behera, H.S.: A study on leading machine learning techniques for high order fuzzy time series forecasting. Eng. Appl. Artif. Intell. **87**, 103245 (2020)
16. Quadrana, M., et al.: Personalizing session-based recommendations with hierarchical recurrent neural networks. In: Proceedings of the 11th ACM Conference on Recommender Systems, pp. 130–137 (2017)
17. Sadaei, H.J., et al.: Short-term load forecasting by using a combined method of convolutional neural networks and fuzzy time series. Energy **175**, 365–377 (2019)
18. Sammut, C., Webb, G.I. (eds.): Encyclopedia of Machine Learning. Springer, Boston (2010). https://doi.org/10.1007/978-0-387-30164-8
19. Ben Schafer, J., et al.: Recommender systems in e-commerce. In: Proceedings of the 1st ACM Conference on Electronic Commerce, pp. 158–166 (1999)
20. Silva, P.C.L., et al.: An open source library for Fuzzy Time Series in Python (2018)
21. de Souza Pereira Moreira, G., et al.: News session-based recommendations using deep neural networks. In: Proceedings of the 3rd Workshop on Deep Learning for Recommender Systems, pp. 15–23 (2018)
22. Srilakshmi, M., et al.: Improved Session based Recommendation using Graph-based Item Embedding (2020)
23. Wang, C.-S., Chiang, J.-H.: FuzzAttention on session-based recommender system. In: 2019 IEEE International Conference on Fuzzy Systems (FUZZ-IEEE), pp. 1–6 (2019)

24. Zhang, J., et al.: Recurrent convolutional neural network for session-based recommendation. Neurocomputing **437**, 157–167 (2021)
25. Zhang, S., et al.: Deep learning based recommender system: a survey and new perspectives. ACM Comput. Surv. **52**(1), 1–38 (2019)
26. A Comprehensive Guide to Convolutional Neural Networks – the EL15 way. https://toward sdatascience.com/a-comprehensive-guide-to-convolutional-neural-networks-the-eli5-way-3bd2b1164a53. Accessed 15 Sept 2021
27. Understanding AUC-ROC curve. https://towardsdatascience.com/understanding-auc-roc-curve-68b2303cc9c5. Accessed 10 Oct 2021

Feature Extraction and Classification for Emotion Recognition Using Discrete Cosine Transform

Garima[1,2(✉)], Nidhi Goel[1], and Neeru Rathee[2]

[1] Indira Gandhi Delhi Technical University for Women, Delhi, India
[2] Maharaja Surajmal Institute of Technology, Delhi, India

Abstract. In recent years, the rigorous development in tools and techniques for biomedical signal acquisition and processing has drawn interest of researchers towards EEG signal processing. Human emotion recognition using Electroencephalography (EEG) signals has proved to be a viable alternative as it cannot be easily imitated like the facial expressions or speech signals. In this research, authors have explored EEG signals for behavior analysis using Discrete Cosine Transform and classifying the signals using K-Nearest Neighbors. The algorithm is then evaluated on publically available DEAP Dataset. Experimental results are expressed in terms of F1 score, accuracy, precision and recall. The performance metrics evaluation for the classification of the emotional labels of DEAP dataset has further confirmed the effectiveness of the research. Comparison evaluation with the recent state-of-the-art methods further confirms the efficacy of the proposed work.

Keywords: Discrete Cosine Transform · EEG · KNN · Classification

1 Introduction

EEG signal processing plays a vital role in various applications e.g., sleep state classification, seizure detection/prediction, emotion identification, depression detection, and task related activities [1, 2] i.e., motor imagery classification. Processing of EEG signal involves signal acquisition and pre-processing unit, feature extraction/signal processing unit and a decision block responsible for classifying the desired EEG signals as shown in Fig. 1.

EEG signals can be acquired through the electrodes connected to brain interior or brain surface or scalp which serves as the input signals for the whole system. Feature extraction/signal processing unit is responsible for filtering out the discriminative features from the channels. In Brain Computer Interface (BCI), the decision unit serves as a hybrid unit which executes the task of signal classification and decision modelling [3, 4]. An ideal BCI effectively detect the EEG signals on the basis of affective state as perceived by the user. Interfacing of brain and computer (or a gadget) can be accomplished either through invasive technology or via non-invasive technology. Despite being the promising technology in various applications by achieving large values of accuracy

© Springer Nature Switzerland AG 2022
A. Dev et al. (Eds.): AIST 2021, CCIS 1546, pp. 447–454, 2022.
https://doi.org/10.1007/978-3-030-95711-7_37

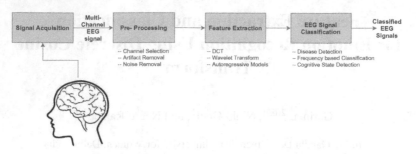

Fig. 1. Steps involved in processing EEG signals

and low-noise signals, invasive technology is not prevalent in most researches. Non-invasive technologies are being used on an enormous scale as it involves addition of some signal processing techniques in order to address the issues related to the noise and resolution. EEG signal acquisition via scalp electrode placement are the most preferred devices as they offer various advantages such as high temporal resolution, portability and usability. EEG signals can be acquired via scalp signal acquisition either by unipolar mode or bipolar mode. International 10–20 systems which is an approach used to place electrodes on the scalp, was suggested by the International Federation of Societies for Electroencephalography and Clinical Neuro- physiology (IFSECN) [7] and has been used extensively for EEG signal acquisition.

Five crucial brain waves, which mainly conveys all information related to functional state of the human brain have been categorically divided in different frequency bands. There are majorly five frequency bands which depicts the human emotional states effectively these band are:

- Delta band (0 Hz to 4 Hz): These are slowest waves and usually represents the grey matter of the brain.
- Theta band (3.5 Hz to 7.5 Hz): These waves tends to have slow activity rate.
- Alpha band (7.5 Hz to 13 Hz): These waves are majorly representing brain rhythm in normal relaxed adults.
- Beta band (13 Hz to 26 Hz): These waves depicts fast activity rate. These waves represent the normal rhythm of the brain.
- Gamma band (26 Hz to 70 Hz): These brain waves are associated with the consciousness of the human mind.

Delta waves are responsible for detecting the deep sleep state [8]. Theta waves depicts the information related to the alertness of mind. Alpha waves relate to the relaxed state of mind. Among all beta wave is the dominant one which shows the information related to the alertness of mind and also these waves are more prevalent in subjects having their eyes open. Gamma waves contain information related to the analysing/decision-making capability of the human mind. Any unexpected disturbances in these brain waves accounts for mental state illness. Therefore, EEG turns out to be the effective technique for screening such brain related problems. As depicted in Fig. 1 after EEG signal acquisition, next stage involves pre-processing of the acquired EEG signals which mainly involves artifact removal. This is the most challenging task while monitoring EEG signals. Artifacts usually arise due to eye movements, sweating (subject-related artifacts) or electrode paste or cable movements (technical artifacts).

One of the most crucial challenge in BCI is emotion detection. Emotion detection/recognition involves the study of different human moods. Emotion plays a vital role in human decisions and behaviour. Many studies have been carried out in recent past on emotion recognition [9, 10]. One of the most important characteristic of EEG signals in emotion recognition is that they cannot be altered. However, in order to hide actual emotion, humans can easily change their speech or facial expressions. First step in studying EEG signal involves signal acquisition. The acquired EEG signals are usually obtained in of multiple channels. In order to classify such multi-channel EEG signals, two approaches have been used commonly: selecting a portion of channels based on some pre-defined principles or to make use of all the channels. The signal processing step involves reduction in the channels as processing of huge number of channels is quite tedious. Also, it further exhausts the computational efficiency of the system.

In the presented work, authors have devised an algorithm for emotion recognition which mainly comprises of two steps: first step involves feature extraction using Discrete Cosine Transform (DCT) and in the second step the extracted features are classified using K-Nearest Neighbour Technique as shown in Fig. 2. KNN is used in this work due to its inherent capability to adapt to the new set of training data i.e., it is a memory based machine learning algorithm. Authors have evaluated the proposed algorithm on publically available DEAP dataset.

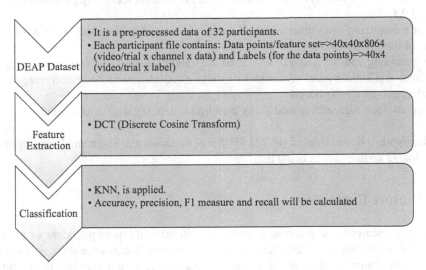

Fig. 2. Sequence of flow for the proposed method

Organization of the rest of the paper is as follows. Section 2 presents the feature extraction technique i.e., Discrete Cosine Transform. Section 3 describes the DEAP dataset used in this research. Experimental setup and results are presented in Sect. 4. Conclusion is drawn in Sect. 5 along with future scope.

2 Dataset Description

DEAP (A Database for Emotion Analysis using Physiological Signals) dataset [11] is being utilized in this work. It is a pre-processed data. In this dataset the peripheral physiological signals and electroencephalogram (EEG) signals were recorded for 32 participants, while each of them watched 40 one-minute long music video. Every participant was supposed to rate each video in five dimensions: valence, arousal, like/dislike, familiarity and dominance. Out of 32 participants, 22 participants were also selected for the recording of their frontal face video.

The DEAP dataset comprises of following two parts:

- Ratings of the subject from an online self-assessment where 14–16 volunteers rated 120 one-minute video excerpts on the scale of valence, arousal and dominance.
- Ratings of the participants, face video of the experiment and physiological recordings where 32 subjects (containing 50% females), in the age group of 19 to 37 (where, mean age $= 26.9$), where they observed a selected subset of 40 of the above music videos. Each subject rated the above videos as well and physiological and EEG signals of every participant were also recorded.

Few important features of DEAP dataset are:

- Recording of peripheral physiological signals and EEG was accomplished by using a Biosemi ActiveTwo System on a standalone PC used for recording purpose (Pentium 4, 3.2 GHz).
- For minimizing eye movements, all music video used as a stimuli were shown at a resolution of 800×600.
- A sampling rate of 512 Hz was used for recording these EEG signals using 32 active AgCl electrodes, placement of these electrodes were done according to the international 10–20 system.
- Eye artefacts were eliminated using the blind source separation technique.

In this work, a downsampled (to 128 Hz), pre-processed and segmented version of the data for 32 participants is being used.

3 Feature Extraction

In recent researches on machine learning classification its quite prevalent to work to hundreds or thousands of data features. If more similar features are there in a dataset than the total number of observations present in a dataset, then it may lead to overfitting in the machine learning model. Therefore, in order to get rid of this problem there is a need to apply feature extraction techniques.

Feature extraction is the most crucial step before applying machine learning classification algorithm to the available dataset. It is a part and parcel of dimensionality reduction techniques as it involves dividing of original data into a manageable group in order to effectively process the information contained in the original dataset. In this work, Discrete Cosine Transform (DCT) is being utilized due its inherent capability of signal compression. DCT offers following advantages: (1) Reduction in the size of the dataset (2) filtering of high frequency noise (3) reduction in time for data training and classification.

3.1 Discrete Cosine Transform (DCT)

DCT is the transformation method used for the conversion of a time series signal to its fundamental frequency elements [9]. First few coefficients of DCT contains the low frequency components and the last DCT coefficients contains information related to high frequency components. For a series of N real numbers, one-dimensional DCT is expressed using the following equation:

$$Y(u) = \sqrt{\frac{2}{N}} x(u) \sum_{a=0}^{N-1} f(x) \cos\left(\frac{pi(2a+1)}{2N}\right) \qquad (1)$$

where $u = 0, 1, 2, \ldots, N-1$
$x(0) = 1\big/\sqrt{2}$
$x(j) = 1, \, j \neq 0$

The input contains a set of N data values, in the proposes work it is EEG features, and the output ($Y(u)$) shows the generated N DCT coefficients. Average signal value is contained in the first coefficient i.e., $Y(0)$ also known as DC coefficient. Rest of the DCT coefficients are termed as AC coefficients [10].

For highly correlated signals, DCT provides quality energy compaction. In case the input signals comprise of correlated features, then most of the N DCT coefficients have either zero value or smaller values, and only the first few coefficients have a larger value. Therefore, feature extraction by DCT involves quantization of the coefficients. The smaller DCT coefficients are being quantized coarsely (near about to zero) and the larger DCT coefficients are quantized to the nearest integer.

This feature extraction technique allows compression of useful EEG signals into first few coefficients. Consequently, only these first few coefficients are being utilized for EEG signal classification by applying machine learning classification algorithm. Such kind of feature extraction technique is responsible for responsible for drastically reducing the input vector size and decreasing the time required for data feature training and feature classification.

4 Results and Discussion

This paper aims at investigating the application of computational statistics and machine learning in emotion recognition using different classification algorithms. In this work, different assessment measures of accuracy, recall, precision and F1 score have been used. Calculation of accuracy is carried out as the mean of the binary measurements in which score of each class has been weighted by its accessibility in the actual data. Mathematically it is represented as:

$$Accuracy = \frac{Total\ correct\ predictions}{Summation\ of\ all\ predictions} \qquad (2)$$

Precision is calculated as the percentage of (liked) preference predictions that were actually correct, as sown below:

$$Accuracy = \frac{TP}{TP + FP} \tag{3}$$

Where TP = True Positive, FP = False Positive and FN = False Negative. Recall is calculated as the percentage of real (like) preferences that has been predicted correctly, computed as:

$$Accuracy = \frac{TP}{TP + FN} \tag{4}$$

F1 score is which merges recall and precision, good F1 score depicts smaller false negatives and low false positives. Model is a total failure if F1 score is zero.

The implementation on publically available DEAP dataset involves two main steps: first step is to extract features from the original data using Discrete Cosine Transform and the second step involves applying KNN as the machine learning classification algorithms). Accuracy, recall, precision and f1-score, these are the few important performance metric that were tested throughout the experiment. Higher values of these metrics indicates a better model. Table 1 depicts the values of performance metrics of this work. In order to prove the efficacy of the this work a fair comparison with the existing techniques comparison has been drawn in Table 2.

Table 1. Performance metrics of the proposed algorithm

	Valence	Arousal	Dominance	Liking
Accuracy	0.5937	0.5859	0.5664	0.6172
Precision	0.63	0.66	0.61	0.69
Recall	0.65	0.68	0.71	0.77
F1-score	0.64	0.67	0.66	0.73

Table 2. Comparison analysis with the previous methods

Article	Methodology	Accuracy
Lan et al. [12]	Differential Entropy + Domain Adaptation	48.93% (Valence)
Ganpathy et al. [13]	Phasic component of EDA + SVM	51.51% (Valenec) 51.48% (Arousal)
Chaen et al. [14]	Auto regression + SVM	54.6% (Valence) 53.8%(Arousal)
Proposed	DCT + KNN	59.73% (Valenec) 58.48% (Arousal

5 Conclusion

In this paper, we have implemented feature extraction technique namely Discrete Cosine Transform (DCT) alongwith machine learning classification algorithm (KNN) for multi-channel EEG emotion recognition. We have evaluated various performance measures (accuracy, recall, precision and F1 score) on DEAP dataset to test the classifiers' performance. We have achieved an accuracy of 61.72% for liking label classification. While choosing the dataset, authors faced many challenges, as in the recent researches no standard dataset is there for EEG-based preferences. As the DEAP dataset is not labeled, we have ascertained the preference values by employing the knowledge of the emotion domain.

References

1. Subasi, A., Kevric, J., Canbaz, M.A.: Epileptic seizure detection using hybrid machine learning methods. Neural Comput. Appl. **31**(1), 317–325 (2019)
2. Braga, R.B., Lopes, C.D., Becker, T.: Round cosine transform based feature extraction of motor imagery EEG signals. In: Lhotska, L., Sukupova, L., Lacković, I., Ibbott, G.S. (eds.) World Congress on Medical Physics and Biomedical Engineering 2018. IP, vol. 68/2, pp. 511–515. Springer, Singapore (2019). https://doi.org/10.1007/978-981-10-9038-7_94
3. Rashid, M., et al.: Current status, challenges, and possible solutions of EEG-based brain-computer interface: a comprehensive review. Front. Neurorob. **14**, 25 (2020)
4. Papanastasiou, G., Drigas, A., Skianis, C., Lytras, M.: Brain computer interface based applications for training and rehabilitation of students with neurodevelopmental disorders. A literature review. Heliyon **6**(9), e04250 (2020)
5. Bastos-Filho, T.F., (ed.): Introduction to Non-invasive EEG-Based Brain-Computer Interfaces for Assistive Technologies. CRC Press (2020)
6. Fernandez, L., et al.: Cerebral cortical activity following non-invasive cerebellar stimulation—a systematic review of combined TMS and EEG studies. Cerebellum **19**(2), 309–335 (2020)
7. Babiloni, C., et al.: International Federation of Clinical Neurophysiology (IFCN)–EEG research workgroup: recommendations on frequency and topographic analysis of resting state EEG rhythms. Part 1: applications in clinical research studies. Clin. Neurophysiol. **131**(1), 285–307 (2020)
8. Atangana, R., Tchiotsop, D., GodpromesseKenne, L.C., Nkengfack, D.: Suitable mother wavelet selection for EEG signals analysis: frequency bands decomposition and discriminative feature selection. Sig. Image Process. Int. J. **11**(1), 33–49 (2020)
9. Alhagry, S., Fahmy, A.A., El-Khoribi, R.A.: Emotion recognition based on EEG using LSTM recurrent neural network. Emotion **8**(10), 355–358 (2017)
10. Song, T., Zheng, W., Song, P., Cui, Z.: EEG emotion recognition using dynamical graph convolutional neural networks. IEEE Trans. Affect. Comput. **11**(3), 532–541 (2018)
11. Gupta, A.K., Chakraborty, C., Gupta, B.: Secure transmission of EEG data using watermarking algorithm for the detection of epileptical seizures. Traitement du Signal **38**(2), 473–479 (2021)
12. El-Fequi, N., Ashour, A.S., Gemeaa, E.S., Abd El-Samie, F.E.: Prediction of epileptic seizures: a statistical approach with DCT compression. In: 2020 37th National Radio Science Conference (NRSC), pp. 302–313. IEEE (2020)
13. Koelstra, S., et al.: DEAP: a database for emotion analysis; using physiological signals. IEEE Trans. Affect. Comput. **3**(1), 18–31 (2011)

454   Garima et al.

14. Lan, Z., Sourina, O., Wang, L., Scherer, R., Müller-Putz, G.R.: Domain adaptation techniques for EEG-based emotion recognition: a comparative study on two public datasets. IEEE Trans. Cogn. Dev. Syst. **11**(1), 85–94 (2019)
15. Ganapathy, N., Veeranki, Y.R., Swaminathan, R.: Convolutional neural network based emotion classification using electrodermal activity signals and time-frequency features. Exp. Syst. Appl. **159**, 113571 (2020)
16. Chen, J.X., Jiang, D.M., Zhang, Y.N.: A hierarchical bidirectional GRU model with attention for EEG-based emotion classification. IEEE Access **7**, 118530–118540 (2019)

Sarcasm Detection in Social Media Using Hybrid Deep Learning and Machine Learning Approaches

Tanya Sharma$^{(\boxtimes)}$, Neeraj Rani, Aakriti Mittal, and Nisha Rathee

Indira Gandhi Delhi Technical University for Women, Delhi, India
nisharathee@igdtuw.ac.in

Abstract. Sarcasm refers to the use of ironic language to convey the message. It is mainly used in social sites like Reddit, Twitter, etc. The identification of sarcasm improves sentiment analysis efficiency, which refers to analyzing people's behavior towards a particular topic or scenario. Our proposed methodology has used a hybrid supervised learning approach to detect the sarcastic patterns for classification. The supervised machine learning approaches include Logistic Regression, Naïve Bayes, Random Forest, and hybrid deep learning models like CNN and RNN. Before implementing the models, the dataset has been preprocessed. The data in the dataset is usually not fit for extracting features as it contains usernames, empty spaces, special characters, stop words, emoticons, abbreviations, hashtags, time stamps, URLs. Hence null values, stop words, punctuation marks, etc., are removed, and lemmatization is also done. After preprocessing, the proposed methodology has been implemented using various supervised machine learning models, hybrid neural network models, ensemble hybrid models, and models implementation by using word embeddings. The models have been implemented on two datasets. The outcome revealed that the hybrid neural network model RNN worked the best for both datasets and got the highest accuracy compared to other models.

Keywords: Sarcasm detection · CNN · RNN · Naïve Bayes · Logistic Regression · Random Forest · Deep Learning Models

1 Introduction

Sarcasm is a form of language that detects the real meaning rather than its surface meaning. It can also be called an ironic language wherein an opposite meaning is identified. Humans express their views vocally, and it is always easy to detect sarcasm in this scenario as the person's tone works as a good indication [1]. However, it is not the case while dealing with written text. It is difficult for humans as well as machines to identify sarcasm in text. There can be many different ways of writing text by various individuals, and noise can also be present in text like punctuations, stop words, and sentence expressionlessness. Sometimes emojis present in a sentence can reflect its actual meaning, but if emojis are not present, then it becomes challenging to find out sarcasm in that plain

© Springer Nature Switzerland AG 2022
A. Dev et al. (Eds.): AIST 2021, CCIS 1546, pp. 455–464, 2022.
https://doi.org/10.1007/978-3-030-95711-7_38

sentence. Sarcasm detection nowadays has become a popular research topic. When sentiment analysis performs on some data, it misses the importance of sarcasm, leading to a negative sentiment being detected as a positive one. For example, "It is so much fun to visit a doctor" this sentence has a surface meaning different from what it implies. In a real sense, the sentence is sarcastic, but one can identify it to be a positive sentiment sentence if sarcasm is not detected correctly.

Similarly, sarcastic sentences can have negative surface meanings. For example, "Performance of Kohli was terrible in the match anyway" in this sentence, a response is given to a player's performance as criticism.

It is crucial to detect sarcasm in text and is helpful in various aspects. Online platforms like microblogging, e-commerce websites, etc., are acceptable for people to express their judgments about something or give reviews and feedback [2]. The customer relationship management model is a primary model for any organization, and sarcasm detection can help analyze customers' reviews. Sarcasm detection may help in overcoming the problem of the wrong classification of sentences based on their sentiment.

The initial step in our proposed methodology includes the usage of Machine Learning (ML) techniques with various feature-based approaches for sarcasm detection. This task is performed by training different proportions of data and then analyzing which one gives the better result. The next phase of the proposed methodology uses hybrid Deep Learning (DL) models. These models do not need any manual feature engineering. The models used in the proposed method are hybrid RNN, hybrid CNN, and hybrid LSTM. After applying these algorithms, a comparative analysis of ML models and hybrid DL models has been done with various parameters.

2 Related Works

Many researchers are working on classifying text based on various features like sentiment, sarcasm, etc. They are using multiple machine learning and deep learning models.

Wicana et al. [3] represent numerous challenges while detecting sarcasm. They presented various supervised and hybrid algorithms to detect sarcasm. Hiai et al. [4, 5] had focused on features that are based on indicators and roles. They had used Twitter data and considered only two types of feature words. The first one is affected by the indicator and the additional in which words express role. The words that are extracted from Twitter are used in their model-like features. They applied an ensemble of two classifiers of an SVM model trained with various features. Erik et al. [6] showed how sarcasm detection correlated with sentiment analysis, used a multitasking learning-based framework, and applied a neural network to improve accuracy by modeling the Correlation. Razali et al. [7] presented the significance of multimodality in the classification of sarcasm and expressed the need to detect sarcasm in sentiment analysis. Pyae et al. [8] experimented lexicon-based approach for extracting emotional features. They had used the ensemble bagging technique as the solution to the problem, record accuracy of 84%. Norman et al. [9] represented various models that are commonly used for detecting sarcasm. They presented different feature extraction-based techniques: n-grams, part of speech, TF. These techniques are used for extracting features in various ways that can help in providing good results. They used different techniques: SVM, Random Forest, and Naive Bayes.

3 Methodology

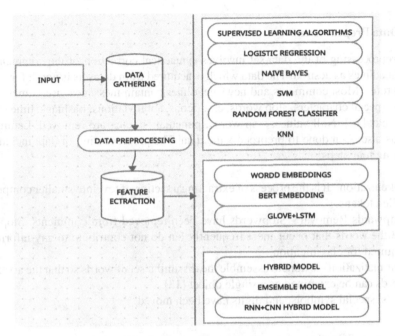

Fig. 1. Proposed methodology

As shown in Fig. 1, the data has been gathered from the Kaggle website https://www. kaggle.com/, an open-source dataset website. These datasets have gone through various steps of Preprocessing to make it more flexible for machines. Then for extracting the features, TFIDF vectorizer has been used as it is used to transform the textual data into numerical data. Some feature selection techniques have also been implemented to select the best features, like Anova and Correlation methods. After the feature selection process, the proposed methodology implements various models using supervised machine learning algorithms (Logistic Regression, Naïve Bayes, KNN, etc.), models using word embeddings (glove and Bert Embeddings), and Hybrid models (Ensemble hybrid, neural network hybrid models).

3.1 Data Collection

The primary goal of gathering data is to get valuable data easily interpreted to examine wealthy data evaluation, resulting in reliable answers to questions essential to be posted. Two datasets have been downloaded using the Kaggle website https://www.kag gle.com/. The first dataset is the Reddit dataset [10]. It has ten attributes like the label, comment, author, etc. The label attribute means whether the statement is sarcastic (1) or nonsarcastic (0). The second is the News headlines dataset [11]. It has three attributes which are article_link, headline, andis_sarcastic. 'Article_link' is the link through which the headline is taken. The 'headline' is the news headline, which is to be classified as sarcastic or nonsarcastic and 'is_sarcastic' is the label of the dataset.

3.2 Data Preprocessing

The preprocessing of the data set involves syntactical correction of the comments and news headlines as desired. The data which is acquired from datasets is not fit for extracting features. Most comments and news headlines contain messages, usernames, empty spaces, special characters, stop words, emoticons, abbreviations, hashtags, time stamps, URLs, etc. [12]. Null values, stop words, punctuation, etc., are removed. Lemmatization has also been done to preprocess the data. The preprocessing of data includes the following four steps:

1. Tokenization - It is the process of extracting a section of text into smaller components called tokens.
2. Stopwords Removal - Stopwords have been removed from comments. Stopwords are the words that occur most frequently but do not contribute to any information required for classification.
3. Lemmatization - is doneto assemble the dissimilar set of words so that the assembled words can be examined as a single object [13].
4. Url's, special symbols, and digits have been moved.

3.3 Feature Selection

The feature selection approach is used to determine the most relevant features of the data set, which helps build the most valuable models with reasonable accuracy. The downloaded data sets might contain unnecessary features that do not contribute to the prediction of models; therefore, feature selection helps identify the features that will contribute best to the output. ANOVA and Correlation approaches have been used for selecting features.

3.4 Models

3.4.1 Supervised Models

Logistic Regression: Logistic Regression also comes under Supervised Learning. This algorithm is used in problems where binary classification is needed having the main aim to create a decision boundary that is linear to separate the data points of two classes. It is a classification algorithm used to assign categories or observations to a discrete set of classes. This algorithm classifies the comments in our proposed methodology as Sarcastic (1) or Non-sarcastic (0).

Naive Bayes: Naive Bayes is an algorithm that comes under supervised learning. It is a probabilistic model that is wholly based on the Bayes theorem. The class with the highest probability wins, i.e., the given sentence will belong to that class.

Linear Support Vector Classifier

Support Vector Machine(SVM) is also a supervised learning algorithm [9]. This algorithm' gives fast and good results with a limited amount of data [9]. SVM is based on the hyperplane parameter. While classifying data based on two classes, a hyperplane is drawn. This hyperplane classifies the data so that the distance of the hyperplane with the nearest data point of both sides of the hyperplane is maximum, i.e., the margin is to be foremost. A hyperplane can be any plane in 2D or 3D space. It could be a line or a different plane in 3D space [14].

Random Forest Classifier

This supervised learning algorithm tries to generate a forest [15] randomly. The algorithm constructs a forest that is part of the whole Decision Trees. Random Forest also enhances more randomness to the model. Rather than identifying the utmost critical feature while splitting the node, it identifies the best feature among the random subset of features, resulting in an extensive diversity that mainly results in an improved model [16].

KNN

KNN (K Nearest Neighbor) is a classification machine learning algorithm that classifies new data points based on the similarity function of the previously stored data points. Here, K in KNN means the number of the nearest neighbors used to classify new data points. Euclidean distances are used to calculate the distance between two data points in the dataset [17].

3.4.2 Models Using Word Embeddings

BERT: Bidirectional Encoder Representation from Transformer was released by the Google research team [18]. BERT is pre-trained on a massive corpus of data sources. BERT is a "bidirectional" transformer-based language model using an encoder rather than a decoder. By Bidirectional, it means that BERT reads information from both sides from left to right side and right to the left side of a token's context during the training phase.

BERT-Random Forest Classifier: The proposed approach has used a random forest classifier with the best sentence embeddings.

GLOVE+LSTM: Glove-(Global Vectors for word representation) is a way to create word embeddings. It is an extension of the word2vector method for efficient learning of word vectors. It captures both the global and local statistics of the corpus. It is based on matrix factorization. It is an unsupervised learning technique for obtaining word vector representations. The matrix has been divided into the lower dimensional matrix in which every row represents a word's vector. The proposed methodology has used a pre-trained 100 dimension glove vector. The main idea behind using this is to convert the words into numbers. When we flip the words into vectors, we have a series of vectors instead of a particular sentence. Then pass the vector sequence to LSTM. For the classification task, *softmax* [19] is required. Therefore the resultant of LSTM has been fed to softmax, which produced a number, and that number tells us the probability of that particular text belonging to sarcasm class and non-sarcasm class.

LSTM is an algorithm that works for solving text-based problems and has the property of memorizing long sequences. In this project, Keras API is used to build this model. First tokenization is performed by using the Tokenizer API of python. The value of num words is taken 10000. After tokenization, the text has been converted to sequences then these sequences are padded using the maximum length of 100, i.e., all the word vectors are padded to an equal length of 100. After tokenization, word embedding is performed to reduce the data in low dimensions. GlOVE embedding has been used. The size of word embedding is 100. The LSTM sequential model is set up using the sequential class of Keras API to build the model. It helps to create a basic neural network model.

3.4.3 Hybrid Models

Ensemble Hybrid Model: In this model, individual models have been combined to boost the model's stability and predictive power. The ensemble method is a machine learning technique that combines several base models to produce one optimal predictive model [20, 21]. The proposed methodology has used LinerSvc, Naive Bayes, Random Forest classifier, Logistic Regression models and ensembled them. The proposed method has used LinearSVC, Naive Bayes, Logistic Regression, KNN on Reddit dataset and LinearSVC, Naive Bayes, Random Forest Classifier, and Logistic Regression on News Headline Dataset. LSTM+RNN hybridization has also been used in the proposed methodology.

RNN With GRU

RNN is the type of artificial neural network which uses sequential data. The algorithm is used to dealwith language-based problems. The main feature of RNN is that while computing output at the time 't', it will have some relation with output at the time 't−1'. RNN behaves like human brain function. The networks inRNN have a memory that stores knowledge about the data seen, but their memory is short-term and cannot maintain long-term time series [22–24].

GRU(Gated Recurrent Unit) is a type of RNN that solves vanishing gradients. It can process the memory of sequence data by storing previous input in an internal state. It has two gates that are reset and updated.

BI-RNN With LSTM

Bidirectional recurrent neural networks (RNN) means putting the two independent RNNs together. In this model, the input sequence is given in ordinary time order for one network and reverse time order for another [25].

CNN (Convolutional Neural Network)

Convolutional Neural Network (CNN) is used for image processing tasks, but this algorithm is also used for language-based tasks. The results of this algorithm on NLP tasks are outstanding. In this proposed methodology, CNN is applied using Keras, a Deep Learning API of python. First, the data is tokenized. For this, the Tokenizer API of Keras is used. It helps to encode the data in the form that it can be processed [26].

4   Results and Discussions

On Reddit corpus, the performance of the LSTM+Glove model works quite impressive. As features, different combinations of the 'comment' column, 'parent-comment' column were used. However, taking the 'comment' column as a feature solely produced the best result. Testing models with and without preprocessing steps has also been done. However, adding the preprocessing step did not show a significant change in the results. Various models have been built to achieve the best accuracy in both datasets. As expected, the hybrid Deep learning models RNN+GRU and RNN+LSTM achieved the best position on both datasets. Feature selection techniques such as Anova and Correlation have also been tried, but the results are not up to the mark. The complete results with more details are shown in the bar graphs in Figs. 2 and 3. Figure 2 displays the outcomes of the Reddit dataset, and Fig. 3 displays the outcomes of the News headlines dataset (Tables 1 and 2).

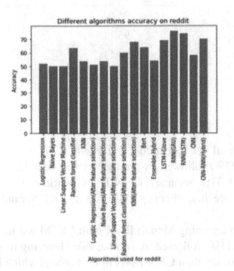

Fig. 2. Accuracy graph of Reddit dataset   **Fig. 3.** Accuracy graph of News Headlines dataset

Table 1. Accuracy score of Reddit dataset after feature selection

Method	Score
Logistic Regression (after feature selection)	53.42
Naive Bayes (after feature selection)	53.57
Linear Support Vector Machine (after feature selection)	49.91
Random forest classifier (after feature selection)	59.8
KNN (after feature selection)	68

Table 2. Models performance between Reddit dataset and News Headline dataset

Methods	Reddit dataset (accuracy score)	News headline dataset (accuracy score)
Logistic Regression	51.76	56.08
Naive Bayes	50.07	56.08
Linear Support Vector Machine	50.07	56.08
Random forest classifier	63.46	66.77
KNN	51	68
Bert	64	72
Ensemble Hybrid	54	56
LSTM+Glove	69	83
RNN+GRU (Hybrid)	76.13	95.64
RNN+LSTM (Hybrid)	74.31	96.11
CNN	57.90	94.11
CNN-RNN (Hybrid)	70.04	90.08

5 Conclusion

For the Reddit dataset, the Hybrid Neural network model RNN with GRU works the best. It got the highest accuracy of 76.13%, followed by another hybrid deep learning model that is RNN with LSTM, with 74.31% accuracy. CNN-RNN hybrid model has 70.04%, and these accuracies are much more than other supervised models KNN, random forest Classifier, Bert embeddings, etc.

For News Headlines Dataset, Deep Learning Model: RNN with LSTM works the best as it got the highest accuracy of 96.11%, followed by another deep learning model RNN with GRU, which has 95.64% accuracy then CNN-RNN hybrid model which has 90.08% and these accuracies are much more than other supervised models KNN, random forest Classifier, Bert embeddings, etc.

So, it has been observed that the News Headlines Dataset has achieved more accuracy than Reddit Dataset. The highest accuracy achieved in Reddit Dataset is 76.13, and in the News Headlines dataset, it is 96.11. Future work will be using bio-inspired evolutionary algorithms for feature extraction in the dataset to improve the accuracy of the classification models.

References

1. Szewczyk, P., Baszun, M.: The learning system by the least squares support vector machine method and its application in medicine. J. Telecommun. Inf. Technol., 109–113 (2011)
2. Krithika, V, Priya, V.: A detailed survey on cyberbullying in social networks. In: International Conference on Emerging Trends in Information Technology and Engineering (ic-ETITE) (2020)

3. Wicana, S.G., İbisoglu, T.Y., Yavanoglu, U.: A review on sarcasm detection from a machine-learning perspective. In: 2017 IEEE11th International Conference on Semantic Computing (ICSC). IEEE (2017)
4. Hiai, S., Shimada, K.: Sarcasm detection using features based on indicator and roles. In: Ghazali, R., Deris, M.M., Nawi, N.M., Abawajy, J.H. (eds.) Recent Advances on Soft Computing and Data Mining, pp. 418–428. Springer, Cham (2018). https://doi.org/10.1007/978-3-319-72550-5_40
5. Ghazali, R., Deris, M.M., Nawi, N.M., Abawajy, J.H. (eds.): Recent Advances on Soft Computing and Data Mining. AISC, vol. 700. Springer, Cham (2018). https://doi.org/10.1007/978-3-319-72550-5
6. Majumder, N., et al.: Sentiment and sarcasm classification with multitask learning. IEEE Intell. Syst. **34**(3), 38–43 (2019)
7. Razali, M.S., Halin, A.A., Norowi, N.M., Doraisamy, S.C.:. The importance of multimodality in sarcasm detection for sentiment analysis. In: 2017 IEEE 15th Student Conference on Research and Development (SCOReD) (2017)
8. Thu, P.P., Anug, T.N.: Implementation of emotional features on satire detection. In: 2017 18th IEEE/ACIS International Conference on Software Engineering, Artificial Intelligence, Networking and Parallel/Distributed Computing. IEEE (2017)
9. Eke, C.I., Norman, A.A., Shuib, L., et al.: Sarcasm identification in textual data: systematic review, research challenges and open directions. Artif. Intell. Rev. **53**, 4215–4258 (2020). https://doi.org/10.1007/s10462-019-09791-8
10. https://www.kaagle.com/danofer/sarcasm
11. https://www.kaggle.com/rmisra/news-headlines-dataset-for-sarcasm-detection
12. https://medium.com/@adamstueckrath/correlations-among-unclassified-social-media-dat ato-structured-event-data-during-the-Syrian-civil-bd4b879f3aa7
13. Maragoudakis, M., Lyras, D.P., Sgarbas, K.: Bayesian retrieval using a similarity-based lemmatizer. Int. J. Artif. Intell. Tools **21**(05), 1250024 (2012). https://doi.org/10.1142/S02182 13012500248
14. Zainuddin, N., Selamat, A.: Sentiment analysis using support vector machine. In: 2014 International Conference on Computer, Communications, and Control Technology (I4CT), pp. 333–337. IEEE (2014)
15. Chaves, L., Marques, G.: Data mining techniques for early diagnosis of diabetes: a comparative study. Appl. Sci. **11**(5), 2218 (2021). https://doi.org/10.3390/app11052218
16. https://builtin.com/data-science/random-forest-algorithm
17. https://towardsdatascience.com/knn-algorithm-what-when-why-how-41405c16c36f
18. Eke, C.I., Norman, A.A., Shuib, L.: Context-based feature technique for sarcasm identification in benchmark datasets using deep learning and BERT model. IEEE Access **9**, 48501–48518 (2021)
19. Murthy, G.S.N., Allu, S.R., Andhavarapu, B., Bagadi, M., Belusonti, M.: Text based sentiment analysis using LSTM. Int. J. Eng. Res. Technol. **9**(05), 299–303 (2020)
20. https://blog.statsbot.co/ensemble-learning-d1dcd548e936
21. Ranjini, K., Suruliandi, A., Raja, S.P.: An ensemble of heterogeneous incremental classifiers for assisted reproductive technology outcome prediction. IEEE Trans. Comput. Soc. Syst. **8**(3), 557–567 (2021)
22. Bengio, Y., Simard, P., Frasconi, P.: Learning long-term dependencies with gradient descent is difficult. IEEE Trans. Neural Netw. **5**(2), 157–166 (1994)
23. Kratzert, F., Klotz, D., Brenner, C., Schulz, K., Herrnegger, M.: Rainfall–runoff modelling using Long Short-Term Memory (LSTM) networks. Hydrol. Earth Syst. Sci. **22**, 6005–6022 (2018)

24. Apaydin, H., Feizi, H., Sattari, M.T., Colak, M.S., Shamshirband, S., Chau, K.-W.: Comparative analysis of recurrent neural network architectures for reservoir inflow forecasting. Water **12**(5), 1500 (2020)
25. https://towardsdatascience.com/understanding-bidirectional-rnn-in-pytorch-5bd25a5dd6
26. Jiuxiang, G., et al.: Recent advances in convolutional neural networks. Pattern Recogn. **77**, 354–377 (2018)
27. Rathee, N., Joshi, N., Kaur, J.: Sentiment analysis using machine learning techniques on Python. In: 2018 2nd International Conference on Intelligent Computing and Control Systems (ICICCS), pp. 779–785 (2018). https://doi.org/10.1109/ICCONS.2018.8663224

An Effective Machine Learning Approach for Clustering Categorical Data with High Dimensions

Syed Umar[1], Tadele Debisa Deressa[1], Tariku Birhanu Yadesa[1],
Gemechu Boche Beshan[2], Endal Kachew Mosisa[3], and Nilesh T. Gole[4]([✉])

[1] Department of Computer Science, Wollega University, Nekemte, Ethiopia
[2] Department of Information Technology, Wollega University, Nekemte, Ethiopia
[3] Department of Mechanical Engineering, Wollega University, Nekemte, Ethiopia
[4] Department of Computer Science and Engineering, RTMNU, Nagpur, India

Abstract. Many modern real world databases include redundant quantities of categorical data that contribute in data processing and efficient decision-making with their advances in database technology. However, for the reasons that they are identical to measurements the clustering algorithms are only devised for numerical results. An immense amount of work is being performed on the clustering of categorical data using a specifically defined similarity measure over categorical data. Thereby, the dynamic issue with real-world domain, which does not clearly take the predictive form, is the inner function. The function is based on both unseen and transonic perspective. This then offers a detailed and inventive collaboration with categorical results. The paper describes a stratified, immune-based approach with a new similarity metric, in order to reduce distance function, for clustering CAIS categorical data. For successful exploration of clusters over categorical results, CAIS adopts an immunology focused approach. It also selects subsistent nomadic characteristics as a representative entity and organize them into clusters that quantify affinity. To minimize database throughput, CAIS is segmented into several attributes. The analytical findings show that the proposed solution yields greater mining performance on different categorical datasets and outperforms EM on categorical datasets.

Keywords: High dimensional data · Categorical data · Immune based clustering · Maximization

1 Introduction

Web Mining is a tool for collecting valuable knowledge from the web, including implicit patterns unfamiliar to the observer. Web mining is a terrific application and technology for website design, personalization and other related features. The rapid bound and superior amount of knowledge available in online uses data mining techniques to evaluate user profiles by clustering. As clustering is a technique that takes advantage of how data points cluster together, and are contained in clusters. These views include numerous

© Springer Nature Switzerland AG 2022
A. Dev et al. (Eds.): AIST 2021, CCIS 1546, pp. 465–474, 2022.
https://doi.org/10.1007/978-3-030-95711-7_39

sets of landscapes with various characteristics with uncompromised data at the fore. Analyses like CACTUS, STIRR, and ROCK are helpful in understanding how values of categorical data shift with time. STIRR is indicated in categorical data by repeating the grouping of circles for each group. The system for grouping data by similarity is hierarchical, and it's defined by the number of ties among the classes. The dataset is clustered by mining closest neighbors in the resulting proximity matrix. CACTUS offers a straightforward view of how such data values will cluster together, but requires a vector space to ensemble objects of data into clusters. A variety of heuristic approaches were suggested for categorical data clustering. The key determinant of memory use and cluster accuracy is the size of the storage and the number of attribute values being stored. Algorithms verified to deliver fully fair performance results on numerical data. This weakness is ideal for researchers to use because the task of calculation of the categorical values is challenging. Therefore, a stratified immune based algorithm was developed to cluster categorical data called CAIS. The complex logic of CAIS is to decide how antibodies are paired instead of matching data objects. In an analysis of the dataset, the affinity information is computed over the matrix, which does not entail substantial creation in the main memory, and increases the output over previous recorded methods. The total scheme of CAIS is outlined below.

1. Compute the centroid of antibodies in the dataset.
2. Using an immune-based algorithm, I manage to find the right cluster for categorical data.
3. Use CAIS to discover misclassified attribute incidence across large datasets.
4. An investigational learning algorithm for case-based inference to analyses and compare its implementation to artificial and real datasets.

A cluster is a set of information substances such that:

(1) Among various classes, such knowledge is correlated with persons.
(2) Information compounds are not equivalent to each other.

1.1 Categorical Field and Attributes

The A1, Am A2, A2… Am, and DOM (A1), DOM (A2)… DOM, are the attribute fields related to inter terrestrial. An ordered delimited set is certainly a field of mathematics. Ajis was a probabilistic trait. Provided that all the A1, A2…Am are categorical, Ω is categorical space.

The relation X represents a set of objects and xi be an entity characterized by m attributes. Let k be an integer. The aim of clustering X is to discover a dividing line which divides X into k separate Cluster.

2 Related Work

Web The efficient cluster-based algorithm for selecting sub-sets for high-dimensional results proposed in Magendiran and Jayaranjani [9]. The efficient collection of Quick subsets mainly thanks to the MST construction. These are the moves taken in the algorithm of Kruskal. The benefits are the precision and dimensionality increased. The FAST-based selection functional algorithm for high dimensional data improved by Godase and Gupta [13]. This paper offers the best results on reduced redundant data. Predict linked data Minimum cover tree used (MST). Dice coefficient calculation often carried out for the deletion of unnecessary data in the Quick algorithm. High dimensionality reduced, better runtime, Wu et al., [13]. The combined method of the enhanced Potential C-means clustering (IPCM) and KHM was hybrid k-harmonic mean (HFKHM). KHM has noise sensitivity issues, and Liu and Li [7] have resolved IPCM membership issue by incorporating high-dimensional cluster algorithm based on restriction. This article primarily conducts three main tasks, i.e. 1) dimension collection, 2) weighted dimension representation and 3) data representation assignments. Collection of dimensions and dimensional weighting by the CDCDD algorithm and by the data assignment method. It eventually included scientific optimization. The Jensen-Shannon divergence approach used in this paper in order to solve problems in the J-divergence method used for the similitude of uncertain data decides. The K-Medoid method for the clustering of uncertain data is a novel K-Medoids method. The algorithm that is proposed is UK-Medoids. In the K-mode algorithm, Cao, et al. is suggested. This algorithm is used to cluster categorical data in subspace. Just some of the clustering process worked for high-dimensional data effectively and many are inappropriate. It is very difficult to find interesting clusters in the entire data field since the data space is essentially sparse. A novel K-Modes algorithm for the clustering of the categorical data sub-space objects into the entropy complement. In this algorithm, the cluster has different sizes with different weights. The clustering algorithm had to be modified for high-dimensional data. The hardest challenge was to classify the cluster based on the intrinsic sparseness of artifacts for the whole data space. We spoke about subspace clusters with categorical data problems and used K-Modes via supplementary entropy weighting attributes. The clusters are based on the K-mode algorithm with different weights and dimensions.

3 Methodology

3.1 Immune Dependent Clustering Algorithm for Categorical

The clustered algorithms K-Means and K-Modes are most important and are crammed into the optimum local solution if the original cluster core is not properly selected. The major weakness of the clustering methodology in the planning is minimal use of implementations. Genetic algorithms are said to be a sort of technique that begins to create life-form processes; they are a universal science technology that is used in combination with them. Clustering K-Means and K-Modes is used to refine the cost feature in the GA where the inspectors are efficiently exploited. Since GA experiences such problems such as decay that raises GA output to an unacceptable amount, the cluster centers do not point out them. A modern quest methodology is used to achieve the high immune system model and also to reduce global solution costs.

3.2 Immune system

Outstanding cells, proteins, muscles and structures are part of the immune system and are used to protect humans from germs and microorganisms. It acts and attacks the pathogens that cause infections, toxic substances. The covered scheme gives b-cell clusters for hiding the antibodies, which are used to classify antigens to avoid infections and to repair them. The power of antigens' antibody interaction is also called "seamlessness" here between antigen as well as the antibody. The antigen is bound as the antigen's similarity is enhanced. A b-cell generation has been supported by a community of immune pathways to repair anti genes. Arbitrarily, the covered mechanism formed more b cells with a broader resemblance to duplicate antigens. These cloned cell types certainly know the fixed antigens called memory cells. Therefore, the clone selection is called this form of memory cell generation. Souvenir cells need longer life than ordinary B cells, useful when an equivalent infection occurs in the next century. The B-cells have slight similarities in the antigen and have to be directly extracted or converted in either direction.

Many researchers have also demoralized immune expertise and overcome many issues with data mining. The theory of the safe network states that the resistant mechanism involves antibody contact with distinct antibodies and the interaction with anticorps. The contact of antibodies that are expressed as, $C = C - \propto (C - X)$ Where C represents the antibody, X containing the antigen, which is said to be a developmental rate that ensures an antigen studies are retained in the algorithm as an antigen and thus as separate data point.

3.3 Encoding

It has been found that the cost function of two encoders, whether they start encoding the W matrix or Q matrix, would be constant. If the clustering algorithm efficiently operates on larger and larger datasets, the search space expands exponentially.

3.4 Initial Antibodies

Random selection is one of the most effective ways to begin an antibody selection process. The starting antibodies are generated by measuring the centers of the clusters which are randomly classified.

3.5 Evaluation Rate

The evolutionary rate is the most important parameter in the immune system and helps with the affinity between the antigens and antibodies. Authentic meaning is measured by problems a job faces. A stronger reliance on the algorithm's ability to quickly exit out of the local optimum contributes to a decreased efficacy.

4   Implementation Methodology

4.1   Authors and Affiliations. The Stratified Immune Dependent Clustering on Categorical Evidence

Random selection. The method of grouping related antigen groups into monoclonal antibodies for detection of a single antibody. In previous algorithm, the collection of cluster k values was far too random and the algorithm took way too long to complete. Due to this difficulty, cluster creation is complicated in a multitude of applications. In the earlier cited work, clustering was presented involving categorical data by the predefined presumption of initial clusters. The latest algorithm fails in how it represents clusters and how correctly it calculates the clusters. According to the CAIS group, the principle of affinity during computation of antibody clusters is something to remember. CAIS built on RAI that used an algorithm called k-means clustering. Details concerning the antibodies used in the receptor assays are known as the "representative antibodies". Discover the mixture of affinity measures from the new collection of entrants was most common and then use that information to calculate the RAI information that was used in the clustering process. The algorithm is discovered by evaluating a conceptual scenario and by showing how the different steps in the algorithm operate.

4.2   Representative Antibody Identification (RAI)

The key aim of RAI is to identify a group of antibodies that better reflect the distribution of consistency. The average cumulative cost for each antibody in a cluster is:

1. If there is an excess of this antibody in the cluster then RAI is also essential.
2. When the antibody is contained in the same cluster instead of in another.

The clustering algorithm was extended to the first subset S1 resulting in two clusters C11 and C12. Once the RAI for each of the components is determined, the value for each component is the same. The determined Reflection coefficient (RAI) for C2 is 1 and for the second iteration C1 and C2 are divided into C11 and C21. The C3 and C4s are separated and are numbered as C31 and C41 in (Figs. 1 and 2).

There are three data points in C11. The object A1 = 1 appears in X1, X2 and X3, but not in X4, X5 and X6. The frequency function is determined to be 1. Therefore, the average RAI of A1 in C11 is 0.66, and the average Adjusted ROI of C21 is 0. The frequency of A2 = 2 in C21 is 0.029, but the RAI for A2 in C31 is 0.66.

For Tmax, 0.66% is 0.029% The C41 has the lowest respective REI on A1, A2, and A3. In short, C cluster will not be pursued for future launches. Finally, the data is grouped into just 3 classes of strong RAI values.

4.3   Clustering for Similarity

The primary aim of maintaining a stable immune system is to efficiently assemble cells and strengthen the immune system against outside threats. The similarity measure indicates how many objects are shared with other objects throughout the dataset due

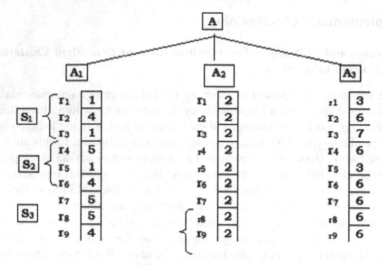

Fig. 1. Example dataset

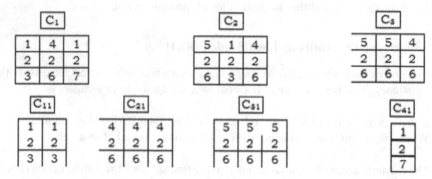

Fig. 2. The RAI of clusters

to their identical characteristics. For distance tests, similarity before clustering is used. The choosing of sufficient similarity measure for such types of clustering algorithms are always difficult. The text categorization method is exactly defined as the process of sorting documents based on pre-existing categories. Compute the similarities of all the various groups, then group the categories according to their similarity. The similarity test is used to evaluate how many two vectors have in common. In order to ensure fair classification performance, it is often required that the larger values be allocated to documents which belong to the same class with smaller values.

In order to achieve the best precision, the dataset is transferred into distinct and disjoint categories. In order to validate the suggested solution, revised immune methods and the current similarity measure of data must be implemented. The method of identifying possible clusters of data is discussed in depth.

5   Algorithm

Step 1 Giving data 'X' of size 'n' such where each data object represents a particular antigen throughout the dataset.

Step 2 Start generating the "K" antibody using the generic antibody identification.

Step 3 The antigen binding and neutralizing properties of the corresponding antibodies. For of particular categorical attribute, the calculation of "affinity" of the attribute is determined.

$Aij(d) = \sqrt{1} - (xid - xjd)2/ |xi - xj|2$

Let D be a database of N entities and d antibodies. Let Xi, Xj be the two instances of same antibody.

If $(xid - xjd)2$ is dominates

$|xi - xj|$ then the affinity Aij(d) is close to '0' and having both Xi and Xj are similar. Categorize the forms of resemblance rendering to the degree of similarities.

Step 4 Separately remove the antigen and the antibody.

Duplicate step 3 through step 4 and alert the affinity matrix allowing of incidences of afterward antigen value from its consistent constellation.

Step 5 Compute the most significant clusters.

Step 5.1 The neutralizing antibodies amount, modifying the antibodies to get an original antibody, being the sum of similarity among the antibodies and the antigen becomes serious.

This can be generated as follows. Let A1 and A2 signify two distinct antibodies and A2, which is substituted for the cluster Ci, provide the distance feature.

$\Phi (a1, a2) = \sum mi=1 \emptyset(a1, i, a2, i)$.

Step 5.2 Within each affinity pair, select the maximum affinity value from the remaining choices and exclude the other options that are less than the threshold given.

Step 5.3 Determines miscluster proportions. The formula is as follows.

miscluster rate $= Nm /N$

where N represents the number of instances and Nm represents the number of categorical objects.

Step6: Verify for stop condition

Step 7: End.

6   Performance Evaluation

Throughout the performance assessment, all measurements of precision for the CAIS are listed, including data extracted from synthetic and actual data sets. The suggested solution was focused on the time elapsed and miscluster incidence, and even different output metrics are used to calculate the accuracy including its clustering operation. The evaluations are mainly concerned with the suggested algorithm's efficiency. A research was performed on a simulated dataset and a sample dataset generated by the Machine Learning Registered Repository.

6.1   Expectation and Maximization

An iterative approach is used. It begins with a proposed parameter value. The parameters act as inputs for the expectation step which is used to calculate the probability. The values for the parameters are recomputed to try to increase the probability of the model being predictive. The new parameter values are being used to calculate a new expectation that maximizes the probability, and then the optimum value is optimized. The iteration proceeds until the model converges.

6.2   Model CAIS Performance Evaluation on Synthetic Dataset

In this segment, the simulated dataset is evaluated by CAIS. The clustering data was used to produce the synthetic datasets. Each proprietary data is represented with fixed instances, and the attributes. From Table 1 it can be shown that F-measure and accuracy values are high because there are relatively few antibodies.

Table 1. Performance of CAIS on synthetic dataset

Dataset name	No of attributes	No of antibodies (RAI)	Min Affinity threshold	No of instances =100			
				Precision	Recall	F-Measure	Accuracy
Synthetic1	100	37	0.2	83.1	80.1	81.57	80
Synthetic2	200	38	0.2	69	69.7	69.31	69
Synthetic3	300	48	0.2	80.7	81	80.84	80
Synthetic4	400	47	0.2	78.6	77	77.79	77

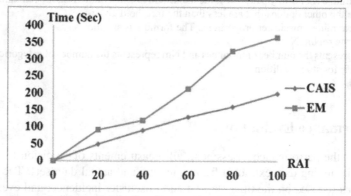

Graph 1. Elapsed time for discovering k=20 with varying RAI

7   Conclusion

This paper provides a research method for classifying categorical data using a nonlinear correspondence measure. In addition, incredibly difficult problems with real time domain guiding the characteristics of data that rely on hidden and transonic interpretation do not occur in the defined form of stable structures. Subsequently this categorization was well executed and precise. Thus, a stratified immune-based method is proposed to compare two categorical data sets for clustering. An approach that utilizes CAIS devices and immuno-diagnostic techniques for the identification of clusters in categorical results. It picks the most predominant attribute and uses it to classify the best selection of clusters. CAIS is generic for the vast number of characteristics in the samples. For a particular attribute or antigen, the conceptual object is designated as a distribution of frequency feature over the attributes, application of represe… Thus, proper CAIS methods minimize the misclassification rate present in the results. The CAIS is contrasted with EM in various settings that include: Concerning EM algorithms, the analytical study shows that CAIS greatly outperforms with EM algorithm. The key difference in the proposed work is the measurement of miscluster rate of categorical data in comparison to current clustering techniques. It is shown that the miscluster incidence is equivalent to 0.05 and 0.07 in varying settings. The elapsed time is eliminated when scaled with greater size attributes and number of clusters, and also outperforms the use of EM algorithm with respect to this metric.

References

1. Zhao, Z., Wang, L., Liu, H., Ye, J.: On similarity preserving feature selection. IEEE Trans. Knowl. Data Eng. **25**(3), 619–632 (2013)
2. Alam, S., Dobbie, G., Koh, Y.S., Riddle, P., Rehman, S.U.: Research on particle swarm optimization based clustering: a systematic review of literature and techniques. Swarm Evol. Comput. **17**, 1–13 (2014)
3. Kameshwaran, K., Malarvizhi, K.: Survey on clustering techniques in data mining. Int. J. Comput. Sci. Inf. Technol. **5**(2), 2272–2276 (2014)
4. Verma, A., Kaur, I., Kaur, A.: Algorithmic approach to data mining and classification techniques. Indian J. Sci. Technol. **9**(28), 1–22 (2016)
5. Jiang, B., Pei, J., Tao, Y., Lin, X.: Clustering uncertain data based on probability distribution similarity. IEEE Trans. Knowl. Data Eng. **25**(4), 751–763 (2013)
6. Sood, M., Bansal, S.: K-Medoids clustering technique using Bat algorithm. Int. J. Appl. Inf. Syst. **5**(8), 20–22 (2013)
7. Cao, F., Liang, J., Li, D., Zhao, X.: A weighting K-modes algorithm for subspace clustering of categorical data. Neurocomputing **108**, 23–30 (2013)
8. Mudaliar, P.U., Patil, T.A., Thete, S.S., Moholkar, K.P.: A fast clustering based feature subset selection algorithm for high dimensional data. Int. J. Emerg. Trend Eng. Basic Sci. **2**(1), 494–499 (2015)
9. Magendiran, N., Jayaranjani, J.: An efficient fast clustering-based feature subset selection algorithm for high-dimensional data. Int. J. Innov. Res. Sci. Eng. Technol. **3**(1), 405–408 (2014)
10. Yun, U., Ryang, H., Kwon, O.-C.: Monitoring vehicle outliers based on clustering technique. Appl. Soft Comput. **49**, 845–860 (2016)
11. Tabakhi, S., Moradi, P., Akhlaghian, F.: An unsupervised feature selection algorithm based on Ant colony optimization. Eng. Appl. Artif. Intell. **32**, 112–123 (2014)
12. Saha, A., Das, S.: Categorical fuzzy K-modes clustering with automated feature weight learning. Neurocomputing **166**, 422–435 (2015)
13. Godase, A., Gupta, P.: Improvised method of FAST clustering based feature selection technique algorithm for high dimensional data. Int. J. Appl. Innov. Eng. Manage. **4**(6), 135–140 (2015)
14. Wu, X., Wu, B., Sun, J., Qiu, S., Li, X.: A hybrid fuzzy K-harmonic means clustering algorithm. Appl. Math. Model. **39**(12), 3398–3409 (2015)

15. Liu, X., Li, M.: Integrated constraint based clustering algorithm for high dimensional data. Neurocomputing **142**, 478–485 (2014)
16. Kamakshaiah, K., Seshadri, R.: Prototype survey analysis of different information retrieval classification and grouping approaches for categorical information. In: 2017 International Conference on Intelligent Computing and Control (I2C2), Coimbatore, pp. 1–7 (2017). Part of ISBN 9781538603741. https://doi.org/10.1109/I2C2.2017.8321825
17. Zhou, J., Pan, Y., Chen, C.P., Wang, D., Han, S.: K-Medoids method based on divergence for uncertain data clustering. In: 2016 IEEE International Conference on Systems, Man, and Cybernetics, pp. 002671–002674 (2016)
18. Guha, S., Rastogi, R., Shim, K.: ROCK: a robust clustering algorithm for categorical attributes. In: 1999 International Conference on Data Engineering, pp. 512–521 (1999)
19. Narayana, G.S., Kolli, K.: Fuzzy K-means clustering with fast density peak clustering on multivariate kernel estimator with evolutionary multimodal optimization clusters on a large dataset. Multimedia Tools Appl. **80**(3), 4769–4787 (2021). ISSN 1380-7501. https://doi.org/10.1007/s11042-020-09718-4
20. Babu, A.G., et al.: An experimental analysis of clustering sentiments for Opinion Mining. In: Proceedings of the 2017 International Conference on Machine Learning and Soft Computing (ACM International Conference), ICMLSC 2017, Ho Chi Minh City, Vietnam, 13–16 January 2017, pp. 53–57 (2017). Proceeding Series. ISBN 978-1-4503-4828-7. EID: 2-s2.0-85018707408. https://doi.org/10.1145/3036290.3036318

Identification of Disease Resistant Plant Genes Using Artificial Neural Network

Tanmay Thareja, Kashish Goel, and Sunita Singhal[✉]

Manipal University Jaipur, Jaipur 303007, India
{tanmay.189301081,kashish.189301023}@muj.manipal.edu,
sunita.singhal@jaipur.manipal.edu

Abstract. Much like animals have their defenses against disease-causing pathogens, plants have their own mechanisms to identify and defend against pathogenic microorganisms. Much of this mechanism depends upon disease-resistant genes, also known as 'R' genes. Early identification of these R genes is essential in any crop improvement program, especially in a time when plant diseases are one of the biggest causes of crop failure worldwide. Existing methods operate on domain dependence which have several drawbacks and can cause new or low similarity sequences to go unrecognized. In this paper, a Machine Learning method, employing a domain-independent approach, was developed and evaluated which improves upon or eliminate the drawbacks of existing methods. Data sets were obtained from publicly accessible repositories, and feature extraction generated 10,049 number of features. Batch Normalization was used on the models, and we were able to achieve a 97% accuracy on the test dataset which is greater than anything else in the literature that uses the same approach.

Keywords: Disease resistant genes · Plants · Artificial Neural Network · Deep Learning

1 Introduction

Plants, like all living organisms, must deal with the constant threat of disease-causing pathogens, including bacteria, viruses, fungi, oomycetes, nematodes, and insects. These pathogens inhibit the normal growth and reproduction process in plant tissue resulting in crop loss and reduced yield. Plant pests and diseases are estimated to cause between 20 and 40% of global crop yield reductions each year [1]. Crop loss due to invasive plant pathogens was estimated by Rossman et al. (2009) [2] to be around $21 billion dollars a year, for the United States alone. To fight off these disease-causing pathogens, plants have developed a complex and adaptive defense mechanism.

Much of this mechanism depends upon disease-resistant genes, or 'R' genes, which allow the production of proteins that act as receptors of direct, or indirect products of pathogen's Avirulence (avr) genes. These interactions are very specific that modify or inactivate avr genes which allow the pathogen to avoid detection (Ellis et al., 2000) [3].

© Springer Nature Switzerland AG 2022
A. Dev et al. (Eds.): AIST 2021, CCIS 1546, pp. 475–484, 2022.
https://doi.org/10.1007/978-3-030-95711-7_40

Considering the importance of these R genes, early identification of them combined with selective breeding offers promising pathways to increased worldwide agriculture yields along with lower magnitudes of crop loss. Attempts have been made in identifying R proteins, Yoon B. J. [4] analyzed Hidden Markov Models for this classification problem, but the problem with most, if not all, of these methods is that they attempt to identify by classifying the protein sequence in domains, or by sequence similarity. This domain-dependent approach might skip unrecognized or even low-similarity proteins. A study [5] proposed a SVM based tool deployed on the web that is domain independent. Reviewing these methods, we felt that, with the new innovations and tools developed in Machine Learning and Deep Learning fields and their applications in plant molecular biology, there is a need to develop a novel prediction method that is domain and alignment independent and boasts very high accuracy, speed, and reliability.

Machine learning as a field is being increasingly used to solve various problems [14] and has recently emerged in molecular biology and allowed us to use Big Data exploits for plant genomics [15]. Studies by A. F. Bent (1996) [6] have presented a systematic review of Machine Learning approaches to various applications in plant biology. It discusses the various tools available for different approaches, the various public databases for sourcing data and the merits and drawbacks of various algorithms.

The study presented here in this paper aims to develop, analyses, and evaluate the best methods or techniques to use for the identification of disease resistant plant genes while following a domain independent approach to cover the drawbacks of existing methods. For investigation and development of this novel technique, we followed a standard machine learning pipeline shown in Fig. 1.

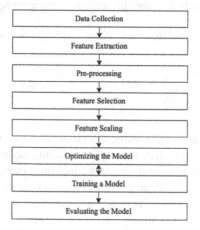

Fig. 1. A flow chart of the machine learning workflow

The steps and techniques used to obtain the final classification model are detailed in this paper. The layout of the paper is as follows: Sect. 2.1 describes the details regarding our dataset and from where we obtained the data. Section 2.2 to 2.4 describes all the steps we performed to pre-process the data and extract all the necessary information to train our model, including feature selection, feature extraction, and feature scaling.

Section 3 describes the Artificial Neural Network model used for classification and in Sect. 4 we evaluate our model using a variety of estimators and then discuss the results and their implications.

2 Developing the Model

2.1 Data Collection and Processing

All Machine Learning approaches rely on data to train the models. For the purposes of our study, we needed plant genomic data, specifically resistant protein sequences in the appropriate format. We found that there were not many databases hosting standardized genome sequences of disease resistant plant genes since the process of encoding DNA sequences (containing more than 3 billion base pairs) for research purposes is painstakingly time consuming. The best and most reliable repository is PRGdb [7]. It is an open and updated platform in which information about Pathogen Receptor Genes (PRGs) is stored, maintained, and discussed. At the time of our data collection the PRGdb database contained 152 Reference Resistant Genes from 34 different species where each were associated with a PRGdb ID, Gene Name, Class, Agent, AVR, and the disease against which it had resistance. This acted as our positive dataset for the purposes of training our models. For the other half of our dataset, we used National Centre for Biotechnology Information [NCBI] online data repository of protein sequences to obtain all protein sequences available for the same 34 species, for a total of 2060354 sequences. The list of the species and the number of sequences for each are listed below in Table 1.

Table 1. Number of sequences for each species

S. no.	Name of species	Number of sequences
1	Aegilops tauschii	4213
2	Arabidopsis thaliana	319200
3	Beta vulgaris	647
4	Capsicum annuum	157749
5	Capsicum chacoense	289
6	Capsicum chinense	35696
7	Cucumis melo	30635
8	Glycine max	168200
9	Helianthus annuus	161301
10	Hordeum vulgare	61535
11	Lactuca sativa	85267
12	Linum usitatissimum	3046

(continued)

Table 1. (*continued*)

S. no.	Name of species	Number of sequences
13	Nicotiana benthamiana	983
14	Nicotiana glutinosa	184
15	Nicotiana tabacum	92425
16	Oryza sativa Indica	47430
17	Oryza sativa Japonica	328712
18	Oryza sativa	61744
20	Phaseolus vulgaris	73017
21	Solanum acaule	216
22	Solanum bulbocastanum	618
23	Solanum demissum	1125
24	Solanum habrochaites	1195
25	Solanum lycopersicum var. cerasiforme	235
26	Solanum lycopersicum	45957
27	Solanum peruvianum	1255
28	Solanum pimpinellifolium	1024
29	Solanum tuberosum subsp. andigenum	494
30	Solanum tuberosum	45811
31	Triticum aestivum	23600
32	Triticum dicoccoides	88505
33	Triticum monococcum	230
34	Zea mays	217800

The sequences obtained were in fasta format, which is the format used for electronically representing plant genomic sequences. Since working with Machine Learning would require us to use tabular form of this data, we used 'Biopython' library [8] which provides a set of tools for computational molecular biology in python. Using this library, we parsed the data into a dictionary which was then converted into a Pandas Data Frame and stored for analysis and manipulations. Further, we randomly selected 152 sequences from the full negative dataset. This was done to prevent bias in our model due to the vast difference in number of sequences between the positive and negative datasets.

2.2 Feature Extraction

For machine learning approaches we require numerical descriptors with which to train our models. Thus, we needed to extract relevant and important information, in the form of numbers, from our protein sequences. We used the iLearn package [9] for python to generate our features. iLearn can generate descriptors from DNA, RNA, and protein sequences specifically for use in genomic bioinformatics. We obtained several important feature groups from this method including Autocorrelation, Quasi Sequence Order, Conjoint Triad, Amino Acid Composition, Pseudo Amino Acid Composition, as well as many more. Through feature extraction we were able to generate 10046 biological descriptors for each sequence. A summary of features extracted is given below in Table 2.

Table 2. Number of descriptors for each feature group

S. no.	Feature name	Number of descriptors
1	Amino Acid Composition	20
2	Dipeptide Amino Acid Composition	400
3	Tripeptide Amino Acid Composition	8000
4	Normalized Moreau-Broto Autocorrelation	240
5	Moran Autocorrelation	240
6	Geary Autocorrelation	240
7	Composition Descriptor	39
8	Transition Descriptor	39
9	Distribution Descriptor	195
10	Conjoint Triad Descriptor	343
11	Quasi-Sequence Order	100
12	Sequence-Order-Coupling-Number	60
13	Pseudo Amino Acid Composition	50
14	Amphiphilic Pseudo Amino Acid Composition	80

2.3 Pre-processing

After feature extraction, we combined our positive and negative datasets into one complete dataset, adding target value, or independent variable, for each sequence with positive reference sequences having value 1 and the rest having value 0. This dataset contained 304 examples with each having 10047 features. We analyzed this dataset to fix missing values if any, explore the data and its features to recognize needed steps to perform before feeding the dataset to our models, and finally to split the dataset after shuffling randomly into train and test with a 75:25 ratio.

2.4 Feature Scaling and Selection

In our analysis we found that many descriptors had different scales which could influence the weights, and this error would be propagated forward and therefore impact the accuracy of our model. To solve this, we used MaxAbsScaler from the sklearn package to scale all our features into a range from −1 to +1. Figure 2 and 3 below show the first 140 features before and after they were scaled respectively.

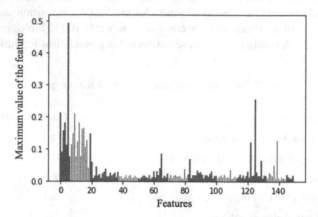

Fig. 2. The maximum values of the first 140 features before Feature Scaling

It was also imperative for us to evaluate the effectiveness of each of the 10046 descriptors we had (not counting the target value feature) because redundant features, as well as features with high correlation, can affect our model's predictive power. Karabulut et al. (2012) [10] tried to map out a relation between feature selection and accuracy of various algorithms in machine learning. We used Variance Threshold and Pearson's Correlation methods to select which features were not useful for us. Using them we dropped a total of 1113 features and ended up with a total of 8933 features for each sequence.

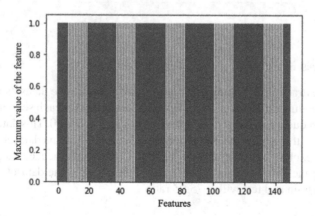

Fig. 3. The maximum values of the first 140 features after Feature Scaling

3 Artificial Neural Network

To build a model with better results we explored other techniques in the machine learning domain, with the best results obtained from the models built using an Artificial Neural Network (ANN). ANNs are inspired by the way in which our own human brain learns, and processes information and they are being used successfully in a wide array of bioinformatic applications because of their ability to cope with high dimensionality of complex datasets [11] to generalize and predict accurately (Fig. 4).

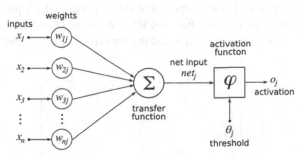

Fig. 4. Artificial neuron

We implemented a feed-forward Artificial Neural Network using a Sigmoid activation function, which is especially good for our classification problem since it outputs a value between 0 and. The function S(x) can be described in Eq. 1

$$S(x) = \frac{1}{1 + e^{-x}} \tag{1}$$

For our loss function we used the BCE loss function (called Binary Cross Entropy Loss) which calculates an error for a predicted example considering the true class or label of that training example as given in Eq. 2

$$H_p(q) = -\frac{1}{N} \sum_{i=1}^{N} y_i \cdot \log(p(y_i)) + (1 - y_i) \cdot \log(1 - p(y_i)) \tag{2}$$

Finally, we used Adam optimizer for our neural network. Adam stands for adaptive moment estimation which seemed to perform better in our classification problem when compared to other optimizers like SGD (called Stochastic Gradient Descent). We used a sequential model in the Keras library of Tensorflow [12] to build our Neural Network containing 3 dense layers (2 hidden layers and 1 output layer), with each layer containing 8933 number of artificial neurons. After creating the dense layers, we added a Batch Normalization layer to the first hidden layer in the network, which as described by Ioffe et al. (2015) [13], works so that any weights that might be numerically large may be normalized. The Batch Normalization was applied across columns of the dataset and its optimal set of parameters was learned by the network during the training loop. During training, outputs for each neuron were feed-forwarded to the next layer and the output of the final layer was then compared to the true label. The error between the two was back propagated and the difference was used to adjust the weights using the Adam optimizer. To test our ANN model, we divided our test dataset into 2, test and validation dataset, which was used to detect overfitting if any. The model achieved a test accuracy of 97.36%, which is highest in literature yet.

4 Results

We used several methods to evaluate our model. The first evaluation technique we used was a Receiver operating characteristic curve (ROC curve), which plots True Positive Rate (TPR) against False positive Rate (FPR) at different classification thresholds. It shows the trade-off between specificity and the sensitivity of the model (Fig. 5).

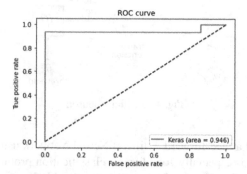

Fig. 5. ROC curve for Artificial Neural Network

We also evaluated the confusion matrix for the model and evaluated the model on a variety of parameters, a table of which is given below. Note that TP, FP, FN, and TN stand for True Positive, False Positive, False Negative and True Negative respectively. The evaluation parameters are listed in Table 3.

Table 3. Various parameters for both models

Parameter	Formula	ANN
Specificity	$\frac{TN}{TN+FP}$	1.0
Sensitivity	$\frac{TP}{TP+FN}$	0.937
Accuracy	$\frac{TP+TN}{TP+TN+FN+FP}$	0.973
Precision	$\frac{TP}{TP+FP}$	1.0
FPR	$\frac{FP}{TN+FP}$	0.0
FNR	$\frac{FN}{TP+FN}$	0.062

(*continued*)

Table 3. (*continued*)

Parameter	Formula	ANN
NPV	$\frac{TN}{TN+FN}$	0.956
FDR	$\frac{FP}{FP+TP}$	0.0
F1-Score	$\frac{TP}{TP+\frac{1}{2}(FP+FN)}$	0.967
MCC	$\frac{TP.TN-FP.FN}{\sqrt{(TP+FP)(TP+FN)(TN+FP)(TN+FN)}}$	0.946

5 Conclusion

In this paper, a ANN model is used to identification plant disease with domain-independent approach. Total, we had 152 sequences for both positive and negative datasets, both with 8933 features each. We ran the trained ANN model on the test dataset and achieved a 97.36% accuracy of prediction without overfitting.

The percentages achieved indicate that our model is accurate for most sequences, this accuracy is also the highest achieved in literature for a domain-independent approach in the identification of disease-resistant plant genes. In future, this model can be updated with the inclusion of more positively identified R genes to further enhance the efficiency of the model.

References

1. Food and Agriculture Organization of United States. http://www.fao.org/news/story/en/item/409158/icode/. Accessed 23 Aug 2021
2. Rossman, A.Y.: The impact of invasive fungi on agricultural ecosystems in the United States. Biol. Invasions **11**(1), 97–107 (2009)
3. Ellis, J.: Structure, function, and evolution of plant disease resistance genes. Curr. Opin. Plant Biol. **3**(4), 278–284 (2000)
4. Yoon, B.J.: Hidden Markov models and their applications in biological sequence analysis. Curr. Genomics **10**(6), 402–415 (2009)
5. Pal, T., Jaiswal, V., Chauhan, R.S.: DRPPP: a machine learning based tool for prediction of disease resistance proteins in plants. Comput. Biol. Med. **78**, 42–48 (2016)
6. Bent, A.F.: Plant disease resistance genes: function meets structure. Plant Cell **8**(10), 1757–1771 (1996)
7. Sanseverino, W., et al.: PRGdb: a bioinformatics platform for plant resistance gene analysis. Nucleic Acids Res. **38**, D814–D821 (2010)
8. Cock, P.J.A., et al.: Biopython: freely available Python tools for computational molecular biology and bioinformatics. Bioinformatics **25**(11), 1422–1423 (2009)
9. Chen, Z.: iLearn: an integrated platform and meta-learner for feature engineering, machine-learning analysis and modelling of DNA, RNA and protein sequence data. Brief. Bioinform. **21**(3), 1047–1057 (2020)
10. Karabulut, E.M., Özel, S.A., İbrikçi, T.: A comparative study on the effect of feature selection on classification accuracy. Procedia Technol. **1**, 323–327 (2012)

11. Lancashire, L.J., Lemetre, C., Ball, G.R.: An introduction to artificial neural networks in bioinformatics–application to complex microarray and mass spectrometry datasets in cancer studies. Brief. Bioinform. **10**(3), 315–329 (2008)

12. Abadi, M., et al.: TensorFlow: a system for large-scale machine learning. In: Proceedings of the 12th USENIX Symposium on Operating System Design and Implementation, pp 1–14. USENIX: The Advanced Computing Systems Association, California (2016)

13. Ioffe, S.: Batch normalization: accelerating deep network training by reducing internal covariate shift. In: Proceedings of the 32nd International Conference on Machine Learning, vol. 37, pp. 448–456 (2015)

14. Jha, M., Singhal, S.: GA with repeated crossover for rectifying optimization problems. In: Haldorai, A., Ramu, A., Khan, S.A.R. (eds.) Business Intelligence for Enterprise Internet of Things. EICC, pp. 195–202. Springer, Cham (2020). https://doi.org/10.1007/978-3-030-44407-5_11

15. Morgunov, A.S., Saar, K.L., Vendruscolo, M., Knowles, T.P.J.: New frontiers for machine learning in protein science. J. Mol. Biol. **433**(20), 167232 (2021)

A Comparative Study on a Disease Prediction System Using Machine Learning Algorithms

S. Rama Sree[1]($\boxtimes$), A. Vanathi[1], Ravi Kishore Veluri[1], and S. N. S. V. S. C. Ramesh[2]

[1] Aditya Engineering College, Surampalem, India
{ramasree_s,vanathi.andiran,ravikishore1985}@aec.edu.in
[2] Aditya College of Engineering and Technology, Surampalem, India
ramesh.snsvsc@acet.ac.in

Abstract. One of the most essential and fundamental factors that motivates people to seek assistance is their physical well-being. A vast range of ailments affect people nowadays, making them extremely vulnerable. Thus, disease prediction at an early stage has now become increasingly relevant as a result of these developments. Machine Learning is a relatively new technique that can aid in the prediction and diagnosis of diseases. To diagnose respiratory difficulties, heart attacks, and liver disorders, this study employs machine learning in conjunction with symptoms. All these diseases are the focus of our investigation because they are extremely prevalent, incredibly expensive to treat, and impact a significant number of people at the same time. A variety of supervised machine learning methods, including Naive Bayes, Decision Trees, Logistic Regression, and Random Forests, are used to forecast the disease based on the provided dataset. The discussion of learning categorization based on correctness ends with this conclusion. Flask is also used to construct a platform that allows visitors to forecast whether they will contract a specific illness and take appropriate precautions if they do contract the illness. Among the most important aspects of healthcare informatics is the prediction of chronic diseases. It is critical to diagnose the condition at the earliest possible opportunity. Using feature extraction and classification methods for classification and prognosis of chronic diseases, this study gives a summary of the current state of the art. The selection of elements that are appropriate for a classification system is critical in improving its accuracy. The decrease of dimensionality aids in the improvement of the overall performance of the machine learning system. The use of classification algorithms on disease datasets gives promising results in the development of adaptive, automated, and smart medical diagnostics for chronic diseases, according to the researchers. Using parallel classification systems, it is possible to speed up the process while also increasing the computing efficiency of the final findings. This paper provides a complete analysis of several feature selection strategies, as well as the advantages and disadvantages of each method.

Keywords: Asthma prediction · Heatstroke prediction · Liver disease prediction · Naive Bayes · Logistic regression

© Springer Nature Switzerland AG 2022
A. Dev et al. (Eds.): AIST 2021, CCIS 1546, pp. 485–499, 2022.
https://doi.org/10.1007/978-3-030-95711-7_41

1 Introduction

These days, the health industry is vastly improving. To preserve better health, several vital procedures and measures are being performed in preparation. People today are very susceptible to a variety of ailments because of their living habits and their surroundings. As a result, predicting sickness at an early stage becomes a critical task. There are various symptoms that are prevalent and pose a higher risk [1]. Machine Learning is a prominent subject of research that aids in the resolution of major issues in the healthcare business. Machine learning has a wide range of applications, one of the most well-known of which is in the field of healthcare. Predicting an illness at an earlier stage improves the healthcare business by eliminating or reducing the severity of diseases and lowering the death rate. A large majority of medical datasets are also available on the internet, making it easier for researchers to construct support systems for any type of disease prediction. Machine Learning makes predictions based on the dataset's past data. This study is focused on diseases that are especially worrisome in the current climate. Prediction of Asthma as a side effect following immunizations, Prediction of Heart Stroke, and Liver Patient Analysis are some of the ailments that this study focuses on since they are common, expensive to treat, and affect a huge number of people who are unable to recover. Medical physicians face numerous obstacles in effectively analyzing symptoms and detecting disease at an early stage due to massive volumes of data. However, supervised machine learning algorithms have already shown tremendous promise in outperforming traditional systems that take a long time to diagnose diseases and in assisting people in the early detection of high-risk conditions [2].

To begin the task, we selected several datasets that contain various traits/attributes associated to that specific condition. The datasets collected must be further evaluated in order to obtain the datasets needed for our paper. To generate final findings, the characteristics available in the dataset are employed. After selecting the datasets, we must clean and modify the data, which includes filling in missing values, converting strings to integers utilizing label encode if appropriate, and scaling the data to fit into a single range. Data pre-processing refers to the complete procedure.

Parting the datasets via preparing stage the model is assembled utilizing the preparation information and afterward assesses our model utilizing the testing information. We use various classification algorithms that fall under supervised machine learning algorithms for model building, such as Naive Bayes, Decision Trees, Logistic Regression, and Random Forest, are used to predict the disease using the data provided [6]. After we've finished developing the model, we'll evaluate it to see which approach is best for our needs. All of the disorders discussed in the paper are treated in the same way.

To develop the website, a more accurate algorithm was applied. Flask (a Web development framework) is used to create the website, which serves as an interface between the front-end official site and the machine learning model. The website allows the user to access data that forecasts whether a person is susceptible to a specific disease based on the medical history they have indicated.

2 Literature Review

Machine learning algorithms have recently been found to be effective in predicting pharmaceutical adverse effects [1]. Huang used pharmacological targets, gene ontology annotations, including binding proteins as drug features, as well as support vector machine or regression, to produce the prediction. To train the model with chemical structures of medications. Toxicology research can improve drug safety profile. "Systems pharmacology" is a promising field of study in molecular systems biology. Systems pharmacology combines clinical and molecular data. This approach seems to be new, and there are very few instances of how it would accurately predict adverse drug reactions.

Medication incidental effects, or unfriendly medication responses, have turned into a significant general wellbeing concern [2]. It is one of the primary drivers of disappointment during the time spent medication advancement, and of medication withdrawal whenever they have arrived at the market. Subsequently, in silico forecast of potential incidental effects from the get-go in the medication disclosure measure, prior to arriving at the clinical stages, is of incredible interest to work on this long and costly interaction and to give new proficient and safe treatments for patients.

The utilization of clinical datasets has drawn in the consideration of analysts around the world. Information mining strategies have been generally utilized in creating choice emotionally supportive networks for illnesses expectation through a bunch of clinical datasets. In this paper [3], we propose another information-based framework for sicknesses forecast utilizing bunching, commotion expulsion, and expectation strategies. We use Classification and Regression Trees (CART) to produce the fluffy standards to be utilized in the information-based framework. We test our proposed strategy on a few public clinical datasets. Results on Pima Indian Diabetes, Mesothelioma, WDBC, Stat-Log, Cleveland and Parkinson's telemonitoring datasets show that proposed strategy strikingly further develops the illnesses expectation precision. The outcomes showed that the mix of fluffy guideline based, CART with commotion evacuation and grouping strategies can be viable in infections forecast from certifiable clinical datasets. The information-based framework can help clinical professionals in the medical care practice as a clinical logical strategy.

In this paper [4] we present DrugClust, an AI calculation for drugs incidental effects expectation. DrugClust pipeline functions as follows: first medications are grouped regarding their provisions and afterward incidental effects expectations are made, as indicated by Bayesian scores. Organic approval of coming about bunches should be possible by means of advancement investigation, one more usefulness executed in the approach. This last apparatus is of outrageous interest for drug disclosure, considering that it tends to be utilized as an approval of the bunches got, just as for the investigation of new potential connections between specific incidental effects and nontargeted pathways.

Data classification based on liver problems. The outcomes of the Naive Bayes, FT Tree, and K-Star algorithms in the field of data classification are discussed in this study [5].

In the first phase, the ANN taxonomy is utilized to classify underlying liver illness. In the second step, rough set rule induction utilizing the LEM (Learn by Example) method is utilized to create categorization rules [6]. Fuzzy criteria are employed in the third step to determine the various types of liver disease.

Stroke prediction was performed using 5 machine learning approaches on the Cardio-vascular health Study (CHS) datasets in [7]. A mix of Decision Tree with C4.5 algorithm, Feature Extraction, Artificial Neural Networks, with Support Vector Machine are uti-lized to achieve the best results. This was done with a dataset with a lesser number of input characteristics.

The healthcare business collects large amounts of data that are not "mined" for effective decision making. This article suggests windows as the predictive application for heart disease [10]. The user is guided for heart illness by the sophisticated prediction system. The application receives various heart disease symptoms. The user first checks the symptoms and details of the heart ailment. Data mining techniques such as decision trees and Naive Bayes are utilized to gather patient details. The system's performance is assessed based on accurate outcome prediction.

M.M., Paul, B.K., Ahmed, K, Quinn, J.M.W., Moni [11] It is difficult to build machine learning and data mining-based techniques to predict and detect cardiac disease. Devel-oping effective and precise initial heart disease prediction through fill up the form of medical decision with digital patient data could solve the shortage of cardiovascular knowledge and high rate of wrong diagnosis in most nations. This study sought to find the most accurate machine learning classifiers for diagnostic applications. Many unsu-pervised machine-learning algorithms were used to predict cardiac disease. Except for MLP and KNN, all applied algorithms calculated feature importance scores. The impor-tance of each factor was prioritized to determine those that predicted high heart disease. The RF technique obtained 100% accuracy, sensitivity, and specificity using a Kaggle dataset of heart illness. We discovered that a basic supervised machine learning method may accurately predict cardiac disease with great potential value.

Cardiovascular diseases (CVD) kill most individuals worldwide. Early detection of sickness reduces mortality. Machine learning (ML) techniques are now widely regarded by medical specialists as a clinical decision support [12]. The most prominent ML models for prediction of heart disease are explored and compared using various criteria. Heart disease predictors include Support Vector Machines (SVM), Logistic Regression, Naive Bayes, Decision Trees, and K Nearest Neighbor. In this paper, individual classifiers are bagged and boosted to increase the system's performance. Individual Naive Bayes classifiers had maximum accuracy of 85.13 percent and 84.81 percent on the Cleveland and Fact that many people datasets. The bagging strategy enhances the decision tree's accuracy by 7%, which is significant in diagnosing CVD.

Heart disease early detection is difficult in today's reality. If not detected in time, this can lead to death. In remote, quasi, and rural areas of developing countries, where heart specialists are scarce, an effective decision assistance system can help diagnose heart disease early [13]. The authors suggest a hybrid decision-making support system that will help detect cardiac disease depending on the patient's clinical characteristics. The authors handled missing values using multivariate imputation via chained equations. The accessible dataset was selected using a hybridized feature selection approach com-bining GA and recursive feature removal. For pre-processing data, SMOTE and normal scalar methods were utilized. The authors used support vector machines, Naive Bayes, regression models, random forest, and gradient boosting classifiers to finish the hybrid system. The algorithm produced the most reliable data with classifier. The proposed fusion system was evaluated in a Python simulation environment.

Machine learning is used to solve numerous challenges in data science. Machine learning is often used to predict outcomes based on historical data [14]. For prediction, the computer learns patterns from an existing dataset and applies these to an unknown dataset. Classification is a popular machine learning technique for prediction. Some categorization algorithms forecast accurately, whereas others do not. This study studies ensemble classification, which combines many classifiers to improve the accuracy of weak algorithms. This tool was tested on a heart disease data. A comparison analysis was used to examine how well the team approach can improve heart disease prediction accuracy. This research aims to improve weak classification algorithms' accuracy while also demonstrating their utility in predicting disease early on. The study's findings show that ensemble techniques like bagging and boosting can improve poor classifier prediction accuracy and identify heart disease risk.

Co morbidity is a significant aspect to consider when estimating asthma treatment costs. The cost of treating an asthmatic patient with co morbidity depends on the co morbidity [15]. The lack of detection of co morbidity in asthmatic patients makes treatment cost prediction difficult. In this work, we suggested a co morbidity portfolio architecture that enhances asthma patient treatment cost prediction by combining common co morbidities into cost categories. Experiments used logistic regression, random forest, support vector machine, classification regression, and back propagation neural network to predict asthmatic patients in a Chinese city from 2012 to 2014.

3 System Proposed

Several approaches are incorporated into our proposed system, including the following:

- Logistic Regression
- Naïve Bayes
- Decision Tree
- Random Forest

The disease predictive model is a proposed model for forecasting a range of diseases, include asthma as a risk factor of vaccination, stroke prediction, including patient analysis of liver disease [5]. The architecture model of the prediction model is shown in Fig. 1. The user interface has been developed that will allow users to foresee certain types of ailments from which they are now experiencing. The ideal algorithm is picked and applied in the web application to use all four of a supervised learning techniques covered before in machine learning. The system methodology for this study was developed using Jupyter Notebook, Sublime Text, and Spyder.

Jupyter Notebook – A Jupyter notebook is a bunch of cells in that we can write code and run it concurrently or in parallel. It is a dependable source for executing machine learning algorithms tasks, as it loads the necessary libraries. We take all essential procedures to ensure that our data pre-processing, model creation, and model evaluation are successful. Later, we save and use the most precise estimation in our web-based application.

Sublime Text – Using sublime text editor, we create the front-end HTML and CSS code for the web application. We create our web application with HTML and CSS in way to lure users and make is user-friendly.

Spyder – The flask code for the web application is created using the Spyder IDE. Flask is written in Python. The flask code retrieves the values given in the web application, as well as the Jupyter notebook models. When the guess switch is clicked, they generate predictions using the user-supplied values.

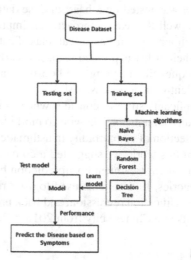

Fig. 1. Architecture diagram for performance prediction of disease

4   Implementation

The This investigation is carried out in utilizing the machine learning calculations to fostering a web application for a superior user interface.

4.1   Machine Learning

The next steps are taken

Step 1: Importing libraries as well as datasets: – Pandas and NumPy libraries for importing datasets and carrying out different dataset operations.

Step 2: Data Visualization: – Converting raw data in usable representation through the visualization process. Different plots such as scatter plot, counter plot and heat map are implemented.

Step 3: Preprocessing of data: – Splitting independent variables, label encryption, scaling (if necessary)

Step 4: Model Construction: – The dataset will be initially partitioned into training data (80%) and testing data (20%). Here, models are constructed for each method and fitted to the training data with each disease. The methods used for supervised machine learning include Logistic Regression, Decision Tree, Random Forest, and Naive Bayes. The process of data processing for predicting the disease is shown in Fig. 2.

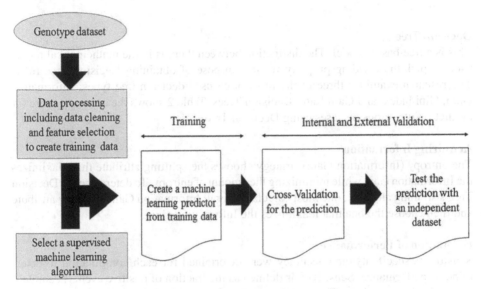

Fig. 2. Data processing for predicting the disease

Formulae to predict the accuracy is defined as the percentage of correct predictions for the test data. It can be calculated easily by dividing the number of correct predictions by the number of total predictions.

$$\text{Accuracy} = \frac{\text{correct predictions}}{\text{all predictions}}$$

Logistic Regression: This approach is used to solve problems involving classification. We import sklearn logistic regression algorithm and fit the model using the training data. Logistic Regression is a classification and machine-learning technique [7] for classifying records in a dataset according to their values in input fields. It makes predictions about a dependent variable using one or more sets of independent variables. The dataset is freely available mostly on Kaggle website and comes with an ongoing illness study involving residents of Framingham, Massachusetts [9]. The categorization objective is to forecast a patient's 10-year risk of developing disease. The dataset contains information on the patients. It has about 4,000 records with a total of 15 qualities. The accuracy score indicates the model's accuracy from Table 1.

Table 1. Accuracy score indicates the disease prediction

Disease	Accuracy score
Asthma	96.99%
Heart attack	79.00%
Liver disorder	70.09%

Decision Tree

This is a tree-based model. The distinction between them is in the mathematical model used to pick the dividing property for the purpose of obtaining Decision Tree rules. The research examines three of the most often used decision tree types: Information Gain, Gini Index, and Gain Ratio Decision Trees. Table 2 shows the accuracy score for prediction of various diseases using Decision Tree.

Acquiring Information

The entropy (Information Gain) strategy chooses the splitting attribute that maximizes the Information Gain while minimizing the amount of entropy. To determine the Decision Tree's splitting attribute, one must calculate overall Information Gain for every attribute and then choose the one that maximizes the Information Gain.

Evaluation of Performance

Sensitivity, specificity, and accuracy were determined for each combination to determine its performance. Sensitivity is defined as the fraction of positive events accurately categorized as positive. "The specificity of an instance is defined as the proportion of instances that are accurately identified being negative." Accuracy is defined as the proportion of correctly classified instances. To determine the stability of the suggested model's performance, the data is trained and tested sets and cross validated tenfold.

Table 2. Accuracy score indicating the disease prediction using decision tree

Disease	Accuracy score
Asthma	96.98%
Heart	77.00%
Liver	64.96%

Naive Bayes: It is a basic yet effective classification method that generates accurate and timely results using probability. The accuracy score indicates the model's accuracy. The Naive Bayes classifier evaluates the information included in each protein sequence and determines whether the sequence is sick or normal. The classifier begins by calculating the probability values for the normal and sick sequences using the training data.

Classification Algorithms are among the simplest and most successful classification systems available. This method is based on the concept of Bayesian Networks, which are probabilistic graphical models that represent a collection of random variables and their conditional independencies. There are various efficient algorithms for inference and learning in Bayesian Networks. The only stipulation is that the dataset's features be independent. The characteristics throughout the dataset are interdependent due to species evolution however the interdependence does not appear to be substantial. As a result of the independent nature of the dataset's features, the classification is performed using the Naive Bayes approach. This approach begins by generating a probability value by each sequence throughout the sequence database. When an input dataset is provided, a probability value for each patient's sequence is determined. This voltage is calculated to the chance of occurrence.

In the database, this is a value. Thus, sequences are categorized according to the value of a probability associated with them sequences. The Naive Bayes classifier is just a straightforward classification algorithm based on the application of Bayes' theorem with High assumption of independence. Table 3 shows the accuracy score for prediction of various diseases using Naïve Bayes.

Table 3. Accuracy score indicates the disease prediction using Naive Bayes.

Disease	Accuracy score
Asthma	96.76%
Heart	82.00%
Liver	60.68%

Naïve Bayes' Rule: The Naïve Bayes algorithm is a classification-supervised learning system that uses supervised learning techniques. The category of a new feature vector can be determined by applying the conditional probability theory to the feature vector. For each class of vectors, the NB employs the training data to determine the dependent probability value of each vector. Following the computation of the chance conditional value of each vector, the new vector class was computed based on the chance conditional value of each vector computed previously. NB is an issue classification algorithm that is concerned with text.

The optimal model for each disease is provided below, along with its Receiver Operating Characteristic (ROC) curve identifies alternative solutions to decisions depending on the situations. Table 4 shows the Accuracy score indicating the disease prediction using Receiver operating characteristic (ROC).

Random Forest: It is an ensemble approach that employs several decision trees during the training phase and generates the output, which would be the median of the trees in classification and the mean of a individual trees in regression.

Table 4. Accuracy score indicating the disease prediction using receiver operating characteristic (ROC)

Disease	Accuracy score
Asthma	96.96%
Heart	70.00%
Liver	67.52%

While the Random Forest is an extremely effective tool for solving classification problems, as is the case with several machine learning algorithms, it might take some time to understand precisely what has been predicted as well as what it means in context. Fortunately, Scikit-Learn make it relatively simple to execute and evaluate a Random Forest. The process of training and testing a simple Random Forest model utilizing confusion matrix is also experimented.

For Asthma Prediction:

- The ROC curve for Asthma Prediction using Logistic Regression is shown in Fig. 3.

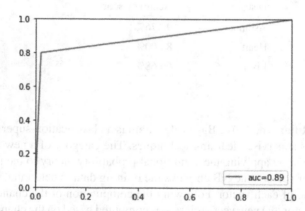

Fig. 3. ROC curve for Asthma Prediction using Logistic Regression

For Heart Stroke Prediction:

- The ROC curve for Heart Stroke Prediction using Naïve Bayes is shown in Fig. 4.

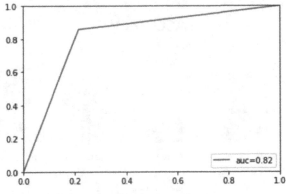

Fig. 4. ROC curve for Naive Bayes

For Liver Disease Prediction:

• The ROC curve for Liver Disease Prediction using Logistic Regression is shown in Fig. 5.

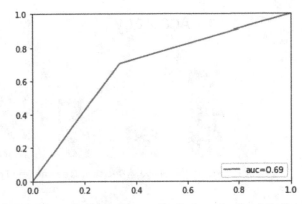

Fig. 5. ROC curve for Liver Disease Prediction using Logistic Regression

Model Evaluation: After a model has been developed using various techniques, it is evaluated to establish its accuracy. The correctness of the model is determined by comparing its output to the output of the data set. It helps us to evaluate what model is the greatest fit for the task and how the suggested scheme will perform with in future. There are a variety of model evaluation metrics available, along with an accuracy score, a classification error, and a categorization report. It validates the model's correctness using test data. It is a fundamental step in the process of growth [8].

Predictions for Asthma: The following Fig. 6 compares the accuracy of various algorithms that are used to construct our model for asthma illness prediction.

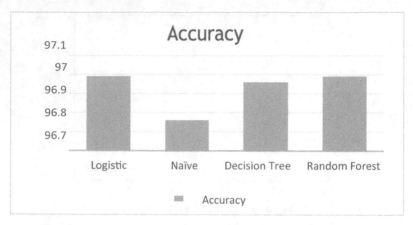

Fig. 6. Comparison between various algorithms of asthma prediction

Heart Stroke Prediction: The below presented Fig. 7 shows the comparison of accuracy between various algorithms used to build our model for heart stroke prediction.

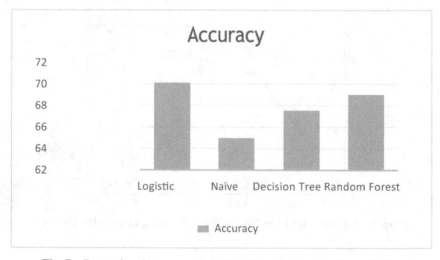

Fig. 7. Comparison between various algorithms for heart stroke prediction

Liver Disease Prediction: The below presented Fig. 8 shows the comparison of accuracy between various algorithms used to build our model for liver disease prediction.

The Confusion Matrix for liver disease prediction using Logistic Regression is shown in Table 5. Similarly, Confusion Matrix can also be obtained for the other algorithms.

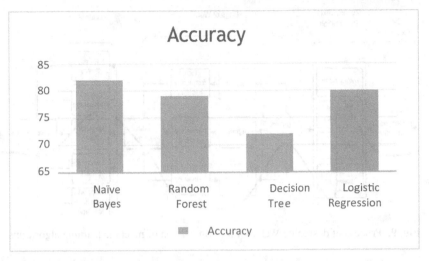

Fig. 8. Comparison between various algorithms for liver disease prediction

Table 5. Confusion matrix of logistic regression for liver disease prediction.

	Actual positive (1)	Actual negative (0)
Predicted positive (1)	TP = 74	FP = 4
Predicted negative (0)	FN = 31	TN = 8

4.2 Web Application Technologies

All these pages feature several fields that must be filled out by the user; thus, the user has the highest accuracy compared to the other algorithms in predicting asthma as a side effect of vaccination and liver disease. Thus, we determine the logistic regression's confusion matrix with classification report.

A confusion matrix is among the measures used to evaluate classification algorithms' models. It summarizes the categorization model's performance. It describes the logistic regression model's performance in this section. TP denotes True Positives, FP denotes False Positives, FN denotes False Negatives, and TN denotes True Negatives. If they are found to be positive for that disease, they may navigate to the precautions page and so take precautions in advance.

Back-End (Flask): Flask is used to construct the web application's back end. Flask is a web framework written in Python that is used to construct web applications.

This back-end technique enables the most accurate machine learning model to be integrated into the web application. All models with the highest accuracy are included into the flask code via "pickle". The flask's Pickle library must be imported. The process of designing Web tool showing the results of prediction for various diseases is shown in Fig. 9.

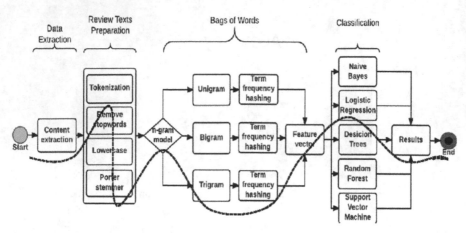

Fig. 9. Process of designing Web tool for comparison of machine learning algorithms

5 Conclusion

The world's health is being harmed by chronic diseases, which are growing and increasing daily. Inadequate or delayed therapy might potentially result in patient mortality. Thus, predicting chronic diseases such as Asthma, Heart, and Liver diseases is a critical responsibility in the medical industry. As a result, it is critical to educate healthcare practitioners about accurate feature selection but also classification approaches that could be successfully applied to medical databases to aid in illness identification. The feature selection process, identified for each feature selection algorithm a new dataset was obtained that comprises only the features considered as most relevant by every algorithm. In the case of principal component analysis, we tested different number of PCs in order to achieve accurate results.

This article provides an overview of current feature selection methodologies and classification systems for the prediction of asthma following immunization, heart attack, and liver illness. To summarize, we utilized logistic regression in the cases of asthma and liver disease, and Naive Bayes in the case of heart attack, because these algorithms are more accurate than most other algorithms in every one of their predictions. Finally, a web tool is designed that people may readily visit to determine their susceptibility to such diseases.

Currently, this system processes textual or numerical data to determine whether the end user has asthma, heart illness, or certain liver ailments. However, by extending this basis, this system can analyze any type of data, including movies and visual data (images, X-rays, and scans). Additionally, we can forecast any other prevalent diseases. Thus, by including a variety of additional machine learning techniques or any other technologies, the system can be significantly enhanced to save lives.

References

1. Huang, L.C., Wu, X., Chen, J.Y.: Predicting adverse side effects of drugs. BMC Genomics **12**(Suppl. 5), S11 (2011)

2. Pauwels, E., Stoven, V., Yamanishi, Y.: Predicting drug side-effect profiles: a chemical fragment-based approach. BMC Bioinform. **12**, 169 (2011)
3. Nilashi, M.I., Bin Ahmadi, O., Leila, H.S.: An analytical method for diseases prediction using machine learning techniques. Comput. Chem. Eng. **106**, 212–223 (2017)
4. Dimitri, G.M., Lio, P.: DrugClust: a machine learning approach for drugs side effects prediction. Comput. Biol. Chem. **68**, 204–210 (2017)
5. Rajeswari, P., SophiaReena, G.: Analysis of liver disorder using data mining algorithm. Global J. Comput. Sci. Technol. **10**(14), 48–52 (2010)
6. Karthik, S., Priyadarishini, A., Anuradha, J., Tripathy, B.K.: Classification and rule extraction using rough set for diagnosis of liver disease and its types. Adv. Appl. Sci. Res. (2011)
7. Rama Sree, S., Ramesh, S.N.S.V.S.C.: Artificial intelligence aided diagnosis of chronic kidney disease. J. Crit. Rev. **7**(12), 909–923 (2020)
8. A Comparative Analysis for Various Stroke Prediction Techniques. www.researchgate.net/publication/340250948
9. https://www.kaggle.com/uciml/indian-liver-patient-records
10. Maheswari, S., Pitchai, R.: Heart disease prediction system using decision tree and Naive Bayes algorithm. Curr. Med. Imaging Rev. **15**(8), 712–717 (2019). https://doi.org/10.2174/1573405614666180322141259
11. Ali, M.M., Paul, B.K., Ahmed, K., Bui, F.M., Quinn, J.M.W., Moni, M.A.: Heart disease prediction using supervised machine learning algorithms: performance analysis and comparison. Comput. Biol. Med. **136**, 104672 (2021). https://doi.org/10.1016/j.compbiomed.2021.104672
12. Balakrishnan, B., Vinoth, K.C.N.S.: A comprehensive performance analysis of various classifier models for coronary artery disease prediction. Int. J. Cogn. Inform. Nat. Intell. **15**(4), 1–14 (2021). https://doi.org/10.4018/IJCINI.20211001.oa36
13. Rani, P., Kumar, R., Ahmed, N.M.O.S., Jain, A.: A decision support system for heart disease prediction based upon machine learning. J. Reliable Intell. Environ. **7**(3), 263–275 (2021). https://doi.org/10.1007/s40860-021-00133-6
14. Latha, C.B.C., Jeeva, S.C.: Improving the accuracy of prediction of heart disease risk based on ensemble classification techniques. Inform. Med. Unlock. **16**, 100203 (2019). https://doi.org/10.1016/j.imu.2019.100203
15. Li, L., Yu, X., Yong, Z., Li, C., Gu, Y.: Design comorbidity portfolios to improve treatment cost prediction of asthma using machine learning. IEEE J. Biomed. Health Inform. **25**(6), 2237–2247 (2021). https://doi.org/10.1109/JBHI.2020.3034092

Leaf Disease Identification Using DenseNet

Ruchi Verma[✉] and Varun Singh

Department of Computer Science and Engineering, Jaypee University of Information Technology, Solan, India
ruchi.verma@juit.ac.in

Abstract. To maintain a promising status of global food security, it is imperative to strike a congruous balance between the estimated alarming growth in the global population and the expected agricultural yield to cater to their needs appropriately. An agreeable balance has not been acquired in this respect which could be the cause of the origin of food crisis across the world. Therefore it is crucial to prevent any direct or indirect factors causing this. Proper growth of plants and protection against diseases is a very instrumental factor towards meeting the quality and quantity of food requirements globally. Deep learning Methods have gained successful results in the spheres of image processing and pattern recognition. We have made an effort in implementing the methods of deep learning for analyzing leaves of plants for prediction and detection of any diseases. Here, we have considered two majorly grown crops in Himachal Pradesh i.e. tomato and potato, for performing various experiments. In our result analysis, we have achieved an accuracy of 96.24% while identifying the diseases in the leaves.

Keywords: Leaf disease · Deep learning · DenseNet · Algorithm · Plants · Detection

1 Introduction

Global food safety and it's requirement is among the most questioned issue all across the globe. According to UN published article of UN by John Holmes [5] more than 25,000 people including children's die because of hunger. Around 854 million people are undernourished globally, and exponential increase in food prices may drive another 100 million people into hunger and poverty. And one of the leading factor for food crisis is plant diseases and pests which often threatens the accessibility of plants for consumption. According to DM Rizzo [9] Yield losses of important staple crops can go up to 30% globally. Plant diseases have significantly affected agricultural fields and crop production worldwide. Due to the rapid increase in world population demands for foods increasing exponentially. In order to meet the demands crops need to be produced significantly on a large scale, but due to changing weather conditions, chemicals, pesticides, etc. are slowing the process of crop production at a large scale.

© Springer Nature Switzerland AG 2022
A. Dev et al. (Eds.): AIST 2021, CCIS 1546, pp. 500–511, 2022.
https://doi.org/10.1007/978-3-030-95711-7_42

Detection of diseases in plants has been a very subjective process. To prevail over this issue, swift and effectual methods need to be discovered. Image based automated systems are proving to contribute very constructively in the agricultural domain. In this paper, we have proposed a deep learning based model that helps in identification and prediction of diseases in Tomato and Potato plants, by predicting the probability of occurrence of a particular disease in the plant. We have collected the dataset form plant village dataset available. The given dataset contains the various classes of unhealthy and healthy plants in order to calculate the accuracy. We have studied the patterns in the leaves of plants through the healthy set and unhealthy set of plants to understand the minute patterns that could identify the diseased plant at an early stage. In the proposed model, we have used the DenseNet-121 and achieved the accuracy of 96.24% on tomato and potato plants.

2 Literature Survey

Here, we have studied the patterns in the leaves with the help of DenseNet 121 a deep learning model that helped us to classify leaves as diseased or healthy. R. Sujatha et al. [14] have done a comparison of the ML and DL techniques of citrus plants. The ML methods used in this performance analysis are Support Vector Machine, Random Forest, Stochastic Gradient Descent and the DL methods used are Inception V3, VGG -16 and VGG -19. The analysis led to the results that VGG-16's performance was the highest in CA and RF records. In [6] many experiments and analysis have been done to detect diseases on banana leaves by implementing convolution neural networks. The accuracy of the various deep learning approaches has been compared using varied patterns of plant leaf images. Techniques like segmentation features, extraction and classification are used to achieve the objective. In a study [1], the success of Efficient Net Deep Learning Architecture was measured against the results accomplished by the advanced CNN architectures. The architecture taken for the comparative analysis were Alex Net, Res Net 50, VGG16 and Inception V3. To achieve better accuracy the original and the augmented version of the plant village dataset was used. The accuracy achieved by the B4 and B5 model was higher for both the original and augmented dataset. In [10], the CNN model was trained to detect the Cassava diseases by studying its plant leaves. The major challenges faced in this study were the small size of the dataset and the asymmetry towards CMD Cassava Mosaic Disease and CBB (Cassava Brown Streak Virus Disease virus Disease) classes. It was brought to light that the efficiency of the model performance could be enhanced by increasing the size of the images, SMOTE and some other parameters [7]. Introduces the concept of IOT innovation in agriculture. A novel IOT based plant detection technique has been proposed to contribute to the agricultural sector. The plant disease is detected with the help of the proposed SCA based RIDE NN optimizer [3] highlights the utility of deep learning methods and computer vision in agriculture and application for the plant disease detection using image detection techniques. A classification framework is proposed where the model is applied on reconstructed images after applying LAPLACIAN and SOBEL filter to the captured image in RGB format. Diseases like Anthracnose, Algal leaf and others are identified in the guava plant using convolution neural networks in [13]. The model developed is trained on a dataset created with sample images of leaves from neighboring regions. In study of the proposed work of Prajwala TM [15] was to find a solution to a problem disease identification in tomato leaf using the easiest approach while using minimal computational resources to get the results. Research study by X.E.Pantazi [8] gave us highlights that how local binary pattern of diseased leaves can be used to identify the condition of a plant.

An image based classification approach for rice plant disease detection has been proposed in [12]. Color has been used as a major determinant to identify the disease. Performance of seven classifiers have been compared achieving an accuracy of 94.65% by analyzing 14 color spaces and extracting four features per color to leading to 172 feature analysis. In [4] a Bayesian learning technique is has been used to establish a probabilistic programming approach with uncertainty taken as a misclassification measurement. It also proximate the posterior density and calibrates the uncertainty of the predictions. As per a survey done in deep learning in precision agriculture it was evaluated that the deep learning models surpasses the traditional machine learning models in performance. It was concluded that deep learning hugely promotes precision agriculture and autonomous systems as ace technologies for the future of the food industry. Melike Sardogan [11] cited that the early stage detection of diseases in plant is important in agricultural fields for an efficient yield. The late blight, bacterial spot, yellow curved leaf and septoria leaf spot diseases affect the quality of tomato crops. In the paper by Gittaly Dhingra [2], we found a comprehensive study of disease detection and classification of leafs using different methods of image processing.

3   Model Description

As we know Deep Learning Techniques are more efficient than Machine Learning Models, because Deep Learning Algorithms are optimized and are able to solve complex problems, they can easily detect the hidden patterns in a dataset by themselves, and hence they compute the result accordingly which make them more efficient. DenseNet is one of latest discoveries in Deep learning used for recognition of visual objects. There is a lot of similarity between ResNet and DenseNet, the only fundamental difference being that ResNet merges the output of previous layers with upcoming layers using additive method, while DenseNet concatenates it. DenseNet also improves the vanishing gradient in a very dense neural networks. DenseNet also known as Densely Connected Convolutional Networks, is a network widely used for visual object recognition. Densenet is a convolutional nueral network which mainly comprises of dense blocks and transition layers. A DenseBlock is composed of several convolutional blocks. These blocks utilize the same number of output channels. Each layer is connected to every other layer in a feed forward fashion. Some of the glaring advantages of

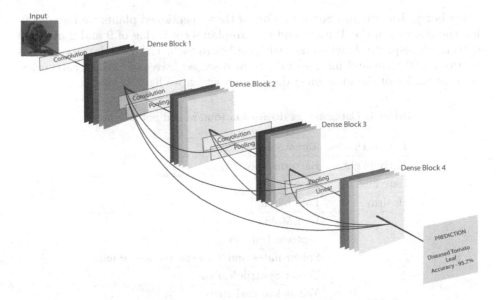

Fig. 1. DenseNet Architecture showing a 4 layered dense block

DenseNet Model are that it bolsters features propagation, enables feature reuse and minimizes the parameters.

From Fig. 1, we can see that the output of previous layer is acting as an input for upcoming layers by using Composite operation which consists of pooling layer, convolution layer, batch normalization and non-linear activation layer. DenseNet-121 is a version of DenseNet and it is calculated as follows:

- 5-Convolution and pooling layers
- 2-DenseBlock (of dim 1×1 and 3×3)
- 1-Classification Layer (16)
- 3-Transition layers (6,12,24)

DenseNet-121 = 5 + (6 + 12 + 24 + 16) * 2 = 121

In Dense block there are different number of filters have the same dimension within the block. Classification Layer accepts the feature maps of all layers to perform classification in the given network. In our DenseNet model we have used the Input Size of 64, Dropout of 0.7 activation function as softplus and sigmoid in inner and output layer respectively. The model is optimized using Adam optimizer with a learning rate of 0.002. The model is fitted on batches with Real-time data augmentation having random rotations, random horizontal/vertical shifts, random zoom and random flips.

4   Dataset Description

Plant village Dataset consists of Images of various plant leaves named Blueberry, Cherry, Apple, Orange, Peach, Pepper, Corn, Grape, Potato, Squash,

Strawberry, Tomato and Soybean. Out of these mentioned plants we have studied the diseases in the Tomato and Potato plants consisting of 9 and 2 diseased sub classes respectively with one healthy subclass each. The total dataset consists of around 20 thousand images of different diseased leaves of various categories. Sub categories of the mentioned diseases on which we have worked are:

Table 1. Categories of diseases in tomato and potato plants.

Potato Disease	Tomato disease
Early blight	Bacterial spot
Late blight	Early blight
Healthy	Late blight
	Leaf Mold
	Septoria leaf spot
	Spider mites and Two spotted spider mite
	Target Spotria leaf spot
	Yellow leaf curl virus
	Mosaic virus
	Healthy

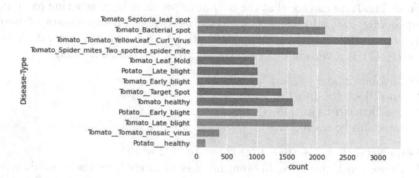

Fig. 2. Distribution of dataset across each category

5   Preprocessing Data

Preprocessing is one of the most important and useful method to ensure enhanced performance of the model. It involves data cleaning, data transformation and data reduction. We have used normalization technique to enhance the efficiency of our model. We normalized the dataset dividing it by 255, which resulted in improved performance of activation functions that leads to easy identification of local or global minimum by cost function.

Fig. 3. Sample images of leaves taken from dataset

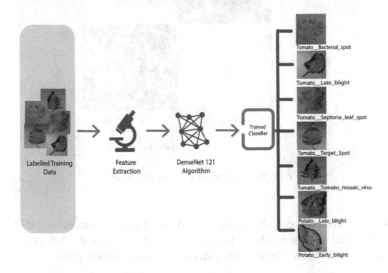

Fig. 4. Workflow of disease detection in tomato and potato plants

---

Algorithm 1: Algorithm used to detect diseased plants

Input   : D_{name} ⟵ Disease name
              D_{id} ⟵ Disease id
              D_{type} ⟵ Disease type
Output: D_{pred} ⟵ Disease Predicted
BEGIN;
1. train ⟵ data trained with random seed of 42 having D_{name}, D_{id}, D_{type}
2. X_{train} ⟵ normalized train data having columns Disease type, Disease name
3. Y_{train} ⟵ normalized train data having column Disease id
4. model$_{DenseNet121}$ ⟵ Created DenseNet121 model with adam optimizer of lr=0.0002
5. fit model$_{DenseNet121}$ with X_{train}
END;
BEGIN RESULTS ;
6. D_{pred}=Y_{pred} ⟵ model$_{DenseNet121}$.preidct($X_{validate}$)
END;

---

6   Result

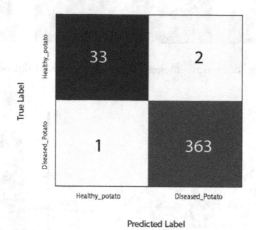

Fig. 5. Confusion matrix for potato

Confusion matrix in Fig. 5 shows how the data of potato leaves is classified. The leading diagonal elements show the correctly classified data for potato, while values above and below the diagonal denote miss-classified data.

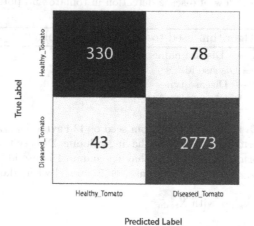

Fig. 6. Confusion matrix for tomato

Confusion matrix in Fig. 6 shows how data of tomato leaves is classified. It can be clearly seen that miss-classified data are more in tomato which is equal to the sum of 78 miss-classified diseased and 43 miss-classified healthy tomato leaves .

Figure 5 and Fig. 6 depict how our trained model accurately identifies whether a given potato and tomato plant is healthy or diseased. In Fig. 5 we can see how our model correctly identified 33 potato leaves as healthy and 363 potato leaves diseased. It also erroneously identified one healthy leaf as a diseased leaf and two diseased leaves as healthy leaves. Similarly, in the tomato dataset the model correctly identified 330 healthy leaves and 2773 unhealthy leaves, the rest were identified incorrectly. We can see that the accuracy achieved for disease detection in potato plant is more than in the tomato plant because the sum of TP and TN values is very large, while the sum of FP and FN values is relatively small .Therefore the accuracy achieved for the potato plant is 99.24% and for Tomato plant the FP and FN are relatively larger resulting in accuracy of 96.24%

Fig. 7. Healthy leaves

The proposed model helps in identification of disease in plants especially in Tomato and Potato plants, which reveals the probability of occurrence of the particular disease a plant is suffering from. We have used Densenet121 and in our training model and have achieved 96% of accuracy. For further analysis, we can create some defensive mechanism against the occurrence of the diseases which can be of utility in the agricultural sector.

Fig. 8. Infected leaves

Performance matrix helps us decide the quality of prepared model, it shows how our test dataset is distributed across four different sections called False positive(FP), False Negative(FN), True Positive(TN) and True Negative(TN). The following values help us calculate the accuracy, precisions and F1 score of our models as shown below.

$$Accuray = \frac{TP + TN}{TP + TN + FP + FN} \tag{1}$$

$$Precision = \frac{TP}{(TP + FP)} \tag{2}$$

$$Recall = \frac{TP}{(TP + FN)} \tag{3}$$

$$F1Score = \frac{2 * TP}{(2 * TP + FP + FN)} \tag{4}$$

Calculating Accuracy using Confusion Matrix for Tomato and Potato:

$$TomatoAccuracy = \frac{(330 + 2773)}{(330 + 2773 + 43 + 78)} = 0.9624$$

$$PotatoAccuracy = \frac{(33 + 363)}{(33 + 363 + 2 + 1)} = 0.9924$$

Calculating Precision using Confusion Matrix for Tomato and Potato:

$$TomatoPrecision = \frac{(330)}{(330 + 78)} = 0.8088$$

$$PotatoPrecision = \frac{(33)}{(33 + 2)} = 0.9429$$

Here precision is the ratio of correctly predicted positive data Calculating Recall using Confusion Matrix for Tomato and Potato:

$$TomatoRecall = \frac{(330)}{(330 + 43)} = 0.8847$$

$$PotatoRecall = \frac{(33)}{(33 + 1)} = 0.9705$$

Calculating Accuracy using Confusion Matrix for Tomato and Potato:

$$TomatoF1Score = \frac{(2 * 330)}{(2 * 330 + 43 + 78)} = 0.8450$$

$$PotatoF1Score = \frac{(2 * 33)}{(2 * 33 + 2 + 1)} = 0.9565$$

It can be clearly seen that model accurately predicts the diseased category in plants, F1 score for Potato is high as compared to Tomato, and it clearly signifies that our model more accurately identifies the diseases in Potato plants.

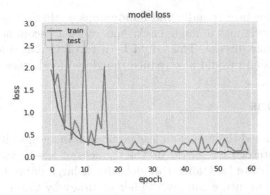

Fig. 9. Loss encountered as compared to test and train data after each epoch

Fig. 9 and Fig. 10 clearly signify the loss and accuracy achieved respectively, while training the models after each epoch. We can see that at the initial stage of training the model from 0–20 epoch, due to lots of noise and outliers, loss was varying and was relatively high as compared to latter part i.e. from 20–60 epochs. We know that the model accuracy is inversely dependent on model loss, therefore in the initial part, loss was higher and as a result accuracy was low as compared to latter.

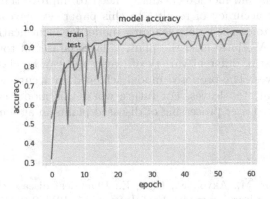

Fig. 10. Model accuracy after each epoch when compared between train and test data

7 Future Work

World is emerging in the era of AI, as a result need of such algorithms and models are required for setting up a balanced workflow of ecosystem. Through this paper we planned to create a defensive mechanism for diseased plants by training the dataset on different deep learning models. In future there is high chances that we can create some user friendly and handy apps so that anyone can detect the diseased plants with just a single click, and can get recommendations how to treat the particular disease. This could be a revolutionary tool for farmers in agricultural fields and would also reduce the global food crisis at some extent.

8   Limitations

Since we have trained the model on less number of images, so it is expected that for very large dataset there could be the chances of less accuracy, which could be overcome in future by training model with a large dataset. There could be also chances that in future can give higher accuracy by tuning the parameters.

9   Conclusion

Artificial Intelligence(AI) has revolutionized the world with it's predictive capability of crucial events at remarkable accuracy. Majorly Researchers are focusing on solving the issues that could be the possible cause of crisis globally, and one such issue is global food safety and security. AI in agriculture has enabled many ways in order to prevent food crisis, and one of it's aspect is early detection of diseases in plants, so that an optimal approach is created using results of deep learning methods for creating a defensive mechanism against diseased plants. With time models and methods available need to improve the decision-making power for higher accuracy of results. In this paper, we have used Dense Net-121 architecture to create a deep learning model for identification of diseases in the plant leaves. We have used the plant village dataset of tomato and potato leaves that consist of different variety of leaves and can be classified as healthy or unhealthy leaves. The proposed model achieved an accuracy of 96.24% while identifying the infected leaves. For future work, this model can be integrated with hardware for faster processing of diseased plants in agricultural fields.

References

1. Atila, Ü., Uçar, M., Akyol, K., Uçar, E.: Plant leaf disease classification using efficientnet deep learning model. Ecol. Inform. **61**, 101182 (2021)
2. Dhingra, G., Kumar, V., Joshi, H.D.: Study of digital image processing techniques for leaf disease detection and classification. Multimedia Tools Appl. **77**(15), 19951–20000 (2017). https://doi.org/10.1007/s11042-017-5445-8
3. Francis, M., Deisy, C.: Mathematical and visual understanding of a deep learning model towards m-agriculture for disease diagnosis. Arch. Comput. Meth. Eng. **28**(3), 1129–1145 (2021)
4. Hernández, S., Lopez, J.L.: Uncertainty quantification for plant disease detection using Bayesian deep learning. Appl. Soft Comput. **96**, 106597 (2020)
5. Holmes, J.: Losing 25,000 to hunger every day. UN Chronicle **45**(3), 14–20 (2009)

6. Jogekar, R.N., Tiwari, N.: A review of deep learning techniques for identification and diagnosis of plant leaf disease. In: Zhang, Y.-D., Senjyu, T., SO–IN, C., Joshi, A. (eds.) Smart Trends in Computing and Communications: Proceedings of Smart-Com 2020. SIST, vol. 182, pp. 435–441. Springer, Singapore (2021). https://doi.org/10.1007/978-981-15-5224-3_43

7. Mishra, M., Choudhury, P., Pati, B.: Modified ride-NN optimizer for the IoT based plant disease detection. J. Ambient Intell. Humanized Comput. **12**, 691–703 (2021)

8. Pantazi, X.E., Moshou, D., Tamouridou, A.A.: Automated leaf disease detection in different crop species through image features analysis and one class classifiers. Comput. Electron. Agri. **156**, 96–104 (2019)

9. Rizzo, D.M., Lichtveld, M., Mazet, J.A., Togami, E., Miller, S.A.: Plant health and its effects on food safety and security in a one health framework: four case studies. One Health outlook **3**(1), 1–9 (2021)

10. Sambasivam, G., Opiyo, G.D.: A predictive machine learning application in agriculture: Cassava disease detection and classification with imbalanced dataset using convolutional neural networks. Egypt. Inform. J. **22**(1), 27–34 (2021)

11. Sardogan, M., Tuncer, A., Ozen, Y.: Plant leaf disease detection and classification based on CNN with LVQ algorithm. In: 2018 3rd International Conference on Computer Science and Engineering (UBMK), pp. 382–385. IEEE (2018)

12. Shrivastava, V.K., Pradhan, M.K.: Rice plant disease classification using color features: a machine learning paradigm. J. Plant Pathol. **103**(1), 17–26 (2020). https://doi.org/10.1007/s42161-020-00683-3

13. Srinivas, B., Satheesh, P., Rama Santosh Naidu, P., Neelima, U.: Prediction of guava plant diseases using deep learning. In: Kumar, A., Mozar, S. (eds.) ICCCE 2020. LNEE, vol. 698, pp. 1495–1505. Springer, Singapore (2021). https://doi.org/10.1007/978-981-15-7961-5_135

14. Sujatha, R., Chatterjee, J.M., Jhanjhi, N., Brohi, S.N.: Performance of deep learning vs machine learning in plant leaf disease detection. Microprocess. Microsyst. **80**, 103615 (2021)

15. Tm, P., Pranathi, A., SaiAshritha, K., Chittaragi, N.B., Koolagudi, S.G.: Tomato leaf disease detection using convolutional neural networks. In: 2018 Eleventh International Conference on Contemporary Computing (IC3), pp. 1–5. IEEE (2018)

A Pilot Study on FoG Prediction Using Machine Learning for Rehabilitation

Kartik Kharbanda and Chandra Prakash[(✉)]

National Institute of Technology, Delhi 110040, India
{191220027,cprakash}@nitdelhi.ac.in

Abstract. Walking has a significant impact on one's quality of life. Freezing of Gait (FoG) is a typical symptom of Parkinson's disease (PD). FoG is characterised by quick and abrupt transient falls, as a result of which the patient's mobility is limited and their independence is lost. Thus, early detection of FoG in PD patients is necessary for diagnosis and rehabilitation. The present strategies for early detection of FoG are ineffective and have a low success rate. This study illustrates the comparative analysis of ML techniques (K Nearest Neighbors (KNN), Decision Trees, Random Forest, Support Vector Classifier (SVC), and Ada Boost Classifier), using time and statistical features to perform detection and prediction tasks on the publicly available DaphNet database. FoG prediction is highly patient dependent and achieved a peak F1 - score of 80% for one of the patients. The paper also present a combined analysis of all the patients which may aid in designing wearable sensors for detection. This system detects FoG with a precision value of about 81%.

Keywords: Freezing of Gait (FoG) · Machine learning techniques · Prediction · Detection · Parkinson's Disease

1 Introduction

Freezing of gait is one of the most disturbing repercussions of Parkinson's Disease (PD). About 50% of patients in the advanced stages of the PD are affected by the freezing of gait (FoG) symptom [1,2]. 10% of PD patients show mild symptoms and 80% of those severely affected regularly experience freezing. During FoG, the patient often perceives the inability to continue with motion. Patients, who experience FoG, report that during the freezing episode their feet are inexplicably glued to the ground [2,3] and patients feel an abrupt inability to practice any locomotion for a brief period of time. Freezing of Gait is described as the gait disturbance, irregular walking with a "sudden and transient" nature which may occur in patients suffering from Parkinson Disease and is seriously incapacitating. FoG episodes increase the risk of falls, and have an undesirable impact on the quality of life, and due to these scenarios in the worst case, it may lead to the death of a patient.

Health care professionals had developed methods to overcome such aforementioned freezing attacks (such as moving forward to a command, walking to a

© Springer Nature Switzerland AG 2022
A. Dev et al. (Eds.): AIST 2021, CCIS 1546, pp. 512–529, 2022.
https://doi.org/10.1007/978-3-030-95711-7_43

beat, and shifting body weight) For this reason, observing the spatial-temporal gait parameters is essential. There is no dispassionate test, like a bio-marker, for Parkinson's disease [4].

Parkinson's Disease is typically a chronic neuro-degenerative disorder distinguished by the factor of freezing of Gait. We comprehend Parkinson's disease to be disarray of the central nervous system that results from the deficit of cells across different sections of the brain, which includes a structure called the substantia nigra. The cells of substantia nigra produce dopamine, a chemical messenger responsible for the transmission of signals in the brain that facilitates the movement. Low levels of dopamine results in the firing of neurons without normal control, which results in patients inability to direct or control their movement [5].

FoG (Freezing of Gait) is a very common symptom of Parkinson Disease as well as some high-level gait disorders. It mostly happens in higher stages of Parkinson's Disease. Such episodes of freezing show a special form of disturbance in movement which can only be seen in PD. During gait, freezing may occur at times while talking, repetitive movement such as handwriting. It can be considered as one of the most disabling and at the very least understood symptoms found in PD patients and is generally observed in the advanced or end stage of the illness. Men experience this disease more frequently than women, especially those who experience tremor symptoms. It is one of the major symptom in PD patients and thus dependent on others for the day to day work [10].

In this neurological Disorder, Parkinson's disease, there is a treatment that provides indicative benefit but no contemporary treatment has been proven to impede disease progression. Therefore the need of an hour is to assess the ability of day today tasks and symptotic response to medication. Proper evaluation is required for managing FoG and to assign participants in FoG research. In the medical field, the initial phase of diagnosis is to physically examine the patient and assigning grade to his postural and gait activity. The Freezing of Gait cannot be predicted easily as it is the sudden resistant towards the forward progression of gait. Therefore the detection of FoG can be done; it can help in rehabilitation or treatment. Prediction of freezing of Gait(FoG) that is pre-FoG(knowing at which instance FoG is going to happen) is more important as it proactively provides the precaution for falling. Parkinson is such a chronic neuro-degenerative disorder that gets worse by time, so proper monitoring is required for analyzing the gait pattern and parameters for its detection. Patients suffering from Parkinson's Disease are monitored either by placing sensors on their body parts, or they are observed under an environment having 2-D and 3-D Cameras [11].

There are two types of approaches for detection of FoG using Machine Learning techniques as illustrated in Fig. 1. The first one is vision based where 2-D and 3-D cameras are used to capture the gait patterns and applying Machine Learning techniques on the same and then interpreting FoG [12]. On the other hand, the next approach is a wearable assistant in which a device having sensors are placed on some body parts of the patients as in accelerometers to measure the frequency of patient's gait movements.

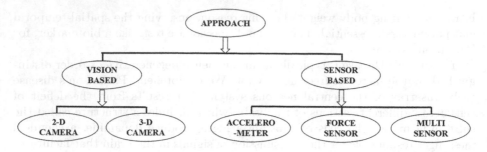

Fig. 1. Approach for Detection of FoG Rehabiliation

The existing work based on different approaches techniques and machine learning techniques with the input used along with data-set used in FoG are summarized in a Table 1.

Vision Based: In Vision based or Camera-based approach, the gait analysis is performed without any physical contact with wearable devices. Cameras are placed at fixed locations in the environment and are used for capturing the input image. To identify human gestures, images are analyzed to produce visual features which can be used to interpret human activity. In this approach, the video can be recorded from 2d and 3d cameras, analyzing such videos to interpret the outputs [13]. Vision-Based approach is the technique in which monitoring is done manually, the researchers used this approach to find the probability of occurrence of FoG. The three main tasks of the Vision system:
a) Tracking module: Tracking and identification of the patient.
b) Scene Model module: observed scene automatic analysis.
c) Context Interpretation module: Inference on how GPS location of the user affects the FoG state of the user.

Sensor Based: A model wearable body sensor network constitutes several types of bio medical gateway and sensors (example, smart phones) that can club the data from devices like sensors and the data gets transmitted to remote control servers. There are many devices which have sensors that are placed on the body to measure the body movements such as accelerometers, gyroscopes, etc. Wearable devices embedded with body sensor networks to measure the body movements are used. In Freezing of Gait Detection, the existing work which used such an approach is as follows. Researchers have worked in the detection of Freezing of Gait using acceleration sensors on the body to measure body motion and reaction of Parkinson's Disease patients. They measure the signals from the most commonly used accelerometers and gyroscopes. In existing works, the researchers extract a standard feature extracted from raw signals captured by accelerometers termed as freezing index(FI) [11,14–16]. Then signals are processed using fast Fourier transform(FFT) to detect FoG. In all these existing work, the main goal was to attain early detection of Freezing of Gait from brain activity using frequency bands.

For detecting the FoG, different approaches are that some observers evaluate the forces experienced by PD patients under their feet. It can be done by using force sensing resistors [17].

Researchers used the sensor based approach for monitoring the Parkinson's Patients [6,29]. The two of them uses both wearable, wireless, small scale tri-axial accelerometer, and electromyographic sensor outcomes as the input characteristics of a known dynamic neural network to observe FoG instances. Parkinson's Disease patients executed their daily life activity by wearing these sensor devices on their body. The signals captured by these sensors are further used in algorithms to give output.

One of the main reasons for utilizing Machine Learning techniques for detecting and predicting FoG is to aid patients because in majority of the cases, pharmacological treatment proves ineffective. This treatment is not only difficult to achieve, it is also ineffective in alleviating FoG. Levodopa, a dopamine precursor, is often used in the management of Parkinson's disease, sometimes in combination with other drugs. Even though Levodopa is the most effective treatment against PD, it only has short term gains as the body becomes immune and develops "dopa resistant" motor signs [2]. These problems are very difficult to prevent. Other complications include nausea and vomiting. It is clear that this treatment is not entirely effective and needs to be improved further so that it can be used in combination with other therapeutic techniques to help patients deal with FoG and soothe their symptoms and drastically improve their mobility and locomotory skills.

ML techniques help us to detect FoG and classify PD patients as freezers and non-freezers with classification algorithms. The primary concern for such a diagnosis is to prevent falling. These falls can be controlled by giving rhythmic sounds in the patient's ear that eventually helps them to maintain balance and makes them context-aware. In [14], window length was set to 1s (64 samples) with 0.25s of overlap (16 samples) empirically and decision tree was implemented. In [21], SVM techniques was applied on the six input features extracted from a wireless gait analysis sensor (WGAS) system. The system specificity and sensitivity was 99.5 % and 97.0% respectively. In [14] Mazilu et al. applied PCA on 192-dimensional features. Zia et al. [20] and Vishwas G et al. [18] explore the deep recurrent neural network (RNN) and Long Short-Term Memory networks (LSTMs) respectively to predict FoG on the Daphent Freezing of Gait dataset. LSTM outperform RNN by 10%.

The main idea for the detection of freezing of gait involves the approach that is vision based or sensor based in data collection for gait analysis in PD patients. If Sensor approach is used, then signals collected by accelerometers are quite noisy, so filtering is essential. It can be done either by Fast Fourier transform (FFT) or wavelet filter so after applying feasible machine learning classification algorithm the PD patients can be classified as freezer or non- freezer.

Table 1. Machine Learning techniques used in FoG

Year	M.L technique	Approach	Data-set	Features	Accuracy	Comment
2018 [18]	Sensor based	LSTM	Daphnet dataset	Accelerometers and gyroscopes	80–87%	
2018 [19]	Correlation	Sensor based		Spatio-temporal gait parameters of PD		study identifies quantitative gait parameters differences in APD and IPD patients.
2016 [20]	Sensor based	RNN	Daphnet dataset	Accelerometers and gyroscopes	61–68%	
2015 [21]	Support Vector Machine classifier(SVM)	sensor based		Accelerometers and gyroscopes	Specificity-99.5% and sensitivity 97.05%	Six features were detected for fall classification using SVM
2013 [14]	Decision Tree	Sensor based	Daphnet dataset ten patients one healthy	Accelerometers and gyroscopes		Detection and prediction of FoG using feature extraction.
2013 [22]	Naive Baye's, Decision Trees, Random Forest	Sensor based		Data from six accelerometers and two gyroscopes	Specificity - 98.7% and sensitivity - 81.4%	Automatic detection of FoG using four classifier algorithm.
2013 [23]		Vision based				A Review on four different models for FoG detection.
2012 [24]	Random Forest, Naive Baye's	Sensor based	Daphnet dataset	Accelerometers and gyroscopes	Specificity-95% and sensitivity-95%	Detection of FoG using smartphone and ML techniques.
2010 [25]	Linear model	Vision based	EMG of 25 PD patients (13-FoG, 12- without FoG	Gait Parameters		Altered activity of brain were shown in freezers involved in step amplitude.
2010 [11]	Moore machine	Sensor based	Daphnet dataset (10 patients 01 Healthy)	Accelerometers and gyroscopes	Specificity - 81.6% and Sensitivity -73.1%	Model based .
2010 [26]	Decision Tree, Neural Network	Sensor based	Parkinson disease dataset		92.9% accuracy with neural networks	comparsion of classification algorithms in detection of parkinson disease
2004 [27]		Hybrid	Daphnet dataset (tenPd Patients one healthy)	Accelerometers and gyroscopes		Difference between falls and freezing.
2003 [28]	Matlab data analysis	Sensor based	two U-AMS on each ankle of 5 normal and 2 PD patients	Signals using U-AMS		Unconstrained- Activity Monitoring system(U-AMS)

Most of the research works focus on detection (FoG and No-FoG). FoG detection is a two class problem (Walk and FoG Class). while in this study the prediction of FoG has been explored, thus it is a three class problem (Pre-FoG, FoG, No-FoG). Making it a three class problem enhances the complexity of the task but predicting the onset of FoG before it occurs is an important task to aid patients.

2   Proposed Methodology for FoG Detection and Prediction

This study illustrates the comparative analysis of ML techniques (K Nearest Neighbors (KNN), Decision Trees, Random Forest, Support Vector Classifier (SVC), and Ada Boost Classifier), using time and statistical features to perform detection and prediction tasks.

The proposed methodology is shown in 2.

2.1   Dataset

There are limited datasets available for Freezing of gait. The dataset used for the experiment is the publicly available DaphNet dataset. DaphNet is a Future and

Emerging Technologies (FET) project supported by the European 6th Framework Program [11]. It contains records of 10 idiopathic PD patients (7 males, 3 females, 66.5 ± 4.8 years). In the experiment, three motion sensors were attached to the body of the patient. The first sensor was attached to the ankle, the second one was attached to the thigh while the last sensor was attached to the torso of the patient. Each patient had to perform three basic tasks [3]: 1. Walk in a straight line including several back and forth 180-degrees turns. 2. Random walking in a free space including several 360-degree turns, 3. Imitating the walking patterns of normal human and simulating daily walking patterns.

The results obtained from the DaphNet experiment are as follows: 1. Eight of the ten patients exhibited FoG conditions while the remaining two patients did not. 2. The dataset contains a video recording of about 8 h 2 0 min consisting of about 237 FoG episodes which were detected by the recording device. 3. The length of FoG episodes ranged from 0.5 to 40.5 s (mean 7.3 s [S.D. 6.7 s]). 4. 50% of the FoG episodes lasted less than 5.4 s and majority of them were less than 20 s long.

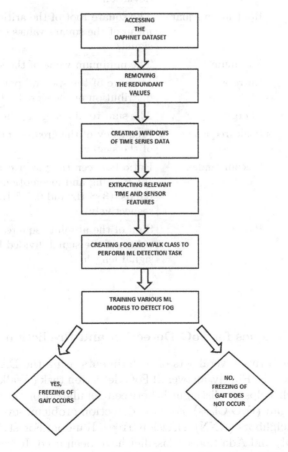

Fig. 2. Flow diagram for detection and prediction of freezing of Gait using machine learning technique

2.2   Feature Selection

For the purpose of our experiment, we extract several features from the dataset as shown in Table 2. These features are statistically significant and some of them can also be retrieved from the sensor. For extracting the features, the window length was set to 1 s and each window contained 64 samples. There is no overlap between any samples. Hence, distinct windows of length 1s with absolutely no overlap are generated.

Table 2. Extracted features from the DaphNet dataset

Feature type	Feature	Description
Time	Mean	Average value of the signal.
Time	Standard deviation	It is a measure of how much the signal fluctuates/varies from the mean.
Time	Variance	It is the squared value of standard deviation.
Time	Root mean square	The square root of the arithmetic mean of the square values of the signal.
Time	Minimum	The minimum value of the signal
Sensor	Entropy	Measure of the spectral power distribution of the signal.
Sensor	Energy	The sum total energy of the signal
Sensor	Peak frequency	Frequency of the greatest amplitude of the system.
Sensor	Freezing index	Ratio between the power contained in the freezing and locomotion frequency bands. (3–8 Hz and 0.5–3 Hz respectively)
Sensor	Power	Sum of the absolute squares of the values of the signal divided by the signal length.

2.3   ML Techniques for FoG Detection and Prediction

The research performs several sets of experiments using the DAPHNet dataset described previously. Firstly, an overall FoG detection task (Walk and FoG class) is created which helps us distinguish between regular locomotion (Walk Class) and freezing of gait (FoG Class). For FoG detection problem, several models such as K Nearest Neighbors (KNN), Decision Trees, Random Forest, Support Vector Machines (SVM) and Ada Boost Classifier have been used. It was observed that

Random Forests significantly outperform the other machine learning algorithms and display a significant recall value of 96% in gait detection.

Next, the paper presents an individual patient analysis for a 3 class problem (Walk, PreFoG, FoG) in which it is shown how FoG prediction is highly patient dependent. For this prediction task, Decision Trees are used as our base model for performing our experiment.

For prediction problem, (3 classes) Decision Trees (DT) are used to perform our evaluations while 5 models mentioned above for detection task (2 classes).

K Nearest Neighbors (KNN): KNN is a simple algorithm which is established on the mere principle that similar things or things which are related to each other exist in close proximity to each other. This algorithm is extensively used in supervised learning problems. It simply works by finding 'K' data values close to each other. By choosing the right value of K, this algorithm can be highly optimized to give efficient results.

Decision Trees: For classification and regression problems, decision trees can be used. Decision tress often copies the thinking capability of a human level, so it's not that much complex to expedite the data and interpret the proper observations. The functionality of complex algorithms such as SVM, NN is easily interpreted by decision tree classifier. In a decision tree, every node shows a feature or an attribute; every branch indicates a decision and each leaf interprets to a decision or labelled class.

Random Forest: Random forests constitute what is known as, ensemble learning technique. They are simply a combination of a large number of decision trees. Random forests tend to be highly efficient in dealing with missing values. For training a random forest model, data is fed to numerous decision trees and the output of each tree is present at the leaf node. Deciding the right output is done by voting system. The output of a random forest model is the majority of the output given by each decision tree.

Support Vector Machine (SVM): Support Vector Machines are based on a very simple principle. The idea is to arrange the data in a N-dimensional hyperplane where N represents the number of features and distinctly classifying the points on it. With the help of the hyper-plane, data points lying on either sides belong to different labelled classes.

Ada Boost Classifier: Ada Boost Classifiers or Adaptive Boosting Classifiers also follow the idea of ensemble learning. In this technique, the main principle is to combine several weaker models which attempt to improve the errors of the previous models by adding subsequent weaker models. With the help of this boosting technique, over fitting can be avoided by a great extent.

3 Result and Discussion

The research presents its results in terms of F1-scores, recall values for each patients varying with the number of features and tries to showcase the ideal number of features to be selected by displaying a mean comparison chart computed through mean of the patients.

The top ranked features are illustrated in Table 3

Table 3. The top ranked features

Feature rank	Feature	Sensor	Axis
1, 2, 3	Mean	Ankle	X, Y, Z
4, 5, 6	Mean	Thigh	X, Y, Z
7, 8, 9	STD	Ankle	X, Y, Z
10, 11, 12	STD	Thigh	X, Y, Z
13, 14, 15	Variance	Ankle	X, Y, Z
16, 17, 18	Variance	Thigh	X, Y, Z
19, 20, 21	RMS	Ankle	X, Y, Z
22, 23, 24	RMS	Thigh	X, Y, Z
25, 26, 27	Minimum	Ankle	X, Y, Z
28, 29 , 30	Minimum	Thigh	X, Y, Z
31, 32, 33	Entropy	Ankle	X, Y, Z
34, 35, 36	Entropy	Thigh	X, Y, Z
37, 38, 39	Entropy	Torso	X, Y, Z
40, 41, 42	Energy	Thigh	X, Y, Z
43, 44, 45	Energy	Ankle	X, Y, Z
46, 47, 48	Energy	Torso	X, Y, Z

For performing each of the above mentioned experiments, the number of features are varied from 5 to 45 with a increment of 5 features each time. Since our evaluations are performed on a patient dependent basis, it is observed that the WALK class was highly over-represented in the dataset [4]. To overcome this obstacle, th research chose to balance the dataset by selecting the size of walk class as n times the size of FoG where, n = 1.5, as illustrated in following equation.

$$sizeofwalk = 1.5 * (SizeofFoG) \qquad (1)$$

3.1 FoG Detection

For detection being a two class problem, several machine learning algorithms are used and concluded that the best algorithms for this classification problem are Random Forests and Decision Trees in terms of performance. However, the model size of Random Forests is relatively higher when compared to others and is a trade-off for performance. We select top 50 features (from our list of features) with the help of recursive feature elimination for each of our model in order to optimize the model. We also normalize the data in each model. This lowers the redundancy of our data. The technique we use to normalize the data is illustrated in following equation.

$$X' = \frac{X - X_{MEAN}}{X_{STD}} \tag{2}$$

where:
N_{avg} = average number of pixels
N_{gray} = number of gray level in contextual region
N_{CR-X_p} = number of pixels in X direction of contextual region
N_{CR-Y_p} = number of pixels in Y direction of contextual region

3.2 FoG Prediction

In FoG Prediction, we have consider three class (Walk, Pre-FoG and FoG). This section presents findings for each relevant patient record present in the dataset. The evaluation parameters considered are Accuracy, Recall and Precision and F1 score. Figure 3 present the accuracy, Recall and Precision .

The highest accuracy, recall and precision achieved by random forest as 92.67%, 96% and 96% respectively . The research concludes that preFoG detection is highly patient dependent and a maximum F1-score of 83% was observed for one of the patients who displayed enough gait deterioration. The recall values for prediction vary around the 50% mark as the different number of features used for evaluation are changed. In one particular case, a recall value of 100% was observed as illustrated in Figure 5(f). High F1 score is obtained when the no. of features selected are 15–25.

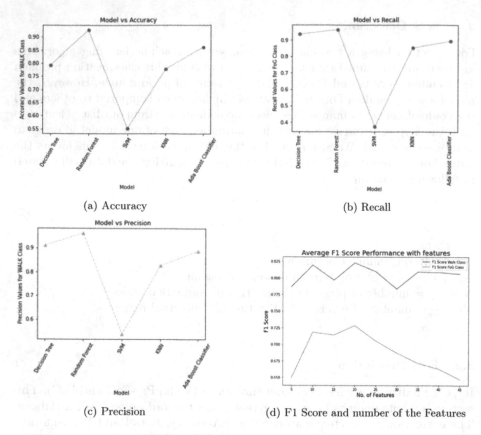

(a) Accuracy

(b) Recall

(c) Precision

(d) F1 Score and number of the Features

Fig. 3. Comparative analysis of the Decision Tree, Random Forest, SVM, KNN and Ada Boost Classifiers

Table 4 and 5 illustrates the output based on F1 and Recall or specificity respectively. Inferring from Table 4 and 5, patient S03R02 exhibited significant gait deterioration and achieved high F1 and Recall scores in FoG prediction. While a majority of the patients do not show preFoG detection, they exhibit high values (60% – 90%) of F1 and Recall Score in detecting the FoG Class as well as the Walk Class. A recall value of 100% was achieved for S07R02 when the number of features selected exceeded 20.

Summing up the individual patient analysis and producing an overall comparison, the research concludes that the ideal number of features for our 3-class problem vary in the range 15–25 since the average F1 scores for both FoG class and Walk class peak in this range. In order to support this observation, if we talk about one class:

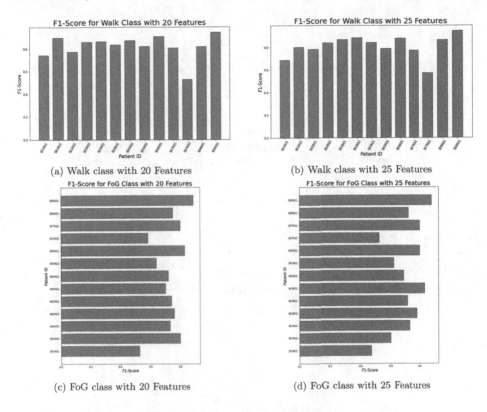

(a) Walk class with 20 Features

(b) Walk class with 25 Features

(c) FoG class with 20 Features

(d) FoG class with 25 Features

Fig. 4. F1 Score for each subject

Walk Class: By selecting number of features as 20 and 25, and observing the F1 Score for each patient, it was concluded that the results are promising with some patients exhibiting an F1-Score greater that 80% for both of the graphs as illustrated in Fig. 4(a) and (b) . The performance of our model the not vary much when the number of features are in this range but it is much superior to other number of features.

FoG Class : The research also focuses on the the F1 Score for each for another class: FoG Class In this evaluation , by selecting the same number of features and observing the scores with respect to each patient. Once again, several patients score a high F1-Score for FoG class as well is illustrated in Fig. 4(c) and (d) . The research concludes that by believe selecting our top 20–25 features envision great machine learning models with high metrics and great performance.

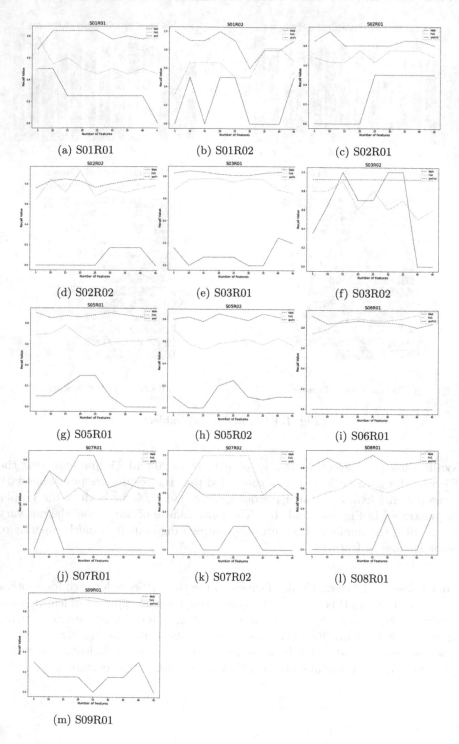

(a) S01R01

(b) S01R02

(c) S02R01

(d) S02R02

(e) S03R01

(f) S03R02

(g) S05R01

(h) S05R02

(i) S06R01

(j) S07R01

(k) S07R02

(l) S08R01

(m) S09R01

Fig. 5. Result of Recall score for subjects

Table 4. F1 output for walk, FoG and PreFoG CLASS

		5	10	15	20	25	30	35	40	45
WALK CLASS	S01R01	0.79	0.744	0.743	0.743	0.687	0.741	0.739	0.732	0.738
	S01R02	0.82	0.84	0.8	0.9	0.8	0.62	0.76	0.76	0.89
	S02R01	0.81	0.867	0.841	0.775	0.783	0.816	0.85	0.85	0.812
	S02R02	0.77	0.766	0.868	0.862	0.841	0.827	0.879	0.871	0.8
	S03R01	0.8	0.874	0.963	0.866	0.868	0.846	0.863	0.84	0.842
	S03R02	0.84	0.8849	0.867	0.837	0.885	0.873	0.891	0.823	0.891
	S05R01	0.85	0.853	0.753	0.875	0.842	0.844	0.845	0.841	0.869
	S05R02	0.83	0.787	0.75	0.821	0.787	0.763	0.83	0.814	0.779
	S06R01	0.88	0.845	0.89	0.911	0.88	0.887	0.883	0.867	0.873
	S07R01	0.64	0.77	0.64	0.81	0.772	0.65	0.708	0.692	0.662
	S07R02	0.55	0.666	0.53	0.53	0.57	0.61	0.537	0.666	0.54
	S08R01	0.76	0.825	0.82	0.82	0.867	0.782	0.813	0.834	0.856
	S09R01	0.89	0.93	0.947	0.947	0.947	0.93	0.925	0.925	0.93
FoG CLASS	S01R01	0.73	0.5	0.531	0.526	0.473	0.681	0.342	0.386	0.386
	S01R02	3.433	0.8	0.8	0.8	0.6	0.55	0.788	0.788	0.662
	S02R01	0.77	0.727	0.668	0.731	0.729	0.783	0.816	0.816	0.782
	S02R02	0.63	0.76	0.7	0.76	0.781	0.643	0.7	0.673	0.724
	S03R01	0.67	0.732	0.75	0.741	0.713	0.728	0.736	0.67	0.667
	S03R02	0.84	0.838	0.881	0.7	0.836	0.7	0.784	0.522	0.591
	S05R01	0.748	0.739	0.8	0.719	0.686	0.7	0.712	0.675	0.675
	S05R02	0.68	0.6	0.546	0.638	0.62	0.627	0.631	0.638	0.573
	S06R01	0.768	0.771	0.818	0.829	0.8	0.818	0.822	0.811	0.786
	S07R01	0.43	0.678	0.462	0.583	0.526	0.462	0.45	0.62	0.586
	S07R02	0.35	0.666	0.8	0.8	0.8	0.73	0.4	0.45	0.4
	S08R01	0.55	0.654	0.72	0.75	0.72	0.646	0.687	0.725	0.75
	S09R01	0.844	0.87	0.88	0.89	0.88	0.86	0.86	0.842	0.824
PreFoG CLASS	S01R01	0.5	0.57	0.2	0.2	0.2	0.19	0.18	0.25	0
	S01R02	0	0.4	0	0.5	0.5	0	0	0	0.5
	S02R01	0	0	0	0	0.2	0.25	0.25	0.25	0.2
	S02R02	0	0	0	0	0	0.225	0.175	0.225	0
	S03R01	0.157	0	0.075	0.1	0.075	0	0	0.25	0.2
	S03R02	0.5	0.8	0.9	0.7	0.7	0.9	0.9	0	0
	S05R01	0.1	0.075	0.175	0.25	0.2	0.1	0	0	0
	S05R02	0.1	0	0	0.2	0.2	0.1	0.1	0.1	0.1
	S06R01	0	0	0	0	0	0.4	0.4	0	0
	S07R01	0	0.225	0	0	0	0	0	0	0
	S07R02	0.3	0.325	0	0	0.325	0.325	0	0	0
	S08R01	0	0	0	0	0	0.25	0	0	0.25
	S09R01	0.25	0.15	0.125	0.175	0	0.15	0.175	0.275	0

Table 5. Recall output for walk, FoG and PreFoG CLASS

		5	10	15	20	25	30	35	40	45
WALK CLASS	S01R01	0.68	0.85	0.85	0.85	0.85	0.77	0.8	0.77	0.81
	S01R02	1	0.9	0.9	1	0.9	0.6	0.8	0.8	0.9
	S02R01	0.85	0.95	0.8	0.8	0.8	0.8	0.85	0.85	0.8
	S02R02	0.76	0.83	0.85	0.83	0.77	0.8	0.83	0.85	0.85
	S03R01	0.83	0.85	0.84	0.82	0.81	0.81	0.83	0.84	0.85
	S03R02	0.92	0.92	0.92	0.92	0.92	0.92	0.92	0.92	0.92
	S05R01	0.9	0.85	0.87	0.86	0.88	0.9	0.88	0.86	0.87
	S05R02	0.8	0.82	0.78	0.85	0.82	0.79	0.85	0.82	0.79
	S06R01	0.912	0.837	0.85	0.867	0.85	0.85	0.837	0.8	0.837
	S07R01	0.48	0.7	0.6	0.84	0.84	0.55	0.6	0.55	0.55
	S07R02	0.42	0.7	0.58	0.58	0.58	0.58	0.58	0.7	0.58
	S08R01	0.82	0.9	0.82	0.85	0.93	0.84	0.84	0.86	0.87
	S09R01	0.875	0.935	0.915	0.935	0.935	0.905	0.896	0.89	0.9
FoG CLASS	S01R01	0.79	0.54	0.6	0.5	0.45	0.5	0.45	0.5	0.45
	S01R02	0.32	0.66	0.66	0.66	0.5	0.5	0.82	0.82	0.68
	S02R01	0.68	0.63	0.63	0.75	0.63	0.75	0.75	0.75	0.68
	S02R02	0.64	0.85	0.72	0.93	0.68	0.75	0.72	0.76	0.79
	S03R01	0.68	0.77	0.78	0.78	0.75	0.78	0.77	0.68	0.65
	S03R02	0.8	0.8	0.9	0.6	0.8	0.6	0.7	0.5	0.6
	S05R01	0.69	0.7	0.78	0.67	0.58	0.62	0.63	0.63	0.65
	S05R02	0.71	0.58	0.53	0.58	0.6	0.62	0.57	0.63	0.57
	S06R01	0.74	0.785	0.87	0.89	0.87	0.87	0.89	0.925	0.87
	S07R01	0.45	0.7	0.45	0.55	0.45	0.45	0.45	0.65	0.63
	S07R02	0.5	0.75	1	1	1	1	0.58	0.58	0.58
	S08R01	0.5	0.56	0.6	0.7	0.6	0.56	0.62	0.67	0.7
	S09R01	0.86	0.875	0.905	0.93	0.9	0.9	0.915	0.89	0.86
PreFoG CLASS	S01R01	0.5	0.5	0.25	0.25	0.25	0.25	0.25	0.25	0
	S01R02	0	0.5	0	0.5	0.5	0	0	0	0.5
	S02R01	0	0	0	0	0.5	0.5	0.5	0.5	0.5
	S02R02	0	0	0	0	0	0.175	0.175	0.175	0
	S03R01	0.157	0	0.075	0.075	0.075	0	0	0.25	0.2
	S03R02	0.35	0.65	1	0.7	0.7	1	1	0	0
	S05R01	0.1	0.1	0.2	0.3	0.3	0.1	0	0	0
	S05R02	0.1	0	0	0.2	0.25	0.1	0.075	0.1	0.1
	S06R01	0	0	0	0	0	0			
	S07R01	0	0.35	0	0	0	0	0	0	0
	S07R02	0.25	0.25	0	0	0.25	0.25	0	0	0
	S08R01	0	0	0	0	0	0.35	0	0	0.35
	S09R01	0.3	0.15	0.15	0.15	0	0.15	0.15	0.3	0

4   Conclusion

In this work, several feature learning techniques are used in order to best detect and predict the occurrence of freezing of gait. Several features based on time-domain and even sensor derived features were used. These features were derived from the DaphNet dataset available publicly on UCI Machine Learning repository. Using this dataset, the research attempted an individual patient analysis to show that FoG prediction is highly patient dependent and achieved a peak F1 - score of 80%. While performing FoG detection, we observed that Decision Trees and Random Forests are the top algorithms for this task, since they have a higher accuracy. However, the size of Random Forests models is a trade-off for its accuracy. Such FoG detection models are great for understanding the onset of FoG and they lead the pathway for further exploration in this field. Numerous statistical features have been identified that can have an impact on further research by utilizing them for further development. In the future, we aim to incorporate the use of Neural Network to this work and improve the results obtained. We hope to solve this problem and design small devices with an incorporated Machine Learning model which can predict the onset of freezing of gait to help patients in their ailment.

References

1. Bächlin, M., et al.: Wearable assistant for Parkinson's disease patients with the freezing of gait symptom. IEEE Trans. Inf. Technol. Biomed. **14**(2), 436–46 (2010)
2. Bächlin, M., Plotnik, M., Roggen, D., Giladi, N., Hausdorff, J.M., Tröster, G.: A wearable system to assist walking of Parkinson's disease patients. Meth. Inf. Med. **49**(01), 88–95 (2010)
3. Schaafsma, J.D., et al.: Characterization of freezing of gait subtypes and the response of each to levodopa in Parkinson's disease. Euro. J. Neurol. **10**(4), 391–398 (2003)
4. Bissessur, S., Tissingh, G., Wolters, E.C., Scheltens, P.: rCBF SPECT in Parkinson's disease patients with mental dysfunction. In: Riederer, P., Calne, D.B., Horowski, R., Mizuno, Y., Poewe, W., Youdim, M.B.H. (eds.) Advances in Research on Neurodegeneration. Journal of Neural Transmission. Supplementa, vol. 50, pp. 25–30. Springer, Vienna (1997)
5. Gewirtz, J.C., Falls, W.A., Davis, M.: Normal conditioning inhibition and extinction of freezing and fear-potentiated startle following electrolytic lesions of medial prefrontal cortex in rats. Behav. Neurosci. **111**(4), 712 (1997)
6. Oung, Q.W., et al.: Technologies for assessment of motor disorders in Parkinson's disease: a review. Sensors **15**(9), 21710–21745 (2015)
7. Elbaz, A., et al.: Risk tables for parkinsonism and Parkinson's disease. J. clin. Epidemiol. **55**(1), 25–31 (2002)
8. Sung, M., Marci, C., Pentland, A.: Wearable feedback systems for rehabilitation. J. Neuroeng. Rehabil. **2**(1), 17 (2005)
9. Van Den Eeden, S.K., et al.: Incidence of Parkinson's disease: variation by age, gender, and race/ethnicity. Am. J. Epidemiol. **157**(11), 1015–1022 (2003)
10. Segev-Jacubovski, O., Herman, T., Yogev-Seligmann, G., Mirelman, A., Giladi, N., Hausdorff, J.M.: The interplay between gait, falls and cognition: can cognitive therapy reduce fall risk? Expert Rev. Neurother. **11**(7), 1057–1075 (2011)
11. Bachlin, M., et al.: Wearable assistant for Parkinson's disease patients with the freezing of gait symptom. IEEE Trans. Inf. Technol. Biomed. **14**(2), 436–446 (2010)

12. Handojoseno, A.M.A., et al.: The detection of freezing of Gait in Parkinson's disease patients using EEG signals based on Wavelet decomposition. In: Engineering in Medicine and Biology Society (EMBC), 2012 Annual International Conference of the IEEE, pp. 69–72. IEEE (2012)

13. Takač, B., Català, A., Rodríguez, D., Chen, W., Rauterberg, M.: Ambient sensor system for freezing of gait detection by spatial context analysis. In: Bravo, J., Hervás, R., Rodríguez, M. (eds.) IWAAL 2012. LNCS, vol. 7657, pp. 232–239. Springer, Heidelberg (2012). https://doi.org/10.1007/978-3-642-35395-6_32

14. Mazilu, S., et al.: Feature learning for detection and prediction of freezing of Gait in Parkinson's disease. In: Perner, P. (ed.) MLDM 2013. LNCS (LNAI), vol. 7988, pp. 144–158. Springer, Heidelberg (2013). https://doi.org/10.1007/978-3-642-39712-7_11

15. Jovanov, E., Wang, E., Verhagen, L., Fredrickson, M., Fratangelo, R.: deFoG-A real time system for detection and unfreezing of gait of Parkinson's patients. In: 2009 Annual International Conference of the IEEE Engineering in Medicine and Biology Society, EMBC, pp. 5151–5154. IEEE (2009)

16. Moore, O., Peretz, C., Giladi, N.: Freezing of gait affects quality of life of peoples with Parkinson's disease beyond its relationships with mobility and gait. Mov. Disord. Offic. J. Mov. Disord. Soc. 22(15), 2192–2195 (2007)

17. Saad, A.: Detection of Freezing of Gait in Parkinson's disease. Université du Havre, PhD diss. (2016)

18. Torvi, V.G., Bhattacharya, A., Chakraborty, S.: Deep Domain Adaptation to Predict Freezing of Gait in Patients with Parkinson's Disease. In: 2018 17th IEEE International Conference on Machine Learning and Applications (ICMLA), pp. 1001–1006. IEEE (2018)

19. Raccagni, C., et al.: Sensor?based gait analysis in atypical parkinsonian disorders. Brain Behav. 8(6), e00977 (2018)

20. Zia, J., Tadayon, A., McDaniel, T., Panchanathan, S.: Utilizing neural networks to predict freezing of gait in parkinson's patients. In: Proceedings of the 18th International ACM SIGACCESS Conference on Computers and Accessibility, pp. 333–334. ACM, October 2016

21. Shibuya, N., et al.: A real-time fall detection system using a wearable gait analysis sensor and a support vector machine (SVM) classifier. In: 2015 Eighth International Conference on Mobile Computing and Ubiquitous Networking (ICMU), pp. 66–67. IEEE (2015)

22. Tripoliti, E.E., et al.: Automatic detection of freezing of gait events in patients with Parkinson's disease. Comput. Meth. Program. Biomed. 110(1), 12–26 (2013)

23. Nieuwboer, A., Giladi, N.: Characterizing freezing of gait in Parkinson's disease: models of an episodic phenomenon. Mov. Disord. 28(11), 1509–1519 (2013)

24. Mazilu, S., et al.: Online detection of freezing of gait with smartphones and machine learning techniques. In: 2012 6th International Conference on Pervasive Computing Technologies for Healthcare (PervasiveHealth), pp. 123–130. IEEE (2012)

25. Snijders, A.H. et al.: Gait-related cerebral alterations in patients with Parkinson's disease with freezing of gait. Brain 134(1), 59–72 (2010)

26. Das, R.: A comparison of multiple classification methods for diagnosis of Parkinson disease. Expert Syst. Appl. 37(2), 1568–1572 (2010)

27. Bloem, B.R., Hausdorff, J.M., Visser, J.E., Giladi, N.: Falls and freezing of gait in Parkinson's disease: a review of two interconnected, episodic phenomena. Mov. Disord. Offic. J. Mov. Disord. Soc. 19(8), 871–884 (2004)

28. Han, J.H., Lee, W.J., Ahn, T.B., Jeon, B.S., Park, K.S.: Gait analysis for freezing detection in patients with movement disorder using three dimensional acceleration system. In: Proceedings of the 25th Annual International Conference of the IEEE Engineering in Medicine and Biology Society (IEEE Cat. No. 03CH37439), vol. 2, pp. 1863–1865. IEEE (2003)
29. Cole, B.T., Roy, S.H., De Luca, C.J., Nawab, S.H.: Dynamic neural network detection of tremor and dyskinesia from wearable sensor data. In: 2010 Annual International Conference of the IEEE Engineering in Medicine and Biology Society (EMBC), pp. 6062–6065. IEEE (2010)
30. Bachlin, M., et al.: Wearable assistant for Parkinson's disease patients with the freezing of gait symptom. IEEE Trans. Inf. Technol. Biomed. **14**(2), 436–446 (2010)

Comparing the Accuracy and the Efficiency in Detection of Coronavirus in CT Scans and X Ray Images

C. V. Sagar and Sumit Bhardwaj[✉]

Department of Electronics and Communication Engineering, Amity University, Noida, India

Abstract. The Coronavirus pandemic, also known as the Covid pandemic, is a global disease (Coronavirus) pandemic caused by SARS Covid 2019 that causes severe respiratory illness (SARS-CoV-2). Side effects differ incredibly in seriousness, going from subtle to perilous. Individuals who are old or have basic clinical issues are more inclined to foster serious infection. Coronavirus is spread by means of the air when beads and small airborne particles dirty it. In this project we would be analyzing the data set images of Chest CT Scans and Chest X Rays for the Detection of Corona Virus using the different kind of deep learning algorithms and checking the efficiency of both of them as to which is more accurate and beneficial for detection of the corona virus pandemics so that this study can be used for future detection of COVID in the patients.

Keywords: Coronavirus · X ray · CT scans · Machine learning

1 Introduction

Covid sickness (Coronavirus) is a recently found Covid that causes an irresistible ailment. Most of patients infected with the Coronavirus will have gentle to direct respiratory demonstration and will recuperate without requiring a particular treatment. Coronavirus spreads by the nasal discharge and the saliva droplets whenever that person sneezes or coughs. Because the symptoms of COVID-19 – fever, cough, trouble breathing, and muscular discomfort – are similar to those of many other illnesses, such as influenza, diagnostic tests are required to determine who has COVID-19. Furthermore, these tests may be used to assess who has recovered from COVID-19, increase our understanding of how the virus spreads, and track the success of control efforts. Some tests seek for the virus's RNA (genetic blueprint), which is found in the SARS-CoV-2 virus that produces COVID-19.

These tests, on the other hand, are ineffective in establishing if someone has recovered from the virus, and they may even miss the virus if it is present in extremely low quantities in a patient's body. Antibodies to the virus are found in other tests, indicating that the body has created an immunological response to it. Because such antibodies take longer to develop, antibody testing aren't very useful in determining if someone hasCOVID-19 in the first few days after infection.

© Springer Nature Switzerland AG 2022
A. Dev et al. (Eds.): AIST 2021, CCIS 1546, pp. 530–546, 2022.
https://doi.org/10.1007/978-3-030-95711-7_44

Therefore new techniques are emerging using artificial intelligence and machine learning so that COVID -19 can be detected and treatment can be given to the concerned patient. The organs and structures of the chest are imaged using X-rays or scans. Radiation is used in X-rays (radiography) to create a two-dimensional picture. They are usually performed in hospitals by a radiographer using fixed equipment, although they can also be performed using portable devices. CT scans combine two-dimensional X-ray pictures into a three-dimensional picture using a computer. They require specialised equipment and are performed by a trained radiographer in a hospital setting. CT scans of the chest may be useful in diagnosingCOVID-19 in those who have a strong clinical suspicion of infection. Early infection is characterised by respective multi-lobar groundglass opacities with a fringe, deviated, and back in circulation. As the disease progresses, subpleural predominance, insane clearing (lobular septal thickening with fluctuating alveolar filling), and solidification may create.

Evaluate and discuss how artificial intelligence (AI) can assist us in combating the continuing epidemic. Detection technologies targeted to infectious animal illness situations can help avoid any cross-species transmission of a viral illness. There is still time for research to increase the overall AI assistance for the present epidemic. Advances in AI's contribution to healthcare systems in the future. There are still some conditions that AI is unable to meet. Indeed, there are three well-known characteristics of AI that might lead to failure: the lack of strong AI, its inability to perform without domain expertise, and the necessity for adequate data quality and flow. Furthermore, ML and DL methodologies must be analyzed in order to find the best present solutions, as well as future advances and research possibilities, while avoiding ethical considerations (such as trust and privacy) that now impede AI use in our society [1]. In order to acquire detection results, the Datasets are assessed using techniques like CLAHE and Convolutional Neural Networks. Future scientists could utilize extra datasets, to accumulate different varieties when conducting further research. The expansion of the pneumonia data can upgrade the exactness, accuracy, review, and F1 scores significantly further, allowing for more distinct distinctions to be noticed. The use of CLAHE is thought to have an impact on the correctness of the generating evaluation model. The detection of Covid-19 had no effect on the precision, recall, or F1 in this study since it looks at a tiny dataset of 40 photos [2].

To increase the quality of CT (Computed Tomography) Scan pictures of COVID-19 lungs, Limited Adaptive Histogram Equalization (CLAHE) contrast will be employed, as well as Convolutional Neural Network (CNN) for image classification. 698 RGB photos were utilised in the study. The number of epochs and data set ratios can impact the accuracy outcomes, according to this study [3]. There is a novel clustering approach provided in this paper. For obtaining ideal clusters, this technique employs a unique variation of a gravitational search algorithm. A comparison of contemporary metaheuristic algorithms is undertaken to validate the performance of the suggested variation. The exploratory investigation contains two arrangements of benchmark capacities, standard capacities and CEC2013 capacities, which are isolated into three classifications: unimodal, multimodal, and unconstrained improvement capacities. The mean wellness esteem, Friedman test, and box-plot are utilized to investigate and measurably approve the exhibition examination. The proposed grouping calculation was additionally considered in contrast to three particular sorts of publically open CoVID19 clinical pictures, specifically X-beam, CT output, and ultrasound pictures. Trials show that as far as exactness, accuracy, affectability, explicitness, and F1-score, the proposed system beats the opposition. Continuous datasets might be explored later on to improve the effectiveness of the proposed approach. Ongoing datasets might be explored later on to improve the proficiency of the recommended approach. Also, utilizing systems like Spark or Hadoop, an equal rendition of the proposed approach may be researched to deal with enormous datasets. A parallel version of the recommended methodology might also be examined utilising frameworks such as Spark or Hadoop to handle massive datasets [4].

This COVID-19 identification model was made with the issues that exist in the space of COVID-19 location using information assembled from various sources as a top priority. The identification of this viral infection necessitates the examination of uncommon characteristics in the photos. The sooner we diagnose a viral infection, the more lives we can save. Further data may be incorporated for improved outcomes, bolstering the proposed model even more [5]. Early diagnosis is critical for both the patient's treatment and the prevention of disease spread. Chest x-ray pictures from Corona virus and non-Covid-19 people were utilized for this investigation. The exchange learning model ResNet 50 is used to classify these photos. Moreover, despite the limited sample size, the findings are positive in terms of the utilisation of computer-aided pathology. It can also be utilized in instances where there aren't enough options (RT-PCR test, doctor, radiologist). It can aid in clinical practice since the categorization accuracy is determined with a high accuracy rate of 99.5%. Moreover, despite the limited sample size, the findings are positive in terms of the utilization of computer-aided pathology. It can also be utilized in instances where there aren't enough options (RT-PCR test, doctor, radiologist). More successful deep learning models can be developed in the future. Furthermore, it can handle bigger data sets [6].

To date, deep learning approaches have been used to multiple X Ray picture for the detection of COVID-19. The data augmentation methodology has boosted this figure. To date, deep learning approaches have been used to analyze 657 chest X-beam pictures for the determination of COVID-19. The information expansion methodology has boosted this figure. VGG19 is the best model, with a 95% exactness rate. The VGG19 model accurately groups COVID-19 patients, solid individuals, and viral pneumonia cases. The relevance of the COVID-19 epidemic is highlighted in this article. The success ratio of future investigations can be improved by expanding the data collection. In addition to chest radiography, lung tomography can be employed. Success ratios and performance may be improved by building various deep learning models. The dataset's most failed approach is InceptionV3 [7]. This model demonstrates that computer vision has the potential to revolutionise radiological image analysis. As a result, a time-saving approach for detecting and isolating contaminated patients may be devised. The suggested model achieves an extraordinary result with a validation accuracy of 84% on a short dataset, compared to 71% for the InceptionV3 model. As the size of such a dataset grows over time, the model will get increasingly accurate and resilient [8].

We proposed a cGAN-basedCOVID-19 CT picture combination approach that can make reasonable CT pictures with ground-glass darkness and solidification, just as other contamination sorts. The recommended strategy utilizes the semantic division guide of a lung CT picture as info, and the cGAN structure learns the CT picture's properties and data. To appropriately offset worldwide data with neighborhood highlights in the CT picture, a worldwide nearby generator and a multi-goal discriminator are utilized. Besides, the discoveries of the semantic division appraisal showed that the manufactured CT pictures' high picture quality and loyalty take into account their utilization in picture amalgamation for COVID-19 finding using AI models. The researchers need to utilize top notch syntheticCOVID-19 CT pictures in future exploration to foster certain PC vision innovations that can help in the fight against COVID-19, for example, lung CT picture semantic division and fast COVID-19 analysis dependent on lung CT pictures [9]. We looked into two different techniques to address the shortage of COVID-19-related data. To start, train a custom CNN utilizing an immense informational collection of non-COVID-19 X-beam chest pictures (ChexPert).Then, using the limitedCOVID-19 data, fine-tune the model. This method yielded Model1, which failed to detect COVID-19-infected individuals reliably. The second option was to use the COVID-19 data to fine-tune pre-trained deep learning models. This method yielded Model 1, which failed to detect COVID-19-infected individuals reliably. This intriguing research paves the path for a novel method of testing and detecting COVID-19-infected people. Despite the fact that the model is of higher quality than Model1, it produces much too many incorrect positive or negative predictions [10].

We created the K-COVID dataset from a variety of chest X-rays in this study. Beam pictures, just as the K-EfficientNet engineering, which depends on and expands the EfficientNet Deep Learning Network plan. We likewise utilize the reformist resizing standard, just as information expansion and move learning, to accomplish high precision in the wake of preparing. It would be much great if we could enhance with a larger database [11]. The proposed 2D convolution methodology, which was used to classify Lung Images by Chest Xray in order to identifyCOVID-19, produced notable results quickly and with greater than 99% accuracy. As part of a future development plan, a large dataset will be used to test for high figuring velocity, execution, and effective implementation of deep learning algorithms utilising GPU [12].

Five layers make up the arranged profound multifaceted CNN. In each layer, 3×3-bit convolution tasks were finished with a unit step sliding window and single cushioning. The enactment work was the Amended, straight unit (ReLU). A 2×2 max-pooling strategy was likewise used to join the yield of each layer's convolution activity into a tensor that is more In the recommended framework, the three-dimensional tensors were changed to one-dimensional component vectors with 4096 neurons after the muddled advancement. Then, at that point there's a thick layer of 128 neurons, a dropout layer with a half-dropout rate, lastly a dropout layer with a half-dropout rate and a yield layer with 3 neurons were used. In the thick layer and yield layer, individually, ReLU and Softmax were employed as activation functions. In the future, data augmentation with a Generative Adversarial Network might be employed to enhance the amount of training photos for improved classification performance. The suggested methodology has achieved a blind test accuracy of 99.1%. As a result, medical practitioners can utilize the suggested technique as a second opinion when makingCOVID-19 diagnostic predictions [13].

The proposed study uses the notion of transmit Learning to characterize chest X-beam pictures to decide whether a patient has been tainted with COVID-19 or not. In the study, two approaches for categorizing the photos were offered. The first technique categorizes people's ages as COVID-19 or Non-COVID-19.The second method divides data into three categories; assessment metrics and might be incredibly effective in detecting the illness quickly and accurately. The VGG-19 delivered the best consequences of the relative multitude of models inspected. This model has the potential to be a critical and rapid technique for detecting COVID-19 in patients, allowing for more prompt and effective treatment. When dense models are developed from the ground up with a limited amount of data, the metrics aren't the best. According to the various approaches for training the classifier. As a result, transfer learning has been demonstrated to be an excellent method for generating cutting-edge models [14]. This research makes use of deep learning technologies COVID-19 was diagnosed in participants using a chest CT scan with an accuracy of 0.897, F1 score of 0.896, and AUC of 0.895, the EfficientNet profound learning engineering is used to quickly and effectively recognize Covid. Bringing down the learning rate (decrease on level), cyclic learning rate, and ceaseless learning rate are three particular learning rate systems that can be utilized when model execution arrives at a level. The model will be prepared on the equivalent dataset that was utilized in this exploration, and it will be tried on an alternate dataset that has been assembled because a short dataset for training might lead to over-fitting, the dataset is extended utilizing transfer learning to expand the amount of images. Because no additional COVID CT-scan dataset is publically accessible, domain generic transfer learning is employed in this technique. To stay away from pre-learning on typical CT-filter pictures, we would prefer not to prepare on sound CT-check photographs. This may prompt weight moving towards the ordinary class [15]. The article's figures, subtitles, and appropriate figure depictions were recovered, and complex considers were partitioned along with subfigures. We made a profound learning model to perceive CXR and CT figures from other figure types and arrange them appropriately because they make up a major component of COVID19 articles. There are 1,327 CT and 263 CXR pictures in the final database. We anticipate that the public dataset will aid in the development of deep learning models, educate medical students and residents, aid in the evaluation of radiologists' results, and give further insights for COVID-19 diagnosis [16].

It is proposed to use a altered profound neural organization. The recommended model depends on Xception models, with two thick layer stacks and batch normalisation in the model's final layer. o keeps away from overfitting in the model, the thick layer and group normalization are utilised. On the basis of chest Xray pictures, the suggested model is employed to identify COVID 19.Dataset's data is categorized into normal, pneumonia and pneumonia caused by COVID-19 The inclusion of layers lengthens the training period [17]. Coronavirus GATNet is it is a network that is used to detect corona virus positive cases in CXR Pictures. This neural organization model had the option to group CXR pictures into three classifications: typical, pneumonia, and COVID-19 positive, making it simpler for radiologists to screenCOVID-19 positive patients. We likewise made a COVID CXR composite informational index making use of three open-get entry to information units and utilized statistics expansion to amplify the scale of 399 CXR pictures of COVID-19 patients. Future exploration will zero in on the most proficient technique to improve the version's identity execution for COVID-contaminated sufferers with the aid of using the whole lot of the pictures' semantic statistics and joining regular language coping with to offer an outline or picture indicative document for the COVID-19 CXR images [18].

2 Methodology

Following are considered for comparison of CT Scan with Xray images (Figs. 1 and 2).

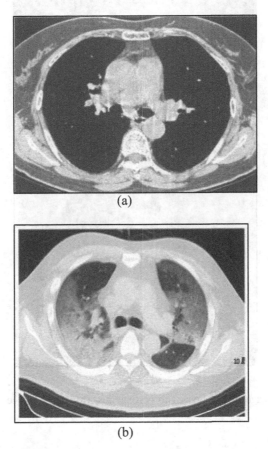

(a)

(b)

Fig. 1. (a) CT scan of a patient with coronavirus, (b) CT scan of a patient without coronavirus

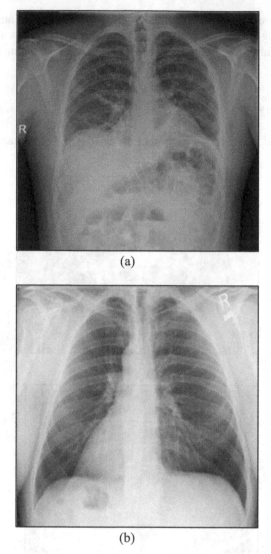

(a)

(b)

Fig. 2. (a): X ray image of a patient with coronavirus, (b): X ray image of a patient without coronavirus

2.1 Epochs

Every training sample has been passed through the model at least once in one epoch. For instance if your epoch is set to 50 it means that the model that is being trained will work through the entire training data sets 50 times.

2.2 Confusion Matrix

A confusion matrix is a system for estimate machine learning categorization presentation. It is a kind of a table that shows how well a categorization representation works on a compilation of test data with known definite values. It summarizes how accurate one's model predictions are. The y axis represents the class of your sample and the x axis represent the class that the model, after learning guesses that sample belong to.

2.3 Different Outcomes of Confusion Matrix

In this section we would be discussing about the Confusion Matrix and its possible outcomes (Fig. 3):

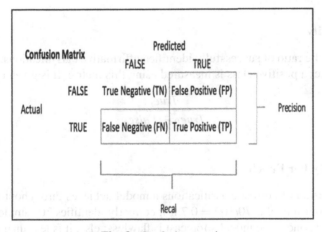

Fig. 3. Confusion matrix

True Positive: Predicted values were right in predicting that the outcome would be positive i.e. you predicted something that it would happen and it came out to be correct.
False Positive: The anticipated values were inaccurate in predicting a favorable outcome i.e. you predicted something that it would happen and it came out to be incorrect.
True Negative: Predicted values were properly predicted as a negative number i.e. you predicted something that it would not happen and it came out to be correct.
False Negative: Positive numbers are anticipated to be negative i.e., you predicted something that it would not happen, and it came out to be incorrect.

Accuracy test of the Confusion Matrix is given by:

$$\frac{True_P + True_N}{True_P + True_N + False_P + False_N} \tag{1}$$

2.4 ROC Curve

The positive rate points which are true are compared to the positive rate points which are false at various cut points on the ROC curve. Its displays a relation between accuracy and sensitivity.

2.5 Precision

It shows how precise is the positive class. It also provides the information how accurate is the forecast of the positive class.

$$\frac{True_P}{True_P + False_P} \tag{2}$$

2.6 Sensitivity

Sensitivity is the ratio of successfully identified affirmative classifications. The model's ability to detect a positive class is measured using this metric. It is given by:

$$\frac{True_P}{True_P + False_N} \tag{3}$$

2.7 Accuracy Per Epoch

It's the proportion of correct classifications a model achieves throughout training. The accuracy of your model is $70/100 = 0.7$ if it correctly identifies 70 samples out of 100. The accuracy is one if the model's forecast is flawless; else, it is less than one.

2.8 Loss Per Epoch

It's a metric for determining how successfully a model has learned to predict the correct classifications for a batch of data. The loss is 0 if the model's predictions are flawless; otherwise, the loss is larger than zero. Imagine you have two models, A and B, to get a feel of what this measures. Model A predicts the correct categorization for a sample, but only with a 60% confidence level. Model B likewise predicts the correct categorization for the same sample, but with a 90% confidence level. Models A and B are equally accurate, however Model B has a smaller loss value.

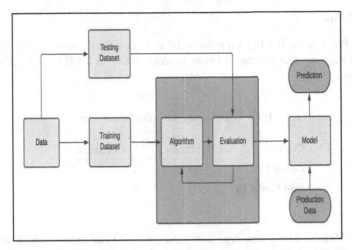

Fig. 4. Shows how machine learning works

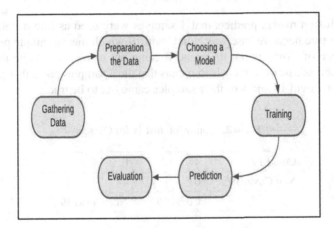

Fig. 5. Flow of work of the model

2.9 Batch

A batch size is a collection of samples utilised in a single training iteration. Consider the following scenario: you have 80 pictures and a batch size of 16. This implies the data will be divided into five batches of $80/16 = 5$. The model will be complete after all 5 batches have been passed through it exactly on epoch (Figs. 4 and 5).

3 Result

In this section we would be discussing about the Accuracy per class and the Confusion Matrix of CT Scans and X Ray Images.

3.1 CT Scans

***Accuracy Per Class*:** It's the proportion of correct classifications a model achieves throughout training. The accuracy of your model is 100/100 = 1.00. It correctly identifies all the samples.

Table 1. Accuracy per class for CT scan

Class	Accuracy	No. of samples
Covid 19	1.00	4
Non Covid 19	1.00	4

Confusion Matrix: The y axis represents the class of your sample which are the Non Covid 19 and Covid 19 and the x axis represent the class that the model which is to predict Non Covid 19 and Covid 19, after learning guesses that sample of CT Scans belong to.

The confusion matrix predicts that 4 samples were used as true negative and true positive. The true negative case was Non Covid 19 which means sample predicted that the occurrence of Covid is not there and it came out to be true. While the Covid 19 class was taken as true negative which means that the 4 samples taken that predicted the occurrence of Covid 19 and 4 of their samples came out to be true.

Table 2. Confusion matrix for CT scan

Covid 19	4	0
Non Covid 19	0	4
	Covid 19	Non Covid 19

Graphs related to Table 1, i.e., graph of accuracy per epoch and graph of loss per epochs of CT scans are represented in Fig. 6 and in Fig. 7 (Table 2).

3.2 For X rays

Accuracy Per Class

It's the proportion of correct classifications a model achieves throughout training. The accuracy of your model is 100/100 = 1.00. It correctly identifies all the samples for Covid 19 while it is 0.75 for Non Covid 19 samples.

Confusion Matrix

The y axis represents the class of your sample which is the Non Covid 19 and Covid 19 and the x axis represent the class that the model which is to predict Non Covid 19 and Covid 19, after learning guesses that sample of CT Scans belong to.

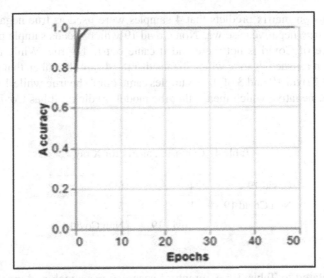

Fig. 6. Graph of accuracy per epoch of the CT scan images

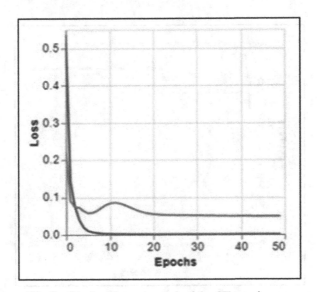

Fig. 7. Graph of loss per epoch of the CT scan images

Table 3. Accuracy per class for X ray

Class	Accuracy	No. of samples
Covid 19	1.00	4
Non Covid 19	0.75	4

The confusion matrix predicts that 4 samples were used as true negative and true positive. The true negative case was Non Covid 19 which means sample predicted that the occurrence of Covid is not there and it came out to be true. While the Covid 19 class was taken as true negative which means that the 4 samples taken that predicted the occurrence of Covid 19 and 3 of their samples came out to be true while 1 sample came out to be false negative which means that the model predicted it has Covid 19 while it doesn't.

Table 4. Confusion matrix for X ray

Covid 19	4	0
Non Covid 19	1	3
	Covid 19	Non Covid 19

Graphs related to Table 3, i.e., graph of accuracy per epoch and graph of loss per epochs of X ray images are represented in Fig. 8 and in Fig. 9 (Table 4).

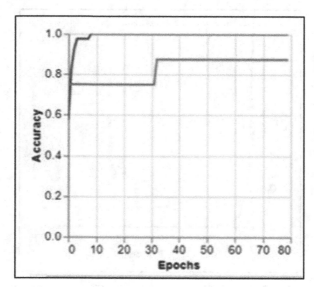

Fig. 8. Graph of accuracy per epoch of the X ray images

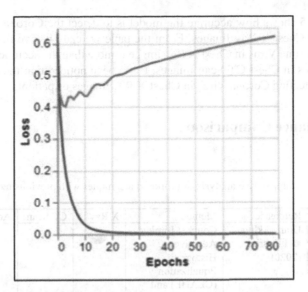

Fig. 9. Graph of loss per epoch of the X ray images

Table 5. Accuracy table to identify coronavirus in chest CT scan and chest X rays

	COVID CT	NON COVID CT	COVID X RAY	NON COVID X RAY
PERSON A	100	100	100	95
PERSON B	100	13	74	100
PERSON C	100	13	72	98
PERSON D	13	1	99	100
PERSON E	1	0	100	98
PERSON F	2	0	100	100
PERSON G	27	0	100	100
PERSON H	1	0	0	16
PERSON I	0	89	25	65
PERSON J	1	89	100	96
PERSON K	1	100	100	100
PERSON L	0	98	14	94
PERSON M	1	19	43	0
PERSON N	1	39	74	4
PERSON O	14	99	100	96
PERSON P	0	100	100	99
PERSON Q	0	100	100	93
PERSON R	3	98	96	98
PERSON S	0	89	86	94
PERSON T	0	100	100	100

The Table 5 shows how accurate the model is to detect the Corona Virus in Chest CT Scans and Chest X Ray Images. From the table we can observe that accuracy for detection of Corona Virus in Chest X Ray image is more than the accuracy for detection of Corona Virus in Chest CT Scan Images. It has been noticed that the model is more efficient in Detecting Corona Virus in Chest X Ray images of patients.

4   Performance Comparison

Table 6. Comparative analysis of proposed techniques with previous techniques

S.No	Reference	Method	X Ray	CT Scan	Accuracy
1.	Umri, Akhyari and Kusrini (2020)	Contrast Limited Adaptive Histogram Equalization (CLAHE) and Convolutional Neural Networks (CNN)	●		
2.	Bhadra and Kar (2020)	Multi-layered CNN having 5 layer	●		
3.	Anwar and Zakir (2020)	deep learning technology	●		89.7%
4.	James and Sunyoto (2020)	Limited Adaptive histogram equalization (CLAHE)		●	83.28%
5.	Mittal, Pandey and Pal (2021)	New clustering method		●	
6.	KARHAN and AKAL (2020)	Transfer learning model ResNet 50	●		99.5%
7.	Padma and Kumari (2020)	2D convolution method	●		99%
8.	Sevi and AYDIN (2020)	Data augmentation technique using VGG19	●		95%
9.	Santoso and Purnomo (2020)	Modified deep neural network		●	
10.	Proposed Model	Machine Learning	●	●	80.725%

The Table 6 interprets and provides a comparative analysis of the Technique Used in the paper and the techniques used earlier for detection of the Coronavirus and their efficiency in detecting the Coronavirus. The dots that are present in the Column 4 and

5 denotes the Image that have been used for modeling. We can notice that most of the earlier study and models were either based for the Chest X Rays or Chest CT Scan while the model proposed contain the information which can be used to detect in both Chest X Rays and Chest CT Scans.

5 Conclusion

We took 24 samples of Corona Positive cases as well as Corona Negative Cases of both Chest X Ray and Chest CT Scans for training the model for the detection of COVID 19. We took 20 patients chest CT Scan and Chest X Ray images who were diagnosed with COVID 19 and after they recover from it for testing the model that was created. It has been witnessed that detection of Corona Virus in Chest X Ray is more accurate that detection of Chest CT Scan via this model. In future there will be more data sets available that will help in training of the model more efficiently and then the model would be trained for detection of Corona Virus more accurately and efficiently for Both CT scans and X Ray Images.

References

1. Piccialli, F., di Cola, V.S., Giampaolo, F., Cuomo, S.: The role of artificial intelligence in fighting the covid-19 pandemic. Inf. Syst. Front. 23(6), 1467–1497 (2021). https://doi.org/10.1007/s10796-021-10131-x
2. Umri, B.K., WafaAkhyari, M., Kusrini, K.: Detection of Covid-19 in chest X-ray image using CLAHE and convolutional neural network. In: 2020 2nd International Conference on Cybernetics and Intelligent System (ICORIS), pp. 1–5 (2020). https://doi.org/10.1109/ICORIS50180.2020.9320806
3. James, R.M., Sunyoto, A.: Detection Of CT-scan lungs COVID-19 image using convolutional neural network and CLAHE. In: 2020 3rd International Conference on Information and Communications Technology (ICOIACT), pp. 302–307 (2020). https://doi.org/10.1109/ICOIACT50329.2020.9332069
4. Mittal, H., Pandey, A.C., Pal, R., Tripathi, A.: A new clustering method for the diagnosis of COVID 19 using medical images. Appl. Intell. 51(5), 2988–3011 (2021). https://doi.org/10.1007/s10489-020-02122-3
5. Perumal, V., Narayanan, V., Rajasekar, S.J.S.: Detection of COVID-19 using CXR and CT images using transfer learning and Haralick features. Appl. Intell. 51(1), 341–358 (2020). https://doi.org/10.1007/s10489-020-01831-z
6. Karhan, Z., Akal, F.: Covid-19 classification using deep learning in chest X-ray images. In: 2020 Medical Technologies Congress (TIPTEKNO), pp. 1–4 (2020). https://doi.org/10.1109/TIPTEKNO50054.2020.9299315
7. Sevi, M., Aydin, İ.: COVID-19 detection using deep learning methods. In: 2020 International Conference on Data Analytics for Business and Industry: Way Towards a Sustainable Economy (ICDABI), pp. 1–6 (2020). https://doi.org/10.1109/ICDABI51230.2020.9325626
8. Dutta, P., Roy, T., Anjum, N.: COVID-19 detection using transfer learning with convolutional neural network. In: 2021 2nd International Conference on Robotics, Electrical and Signal Processing Techniques (ICREST), pp. 429–432 (2021). https://doi.org/10.1109/ICREST51555.2021.9331029

9. Jiang, Y., Chen, H., Loew, M., Ko, H.: COVID-19 CT image synthesis with a conditional generative adversarial network. IEEE J. Biomed. Health Inform. **25**(2), 441–452 (2021). https://doi.org/10.1109/JBHI.2020.3042523

10. Hernandez, D., Pereira, R., Georgevia, P.: COVID-19 detection through X-ray chest images. In: 2020 International Conference Automatics and Informatics (ICAI), pp. 1–5 (2020). https://doi.org/10.1109/ICAI50593.2020.9311372

11. Diallo, P.A.K.K., Ju, Y.: Accurate detection of COVID-19 using K-EfficientNet deep learning image classifier and K-COVID chest X-ray images dataset. In: 2020 IEEE 6th International Conference on Computer and Communications (ICCC), pp. 1527–1531 (2020). https://doi.org/10.1109/ICCC51575.2020.9344949

12. Padma, T., Kumari, C.U.: Deep learning based chest X-ray image as a diagnostic tool for COVID-19. IN: 2020 International Conference on Smart Electronics and Communication (ICOSEC), pp. 589–592 (2020). https://doi.org/10.1109/ICOSEC49089.2020.9215257

13. Bhadra, R., Kar, S.: Covid detection from CXR scans using deep multi-layered CNN. In: 2020 IEEE Bombay Section Signature Conference (IBSSC), pp. 214–218 (2020). https://doi.org/10.1109/IBSSC51096.2020.9332210

14. Shankar, A., Sonar, Y., Sultanpure, K.A.: Detection of COVID-19 using chest X-ray scans. In: 2020 IEEE Bangalore Humanitarian Technology Conference (B-HTC), pp. 1–6 (2020). https://doi.org/10.1109/B-HTC50970.2020.9297910

15. Anwar, T., Zakir, S.: Deep learning based diagnosis of COVID-19 using chest CT-scan images. In: 2020 IEEE 23rd International Multitopic Conference (INMIC), pp. 1–5 (2020). https://doi.org/10.1109/INMIC50486.2020.9318212

16. Peng, Y., Tang, Y., Lee, S., Zhu, Y., Summers, R.M., Lu, Z.: COVID-19-CT-CXR: a freely accessible and weakly labeled chest X-ray and CT image collection on COVID-19 from biomedical literature. IEEE Trans. Big Data **7**(1), 3–12 (2021). https://doi.org/10.1109/TBDATA.2020.3035935

17. Santoso, F.Y., Purnomo, H.D.: A modified deep convolutional network for COVID-19 detection based on chest X-ray images. In: 2020 3rd International Seminar on Research of Information Technology and Intelligent Systems (ISRITI), pp. 700–704 (2020). https://doi.org/10.1109/ISRITI51436.2020.9315479

18. Li, J., Zhang, D., Liu, Q., Bu, R., Wei, Q.: COVID-GATNet: a deep learning framework for screening of COVID-19 from chest X-ray images. In: 2020 IEEE 6th International Conference on Computer and Communications (ICCC), pp. 1897–1902 (2020). https://doi.org/10.1109/ICCC51575.2020.9345005

An Analysis of Image Compression Using Neural Network

Mohit and Pooja Dehraj[✉]

Noida Institute of Engineering and Technology, Greater Noida, Uttar Pradesh, India
{0201mai004,drpooja.cse}@niet.co.in

Abstract. Image compression belongs to the area of data compression because the image is itself made up of data and the task of compressing images has become vital in our current life. Because the scenario is that images are required to build more attractive contents, also in today's world smartphones cover large fraction of internet traffic and are having low data bandwidth on average. Due to these factors and restrictions on bandwidth and other computing capabilities it has necessary for developers of websites/applications to reduce either size or resolution or both of an image to improve responsiveness of your websites/apps. For this purpose image compression is divided into two categories these are lossless image compression and lossy image compression. The requirement for lossless image compression is that during the decompression process the image data must be recovered without/with negligible loss in image quality while in lossy image compression certain amount or level of error is allowed in image data to achieve better compression ratios and performance. Neural Networks because of their good performance have been used to implement the task of image compression and there are multiple modified neural networks that are proposed to perform image compression tasks, however the consequent models are big in size, require high computational power and also best suited for fixed size compression rate and some of them are covered in this survey report.

Keywords: Quantization · PSNR · Loss function · Image scaling · Convolution layer

1 Introduction

Over the years researchers have performed studies and researches to thoroughly examine the task of image compression such as the joint Pictures Expert Group, who designed the prevalent JPEG and JPEG 2000 image formats. More recently, google in 2015 developed a webP algorithm to further improve compression rates. An artificial neural network is nearly a human made replica of human brain neural network structure [1]. These artificial neurons are combined and implemented in parallel to simulate and behave like a human brain and to capture structure, attribute, dimensions, of its vision and are adaptable to this behaviour [2].

To perform this task of image compression, first a neural network is trained by following a compression over an image by using some number of intermediate neurons,

© Springer Nature Switzerland AG 2022
A. Dev et al. (Eds.): AIST 2021, CCIS 1546, pp. 547–554, 2022.
https://doi.org/10.1007/978-3-030-95711-7_45

wherein the input of the training set contains raw picture pixels and the output of the intermediate neurons combined with the weights that are attached/associated with the outer layer's output node generates the compressed picture. And to retrieve the uncompressed image, remembered hidden nodes output are in product with the weights that are attached with output layer nodes. To generate a compressed image and again getting a recompressed image can be done in multiple ways as an example done in [3], here high and low frequency parts within an image are considered to generate optimal results using adversarial discriminator (AD) for high frequency region judgment and to perform low frequency region evaluation a method based on structural similarity that can be scaled multiple times and is differentiable, this kind of training give better results with focus on region of interest. This decompressed image in comparison with the original input image gives compression error and ratio among them gives compression ratio (CR) [4]. Image scale is a common assumption adopted by multiple standard compression algorithms. For example, it is assumed that if an image patch is selected from a high resolution image, it is more likely possible that the components of image patch will contain lot of redundant information and it is also possible that a patch selected from a high resolution image might have low frequency details. By using these techniques multiple image codes has performed the task of image compression of an image having high resolution very efficiently.

With high compression ratios the difference between original and decompressed image becomes visible and looks distorted. And this unpleasant visible difference leads to poor performance of low level vision algorithms. In recent years, neural networks have outperformed the tasks that had been performed by heuristics and ad-hoc algorithms [5]. In current scenario neural networks are state-of-art for multiple image recognition, image classifying tasks and also outperformed the task of image compression. And based on different properties of image multiple neural networks are designed to get good results for compressed and decompressed image. In this survey paper it is tried to address some of the researches and conferences that have implemented or brought the ideas of neural network architecture for image compression tasks and showed that neural network can be used as state-of-art in image compression tasks.

2   Approaches to Image Compression

2.1   Variable Rate Compression [6]

In this methodology a better tuned framework is designed for image compression with no retraining and storing none of the encodings of same images. For this mechanism to work convey of incremental selective information is necessary and for this model must consider that image reconstruction is progressive. Here three functions are used.

E – Production of Encoded Images
B – Binarization Function
D – Decoder Function

With these three functions an auto encoder is formed shown in below Eq. (2.1)

$$X' = D(B(E(X)))$$

(2.1)

Here, 8-bit RGB is used as input with scaled and offset to produce a ranged value between -0.9 to 0.9 for compatibility with Tan_h.

For progressive reconstruction of the image further info is made viable to decoder in the form of reducing error between observed and predicted data in reconstruction.

$$F_t(R_{t-1}) = D_t(B(E_t(R_{t-1})) \text{ A residual auto encoder} \tag{2.2}$$

$Fr_0 =$ base input image patch
$F_t =$ residual based auto encoder
$R_t =$ residual error with t stages completed

For non-recurrent LSTM, F_t does not have memory that is why successive prediction/calculation of residual itself is necessary. In this case, a whole recreation is recovered with the addition of the residuals. See in below Eq. (2.3).

$$R_t = F_t(R_{t-1}) - R_{t-1} \tag{2.3}$$

On other side, recurrent LSTM based model structure contains memory to hold states that's why an expectation of the prediction of patch of original image is made in each stage. Residual with respect to the original patch presented in below Eq. (2.4).

$$R_t = F_t(R_{t-1}) - R_0 \tag{2.4}$$

In these two cases, the training of this whole multi stage network is done with the minimization of $\|R^2\|$ for $t = 1$ to n where n is the total residual encoder in model.

Binary Representation: This process involves two parts, first part uses a continuous interval $[-1, 1]$ for the generation of required number output. And second part includes generation of discrete valued output within $\{-1, 1\}$ with the input of real valued data.

In first step of binarization with activation function Tan_h fully connected layers are used. In next part binarization of continuous interval $[-1, 1]$ defined as [6]:

$$b(x) = x + \varepsilon \text{ where } \varepsilon\{-1, 1\} \tag{2.5}$$

$$\varepsilon = \begin{cases} 1 - x, & \text{with probability, } \frac{1+x}{2} \\ -x - 1, & \text{with probability, } \frac{1-x}{2} \end{cases} \tag{2.6}$$

$b(x) =$ binarization function
$\varepsilon =$ quantization noise

Now full function of binary encoder is:

$$B(x) = b\left(\tanh_h\left(W^{bin}x + b^{bin}\right)\right) \tag{2.7}$$

$B(x) =$ full function for binary encodings
$W^{bin} =$ Weights
$b^{bin} =$ Biases

When the networks are fully trained and to get a fixed output for a certain input, b^{inf} is used over b, for most likely output of b(x):

$$b^{inf}(x) = \begin{cases} -1 \text{ if } x < 0 \\ +1 \text{ otherwise} \end{cases} \tag{2.8}$$

Residual encoder with fully connected layers with feed forward network structure.

First weights are shared with all stages. Second, independently learn unambiguous weights with each stage (Fig. 1).

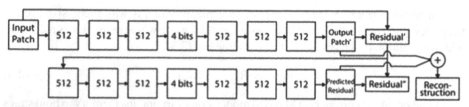

Fig. 1. Residual encoder with fully connected layers with feed forward network structure [6].

Compression based on LSTM.

64-bit output is viable by iterating 16 times with a space of 4 bit each. Blocks with 512 are layers fully connected with each other.

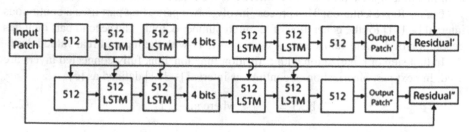

Fig. 2. Compression based on LSTM [6].

A block with 512 contains LSTM contains layers of LSTM with 512 units repeatedly passing residual of output again as input 16 times is done, to construct 64-bit internal representation. A persistent memory is shown as a connection that is a vertical edge between two LSTM cells in the unrolled diagram. The loss used in training over residual is L2 measurement. In this model, every iteration/step actual output is predicted.

A residual encoding with de-convolutional/Convolutional using Feed-Forward.

Rectangles with sharp edges represent convolution layers and with round edges are de-Convolutional.

Previous architecture is extended in a manner that convolution operators are used in encoder E in layer connected in fully connected nature and with de-convolution operators

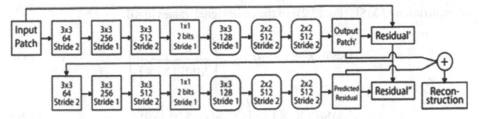

Fig. 3. De-convolutional/convolutional residual based encoder [6].

in D. Decoder in final layer contains convolution of 1×1 with three filters to convert decoded data into RGB values.

Compression using LSTM with De-convolution/Convolution.
In this case, De-convolution/convolution operators are used with LSTM. In this architecture, convolution based layers in Fig. 3 are replaced with LSTM with convolution based layers plus bias. In decoder, to construct a LSTM with de-convolution that are Fig. 2 and Fig. 3 of de-convolution based decoder are replaced with LSTM having de-convolution strategy/based model/embedded.

2.2 Convent Based Image Compression

A Convent based image compression [7] technique is used, here A and D (as shown in Fig. 4) Are the layers with convolution with channels from 1 to 128 and later again to 256, for the deep network? A down sampling to perform resolution change is done at the same time by using a 2×2 filter pooling with average of them with a stride of 2×2. After this data flow through convolution layers with full connection that are $\tilde{D}$, $\tilde{B}$ and also through $\tilde{A}$, following this a 12 layer convent is obtained. Going beyond the accuracy of the stare of the art is fulfilled by bringing down the path length in the network. And to perform this task, the intermediate outcomes of higher dimension namely resolution after fully connected layer of convolution are emphasized in next layer by adding features (low level) extracted beforehand from network with this resolution natively. Instead of performing optimization from Input to output, a lower resolution previously obtained from network and via a single layer of convolution ($\hat{D}$, $\hat{c}$, $\hat{B}$) is constructed. An output here is not abandoned but up scaled by using a 2×2 filter size using NN merging with the feature maps that are yielded by parallel (yellow connection) layer of full convolution.

A PRELu activation function is used in all of the layers that are concerned with the full convolution and convolution. Initial weights and initial biases are obtained through a $(-nin^{\wedge}(-1/2), nin^{\wedge}(-1/2),)$ uniform interval.

Performance Metrics.
Well known metrics that are used to evaluate changes between pictures and other lower and higher frequency signals are MSE and PSNR where MSE is the difference of intensity of pixels referenced and a deformed (obtained) image. PSNR (Eq. (2.1)) is the

normalization of MSE (Eq. (2.2)) to the peak signal values in dB.

$$\text{PSNR}(X, \hat{X}) = 10 \log_{10}\left(\frac{1}{\text{MSE}\left(X, \hat{X}\right)}\right) \tag{2.9}$$

$$\text{MSE}\left(X, \hat{X}\right) = \left(\sum_{p \in P} e(x_p, \hat{x}_p)^2\right) / |P| \tag{2.10}$$

P = pixel index set
X = reference image
x^ = image for evaluation
E = error function per pixel
PSNR = Peak Signal to Noise Ratio
MSE = Mean Squared error

Loss Function.
To improve the results low and high resolution are used within the network. A multi-scale loss used with the contribution of MSE. Minimization of MSE is only perform for the high resolution output and trim the loss function with low resolution images until convergence for fine tuning of the network. This task is performed on QF dataset. Model Overview:

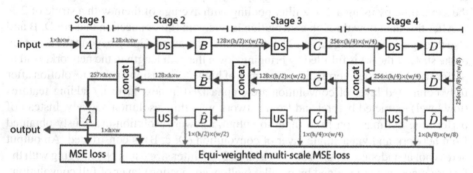

Fig. 4. Structure of the given convolution neural network [7].

The paths are colour coded: main path (blue), Again using multiple time scaled outputs (light yellow), multiple scaled output (green), Low level features are concatenated (red colour) (Tables 1 and 2).

Table 1. Model hyper parameters [7].

Name	Type	#outp. Ch	#inp. Ch	filter size	#param
A(1)	Conv	128	1	3×3	1k
A(2)	Conv	128	128	3×3	147k
B(1)	Conv	128	128	3×3	147k
B(2)	Conv	128	128	3×3	147k
C(1)	Conv	128	256	3×3	295k
C(2)	Conv	256	256	3×3	590k
D(1)	Conv	256	256	3×3	590k
D(2)	Conv	256	256	3×3	590k
$\tilde{D}$	fullconv	256	256	$4 \times 4/2$	1049k
$\hat{D}$	Conv	1	256	3×3	2k
$\tilde{c}$	fullconv	128	513	$4 \times 4/2$	1051k
$\hat{C}$	Conv	1	513	3×3	5k
$\tilde{B}$	fullconv	128	257	$4 \times 4/2$	526k
$\hat{B}$	Conv	1	257	3×3	2k
$\hat{A}$	Conv	1	257	3×3	2k
Total					5144k

Table 2. Results in comparison with other previous works [7].

QF	Algorithm	PSNR[dB]	PSNR-B[dB]	SSIM
10	JPEG	27.77	25.33	0.791
	SA-DCT	28.65	28.01	0.809
	AR-CNN	29.13	28.74	0.823
	L4	29.08	28.7	0.824
	Ours MS Loss	29.36	29.92	0.830
	Ours, W/LossFT	29.44	29.19	0.833
20	JPEG	30.07	27.57	0.868
	SA-DCT	30.81	29.82	0.878
	AR-CNN	31.40	30.69	0.890
	L4	31.42	30.83	0.890
	L8	31.51	30.92	0.891
	Ours, MS Loss	31.67	30.84	0.894
	Ours, W/LossFT	31.70	30.88	0.895
40	JPEG	32.35	29.96	0.917
	SA-DCT	32.99	31.79	0.924
	AR-CNN	32.63	33.12	0.931
	L4	33.77	–	–
	Ours, MS Loss	33.98	32.83	0.935
	Ours, w/LossFT	34.10	33.68	0.937
60	JPEG	33.99	31.89	0.940
	Ours, w/LossFT	35.78	35.10	0.954
80	JPEG	36.88	35.47	0.964
	Ours, w/LossFT	38.55	37.75	0.973

QF = quality factor of JPEG images.

3 Conclusion and Discussion

According to the implementation of image compression with variable rates using RNN [6], the given approach produces remarkable results with small size images in comparison with new codecs, these new codecs may use entropy based coder and likely to improve results on large resolution pictures. As this methodology needs to be further improved to work upon random large size pictures.

In the deep ConvNet based method [6] 12-layer are used to train, according to this methodology better results are achieved in comparison to normal JPEG giving a rise of 1.79 dB in peak signal to noise ratio and improvement of 0.36 dB against previous works but specific compression based JPEG are not tailored with this Net.

References

1. Aaditya, P., Nick, M., Solomon, G., Antonella, D., James, S.: Semantic Perceptual Image Compression using Deep Convolution Networks, pp. 250–252. Brandeis University, New York (2017)
2. Fei, Y., Luis, H., Yongmei, C., Mikhail, G.M.: Slimmable compressive autoencoders for practical neural image compression. In: Proceedings of the IEEE/CVF Conference on Computer Vision and Pattern Recognition, pp. 1–3 (2021)
3. Guo, P., Li, D., Li, X.: Deep OCT image compression with convolutional neural networks. Biomed. Opt. Express 11, 3543–3554 (2020)
4. Saleh, A.A.: neural network technique for image compression. In: IET Image Processing (2016)
5. Nick, J., Elad, E., Ariel, G., Johannes, B.: Computationally Efficient Neural Image Compression. Google Research, pp. 1–2 (2019)
6. George T., et al.: A Conference Paper Variable Rate Image Compression with Recurrent Neural Networks, pp. 1–6 (2016)
7. Lukas, C., Pascal, H., Luca, B.: CAS-CNN: A Deep Convolutional Neural Network for Image Compression Artifact Suppression, pp. 753–755 (2017)

Deep Learning on Small Tabular Dataset: Using Transfer Learning and Image Classification

Vanshika Jain[✉], Meghansh Goel, and Kshitiz Shah

Maharaja Agrasen Institute of Technology, New Delhi, India

Abstract. Deep Learning is a subset of machine learning inspired by the human brain. It uses multiple layers of representation to extract specific knowledge from raw input. It is best suited for large image or sound-based datasets. Deep learning methods are generally avoided for small datasets because they tend to overfit. Transfer learning can be one approach used to solve this problem. However, in the case of tabular datasets, their heterogeneous nature makes transfer learning algorithms inapplicable. This paper aims to discuss a few approaches using a literature review to convert tabular data into images to overcome such limitations. The paper provides a 2-part study wherein we first give a brief overview of transfer learning enhancing the efficiency of deep learning algorithms and drastically reducing the training time for small datasets. Secondly, we provide a detailed study of different techniques available to convert tabular data into images for image classification such as SuperTML, IGTD, and REFINED approach. Furthermore, we propose a novel approach inspired by IGTD to create a blocked image representation of the tabular data on which we apply transfer learning to demonstrate the application of deep learning methods on small tabular datasets (with less than 1000 data points).

Keywords: Deep learning · Resnet · Small tabular datasets · Image classification · Transfer learning

1 Introduction

Deep-learning methods are a subset of machine learning algorithms using artificial neural networks. These neural network layers are obtained by combining non-linear modules, each of which starts with an original input and transforms a level of representation into a higher one. Deep learning algorithms try to mimic the function and structure of the human brain. Deep Learning models are much more efficient than conventional machine Learning (ML) models as they can work on unstructured data. ML models usually require an extra step of data pre-processing, increasing the user load.

A Deep Learning algorithm learns and adjusts itself through methods like back-propagation and gradient descent. Such adaptability leads to greater accuracy on models trained on large datasets. In recent times Deep Learning has taken the world by storm and has found numerous applications in various fields such as Law enforcement, healthcare, banking & finance, agriculture, eCommerce, and many more. Hence, there has been an exponential increase in the number of Deep Learning publications, evident from Fig. 1.

© Springer Nature Switzerland AG 2022
A. Dev et al. (Eds.): AIST 2021, CCIS 1546, pp. 555–568, 2022.
https://doi.org/10.1007/978-3-030-95711-7_46

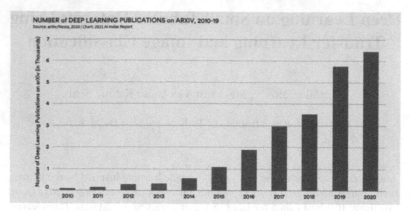

Fig. 1. Chart depicting the increase in number of Deep Learning Publications on ARXIV [1]

While using deep learning has many benefits, such as eliminating feature extraction and delivering excellent results, it faces its limitations. A fundamental limitation of DL models is their inability to deal with small and tabular data. A deep learning model works by tweaking its bias and variance until a good enough compromise is achieved. Research has shown that the more data such models have to train, the higher their accuracy. Hence, deep learning models generally require an extensive dataset. However, data is usually limited in many domains, making building large, high-quality annotated datasets complex and expensive. Also, tabular datasets still exist in numerous fields, like healthcare, finance, bioinformatics and many more.

The problem with using deep learning on small datasets is that deep learning models tend to overfit after several epochs. Consequently, another field of deep learning, known as transfer learning, has evolved and proven to be efficient in drastically reducing the need for extensive training datasets and training time, thereby increasing the accuracy.

In transfer learning, information is transferred from a pre-trained model of a related domain and then by fine-tuning that knowledge on a relatively small dataset of the current task. This paper gives a brief overview of how transfer learning has successfully applied deep learning on smaller datasets.

However, for tabular datasets, the transfer learning and deep learning methods become inapplicable. Hence, researchers tried to develop methods to create image representations of tabular datasets which can be further used for classification using CNNs. Here, we discuss a few approaches for converting tabular data to images: REFINED technique, IGTD and SuperTML.

IGTD transforms tabular data into images by assigning features to pixel positions so that similar features are closer in the image [2]. On the other hand, the REFINED technique considers the similarities between features to generate a concise feature map in the form of a 2-D image by minimizing the pairwise distance values following a Bayesian Metric Multidimensional Scaling Approach [3]. SuperTML, however, borrows the idea of the Super Characters method and two-dimensional embeddings to create image representation of the tabular data and then applies transfer learning on the same for classification [4].

This paper provides a literature review of these three techniques. Finally, we provide our empirical work on a relatively rare field, i.e., the application of deep learning models on small tabular datasets. Inspired by IGTD, we apply a new technique for creating image representations of tabular data. Then we apply transfer learning on the same to improve deep learning results, considering the dataset is very small (796 data points). The idea of using transfer learning on image conversions of tabular data was inspired by SuperTML.

For this practical application, we use the Pima Indians Diabetes dataset for type-2 diabetes prediction. We also compare the results with some conventional machine learning classification algorithms such as KNN, Random Forest, Decision Trees (ID3), SVM, Naive Bayes, and many more. The results highlight how deep learning techniques can be used effectively for small tabular datasets (with less than 1000 data points).

2   Transfer Learning: A Brief Overview

Transfer learning is a technique that creates complex models by using existing pre-trained models. It transfers skills acquired from learning and training in one domain to another related domain [5, 6]. The premise for the Transfer Learning methodology can be witnessed in real life. As illustrated in [5], a person who has a fundamental understanding of music theory because of their experience with the guitar would grasp and learn the piano much faster when compared to a person with no prior knowledge of music.

The need for transfer learning arises due to the limited supply of training data which could be due to the data being expensive to collect and label, the data being rare, or the data being inaccessible. Transfer learning has found success in various fields including text image classification [7–9] multi-language text classification [10–12], software defect classification [13],sentiment classification [14] and human activity classification [15]. Information regarding the nitty-gritty and history of transfer learning is not under this paper's scope but can be read in the paper by Pan [16].

Transfer learning's benefits have been seen in image classification using small datasets. In a paper by Mengying Shu [17]. Shu explores the advantages of transfer learning by using a relatively small image-based dataset containing images of cats and dogs. The dataset consisted of 6,000 images, including 3000 training data, 2,000 validation data, and 1,000 testing data. Shu avoided extreme overfitting by using tabular transfer learning. Shu employed data augmentation, fine-tuning, and Dropout mechanisms before using deep models like VGG16 VGG19, Inception V3, InceptionResNet V2. The accuracy obtained has been shown below in Table 1, from which we can see that the experiment was quite successful.

In another study [18], researchers compared the results of popular CNN models like Alexnet, TCNN [19] and their approach – TLCNN-GAP. The dataset is the Pascal VOC2007 data set consisting of 20 categories and 9963 images. They extracted some of the data to form a small sample data set. They also tested on the Caltech10 dataset, with ten categories totalling 50,000 training pictures and 10,000 test pictures. They randomly selected five categories. The results shown below (Table 2) indicate that transfer learning does help improve the results even when applied to small datasets.

Table 1. Accuracy of various deep learning models trained using transfer learning [17]

	Training accuracy	Validation accuracy	Testing accuracy
Baseline	86%	75%	73.8%
VGG16	95%	89%	83%
VGG16 with Data Augmentation	83%	89%	88.1%
VGG16 with FineTuning	97%	96%	95%
VGG19	95%	89%	83%
VGG19 with Data Augmentation	83%	88%	85.2%
VGG19 with FineTuning	98%	96%	95.3%
Inception V3	99%	96%	93%
Inception V3 with Data Augmentation	80%	95%	94.7%
Inception V3 with FineTuning	88%	95%	95%
InceptionResNet V2	99%	97%	95%
InceptionResNet V2 with Data Augmentation	82%	95%	95.6%
InceptionResNet V2 with FineTuning	90%	97%	96%

Table 2. Accuracy improvement by using transfer learning on small datasets (Caltech10) [18]

Model	Airplane	Automobile	Bird	Cat	Deer
CNN	78.6	80.2	78.3	83.5	80.6
TCNN	80.5	82.1	81.4	85.3	82.8
TLCNN-GAP	81.6	83.7	84.1	86.4	83.0

Transfer learning is a deep learning approach; thus, it shares the pros and cons of a deep learning algorithm. Deep learning has taken over the domain of unstructured data however is inefficient in handling tabular data and does not perform well compared to other neural networks and some conventional machine learning classification algorithms. This paper reviews the following techniques (REFINED, IGDT, and SuperTML) to overcome the limitation mentioned above by converting this 1-dimensional data into 2-dimensional data.

3 Deep Learning on Tabular Datasets

Deep learning techniques have produced excellent results in the field of image classification, computer vision, NLP, speech and audio recognition, and many more, especially with large datasets. With the introduction of transfer learning, they have also overcome their limitations with small datasets. However, transfer learning and deep learning methods are inapplicable for tabular datasets due to their heterogeneous nature. Therefore, to fully exploit deep learning powers for tabular datasets, algorithms have been developed to convert these tabular datasets into image representations. This paper discusses three such algorithms: REFINED (REpresentation of Features as Images with Images NEighborhood Dependencies), IGTD (image generator for tabular data), and SuperTML. A brief literature review of these three methods is given first, and then we will also discuss them in detail in further sections.

3.1 Literature Review

3.1.1 Representation of Features as Images with Neighborhood Dependencies for Compatibility with Convolutional Neural Networks [3]

Omid Bazgir, Ruibo Zhang, Saugato Rahman Dhruba, Raziur Rahman, Souparno Ghosh & Ranadip Pal

In this literature, the authors have proposed a novel method called REFINED (REpresentation of Features as Images with NEighborhood Dependencies) to arrange high-dimensional tabular data in a compact image form for CNN-based deep learning. The authors have proposed to create image datasets by minimizing the pairwise distance values using a Bayesian Metric Multidimensional Scaling Approach for each datapoint.

The technique was applied on drug sensitivity prediction scenarios using synthetic datasets, drug chemical descriptors as predictors from NC160, and both transcriptomic information and drug descriptors as predictors from GDSC [3].

Finally, the paper compares the performance of the REFINED-CNN model with other competing models such as ANN, SVR, Random Forest, and many more, wherein it consistently outperformed others.

3.1.2 Converting Tabular Data into Images for Deep Learning with Convolutional Neural Networks [2]

Yitan Zhu, Thomas Brettin, Fangfang Xia, Alexander Partin, Maulik Shukla, Hyunseung Yoo, Yvonne A. Evrard, James H. Doroshow & Rick L. Stevens

In this literature, the authors have proposed a novel algorithm, Image Generator for Tabular Data (IGTD), to transform tabular data into images by assigning features to pixel positions so that similar features are closer in the image. Their algorithm minimizes the difference between the ranking of distances between features and the ranking of distances between their assigned pixels in the image [2]. They have used gene expression profiles of cancer cell lines (CCLs) and molecular descriptors of drugs as their datasets to predict anti-cancer drug response. One of the motivations for the paper was that for some tabular data, the order of features could be rearranged in 2-D space to explicitly represent relationships between features [2], which CNN can learn and utilize to improve the prediction performance.

The paper also discusses three more approaches in brief and uses the same on their datasets to create a comparison of results. These techniques are DeepInsight [20], REFINED (REpresentation of Features as Images with NEighborhood Dependencies) [3], and OmicsMapNet [21]. Finally, the paper compares the results with three approaches and states that their algorithm successfully overcame the limitations of the other three techniques and provided the best results.

3.1.3   SuperTML: Domain Transfer from Computer Vision to Structured Tabular Data Through Two-Dimensional Word Embedding [4]

Still Under Review by the International Conference on Machine Learning (ICML).

In this literature, the authors take inspiration from the Super Characters method. They propose the SuperTML method in which, for each input of tabular data, the features are first projected into two-dimensional embeddings like an image. Then this image is fed into fine-tuned ImageNet CNN models for classification [4].

As stated in the paper, one of the motivations for this technique was the analogy between TML (transfer machine learning) problems and text classification problems [4]. The algorithm has been applied to three datasets: The Adult dataset, the Wine dataset, and the Iris dataset. Finally, the results have been compared with one of the most popular machine learning techniques, i.e., XGBoost.

4   Methods Used

4.1   REFINED

4.1.1   About

REFINED is a feature representation approach that aids in CNN-based deep learning by arranging vectors of high dimension into compact images. A two-dimensional image is created by generating a feature map using a Bayesian Metric Multidimensional Scaling Approach to minimize the pairwise distance and identify the similarities between various features. REFINED eliminates the need for feature engineering and allows for automatic feature extraction using CNN.

4.1.2   Image Generation Technique

The REFINED technique for image generation comprises three steps. In the first step, a Euclidean Distance matrix of the features is obtained, used as a distance measure to generate 2D images of closely related neighborhood features [3]. The 2D images are generated by using a Multidimensional Scaling (MDS) Approach. The next step is to guarantee that each mapped point has a unique pixel representation in the image and there are no overlaps. This step involves applying the Bayesian version of metric MDS (BMDS), which ensures that each pixel represents a unique feature.

After obtaining the BMDS version of the image, the final step involves finding the optimal configuration of the features, which is achieved by trying all the permutations of features by interchanging the position of central feature position with neighboring features such that the cost function is minimized [3].

4.1.3 Results of REFINED Method

After considering 80% drugs as training set, 10% as test and 10% as validation set, REFINED CNN showed better results on all 17 cell lines when compared with other classifiers. F1-score and AUROC values also indicated REFINED CNN's high discriminative abilities. Accuracies obtained are shown in Table 3.

Table 3. Accuracy of REFINED-CNN compared with other classifiers [3]

Model	Mean accuracy
REFINED-CNN	75.4%
ANN	70.3%
RF	70.0%
SVM	69.0%
LR	67.9%

McNemar's test was also used to compute the variation in performance of different classifiers. For all competing classifiers, it was observed that RANDOM CNN performed significantly better.

4.2 IGTD

4.2.1 About

The IGTD algorithm works by assigning every feature a particular pixel value for the image representation. The pixel intensity is controlled by the value related to that specific feature. It optimizes this process of feature assignment to pixels by reducing the difference between pairwise feature distance ranks and also, between pairwise pixel distance ranks [2].

4.2.2 Image Generation Technique

The objective is to convert each sample data row into a 2-Dimensional image. First, the distance between each two features is calculated. Then all the distances are ranked in ascending order. Next, an N x N matrix is formed. Here, N represents the number of features, in which at the ith row and jth column of the matrix represents rank of the distance between ith and jth features. The larger the rank is, the darker the point in the plot. Similarly, a N x N matrix for pixel pairwise distances is formed. The error function given below is used to calculate the difference between these matrices (Fig. 2).

The algorithm reorders the features to reduce err(R, Q), keeping similar features closer in the image. For this, it selects two features using an iterative process and swaps

$$err(\textbf{R}, \textbf{Q}) = \sum_{i=2}^{N} \sum_{j=1}^{i-1} diff\left(r_{i,j}, q_{i,j}\right)$$

Fig. 2. The formula used to calculate error between two matrices [2]

the position of these two features. Algorithm keeps a track of all the features that have been involved in a feature swap by using a vector and updating it after every iteration with the iteration number for that feature position. Initially every value is negative of infinity. After every iteration, the feature with smallest value in the vector is picked up and then a suitable feature swap resulting in least error function value is identified.

4.2.3 Results of IGTD Method

The results show that compared with REFINED and DeepInsight, the IGTD algorithm produced many promising results. For instance, OmicsMapNet requires domain-specific knowledge, whereas IGTD is a general algorithm that can be used without any domain knowledge. Also, the image representations generated by the DeepInsight method are huge and thus use relatively more training time and storage space than IGTD. Moreover, IGTD generates images preserving the neighborhood structure much better than the REFINED technique (Table 4).

Table 4. Comparing the performance of IGTD method with other models. In R^2 column, value out of parenthesis is the avg. over 20 cross-validation trials. The value in parenthesis is S.D. [2]

Dataset	Prediction model	Data representation	R^2	P-value
CTRP	LightGBM	Tabular data	0.825 (0.003)	8.19E−20
	Random forest		0.786 (0.003)	5.97E−26
	tDNN		0.834 (0.004)	7.90E−18
	sDNN		0.832 (0.005)	1.09E−16
	CNN	IGTD images	**0.856** (0.003)	
		REFINED images	0.855 (0.003)	8.77E−01
		DeepInsight images	0.846 (0.004)	7.02E−10

4.3 SuperTML

4.3.1 About

The SuperTML method solves the problem of classification of tabular datasets by borrowing the concept of the super characters method and 2-dimensional embeddings. The features from the tabular dataset are projected onto a 2-dimensional embedding first and then classified using pre-trained CNN models. The SuperTML method automatically solves the issue of the missing values and categorical type, removing the need for separate numerical conversions [4].

4.3.2 Image Generation Technique

There are two types of SuperTML methods. These are SuperTML_VF and SuperTML_EF. The SuperTML algorithm is a two-step process. Firstly, input text characters are transferred on a blank image. The image conversions for different datasets used in the paper for SuperTML are shown in Fig. 3((a), (b), and (c)). In the second step, these images are fed into fine-tuned CNN models. These convolution neural networks are pre-trained using huge image repositories such as ImageNet.

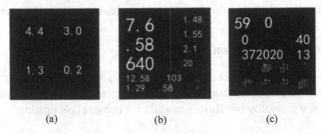

   (a)   (b)   (c)

Fig. 3. (a) SuperTML_EF representations on Iris Dataset. (b) SuperTML_VF representations on Wine Dataset. (c) SuperTML_EF representations on Adult Dataset

4.3.3 Results of SuperTML Method

The results indicate how CNN models successfully classified tabular data after they were pre-trained on large image datasets such as ImageNet. The results are also compared with leading machine learning classification technique: the XGBoost algorithm (Tables 5 and 6).

Table 5. An overview of the datasets used in SuperTML [4]

Dataset	Classes	#Attributes	Train	Test	Total	Data types	Missing
Iris	3	4	NA	NA	150	Real	No
Wine	3	13	NA	NA	178	Integer and Real	No
Adult	2	14	32,561	16,281	48,842	Integer and Categorical	Yes

Table 6. Accuracy of SuperTML compared with XGBoost [4]

Accuracy	Iris (%)	Wine (%)	Adult (%)
XGBoost	93.33	96.88	87.32
SuperTML	93.33	97.30	87.64

5   Application of Deep Learning on Small Tabular Dataset

5.1   About the Dataset

Type II diabetes, a form of diabetes, strikes a person due to insulin resistance and relative insulin deficiency. It can be due to obesity, bad eating habits, lethargy, hereditary diabetes issue, or particular ethnicity. About 90% of the diabetic population has type II diabetes [25, 26]. Thus, for this paper, we aimed to study type II diabetes using the Pima Indians diabetes dataset available on the Kaggle repository having eight variables and 768 data points. All patients included in the dataset are females and at least 21 years old.

5.2   Technique and Application

We followed a two-part approach. In the first part, we work on generating images from the dataset. We use a sigmoid function to generate pixel values for each data point. In the second part, we employ our Resnet models for image classification.

5.2.1   Image Generation Using Sigmoid Function

A *sigmoid* mathematical function has a 'S'-shaped curve. (Fig. 4). Since pixel values in images are positive, a sigmoid function was chosen to map negative values to positive ones.

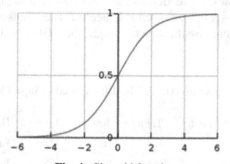

Fig. 4. Sigmoid function

The flow of converting data points to pixel values was as shown below. From these pixel values, we created blocked image representations of each data point shown in the figure below (Fig. 5).

5.2.2   Image Classification Using ResNet34

ResNet [22] stands for residual neural network. It is an extension of ANN that is developed by knowledge gained from pyramidal cells in the human cerebral cortex. ResNet model uses multi-layer skip connections that contain nonlinearities (ReLU) between them (Fig. 6).

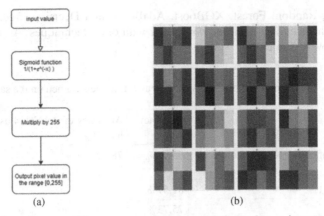

(a)   (b)

Fig. 5. (a) A flow diagram of the process used to convert tabular data to image representations. (b) Blocked image representation obtained from the tabular data

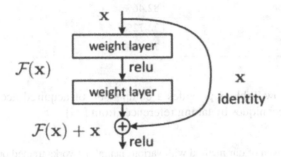

Fig. 6. Architecture of a ReLU unit [22]

ResNet requires a large dataset for optimal weight optimization and good accuracy for training on a new model. Therefore, to increase our accuracy and reduce training times, we employ the use of Transfer Learning. ResNet is trained using ImageNet dataset containing more than 14,000,000 images divided into more than 20,000 categories. We have to tweak the weights a little according to our dataset using transfer learning instead of initializing them from scratch. We tested three variations of Resnet, namely Resnet18, Resnet34, and Resnet50. However, we achieved the best results using Resnet34.

We also employed state-of-the-art training strategies such as Cyclic Learning Rate [23] and One Cycle Learning [24]. One Cycle Learning suggests cycling the learning rate of the model from its smallest value to its highest. Hence, the model was able to provide flatter minima.

5.3   Results and Comparison

Using Transfer Learning and One Cycle Learning, we were able to achieve high accuracy of 78.4% using the Pima Indians Diabetes dataset. We also applied some standard machine learning techniques to the same, such as Logistic Regression, KNN, Naive

Bayes, SVM, Random Forest, XGBoost, AdaBoost, and Decision Tree, to compare the results. The accuracy achieved was at par with other techniques. A comparison is provided below in Table 7.

Table 7. Comparison of our method with various ML models trained on the same dataset

Technique	Accuracy	Accuracy of ResNet34 using transfer learning
K-Nearest Neighbors (KNN) (with K = 5)	75.97%	78.4%
Random Forest	81.57%	
Naïve Bayes	75.73%	
Decision Tree – (ID3)	73.37%	
Support Vector Machine (SVM)	79.22%	
Logistic Regression	82.46%	
XGB Classifier	72.72%	
AdaBoost	77.92%	

Also, the below Table 8 provides a comparison of acquired accuracy with some neural network techniques by taking references from [25].

Table 8. Comparison of our method with various neural networks trained on the same dataset

Year performed	Technique	Accuracy	Accuracy of ResNet34 using transfer learning
2014	Multilayer Feed Forward Neural Network – Back-Propagation Algorithm (ANN) [27]	82%	78.4%
2016	Probabilistic Neural Network (PNN) [28]	81.49%	
2017	Recurrent Deep Neural Network (RNN) [29]	81%	
2017	Two-Class Neural Network [30]	83.3%	

6 Conclusion

Deep Learning techniques are much more efficient than classic machine Learning (ML) algorithms. But their limitations with small and tabular datasets have recently questioned their extensibility. Transfer learning is one approach used to resolve the problem of overfitting with small datasets. However, transfer learning and deep learning methods were still inapplicable for tabular datasets due to their heterogeneous nature.

Hence, researchers tried to develop methods to create image representations of tabular data which can be further used for classification using CNNs. Three such techniques were discussed in this paper: IGTD, REFINED technique, and SuperTML, out of which IGTD has been the best technique as it does not require any domain knowledge, produces compact images, and preserves neighborhood structure better.

Eventually, taking inspiration from IGTD, we proposed a new image generation technique using a sigmoid function. The images generated by this mechanism were in the form of blocked representation on which we further applied transfer learning using the ResNet34 model, which was pre-trained on ImageNet data.

For this practical application, we used the Pima Indians Diabetes dataset for type-2 diabetes prediction. The algorithm obtained an accuracy of 78.4%, highlighting how deep learning techniques can be used effectively for small tabular datasets (with less than 1000 data points).

7 Future Scope

The proposed approach can be applied to other tabular datasets to create a comprehensive comparison of the performance in different cases. The model's accuracy can be improved by representing feature importance in the generated images. For this, the size of the blocks of essential features needs to be increased compared to others. Morcover, compound models like ResNet-SVM or ResNet-XGBoost can also give better results.

References

1. Zhang, D., et al.: The AI Index 2021 Annual Report (2021)
2. Zhu, Y., et al.: Converting tabular data into images for deep learning with convolutional neural networks. Sci. Rep. **11**(1), 11325 (2021). https://doi.org/10.1038/s41598-021-90923-y
3. Bazgir, O., Zhang, R., Dhruba, S.R., Rahman, R., Ghosh, S., Pal, R.: Representation of features as images with neighborhood dependencies for compatibility with convolutional neural networks. Nat. Commun. **11**(1), 4391 (2020). https://doi.org/10.1038/s41467-020-18197-y
4. Sun, B., et al.: SuperTML: Two-Dimensional Word Embedding and Transfer Learning Using ImageNet Pretrained CNN Models for the Classifications on Tabular Data (2019)
5. Weiss, K., Khoshgoftaar, T.M., Wang, D.: A survey of transfer learning. J. Big Data **3**(1), 1–40 (2016). https://doi.org/10.1186/s40537-016-0043-6
6. Tan, C., Sun, F., Kong, T., Zhang, W., Yang, C., Liu, C.: A Survey on Deep Transfer Learning. arXiv (2018)
7. Duan, L., Xu, D., Tsang, I.W.: Learning with Augmented Features for Heterogeneous Domain Adaptation. arXiv (2012)
8. Kulis, B., Saenko, K., Darrell, T.: What you saw is not what you get: domain adaptation using asymmetric kernel transforms. CVPR **2011**, 1785–1792 (2011)
9. Zhu, Y., et al.: Heterogeneous transfer learning for image classification. In: Proceedings of the Twenty-Fifth AAAI Conference on Artificial Intelligence, AAAI (2011)

10. Tianyi Zhou, J., Tsang, I.W., Jialin Pan, S., Tan, M.: Heterogeneous domain adaptation for multiple classes. In: AISTATS (International Conference on Artificial Intelligence and Statistics) (2014)
11. Zhou, J.T., Pan, S.J., Tsang, I.W., Yan, Y.: Hybrid heterogeneous transfer learning through deep learning. In: Proceedings of the AAAI Conference on Artificial Intelligence, vol. 28, no. 1 (2014)
12. Prettenhofer, P., Stein, B.: Cross-language text classification using structural correspondence learning. In: Proceedings of the 48th Annual Meeting of the Association for Computational Linguistics, pp. 11–16 (2010)
13. Nam, J., Kim, S.: Heterogeneous defect prediction. IEEE Trans. Softw. Eng. **44**(9), 874–896 (2015)
14. Wang, C., Mahadevan, S.: Heterogeneous domain adaptation using manifold alignment. In: Proceedings of the 22nd International Joint Conference on Artificial Intelligence, pp. 1541–1546 (2011)
15. Harel, M., Mannor, S.: Learning from Multiple Outlooks. *arXiv* (2011)
16. Pan, S.J., Yang, Q.: A survey on transfer learning. IEEE Trans. Knowl. Data Eng. **22**(10), 1345–1359 (2010)
17. Shu, M.: Deep learning for image classification on very small datasets using transfer learning using transfer learning. Creat. Compon. 345 (2019)
18. Zhao, W.: Research on the deep learning of the small sample data based on transfer learning. AIP Conf. Proc. **1864**, 020018 (2017)
19. Krizhevsky, A., Sutskever, I., Hinton, G.E.: ImageNet classification with deep convolutional neural networks. Commun. ACM **60**(6), 84–90 (2017)
20. Sharma, A., Vans, E., Shigemizu, D., Boroevich, K.A., Tsunoda, T.: DeepInsight: a methodology to transform a non-image data to an image for convolution neural network architecture. Sci. Rep. **9**(1), 11399 (2019)
21. Ma, S., Zhang, Z.: OmicsMapNet: Transforming omics data to take advantage of Deep Convolutional Neural Network for discovery. *arXiv* (2018)
22. He, K., Zhang, X., Ren, S., Sun, J.: Deep residual learning for image recognition. In: 2016 IEEE Conference on Computer Vision and Pattern Recognition (CVPR), pp. 770–778 (2016)
23. Smith, L.N.: Cyclical learning rates for training neural networks. In: 2017 IEEE Winter Conference on Applications of Computer Vision (WACV), pp. 464–472 (2017)
24. Smith, L.N.: A Disciplined Approach to Neural Network Hyper-Parameters: Part 1. Learning Rate, Batch Size, Momentum, and Weight Decay. *arXiv* (2018)
25. Larabi-Marie-Sainte, S., Aburahmah, L., Almohaini, R., Saba, T.: Current techniques for diabetes prediction: review and case study. Appl. Sci. **9**(21), 4604 (2019)
26. American Diabetes Association: Type 2 diabetes in children and adolescents. Pediatrics **105**(3), 671–680 (2000). https://doi.org/10.1542/peds.105.3.671
27. Khashman, A., Ebenezer, O., Oyedot, O., Munawar, S., Olaniyi, E.O., Adnan, K.: Onset diabetes diagnosis using artificial neural network. Int. J. Sci. Eng. Res. **5**(10), 754–759 (2014)
28. Soltani, Z., Jafarian, A.: A new artificial neural networks approach for diagnosing diabetes disease type II. Int. J. Adv. Comput. Sci. Appl. **7**(6), 89–94 (2016)
29. Ashiquzzaman, A., et al.: Reduction of overfitting in diabetes prediction using deep learning neural network. In: Kim, Kuinam J., Kim, Hyuncheol, Baek, Nakhoon (eds.) IT Convergence and Security 2017, pp. 35–43. Springer Singapore, Singapore (2018). https://doi.org/10.1007/978-981-10-6451-7_5
30. Rakshit, S., et al.: Prediction of diabetes Type-II using a two-class neural network. In: Mandal, J.K., Dutta, P., Mukhopadhyay, S. (eds.) CICBA 2017. CCIS, vol. 776, pp. 65–71. Springer, Singapore (2017). https://doi.org/10.1007/978-981-10-6430-2_6

Implementation of a Method Using Image Sequentialization, Patch Embedding and ViT Encoder to Detect the Breast Cancer on RGBA Images and Binary Masks

Tanishka Dixit[1], Namrata Singh[2](✉), Geetika Srivastava[3], and Meenakshi Srivastava[4]

[1] Department of Computer Science and Engineering, NarainaVidhyapeeth Engineering and Management Institute, Panki, Kanpur, India
[2] Department of Computer Science and Engineering, NarainaVidhyapeeth Engineering and Management Institute, Panki, Kanpur, India
[3] Department of Physics and Electronics, Dr. Ram Manohar Lohia Avadh University, Ayodhya, India
[4] Amity Institute of Information Technology, Amity University, Lucknow, India
msrivastava@lko.amity.edu

Abstract. This paper uses an approach where we will be training the unlabelled and labelled datasets into the system and these datasets comprises of: RGBA images and Binary masks. This will be a benefit in order to get a much better result and more accurate also as pre-training method always helps in getting excellent output. We will use a Transformer Model in this paper where we will apply an image sequentialization technique having 51 million parameters which will help us in attaining the smoother images without any noise. At times, this approach could be time consuming due to used datasets and its sizes, however it shows more accurate and efficient results. Further, we will try to figure out the pixel wise label map using patch embedding technique. Once these techniques are applied then CNN-Transformer Hybrid will come into the role which will encode and decode the images to high-level feature extractions and full spatial resolution respectively. This way of doing encoding and decoding is also known as forward pass and back propagation. Also, it will involve the cascaded upsampler where we will try to use self-attention processes into the design of encoder using the transformers. This entire mechanism will involve few of the best evaluation metrics and those are: Pixel accuracy, IoU, Mean-IoU and Recall/Precision/F1 Score giving the effective and best results.

Keywords: Deep learning · Vision Transformer (ViT) · Convolutional Neural Networks (CNNs) · Mammography · Image sequentialization · Upsampler · Breast cancer

1 Introduction

As per the researches, it has been found out that breast cancer is one of the major causes of death around the globe [19, 20] and is becoming a major health issue within the

© Springer Nature Switzerland AG 2022
A. Dev et al. (Eds.): AIST 2021, CCIS 1546, pp. 569–592, 2022.
https://doi.org/10.1007/978-3-030-95711-7_47

human body. It has been told that it generally occurs due to unconstrained growth of breast tissues [20, 24]. An, these tissues tend to form cancer and these can be viewed from the breast region using different techniques of detecting the same [20, 21]. Before studying and detecting the breast cancer we should always have a basic understanding about the methods used to analyse and detect the same [18, 20]. There are few things which forms the women's breasts and they are lobules, ducts, nipples, and fatty tissues [12, 14, 20]. Generally, what happens is that epithelial tumours spread inside the lobes, and also in ducts, and after it form a lump which generates breast cancer [15, 20].

Breast cancer masking aims at finding the benign and malignant tumors before the indications appear and leads towards increasing the life span [13, 20]. At present there are multiple ways to detect the breast cancer such as: Ultrasound, Mammography, MRI and Computed Tomography [11, 17, 20]. All of these help in diagnosing the hidden features of cancer or tumour and out of the above-mentioned modalities, ultrasound and mammogram are the most used screening techniques for detecting cancers before they become presumptuous [3, 20, 22]. However, there is a drawback in mammography that its output depends on the type of the lesion, age of patient, and the density of the breasts [2, 7, 20]. So, in order to avoid these issues ultrasound is used at times in comparison to digital mammography [1–3, 7, 8].

But ultrasound is non-radioactive, non-invasive and real time imaging technique [4, 8, 20] that gives high resolution output in the form of images. These are very time-consuming methods which require manual intervention for better accuracy [20, 23, 24].

So, nowadays self-attention architectures especially in Transformers have become the model way out in NLP (Natural Language Processing) [1, 3, 4, 6, 9]. The presiding approach is to pre-train on a big text entities and then fine tune on small job specific database [1, 10]. With this model it has become easier and more efficient to train models of extraordinary size [1, 25]. In computer perception, however, convolutional structures remain commanding. Motivated by NLP successes [1, 2, 16], multiple tasks tries to combine with CNN architectures with self-attention [1], where few replace the convolutions completely [1, 2, 4] (Fig. 1).

Inspired by the successes of the Transformer in NLP, we will examine it by applying it with the conventional Transformer [2–6]. Also, transformer has shown to succeed on many natural languages that might part in due to capability to structure unpredictable dependencies in a continual no. of layers [2, 4, 6].

However, the storage and statistical needs of such nets enlarges quadratically with respect to sequence length that excludes its usage on long sequences [2, 4, 6].

2   Review of Literature

In [1], the author inspected the undeviating approach of Transformers to image recognition [1]. Earlier attention was applied in coexistence with convolutional networks or applied to put back defined elements of convolutional networks by keeping the entire composition in position [1]. So, he showed this dependency on convolutional networks is not mandatory and filtered transformer put in straight to chain of image patches can execute admirably on image classification assignments [1]. While pre-training it on big

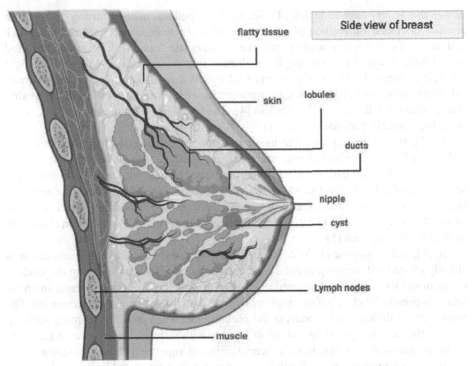

Fig. 1. This scheme represents the anatomy of a woman's breast. Inside the lobes are the zones where the epithelial tumors or cyst grow. Designed by Biorender (2020). Retrieved from https://app.biorender.com/biorender-templates. [20]

data and moved to numerous mid-sized or small image identification standards, Vision Transformer (ViT) obtains amazing outputs matched to state-of-the-art CNN where pre-training is cheap [1].

In [2], author presents sparse articulation of the attention model that reduces and achieves corresponding or fine execution on density framework of long sequences than quality Transformers while needing notably few actions [2]. He uses the similar framework to design images, text and audio from fresh bytes, positioning a new state of the art for mass designing of CIFAR-10, Enwik8 and ImageNet-64 [2]. Further, he demonstrated a framework where he used long term context and creates throughout consistent cases [2].

In [3], the author reviewed few recent deep convolutional network-based techniques for self-monitored image and video characteristic learning from all point of view together with usual network constructions, pretence assignment, algorithms, database, accomplishment collation, conversations, and upcoming commands etc. [3]. The relative synopsis of the techniques, datasets, and presentation in tabular format distinctly display their properties that will be convenient for researchers in the computer vision group [3].

In [4], the author reviewed the work of Caruana and his colleagues where they showed that it is feasible to crush the understanding in an association into an exclusive design that is very easy to deploy [4]. So, he developed this method further by applying another compression method [4]. He received some unexpected outputs on MNIST and showed that we can notably enhance the acoustic framework of a steadily used materialistic system by processing the understanding in a collection of frameworks into a single framework [4]. He also introduced a new way of collecting of one or more full frameworks and many thorough frameworks which absorb to differentiate quality classes that the full frameworks confuse [4]. The best part is that these frameworks can be trained quickly and side by side [4].

In [5], the author explored the usage of knowledge extracting to enhance a multi task DNN for learning text characterization over many natural language interpretation assignments [5]. Though, this kind of learning can enhance the framework execution, serves groups of big DNNs like MT-DNN which can be costly [5]. So, author applies the knowledge extracting procedure in the aggregate learning surrounding [5]. The author shows that the processed MT-DNN notably exceeds the primary MT-DNN on maximum of the GLUE functions [5].

In [6], author proposes a Fix Match which is a method of remarkable analyzation of already existed SSL techniques [6]. It first creates pseudo labels by applying the model's projections on weakly supplemented unlabelled images [6]. So, author retrains an image which is pseudo-label only if the framework gives a high-dependence projection [6]. The framework is then trained to analyse the pseudo label when provided a strong build up class of the same image [6]. In spite of its lucidity author shows that this way it gets state of the art accomplishment beyond a diversity of semi-supervised learning standards [6].

In [7], author introduces a flexible input presentation for neural language designing which expand the flexible SoftMax to input presentations of inconsistent capacity [7]. There are many options on how to articulate the input and output surface, and even if to represent words, sub-words or characters [7]. The author does the comparison of a popular options in a very systematic way for a self-attentional framework [7]. So, his evaluation shows that framework furnished with flexible submerging are more than 2 times as quick to train than the liked character input CNN while possessing a lower no. of criterion [7].

In [8], the author shows that an extensive 64-layer transformer framework with set conditions surpasses RNN variants through a huge margin by attaining state of the art on 2 desired criterions: 1.13 bps on text8 and 1.06 on enwik8 [8]. In order to get great outputs at this depth author shows that its foremost to connect additional deprivation at intermediate network layers and sequence positions [8].

In [9], author investigates the part of situation in an LSTM LM along with sublation work [9]. Particularly, author examines the expansion in confusion when earlier situation words are rearranged, descended and restored [9]. On applying 2 databases author finds out that this framework is efficient of using approx. 200 tokens of context on median, however it also differentiates close by context from the faraway history [9]. The proposed design is very sensitive towards the order of words that is there in the recent statement, however disregard word order in the broad range circumstances [9]. He also found that neural caching framework helps out the LSTM to duplicate words from inside faraway factors [9]. So, in total this approach gives the better clarity of how the neural LM's apply their factors [9].

In [10], author shows the new design i.e., VDCNN for text transforming that utilizes straight at the character level where he makes sure that he uses small convolutions and amalgamated tasks [10]. The author is showing the increase in the model performance with depth where he uses approx. 29 convolutional layers [10]. Further, he reports the improvements on many public text classifications over the state of the art [10].

In [11], the author is motivated by the victory of DNNs in acoustic framework and he explores DNN language frameworks over here [11]. It has been shown that improvements are there over a unique concealed layer NNLM [11]. Further, prior outputs are aggressive with a framework M language considering to be the present state of the art methods for language framework [11].

In [12], author finds out that to learn complicated functions which can show high level absorptions for example, language, vision and other AI level tasks needs deep frameworks [12]. It includes many levels of non-linear functioning, for example neural nets having many unseen surfaces or complex propositional formula where it reuses the many subs formula [12]. Hence, in this paper author discusses the inspiration and fundamentals with respect to learning algorithms for deep frameworks particularly those utilizing as constructing blocks unsupervised learning of 1-layer structures for example, Restricted Boltzmann Machines which is used to build deeper frameworks such as deep belief networks [12].

In [13], author shows an organised collation and train huge lexicons which includes hierarchical SoftMax, target sampling, SoftMax, self-normalization and contrastive estimation which behaves as an estimator of probability and initiates a well organised variant of soft max [13]. Further, author evaluates every method on 3 famous criterions, inspecting presentation on rare words, the speed/precision trade-off and interdependence to Kneser-Ney [13].

In [14], author proposes easy and flexible detection method that enhances mean average precision over and above 30% respective to the earlier finest result on VOC 2012 which achieves a mAP of about 53.3% [14]. The approach is combined of 2 key observations [14]: 1. We can use high-column CNN's to bottom area approaches in place to localize and fragmented objects, and 2. labelled training details is insufficient, supervised pre-training is used as an additional method which is followed by area related fine tuning [14]. This shows a good boost in performance [14]. The author has named his work as R-CNN which means it is a method where region is involved with CNN characteristics [14].

In [15], the author proposes a work where he will learn from the unlabelled data which is generated by soft pseudo-labels which uses network projections [15]. Further, he shows the simple pseudo labelling which is over fitting wrong pseudo labels due to the reason which is called confirmation bias [15]. It demonstrates that scrambled enhancement and locating a less count of labelled samples for every productive regulation method to lessen it [15]. Hence, this method reaches state of the art outputs in SVHN, Mini image net and CIFAR-10/100 which are much simple than other ways [15].

In [16], authors show a balance in between accuracy and speed by creating a productive and well-organized video classifying system by orderly inspection of critical network framework options [16]. He shows that it is possible to change many of 3D convolutions by less cost 2d convolutions [16]. And, unexpectedly good result is achieved when this replacement happens by suggesting secular presentation learning on high level semantic characteristics that is more useful [16]. As a result, he generalizes the database with distinct properties and show that this system is an effective video classifying system that gives very great results on various action classifying standards along with 2 action detection standards [16].

In [17], the author transposes batch normalization to layer normalization by calculating the variance and mean which is applied for normalization from all the concluded inputs to neurons in a surface on one training case [17]. He also tries to give every neuron its own flexible bias and gain that are given after normalization acts the same calculation but prior to non-linearity [17]. So, this method proves to be the more effective for stabilizing the invisible state kinetics in recurring networks [17]. Theoretically, author shows that his normalization can significantly lessen the training time as compares to earlier published methods [17].

In [18], author represents a work where only initial analysis has been shown as a benefit of complementary supervised pretraining [18]. Further, in this work author uses four examples in between training jobs where a significant improvement was shown by applying STILTS to other 3 encoders such as GPT, BERT and ELMo, adding to it setting the state of the art on GLUE [18] standards along with BERT on STILTs [18]. This helps in remarkably balancing training in unsteady training contexts such as while applying BERT on given tasks having less data [18]. At the end it shows that in data inhibited arrangement, the advantages of applying STILTs [18] are more noticeable showing up to 10-point score boost on few task pairs [18].

In [19], author proposes an approach where neural network structure known as RNN encoder and decoder that involves of 2 recurring neural networks [19]. One of it enciphers a chain of symbols to a specified length vector presentation and deciphers the presentation into different chain of a specified symbols [19]. Both the encipher and decipher of the suggested model are trained together to increase the conditional possibility of a chosen sequence given an origin series [19]. Conditionally, the author shows that the suggested model absorbs a meaningful presentation of linguistic expressions [19].

In [20], the author provides an analytical evaluation of the writings on deep learning implementations in breast malignancy diagnosis that uses mammography images and ultrasound [20]. Further, it summarizes the recent proceedings in CAD systems that makes use of newly described deep learning techniques to recognize the images automatically and improving the efficacy of diagnoses that are done by radiologists [20]. This entire procedure reveals the new DL-CAD techniques that are useful and constructive masking tools for the cancer which reduces the manual work [20].

In [21], the author uses a simple MRI HIFU [21] breast excision system to improve on earlier issues [21]. The system consists of the ring HIFU transducer which acts as a commercial amplifier, graphical user interface and mechanical positioner [21]. Adding to it, accuracy of the positioner which moves the HIFU focal area has been within 6% error below MRI occurrences [21]. This system ablates the biceps femur of a rabbit which has no skin burn to create a lesion 2.5 mm under the skin [21].

In [22], the author has introduced completely new breast mass segmentation technique which is fully automated from dynamic contrast enhanced MRI [22]. This process is based on overall ideal inference in an uninterrupted space which uses a shape prior assessed from a semiotic segmentation build by a DL method [22]. The author proposes this approach because restricted amount of explicated training samples don't allow the execution of a vigorous DL model that gives an accurate result by its own [22].

In [23], the author proposes a method where he uses an optimization based super pixel clustering method for an automatic segmentation of a nuclei cell [23]. So, for this to happen author acquires the histopathological images datasets from a suitable database [23]. Post this normalization method is applied in order to remove the noise from all images [23]. Post denoising, the segmentation method is applied using an optimized clustering algo so that it can separate the non-nuclei and nuclei cells [23]. The main motive of this method is to get an efficient method of segmentation to overcome the problems of overlapping cells [23].

In [24], author focuses on deterministic clustering methods and this should result in same clustering solution through runs and toolkits [24]. For every algo, authors were able to get the diverse main causes of non-determinism and inconsistency, and it brings them more together with each other [24].

In [25], author develops a new prediction method and also tries to explore diverse factors related to risk [25]. The machine learning algorithms are not restricted to a particular number of factors related to risk but have the resilience to change extra ones [25]. As per author the improvement shown in this predictive accuracy will be explored with proposed databases and some more added risk factors [25].

In [26], author finds out that NAC treatment is becoming the main option for treating the breast cancer [26]. Also, he finds out that the severe drug reactions make it more painful both ways that is psychologically and physiologically [26]. The further factor i.e., pCR which is a kind of complete remission which explains how a continuous series of chemotherapeutic works on the patients [26]. So, this research has done investigation on finding out the pCR by applying nodal sizes of the treatments [26]. Authors evaluated through the metrics Avc which is equal to the sum of sensitivity and specificity which if further divided by 2. So, they are estimating that patient having triple negative (TN) breast cancer may have Avc = 0.8696 [26].

In [27], the authors find out that microwave imaging that is based on radar is being used widely for detecting the breast cancer [27]. So, they have proposed the antennas which are designed to work in a range of frequency which is 2–4 Ghz where reflection coefficient will be below −10 dB [27]. Post working on this method authors find out that it has good impedance which matches when it is in different positions with different curvature around the breast [27]. They also used reflector for the arrays and the penetration of the waves of electromagnetic getting generated from the antennas in the breast can helps us to improve it by 3.3 and 2.6 factors each [27].

In [28], authors got to know that an automated breast ultrasound is one of the innovative and promising way to do screening for examining the breast [28]. So, in this study authors have offered a creative way for 3D convolutional network and this is being used for the above-mentioned technique of detection so that we can get high rate of detection sensitivity having FP's which is known as False Positives [28]. The authors have also used the multi-layer concept very efficiently and suggested a loss in threshold so that they can get voxel-level adaptive threshold to find out the cancerous and non-cancerous areas and this will show high sensitivity having low FP's [28]. The authors have got the sensitivity of 95% having 0.84 FP/volume [28].

In [29], the authors have proposed a method where they have presented a technique that helps in combining high frequency excitation and thermography techniques [29]. So, it uses variation and distribution of temperature on the surface of breast so that they can estimate the location and size of a cancerous tissue [29]. This work has come out by analysing the effects of RF radiation on human body [29]. So, over here they have provided the description of RF effects on a human and providing the results of simulation [29]. In order to verify they have used multi-layer 3D model of breast which is simulated. Further, towards the end both specific absorption rate and temperature increases as defect gets closer or bigger to the surface. Finally, these kind of responses of many defect areas have been employed to find out whether area is benign or malignant [29].

In [30], author proposes a method which used Stacked Sparse Autoencoder also known as SSAE which is an instance of a strategy that involves deep learning [30]. It is presented for detection accurate nuclei over the high-resolution images of histopatholog-ical [30]. This method identifies distinguishing features where high-level features learns from pixel intensities alone [30]. Further, authors apply a sliding window operation to every image so that they present patches of image through high-level features which are received from the autoencoder and later it is fed into a classifier that helps in dividing every patch of an image as either nuclear or non-nuclear [30]. This approach has shown a good and improved F-measure and Precision-Recall curve [30].

In [31], the authors have proposed a method where they will directly extract tumour through EEMD that is Ensemble Empirical Mode Decomposition so that it can be detected at an early stage by Ultra-Wide Band (UWB) which is a microwave imag-ing [31]. Using this method, the reconstruction of an image for detection of cancer can be done with extracted signals which are as detected waveforms [31]. So, authors tes-tified this successfully by finding a 4mm cancer located into the region of glandular that too in a breast model [31]. Also, authors checked its reliability by differentiating a cancer/tumour that has been buried into the tissue of glandular which has a dielectric constant as 35 [31]. Its feasibility is checked by right information of tumour in both experimental as well as simulation results for real 3D breast phantom [31].

In [32], the authors focused more on improving millimeter waves perforation for imaging of breast cancer [32]. They used a technique which is field focusing that too on convex optimization method which is capable of growing the level of field in a breast imitating lamination [32]. The results have been verified in digits through the design and reflection of antennas that are polarized in a round manner [32]. So, the designed antennas are verified experimentally where they have used tissue mimic phantoms which is provided in good agreement with theoretical projections [32].

In [33], authors find out that breast cancer has become one of the most minacious diseases and 2nd highest reason for the cause of female death due to cancer [33]. So, over here authors will work on deep learning concept which is supported by DLA-EABA for detecting the breast cancer using advanced techniques of computation [33]. It starts by observing CNN based transfer learning in order to distinguish masses of breast for distinct diagnostic, some tasks which are predictive and few other imaging modalities which can be Ultrasound, MRI, etc. [33] This DNN framework has many convolutional layers i.e., LSTM and Max-pooling layers [33]. It has paid more attention to the combination of ML approaches with techniques of selected characteristics and then taking it out through output evaluation. In this way they have used classification and segmentation methods to get the best result [33].

In [34], the authors have presented a DNN for screening the breast cancer then they have trained and also, evaluated on approx. 200,000 exams [34]. There architecture gets an AUC as 0.895 to predict the cancer in breast [34]. The authors have conducted a study with approx. 14 readers which were reading 720 screening mammograms [34]. Also, it shows that this approach is perfect as knowledgeable radiologists when same data is being shown [34]. Towards the end authors shows that there is one Hybrid Model and by averaging the probability of malignancy is being detected with a detection of a hybrid model [34].

In [35], the author found out that CAD systems are giving unsatisfactory answer [35]. So, over here they have explored a breast CAD technique based on future fusion with CNN [35]. In this approach the accuracy and efficiency demonstrate given technique mass detection and classifying the breast cancer [35].

In [36], the authors have presented a clinal decision which support tool and this tool is efficient of helping doctors to make diagnostics decisions [36]. This method has been improved the specificity of breast cancer and finding it out. This system has been using clinical context so that FP's can be reduced while it avoids the FN's [36]. An online contextual based learning algorithm is using to work on the strategy which is presented to the doctors on time. So, adding to it this technique has important merit, then it can give us individualized confidence regarding the preciseness, hence, most value information in reducing the errors of diagnostics [36]. This outperforms the current clinical by 36% w.r.t. 36% which is given to 36% [36].

In [37], the author aims at developing a process so that automatic detection can take place through histological slides which uses a deep learning framework that is supervised partially [37]. However, earlier researched focused on getting the solution of the problem i.e., detection of mitosis in the weak elucidated datasets through labels that are weak [37]. Over here author is trying to make a structure which is supervised partially over 2 parallel DNN's [37]. One has gone under training using labels that are weak and second has been trained with strong one's that too with a function weight transfer [37]. During the phase of detection, author tried to combine segmented maps which were produced by 2 different networks [37]. This kind of approach has proven much more efficient in comparison to earlier applied techniques by getting F-scores of 0.575 and 0.698 of 2 different datasets [37].

In [38], authors are trying to get a way where very efficient CAD system that is constructed on a 3-D CNN and highlighted candidate aggregation [38]. It is suggested to speed up this review. Initially an effective method of sliding window is used to get the VOI's and then every VOI is approximated the cancer chances with 3D CNN and VOI's with high approximated possibility are chosen as its candidates [38]. The author has found out that they might overlap over each other so, a proper structure is made to aggregate them and they are also prioritized at this time depending on possibility of getting a tumor [38]. The size of VOI and targeted tumor is exploited in such a way that it performs efficiently for every algorithm of detection. In short, author claims that this way is faster that earlier works and gives good results [38].

In [39], authors are proposing a new way of identifying breast cancer where they have used ML algorithms and clinical data [39]. Further, they have used 2 techniques i.e., supervised and unsupervised for attributes selection from given dataset and once they get selected then these are used for training and testing [39]. Adding to it the authors have initiated a method K-Fold Cross validation that is used for validating model and choosing good hyperparameters [39]. For evaluating the performance of model, the metrics which does the same are used and datasets are used for testing [39]. Hence, the method has received the great results in accuracy over selection of feature using Relief Algorithm and getting up to 99.91% accuracy [39].

In [40], authors present a technique which detects objects in images that use Single DNN [40]. Further, their approach is named as SSD which separates the space of output of leaping boxes over distinct aspect ratios and it scales map location per feature [40]. Also, many times network creates scores for every object class presence in every default box that generates adaptations to better match its shape [40]. Further, this makes SSD very easy to train and uncomplicated to combine into systems that really need a component of detection [40]. Post applying the entire technique and after comparing the single stage process SSD has got the much good accuracy even with small size of an input image [40].

3 Materials and Methods

3.1 Methodology

In the proposed method we will use a vision transformer encoder for the feature extraction and will use up-convolution for reconstruction.

Let us take an example that there is an image of dimensions [H*W*C] which have a spatial resolution of about [H*W] and no. of channels to be as "C".

So, our aim is to anticipate the corresponding pixel wise label map which have a size of [H*W]. One of the most common method is to directly train a CNN for an example, UNet, to first encipher the images (encode) into high level attributes representations which are then deciphered (decoded) back to the complete spatial resolution.

Unlike the existing ones, we will use self-attention mechanisms into the encoder design through usage of Transformers.

The whole pipeline has the below mentioned four steps.

1. Image Sequentialization
2. Patch Embedding -: map the vectorized patches into a latent D-dimensional embedding space
3. CNN-Transformer Hybrid as Encoder
4. Cascaded Up sampler

And, we will be using the below written evaluation metrics for better accuracy and efficacy:

(i)   Recall, Precision and F1 score
(ii) Pixel Accuracy
(iii) Intersection over Union
(iv) Mean-IoU

3.2 Algorithm

To examine and detect the breast cancer we have used the following method:

(i)   We will initiate the process by giving the dataset as an input and further this dataset has two folders, which are:

    (a) RGBA Images
    (b) Binary Masks
        where image and image labels are used.

(ii) We will process the dataset/images using an Image Sequentialization where an iterator is being created.
(iii) Post this we will apply Patch Embedding which will map the vectorized patches into a latent D-dimensional embedding space.
(iv) Once data has gone under the above-mentioned step then we will use an encoder i.e. CNN-Transformer Hybrid.
(v)   Then we will use the Cascaded-Up-Sampler to increase the sampling rate.
(vi) And, we will train the datasets which will help us in getting the error of deviation.
(vii) At last, we will use the below evaluation metrics to detect malignancy and check which is the best metric:

    (a) Recall, Precision and F1 score
    (b) Pixel Accuracy
    (c) Intersection over Union
    (d) Mean-IoU

3.3 Flowchart

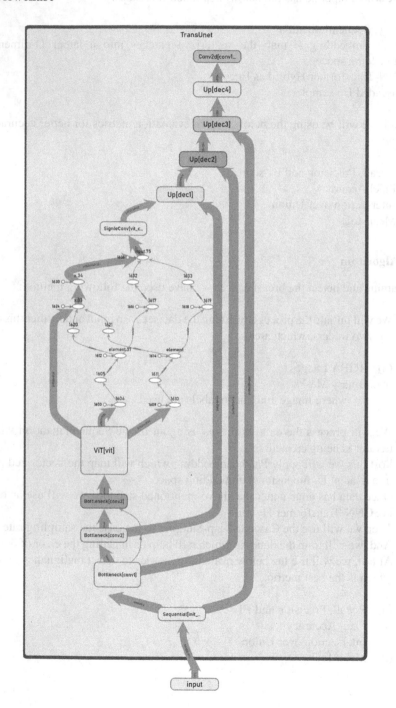

4 Observations

The total number of trainable parameters used is 51.078284 million. So, below table will show the results achieved post applying the evaluation metrics (Table 1).

Table 1. Here are the evaluation results of our model on the cancer cell segmentation task

Metrics	Value (%)
Mean Intersection-over-Union (mIoU) averaged across classes	92.48536975
Frequency Weighted IoU (fwIoU)	96.62835867
Mean Pixel Accuracy averaged across classes (mACC)	96.38648278
Pixel Accuracy (pACC)	98.24153252
Dice Similarity Coefficient (DSC)	95.22226733

Also, below graphs are obtained post using the above-mentioned approaches and it shows the evaluation metrics percentage with respect to Smoothening, Value, Step, Time and Relativity.

4.1 Scalar Graphs-

Figures 2, 3, 4, 5, 6 and 7.

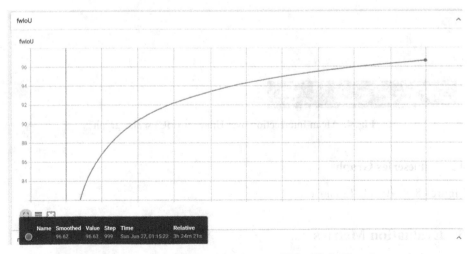

Fig. 2. Frequency Weighted Intersection over Union (fwIoU) scalar graph

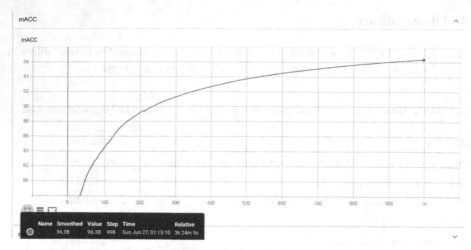

Fig. 3. Mean Accuracy (mACC) scalar graph

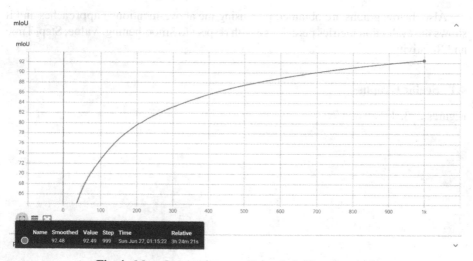

Fig. 4. Mean Intersection over Union (mIoU) scalar graph

4.2 Timeseries Graph-

Figures 8, 9, 10, 11, 12 and 13.

5 Evaluation Metrics

A. Recall, Precision and F1 score-

(i) **Precision:** This metric helps us in computing the number of "True Positives" i.e., positive class projections which actually belong to positive class [14, 16, 20, 21].

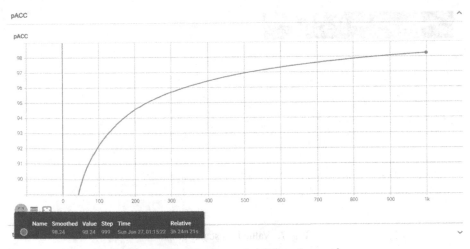

Fig. 5. Pixel Accuracy (pACC) scalar graph

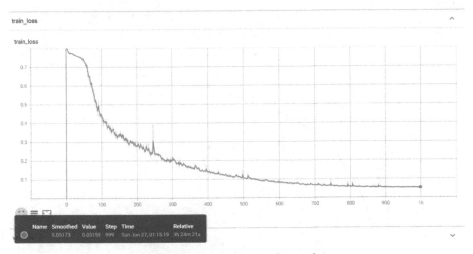

Fig. 6. Training loss scalar graph

   [Precision = True Positives/(True Positives + False Positives)] [14, 16, 20, 21].

(ii) **Recall:** This metric helps us in computing the number of "True Positives" i.e., positive class projections which are made out all the existing positive examples in the dataset [14, 16, 20, 21].

   [Recall = True Positives/(True Positives + False Negatives)] [14, 16, 20, 21].

(iii) **F-Measure:** This metric helps us in providing a single score that balances both i.e., precision and recall in one go [14, 16, 20, 21].

   [F-Measure = (2 * Precision * Recall)/(Precision + Recall)] [14, 16, 20, 21].

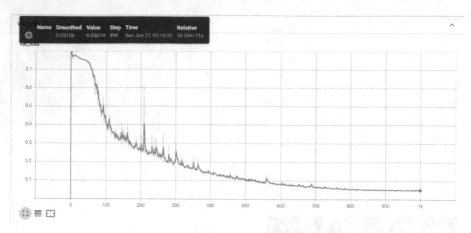

Fig. 7. Value loss scalar graph

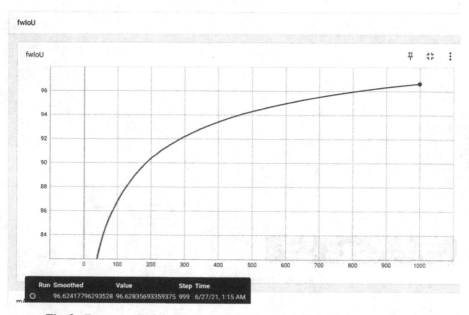

Fig. 8. Frequency Weighted Intersection over Union (fwIoU) timeseries graph

B. Pixel Accuracy-

This is one of the easiest methods to find out an image segmentation model executes. So, for this method to be executed first we need to figure out the True Positive (TP), True Negative (TN), False Positive (FP) and False Negative (FN) values [14, 16, 20, 21].

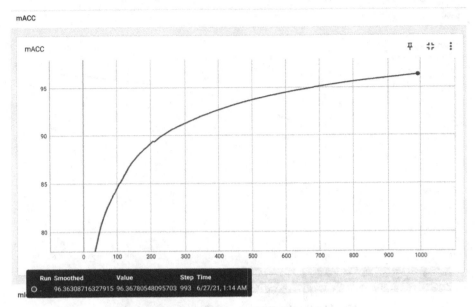

Fig. 9. Mean Accuracy (mACC) timeseries graph

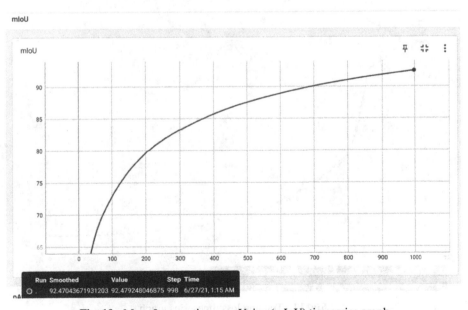

Fig. 10. Mean Intersection over Union (mIoU) timeseries graph

pACC

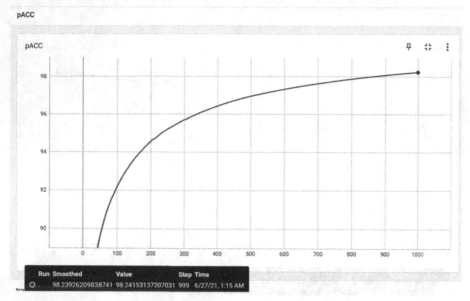

Fig. 11. Pixel accuracy (pACC) timeseries graph

train_loss

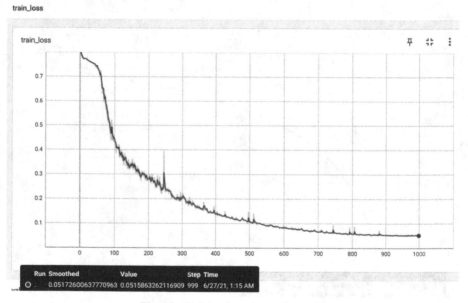

Fig. 12. Training loss timeseries graph

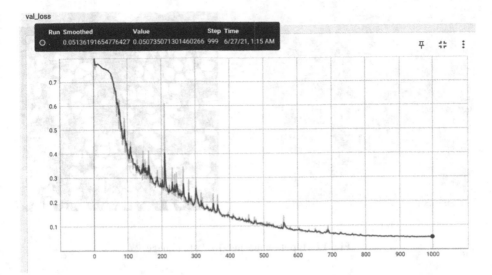

Fig. 13. Value loss timeseries graph

For the above mentioned, below gives the basic idea-

- **True Positive (TP):** pixel analysed accurately as X
- **False Positive (FP):** pixel analysed inaccurately as X
- **True Negative (TN):** pixel analysed accurately as not X
- **False Negative (FN):** pixel analysed inaccurately as not X

And, below is the formula to calculate the pixel accuracy:

[Pixel Accuracy = (TP + TN)/(TP + TN + FP + FN)] [14, 16, 20, 21].

C. Intersection over Union-
This is one more way of evaluating the projections from an image segmentation model. In this method performance is calculated by intersection and union in between the ground truth and prediction [14, 16, 20, 21].

[IoU = (T P)/(F P + T P + F N)] [14, 16, 20, 21].

D. Mean-IoU-
This is a metric that takes intersection over union (IoU) over all the classes and then take out the mean of it. This is somehow a good sign of how your image segmentation model is performing over all other classes that a model will want to detect [14, 16, 20, 21].

6   Results

Figures 14, 16 and 17.

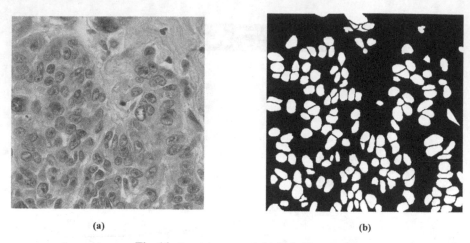

(a)   (b)

Fig. 14. Input image and (b). Label image

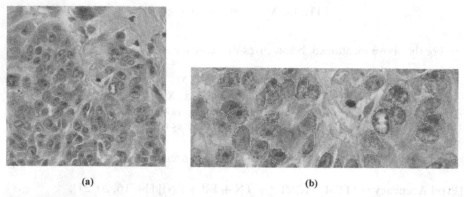

(a)   (b)

Fig. 15. Ground truth predicted image and (d). Zoomed view of ground truth predicted image

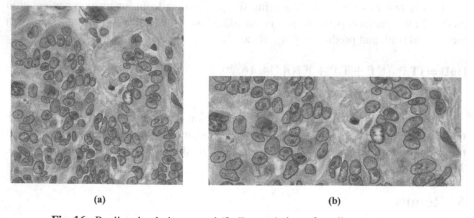

(a)   (b)

Fig. 16. Predicted only image and (f). Zoomed view of predicted only image

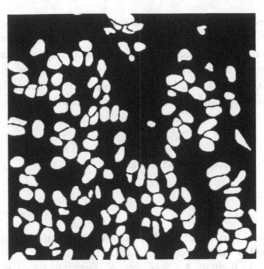

Fig. 17. Segemented image

7 Conclusion

We have tried to explore the straight application using transformers (ViT) to detect the breast cancer. Unlike, the earlier works here we have proposed a way in which we have used RGBA images and binary masks. In order to do the feature extraction, we have used a vision transformer which acts like an encoder and for reconstructing purposes we have been using up-convolution. So, we have trained the datasets so that they can be represent features to a high-level and later we have decoded them back to complete spatial resolution. Adding to it we have tried to use self-attention approach into this design of encoder through use of transformers. This entire process included: Image sequentialization, Patch embedding, CNN-Transformer Hybrid (acting as an encoder) and cascaded up sampler. We have received an amazing result in terms of accuracy and efficacy. All the used evaluation metrics have shown good value in percentage wherein lowest has been shown by Mean IoU i.e., 92.48% and maximum has been shown by Pixel Accuracy i.e., 98.24%. Other used evaluation metrics have also shown good results up to 95.22% and approximately 96%. Also, as we can see in the above-mentioned results that labelled image is matching with the segmented image that means we have applied a good approach for detecting the cancer in breasts and more detail view can be seen in Fig. 15.

8 Discussion and Future Work

This time we have taken limited datasets, however in future we will be working on large datasets and also will work on real time datasets. This time we have applied the techniques to detect cancer in breasts, moreover adding to it in future we will try to do detect the cancer in lungs, chest, etc.

Till now we used to consider convolutional neural network to be the best technique to detect the cancer in breasts, however post researching in detail and reviewing current papers got to know that transformer is one of the efficient and accurate method to detect the cancer. And, going ahead will try to work on much better technique depending on current scenario. This time we have only worked on detection method but looking forward to apply some classification techniques in future wherein we will try to use multi-modalities.

Conflict of Interest. There is no conflict of interest.

References

1. Dosovitskiy, A., et al.: An Image is Worth 16X16 Words: Transformers for Image Recognition at Scale. Published as a conference paper at ICLR (2021)
2. Child, R., Gray, S., Radford, A., Sutskever, A.: Generating long sequences with sparse transformers. arXiv:1904.10509v1 [cs.LG] (2019)
3. Jing, L., Tian, Y.: Self-supervised visual feature learning with deep neural networks: a survey. arXiv:1902.06162v1 [cs.CV] (2019)
4. Hinton, G., Vinyals, O., Dean, J.: Distilling the knowledge in a neural network. arXiv:1503.02531v1 [stat.ML] (2015)
5. Liu, X., He, P., Chen, W., Gao, J.: Improving multi-task deep neural networks via knowledge distillation for natural language understanding. arXiv:1904.09482v1 [cs.CL] (2019)
6. Sohn, K., et al.: FixMatch: Simplifying semi-supervised learning with consistency and confidence. In: 34th Conference on Neural Information Processing Systems (NeurIPS 2020), Vancouver, Canada (2020)
7. Baevski, A., Auli, M.: Adaptive input representations for neural language modelling. arXiv:1809.10853v3 [cs.CL] (2019)
8. Al-Rfou, R., Choe, D., Constant, N., Guo, M., Jones, L.: Character-level language modeling with deeper self-attention. arXiv:1808.04444v2 [cs.CL] (2018)
9. Khandelwal, U., He, H., Qi, P., Jurafsky, D.: Sharp nearby, fuzzy far away: how neural language models use context. Association for Computational Linguistics (2018)
10. Conneau, A., Schwenk, H., Cun, Y.L., Barrault, L.: Very deep convolutional networks for text classification. arXiv:1606.01781v2 [cs.CL] (2017)
11. Arısoy, E., Sainath, T.N., Kingsbury, B., Ramabhadran, B.: Deep neural network language models. Association for Computational Linguistics (2012)
12. Bengio, Y.: Learning deep architectures for AI. Technical Report 1312 (2009)
13. Cheny, W., Grangier, D., Auli, M.: Strategies for training large vocabulary neural language models. arXiv:1512.04906v1 [cs.CL] (2015)
14. Girshick, R., Donahue, J., Darrell, J., Malik, J., Berkeley, U.C.: Rich feature hierarchies for accurate object detection and semantic segmentation Tech report (v5). arXiv:1311.2524v5 [cs.CV] (2014)
15. Arazo, E., Ortego, D., Albert, P., O'Connor, N.E., McGuinness, K.: Pseudo-labeling and confirmation bias in deep semi-supervised learning. arXiv:1908.02983v5 [cs.CV] (2020)
16. Xie, S., Sun, C., Huang, J., Tu, Z., Murphy, K.: Rethinking Spatiotemporal feature learning: speed-accuracy trade-offs in video classification. arXiv:1712.04851v2 [cs.CV] (2018)
17. Ba, J.L., Kiros, J.R., Hinton, G.E.: Layer normalization. arXiv:1607.06450v1 [stat.ML] (2016)

18. Phang, J., F´evry, T., Bowman, S.R.: Sentence encoders on STILTs: supplementary training on intermediate labeled-data tasks. arXiv:1811.01088v2 [cs.CL] (2019)
19. Cho, K., et al.: Learning phrase representations using RNN encoder–decoder for statistical machine translation. arXiv:1406.1078v3 [cs.CL] (2014)
20. Jiménez-Gaona, Y.: María José Rodríguez-Álvarez and Vasudevan Lakshminarayanan; Deep-learning-based computer-aided systems for breast cancer imaging: a critical review. Appl. Sci. **10**, 8298 (2020). https://doi.org/10.3390/app10228298
21. Gamil, M.E., Fouad, M.M., Abd El Ghany, M.A., Hoflman, K.: Fully automated CADx for early breast cancer detection using image processing and machine learning. In:30th International Conference on Microelectronics (ICM). IEEE (2018). 978-1-5386-8167-l/18/$31.00 ©2018
22. Maicas, G., Carneiro, G., Bradley, A.P.: Globally Optimal Breast Mass Segmentation from DCE-MRI Using Deep Semantic Segmentation as Shape Prior. IEEE (2017). 978-1-5090-1172-8/17/$31.00 ©2017
23. Saturi, R., Prem Chand, P.: Implementation of efficient segmentation method for histopathological images. In: Proceedings of the Fifth International Conference on Inventive Computation Technologies (ICICT-2020). IEEE (2020). 978-1-7281-4685-0/20/$31.00 ©2020
24. Yin, X., Neamtiu, I., Patil, S., Andrews, S.T.: Implementation-induced inconsistency and nondeterminism in deterministic clustering algorithms. In: 2020 IEEE 13th International Conference on Software Testing, Validation and Verification (ICST). IEEE (2020). 978-1-7281-5778-8/20/$31.00 ©2020
25. Chang, M., Viassolo, V., Probst-Hensch, N., Chappuis, P.O., Dinov, I.D., Katapodi, M.C.: Machine learning techniques for personalized breast cancer risk prediction: comparison with the BCRAT and BOADICEA models. Breast Cancer Res. (2019). https://doi.org/10.1186/s13058-019-1158-4
26. Feng, X., et al.: Accurate prediction of neoadjuvant chemotherapy pathological complete remission (pCR) for the four sub-types of breast cancer. Digital Object Identifier. IEEE ACCESS (2019). https://doi.org/10.1109/ACCESS.2019.2941543
27. Bahrami, H., Porter, E., Santorelli, A., Gosselin, B., Popović, M., Rusch, L.A.: Flexible sixteen antenna array for microwave breast cancer detection. In: IEEE Transactions on Biomedical Engineering, 0018-9294 (c) 2015. IEEE (2014). https://doi.org/10.1109/TBME.2015.2434956
28. Wang, Y., et al.: Deeply-supervised networks with threshold loss for cancer detection in automated breast ultrasound. In: IEEE Transactions on Medical Imaging, 0278-0062 (c) 2019. IEEE (2019). https://doi.org/10.1109/TMI.2019.2936500
29. Rahmatinia, S., Fahimi, B.: Magneto-thermal modeling of biological tissues: a step towards breast cancer detection. In: IEEE Transactions on Magnetics, 0018-9464 © 2015. IEEE (2017). https://doi.org/10.1109/TMAG.2017.2671780
30. Xu, J., et al.: Stacked sparse autoencoder (SSAE) for Nuclei detection on breast cancer histopathology images. IEEE Trans. Med. Imaging (2016). https://doi.org/10.1109/TMI.2015.2458702
31. Li, Q., et al.: Direct extraction of tumor response based on ensemble empirical mode decomposition for image reconstruction of early breast cancer detection by UWB. IEEE Trans. Biomed. Circuits Syst. **9**(5), 710–724 (2015)
32. Iliopoulos, I., et al.: Enhancement of penetration of millimeter waves by field focusing applied to breast cancer detection. IEEE Trans. Biomed. Eng. (2021). https://doi.org/10.1109/TBME.2020.3014277
33. Zheng, J., Lin, D., Gao, Z., Wang, S., He, M., Fan, J.: Deep learning assisted efficient AdaBoost algorithm for breast cancer detection and early diagnosis. IEEE Access **8**, 96946–96954 (2020). https://doi.org/10.1109/ACCESS.2020.2993536

34. Wu, N., et al.: Deep neural networks improve radiologists' performance in breast cancer screening. IEEE Trans. Med. Imaging **39**(4), 1184–1194 (2020)
35. Wang, Z., et al.: Breast cancer detection using extreme learning machine based on feature fusion with CNN deep features. IEEE Access (2019). https://doi.org/10.1109/ACCESS.2019.2892795
36. Song, L., Hsu, W., Xu, J., van der Schaar, M.: Using contextual learning to improve diagnostic accuracy: application in breast cancer screening. IEEE J. Biomed. Health Inf. (2016). https://doi.org/10.1109/JBHI.2015.2414934
37. Sebai, M., Wang, T., Al-Fadhli. S.A.: PartMitosis: a partially supervised deep learning framework for mitosis detection in breast cancer histopathology images. Digital Object Identifier (2020). https://doi.org/10.1109/ACCESS.2020.2978754
38. Chiang, T.-C., Huang, Y.-S., Chen, R.-T., Huang, C.-S., Chang, R.-F.: Tumor detection in automated breast ultrasound using 3-D CNN and prioritized candidate aggregation. IEEE Trans. Med. Imaging. https://doi.org/10.1109/TMI.2018.2860257
39. Haq, A.U., et al.: Detection of breast cancer through clinical data using supervised and unsupervised feature selection techniques. Digital Object Identifier (2021). https://doi.org/10.1109/ACCESS.2021.3055806
40. Liu, W., et al.: SSD: Single shot MultiBox detector. In: Leibe, B., Matas, J., Sebe, N., Welling, M. (eds.) ECCV 2016. LNCS, vol. 9905, pp. 21–37. Springer, Cham (2016). https://doi.org/10.1007/978-3-319-46448-0_2

An Ensemble Model for Face Mask Detection Using Faster RCNN with ResNet50

M. DhivyaShree[✉], K. R. Sarumathi, and R. S. Vishnu Durai

Sri Ramakrishna Engineering College, Coimbatore, Tamil Nadu, India
{dhivyashree.m,sarumathi.k.r,vishnudurai.rs}@srec.ac.in

Abstract. The computer vision which is an important aspect of Artificial Intelligence. The object detection is the most researchable area with deep learning algorithms. Now in the current COVID – 19 pandemics, the social distancing is a mandatory factor to prevent this transmission of this deadly virus. The government is struggling to handle the persons without wearing masks in public places. Our work concentrates on the object detection of face masks using the state-of-the-art methodologies like YOLO, SSD, RCNN, Fast RCNN and Faster RCNN with different backbone architectures like ResNet, MobileNet, etc. This paper brings out various ensemble methods by combining the state of art methodologies and compare those combinations to identify the best performance, in choice of the dataset of the application. We have obtained the highest performance benchmark with the usage of Faster RCNN – ResNet50 among the other ensemble methods. All the performance evaluation metrics are compared with one other with the same face mask detection image dataset. In this paper, we present a balancing collation of the ensemble methods of object detection algorithms.

Keywords: Face mask · Neural networks · Object detection · Faster RCNN · Resnet

1 Introduction

Coronavirus (COVID – 19) [1] is the disease caused by rare coronavirus called serious acute respiratory syndrome. Corona virus 2(SARS-COV-2) which was firstly spotted amid an upsurge of respiratory sickness occurrences in Wuhan city, China. In common, these viruses don't affect all people with mortality, most of the people gets affected and survived without medical assistance, whereas senior public with or without medical problems are most likely to evolve with the disease. The Covid-19 virus propagates firstly through saliva droplets or a nose discharge, when an affected person coughs or sneezes. Hence it is vital that we follow proper respiratory conduct. Out of many recommendations suggested by WHO and the governments, wearing masks, sanitization and vaccinations are most important to stay away from this virus.

We have variety of face mask applications like banking systems, security checks, bio metric systems, etc. In all face mask applications, identification of facial feature details is observed. The surveillance system nowadays operate along with artificial intelligence

© Springer Nature Switzerland AG 2022
A. Dev et al. (Eds.): AIST 2021, CCIS 1546, pp. 593–603, 2022.
https://doi.org/10.1007/978-3-030-95711-7_48

models together to identify the objects. Due to current pandemic situation, the government imposes various rules and regulations to handle the outbreak of virus transmission. So, the existing surveillance system can include additional features to differentiate between masked and unmasked person, thereby to reduce the risk of transmission of virus.

So, our research in this paper first collects data from the available surveillance systems, which can be images, videos and live updates. The data preprocessing steps highly depends on feature extraction method [2] and the type of input data. Next the data annotation part helps to have a labelling process done to the image. The data augmentation step follows to have multiple variations of the same image [3] dataset.

2 Related Works

A significant research has been done with many algorithms for object detection YOLO with detection, localization and recognition regions of interest in real time of video data from surveillance systems where actions of persons are detected, it is said that a single frame could be helpful for identifying the action [4].

An upgraded network structure of YOLOV2 is proposed for performing object detection [5]. They had come up with an improvisation of accuracy through convolutional layer, feature extraction by changing the output layers and optimization of loss function on VOC2007 dataset.

MS-CNN [6] in terms of sub-network, where detection is performed at multiple layers and detection network, it helps to provide a powerful Multi scale object detector where if a picture contains many persons are into a single frame where multiple objects are detected.

A PCA method [7], which explores accuracy rate in face recognition based on face mask wearing and non-mask face. The faces with no mask are identified with better feature extraction mechanisms than masked faces. The mask can be due to the makeup, sunglasses they wear and also hair texture and color.

A new model is developed for localization of objects in an image [8], which can predict multiple bounding boxes at the same time which could be helpful in recognition and localization of objects through bounding box when an image contains multiple objects to be detected.

There was another idea to compute finely sampled feature pyramids at a fraction of cost, without comprising the performance [9]. They had visualized the results with fast feature pyramid by modifying the visual recognition systems where detection rates are not affected and there is also a decrease in the computational cost.

For accurate object detection and semantic segmentation [10], the algorithms combine two steps, one which uses high-capacity CNN to bottom-up region proposals in order to locate and segment objects and the second, is for training large CNNs, when labelling is scanty. Region based segmentation is done which gives an easy and scalable object detection algorithm that gives more than 50% relative improvement over previous best results.

YOLOV2 algorithm [11], which is faster than other detection systems and YOLO9000 uses a detection for more than 9000 object categories and thereby improving detection and classification using word tree representation.

AdaBoost with Haar cascade [12] to detect human faces and to recognize the detected faces using fast PCS and LDA. The experiment is used to mark attendance in the laboratory for face recognition which gets an increased accuracy.

A mask R-CNN [13] is used for detecting images for evaluating residual nets with many layers to perform detection and opens a new research area for instance level recognition.

The techniques used in the above algorithms are considered for our research work and implicated with various dimensions of comparisons, thereby we provide a complete analysis study of various object detection and recognition algorithms.

3 Methodology

3.1 Motivation

The main part of computer vision [14] approach is object detection [15]. The object detection helps to recognize and pinpoint objects in an image or a video. The main work of computer vision is pattern learning and object recognition, which are the building blocks. The object recognition algorithms are employed in existing surveillance systems to detect objects with the mask over the face. Usually, the object recognition and object detection come in handy, so people will get confused.

The object detection [16] helps to forecast where a particular object is in the frame of an image or video and what label name has to be applied for identification purpose. The object detection provides information about the input to a greater recognition extent than image recognition algorithms. The main challenges of object detection [17] in computer vision are variations in view point, difference in illumination, hidden parts of images, background clutter, etc. We are preprocessing the images to handle these challenges.

3.2 Dataset

In this work, we have chosen data from various datasets like FMD, LFW SMFD, MFDD, MS COCO, PASCAL VOC, and RMFRD which comprises of around 55000 images. Out of which 30000 images are training images, 10000 are validation images and 10000 are testing images. We are dealing three main categories of face mask detection [18, 19] namely:

- Faces with mask
- Faces without mask
- Faces with incorrect face mask wearing

3.3 Data Preprocessing

The data preprocessing techniques helps to convert the raw input data into any under-standable format. It is the first and the foremost step in the process of knowledge discovery. The main process of data preprocessing are data cleaning, transformation and reduction. Through the preprocessing step, we can make our dataset highly perfect and improves the consistency of the dataset (Figs. 1, 2 and 3).

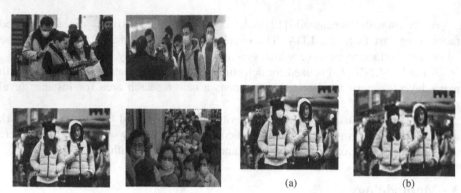

Fig. 1. Sample images from the dataset

Fig. 2. a. Normalization effects before preprocessing. b. Normalization effects after preprocessing

Fig. 3. Images with bounding box

When the dataset grows in size, the dimensionality reduction problem comes into action. In such cases, feature extraction method helps to minimize the number of features from the already available features. The most preferred feature extraction methods are PCA, ICA, LDA, LLE, t-SNE, AE, etc.

Another method to minimize the number of features in a dataset is feature selection, which hugely impacts the performance of our model. The popularly used feature extraction techniques like univariate selection and feature importance correlation matrix with heat map.

3.4 Data Augmentation

The data augmentation is the method which helps the users to have a remarkable rise in the variety of dataset available for training models, without literally gathering advanced data.

This technique can be employed to any form of data. The performances are compared with and without augmentation process mentioned in Table 1.

Table 1. Performance comparison table for data augmentation

Process	Augmentation method	Performance without augmentation	Performance with augmentation
Image classification	Simple image based	58.5%	79.2%
	GAN based [20]	58.1%	86.3%

3.5 Object Detection

The object detection tools apply algorithms to input data with the idea of obtaining regions of interest. The final step of detection is to do object classification based on models, apply probability distributions and return the classes (Figs. 4 and 5).

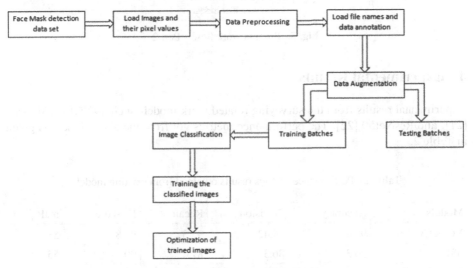

Fig. 4. Process work flow – Part 1

When it comes into technical part, the face detection and face recognition have many similarities. Both these techniques help to classify and locate objects in a frame.

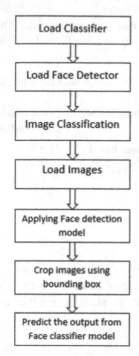

Fig. 5. Process work flow – Part 2

4 Experimental Results

Experimental results from the surveying related work models such as YOLO [5], SSD [21], and ResNet50 [22]. The performance metrics got from the above model is given in Table 2.

Table 2. Performance metrics results obtained from existing models

Models	Accuracy	Precision	Recall	F1 score	maP
YOLO 3	93.2	94.42	92.3	91.8	53
SSD	90.3	86.3	87.4	90	55
RESNET 50	95.3	98.9	98.24	91	79.2

In this experiment, we combined and compared various model architectures with different backbones such as YOLO-SSD, YOLO-RESNET 110, YOLO V2-RESNET 50, SSD-RESNET, SSD-MOBILENET V2 [23], RCNN-RESNET, RCNN-RESNET 50, and Faster RCNN-RESNET 50 [24] against the various performance metrics [25] as accuracy, precision, recall, F1 score and maP in a simulated dataset, where we had trained the model with the chosen dataset for over 50 epochs.

$$precision = \frac{TP}{TP + FP}$$

$$recall = \frac{TP}{TP + FN}$$

$$F1 = \frac{2 \times precision \times recall}{precision + recall}$$

$$accuracy = \frac{TP + TN}{TP + FN + TN + FP}$$

$$specificity = \frac{TN}{TN + FP}$$

The results obtained as shown in Table 3.

Table 3. Experimental results of the comparison of the ensemble models

Models	Accuracy	Precision	Recall	F1 Score	maP
YOLO-SSD	91.3	82.3	87.5	88	83
YOLO-RESNET 110	90.2	81.6	82.5	84	80.5
YOLO V2-RESNET 50	92.5	81	83.2	91	82
SSD-RESNET	87.5	70.3	77.4	83.2	72.4
SSD-MOBILENET V2	92.64	90.1	92.3	93	93.3
RCNN-RESNET50	91.1	90.8	91.3	86	91
Fast RCNN-RESNET 50	92.8	92.5	92.2	92	90.6
Faster RCNN-RESNET 50	98.2	95.2	98.5	95	95

From the results obtained from our experiment in comparison with the different model architecture with various backbones is found that the Faster RCNN ResNet50 outperforms other combined models in terms of the performance metrics. The graph of comparison for accuracy metric is given in the Fig. 6, Precision graph in Fig. 7, Recall in Fig. 8, F1 score in Fig. 9 and maP in Fig. 10.

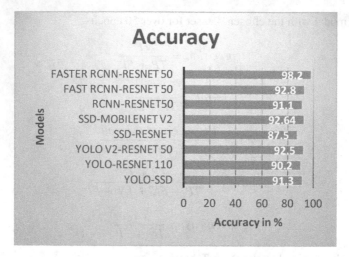

Fig. 6. Accuracy

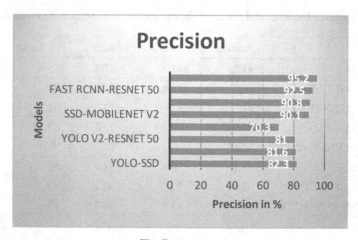

Fig. 7. Precision

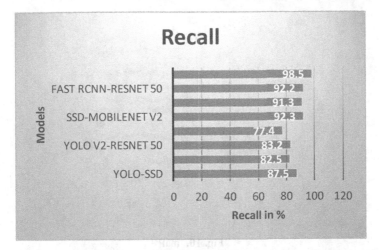

Fig. 8. Recall

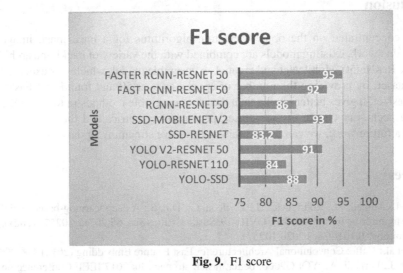

Fig. 9. F1 score

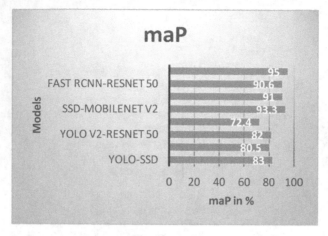

Fig. 10. maP

5 Conclusion

This work concentrated on the object detection algorithms for a Face mask image datasets. In this work, existing models are combined with the variety of backbone architectures like ResNet50, MobileNet and created an ensemble model, which was executed with the dataset, by providing the number of epochs as over 50 and found that Faster RCNN – ResNet50 gives better results than the other ensemble methods in terms of the following aspects, our choice of the dataset, performance metrics and the number of epochs. As a future work, we can extend this work to live streaming of data.

References

1. Ahmed, I., Ahmad, M., Rodrigues, J.J.P.C., Jeon, G., Din, S.: A deep learning-based social distance monitoring framework for COVID-19. Sustain. Cities Soc. **65**(2021), 102571 (2021). https://doi.org/10.1016/j.scs.2020.102571
2. Jia, Y., et al.: Caffe: Convolutional Architecture for Fast Feature Embedding (2014)
3. Redmon, J., Farhadi, A.: YOLO9000: better, faster, stronger. In: 2017 IEEE Conference on Computer Vision and Pattern Recognition (2017). https://doi.org/10.1109/CVPR.2017.690
4. Shinde, S., Kothari, A., Gupta, V.: YOLO based human action recognition and localization. Procedia Comput. Sci. **133**, 831–838 (2018). https://doi.org/10.1016/j.procs.2018.07.112
5. Dong, E., Zhu, Y., Ji, Y., Du, S.: An improved convolution neural network for object detection using YOLOv2. In: Proceedings of 2018. IEEE (2018)
6. Leibe, B., Matas, J., Sebe, N., Welling, M. (eds.): ECCV 2016. LNCS, vol. 9908. Springer, Cham (2016). https://doi.org/10.1007/978-3-319-46493-0
7. Ejaz, S., Islam, R., Sifatullah, Md., Sarker, A.: Implementation of Principal Component Analysis on Masked and Non-masked Face Recognition. In: 1st International Conference on Advances in Science, Engineering and Robotics Technology 2019 (ICASERT 2019) (2019)
8. Erhan, D., Szegedy, C., Toshev, A., Anguelov, D.: Scalable object detection using deep neural networks. In: IEEE Conference on Computer Vision and Pattern Recognition (2014). https://doi.org/10.1109/CVPR.2014.276

9. Dollar, P., Appel, R., Belongie, S., Perona, P.: Fast feature pyramids for object detection. IEEE Trans. Pattern Anal. Mach. Intell. **36**(8) (2014)
10. Girshick, R., Donahue, J., Darrell, T., Malik, J.:Rich feature hierarchies for accurate object detection and semantic segmentation. In: 2014 IEEE Conference on Computer Vision and Pattern Recognition (2014). https://doi.org/10.1109/CVPR.2014.81
11. Redmon, J., Divvala, S., Girshick, R., Farhadi, A.: You only look once: unified, real-time object detection. In: 2016 IEEE Conference on Computer Vision and Pattern Recognition (2016). https://doi.org/10.1109/CVPR.2016.91
12. Kumar, K.S., Semwal, V.J., Tripathi, R.C.: Real time face recognition using adaboost improved fast PCA algorithm (2011)
13. He, K., Zhang, X., Ren, S., Sun, J.: Deep residual learning for image recognition. In: 2016 IEEE Conference on Computer Vision and Pattern Recognition (2016). https://doi.org/10.1109/CVPR.2016.90
14. Roh, M.-C., Lee, J.-Y.: Refining faster-RCNN for accurate object detection. In: 15th IAPR International Conference on Machine Vision Applications (MVA). Nagoya University, Nagoya, Japan (2017)
15. Girshick, R., Donahue, J., Darrell, T., Malik, J.: Region-based convolutional networks for accurate object detection and segmentation. IEEE Trans. Pattern Anal. Mach. Intell. (2016). https://doi.org/10.1109/TPAMI.2015.2437384
16. Nguyen, N.-D., Do, T., Ngo, T.D., Le, D.-D.: An evaluation of deep learning methods for small object detection. J. Electr. Comput. Eng. **2020**, 1–18 (2020). https://doi.org/10.1155/2020/3189691
17. Wu, X., Sahoo, D., Hoi, S.C.H.: Recent advances in deep learning for object detection. Neurocomputing **396**(2020), 39–64 (2020). https://doi.org/10.1016/j.neucom.2020.01.085
18. Zhan, S., Tao, Q.-Q., Li, X.-H.: Face Detection using representation learning. J. Neurocomput. **187**(2016), 19–26 (2016). https://doi.org/10.1016/j.neucom.2015.07.130
19. Loey, M., Manogaran, G., Mohamed, H.N., Taha, N.E., Khalifa, M.: A hybrid deep transfer learning model with machine learning methods for face mask detection in the era of the COVID-19 pandemic. J. Int. Meas. Confed. (2021). https://doi.org/10.1016/j.measurement.2020.108288
20. Din, N.U., Javed, K., Bae, S., Yi, J.: A novel GAN-based network for unmasking of masked face. IEEE Access **8**, 44276–44287 (2020)
21. Liu, W., et al.: SSD: single shot multibox detector. In: Leibe, B., Matas, J., Sebe, N., Welling, M. (eds.) ECCV 2016. LNCS, vol. 9905, pp. 21–37. Springer, Cham (2016). https://doi.org/10.1007/978-3-319-46448-0_2
22. Loey, M., Manogaran, G., Tahad, M.H.N., Khalifa, N.E.M.: Fighting against COVID-19: a novel deep learning model based on YOLO-v2 with ResNet-50 for medical face mask detection (2021)
23. Nguyen, H.: Fast object detection framework based on mobilenet V2 architecture and enhanced feature pyramid. J. Theor. Appl. Inf. Technol. **98**,(05) (2020). ISSN: 1992-8645
24. Jiang, H., Learned-Miller, E.: Face detection with the faster R-CNN. In: 2017 IEEE 12th International Conference on Automatic Face & Gesture Recognition. IEEE Computer Society (2017). https://doi.org/10.1109/FG.2017.82
25. Padilla, R., Netto, S.L., da Silva, E.A.B.: A survey on performance metrics for object-detection algorithms. In: Proceedings of the IWSSIP 2020. IEEE Explore (2020)

A Novel Approach to Detect Face Mask
in Real Time

Sumita Gupta[1], Rana Majumdar[2(✉)], and Shivam Deswal[1]

[1] Department of CSE, Amity School of Engineering and Technology, Amity University, Noida, India
[2] School of Computer Science and Engineering, Swami Vivekananda University, Kolkata, India

Abstract. COVID-19, a deadly virus outbreak in the entire world, infected count-less number of people and leads to death of millions of people. Economy of coun-tries halted, people are stuck up, the situation is becoming worse day by day that no one expected. The COVID-19 can be spread through airborne droplets, aerosols and other carriers. So, the guidelines are released which promotes 3 key points for its prevention: (a) maintain social distancing, (b) sanitization, and (c) most important, wearing of mask in public places. But unfortunately, people are avoid-ing these measures leading to spread of the disease. So, there is need of some sort of security guards on ground that ensures people would strictly follow the guide-lines. But, it's too risky for the lives of security guards. Fortunately, we live in 21st century. There are so powerful technologies like Machine Learning, Artificial Intelligence, Deep Learning and many more. So, it is possible to develop a way where machines will help us to ensure the guidelines to be followed. There is no need for a physical person to watch over crowd. This research paper proposed a work to implement machine-learning algorithm to ensure people wear the proper face mask or not. It can be used in public places like airports, railway stations or at main gate of societies to ensure that no one without mask may enter the society and similarly can be used at stores.

Keywords: COVID-19 · Face detection · Mask detection · Machine learning · SVM · Viola-Jones algorithm

1 Introduction

COVID-19 is an infectious disease caused by a newly discovered virus coronavirus. Every single nation is fighting against the virus and no one is safe. Country's economy collapsed, countless people were infected, millions of them died, shortages of equipment in hospitals, and the situation is becoming worse day by day that no one expected. Older people, and those with chronic diseases like cancer, blood pressure, Tuberculosis, Thyroid, etc. are more likely to develop serious illness. The best way to prevent and slow down transmission is to follow the guidelines regulated by World Health Organization (WHO) and by the government of the country. 3 key points to remember is to keep social distancing, sanitization and wear proper face mask. The COVID-19 virus spreads

© Springer Nature Switzerland AG 2022
A. Dev et al. (Eds.): AIST 2021, CCIS 1546, pp. 604–615, 2022.
https://doi.org/10.1007/978-3-030-95711-7_49

primarily through droplets of saliva or discharge from the nose when an infected person sneezes [1].

It's a deadly virus and prevention is needed from it, as prevention is better than cure. But still many people are not following the guidelines issued. For example, still many people not wear masks properly; don't stay socially distanced and other negligence. So, in order to ensure the guidelines are followed or not, there is need to have some security guards present at the place physically. But it increases the risk of infection in them [2]. But fortunately, it is 21st century. There are so powerful technologies like Machine Learning, Artificial Intelligence, Deep Learning and many more. So, it is possible to develop a way where machines will help us to ensure the guidelines to be followed. There is no need for a physical person to watch over crowd.

In this paper, implementation of face mask detection system is proposed which helps to check and detect the person who has wear the mask i.e. yes or no and who has not wear the mask properly. This system enables to help all the shop owners, offices, banks or any other public areas like airports, railway stations, bus stops, metro, etc. [3].

In this research paper, Sect. 2 is describing literature review of different research papers. Section 3 is describing the different steps used in implementing the working model. It thoroughly explains face detection through Viola-Jones algorithm [13], OpenCV used for converting images into array [14], Classification technique under Machine Learning through support vector machine. Further Sect. 4 is about implementation analysis and Sect. 5 includes result.

2 Literature Survey

This section discusses about various methodologies proposed till now for mask detection.

MobileNet and Global Pooling Block [4] are used for detecting face mask. Mobilenet is pretrained and considered the input image without accepting the output layer. It generates a feature map. Global pooling block is used to transform a multi-dimensional feature map into a 1D vector having 64 features which are further forwarded to a softmax layer for performing binary classification. In [5], YOLOv3 method is used. During preprocessing, the input image quality is enhanced by using auto white balance and edge enhancement using unsharp filter. In this paper, system detected the face mask on the face through YOLOv3 algorithm. The main advantage of using YOLOv3 is speed of detection, accuracy and meets the real-time requirements for ship detection.

In [6], the author used improved retina face algorithm. Retina face algorithm is only used for face detection. It creates point on different places of face and identifies a face through those points like nose, mouth, eyes, etc. So, this research paper improved the working of retina face algorithm and used this algorithm to further detect masks on the face. Improved the working of Retina Face algorithm. Retina Face algorithm is very accurate for detection. The algorithm used is not compatible for all system. Thus increasing the cost factor in order to implement the system in practice.

In [7], the author used Cosine Distance algorithm. Image preprocessing is done. With transfer learning, it accomplished the last convolution. A trained network is used for fine-tuning and then further forwarded for re training by using a new dataset. Facenet uses 128-neuron fully connected layer as the last layer. The cosine similarity measure is considered for capturing the orientation (the angle) of the data objects. But the main drawback is that the magnitude of vectors is not considered into account.

In [8], the author used transfer learning algorithm. VGG19, Xception, MobileNetV2 is primarily used. Support Vector Machine are a set of supervised learning methods used to recognize classes of objects. KNN is one of the simplest algorithms used in machine learning for regression and classification problems. The proposed model outperforms existing models in the number of parameters as well as training time. In order to minimize the time complexity, the models have now very high space complexity.

In [9], Multi Task Cascade Convolution Neural Network method is used to detect face masks from videos. For detecting the face mask in given facial images, a distinct facial classifier is built. It had better accuracy than the OpenCV, Haar-Cascade method. It has high run time. In [10], Color information is considered for extracting discriminant features of the image. This can be achieved by using color quotient algorithm. It can be used with low quality images/videos. It has low accuracy. In [11], the author used Convolutional Neural Network. CNN's can perform person and face mask classification with high accuracy. It first detects the person, then the face, and then the mask. So, it is basically meant for the purpose of pedestrians, able to detect masks even when camera is installed at a certain height. It has high run time.

3 Proposed Work

A system for face mask detection is implemented using Machine Learning. A dataset of 14 thousand images was used; half of them is with face mask and other half without face mask. Then loaded the images into data model and trained the model for face mask detection. The loaded images are converted into array. The array consists the information about RGB values of every index of the images. For face detection, Viola-Jones algorithm is used. It then takes an input of an image or a video and converts that image or every frame of a video into an array of RGB values of every index, which is further compared with the trained data model and shows the output accordingly. Architecture of the work is shown in Fig. 1.

A detailed description of each step is given below.

3.1 Dataset Collection

This model collected data through two different areas. First is from Kaggle [11], Twelve (12K) thousand images are taken from kaggle of which six (6K) thousand are of with face masks and rest without face mask, second from webcam of laptop where I provided 1,000 images with face mask and 1,000 without face mask. Images with mask consist of all the people wearing face mask correctly, while images without face mask consist of images where either people are not wearing face mask or wearing it incorrectly.

3.2 Image Processing

Image processing is a method to perform some operations on an image or to identify an image. It is primarily used for object detection and recognition and there are so many pre-existing algorithms and that too in numerous areas of application. For example; in healthcare for cancer detection, at toll booths for number plate detection, in self driving cars for detection of everything around, every smartphone comes with a feature of facial unlock and many more.

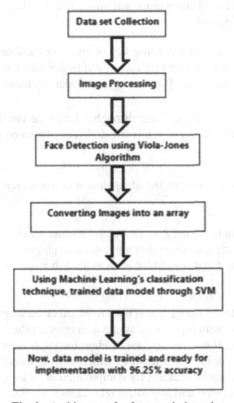

Fig. 1. Architecture for face mask detection

3.3 Face Detection Using Viola-Jones Algorithm

For facial detection, this model will be using Viola-Jones algorithm in this model [13]. This algorithm works on frontal face detection. The characteristics of Viola-Jones algorithm that makes it a good detection algorithm are:

- It is robust, that is high detection rate and low false positive rate.
- It is possible to implement in real time.
- It is used for face detection, not face recognition.

The algorithm is divided into four phases as described below in details:

The Viola-Jones algorithm is meant for the detection of face through rectangular areas. It makes small window, and start searching for haar features in it. It adds all white and black pixel respectively and find the difference between the two. If it is nearer to one, it is a haar feature. Else if it is nearer to zero, it is not considered as haar feature. Same process repeats for all the windows it virtually created and tells the result at the end for all the faces detected.

Haar Features: Every human has some key points over the face like eyes, eyebrows, nose, lips, etc. It searches for it and tells the result as described in Fig. 3. Eyes and nose are identified through rectangle. The procedures to identify them are as:

- Exact location and size are identified through different rectangles shown in Fig. 2.
- These rectangles are nothing, but just the difference between the sum of white and black pixels.

If any Haar feature is found by the algorithm, it is considered as a face.
Rectangle Features:

- Value $= \Sigma$ (pixels in black area) $- \Sigma$ (pixels in white area)
- Three types: two-rectangle, three-rectangle, four rectangles.
- Each feature is related to a special location in the sub-window.

Integral Image:

In Fig. 2 represents integral image that is used to calculate rectangular features shown in Fig. 2 in constant time, which provides an advantage over other features by enhancing the speed performance. If one rectangular or Haar feature is found, then it searches for other remaining rectangles or Haar features which will comprise as a face. The system considers any two rectangular features for computation in six array references, any three rectangular features in eight, and four-rectangle feature in nine.

Adaboost Training and Cascading Classifiers:

Adaboost training is used to choose sub window which is by default of size 24×24. It trains the classifiers at a cheaper rate as compared to other methods and is considered as strong classifier, not weak classifier. This single classifier helps in reducing the evaluation time of entire cascade by half approximately. In cascading, a strong classifier is used at every stage so that all the features on every stage are grouped together. Each stage checks whether a given sub-window is representing a face or not. If at any stage, it detects there is no face, then it immediately discards the given sub-window.

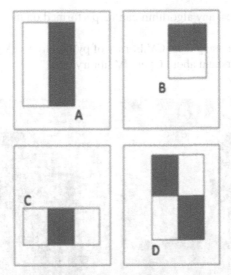

Fig. 2. Example of rectangle feature

Haar-like feature applied on the eye region

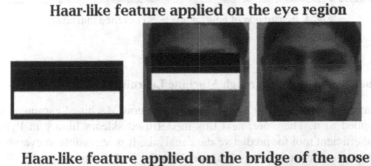

Haar-like feature applied on the bridge of the nose

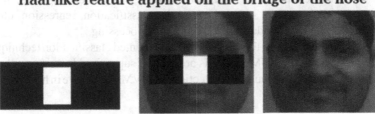

Fig. 3. Example of Haar features

3.4 Converting Images into an Array

In order to detect face masks accurately, this model will be following the following steps:

- Load images using pre-defined data set into python.
- Convert images into array. These arrays will contain the RGB value ranging from 0 to 255 for every pixel of every image. Pictorial representation is shown in Fig. 4.

- After loading images, any algorithm can be performed on the array we have.

  This model will be using OpenCV library of python for working on mask detection. So, let's first understand about OpenCV library.

Fig. 4. Illustration of how an image is converted into array.

3.5   Training Data Model Through Machine Learning:

Once, dataset is converted from images to an array, now Machine Learning algorithms can be applied to it. Therefore, next this model used sklearn library in Python. It's simple and efficient tool for predictive data analysis. It is accessible to everybody, and reusable in various contexts. It is built on NumPy, SciPy and matplotlib. It is open source, commercially usable. It can be used for classification, regression, clustering, dimensionality reduction, model selection and pre-processing.

Specifically, under sklearn this model has implemented classification technique using Support Vector Machines (SVMs). SVMs are a set of supervised learning methods used for classification, regression, outliers' detection. As SVM is effective in high dimensional spaces.

4   Implementation and Analysis

This model used a combined dataset from kaggle and from webcam. The images are first converted into an array using OpenCV, which stores the RGB (Red, Green, Blue) values of every pixel of every image. Further, Viola-Jones algorithm is used to detect faces. It can detect multiple faces in an image or a video. Then, trained the model through Machine Learning. Sklearn is used for training. Specifically, under sklearn we have implemented classification technique using Support Vector Machines. Now, our model is ready to take input and providing the output with an accuracy of 96.25%.

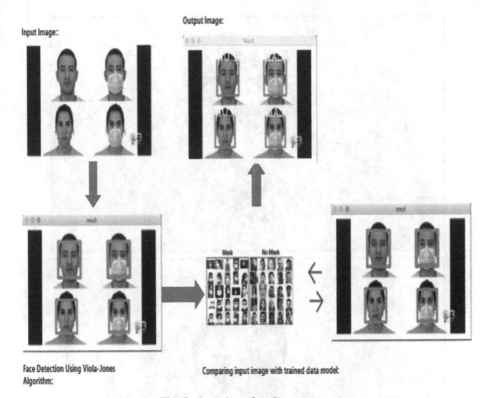

Input Image::

Output Image:

Face Detection Using Viola-Jones
Algorithm:

Comparing input image with trained data model:

Fig. 5. Snapshot of each step output

First, input is provided through a webcam, CCTV cameras or any link (as shown in Fig. 5) and it will scan the image or any frame of a video for faces through Viola-Jones algorithm. Then it ignores the background details and works for faces detected in the image if any. Then it uses pre-trained model to recognize whether the person is wearing a face mask or not. If person is wearing a face mask, it will show "MASK" written, else if mask is absent or not properly worn, it will show "NO MASK" written. The screenshot of images with or without mask are shown in Figs. 6 and 7.

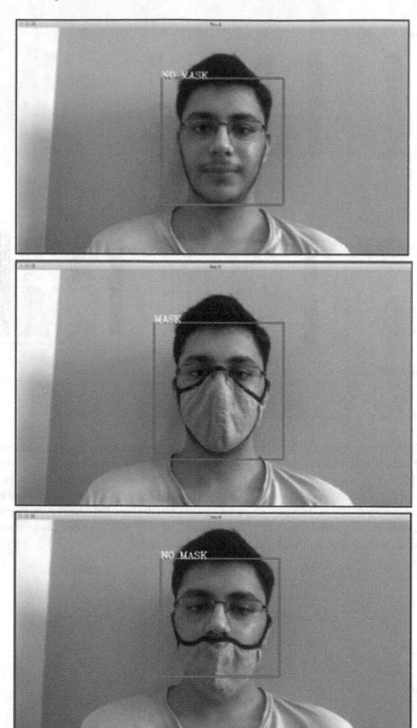

Fig. 6. Screenshot of working model through a webcam. It is showing "NO MASK" for (a) no face mask worn and (b) improper face mask, and showing "MASK" for (c) proper worn face mask.

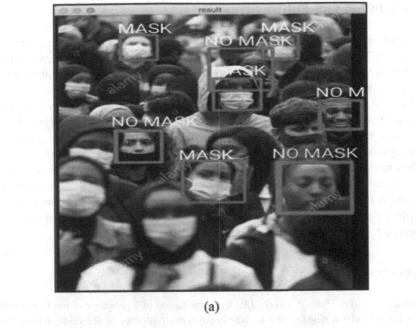

(a)

(b)

Fig. 7. (a) & (b) Face masks detection for an image with multiple faces in a crowd.

5 Conclusion and Future Scope

This paper presents a method for face mask detection system to reduce the spread of coronavirus. This model uses Viola-Jones algorithm for face detection, then comparing the detected faces with the trained data model and finally showing the output with an accuracy of 96.25%.

This model can be helpful for all the shop owners, offices, banks or any other public areas like airports, railway stations, bus stops, metro, etc. because if anyone is not wearing a face mask then he or she must not be allowed in that area. This model replaces the security guards that we need to ensure that guidelines were followed or not.

This model works well if the face is clearly visible and could be detected. This algorithm uses a technique of detecting the face through key points that everyone has in common. But there are situations when face's features are not visible in the image. For example, a person wearing a face mask, sunglasses, and a hat. Because of this, face is not detected. In future, this thing can be improved.

References

1. Draughon, G.T.S., Sun, P., Lynch, J.P.: Implementation of a computer vision framework for tracking and visualizing face mask usage in urban environments. In: IEEE International Smart Cities Conference, pp. 1–8 (2020). https://doi.org/10.1109/ISC251055.2020.9239012
2. Susanto, S., Putra, F.A., Analia, R., Suciningtyas, I.K.L.N.: The face mask detection for preventing the spread of COVID-19 at Politeknik Negeri Batam. In: 3rd International Conference on Applied Engineering, pp. 1–5 (2020). https://doi.org/10.1109/ICAE50557.2020.9350556
3. Din, N.U., Javed, K., Bae, S., Yi, J.: A novel GAN-based network for unmasking of masked face. IEEE Access **8**, 44276–44287 (2020). https://doi.org/10.1109/ACCESS.2020.2977386
4. Venkateswarlu, I.B., Kakarla, J., Prakash, S.: Face mask detection using MobileNet and global pooling block. In: IEEE 4th Conference on Information & Communication Technology, pp. 1–5 (2020). https://doi.org/10.1109/CICT51604.2020.9312083
5. Vinh, T.Q., Anh, N.T.N.: Real-time face mask detector using YOLOv3 algorithm and Haar cascade classifier. Int. Conf. Adv. Comput. Appl. (2020). https://doi.org/10.1109/ACOMP5 0827.2020.00029
6. Xue, B., Hu, J., Zhang, P.: Intelligent detection and recognition system for mask wearing based on improved RetinaFace algorithm. In: 2nd International Conference on Machine Learning, Big Data and Business Intelligence, pp. 474–479 (2020). https://doi.org/10.1109/MLBDBI 51377.2020.00100
7. Maharani, D.A., Machbub, C., Rusmin, P.H., Yulianti, L.: Improving the capability of real-time face masked recognition using cosine distance. In: 6th International Conference on Interactive Digital Media, pp. 1–6 (2020). https://doi.org/10.1109/ICIDM51048.2020.933 9677
8. Oumina, A., El Makhfi, N., Hamdi, M.: Control the COVID-19 pandemic: face mask detection using transfer learning. In: 2nd International Conference on Electronics, Control, Optimization and Computer Science, pp. 1–5 (2020). https://doi.org/10.1109/ICECOCS50124.2020. 9314511
9. Joshi, A.S., Joshi, S.S., Kanahasabai, G., Kapil, R., Gupta, S.: Deep learning framework to detect face masks from video footage. In: 12th International Conference on Computational Intelligence and Communication Networks, pp. 435–440 (2020). https://doi.org/10.1109/CIC N49253.2020.9242625

10. Buciu, I.: Color quotient-based mask detection. In: International Symposium on Electronics and Telecommunications, pp. 1–4 (2020). https://doi.org/10.1109/ISETC50328.2020.930 1079

11. Jangra, A.: Face Mask Detection ~12K Images Dataset, kaggle. https://www.kaggle.com/ash ishjangra27/face-mask-12k-images-dataset

12. Rahman, M.M., Manik, M.M.H., Islam, M.M., Mahmud, S., Kim, J.-H.: An automated system to limit Covid-19 using facial mask detection in smart city network. In: IEEE International IOT, Electronics and Mechatronics Conference, pp. 1–5 (2020). https://doi.org/10.1109/IEM TRONICS51293.2020.9216386

13. Vikram, K., Padmavathi, S.: Facial parts detection using Viola Jones algorithm. In: 4th International Conference on Advanced Computing and Communication Systems, pp. 1–4 (2017). https://doi.org/10.1109/ICACCS.2017.8014636

14. Adusumalli, H., Kalyani,D., Sri, R.K., Pratapteja, M., Rao, P.V.R.D.P.: Face mask detection using OpenCV. In: Third International Conference on Intelligent Communication Technologies and Virtual Mobile Networks, pp. 1304–1309 (2021). https://doi.org/10.1109/ICICV5 0876.2021.9388375

15. Batagelj, B., Peer, P., Štruc, V., Dobrišek, S.: How to correctly detect face-masks for COVID-19 from visual information? Appl. Sci. 11(5), 2070 (2021). https://doi.org/10.3390/app110 52070

16. Zhang, J., Han, F., Chun, Y., Chen, W.: A novel detection framework about conditions of wearing face mask for helping control the spread of COVID-19. IEEE Access 9, 42975–42984 (2021). https://doi.org/10.1109/ACCESS.2021.3066538

A Novel Approach for Detecting Facial Key Points Using Convolution Neural Networks

Rishi Kakkar⬤ and Y. V. Srinivasa Murthy⁽⊠⁾⬤

Department of CSE, VIT University, Vellore, Tamil Nadu 632 014, India
rishi.2018@vitstudent.ac.in, vishnu.murthy@vit.ac.in

Abstract. The task of face recognition is having many real-time applications in which the process of facial keypoint detection is considered to be an intermediate and crucial step. The amount of keypoints that are using for face recognition decides the computational requirements of the algorithm. In this paper, an effort has been made to detect the useful 15 facial key points using convolutional neural networks and compared with the state-of-the-art system with 30 facial key points. We made an effort to identify the 15 facial key points (6 points from eye +4 points from eyebrows +4 points from lips +1 point from the nose) by using the proper hyperparameters for convolutional neural network. It is found that the performance of the proposed system is quite similar when compared to the system with 30 facial key points.

Keywords: Batch size · Convolutional neural networks · Dropout layer · Facial keypoint detection · Face recognition

1 Introduction

There are many practical uses of facial features, which might help to shape the future of biometric-based applications. Exhaustive research has been conducted on the frontal profile of the face and found to represent the maximum number of features. Thus, a human face can be represented with a few coordinates in the facial profile, which reduces the information by keeping the integrity and representation of data intact. Furthermore, the advancements in deep learning techniques have led to the improvement in the process of extracting biometric-based features, especially facial key points. With this, it possible to obtain more practical usage to recognition and identification.

There are enormous number of applications by extracting the facial key points from the human face. The foremost application could be the process of face recognition with less computational complexity. Also, facial features can be used in crime investigation by determining the suitable facial key points. They are unique from person to person. It can be achieved even a person does morphing. Facial features can be used to identify criminals in video-based crime investigations.

Usage of facial features in pedestrian detection by just reducing the search space even on a large number of human faces [11]. It can be also applied in knowing how faces can be used to detect intruders to restricted or high-security areas and help in minimizing human error [12]. Also, it is possible to design smart spectacles that blind people can maintain to detect known human faces since it takes less computational time [4].

The facial-key feature extraction model requires two things: (i) processing power and (ii) memory which makes it hard for embedded systems to use in small-scale applications. Moreover, the process of training with correct data, i.e., grayscale images, is tricky as color-based information is lost. Also, features that are to be identified may reduce from 65 to 15 that required basic analysis and important classification based on experts suggestions [6]. Identifying the correct layers of convolutions with their relations with average pooling for getting correct parameters to the next layer for feature extraction was a significant challenge.

In regard to applications and motivational outcomes of facial-key features identification, a new improved and innovative model is need of the hour. This paper introduces a new deep learning model, which is based on convolutions and helps to better understand and extract the facial features from the given image. It also aims at setting up better performance benchmarks in reducing the number of key points required to describe a face. With reduced key points and a better performing model, new light could be shed towards face identification or recognition tasks.

The rest of the paper is organized as follows: Sect. 2 details the exhaustive literature done in this field. Section 3 gives the detailed flow diagram with appropriate explanation. The dataset considered for the work is explained in Sect. 4. Section 5 details the results obtained with the proposed methodology. At the verdict, conclusions drawn out of this work along with feasible future directions are listed in Sect. 6.

2 Literature Survey

Recognition and identification are having 20 years of development in various domains. In this work, we are focusing on the process of face recognition based on facial key features. Also, it has started to yield some amazing results. However, there are many things to quantify and analyze that bring into active commercial and general-purpose usage. In the early 1950s, there are first signs of facial recognition that are found in psychology, and in the late 1960s, it was entered into the engineering field.

Extensive research has led to the implementation of the suggested method for practical purposes. However, there are still far from satisfactory results in real-time scenarios. One notable application is that face recognition can be used in biometrics. Also, it has numerous applications that often lead to information extraction of a person beyond realization. Dantcheva et al., 2015 [4], detailed the analytical works carried out to identify the age, gender, and ethnicity of a person from just facial features. Also, they establish how other metrics can be used to construct an information chart. Implementation of facial recognition can be easily done, which is shown by Khan *et al.*, 2019 [7], suggesting smart glasses which can recognize and identify the person with 98.3% accuracy.

As a first step towards face recognition, algorithms related to image processing and computer vision are prominently used [14]. A survey paper presented by [14] details the same. Also, it details the importance of psychological point of views.

In the early years of 21st century, new techniques such as principle component analysis (PCA), independent component analysis (ICA), linear discrimination analysis (LDA), support vector machines (SVM) are introduced to identify the suitable features from the large dimensional feature vector. They are succeeded in providing efficient results with low dimensional feature vectors. Further, there are many works that are focused on feature dimensionality reduction for recognizing the face with a minimal number of features. It obviously reduces the complexity issues and suitable for low-end devices. For instance, PCA with eigenfaces was a successful attempt to prioritize the features and reconstruct the face so that it can be identified later, giving consistent promising results [14].

Research on feature identification and prioritization made it easy to identify important key points in a person's face, which helped reduce the extensive data for facial features to some coordinates. In early 1996, neural networks were introduced to locate three facial features, eyes, nose, and mouth, focusing on microfeatures of each of these rather than as a single entity. It had shown considerable improvement in detecting features [15]. Latha *et al.*, 2009 used backpropagated neural networks to recognize 200 faces from the yale database and compared it with PCA-based neural networks obtaining considerable improvement when compared to the original feature vector [9].

The introduction to the convolutional neural networks (CNNs) has been started in the early days of 2011. However, it has outperformed many traditional approaches and occupies the top position in 2015. They are popularized in the field of image processing especially. The face recognition with the CNN model outperforms all the traditional feature-based approaches. CNN is a convolution matrix-based neural network that helps extract information by applying a convolution function. It is found to be 90% accurate on image models with different parameters. Chauhan *et al.*, 2018 described how CNN's performed on image recognition and detection datasets using data augmentation and dropout. Further, CNN was explored into biometric-based recognition systems based on the score obtained as output, which sets the basic requirements for biometrics identification systems. Features can be extracted from a CNN-based model and used further for any classifier function for identification [3].

The task of face recognition is achieving better accuracy with CNN. However, feeding the whole face to CNN consumes more computational power. Hence, it grabs less attention due to its ineffectiveness for low-end products. It is highly essential to reduce the feature dimensional length to make it useful for the products with less computation power. Hence, we have proposed a method to extract the suitable and prominent facial key points from the given face. A total number of 15 facial key points are identified in this work. They are far less than 30 and 65 facial key points used in many state-of-the-art approaches [19]. A reduction of 50% is observed with the proposed approach.

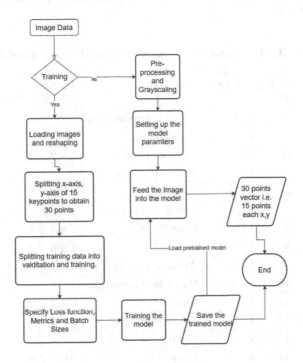

Fig. 1. Flow chart depicting the process of model

3   Proposed Methodology

There have been several works that identify batches of the image dataset. Each work has been developed to improve the accuracy or to reduce the computational complexity issues. Some works have mentioned with valid proof that the increase in batch size while training the convolutional neural network model may surely improve the performance of the face recognition system [13]. However, it depends on the type of model developed. It also states that the type of batch size is yet not confirmed and is highly dependent on the task at hand.

Explicitly focusing on small-batch training, a more generalized model with a smaller memory footprint is obtained at once. Also, another benefit is the accuracy comparison with base learning rate, which increases with an increase in batch size by looking at well-established CNN models [10].

Moreover, the usage of smaller batch sizes with standard learning rates can provide better results to any deep learning model with convolutions. Based on this, a novel model based on CNN is introduced, given in Fig. 1. The information related to batch and tensor sizes is given in Table 1. The columns of the table represents number of layers considered for experimentation, the type of layer (*also called* layer name), and the details of tensor size mentioned ($R \times C \times S$). For instance, row number 5 is with one layer, Conv2D type, and the tensors are equal to $2 \times 2 \times 1$.

Table 1. Hyper parameters considered for the experimentation.

Row ID	# Layers	Layer type	Tensors $(R \times C \times S)$
1	1	Batch normalization	
2	2	Conv2D	$5 \times 5 \times 2$
3	1	Average pooling	$2 \times 2 \times 1$
4	1	Batch normalization	
5	1	Conv2D	$2 \times 2 \times 1$
6	1	Batch normalization	
7	1	Conv2D	$3 \times 3 \times 1$
8	1	Conv2D	$3 \times 3 \times 2$
9	1	Average pooling	$2 \times 2 \times 1$
10	1	Batch normalization	
11	1	Conv2D	$2 \times 2 \times 2$
12	1	Average pooling	$2 \times 2 \times 1$
13	1	Flatten	
14	2	Dense	1024, 256
15	1	Dense(Output layer)	30

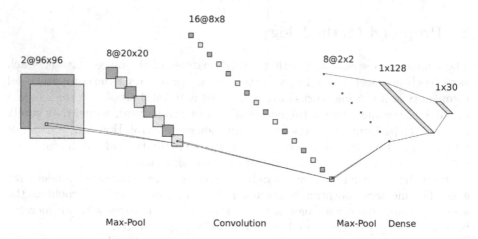

Fig. 2. Representational architecture of CNN model

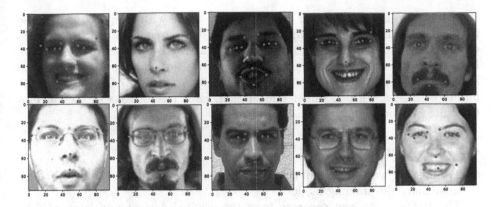

Fig. 3. A few set of images with facial key points. Each image is of size 96×96 pixels.

Batch normalization can alleviate many of the common pitfalls in neural network training. Increased learning rates that would cause a vanilla model to diverge can be beneficial in normalized batch models and even accelerate their convergence[16]. That is why after every pooling layer, it is practically feasible to use the normalization layer so that "zeros" from the activation function can be cut off and represent more information in whole [18]. This model has 10million parameters that are trainable and are trained on the dataset. The proposed model is compiled with an Adam optimizer; the mean absolute error was used as a loss function and accuracy using "R-squared" metric with "Root-mean-squared-error". Adam optimizer is identified as a momentum-shifting algorithm, which is suitable for non-convex optimization problems in machine learning tasks [8].

4   Dataset

4.1   Description

The data set chosen to train the model is collected from **Kaggle** competition-facial key points detection challenge[1]. In this work, a prominent set of 15 facial key points are identified per face image as shown in Fig. 3. The characteristics of each image and the main features extracted from the face are given in the following points:

- Each eye has three divisions namely center, left, right. Hence, six points for both eyes.
- Lips have four points are defined as upper, left, right and bottom.
- Center point on the nose represents orientation.
- Other four points are placed at eye brow where each eye brow carries two points.

---

[1] https://www.kaggle.com/c/facial-keypoints-detection.

The set of images taken for dataset are grayscale with size 96 × 96 and the pixel values ranges from [0–255]. The training dataset consists of 7,049 images, with 30 targets representing individually for x and y coordinates of 15 features. It also consists of missing target values for many key points positions for face images. The imputation of missing values are discussed in 4.3. The test dataset has 1,783 images with no target information. Each test image was present in a CSV file with no target information.

4.2 Splitting Training Set

- Training set was further split into (90, 10) sets and reshuffled every 5 epochs to validate the training model.
- The test set was kept separate from the original dataset and later used to determine the error.

4.3 Imputing Missing Values

Missing values are a drawback on any machine learning task as the target variables cannot be properly identified from the missing values. Using covariance matrix and correlation coefficients it is possible to calculate revised variance and covariance matrices [1]. A strategy for imputing missing values by modeling each feature with missing values as a function of other features in a round-robin fashion is the method for iterative imputation [2].

The framework used for imputation is defined by sklearn called iterative imputer, which is still under experimental stages but works well with missing data.

After the imputation the dataset is ready to be used for regression tasks. As for the test dataset there were no missing values found to impute. Both sets required a conversion of string based image in an array based image representation for model inputs.

5   Result Analysis

The introduced model was used to determine 15 facial key points to identify the face introduced in the image. with CUDA enabled.

These results were obtained from an i7 8750H processor with 2.2 GHz clock speed, 16 GB of RAM and 16 GB NVidia K80s GPU. To present the results, a virtual environment with python programming language was setup with frameworks tensorflow 2.0, keras 2.5, scikit-learn 0.25.2 and numpy 1.19.2 installed on it. Trained on 100,150 epochs. In 100 epochs with using an early stopping method with six iterations to analyze performance.

With simple 150 epochs training accuracy is reached above 90% provided in Fig. 4 (a), whilst looking at Fig. 4 (b), as epochs exceeds 50 we obtain almost plateau on loss thus reducing the number of epochs can help us obtain better accuracy values. Moreover validation loss follows the accuracy which shows accuracy improvements.

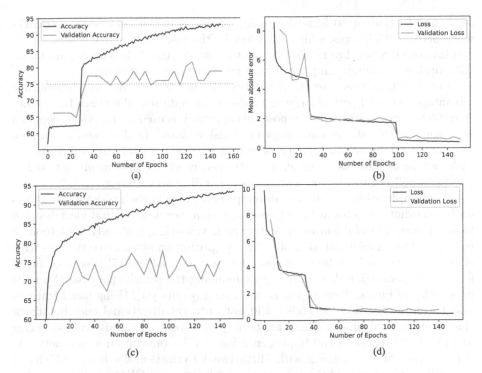

Fig. 4. Accuracy and loss values obtained. (a) Accuracy values observed for 150 epochs, (b) Mean absolute error observed for 150 epochs, (c) Accuracy observed for six iterations using early stopping each iteration with 100 epochs, and (d) Mean absolute error for six iterations 100 epochs each with early stopping.

Noticing validation accuracy stays above 75% and reaches 83% on 150 epochs indicating there is no over fitting in the model.

In Fig. 4(c), i.e. 100 epochs for six iterations with using early stopping which brings the total training epochs to 150. Thus, provides evidence that 150 is optimum epochs for training the model in one go.

It can be seen from Fig. 4 that we have clearly reduced the error with each epoch and obtained a near similar result to training loss. Obtaining a mean absolute error in range 4–5 with 30 target vectors, translates to 0.133–0.166 for each feature.

Comparing the results attained, simple 150 epochs performs better than using "early stopping" with six iteration 100 epoch each. The above figures also indicates that there is less over fitting with 150 epochs rather than Second approach.

These results may vary with using different batch sizes and epochs [10].

6   Conclusion and Future Work

This paper has focused on introducing a novel method for identifying facial key points. It is found that the proposed approach is giving better accuracy when compared to that of 30 facial key points. Since convolutional neural networks work better with images, which is evident by the results presented above. CNNs can improve if a new layer called dropout is added. Also, if batch sizes are found with optimal training, the performance may improve significantly.

The fact that there are 15 facial key points for each face is a significant advantage to model performance and reduces the data stored for each face rather than 65 features as well [19]. Suppose this approach is used for practical scenarios with some modifications according to the task at hand. In that case, it can help to provide a benchmark for face detection with a minimal data overhead. In tasks where memory is an issue, a pre-trained model is used to predict 30 key points. It will reduce the memory issues depending on the data.

Many applications are already developed for facial keypoints detection as it is an intermediate step towards all face recognition, verification, and identification tasks. The use of facial features to detect pedestrians [20] is already a hot topic of research. Also, implementation of facial recognition on attendance systems with eigenfaces returns 70%–90% accuracy for genuine images [17]. Usage of facial features in pedestrian detection by just reducing the search space based on the proportion of human faces has some promising results [11]. Using facial features and feature extraction methods could not only get directional cues but track the face [5]. Real-time testing and performance-based analysis will be better identified with research and implementation of this convolution neural network. It has a scope of improvement with a little tweak to the neural network, which can be a different partition of the same base model. However, CNN-based approaches can be used to detect features but can carry out the tasks of recalling features for the same image.

References

1. Buck, S.F.: A method of estimation of missing values in multivariate data suitable for use with an electronic computer. J. R. Stat. Soc. Ser. (Methodological) 22(2), 302–306 (1960)
2. Buitinck, L., et al.: API design for machine learning software: experiences from the scikit-learn project. arXiv preprint arXiv:1309.0238 (2013)
3. Mehdi Cherrat, E., Alaoui, R., Bouzahir, H.: Convolutional neural networks approach for multimodal biometric identification system using the fusion of fingerprint, finger-vein and face images. Peer J. Comput. Sci. 6, e248 (2020)
4. Dantcheva, A., Elia, P., Ross, A.: What else does your biometric data reveal? a survey on soft biometrics. IEEE Trans. Inf. Forensics Secur. 11(3), 441–467 (2015)
5. Gupta, K.D., Ahsan, M., Andrei, S., Alam, K.M.R.: A robust approach of facial orientation recognition from facial features. BRAIN. Broad Res. Artif. Intell. Neurosci. 8(3), 5–12 (2017)
6. Karczmarek, P., Pedrycz, W., Kiersztyn, A., Rutka, P.: A study in facial features saliency in face recognition: an analytic hierarchy process approach. Soft Comput. 21(24), 7503–7517 (2016). https://doi.org/10.1007/s00500-016-2305-9
7. Khan, S., Javed, M.H., Ahmed, E., Shah, S.A., Ali, S.U.: Facial recognition using convolutional neural networks and implementation on smart glasses. In: 2019 International Conference on Information Science and Communication Technology (ICISCT), pp. 1–6. IEEE (2019)

8. Kingma, D.P., Ba, J.: Adam: A method for stochastic optimization. arXiv preprint arXiv:1412.6980 (2014)
9. Latha, P., Ganesan, L., Annadurai, S.: Face recognition using neural networks. Signal Process. Int. J. (SPIJ) **3**(5), 153–160 (2009)
10. Masters, D., Luschi, C.: Revisiting small batch training for deep neural networks. arXiv preprint arXiv:1804.07612 (2018)
11. Min, W., Fan, M., Li, J., Han, Q.: Real-time face recognition based on pre-identification and multi-scale classification. IET Comput. Vis. **13**(2), 165–171 (2019)
12. Owayjan, M., Dergham, A., Haber, G., Fakih, N., Hamoush, A., Abdo, E.: Face recognition security system. In: Elleithy, K., Sobh, T. (eds.) New Trends in Networking, Computing, E-learning, Systems Sciences, and Engineering, pp. 343–348. Springer (2015). https://doi.org/10.1007/978-3-319-06764-3_42
13. Radiuk, P.M.: Impact of training set batch size on the performance of convolutional neural networks for diverse datasets. Inf. Technol. Manag. Sci. **20**(1), 20–24 (2017)
14. Rajni, D.K.: An efficient method of PCA based face recognition using simulink (2014)
15. Reinders, M.J., Koch, R., Gerbrands, J.J.: Locating facial features in image sequences using neural networks. In: Proceedings of the Second International Conference on Automatic Face and Gesture Recognition, pp. 230–235. IEEE (1996)
16. Schilling, F.: The effect of batch normalization on deep convolutional neural networks (2016)
17. Siswanto, A.R.S., Nugroho, A.S., Galinium, M.: Implementation of face recognition algorithm for biometrics based time attendance system. In: 2014 International Conference on ICT For Smart Society (ICISS), pp. 149–154 (2014). https://doi.org/10.1109/ICTSS.2014.7013165
18. Xu, B., Wang, N., Chen, T., Li, M.: Empirical evaluation of rectified activations in convolutional network. arXiv preprint arXiv:1505.00853 (2015)
19. Yarlagadda, V., Koolagudi, S.G., Kumar, M., Donepudi, S.: Driver drowsiness detection using facial parameters and RNNS with LSTM. In: 2020 IEEE 17th India Council International Conference (INDICON), pp. 1–7. IEEE (2020)
20. Zheng, J., Peng, J.: A novel pedestrian detection algorithm based on data fusion of face images. Int. J. Distrib. Sens. Netw. **15**(5), 1550147719845276 (2019)

Effective Hyperspectral Image Classification Using Learning Models

Sushmita Gautam[✉] and Kailash Chandra Tiwari

Multidisciplinary Centre for Geoinformatics, Delhi Technological University, Delhi, India

Abstract. Recently, machine learning has produced appreciable performance results on various visual computing related studies, including the classification of common hyperspectral images. This study aims to compare the results of different machine learning models for the classification of a hyperspectral image dataset. The hyperspectral data captured from AVIRIS sensor covering scene over the Indian Pines test site in North-western Indiana and consists 224 spectral reflectance bands. The ground truth has sixteen classes including vegetation crops, built structures, etc. Accuracy assessments and confusion matrices were used to evaluate classification performance. The study includes classification results of mainly three learning models including dimensionally reduced data via PCA for SVM classification, CNN and k-NN. The overall accuracy in PCA-SVM results was 72.38%, CNN was 85% and k-NN was 66.21% concluding the better efficiency of CNN classification for the hyperspectral dataset. Hence CNN classification technique succeeded in the hyperspectral image classification.

Keywords: Hyperspectral · Classification · Accuracy · Support vector machines · CNN · k-NN

1 Introduction

In remote sensing, hyperspectral imaging is a rapidly expanding field. It is a step forward from multispectral image analysis. The 224-band AVIRIS (Airborne Visible/Infrared Imaging Spectrometer) and the 210-band HYperspectral Digital Imagery Collection Experiment are two hyperspectral sensors now in use and operated on an airborne platform (HYDICE). They use hundreds of contiguous spectral channels to uncover elements that multispectral sensors can't normally resolve [1]. Since the hyperspectral image has information about the fine spectra, it is continuously in use in various applications such as mining [2], medical image analysis [4], agriculture [3], military [5] etc.

A significant body of research shows that machine-learning techniques (especially decision trees and neural networks) are capable of dealing efficiently with multidimensional data challenges (e.g., hyperspectral). Deep learning is recognised as the effective and powerful tool for feature- extraction and widely used in tasks involving image processing.[6].

Artificial Neural Networks (ANN) were one of the first learning machines developed in the 1940s, based on the human brain's biological neuron system. Artificial

© Springer Nature Switzerland AG 2022
A. Dev et al. (Eds.): AIST 2021, CCIS 1546, pp. 626–640, 2022.
https://doi.org/10.1007/978-3-030-95711-7_51

neural network is applicable in various applications like pattern recognition, business applications, bankruptcy application, speech recognition. A favorable point associated with neural network is tolerance to noisy data, parallelism, and learning from example.

The parallelism increases the speed of network. It was first employed in the 1980s and has since been used for a variety of engineering-related applications, owing to its capacity to extract complicated and non-linear correlations between aspects of various systems. Besides these favorable points it has also many limitations. Training of the neural network is time consuming and expensive. Training of neural network plays an important role in classification accuracy [7]. However, it has since been discovered that the ANN can only produce trustworthy results when a large amount of data is available for training.

Support vector machines (SVMs) are another type of machine-learning software that can be used for remote sensing classification. SVMs have been used to define a space in which the different classes are maximally separable. SVM works well with smaller and cleaner datasets and is effectively useful for both non-linearly separable and linearly separable data. However, it is less effective on noisy and overlapping classes datasets and the computational time might be slow depending upon the kernel used [8].

Because it is typically helpful to include more than one neighbour, the technique is also known as k-Nearest Neighbour (k-NN). Classification in which the class is determined by the number of nearest neighbours (k). Memory-Based Classification is named after the fact that the training examples are needed at run-time, i.e., they must be in memory at that moment. As induction is delayed to run time, it is known as a Lazy Learning technique.

Deep feature extraction and classification for HSIs was developed using CNN [9], which achieved state-of-the-art performance due to its capacity to extract local spatial relationships. The CNN structure's versatility makes it ideal for computer vision tasks like picture classification and object recognition [10, 11].

2 Experiment Dataset

The AVIRIS sensor acquired the scene used in the study over the Indian Pines test site in northwestern Indiana. There are 145×145 pixels and 224 spectral reflectance bands in this image. The bands have wavelengths ranging from 0.4 to 2.5×10 (-6) metre. The scene is a part of a bigger picture. Two-thirds of the scene in Indian Pines is agriculture, one-third is woodland, and the remainder is natural permanent vegetation. Two main lane highways, a rail line, and some low-density housing, minor roads, and manmade structures are all present. The sensor captured the view in June, and some of the crops present, such as corn and soybeans, are still in their early phases of growth, with less than 5% coverage. The available ground truth is divided into sixteen categories. By deleting bands encompassing the water absorption region, the number of bands was reduced to 200: [104–108], [150–163], 220.

Figure 2 shows the ground truth classes for the Indian Pines scenario, along with their respective sample numbers (Fig. 1).

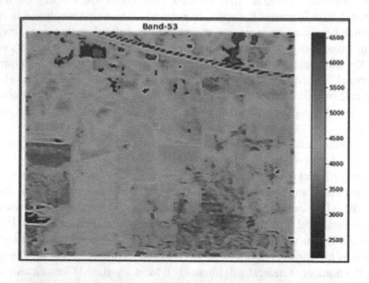

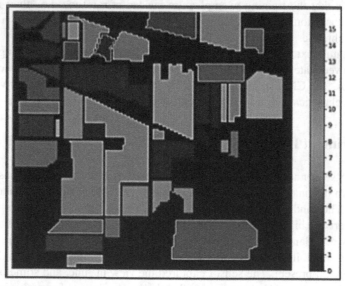

Fig. 1. The visualization of band 53 of the hyperspectral dataset of Indian pines (top) and ground truth visualization (bottom).

#	Class	Samples
1	Alfalfa	46
2	Corn-notill	1428
3	Corn-mintill	830
4	Corn	237
5	Grass-pasture	483
6	Grass-trees	730
7	Grass-pasture-mowed	28
8	Hay-windrowed	478
9	Oats	20
10	Soybean-notill	972
11	Soybean-mintill	2455
12	Soybean-clean	593
13	Wheat	205
14	Woods	1265
15	Buildings-Grass-Trees-Drives	386
16	Stone-Steel-Towers	93

Fig. 2. A figure giving information about the various ground truth classes and their samples present in the Indian Pines dataset.

3 Classification Strategies

3.1 Principal Component Analysis and the Support Vector Machine

PCA (Dimensionality Reduction): Data dimensionality refers to the number of spectral bands connected with a remote sensing device. Principal component analysis is a technique which has the capability to transform the original remote sensing dataset into smaller interpretable set of uncorrelated variables representing information present in the original dataset. Principal components are retrieved from raw data in such a way that the first principal component accounts for the greatest proportion of the original dataset's variance and orthogonal components account for the greatest proportion of the remaining variance (Zhao and Maclean, 2000; Viscarra-Rossel and C hen, 2011). The PCA analysis has been widely employed in remote sensing for a variety of applications. In this paper, we offer a historical overview as well as a mathematical derivation pertinent to PCA (Gonzalez and Woods 1993). There are also some brief debates in (Lillesand and Kiefer 2000; Campbell 1996). To shorten classification time, the practice of examining a few primary components initially and then training with a Support Vector Machine is used.

An image pixel vector can be expressed as:

$$\mathbf{x}_i = [x_1, x_2, \ldots x_N]_i^T \tag{1}$$

where,

$x_1, x_2, \ldots z_N$ = Pixel values of Hyperspectral image at corresponding pixel location.
N = The number of the hyperspectral bands equivalent to dimension of the pixel vector.

The mean vector for all image vectors is calculated as:

$$\mathbf{m} = \frac{1}{M} \sum_{i=1}^{M} [x_1, x_2, \ldots x_N]_i^T \tag{2}$$

The covariance matrix of x is defined as:

$$Cov(x) = E\{(x - E(x))(x - E(x))\}^T \tag{3}$$

where,
E = expectation operator;
T = transpose operation; and
Cov = notation for covariance matrix.

The PCA is based on the eigenvalue decomposition of the covariance matrix, which takes the following form:

$$Cx = MDM_T \tag{4}$$

Where $D = \text{diag}(\lambda_1, \lambda_2 ... \lambda_N)$ is the diagonal matrix composed of the eigenvalues λ_1, $\lambda_2 ... \lambda_N$ of the covariance matrix C_X, and M is the orthonormal matrix composed of the corresponding N dimension eigenvectors.

The linear transformation defined by:

$$y_i = M^T x_i (I = 1, 2, ..., K) \tag{5}$$

is the PCA pixel vector, and all these pixel vectors form the PCA (transformed) bands of the original images. the first K PCA bands contain majority of information residing in the original hyperspectral images. These can be used for more effective analyses since the number of bands and the amount of image noise involved are reduced (Figs. 3 and 4).

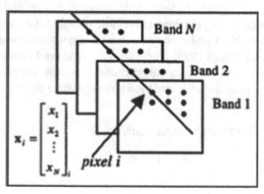

Fig. 3. Pixel vector in principal component analysis [adapted from Gonzales and Woods (1993)].

Support Vector Machines: The main reason for this classifier's selection is due to its properties, which include: a) high generalization ability and high classification accuracies (in comparison to other classifiers); b) effectiveness in addressing ill-posed problems (which are common with hyperspectral data due to the limited number of training samples

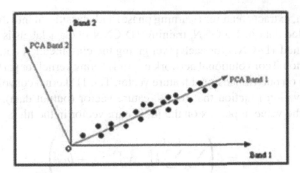

Fig. 4. Geometry of principal component analysis and PCA bands.

relative to the number of features (bands) (Plaza et al. 2009); and c) low effort required for architecture design (Jenson). SVM consists of learning of optimal hyperplane, i.e, separating the hyperplane which provides maximum separation between the classes. Among all separating hyperplanes, the one with largest margin is the optimal hyperplane.

Example of good separating hyperplane is shown in the Fig. 5 below.

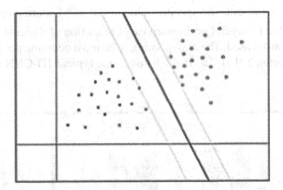

Fig. 5. Examples of hyperplane separating 2 classes.

The ideal separating hyperplane acquired separa-rating two classes by increasing the margin between the class's nearest training samples may be seen in the example above.

The support vectors are the points that lie between the boundaries. The Optimal Separating Hyperplane is located in the centre of the margin (OSH). Negative weights are applied to the training data points on the wrong side of the discriminant margin, reducing their effects. When identifying a linear separator is not possible, the data points are projected onto a higher-dimensional space using the kernel technique. A Support Vector Machine is a program that executes all of these stages.

3.2 Convolutional Neural Network

Convolutional neural network is a standard deep learning algorithm for various image classification and object detection problems. An input image is taken as a array matrix by the algorithm, extracts features (learning phase) and classifies it into different classes. The input labelled data in 1D-CNN, training 1D-CNN in class labels is performed and finally used trained 1D-CNN for each pixel giving the classification output.

One dimensional convolutional network uses a 1D conv kernel for performing convolution operation on one-dimensional feature vector. The 1D kernel convolved input data, go through activation function that forms feature vector (output data). The following equation gives the value at point x on the jth feature vector in the lth layer:

$$v_{l,j}^x = f\left(\sum_m \sum_{h=0}^{H_l-1} k_{l,j,m}^h v_{(l-1),m}^{(x+h)} + b_{l,j} \right) \qquad (6)$$

where,

l = layer number,

j = the feature vector number in the lth layer,

$b_{i,j}$ = bias of the jth feature vector in the lth layer and f() is the activation function.

m = m^{th} feature vector connected to the convolution kernel.

H_i = the length of the one-dimensional convolution kernel.

The term $v_{(l-1),m}^{(x+h)}$ represents the specific value of the mth feature map at the $(x + h, y + w)$ position in the lth layer. For the purpose of reduction of dimensions of the feature vectors, pooling can be used. The max-pooling is the most common pooling (Krizhevsky, Sutskever, and Hinton 2012). The Fig. 6 below is the typical 1D-CNN architecture used in our work.

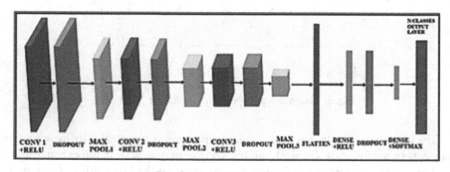

Fig. 6. 1D-CNN architecture.

3.3 k-Nearest Neighbours

The k-Nearest Neighbour algorithm is a supervised machine learning algorithm that can be applied to classification and regression issues. However, it is primarily utilized in industry to solve categorization and prediction problems. It is classified as a nonparametric learning algorithm and a lazy learning algorithm (since it does not have a specialized training phase and uses all of the input for training while categorization) (because it does not assume anything about the underlying data).

The training and testing data are loaded during the first step of the k-NN. The nearest data points are then chosen as the value of k (which can be any integer). The following is done for each point in the test data: 1) Using any approach, such as Euclidean (most widely used), Manhattan, or Hamming distance, calculate the distance between test data and each row of training data. 2) They are sorted in ascending order based on their distance value. 3) The array is sorted, and the top k rows are selected. 4) Based on the most frequent class of these rows, a class is now assigned to the test point.

The value of k that is most commonly used is 5. It is vulnerable to noise when the value of k is too small, and it may incorporate points from other classes when the value of k is too large. For example, if k = 3, it will find the three closest data points, as illustrated in Fig. 7.

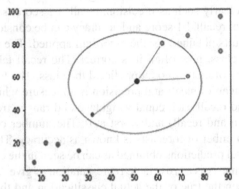

Fig. 7. The 3 nearest neighbours of the data point in black dot. Among the three neighbours, two of them lies in the Red class, hence the black dot will be assigned in the Red class. (Color figure online)

The square root of the sum of the squared differences between a new point (x) and an existing point (y) is used to determine the Euclidean distance (y). The Euclidean distance is calculated as follows:

$$d(x, y) = \sqrt{\sum_{i=1}^{n} (x_i - y_i)^2} \tag{7}$$

Manhattan distance can be calculated as below:

$$d(x, y) = \sum_{i=1}^{n} |x_i - y_i| \tag{8}$$

The Hamming distance is calculated as:

$$\begin{aligned} D_H &= \sum_{i=1}^{k} |x_i - y_i| \\ x = y &\Rightarrow D = 0 \\ x \neq y &\Rightarrow D = 1 \end{aligned} \tag{9}$$

Once the distance of a new observation from the points in our training set has been measured, the next step is to pick the closest points.

It's a straightforward algorithm to grasp and comprehend, and it's the most adaptable because it can be used for both classification and regression, but it's sensitive to data size and irrelevant information. It's a computationally costly theorem because it saves all of the training data and also requires a lot of memory storage compared to other supervised classification approaches.

4 Results and Discussion

4.1 PCA and SVM

The classification map of PCA + SVM, the classification report and the confusion matrix of the classification results are shown in below Fig. 8 and Fig. 9. The classification report contains parameters clearly such as precision, recall, F1 score, support, and accuracy of which the precision, recall, F1 score and accuracy can be considered most important in concluding the results obtained for the algorithm applied. The precision talks about when it predicts the class, how often it is correct. The recall talks about that it was actually the class, how often the model predicted the class. The F1 score, which is the weighted harmonic mean of recall and precision is a measure which gives the balance between precision and recall each equal weightage and ranges from 0 to 1 being best at 1 (perfect precision and recall) and worst at 0. The number of correct predictions divided by the total number of forecasts is known as accuracy. The accuracy obtained for PCA + SVM model predictions obtained as can be seen in the classification report is 72%. The confusion matrix is a cross table representation of give records of the number of occurrences between the true or the actual classification and the predicted one. The elements of correct classification can be found at the diagonal from top left to bottom right corresponding the actual and predicted results agreeing it.

$$\text{Precision} = \frac{TP}{TP + FP} \tag{10}$$

$$\text{Recall} = \frac{TP}{TP + FN} \tag{11}$$

$$\text{F1-Score} = \left(\frac{2}{\text{precision}^{-1} + \text{recall}^{-1}}\right) = 2 \cdot \left(\frac{\text{precision} \cdot \text{recall}}{\text{precision} + \text{recall}}\right) \tag{12}$$

$$\text{Accuracy} = \frac{TP + TN}{TP + TN + FP + FN} \tag{13}$$

Where in above equations the following can be referred:

TP = True positives which are actual positives and the model has labelled them as positive.
FP = False positives which are actual negatives and the model has labelled them as positive.

FN= False negatives which are actual positives and the model has labelled them as negative.

TN = True negatives which are actual negatives and the model has labelled them as negative.

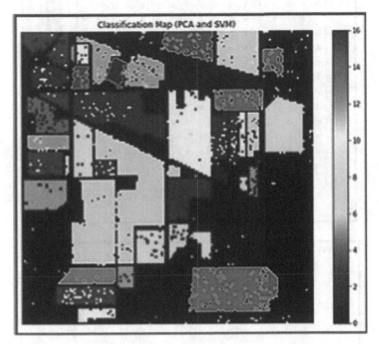

Fig. 8. The PCA with SVM classification map

4.2   CNN

The 85% overall accuracy is obtained for the classification using CNN. The precision value of the different classes can be seen which is 0.79 for Alfalfa class, 0.97 for Wheat class etc., which are measures for correctly classified classes by the model when the class was present actually. The F1- scores can be seen as 0.81, 0.98, 0.95 etc., which are the value close to 1 giving the sign of near accurate measures of precisions and recalls (Fig. 10).

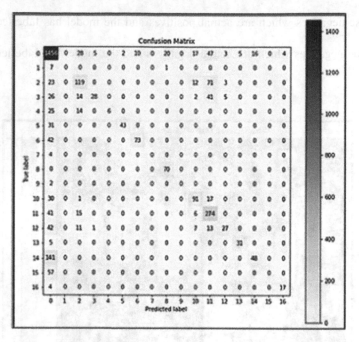

```
Classification report:
              precision    recall  f1-score   support

           0       0.75      0.90      0.82      1613
           1       0.00      0.00      0.00         8
           2       0.59      0.52      0.55       228
           3       0.82      0.24      0.37       116
           4       1.00      0.13      0.24        45
           5       0.96      0.58      0.72        74
           6       0.88      0.63      0.74       115
           7       0.00      0.00      0.00         4
           8       0.77      1.00      0.87        70
           9       0.00      0.00      0.00         2
          10       0.67      0.65      0.66       139
          11       0.59      0.82      0.69       336
          12       0.71      0.27      0.39       101
          13       0.86      0.86      0.86        36
          14       0.75      0.25      0.38       189
          15       0.00      0.00      0.00        57
          16       0.81      0.81      0.81        21

    accuracy                           0.72      3154
   macro avg       0.60      0.45      0.48      3154
weighted avg       0.72      0.72      0.69      3154
```

Fig. 9. The confusion matrix (top) and the classification report (bottom) for the PCA with SVM classification result with an overall accuracy of 72%.

	precision	recall	f1-score	support
1.Alfalfa	0.79	0.85	0.81	13
2.Corn-notill	0.71	0.90	0.80	339
3.Corn-mintill	0.73	0.80	0.76	225
4.Corn	0.72	0.73	0.72	70
5.Grass-pasture	0.92	0.87	0.90	154
6.Grass-trees	0.97	0.93	0.95	228
7.Grass-pasture-mowed	0.62	1.00	0.77	5
8.Hay-windrowed	0.98	0.97	0.98	144
9.Oats	1.00	0.86	0.92	7
10.Soybean-notill	0.83	0.79	0.81	306
11.Soybean-mintill	0.89	0.79	0.84	832
12.Soybean-clean	0.82	0.81	0.82	180
13.Wheat	1.00	0.92	0.96	66
14.Woods	0.97	0.93	0.95	396
15.Buildings-Grass-Trees-Drives	0.59	0.82	0.69	84
16.Stone-Steel-Towers	0.93	1.00	0.96	26
accuracy			0.85	3075
macro avg	0.84	0.87	0.85	3075
weighted avg	0.86	0.85	0.85	3075

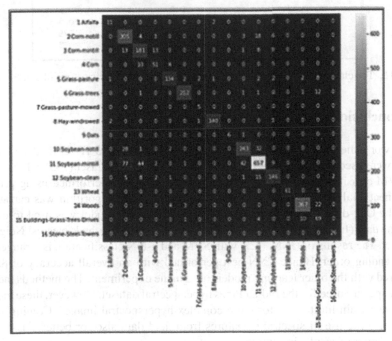

Fig. 10. The classification report (top) and the confusion matrix (bottom) of the 1D-CNN classification results

4.3 k-NN

The overall accuracy of the k-NN classifier was obtained as 66.2% being the lowest as compared to the above algorithm i.e., PCA + SVM algorithm and CNN algorithm used. The F1 scores were varying between near 1 to near 0 for this classifier (Fig. 11).

	precision	recall	f1-score	support
0	0.00	0.00	0.00	0
1	0.67	0.15	0.25	13
2	0.78	0.51	0.62	428
3	0.93	0.42	0.58	257
4	0.81	0.24	0.37	71
5	0.93	0.85	0.89	134
6	0.81	0.95	0.87	218
7	1.00	0.67	0.80	12
8	0.93	0.98	0.95	149
9	0.50	0.12	0.20	8
10	0.82	0.65	0.73	280
11	0.82	0.68	0.74	734
12	0.82	0.33	0.47	183
13	0.93	0.99	0.96	67
14	0.94	0.93	0.94	382
15	0.70	0.23	0.35	111
16	1.00	0.89	0.94	28
micro avg	0.86	0.66	0.75	3075
macro avg	0.79	0.56	0.63	3075
weighted avg	0.85	0.66	0.72	3075
samples avg	0.66	0.66	0.66	3075

Fig. 11. The classification report of kNN classifier consisting precision, recall and F1 score.

5   Conclusions

In this work, the SVM and kNN machine learning models and 1D-CNN deep learning model were used to classify the Indian Pines hyperspectral dataset ($145 \times 145 \times 200$). For SVM classifier, the data dimensionality reduction was performed using principal component analysis and after that the SVM classification algorithm was carried out. Later the One-dimensional Convolutional neural network model was used to classify the same data (Indian Pines hyperspectral image) followed by the k-Nearest Neighbour classifier. The results of CNN, PCA with SVM and k-NN classification is arranged here in descending order. Hence CNN best performed with an overall accuracy of 85% as compared with the other learning models used in the experiment. The methods included in this paper are used for the Indian Pines hyperspectral dataset. However, these methods still have certain limitations for more complex hyperspectral images. Coming studies can involve the use of spectral signatures from field data also for better classification and validation of results in future.

Appendix

Visualization of bands of the Indian Pines Hyperspectral Dataset shown below.

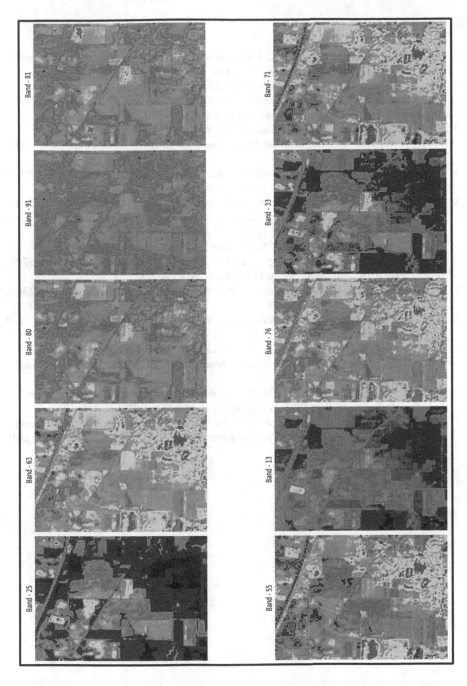

References

1. Chang, C.I.: Hyperspectral Imaging: Techniques for Spectral Detection and Classification. Kluwer Academic/Plenum Publishers, New York (2003)
2. Wan, Y.Q., Fan, Y.H., Jin, M.S.: Application of hyperspectral remote sensing for supplementary investigation of polymetallic deposits in Huaniushan ore region, Northwestern China. Sci. Rep. **11**(1), 440 (2021). https://doi.org/10.1038/s41598-020-79864-0
3. Lu, B., Dao, P.D., Liu, J., He, Y., Shang, J.: Recent advances of hyperspectral imaging technology and applications in agriculture. Remote Sens. **12**(16), 2659 (2020). https://doi.org/10.3390/rs12162659
4. Lua, G., Fei, B.: Medical hyperspectral imaging: a review. J. Biomed. Optics **19**, 010901 (2014). https://doi.org/10.1117/1.JBO.19.1.010901
5. Briottet, X., Boucher, Y., Dimmeler, A.: Military applications of hyperspectral imagery. In: Proceedings of Targets and Backgrounds XII: Characterization and Representation, vol. 6239, p. 62390B (2006). https://doi.org/10.1117/12.672030
6. Li, S., Song, W., Fang, L., Chen, Y., Ghamisi, P., Benediktsson, J.: Deep learning for hyperspectral image classification: an overview. IEEE Trans. Geosci. Remote Sens. **57**(9), 6690–6709 (2019). https://doi.org/10.1109/TGRS.2019.2907932
7. Bala, R., Kumar, D.: Classification using ANN: a review. Int. J. Comput. Intell. Res. **13**(7), 1811–1820 (2017). ISSN 0973–1873
8. Gibbs-Bravo, A., Pennacchia, D.: Evaluating the performance of multilayer perceptrons and support vector machines on an image classification task (2019)
9. Chen, Y., Jiang, H., Li, C., Jia, X., Ghamisi, P.: Deep feature extraction and classification of hyperspectral images based on convolutional neural networks. IEEE Trans. Geosci. Remote Sens. **54**(10), 6232–6251 (2016)
10. Chen, Y., Nasrabadi, N.M., Tran, T.D.: Hyperspectral image classification using dictionary-based sparse representation. IEEE Trans. Geosci. Remote Sens. **49**(10), 3973–3985 (2011)
11. Haut, J.M., Paoletti, M., Plaza, J., Plaza, A.: Cloud implementation of the K-means algorithm for hyperspectral image analysis. J. Supercomput. **73**(1), 514–529 (2016). https://doi.org/10.1007/s11227-016-1896-3

Reinforcing Digital Forensics Through Intelligent Behavioural Evidence Analysis: Social Media Hate Speech Profiling

Barkhashree[✉] and Parneeta Dhaliwal

Manav Rachna University, Faridabad, Haryana, India
parneeta.cst@mru.edu.in

Abstract. Cumulative boom in the use of social media for crime incidents creates a need to achieve improvement in overall efficiency by developing tools and techniques. The present manuscript discusses this issue by proposing a model which offer a feasible solution to escalate the criminal investigation by performing digital criminal profiling using social media hate speeches content. The proposed expert system will consider the hate speech content analysis along with other digital footprints of the suspects. The achieved analysis along with the proofs collected manually will be fed into the knowledge base of expert system. The system will automatically process the dataset to lower down the list of suspects using intelligent machine learning algorithms. Hate speech content analysis achieved using latest intelligent mechanisms, can perform in the boundaries of Behavioural Evidence Analysis-Standardised (BEA-S) model to create criminal profiling which again act as a basc for future investigations. The whole concept and the model are discussed in the paper which surely will upgrade the current investigation process to an innovative stature of digital forensics.

Keywords: Criminal profiling · Expert system · Hate speech · Digital forensics · Intelligent behavioural evidence analysis · BEA

1 Introduction

The rapid technology advancements are revamping the digital devices, from being only "data containers" to "digital diaries". This makes it impossible to leave any mark or evidence of our lifestyle or personal/social habits digitally [1]. The various chat rooms, blogs, forums and social networking sites pretend as a digital memory of suspect's footprints. In order to procure advantage of the free-flowing digital information, the present manuscript proposes a Machine Learning (ML) embedded intelligent expert system which gathers the available information on social media [2]. This will act as a vital artifact in a case, where the system can automatically map, identify and correlate the digital footprints of the suspects. The foremost aim of automation is to narrow down the list of suspects.

The present research considers the behavioural evidence analysis to embed the expert system for digital criminal profiling. Behavioural Evidence Analysis (BEA) integrated in the DF procedure augmented the premature convergence of results [3].

© Springer Nature Switzerland AG 2022
A. Dev et al. (Eds.): AIST 2021, CCIS 1546, pp. 641–650, 2022.
https://doi.org/10.1007/978-3-030-95711-7_52

According to Deepak and Hadi [4], the social media is swiftly sprouting as a cutting-edge technology providing far-fetched fuel in the process of criminal investigations. ML governed by AI, employed unequivocal programming to portray the human-like behaviour. This has significant potential to aid crime investigation by automating the process at different stages of investigation. In the present manuscript an expert system framework is developed. From social media, the hate speech comments posted and other related data collected corresponding to each suspect helps in automation of the process.

The expert system proposed has a wide utility across the digital forensics. The forensic investigators responsible for effectual inspection can easily accumulate, accomplish, and administer the legal social contents. Irony is, to date, very diminutive research has been commenced to embrace progressive digital techniques to accomplish "intelligent" investigations. Thus, the proposed approach encompassing plentiful ML techniques is proficient enough to examine the cases quicker and accurately. Devoid of this notch of computerization, the progression of digital forensics would not plunk a likelihood to endure the ambush of the massive number of crime occurrences and the rising volumes of data they have to deal with.

The paper is organized as follows. Section 2 describes the BEA process along with its extended version BEA-S. The next section focuses on the digital criminal profiling for BEA-S. The need of criminal profiling, the methods to achieve it and role of victimology in the process is also discussed. Last sub-section also confers the need of hate speech for criminal profiling along with the proposed workflow for digital criminal profiling. Section 4 of the research manuscript presents the proposed expert system framework for digital criminal profiling in BEA-S. Last section concludes the research with future direction.

2 Behavioural Evidence Analysis (BEA)

2.1 Overview

According to Turvey [5], BEA is considered as a syllogistic, task-based investigation methodology which intend to examine evidences from the perspective to discover behavioural and individuality distinctiveness of the probable suspects. BEA is believed to be an ideo-deductive process of crime spot analysis which generally lays a foundation for criminal profiling. Being an ideographic approach, it majorly consists of four kind of analysis- equivocal forensic analysis, victimology, identification of crime scene characteristics, and identification of offender characteristics [5]. The process of analyzing behaviour of the criminals mainly include critical thinking, scientific methods and deductive logic, and the outcomes, implications and conclusions obtained are predictions in camouflage totally dependent on physical evidences. Moreover, the BEA is meant for specific case study, similar case studies cannot be grouped together for analysis. Many researchers have successfully integrated the BEA process. However, a gap between the standardization of the functional integration of BEA in criminal investigation has been observed. Different strategies proposed till date concentrate on exclusive evidences as per their requirement. As a result, a novel approach BEA-S, casing all the different aspects has been proposed recently [6]. Next section, pours some light on BEA-S.

2.2 BEA-S

The author [6] developed a framework where the proposed approach was incorporated during the third stage, i.e., Analysis, of the standard flow of forensic process. The author exemplified that all the potential parameters and many aspects are amalgamated mutually in a unified manner to improve the BEA process altogether. Three types of analysis based on behaviour has been carried out stating- Equivocal Forensic Analysis, Victimology and Crime scene Characteristics. Along with this As-Is evidence analysis is also included. The author presented a detailed algorithm and a case study to prove their view-point, which seems to be convincing. Therefore, in the present manuscript, we aim to integrate an Expert system model in BEA-S process.

2.3 Role of BEA and BEA-S in Digital Forensics

After many researches and studies, it has been accentuated that the investigation of behavioural testimony of a criminal is equally important as the inspection of digital evidences. BEA based models are vital for accurate and complete criminal investigation. It creates a better understanding of the individuals involved in the offense, both offenders and sufferers [7]. BEA-S modeling not only assists in recognizing criminal's inspiration, and their connection with victims like BEA, it also considers numerous other factors affecting the assessment of crime. Many practical case studies were carried out by researchers to identify true strength of BEA [5, 8]. Al Mutawa in 2019 [7], presented a detailed case study discussing the ways in which BEA can be applied to the digital forensics investigations.

3   Digital Criminal Profiling and BEA-S

According to Turvey [9], criminal profiling is an investigative psychological profiling tool which assist in tapering the suspect pool of offenders. It is a confront to the personality uniqueness of delinquents by their deportment at crime scenes [10]. The criminal investigation process includes analysis, evaluation and interpretation of tangible evidences found on the crime scene, the nature of the crime and the way it was executed [11]. This section discusses the various phases involves in the process.

3.1   Overview: Digital Criminal Profiling (DCP)

The involvement of digital technology in criminology, unbolt vast sphere for offenders to locate their target victims [12]. On the parallel node, this also makes it easy to process the criminology for investigation. The knowledge of digital criminal profiling is crucial phase in digital forensics. Focused aim is to create a demographic and behavioural profiles of the suspects.

3.2   Methods to Achieve DCP

For DCP, researchers are majorly exploiting statistical analysis methods using the behavioural and psychosomatic data from the convicted criminals to detect a comprehensive behavioural prototype and personality traits of a lawbreaker in identifiable category of criminal cases [13]. The defined characteristics assist to recognize a cluster of latent suspects. Few researchers also adopt deductive DCP profiling which is purely case based

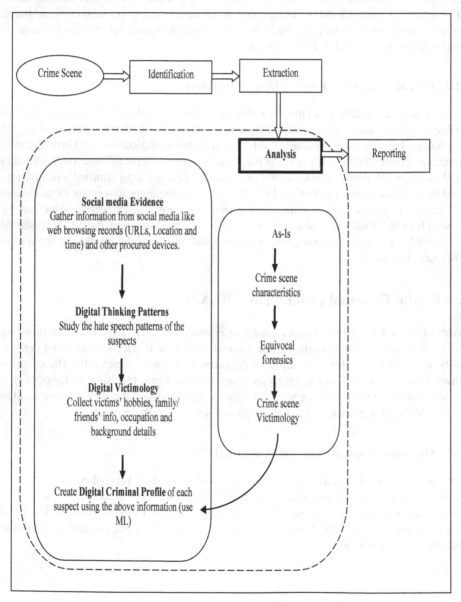

Fig. 1. Workflow of embedded BEA-S with digital criminal profiling

[10]. Chad M. steel [12], also proposed a digital profile framework using idiographic system which inspect a specific subject's digital footprints for abrupt use in an existing investigation. ML techniques were also explored for creating offender's profile [14]. The author proposed a tool to examine and analyse the bad behaviour data specifically. The idea behind is to consider the criminal prosecution during investigation which plays a vital role in improving investigations and cybercriminal finding. Major challenge faced in DCP domain is the legal tests for permissible proficient evidence [15].

3.3 Role of Victimology

With rising number of people stumbling upon and exchanging a few words with each other on the Internet, it is essential to consider the likelihood that the criminal had contacted the victim at some point of time using the Internet. This study will also reveal the conversation or the other exchanged between them [16]. On the contrary, in the case of missing victims, a detailed investigation of their computers, other devices and social profiles might escort to a mutual reprobate. Main aim here is to acquire some indulgent of the victim as a human being from his/her Internet actions. Each facet of the victim's life and behavior provide a better understanding of the reasons to target that particular individual as a victim of a crime [17]. In our case also this holds a major role. The digital victimology holds an important role in the current workflow as well. Through this we can inspect the psychosomatic consequence of crimes on the victims, the connections between victims and the criminal justice system and the associations between sufferers and offenders.

3.4 Role of Hate Speech in DCP

Hate speech is the content/ comments posted online on social media. In digital forensics, hate speech study is a leading process to investigate the criminal and victim behavior [18]. In the proposed workflow, hate speech analysis plays a major role as using this the character and behaviour can be easily depicted, which eventually help in creating the profiles of both criminal and the victim. For this purpose, numerous methods have been exploited till now [19, 22]. Recent techniques include machine learning methodologies, which provide higher accuracy rates. The proposed expert system that will be discussed in the next section must use this to provide better intelligent solutions.

3.5 Proposed Workflow of the Digital Criminal Profiling

The purpose of this research is to investigate the workflow of DCP in BEA-S model as well. This will produce the most significant component of our proposed Expert system. Figure 1 illustrates the details of the proposed work flow. The analysis phase of the standard BEA process will be equipped with ML techniques to fabricate an enhanced profile. Here, the foremost tread is to accumulate the footprints of the criminals as well as the victims. For this, our proposed system will consider social media evidences. It includes their web browsing histories, location and time of various devices in use. Addition to this, we have focused on the assortment and investigation of hate speech patterns which can be effortlessly retrieved from the comments posted on social media platforms. The victimology will also be taken care of, as it will help in the discovery of the associations and connections between the offender and victims. Along with it, our system will consider As-Is operator proposed in BEA-S, which help in analyzing the minute details about the demographic, behavioural and socio-economic patterns of crime. This flow can be empowered using the experiences from other domains such as criminal psychology. The traits which signify criminal's mindset and using that a series of models that would assist in mapping can be developed. This can be achieved using AI based systems. This helps in creating the correlation of artefacts within the intelligent Expert system to develop a holistic evidence locator and collector. More accurate DCP, will result in early detection of criminal and finding out the most appropriate reason behind the offense.

4 Proposed Expert System Model for BEA-S Using Machine Learning

The standardised approach BEA-S [6] leads to more reasonable and apparent depiction of the crime investigation. Accumulating all the potential evidences, both physically and digitally, and investigating them with accurate analysis and recommendations, generate the necessity to automate the tedious task of criminology.

Figure 2 describes the workflow of the proposed expert system framework. The knowledge base of the expert system comprises of two set of evidences. The first suite is produced by collecting the hate speech comments posted across the social media platforms. The data can be collected using the various APIs provided by the social media. The hate words included in the comment will make the statements hate speech. This assist to identify the basic characteristics of the criminal's behaviour in the recent time. The other set of the knowledge base is formed by extracting the other details of the suspect including demographic, geographic, technical and personal/social details available on the social media. For this, the profile knowledge, their current locations and other information available online can be retrieved. This dataset also includes the connection of suspect with the victim. This guides in creating the victimology as well. Proposed expert system essentially focuses on the social platforms to generate the digital profile of the criminal. However, it can be extended by incorporating the crime scene related information in order to automate the whole recommendation process of digital forensics. Once the knowledge base is prepared, the inference engine of the expert system is accountable to produce the criminal profiling and analysis report. Here, the knowledge engineering is carried out by exploiting machine learning algorithms. ML algorithms already revealed their significance in extracting patterns and connections in the datasets. Various ANN and deep learning mechanisms also proved beneficial for create the whole profile for probable suspects. The outcomes will be in the form of profiling with respect to each of the suspects. This creates a good knowledge base of the system containing all the details. This can further be enhanced by incorporating on-site proofs and clues of the suspects. Once this is ready, the results obtained are transmitted to the user interface of the expert system for supplementary processing if required.

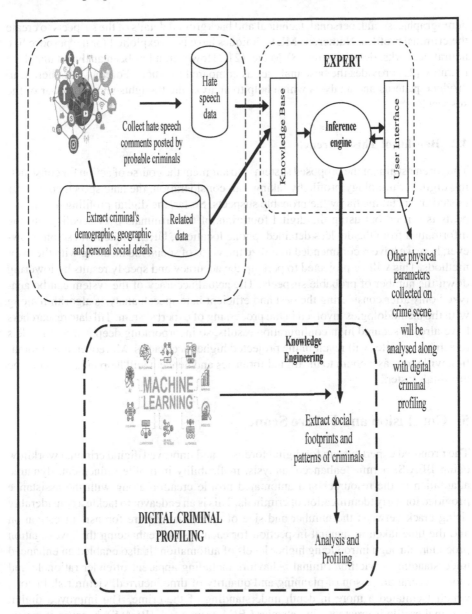

Fig. 2. Proposed Expert system framework for Digital Criminal Profiling in BEA-S

4.1 ML for Digital Criminal Profiling Using Hate Speeches

ML behavioural analytics is the nucleus of modeling, profiling and forecasting in the criminal profiling. The proposed system makes use of hate speech comments posted across the social media by the suspects. The ML techniques aid in detecting the behaviour of the criminal while posting comment. Along with this, the ML technique considers demographic, social, personal, technical and background details of the suspects to create the criminal profiles. Numerous ML techniques have been exploited for the purpose like neural networks, deep learning, SVM etc. [21]. However, it has been analyzed that deep learning [22] provides the best analytics as compared to others. Foremost aim here is to produce patterns and analysis which help to analyze the thoughts and behaviour of the suspects.

4.2 Benefits of This Entrench

The foremost aim of the proposed system is to augment the course of action for constructing digital criminology profile by taking into consideration, the hate speech comments posted on social media by the probable suspects. So far, the digital profiling of the suspects is carried out using the digital footprints of the criminals by wheedling out the information from the devices detained, phone locations, URLs visited and so on. However, here we have recommended to utilize the vigor of social media along with the prior methods. This will be projected to perk up the accuracy and speedy results by lowering down the number of probable suspects. The actual accuracy of the system can be analyzed only after considering the best and efficient hate speech analysis algorithm along with the methodologies involved in the processing of expert system. Till date researchers have already secured high configuration results, so incorporating deep learning models to achieve it better will result in the projected higher accuracies. Moreover, the automation will prove as a boom to the digital forensics and hence it will help in identifying the criminals faster.

5 Conclusion and Future Scope

The proposed expert system for digital forensics and improved digital criminal workflow using BEA-S, permits enhanced analysis, malleability in profile refinement, dynamic adaptation to the resources and automated profile creation along with the assistance provided for early identification of criminals. This is an endeavor to tackle a considerably rising crack between the number and size of cases that require forensic investigation and the time taken in manual inspection for each case by enhancing the investigation procedure through introducing higher levels of automation. It also enabled an enhanced understanding of victim/criminal behaviors including apparent offender rationale and modus operandi, reason of planning and quantity of time incurred, victim risk factors, which facilitated a more in depth understanding of the crime. The improved digital criminal profile is created using standard BEA framework (BEA-S), because it covers all the aspects of forensics and thus can map to broader perspective. ML techniques like deep learning can be utilized to achieve the aimed results. Researchers can also utilize different methods to collect digital data from social medias and other footprints of the victim/crime. This recommendation expert system can be incorporated in the cloud solution to evaluate the intricate cases with the help of similar kind of cases occurred worldwide.

References

1. Anconelli, M.: Introduzione al digital profiling (2010). www.cybercrimes.it
2. Colombini, C.M., Colella, A., Army, I.: Digital scene of crime: technique of profiling users. J. Wirel. Mob. Netw. Ubiq. Comput. Depend. Appl. **3**(3), 50–73 (2012)
3. Al Mutawa, N., et al.: Behavioural digital forensics model: embedding behavioural evidence analysis into the investigation of digital crimes. Digit. Invest. **28**, 70–82 (2019)
4. Deebak, B.D., Zahmatkesh, H.: Forensic analysis in social networking applications. In: Security in IoT Social Networks, pp. 133–17. Academic Press, (2021)
5. Petherick, W.A., Turvey, B.E.: Behavioral evidence analysis. In: Criminal Profiling: An Introduction to Behavioral Evidence Analysis, p. 133 (2011)
6. Shree, B., Dhaliwal, P.: Behavioural evidence analysis: a paradigm shift in digital forensics. Int. J. Digital Crime Forensics (IJDCF) **13**(5), 20–42 (2021)
7. Al Mutawa, N., Bryce, J., Franqueira, V.N., Marrington, A., Read, J.C.: Behavioural Digital forensics model: embedding behavioural evidence analysis into the investigation of digital crimes. Digit. Investig. **28**, 70–82 (2018). https://doi.org/10.1016/j.diin.2018.12.003
8. Al Mutawa, N., et al.: Behavioural evidence analysis applied to digital forensics: an empirical analysis of child pornography cases using P2P networks. In: 2015 10th International Conference on Availability, Reliability and Security. IEEE (2015)
9. Petherick, W.A., Turvey, B.: Behavioural evidence analysis: ideo-deductive method of criminal profiling. In: Criminal Profiling: An Introduction to Behavioural Evidence Analysis, pp. 133–153. Elsevier (2008)
10. Warikoo, A.: Proposed methodology for cyber criminal profiling. Inf. Secur. J. Global Perspect. **23**(4–6), 172–178 (2014)
11. Ainsworth, P.: Offender Profiling Crime Analysis. Willan, London (2013)
12. Steel, C.M.: Idiographic digital profiling: behavioral analysis based on digital forensics. J. Digit. Forensics Secur. Law **9**(1), 1 (2014)
13. Rogers, M.: The role of criminal profiling in the computer forensics process. Comput. Secur. **22**(4), 292–298 (2003)
14. Goyal, A., et al.: Criminal profiling using machine learning. Int. Res. J. Eng. Technol. (IRJET) **07**(06) (2020)
15. Balogun, A.M., Zuva, T.: Criminal profiling in digital forensics: assumptions, challenges and probable solution. In: 2018 International Conference on Intelligent and Innovative Computing Applications (ICONIC). IEEE (2018)
16. Tapley, J., Davies, P.: Victimology: a conversion of narratives.. In: Victimology, pp. 1–16. Palgrave Macmillan, Cham (2020)
17. Jaishankar, K.: Cyber victimology: a new sub-discipline of the twenty-first century victimology. In: Joseph, J., Jergenson, S. (eds.) An International Perspective on Contemporary Developments in Victimology, pp. 3–19. Springer, Cham (2020). https://doi.org/10.1007/978-3-030-41622-5_1
18. Vogel, I., Meghana, M.: Profiling hate speech spreaders on twitter: SVM vs. Bi-LSTM. In: CLEF (2021)
19. Bevendorff, J., et al.: Overview of PAN 2021: authorship verification, profiling hate speech spreaders on twitter, and style change detection: extended abstract. In: Hiemstra, D., Moens, M.-F., Mothe, J., Perego, R., Potthast, M., Sebastiani, F. (eds.) Advances in Information Retrieval: 43rd European Conference on IR Research, ECIR 2021, Virtual Event, March 28 – April 1, 2021, Proceedings, Part II, pp. 567–573. Springer International Publishing, Cham (2021). https://doi.org/10.1007/978-3-030-72240-1_66
20. Iqbal, S., Alharbi, S.A.: Advancing automation in digital forensic investigations using machine learning forensics. Digit. Forensic Sci. **3** (2020)

21. Mullah, N., Zainon, W.: Advances in machine learning algorithms for hate speech detection in social media: a review. IEEE Access **9**, 88364–88376 (2021)
22. Zimmerman, S., Kruschwitz, U., Fox, C.: Improving hate speech detection with deep learning ensembles. In: Proceedings of the Eleventh International Conference on Language Resources and Evaluation (LREC 2018) (2018)

Collaborative Travel Recommender System Based on Malayalam Travel Reviews

V. K. Muneer(✉) 🆔 and K. P. Mohamed Basheer 🆔

Research Department of Computer Science, SS College, Malappuram, Kerala, India

Abstract. Recommender System is an unsupervised machine learning technique used for users to make decisions on their own choices and interests. Travel and Tourism is one of the important domains in this area. Rapid growth of redundant, heterogeneous data and web has created the importance for Recommender system. Travel Recommender System helps to users or travelers to decide on their choices and preferences on their travel. The work proposes a machine learning approach for a personalized travel recommender system in Malayalam Language, one of the prominent languages used in Southern part of India. The system developed using Collaborative Filtering technique, Malayalam Text processing with the help of Cosine similarity and TF-IDF methods. Data has been taken from the largest Malayalam Travel group in Facebook named "Sanchari". A customized scraping algorithm also developed to collect relevant and enough information from social media. The RS could suggest most suitable destinations to each of users with the accuracy of 93%, which is fair result as compared with other algorithms on same domain.

Keywords: Recommender System [RS] · Collaborative filtering · Natural language processing · Malayalam · Cosine similarity

1 Introduction

The use of Social Media platforms is strengthening day by day. With its constant and successful development, it has been contributed huge amount of redundant, heterogeneous data on the web. The popular examples are Amazon, Google, Netflix, Facebook, Instagram, and YouTube. For the integration of data, Recommender System (RS) is a fundamental tool for users to decide on their choices and interests based on available data. There use different kind of recommender system to recommend effective choices to the users. Among them Travel and Tourism is important now-a-days as the increase of travelers. So, Travel Recommender System is a type of recommender system which focus on suggesting or recommending accurate places for users based on available data of similar travelers.

The objective of this work starts from the assumption that the development of a recommender system can contribute to the field of tourism more focuses on regional languages. The recommender system designed by using collaborative filtering method which take an account into high accuracy. Around 44% travel recommendation systems

© Springer Nature Switzerland AG 2022
A. Dev et al. (Eds.): AIST 2021, CCIS 1546, pp. 651–659, 2022.
https://doi.org/10.1007/978-3-030-95711-7_53

using Collaborative filtering [1]. The selection of attributes to develop RS are depending on each person's viewpoint on travel. Like, methodologies also vary with the selection of attributes. For travel and tourism, social filtering widely used which based on likes and comments from social media platforms like Facebook and Instagram [4]. Apart from these, Content based filtering is also an important methodology in which it focuses to provide more on personalized information [2].

Natural language processing remains as a hot topic yet to explore in AI, especially the low resource languages like Malayalam text and speech processing [3], Tamil, Kannada etc. A customized scraping tool has been used here to retrieve data from Facebook, hence dataset contains lengthy travel reviews written in Malayalam language. All conventional preprocessing tools and some additional methods developed exclusively to process malayalam language has also used in this work. The accuracy of Recommendation can considerably be increased by increasing the size of dataset as well as optimizing algorithms.

2 Related Works

In the area of recommendation, there exist numerous methods to build a recommender system of any domain. Users interests and preferences plays vital role in sentiment analysis [5] through Recommendation models. To get most accurate recommender system, always better to study on personalized recommendation rather than general ones. To get personalized recommendation, it is highly suggested for work on location based collaborative filtering [8]. By using various data mining and routing methods, personalized travel sequence recommendation can build [12]. It will provide personalized information as per user's interest and gives a sequence of similar personalized travel recommendation which provide travelers a complete satisfaction. Recommendation by Cosine similarity is an approach suitable for large datasets [14]. Cosine similarity along Rankdiff algorithm make a perfect choice for recommendation. Another algorithm, Markov chains algorithm using matrix factorization provide personalized recommendations which gives importance to user's interest [12]. This approach is considered as expensive.

Hybrid filtering is another type of filtering techniques which tries to provide personalized recommendation. Hybrid filtering preference better results by using social matrix factorization [15]. This combines both user preferences obtained from check-ins and text-based tips and perform sentiment analysis on them. Traditional recommender system always fails to bring precise results rather than it generates highly ranked recommendations. Personalized travel recommender system uses various methods like location based collaborative filtering and similar user mining methods. Concepts of hybridization, machine learning, fuzzy logic, genetic algorithm, and heuristic search are another method lies under personalized recommender system.

The Malayalam text summarization has an important role in research. Since it is a Dravidian language, it requires efficient and accurate summarization system [9]. There are two types of summarization methods: abstractive and extractive. From this, abstractive summarization method needs to undergo heavy computational model to summarize any Malayalam documents. So extractive approach is widely used. It produces summary by time bound with high precision. To improve the quality of summary, improve the sentence scoring stage [10]. The performance can further be improved by stemming process, sentence splitting criteria and adding a greater number of features.

To personalize recommender system, the attribute location is very much helpful. Location based personalized recommendation can be successfully executes by implementing hybrid preference model [11]. Another interesting method used for personalized recommendation is by an author-based topic model collaborative filtering [13]. Here, user's topic preference can be mined from textual description. This textual description is retrieved from the user's photos via author topic model. To recommendation, GPS trajectories [16] means, other people's experience and opinions. Collaborative filtering (CF) methods applied on available GPS trajectories to improve point of interest (POI) recommendation. By using such geotagged images [17], it is helpful for users to find tourist destinations. To find places of user's interest using geotagged photos, there use different methods like GoThere [18]. By using GPS data, a new technique proposed for extracting semantically meaningful geographical locations [19]. Here the relationship between locations gets modeled with a two layered graph. From this demonstration it is found that, this method performs better than other several baseline methods.

For an efficient recommendation, the type of location is more important than any other attributes [20]. It includes locations like, gastronomic, educational or entertainment locations. Users are always interest bound to location type and this change over time and experience. By using matrix factorization [MF] method, it predicts accurate places. Matrix factorization has high accuracy and scalability. Most of the present MF methods are batch models which undergo incremental update [21]. For this Regularized matrix factorization [RMF] model is introduced. To perform RMF, first simplify training rule of RMF to propose this.

By the method sequential pattern mining, the system extracts travel routes based on blog entries of visitors hence multimedia contents get presented accordingly [22]. To present this multimedia contents, there creates a user interface. So, this system can act as an automatically generated tour guide which is portable. In recommendation, user's interests and requirements take primary attention. To meet these peculiarities, currently there using cloud-based trip planning [23]. Among these, an approach called Touch Map is used for recommending places in accordance with user's personal requirements with multiple constraints. For the evaluation, the real dataset Gowalla is used. Here it focusses on multiple constraints as well as cloud computing simultaneously. Touch Map shows excellent performance by recommending desired places.

Like Touch Map, Trip Mine is another mining-based approach to predict travel places with respect to time constraints [24]. Based on trip mine, it further classified three optimization techniques: attraction sorting, low bound checking and score checking. It always needs to note the destination attractions of every places. A skyline query-based attraction recommendation system introduced recommendation on the basis of preferences of user's on location [25]. To attain the efficiency of new algorithm, it was applied to an attraction query system which referred to as demodulation and encoding heritage system. This system was developed to improve the tourism in Taiwan.

3 Dataset

Facebook is one of the most important data providers in social media. Many recommender systems depend social media [6] to predict new suggestions and customer relationships. People all over the world use umpteen groups and pages to share their views and opinions. "Sanchari", a malayalam word meant for travelling, is the largest Facebook travel group in Malayalam Language which contains 7 lakh members all over the world who usually share their travel experiences and engaging in the group actively. The groups contains more than 50K travelogues and each of them gets hundreds of reactions. As the preliminary step, the customized scraping tool fetched 12500 travelogues, public personal information of 3781 travelers and details about 84463 check-in spots around the globe.

4 Methodology

To carry out the work, the primary part is data collection. The conventional data scraping methods were not as good as fetching all required details from Facebook. The native API from Facebook provides only limited information. Hence the customized automatic scraping tool has developed to overcome this issue. The Scraped malayalam travelogue underwent several preprocessing steps before passing to Recommender model. The important steps are given below (Fig. 1).

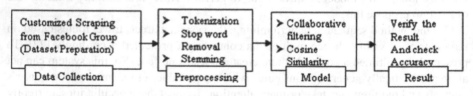

Fig. 1. Steps in Malayalam Travel RS

4.1 Data Collection

This functionality of this scraping algorithm relies on three sequential steps. Targeting the posts returns the messages written in Malayalam, posting time, count of reactions, count of comments, number of shares, and profile_url of author for each post. We did not focus on taking the comments on the post for the time being. With the help of this profile_url, the Second step focuses more on the public personal details like education, hometown, marital and family details, age, and their check-in details. All these raw details are fetched in a JSON format which is then flattened to an excel sheet which is the third stage.

4.2 Malayalam Text Processing

Natural language processing includes several tasks to clean the text data. Malicious details and irrelevant text token to be removed before proceeding to tokenization steps. The prominent task in preprocessing includes,

a) Removal of punctuations and HTML tags
b) Sentence tokenization and Word tokenization
c) Malayalam stop word removal

As any language, malayalam also created a set of tokens which are considered irrelevant in most of the context in text processing. Parsing and syntax analysis can be performed in NLP without such stop words. Few of them are (Fig. 2),

ആയിരുന്നു	വേണ്ടി		മേൽ	ഉണ്ട്	കൂടെ		അവർ	അവൻ	എങ്ങനെ
അതും	ഇതും	അന്നും	ഇന്നും	എന്നു		ഒന്ന്		ഈ	നിന്ന്	കൊണ്ട്
വാക്ക്	പക്ഷേ	എന്ത്		കുറെ		ആകുന്നു		അത്	നിങ്ങളെ	
അഥവാ		ഉണ്ടായിരുന്നു	ഒരു	ലേക്ക്	ഒപ്പം	ഒരു	കഴിയും		പുറത്ത്
മറ്റ്	ആയിരുന്നു	ഏത്	ചെയ്യുക		അവരുടെ	എന്ന	മാത്രം	വരെ	അതിൽ
എങ്കിൽ	ഏറെ	ഉള്ള	അങ്ങനെ		ഇങ്ങനെ	നിന്ന്	എന്നാൽ		പോരെ

Fig. 2. Steps in Malayalam Travel RS

d) Stemming – through root-pack extractor

A language processing module named 'root-pack' specially developed to find out the root words of malayalam tokens. For example,
Given a sample Malayalam inflated word "ഞങ്ങൾക്കെല്ലാവർക്കുമായി"

import root_pack
root_pack.root("ഞങ്ങൾക്കെല്ലാവർക്കുമായി")

The extractor will find out the root word as "ഞങ്ങൾ"

4.3 Feature File Creation

After the successful preprocessing of each of the lengthy travelogues, resulted a structured format of travel details. To move ahead with comparison and similarity check of this text, four document files newly created with specific purposes. They are files for describing destination details, climate details, user type and travelling mode. Another CSV file has been created to map the updated data with comparing the occurrences of each data in these files by comparing it with preprocessed data. After forming this CSV file, it given to the model for performing collaborative filtering by the method of cosine similarity. Before filtering starts, the system will examine user's interests, preferences, and profile for the final recommendation. Table 1 show the format of files.

Table 1. Format and Sample details of 4 files for comparative analysis

Sl. No	Climate	User_type	Travel_mode	Locations
1	മഴ	തനിയെ	കാർ	മണാലി
2	വെയിൽ	സോളോ	ബസ്	ദൽഹി
3	മഞ്ഞ്	കുടുംബം	ബൈക്ക്	ഇടുക്കി
4	തണുപ്പ്	കൂട്ടുകാർ	തീവണ്ടി	കോഴിക്കോട്
5	ചൂട്	ഫ്രണ്ട്സ്	വിമാനം	കശ്മീർ
6	സമ്മർ	ചങ്ങാതി	ഫ്ലൈറ്റ്	ലഡാക്ക്
7	വിന്റർ	സഹപ്രവർത്തകർ	കപ്പൽ	കോവളം
7	ശൈത്യം	ഓഫീസ്	റോഡ്	ഗോവ
8	വസന്തം	ഭാര്യ	കടൽ	വയനാട്
9	മഴ	ഭർത്താവ്	ബോട്ട്	കാസർഗോഡ്
10	വെയിൽ	സഹോദരങ്ങൾ	സൈക്കിൾ	ആലപ്പുഴ
11	മഞ്ഞ്	അമ്മ	നടന്ന്	ബാംഗ്ലൂർ
12	തണുപ്പ്	അച്ഛൻ	സ്കൂട്ടർ	മൈസൂർ

4.4 Preparation of Travel DNA

Collaborative filtering with the help of Cosine similarity mechanism, a user-based recommendation model will be generated. To execute algorithm, the collected data should be in a way the model can recognize. The numerical representation of values of each file constitutes a vector format of each the travelogue.

$$\text{Numerical representation} : [4 \quad\quad 7 \quad\quad 1 \quad\quad 10]$$

Actual representation [തണുപ്പ്   സഹപ്രവർത്തകർ   കാർ   ആലപ്പുഴ].

Each of the item represents feature from climate, user_type, travel_mode and location files respectively. These items are selected based on the highest occurrence in the preprocessed text in comparison with above files.

5 Experimental Result

In this work, collaborative filtering using cosine similarity helped to observe maximum accuracy. To calculate accuracy, first create a list of similar places by manually. Then compare those places with the places found from collaborative filtering. If a match found print it and calculate accuracy. For that, if a match found, increment the variable count by 1. Then calculate accuracy by,

$$Accuracy = count \, / \, len(resultset) * 100$$

Result set contains manually stored data. If the recommended five places are matching with manually written place, then accuracy is more than 90%. Out of the 5 suggestions, if 4 of them are correctly predicted, the accuracy goes 75%. The accuracy depends on the suggestion list, in which previously visited locations should not listed again.

Cosine similarity is a metric used in collaborative filtering to measure similarity of items. Mathematically, define cosine as, the angle between two vectors which projected in a multi-dimensional space. The output can be differed from 0 and 1. 0 implies there has no similarity, where 1 implies similarity of 100%. In other words, larger cosine implies that there is a smaller angle between two users, hence they have similar interests.

$$Cosine\ similarity\ (cos\ \theta) = A.B\ /\ |A|\ |B|$$

First need to preprocess the dataset to perform the algorithm. The new CSV file contains index of maximum value, most occurred data. Then this new CSV file is given to the model. Collaborative filtering is done by finding the Cosine Similarity of values of new CSV file and the data collected from user at the time of execution. Then created a TF-IDF matrix which contains index value of maximum occurred data. By the concept of spatial Euclidean distance formula, calculated cosine similarities of all matrix values. Then sort those obtained values to get the score of five most similar places. Finally, return most similar places obtained. Next, checking those obtained places are accurate or not. For that, first the predicted output by considering user's interests and preferences manually. And give these data as input to the model while the execution begins. Then model will show most similar five places based on cosine similarity. Then compare predicted output with obtained output. The accuracy is also calculated by the percentage of correctness of output. These steps are repeated for multiple users to verify the accuracy.

During the testing phase, various inputs taken from real time user, such as preferred travel mode, user type, expecting season and related information. These input variables undergo the similarity check and succeeding to collaborative filtering to suggest best suitable 5 ranked locations exclusively to that user. A sample of list given below.

Recommended   destinations   are:
[ബ്രഹ്മഗിരി   കൊളുക്കുമല   ചെമ്പ്ര   വയനാട്
ലോണാവാല]

6 Conclusion

Travel recommendation using Malayalam travel reviews is very emerging and demanding in these days. In this work, conducted a Malayalam preprocessing which further used for recommendation purpose to build an accurate and yet another type of recommender system. This system can be used to the peoples who take travel as their passion. The recommendation performed here shows high degree of accuracy with dataset. To get precise recommendation, Collaborative Filtering modeling is used with the help of Cosine Similarity method. A personalized travel recommendation system in Malayalam language could successfully suggest most suitable 5 recommendation to the used by evaluating their preferences and past histories. The model could be upgraded by enhancing dataset and optimizing machine learning algorithms.

References

1. Roopesh, L.R., Tulasi, B.: A survey of travel recommender system. Int. J. Comput. Sci. Eng. 7(3), pp. 356–362 (2019). https://doi.org/10.26438/ijcse/v7i3.356362

2. Hirakawa, G., Satoh, G., Hisazumi, K., Shibata, Y.: Data gathering system for recommender system in tourism. In: Proceedings - 2015 18th International Conference Network-Based Inf. Syst. NBiS 2015, pp. 521–525 (2015). https://doi.org/10.1109/NBiS.2015.78
3. Thandil, R.K.: Automatic speech recognition system for utterances in Malayalam Language. Malaya J. Matematik S(1), 560–565 (2019). https://doi.org/10.26637/MJM0S01/0101
4. Wijaya, N., Furqan, A.: Coastal tourism and climate-related disasters in an archipelago country of indonesia: tourists' perspective. Procedia Eng. 212, 535–542 (2018). https://doi.org/10.1016/j.proeng.2018.01.069
5. Rahul, M., Rajeev, R.R., Shine, S.: Social media sentiment analysis for Malayalam. Int. J. Comput. Sci. Eng. 06(06), 48–53 (2018). https://doi.org/10.26438/ijcse/v6si6.4853
6. Anandhan, A., Shuib, L.: Social media recommender systems: review and open research Issues. In: 2018 IEEE, vol. 6, pp. 2169-3536 (2018)., doi: https://doi.org/10.1109/ACCESS.2018.2810062
7. Ashok, M., Rajanna, S., Joshi, P.V., Kamath, S.S.: A personalized recommender system using Machine Learning based Sentiment Analysis over social data. In: 2016 IEEE Students' Conference on Electrical, Electronics and Computer Science (SCEECS) (2016). https://doi.org/10.1109/SCEECS.2016.7509354
8. Zheng, Y., Zhang, L., Ma, Z., Xie, X., Ma, W.Y.: Recommending friends and locations based on individual location history. ACM Trans. Web 5(1) (2011). https://doi.org/10.1145/1921591.1921596
9. Mubarak, D.M.N., Shanavas, S.A.: Malayalam text summarization using graph based method, vol. 9, no. 2, pp. 40–44 (2018)
10. Krishnaprasad, P., Sooryanarayanan, A., Ramanujan, A.: Malayalam text summarization: an extractive approach. In: 2016 International Conference on Next Generation Intelligent Systems, ICNGIS 2016, pp. 0–3 (2017). https://doi.org/10.1109/ICNGIS.2016.7854008
11. Yang, D., Zhang, D., Yu, Z., Wang, Z.: A sentiment-enhanced personalized location recommendation system categories and subject descriptors. In: 24th ACM Conference Hypertext Social Media, Hypertext 2013, pp. 119–128 (2013)
12. Jiang, S., Qian, X., Mei, T., Fu, Y.: Personalized travel sequence recommendation on multi-source big social media. IEEE Trans. Big Data 2(1), 43–56 (2016). https://doi.org/10.1109/tbdata.2016.2541160
13. Jiang, S., Qian, X., Shen, J., Fu, Y., Mei, T.: Author topic model-based collaborative filtering for personalized POI recommendations. IEEE Trans. Multimed. 17(6), 907–918 (2015). https://doi.org/10.1109/TMM.2015.2417506
14. Clements, M., Serdyukov, P., de Vries, A.P., Reinders, M.J.T.: Personalised Travel Recommendation based on Location Co-occurrence, May 2014 (2011). http://arxiv.org/abs/1106.5213
15. Cheng, C., Yang, H., Lyu, M.R., King, I.: Where you like to go next: Successive point-of-interest recommendation. In: IJCAI International Joint Conference on Artifical Intelligence, January, pp. 2605–2611 (2013)
16. Huang, II., Gartner, G.: Using trajectories for collaborative filtering-based POI recommendation. Int. J. Data Mining, Model. Manag. 6(4), 333–346 (2014). https://doi.org/10.1504/IJDMMM.2014.066762
17. Cao, L., Luo, J., Gallagher, A., Jin, X., Han, J., Huang, T.S.: A worldwide tourism recommendation system based on geotagged web photos. In: ICASSP, IEEE International Conference Acoust. Speech Signal Process. - Proc., April, pp. 2274–2277 (2010). https://doi.org/10.1109/ICASSP.2010.5495905
18. Majid, A., Chen, L., Chen, G., Mirza, H.T., Hussain, I.: GoThere: Travel suggestions using geotagged photos. In: WWW'12 – Proceedings of the 21st Annual Conference World Wide Web Companion, April, pp. 577–578 (2012). https://doi.org/10.1145/2187980.2188135

19. Cao, X., Cong, G., Jensen, C.S.: Mining significant semantic locations from GPS data. Proc. VLDB Endow. **3**(1), 1009–1020 (2010). https://doi.org/10.14778/1920841.1920968
20. Berjani, B., Strufe, T.: A Recommendation System for Spots in Location-Based Online Social Networks (2010)
21. Luo, X., Xia, Y., Zhu, Q.: Knowledge-based systems incremental collaborative filtering recommender based on regularized matrix factorization. Knowledge-Based Syst. **27**, 271–280 (2012). https://doi.org/10.1016/j.knosys.2011.09.006
22. Kori, H., Hattori, S., Tezuka, T., Tanaka, K.: Automatic Generation of Multimedia Tour Guide from Local Blogs, pp. 690–699 (2007)
23. Ying, J., Lu, E.H., Huang, C., Kuo, K., Hsiao, Y., Tseng, V.S.: A Framework for Cloud-based POI Search and Trip Planning Systems, September 2015 (2013). https://doi.org/10.1109/ICOT.2013.6521211
24. Lu, E.H., Lin, C.: Trip-Mine : An Efficient Trip Planning Approach with Travel Time Constraints, September 2015. https://doi.org/10.1109/MDM.2011.13
25. Chen, Y., Loh, C., Chen, W., Ho, W., Chen, Y.: Skyline query-based attraction recommendation system: an example on Design and development of the Demodulation and Encoding Heritage System, pp. 318–321 (2016). https://doi.org/10.1109/ICS.2016.69

Hybrid Framework Model for Group Recommendation

Inderdeep Kaur[1]($\boxtimes$), Sahil Drubra[2], Nidhi Goel[3], and Laxmi Ahuja[4]

[1] Accenture, SEZ, Bldg 7, G to 8 floor, Unitech Infospace, Sec-21, Dundahera, Gurugram, Haryana 122001, India
inderdeepdhanoa@gmail.com

[2] Tata Consultancy Services, SEZ, GG-V, Tower B, 3rd & 11th Floor, Tower C 2nd to 4th and 11th floor, Tower A-4th floor, Building No 6, DLF Cyber City, Sector 24 & 25A, Gurugram, Haryana 122002, India
drubra.sahil@gmail.com

[3] Indira Gandhi Delhi Technical University for Women, Kashmiri Gate, Delhi 110006, India
nidhigoel@igdtuw.ac.in

[4] Amity University, Noida, India
lahuja@amity.edu

Abstract. Group-based recommender systems are known for web-based applications to satisfy the preferences of every user in the group equally. The recommender system aims to identify user-preferred items, such as movies, music, books, and restaurants that tend to satisfy each individual and their collective needs in a group. They have a proclivity to solve the problem of information overload by probing through large volumes of dynamically generated information and provide its users with significant content and services. For better and more pertinent recommendations for a group of users, it is a non-trivial task as there is a huge diversity in tastes and preferences among various members of the group residing at different locations. This paper presents the results computed from traditional filtering approaches and the Hybrid filtering mode. These approaches are evaluated using various offline metrics on Movie-Lens dataset and the proposed model is based on the working efficiency and the quality of recommendations generated. This Hybrid Filtering Model proposed as Hyflix is explored for generating recommendations to a group of users and compared with the existing traditional filtering approaches in a social network.

Keywords: Group recommender system · Movie recommender · Collaborative filtering · Content-based filtering · Hybrid model · Hyflix · Movie-Lens

1 Introduction

A recommender system is capable of predicting the future preference by identifying behaviour of its users based on their preferencesin order to recommend suitable or appropriate items or services. It is a framework that generates and recommends appropriate services such as "which movie to watch?" or "what book to read?" or "which

A. Dev et al. (Eds.): AIST 2021, CCIS 1546, pp. 660–673, 2022.
https://doi.org/10.1007/978-3-030-95711-7_54

music to listen?" or "what product or services to buy?" after learning them from their user's tendencies. They are considered as highly prominent in the field of e-commerce and information technology. There are two types of recommender systems:

1) Personalized recommendation system and
2) Group-based recommendation system.

A high number of recommender systems are available for not only generating personalized recommendations but also group-based recommendations. The group recommender system uses various filtering approach such as collaborative, content-based and technique based on utility known as the hybrid approach [1]. To make more refined recommendations to a group of users, content-based and collaborative filtering approaches [2], n-dimensional analysis are also prominent.

A Personalized and Group-based recommendation system widely uses collaborative filtering and content-based filtering approach. In addition to these approaches, a hybrid recommender system is also prevailing which overcomes the individual drawbacks of the two approaches and proposes better results that satisfy every member of the group [3].

Group-based recommendation systems can be classified based on the types of groups to which the recommendations are made. Broadly, groups are classified into two categories i.e. homogeneous and heterogeneous [1, 2], which uses various filtering approaches such as collaborative, content-based and techniques based on utility known as the hybrid approach. Members of a homogenous group are those with similar tastes and preferences, whereas heterogeneous group members that do not share common interests.

The different approaches for evaluating group recommender systems are based on various evaluation metrics providing relevance based on the domain of an item [4]. Some researchers consider various grouping factors, which comprises of social interactions between various members, level of expertise and some of the dis-similarity of preferences and tastes between members, to recommend movies of preferences and tastes in the group [3]. In Happy Movie [5], a personality profilefor group of users on Facebook was created through a questionnaire survey rates the movies, followed by collaborative filtering approach.

A group-based recommender systems for generating recommendations to the group of users that are predefined incorporate Latent Group Model (LGM) [4, 6]. The traditional group recommender forms the groups in a fully automated fashion, resulting in data sparsity problem in user-item ratings. These models use the k-means clustering algorithm. Groups are also formed based on genre in movies. Therefore, for each group, the latent factor profiles of all the group of users are aggregated together into a group profile. Matrix factorisation approach is also used for generating the recommendations to these groups. These recommendations made to a group of users is calculated by computing group's profile and the component vector that contains all the latent factors based on the user preferences.

Recommendations can be proposed by content-based filtering and collaborative filtering techniques to its each user individually. Top-N Rec [7] recommends the movie using aggregation strategies therefore, movies recommended by collaborative approach are reordered based on the results from content-based approach. This is an intuition-based model, that recommend movies to its users by using both the approaches. Either of the two approaches can be considered more suitable and appropriate than that of movies recommended by personalized techniques. When this model was evaluated on some standard dataset, it was seen that it performed better than the traditional filtering approaches.

The user satisfaction has also been proposed for computing, followed by the Hungarian Aggregated method [3], which is an extension for the least misery strategy. The assessment of the more significant effect of rank-based aggregation approaches i.e. Least Misery Spearman Foot rule and Average strategy, for computing individual preferences using a collaborative filtering technique has also been explored for generating the recommendations for the group [8].

This paper provides a landscape of different traditional recommender system approaches and explores a hybrid filter model, Hyflix for recommending movies to its users. The paper is structured in five sections. Section 2 describes the proposed model and research methodology. Section 3 elaborates about the experiments that are performed on the Movie-Lens dataset. Section 4 discusses the impact of socio-behavioural aspects on group-based recommendations and Sect. 5 concludes with future research options.

2 Proposed Work

The Hyflix (hybrid filter model) is explored in accordance to the other traditional filtering approaches for generating and recommending movies to the members of the groups, based on the preferred genres of the group. Figure 1, describes the research procedure.

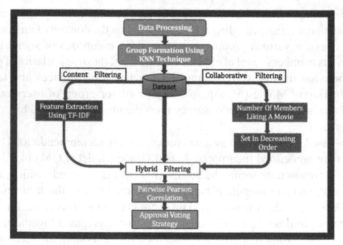

Fig. 1. Diagrammatic representation of proposed recommender system

2.1 Creating a Group Profile

The efficiency of the system can be increased by normalizing each user's rating. The score is calculated for each movie to normalize the ratings that are given to them by each user in the group. The score is equal to the sum of the ratings that each user gives to a particular movie subtracting the average rating of that user and multiplying with some weight. Weight is calculated using cosine similarity. Therefore, the score is:

$$S = \sum_{i=1}^{n} R - A \times W \qquad (1)$$

where, S is score, R denotes sum of ratings by each user, A is the average rating, W is the weight applied.

2.2 Pre-processing Data and Identifying Popular Genres

We know, when it's really cold weather, the engine faces many problems while starting up, but once it reaches its optimal operating temperature, it starts its functioning and runs smoothly. Similarly, the recommendation engines face a cold start [9] i.e., to adapt to a group of users, the engine needs to know what is liked by the members in the past. This simply means that the situation is not optimal yet for the system to recommend the best possible and suitable results [10]. To overcome this problem, we have generated a notion of the neighbourhood. This neighbourhood includes only a set of 30 similar users (K = 30) in each group. Similarly, 30 nearest neighbour for each user can be calculated. Hence, for every group, we have data about their preferred movie and its corresponding genre.

Here in our experiment, we will apply both the approaches i.e., collaborative approach and content-based approach on *group-1*. Now, we will compute the most liked genre for members of group-1 for the recommendation of movies to all the members by satisfying each user's taste (Fig. 2).

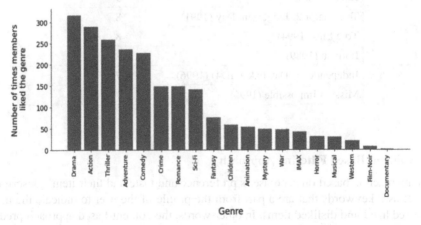

Fig. 2. Most popular movie genres of members of group-1

2.3 Collaborative Filtering Approach

It is a method by which items are recommended among users based on similar tastes and preference. Such a recommender system predicts and recommends items that are majorly preferred by similar kinds of members in a group [10]. This approach is independent of its content as it is a connection-based strategy. Sometimes, we achieve serendipitous recommendation as they are based on the similarity of users instead of item similarity [11]. Generally, a collaborative filtering technique is known as the workhorse of recommendation systems [10].

The ratings were normalized to achieve the top-rated movies satisfying each user's tastes and preferences. Therefore, the most preferred genre among the group of users is achieved. Hence, for the collaborative approach the following algorithm is applied and implemented to all the groups formed:

1. Group each movie according to its corresponding attribute i.e. movie-id, to get the number of users who liked that particular movie.
2. Sort the number in decreasing order, so that the most rated movies in that group is identified (Table 1).

Table 1. Top 10 movies recommended to members of group-1 by the collaborative approach

S No	Titles	Number of Ratings
1	Shawshank Redemption, The (1994)	12
2	Silence of the Lambs, The (1991)	11
3	Pulp Fiction (1994)	10
4	Forrest Gump (1994)	10
5	Jurassic Park (1993)	9
6	Terminator 2: Judgement Day (1991)	8
7	True Lies (1994)	8
8	Batman (1989)	8
9	Independence Day (a.k.a. ID4) (1996)	7
10	Mission Impossible (1996)	7

2.4 Content Based Filtering Approach

This approach is based on each user's preference and taste and their item's description [12]. It uses keywords that are a part from the profile of the user to indicate the user's preferred liked and disliked items. In other words, the content-based approach predicts and recommends those items that were liked by the user in the past. It considers previously rated items and finds the best matching item for a recommendation [9, 12]. To generate appropriate recommendations, the users' profile and its information are compared with the characteristic of the items examined. By normalizing the ratings, top-rated movies are identified and subsequently the most liked genre among the group of users. Hence, for the proposed model which uses Content filtering approach the following algorithm is applied and movies are recommended to the groups.

1. Term Frequency-Inverse Document Frequency (TF-IDF) transforms text to feature vectors and negates the words that are highly occurring for determining the importance of any document (movie). Vector Space Model used by TF-IDF computes the closeness based on the angle formed between feature vectors. In this model, each item is stored as a vector of its features and visualized in an n-dimensional space. Here, the angle formed between the vectors is used to determine the similarity among the feature vectors. Hence, giving the TF-IDF scores to determine which movies are closer to each other, that is closer to the user profile.

2. By using the TF-IDF scores, the dot-product for the scores of two feature vectors is computed, known as cosine similarity. The angle of cosine between any two vectors quantities are projected and are visualized in a multi-dimensional space. Cosine similarity is very useful because if any two similar users lie far apart when projected due to their preferences, tastes, and their profiles, then also they still can be closely oriented to each other. Smaller is the cosine angle, higher is the similarity.

$$\text{similarity} = \cos\theta = \frac{A \cdot B}{||A||\,||B||} = \frac{\sum_{i=1}^{N} A_i B_i}{\sqrt{\sum_{i=1}^{N} A_i^2}\sqrt{\sum_{i=1}^{N} B_i^2}} \tag{2}$$

Where, A_i and B_i are *components of vector A and B* respectively, $\cos\theta$ is *similarity*.

Using the similarity feature, most similar movies based on the cosine similarity score are recommended to the group (Table 2).

Table 2. Top 10 movies recommended to members of group-1 by the content-based approach

S No	Titles
1	Rock, The (1996)
2	Fargo (1996)
3	Time to Kill, A (1996)
4	Independence Day (a.k.a ID4) (1996)
5	Grumpier Old Men (1995)
6	Star Trek: First Contact (1996)
7	Willy Wonka and the Chocolate Factory (1971)
8	Birdcage, The (1996)
9	Twister (1996)
10	Sense and Sensibility (1995)

2.5 Hybrid Filtering Approach (Hyflix Model)

To overcome the limitations of collaborative as well as content-based approaches in terms of accuracy and the effect of appropriate recommendations on the members of the group, the **Hybrid Filtering approach** is explored which is a combination of these approaches in such a way that it is either a result of various recommendations methods of collaborative approach or an amalgam of both collaborative and content-based approach. Therefore, it is considered as a more pertinent way for recommendation of movies to its users. The Hyflix uses a rank aggregation strategy blended with content-based approach to generate better recommendations.

The average strategy when combined with content-based approach for similarity between the content, uses Pearson's Correlation to give the desired results. The projected model works on the stated algorithm:

1. Compute pairwise correlation of the desired movie with every other movie as done in content-based approach by applying Pearson's Correlation, also known as centred-cosine similarity that helps to compute, type of relationship among two quantities. The expected value of the Pearson Correlation Coefficient is significant between the range negative 1 to positive 1 [9]. Therefore, + 1 signifies that users/item are highly correlated with each other whereas zero (0) signifies no correlation, and -1 signifies that a negative correlation is seen. It is denoted by 'r'.

$$r = \frac{\sum(x - \bar{x})(y - \bar{y})}{\sqrt{\sum(x - \bar{x})^2 \sum(y - \bar{y})^2}} \tag{3}$$

Where, *x is standard deviation of x, y is standard deviation of y, $\bar{x}$ is mean of x, $\bar{y}$ is mean of y, r is Pearson's Correlation Coefficient.*

2. Store the movie titles with correlations separately and convert it into a table with index as user-id, attributes as movie titles and the normalized rating.
3. Apply average strategy, which considers all the member in the group with equal importance and therefore compute the average satisfaction of a particular group by any movie.

$$GRi = average(\mathcal{R}i, j) = \frac{\sum_{j=1}^{n} \mathcal{R}i, j}{n} \tag{4}$$

Where, '*n*' is *number of users* in a group, '*R*' is *ratings* by any user '*j*' for any *movie 'I'* (Table 3).

Table 3. Top-10 movies recommended by average strategy to group-1

S No	Titles
1	Shawshank Redemption, The (1994)
2	Silence of the Lambs, The (1991)
3	Pulp Fiction (1994)

(continued)

Table 3. (*continued*)

S No	Titles
4	Forrest Gump (1994)
5	Jurassic Park (1993)
6	Terminator 2: Judgement Day (1991)
7	True Lies (1994)
8	Dances with Wolves (1990)
9	Batman (1989)
10	Independence Day (a.k.a ID4) (1996)

3 Dataset and Experimental Results

3.1 Dataset Description

To evaluate and implement the group recommender system, the Movie-Lens dataset consisting of approximately one lakh movie ratings from 671 users on 9066 movies has been used. Every user in this dataset has rated more than 20 movies. Some of the most popular genres are Action, Comedy, Drama, Romance, and Thriller. The dataset has not been used directly for implementation as there were no groups in the dataset. Hence, first, the grouping was done and then the dataset was used for computation of results. 20 groups each consisting of 30 members has been used, thus maintaining the consistency.

3.2 Evaluation Metrics

The offline accuracy metrics used to examine the performance of the proposed research work were RMSE (Root Mean Square Error), MAE (Mean Absolute Error), Precision and Recall Curve, ROC and AUC.

Root Mean Square Error (RMSE): The RMSE is used to evaluate the accuracy of the recommendations made to groups of users. It is used to measure the average magnitude of error. It is the square root of the average of differences (squared) between actual value and observed value. The RMSE is computed as:

$$RMSE = \sqrt{\frac{\sum_{i=1}^{N}\left(yi - \widehat{yi}\right)^2}{N}} \tag{5}$$

where, yi is *actual value*, $\left(\widehat{yi}\right)$ is *observed value*, $N = total\ cases$ as shown in Fig. 3.

Mean Absolute Error: The MAE evaluation of errors is a method which is direction-less. It is the average of test sample of the absolute differences between prediction and actual observation where all individual differences have equal weight. Smaller the MAE value better is the filtering approach. The MAE is computed as:

$$MAE = \frac{1}{\mathcal{N}} \sum_{i=1}^{\mathcal{N}} \left| yi - \widehat{yi} \right| \tag{6}$$

where, yi is *predicted value,* $\left(\widehat{yi}\right)$ is *actual value,* $\mathcal{N} = total\ cases$ shown in Fig. 3.

ROC and AUC: The Receiver Operating Characteristic (ROC) plot is used to visualize the trade-off between true positives and false positives for binary classification. The Area Under the Curve is used majorly as an evaluation metrics for recommender systems. Models that occupy large area under the ROC curve have better performance (Fig. 4).

Precision and Recall Curve: The Precision and Recall plot is used to visualize the trade-off between precision and recall (Fig. 5) for one class of recommendations.

3.3   Experimental Results

In this era of fast-growing web-based recommendations, a huge number of recommender systems have been developed that are either based on a Content-based filtering approach or Collaborative filtering approach to determine which of the approach is more appropriate for recommending movies to a group of users staying at different locations. The proposed work was thus evaluated using various offline metrics.

The computations from the evaluation metrices and curve plots conclude that the proposed Hybrid model- *Hyflix* for group recommender system provides *better* as well as*pertinent* movies to a group of users than the traditional approaches; content-based and collaborative approach.

4   Impact of Social Behavioral Aspects on Group-Based Recommendations

Sometimes, some members of group are more influential than the other members, so by, incorporating some of the social as well as behavioural factors for recommendations to a group [13] along with each user's taste and preferences, increases the quality of generated recommendations. Social factors such as personality, satisfaction, etc., will give each member's personalised measures [5] to generate pertinent recommendations. Also, negotiation-based strategies can be evolved in which members in the group negotiate for their preferred items/movies by interacting with other members of that group. However, such strategies provide appropriate results only when the group size is small and consistent and fails for larger and inconsistent groups.

The model proposed in [14] used some of the social factors such as dissimilarity-descriptor, social-descriptor and also, designed a rule-based system which incorporated the aforementioned social factors for a group recommendation. In group-based recommender system for heterogeneous groups i.e. group members that do not share common

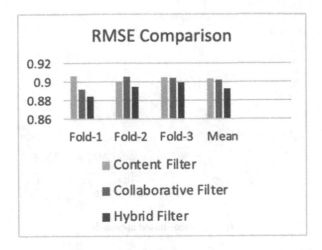

(a) RMSE values

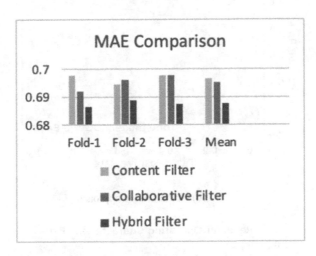

(b) MAE values

Fig. 3. Comparison of Collaborative Approach, Content-based approach, and Hybrid-Model approach (a) RMSE values, (b) MAE values

interests, hence, no social relations will exist among the group members, by incorporating some behavioural aspects along with the preferences by its members will lead to appropriate recommendations. Also, the model proposed in [15] offers weighted-user-collaborative approach along with a social aspect of group's personality to produce better and appropriate recommendations than any other traditional methods used for this purpose.

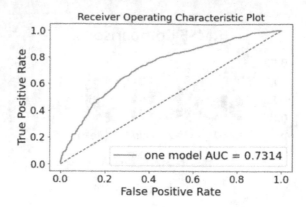

(a)   Content-based approach

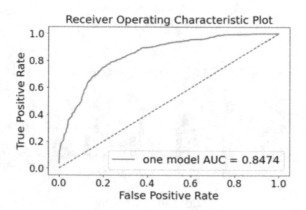

(b) Collaborative approach

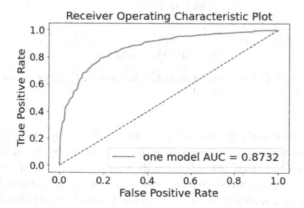

(c) Hybrid Model

Fig. 4. ROC Curve for (a) Content-based Approach, (b) Collaborative Approach and (c) Hybrid Mode.

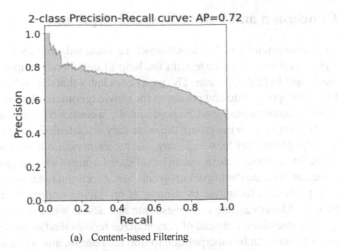

(a) Content-based Filtering

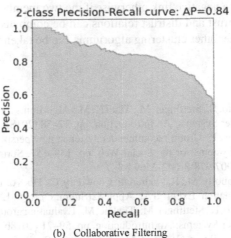

(b) Collaborative Filtering

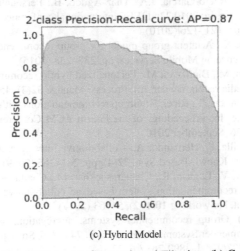

(c) Hybrid Model

Fig. 5. Precision and Recall Curve (a) Content-based Filtering, (b) Collaborative Filtering and (c) Hybrid Model

5   Conclusion and Future Research Options

A group recommender is developed which recommends movies to a group of users, by satisfying each member's taste with the help of collaborative approach, content-based approach, and hybrid approach. The paper concludes that the Hybrid filtering technique used is more appropriate and pertinent for movie recommendations in a group than the other two techniques examined. Experimentally, a common belief is analysed i.e. more a-like are the members in the group, the more they are satisfied with the recommendations made to the group. Hence, we can say, our recommendations are consistent.

In the future, the conclusions can be validated using other aggregation strategies. Further, one can evaluate the impact on group-based recommender system, by collaborative filtering prediction technique by aiming at producing improved and accurate ranking predictions. Moreover, one can investigate and assess when it is convenient to make a group recommendation instead of personalized recommendations. Furthermore, Signed Social Networks can be incorporated to find the relation among various members of the group as a positive or a negative link otherwise if the two members are either friends or foes. Similarly, their trust and distrust relations can be computed. Correspondingly, to enhance the group size, other clustering algorithms can be taken into account.

References

1. Felfernig, A., Boratto, L., Stettinger, M., Tkalčič, M.: Algorithms for group recommendation. Group Recommender Systems: An Introduction, pp. 27–58 (2018)
2. Cantador, I., Castells, P.: Group recommender systems: new perspectives in the social web. In: Recommender Systems for the Social Web, pp. 139–157. Springer, Heidelberg (2012). https://doi.org/10.1007/978-3-642-25694-3_7
3. Agarwal, A., Chakraborty, M., Ravindranath Chowdary, C.: Does order matter? effect of order in group recommendation. Expert Syst. Appl. **82**(Suppl. C), 115–127 (2017)
4. Felfernig, A., Boratto, L., Stettinger, M., Tkalčič, M.: Evaluating group recommender systems. Group Recommender Systems: An Introduction, pp. 59–71 (2018b)
5. Quijano-Sanchez, L., Recio-Garcia, J.A., Diaz-Agudo, B.: Personality and social trust in group recommendations. In: 2010 22nd IEEE international conference on tools with artificial intelligence, vol. 2, pp. 121–126 (2010)
6. Shi, J., Wu, B., Lin, X.: A latent group model for group recommendation. In: 2015 IEEE International Conference on Mobile Services, pp. 233–238 (2015)
7. Kaššák, O., Kompan, M., Bieliková, M.: Personalized hybrid recommendation for group of users: top-n multimedia recommender. Inf. Process. Manage **52**(3), 459–477 (2016)
8. Baltrunas, L., Makcinskas, T., Ricci, F.: Group recommendations with rank aggregation and collaborative filtering. In: Proceedings of the Fourth ACM Conference on Recommender Systems, pp. 119–126, September 2010
9. Bobadilla, J., Serradilla, F., Hernando, A.: Collaborative filtering adapted to recommender systems of e-learning. Knowl.-Based Syst. **22**(4), pp. 261–265 (2009)
10. Subramaniya swamy, V., Logesh, R., Chandrashekhar, M., Challa, A., Vijayakumar, V.: A personalised movie recommendation system based on collaborative filtering. Int. J. High Performance Comput. Networking **10**(1–2), 54–63 (2017)
11. Masthoff, J. (2015). Group recommender systems: aggregation, satisfaction and group attributes. In: Recommender Systems Handbook, pp. 743–776. Springer, Boston (2015). doi: https://doi.org/10.1007/978-1-4899-7637-6_22

12. Christensen, I.A., Schiaffino, S.: Entertainment recommender systems for group of users. Expert Syst. Appl. **38**(11), 14127–14135 (2011)
13. Pujahari, A., Padmanabhan, V.: group recommender systems: combining user-user and item-item collaborative filtering techniques. In: 2015 International Conference on Information Technology (ICIT). IEEE, pp. 148–152, December 2015
14. Quijano-Sanchez, L., Recio-Garcia, J.A., Diaz-Agudo, B.: Happymovie: a Facebook application for recommending movies to groups. In: 2011 IEEE 23rd International Conference on Tools with Artificial Intelligence, pp. 239–244, November 2011
15. Gartrell, M., et al.: Enhancing group recommendation by incorporating social relationship interactions. In: Proceedings of the 16th ACM International Conference on Supporting Group Work, pp. 97–106, November 2010

Author Index

Printed in the United States
by Baker & Taylor Publisher Services